SPIRITUAL UPLIFTS
FOR A RAPIDLY CHANGING WORLD

EUGENE LEITER

ISBN 979-8-88685-282-0 (paperback)
ISBN 979-8-88685-285-1 (digital)

Christian Faith Publishing
832 Park Avenue
Meadville, PA 16335
www.christianfaithpublishing.com

Printed in the United States of America

HOW TO EFFECTIVELY USE THIS BOOK AND INSIGHTS ABOUT THE AUTHOR

In the Word of God, there is significance in the number seven. It derives much of its meaning from being tied directly to creation. The book of Genesis tells us that God created the heavens and the earth in six days, and upon completion, He rested on the seventh day. Furthermore, Jesus performed seven miracles on God's Holy Sabbath. He agonized as He made seven statements from the cross at the end of His earthly duties. The number seven is also associated with promises in the book of Revelation. In particular, we read of seven letters addressed to seven churches. And the references go on and on. Used over 700 times in the Bible, "seven" often symbolizes completeness or perfection.

You will not be surprised to learn it was with some intent that the devotions compiled in this book were written over a seven-year period. This presents the reader with a choice. A complete reading can be accomplished over the course of one year by sequentially reading the daily devotion (specified in the text by the month and day). Or the book can also be used more intensively as a weekly devotional allowing the reader to focus more deeply on the content and reflection questions. In the latter case, the reader will need to follow the Y and D designations at the top of each page. For instance, Y2, D25 represents year 2, devotion 25. Y6, D52 would end the sixth year with devotion 52. You will read every seventh devotion (one each week) for whatever year you are studying. It may sound a little confusing at first, but you will catch on quickly if this is the course you decide to follow. Originally published in blog format, I utilized many sources for my inspiration. In addition to referencing several biblical translations, the writings were stirred from historical occurrences, current events, and personal experiences. Emphases for themes were derived from both the seasonal and Christian calendars and are, therefore, arranged to coincide with annual recognitions and traditional holiday celebrations.

As the author, I have been gifted with a strong sense of servanthood as my life has developed. Frequently, I have been inspired to reflect on the roads I have traveled. At times, I have met others who seem to be on a similar path, and once in a while, our stories get shared. My purpose for these writings is simply to lift up insights from these journeys. I hope this has been done in a manner that will provide a source of hope and encouragement as you progress down your own life pathway. In the end, I have discovered that it's usually not about the destination itself but rather the lessons which surface as the journey unfolds. I am always grateful when God enables me to use these "journey lessons" to support and motivate others.

Together, we are facing a challenging, confusing, and sometimes threatening world out there. I don't know about you, but I have come to realize that it is when we begin to feel that life around us is about to collapse suddenly, the glory of God appears above us. Hence the title, *Spiritual Uplifts for a Rapidly Changing World.* I am blessed to share them with you and pray they bring meaning into your life as you continue your walk with Him.

Eugene Leiter

JANUARY 1
(Y1, D1)

Finding Wisdom By Looking Up

For wisdom is far more valuable than rubies. Nothing you desire can compare with it.

—Proverbs 8:11 (NLT)

A friend of mine was telling me about an annual work evaluation he was given. In discussion with his supervisor, the statement was made that part of my friend's success was that he surrounded himself with good people. He wasn't quite sure whether that was a compliment or a criticism. Did it mean that he hired persons to work with him who enhanced his abilities? Or did it infer that if he hadn't brought these people into his work group that he would otherwise be unsuccessful? When he questioned his boss about it, the supervisor smiled. He further explained that in their particular line of business, those who have a high rate of success are not intimidated to hire others who have skill sets and levels of knowledge different than their own. In fact, he went on to tell my friend that "doing this is a very wise thing." Wisdom can be defined as the ability to think and act using knowledge, experience, understanding, common sense, and insight. In the business world, it is productive if it is both individual and collective.

The American writer and educator, Isaac Asimov, once wrote "The saddest aspect of life right now is that science gathers knowledge faster than society gathers wisdom." We live in the information age, where news pops up on our cellphones and degrees can be obtained online. While there is an abundance of knowledge floating around, there isn't a whole lot of wisdom, especially the godly kind. This kind of wisdom is the capacity to see things from the Lord's viewpoint and respond according to scriptural principles. For most of us, this doesn't always come naturally, but one can develop it gradually over time through prayer and practice. In pursuing the Christian life, we acquire wisdom by absorbing scripture, following what it says, and weighing the result, even when consequences appear to be less than favorable. In doing so, we will soon learn that basic knowledge comes from reasoning, but wisdom comes from revelation. In other words, knowledge is something you learn while wisdom is a gift.

Solomon was young when he became king, succeeding his father, David. When God appeared to him in a dream and asked him what he wanted, Solomon responded by asking for wisdom to rule well over God's people. Solomon knew that he lacked the heart of understanding needed to lead and to judge over them properly. "The Lord was pleased that Solomon had asked for wisdom" (1 Kings 3:10 NLT). He also blessed Solomon with the following words: "I will do what you have asked. I will give you a wise and discerning heart, so that there will never have been anyone like you, nor will there ever be. Moreover, I will give you what you have not asked for—both wealth and honor—so that in your lifetime you will have no equal among kings" (1 Kings 3:12–13 NIV). King Solomon, one of the richest and most successful men who ever lived, had everything he needed and could possibly want in life. Yet he knew that riches, power, and comfort meant nothing if he couldn't make wise decisions. He wanted to honor God who gave him everything he had, so he asked for wisdom to know what to do and how to do it.

Similar to Solomon, God will provide wisdom in our lives so we can relate positively to those around us. By our example, the world needs to see God-given wisdom rooted in humility and not displayed by arrogance. We need to see Christians walking wisely when it comes to being godly friends, neighbors, husbands, wives, parents, bosses, employees, and citizens. Those with whom we come in contact need to see that the gospel has fully equipped and empowered us to live righteous and upright lives in this world. You might ask, "So how do I find such wisdom?" As you study God's Word, seek the Lord's will, observe His principles in action, and apply them to your life. "If any of you lacks wisdom, you should ask God, who gives generously to all without finding fault, and it will be given to you" (James 1:5 NIV). If you approach Him with a willing and obedient heart, God will pour wisdom into your mind and spirit. Bottom line, know that knowledge comes from education; wisdom comes from God. To achieve knowledge, you look around. To inherit wisdom, you simply need to look up, and you will find it!

Reflection

What are some differences between the wisdom that comes from God and the knowledge of the world? Recall some experiences when have you sensed the Lord granting you wisdom as you gave advice to someone or as you made a decision. What are some specific areas in life in which you should be regularly asking for God's wisdom? How might you demonstrate this gift of wisdom to others each day?

JANUARY 2
(Y2, D1)

Putting Away Christmas

Christmas waves a magic wand over this world, and behold,
everything is softer and more beautiful.

—Norman Vincent Peale

It's time to put away Christmas. The outside decorations must come down; the wreath over the fireplace needs to be removed, and the model train and village boxed up for another year. The biggest job, of course, is taking all the individual ornaments off of the live tree. As I do so, there is a certain amount of care given to particular ones because some were given as gifts by folks who are no longer living. Others are remembrances of favorite travel spots or may have been purchased at a significant time or event along my life journey. One of the most significant displays in my home contains the nativity characters. Each shepherd, wise men, as well as Mary, Joseph, and the baby Jesus have separate boxes that protects them from being broken as they are carried off to the storage area for the next eleven months.

I must admit I am not nearly as enthused about the after-Christmas activity as I am when I start decking the halls shortly after Thanksgiving. This year, however, I had an interesting experience which carried over from one Christmas to the next. Last December, I bought a dish garden containing a poinsettia plant. As we transitioned from the holidays and further into the winter season, I placed the mostly green plantings at my window. Piece by piece, the red leaves of the poinsettia began to drop off, but it was many weeks before the last one fell. As spring turned into summer, I fertilized and regularly watered the arrangement. The ivies and other greens flourished over the container and spread across the ledge at my back window. About mid-Summer a new broadleaf plant appeared in the center of it all. Then early in November, several of the leaves began to turn red, exhibiting itself as a rejuvenated poinsettia just in time for another Christmas. The roots of the poinsettia had been there all along and had, in fact, never gone away. That should be the way Christmas is for each of us.

When the excitement of gift giving is over and the garland and tinsel are taken down, the reminder of the emerging of the Christ-child should be a revitalized seed in the hearts of all who know Him. The Apostle Paul stated it this way:

> Then Christ will make his home in your hearts as you trust in him. Your roots will grow down into God's love and keep you strong. And may you have the power to understand, as all God's people should, how wide, how long, how high, and how deep his love is. May you experience the love of Christ, though it is too great to understand fully. Then you will be made complete with all the fullness of life and power that comes from God. (Ephesians 3:17–19 NLT)

Just like the mother of the baby Jesus, we should be so amazed at the spirit of Christmas that we would never want to let go. Scripture says, "But Mary treasured up all these things and pondered them in her heart" (Luke 2:19 NIV).

In all of God's creation, man was the most precious. He intended to always be in fellowship with each of us, and the birth of Jesus reaffirmed His desire and love. "God did this so that they would seek him and perhaps reach out for him and find him, though he is not far from any one of us" (Acts 17:27 NIV). Another new year has dawned, and He waits to be included. By keeping Christ in our hearts all year long, we cannot help but become a blessing to those in the world around us. So continue, my friends, to search for the nearness of Jesus before you speak, before you act, giving this a priority in everything that you do. "Therefore, if anyone is in Christ, the new creation has come: The old has gone, the new is here" (2 Corinthians 5:17 NIV). Consequently, my fellow sojourners, we must let the past behind, walk along the path He provides in the present, and be assured that our future will rest in His loving arms. As you do so, you will find that like my poinsettia—Christmas will never need to be put away.

Reflection

As you take down the decorations in your home, how might you hold on to the joy of Christmas? In doing so, can you identify ways this will enable you to become a more effective witness? What new thing does God want to do in your life this year? How will you enable His Spirit to work within you as you begin the implementation process and work to maintain it in the days ahead?

JANUARY 3
(Y3, D1)

Running on Empty

And the believers were filled with joy and with the Holy Spirit.

—Acts 13:52 (NLT)

One of our family members received an interesting Christmas gift recently. Weeks before the big day, my mother and I went shopping at a major department store. While walking through the housewares department, she saw a condiment caddy which had been reduced to half-price. She remarked that it would be useful to have for picnics on the deck next summer. We paid for the item, and I saved it as one of her Christmas gifts. Since it was rather insignificant, I decided to have her open it first on Christmas. As I handed it to her, I became a little suspicious because the package was very light. Sure enough, when she opened the box, there wasn't anything inside. If nothing else, it did provide us with a few hearty laughs. The event reminded me of another incident that happened to me many years ago when I purchased a new car. A day or so after the acquisition, I decided to take a long-distance drive to get a feel for how the car handled. I chose a familiar destination within an hour from home. When I arrived there, all of a sudden, the car began to chug, sputter, and came to a halt. As anyone would do, I glanced down at the gas gauge to check the obvious. According to the indicator, I still had plenty of fuel. I then proceeded to phone the dealership where I purchased the car. They willingly sent out a tow truck for the car, and it took us back home. The next day, they notified me that the reason for the shutdown was that there was, in fact, no gas in the tank. Apparently, the new car came fully-equipped with a faulty gas gauge. And there I was, trying to run on empty.

Emptiness comes in many forms. Sometimes, when we go too long without eating, we might say that we are "getting a little empty." If the person at work who is responsible for supplies allows the inventory to be depleted, that emptiness can become problematic for the production staff. If both our wallet and our bank account are empty, we are going to have to make some temporary lifestyle changes. And when we feel a sense of emptiness in our soul, then loneliness and despair can quickly lead to depression. At times, Christians may also feel spiritually empty if they have not maintained a vibrant connection with God. Each of us has no doubt experienced seasons when we have felt spiritually dry; we lack joy, and our faith is no longer infectious. The key to overcoming spiritual emptiness is to fill up. Scripture tells us that as a child of God, we possess that capability because we have the Holy Spirit that Jesus promised inside of us. The great evangelist D. L. Moody understood this. When asked why he placed so much emphasis upon being filled with the Holy Spirit, he wisely said, "Because I leak."

Spiritual emptiness is often caused by our own sinfulness or sluggishness in sustaining regular contact with God in our daily lives. We cannot expect much peace if we are always trying to run spiritually on empty. Without a continuously filled spiritual tank, our days are doomed to stress, anxiety, and frustration. When we fill up by spending some quality time with Him, we will become revitalized and discover our faith is renewed. Jesus warned that it is dangerous to allow ourselves to become empty:

> When an evil spirit leaves a person, it goes into the desert, seeking rest but finding none. Then it says, "I will return to the person I came from." So it returns and finds its former home empty, swept, and in order. Then the spirit finds seven other spirits more evil than itself, and they all enter the person and live there. And so that person is worse off than before. That will be the experience of this evil generation. (Matthew 12:43–45 NLT)

So dare to be different than your peers. Those who endeavor to maintain a full spiritual tank strive to be grounded in God's Word and sustain a solid prayer life. If you are entering this new year or any transition in your life, you will want to make sure that you are well-fueled for whatever lies ahead. While it may be misguided to think that just because one year ends and another begins, you will permanently change your course. But when you find yourself presented with an empty box or tank, there's only one way to go. It's only common sense to conclude that you won't get very far when you are trying to face the journey ahead by running on empty. Why not take some time and start refueling today?

Reflection

Do you recognize times when your spiritual life just doesn't seem as full as it once was? Do you have any signs of spiritual dryness in your life at the moment? How long have you felt this way? Think of times in the past when you have experienced a fulfilled life. What are some very practical things you can do this week and throughout this new year to personally reconnect with God?

JANUARY 4
(Y4, D1)

A Fair Exchange

As a fair exchange—I speak as to my children—open wide your hearts also.

—2 Corinthians 6:13 (NIV)

While time for Christmas giving has passed, the season of returns has just begun. Some estimate that up to 2 percent of holiday gifts are returned each year, amounting to billions of dollars in merchandise. What do you do when you receive a gift you can't use? Many folks simply take it back to the store where it was purchased and just exchange it. Or they may simply save it for regifting. The late Johnny Carson is credited with once having said, "The worst gift is fruitcake. There is only one fruitcake in the entire world, and people keep sending it to each other." What if your holiday present happens to be a symbolic fruitcake taking the form of one of those gift cards from a place where you don't even shop? One recent trend has been to go online and do a gift card exchange for cash. While you do not get the full-face value of the card, some sites claim to get you up to 90 percent of what the giver paid. But seller, beware, just like the rest of our society—there are scams out there that are targeting folks who are both buying and selling gift cards, making it not always the fair and easy exchange some might promote it to be.

Sometimes, though, there are gift exchanges done on earth that just may have been a match made in heaven. Here is one such true story. Jay and Jackie met five years before, working for the same nonprofit organization. They fell in love, but their blossoming relationship was clouded by Jay's failing health and need for a kidney transplant. Jackie would have gladly provided a kidney to the love of her life, but she was not genetically compatible. As the couple were about to be married, they found out that a donor had been located for Jay many states away. There, a man named Blake had hoped that he could be a donor for his mother who was also in need of a kidney. While he was not a match for her, he was a perfect match for Jay. But Chandra, Blake's mom, also found her seamless match at another household where, as it turned out, two kidneys would just swap addresses. The newlywed couple would not only receive a kidney for Jay, but his wife, Jackie, would provide one of hers to Chandra. Following the separate surgeries in different states, the two families reconnected to share their gratefulness for each other, realizing that there was a new and somewhat miraculous future in store for each of them.

Jesus had His own take on a fair exchange for giving "new life." He spoke about it with his followers as He predicted His own death.

> Then he called the crowd to him along with his disciples and said: "Whoever wants to be my disciple must deny themselves and take up their cross and follow me. For whoever wants to save their life will lose it, but whoever loses their life for me and for the gospel will save it. What good is it for someone to gain the whole world, yet forfeit their soul? Or what can anyone give in exchange for their soul? If anyone is ashamed of me and my words in this adulterous and sinful generation, the Son of Man will be ashamed of them when he comes in his Father's glory with the holy angels." (Mark 8:34–38 NIV)

Similar recordings are also found in Matthew 16:24–28 and Luke 9:23–27.

These words are particularly emotional in a world where it would seem that those who speak out for Christ are being persecuted more than ever. As we journey through this life and follow the teachings of Christ, we come to find new meaning in the phrase "We all have our own cross to bear." Jesus calls on each of us to lay down our life for Him. Unfortunately, in many parts of the world, this may literally involve violence and suffering. To others, it might simply necessitate giving up those things that Jesus would have despised in order that we might embrace those things that He would love. The call to follow Him is more than that of simple belief; it is rather a call to action. We are, therefore, faced with a choice. We live as the world would have us do for the temporal pleasantries of today. Or we can follow Jesus with the understanding that we may suffer some hardships through the denial of self. In doing the latter, we will inherit everlasting peace, joy, and contentment for all of eternity. Now that seems like a fair exchange at the beginning of a new year—or any time, for that matter.

Reflection

Who is the master of your life? What have you done with the gift that Jesus offers? In order to follow Him, consider those things you might need to exchange. What would be required of you to put your own plans to death and commit yourself to living out His will?

JANUARY 5
(Y5, D1)

The Human Factor

And let us not neglect our meeting together, as some people do, but encourage
one another, especially now that the day of his return is drawing near.

—Hebrews 10:25 (NLV)

Over one holiday break, I decided to watch the movie *Sully*. The 2016 film follows the January 2009 emergency landing of US Airways Flight 1549 on the Hudson River orchestrated by pilots Captain Chelsey "Sully" Sullenberger and First Officer Jeff Skiles. The flight, which had just taken off from New York's LaGuardia Airport, struck a flock of birds, disabling both engines after just three minutes in the air. All 155 passengers and crew survived with only minor injuries, creating a highly publicized event referred to as "The Miracle on the Hudson." What was not significantly emphasized at the time was the subsequent investigation by the National Transportation Safety Board which became the focus of the film. The investigation centered on several computerized simulations demonstrating that the plane could have landed safely without engines at either of two nearby airports. Captain Sully argued that these simulations were unrealistic because they were simplistic views containing preprogrammed knowledge for immediate reaction to the emergency. However, they did not provide any allowance for real-life decision-making. Once additional time was added for these "human factor" considerations, the board concluded the Sully acted responsibly, thus saving the lives of everyone aboard.

In this movie, as with many situations, the age-old question of knowledge versus wisdom comes into play. Alfred Lloyd Tennyson once stated that "Knowledge comes, but wisdom lingers." Computers will only give us the information for which they were programmed, once defined by the expression "garbage in, garbage out." Likewise, the automated digital assistant, Siri, and the voice control system known as Alexa can provide all sorts of data to you, simply for the asking. They are knowledgeable, and their statistics and facts will often enable the immediate gratification required. However, they lack wisdom and, most of all, any warmth exclusive to humankind. Alexa can't hold our hand, give us a hug, or wipe our tears when we are sad. Should it concern us then that there seems to be a trend in our society to move away from personal interactions in order that our needs might be satisfied more expeditiously?

Since we are created in God's image (Genesis 1:27) and He calls us into fellowship with Him (1 Corinthians 1:9), we should be cautious about the depersonalization of our lives which is so pervasive in many aspects of our culture. Not that long ago, it was commonplace to patronize the stores of the local merchants. There you chatted with storeowners who lived in your town and were vested in the community. While you shopped or walked from store to store, you would have a good chance of running into people you knew, perhaps engaging in good conversation. Soon those stores became replaced by larger retailers located in the suburbs. But even then, there were local personalities who continued to provide some level of human interaction. These days, it has become easier to do our shopping online. It can then be picked up curbside or perhaps delivered by a drone. Do we really need most of what we order that quickly? What do we sacrifice in the process of gaining this convenience? When we absent the human factor from more and more of our interactions, we can't help but also move a little further from God.

God's Word provides wise counsel in this regard. The Apostle Paul said, "When we get together, I want to encourage you in your faith, but I also want to be encouraged by yours" (Romans 1:12 NLT). One might argue that encouragement can come via a text or a tweet. While that might seem to be so, there are limitations. Jesus Himself stated, "For where two or three gather in my name, there am I with them" (Matthew 18:20 NIV). The "gathering" is being devalued as the human factor becomes diminished. In the early days of the church, "They devoted themselves to the apostles' teaching and to fellowship, to the breaking of bread and to prayer" (Acts 2:42 NIV). These days, our devotion is to our handheld devices, rationalizing that when we lack information, they will make us wise. James would refute that thought as he tells us, "If you need wisdom, ask our generous God, and he will give it to you. He will not rebuke you for asking" (James 1:5 NLT). Perhaps a novel idea worth considering as we enter a new year!

Reflection

As you look back over recent months and years, consider ways that you have become less interactive with others. Have you restricted your own knowledge base while becoming more reliant on electronic devices? How might you grow through more involvement with others and as you share God's Word and His instruction for making the world around you a better place?

JANUARY 6
(Y6, D1)

Beginnings and Endings

God blesses those who patiently endure testing and temptation. Afterward they
will receive the crown of life that God has promised to those who love him.

—James 1:12 (NLT)

I once heard a story about a man who was shipwrecked. After the sole survivor reached a small, unin-habited island, he prayed for God to rescue him. But help didn't come. As he began to be resigned to his fate, he labored for many hours, building a hut out of driftwood for protection from the elements. One day, as he returned from hunting for food, he saw smoke rising to the sky in the distance. As he drew close, he found his hut in flames. Angrily, he cried out, "God, how could You do this to me?" The next morning, he was awakened by rescuers. "How did you know I was here?" he asked. "We saw your smoke signal," they replied. The story serves to remind us that when we find ourselves seemingly lost and alone from the turmoil of life, we always have someone by our side to calm the storm. Scripture tells us about Jesus in a boat with His disciples when they found themselves in the midst of a turbulent storm.

> Jesus was sleeping at the back of the boat with his head on a cushion. The disciples woke him up, shouting, "Teacher, don't you care that we're going to drown?" When Jesus woke up, he rebuked the wind and said to the waves, "Silence! Be still!" Suddenly the wind stopped, and there was a great calm. Then he asked them, "Why are you afraid? Do you still have no faith?" The disciples were absolutely terrified. "Who is this man?" they asked each other. "Even the wind and waves obey him!" (Mark 4:38–41 NLT)

One early January day in 1809, Louis Braille was born in a small French town. The fourth child of Simon and Monique Braille appeared to be quite frail, so his parents arranged for a quick baptism. The early death that they had feared for him did not happen. Louis quickly showed himself to be a bright and curious lad, often playing in his father's leather workshop. One day, the three-year-old attempted to use an awl to punch holes in a piece of leather when the tool slipped and caught his eye. The eye could not be saved, became infected, and it soon spread to his other eye. From that point on, Louis Braille was blind. A local priest saw potential in the boy and began to teach him. When he was ten, he was enrolled in a special school for blind children in Paris. There, at the age of twelve, he met Charles Barbier, a former soldier, who had invented a system of raised dots which he hoped would enable silent communication for the soldiers at night. The army determined the system was too complex, so Barbier thought the school for the blind might have use for it. Braille was fascinated by this, so he dedicated himself to refining it. Over the next few years, he organized the raised letters into an alphabet. By the time he was fifteen, Louis had created the world's first meaningful structure for blind reading. At the young age of forty-three, as he lay dying of tuberculosis, he said, "God was pleased to hold before my eyes the dazzling splendors of eternal hope. After that, doesn't it seem that nothing more could keep me bound to the earth?"

The Apostle Paul said, "And we know that God causes everything to work together for the good of those who love God and are called according to his purpose for them" (Romans 8:28 NLT). We should pay attention to read this verse in its entirety. Note that this passage does *not* promise that all things work together for the good of all people. It is careful to point out that we must love Him and be called *by* Him. We all know of situations where things work out well for some who seem to not know God at all. But we have to remember we typically only know a small part of the story. Perhaps God is giving that person a second chance or maybe He didn't have His hand in it at all. But for those who know and love Him, we can be certain He allows circumstances to occur. Rick Warren says:

> But God can draw good out of each event in your life. That means every single event, no matter how dark or shameful or how guilty or bitter you feel about it, God can bring good out of it. He can work for your good. The Bible doesn't say all things are good. Not all things in the world are good. There's a lot of bad. But it does say that all things work together for good for those who give God all the pieces and say, "Will you work good out of this?" God will do it. He has an appointed time for everything.

Just as one cannot judge a book by its cover, neither should we predict an end at its beginning but rather judge its beginning only at its end.

Reflection

Is there anything that keeps you from asking God for His help? In what situation do you need to ask God to work for your good? What are the most difficult trials that you have been through? In what ways might God be working through them for an eventual good ending?

JANUARY 7
(Y7, D1)

Readiness for the Storms Ahead

He calmed the storm to a whisper and stilled the waves.

—Psalm 107:29 (NLT)

It doesn't much matter how many resolutions you have made or how many good luck sandwiches you have eaten. One can expect that in this new year, you will likely have some form of unrest in your life. We all experience situations that result in worry, suffering, or loss. We call them the storms of life. When they occur, it's not unusual to ask a question such as, "What did I do to deserve this?" On occasion, even God's most faithful pause to ask where Jesus is when circumstances seem to erupt into one of these powerful storms. God knew we would experience times when we would become overwhelmed by the clouds and lose sight of an escape from a threatening squall. By meditating on His Holy Word, we can find relief from the rain, gaining peace and security, even when the storms swirl around us. For that is when we can learn lessons about how He led His chosen through some truly tumultuous encounters.

One of those is described by three of His disciples—Matthew, Mark, and John. In their gospel writings, each records the events of the feeding of the five thousand. Immediately following this miracle, there is less-observed one when Jesus walks on water in the midst of a fierce windstorm. Each of the writers offer some variation on their perspective as to how this occurred. It is stated that after the crowd was dismissed, "Jesus *made* his disciples get into the boat and go on ahead of him" (Mark 6:45 NIV). This is confirmed by another who says that Jesus "*insisted*" (Matthew 14:22 NLT). Afterward, Jesus went to a mountainside alone to pray. Later that night, there was a storm brewing on the lake where the disciples were. "He saw that they were in serious trouble, rowing hard and struggling against the wind and waves" (Mark 6:48 NLT). The disciples speak of Jesus coming out to find them, "but when they saw him walking on the water, they cried out in terror, thinking he was a ghost" (Mark 6:49 NLT). "Jesus spoke to them at once. 'Don't be afraid,' he said. 'Take courage! I am here!' Then he climbed into the boat, and the wind stopped. They were totally amazed" (Mark 6:51 NLT); "and immediately they arrived at their destination" (John 6:21 NLT).

As we study these accounts, we first become mesmerized with the fact that Jesus walked on the water. But what we may be overlooking are the more important lessons as to how we need to respond when we find ourselves facing a threatening situation. At first, I found it interesting that Jesus would insist that His most devout followers go out onto a lake, knowing He was sending them to face uncontrolled waters. Was He possibly doing this as a test of their faith? Maybe then our first lesson is that the eyes of the Lord are upon us when we encounter one of life's storms, even if He helped to place us there. Sometimes it may appear as though no one notices, but rest assured, Jesus sees. The second lesson is that we should make every attempt to find Jesus in that storm. As with the disciples, things are not always as they seem. Be conscious of the fact that your perspective is often distorted when the storm surrounds you. You have no need to fear; He's right there in the boat with you. And then there's our final lesson. When He is ready to clear your storm, He will do so effectively. He may move to calm the storm immediately; at other times, He will calm His child first. When such a period of waiting occurs, ask God to reveal to you what He wants you to learn in the process. Then "cast all your anxiety on him because he cares for you" (1 Peter 5:7 NIV).

It is during the turbulent stages in our lives that we find a new perspective on the Lord and how He works. Frequently, this awareness will come only after the storm when we are able to look back with renewed vision and see how He brought us through it. Then we are able to better understand that His strength was sufficient, His purpose was good, and we were fulfilled by His support. We realize that any storm He allows is motivated by His love because He wants us to rely on Him. We learn to appreciate that contrary to what we thought, the storm was not when we had to face our enemy; instead, it was in that place where we found our God. As we enter a New Year, isn't it nice to know that in our times of struggle, Jesus is watching over, providing protection, and ready to meet us right where we are? Just one more reason to call Him Savior and Lord as we prepare ourselves for whatever comes our way.

Reflection

Are you experiencing a life storm now? Are its circumstances gathered ominously around you? Do you find yourself consumed by the clouds that seem to be gathering? Or are you actively looking for Him? As you look back on past storms, what has the Lord taught you about Himself and His ways?

JANUARY 8
(Y1, D2)

As Is? Or Change?

For everyone has sinned; we all fall short of God's glorious standard.

—Romans 3:23 (NLT)

If you have ever purchased a used car or bought something at a yard sale, you may have exercised the "as is" principle. Usually, one is given the right to a reasonable inspection. They might take the car for a test drive or ask the person running the yard sale if the piece is in workable condition. But once there is an exchange of title or cash, the item is yours, and you forfeit the right to complain if the item is faulty. Similarly, persons who have not maintained their home may list their property as a "fixer-upper" or might otherwise be tempted to sell to one of those "We Buy Your Home" organizations for a quick cash-on-the-line bargain. The promise of an "as is" sale could be music to one's ears in today's throwaway society, allowing us the opportunity to exercise the old adage "One man's junk is another man's treasure." It is a given that others can sometimes see great value in what you are willing to discard.

This effort to discard is often applied to persons as well. A serious disagreement with a friend or colleague can put a once solid relationship in jeopardy. Marriages are severed, and divorces are frequently granted for reasons of "irreconcilable differences." Political notables and members of the rich and famous are rejected from our list of idolized figures when we discover that they may not represent what we once thought. How blessed we are to have a God who loves us and welcomes us into His loving arms, despite what we have done and who we are. Our culture is often quick to reject those who have become tarnished or are no longer useful to us. Looking down on lost people is perhaps the most hypocritical thing we can do. We must never forget that there have been times in our lives when we, too, were lost. We were broken and sinful, but Jesus came in and changed that. If we had the capability to change it ourselves, then we wouldn't need Him, and He most certainly wouldn't have had to die on the cross. The stark reality is that even those who have accepted Christ aren't perfect all the time in every situation. While we recognize that there are certain standards that apply to the Christian lifestyle, we must also acknowledge that Jesus is about forgiveness first. He forgives us before He helps to change us.

There are two occasions in scripture that Jesus essentially says, "Go and sin no more." This is noted in scripture when He healed an invalid by the Pool of Bethesda (John 5:1–15) and when He failed to pass judgment of a woman accused of adultery (John 8:3–11). While He cautioned them with these words, Jesus was not speaking of sinless perfection here. Instead, He offered an extension of mercy and a warning against a return to sinful lifestyle choices. Jesus was always the perfect balance of "grace and truth" (John 1:14 NIV). With forgiveness comes the expectation that we will not remain on the same path of rebelliousness, for those who know God's love will naturally want to obey Him. We will no doubt continue to be sinful at times, but sin is no longer a thoughtless choice. Christians should understand that the reason God wants us to stop sinning is simply because He desires what is best for us. Sin does not result in God's best. However, acts of sin don't cause Him to turn away from us, reject us, nor cast us out. It should be the goal of every Christian to "sin no more," recognizing the fact that "If we claim we have no sin, we are only fooling ourselves and not living in the truth" (1 John 1:8 NLT).

The "come as you are" philosophy is sometimes misunderstood or misapplied and leads us to think that it makes no difference how we live, as long as we believe. In the mind of one who just believes "God accepts me as I am," there is no objective standard of behavior. We falsely conclude that God accepts us because He is motivated exclusively by love. But if one is not following Jesus, there can be no relationship with Him. Furthermore, without a relationship, there can be no commitment. He requires us to confess and abandon our sins when we come to Him. He receives us just as we are, then begins to change us as we submit to Him in obedience. We reject corruption by walking with Jesus, inviting God into the dark places of our lives, and watching the light of His precious love cast out all sin. "This means that anyone who belongs to Christ has become a new person. The old life is gone; a new life has begun!" (2 Corinthians 5:17 NLT). As we rest on the crossover of another year, it is pertinent for each of us to consider what parts of our life Christ would accept "as is" or what parts He would have us change.

Reflection

As you enter a new year, what aspects of your life do you believe Jesus would ask you to change? As a Christian, do you feel you have the right to allow yourself to judge another person? How can you explain the difference between condemning someone's actions and condemning the individual?

JANUARY 9
(Y2, D2)

Life Is Just Too Short

And he has given us this command: Anyone who loves
God must also love their brother and sister.

—1 John 4:21 (NIV)

A number of years ago, *The Hatfields and the McCoys* aired as a television mini-series. If you don't know the history of these post-Civil War era neighbors separated only by a river in West Virginia and Kentucky, suffice it to say, it's quite a drama. Once close friends, the heads of the two families, explode with hostility after increasing tensions and misunderstandings. And thus, the saga unfolds. It prompts one to ask how many of our own families or neighborhoods are filled with resentments and hatred that have been handed down through the generations? We know that we don't have time for certain folks or can't stand that side of the family. But because years have passed (as well as people), we have no idea why. We just know that they are "no good" because that's what we've always been told. Well, let me tell you, my friend, life is too short. I wonder how many people have gone to their graves, never getting to know a really wonderful person because they were held back by ill-favored sentiments.

During a low time in my life, a friend and I had drifted apart. I had a feeling that she was angry with me. While lesser-known acquaintances had taken the opportunity to reach out to me, there had been no contact from this older friend. I began to develop bitterness and anger because she had not made an effort to get in touch. That year, on her birthday, while engaged in a task of which we were both quite familiar, I was prompted to think of my friend. Without much hesitation, I picked up the phone and called, stating that through my activity that day, I had been reminded of her and accordingly remembered her birthday. The call was short, and my friend seem to be surprised by my call. But at least she came across as gracious. It was a beginning of the healing of my resentment for her inattentiveness.

Today's lead-in scripture passage is preceded with thoughtful and challenging verses. They include this one: "We love each other because he loved us first. If someone says, 'I love God,' but hates a fellow believer, that person is a liar; for if we don't love people we can see, how can we love God, whom we cannot see?" (1 John 4:19–20 NIV). In other words, we cannot love the Creator (whom we *have not* seen) and at the same time hate the Creation (whom we *have* seen). John stresses in verse 21 the fruitless vanity of professing to love the Lord when there is hatred in one's heart for another. The more a true believer is being conformed into the image and likeness of Christ, the greater will be their love toward a brother, sister, and, yes, even one who is considered to be an enemy.

Consider bitterness, jealousy, misinterpretation, stubbornness, lack of forgiveness—they all take you down a path you don't want to go. It's indeed a low road, one that leads to hatred, destruction, and possible woundedness. Worse yet, it may ruin a relationship opportunity that may have otherwise been a blessing. Loving others as Christ loved us is not something that we can easily do with our own human strength. However, it is achievable because God indwells in the heart of those who love Him and are striving to walk in spirit and truth. He works in the lives of those who are living by faith and not by sight. His love is perfected in all who are growing in grace and in a knowledge of the Lord Jesus Christ.

It would serve us well to remember a quote by the late Dr. Martin Luther King Jr. who said, "Let no man pull you so low as to hate him." So move forward. Get through it, get by it, get on with it, for life on this earthly test ground is really far too short.

Reflection

For what person in your life do you hold a grudge, resentment, or hatred? Can you remember why? Would you be willing to take the first step to build a bridge, even if you perceive the problem was caused by the other person? Do you need to seek or offer forgiveness? Consider giving prayerful consideration that God will remove your feelings so that you can begin to repair the damage before it's too late.

JANUARY 10
(Y3, D2)

Return to Sender

All the believers were one in heart and mind. No one claimed that any of
their possessions was their own, but they shared everything they had.

—Acts 4:32 NIV

One day in early January, I went to the mailbox and was going through the various pieces I had received. Among them was a returned Christmas card that I had sent to a friend weeks before. On it, there was a sticker marked "Vacant—Unable to Forward." Knowing that my former work colleague had been in and out of remission for the past decade, I assumed those words most likely meant the worst. A quick search, and I was able to locate an online obituary and came to realize that she had died about four months before. The last time I had visited with her, I could tell that she was failing. But I was with her that day for several hours, and we were able to share a meal together at a local restaurant near her home. She was in good spirits and determined to be here for a while longer. I intended to visit again, but sometimes, life gets in the way. Now a tear ran down my face, and I felt a bit guilty for not having done so.

Quite a few years ago, my friend and I worked for the same company. On one occasion, we needed to attend a conference at the other end of the state. I suggested that we take the training order to avoid the hassle of the drive ending up in a city with which neither one of us was familiar. The trip proved to be a great time together, and as I look back, I now realize it was on that occasion that I first came to call her a friend. Although we shared some homemade sandwiches and laughed together, there were also special moments on that trek when we spoke about our faith. Although the churches we attended were both Christian, there were some very distinct denominational differences. I asked her if she was comfortable talking about her place of worship and some of the variances between her church and the one in which I had been raised. We had a wonderful conversation and gained a new level of understanding for each other's faith journey. Our common experience that day helped me to feel assured in sharing a prayer with her the last time we were together.

19

I may have regrets about not having been in contact with my friend more regularly. But nothing separated us in matters of faith. Even though we may have experienced different styles of worship, I am sure that we knew the same God. Paul said, "So it is with Christ's body. We are many parts of one body, and we all belong to each other" (Romans 12:5 NLT). In worship, one will raise his hands to praise God; another is not comfortable doing this. One is baptized by immersion, still others by sprinkling or pouring. Dipping the bread into a common chalice instead of using a piece of bread and an individual cup may be one's preferred method of receiving the sacrament. These are all variances in the Christian church that can separate us and provide labels such as fundamental, evangelical, or charismatic. The psalmist wrote "How good and pleasant it is when God's people live together in unity!" (Psalm 133:1 NLT).

It is apparent from scripture that in the early church, various groups were in competition and often in disagreement with each other about faith practices. It should not surprise us then that this has persisted through the ages and is true even today. It might be fair to ask if we become divisive and argue about such things, what kind of witness do we become to those who have not yet come to know Jesus as Lord and Savior? "I appeal to you, brothers and sisters, in the name of our Lord Jesus Christ, that all of you agree with one another in what you say and that there be no divisions among you, but that you be perfectly united in mind and thought" (1 Corinthians 1:10 NIV). I am glad I had that journey with my friend when we talked about our faith. As I looked at the card addressed to her one more time, I once again read those words "Return to Sender." I have no doubt that's where she was—with the one who sent her here in the first place. My hope is that one day, I will be able to once again break bread with her as we do so in the presence of our God.

Reflection

Are there times that you have debated with fellow believers over worship practices? The next time this occurs, how can you refocus the discussion on Jesus' words and example? What are ways that we might strive for strong unity, less disagreement, and serve to be a better witness for the world?

JANUARY 11
(Y4, D2)

Oil, Ice Cream, and Living Water

On the last and greatest day of the festival, Jesus stood and said in a loud voice,
"Let anyone who is thirsty come to me and drink. Whoever believes in me, as
Scripture has said, rivers of living water will flow from within them."

—John 7:37–38 (NIV)

In the classic movie *The Wizard of Oz*, the main character, Dorothy, meets a motley cast of misfits as she traverses down the yellow brick road on her way to Emerald City. One of the merry band is the Tin Man who on their first encounter looks like a metallic statue standing in the middle of the woods. A muffled high-pitched sound resonates from the body-like structure as Dorothy and her newly found friend, the Scarecrow, inspect their discovery. A resemblance of a voice from within appears to be saying the words "Oil Can" as the two locate an actual can of oil not too far away. A few squirts to the mouth and the joints, and the silver-plated being begins to speak and then gradually move around. He says that he has been that way for ages, ever since one day when he was chopping down a tree and it began to rain. Now with the oil application, he has found new life.

Not so long ago, I experienced my own oil can story. I was engaged in the process of making homemade ice cream using an old motor contraption that has been in our family for many years. The apparatus has saved a lot of churning-by-hand and has produced hundreds of gallons of frozen delight for many special events. On this particular day, the freezer was not mixing well, and I thought that I had perhaps misconnected something. So I disengaged the freezer from the motor and tried several approaches, but I soon became discouraged. I was left to conclude that after many years of hard work, the old motor had just burned itself out. As a last-ditch effort, I grabbed a can of WD-40 and sprayed any visible moving part that I could find. Reluctantly, I plugged in the machine, and it began to purr like a baby kitten. All it needed was a few drops of oil, and like the Tin Man, it had also found new life.

One day, Jesus encountered a Samaritan woman by a well and asked her for a drink. She was surprised that this Jewish man would make such a request of her, for in that day, Jews did not associate with Samaritans. She was even more shocked to learn that He knew everything about her and concluded that He must be a prophet. Jesus told her, "If you knew the gift of God and who it is that asks you for a drink, you would have asked him and he would have given you living water" (John 4:10). Seeing that she was perplexed, he further explained, "Everyone who drinks this water will be thirsty again, but whoever drinks the water I give them will never thirst. Indeed, the water I give them will become in them a spring of water welling up to eternal life" (John 4:13–14 NIV). Although she may have been naïve about many things, she gave indication that she had some awareness: "The woman said, 'I know the Messiah is coming—the one who is called Christ. When he comes, he will explain everything to us'" (John 4:25 NLT). Then He revealed Himself to her.

Jesus was offering the living water of eternal life that only the Holy Spirit gives. It is a continual source of life that indwells in the heart of all believers, and it's always active and flowing. David understood this need when he spoke these words: "O God, you are my God; I earnestly search for you. My soul thirsts for you; my whole body longs for you in this parched and weary land where there is no water" (Psalm 63:1 NLT). The Tin Man, my family's ice-cream motor, and the Samaritan woman were all given the opportunity to experience new life. The main difference between the three is that Jesus was promising a healing with free-flowing water that would never need replaced. Eventually, the Tin Man and the motor are going to need oil again, and through time, they will both end up in a state of disrepair. And therein lies the choice for each one of us. We can continue to drink from the world's sources as we search for lasting spiritual fulfillment, and we will be sure to thirst again. But one drink from the "living water" that Jesus offers, and we'll never be the same. Jesus told the Samaritan woman all she needed to do was ask. The Tin Man knew what He needed and made it known. We would do best to take their lead.

Reflection

What cultural restrictions do we face today that may keep us from talking with others about Christ? Do you know an individual who you think would not be interested in the gospel? How might you ask for the guidance of the Holy Spirit to bridge your reluctance to approach such a person?

JANUARY 12
(Y5, D2)

Excess Baggage

Give your burdens to the LORD, and he will take care of you.
He will not permit the godly to slip and fall.

—Psalm 55:22 (NLT)

I recall a time when I was checking my luggage at an airport before going to the gate. As I placed my bag on the scale, the associate told me that it exceeded the weight limit by several pounds. I was also informed that if I decided to check the bag as it was, I would have to pay a fee. When I inquired what the fee would be, I was shocked at the amount. Not wishing to delay all those who were in line behind me, I asked if there were any other options. The attendant looked at me as if she wanted to say, "Duh." Then she stated the obvious, "Sir, I suggest that you simply remove a few items from the bag you are checking and place them in your carry on." I did so quickly, and I was good to go. I do remember thinking at the time that this was stupid because I would be taking the same amount of weight on the plane. But I did not express my objection. If transferring some of the weight relieved the burden of paying the extra fee, then all parties would be satisfied.

It's that time of year when we can feel overwhelmed as though we are personally carrying excess baggage. The beginning of the year presents us with new goals with which we have set to challenge ourselves or, even worse, may have been established for us by someone else. It's a time when we realize that we have lived in excess over the holidays. Now we have the additional pounds to lose or the extra fees to pay on our credit cards. Or perhaps both. Routine obligations which have been postponed because of the season are now back on our schedule. Additionally, we may have seen persons we haven't seen in a while. This often reignites old arguments or perhaps connects us with extra responsibilities or concerns. These burdens present themselves in the dullest of the seasons when the weather is gloomy and summer vacation seems a long way off. So we take a deep sigh, and like I did with my overloaded luggage, we take a quick assessment of just what our options might be to relieve some of the burdens at hand.

Enter Jesus, saying, "Come to me, all of you who are weary and carry heavy burdens, and I will give you rest. Take my yoke upon you. Let me teach you, because I am humble and gentle at heart, and you will find rest for your souls. For my yoke is easy to bear, and the burden I give you is light" (Matthew 11:28–30 NLT). Here, Jesus drew a distinct contrast between the Pharisees and Himself. In His time, these religious leaders had established lists of spiritual duties to keep the Jewish people from breaking God's laws. The lists were long and burdensome, often too extensive to be kept, even by the religious leaders themselves. Jesus uses the symbol of a yoke to demonstrate how he will help us carry our burdens. In Jesus' day and for centuries thereafter, a wooden yoke would often be utilized to join two animals together. The result was that their combined strength could pull a load that would have been difficult for one animal to move alone. Unlike the requirements imposed by the Pharisees, Jesus states that His burden on us is light. He asks us simply to believe and trust in Him. He carries the burden meant for us all the way to the cross where His perfect obedience and righteousness are exchanged for our sin.

The Apostle Paul explained it this way: "For God made Christ, who never sinned, to be the offering for our sin, so that we could be made right with God through Christ" (2 Corinthians 5:21 NLT). Jesus never promised that He would remove all the difficulties of our lives. But He did promise that if we followed Him, He would provide the rest and forgiveness we need to face our life's challenges. In that regard, we do not bear our burdens alone. As with my luggage, the weight is still there, but the load has been shifted. So as the song says, just "Give Them All to Jesus"—your "shattered dreams, wounded hearts, broken toys" (Phil Johnson and Bob Benson). When we become yoked with Jesus, the excess baggage we have been trying to carry alone will become oh so much lighter.

Reflection

What are the burdens you are facing or have been trying to carry for a long time? How might you begin to partner with Jesus to lessen your load? If you know someone who seems to be carrying the weight of the world on their shoulders, would you be able to use Jesus' illustration of the yoke as a demonstration of His love for each of us?

JANUARY 13
(Y6, D2)

Underestimating His Power

Now all glory to God, who is able, through his mighty power at work within us, to accomplish infinitely more than we might ask or think.

—Ephesians 3:20 (NLT)

In January of 1815, the War of 1812 was not going well for the United States. When we remember Andrew Jackson's role in the conflict known as the Battle of New Orleans, we seldom hear about his relationship with the Ursuline nuns of that city. But we should. On January 8, 1815, Jackson and his mostly untrained militia of only a few thousand were heavily outnumbered by a British army of veteran soldiers about three times its size. However, the US handed the British the most lopsided defeat in their history, inflicting over 2,000 casualties with minimal American lives lost. The night before the Battle of New Orleans, a large wooden statue of Mary and the child Jesus, known as Our Lady of Prompt Succor, was placed above the chapel entrance. All night long, the Ursuline sisters and New Orleans citizens prayed for an American victory. The mother and nuns were still at prayer on January 8 when a courier arrived at the church, making a dramatic entrance and proclaiming that General Jackson was victorious. After the battle, "Old Hickory" Jackson came to the convent to thank the nuns for their prayers. He stated, "The divine providence of God through the intercession of Our Lady of Prompt Succor has shielded us and granted this stupendous miracle." In later years, whenever Jackson went to New Orleans, he always visited the Ursuline Convent where an annual Mass of Thanksgiving has been held faithfully since 1815.

In God's Word, we are introduced to Gideon, the fifth judge of Israel. He played a small but important role in the history of God's people. An angel spoke to Gideon who was called upon as a reluctant leader to free Israel from its enemy, the Midianites. After testing the Lord in several ways, Gideon came to be convinced of God's power. Even though Gideon's army was greatly outnumbered, the Lord continued to reduce his force from thousands to only 300 through a series of events. "That night, the LORD said, 'Get up! Go down into the Midianite camp, for I have given you victory over them!'" (Judges 7:9 NLT). After overhearing a man in one of the Midianite outposts reveal a dream he had, Gideon was encouraged. He divided his 300 men into three groups of 100 each. Armed with clay jars, torches, and trumpets, they spaced themselves around the enemy camp. When signaled:

> All three groups blew their horns and broke their jars. They held the blazing torches in their left hands and the horns in their right hands, and they all shouted, "A sword for the LORD and for Gideon!" Each man stood at his position around the camp and watched as all the Midianites rushed around in a panic, shouting as they ran to escape. When the 300 Israelites blew their rams' horns, the LORD caused the warriors in the camp to fight against each other with their swords. Those who were not killed fled to places as far away." (Judges 7:20–22 NLT)

In this passage, we learn that God is much more powerful than we ever give Him credit for being. God's power is enough to triumph in any conflict, but so often, we fail to comprehend the mightiness of that power. That is because we try to define who God is by our limited understanding of His divine nature. Jesus was once asked by His disciples, who could receive the gift of salvation? "Jesus looked at them intently and said, 'Humanly speaking, it is impossible. But with God everything is possible'" (Matthew 19:26 NLT). As our journey deepens with Him, we will discover that God hears those who seek His intervention through their prayers. All things are indeed possible with God, and our God does abundantly more than we can ask or imagine. When we trust His power to work in our lives without explanation, our faith is increased. Jesus said, "You may ask me for anything in my name, and I will do it" (John 14:14 NIV). American pastor and author David Platt states it this way: "Nothing is impossible for the people of God who trust the power of God to accomplish the will of God." While we may not be called upon to lead a conflict on the battlefield with seemingly far too few, there undoubtedly will be times when the adversities we face will leave us feeling overwhelmed, without much hope or direction. Then we come to realize that our spiritual victories only ever occur because of God's power and not through our own. We must never underestimate the mighty power of what He can accomplish in our lives.

Reflection

Have you experienced God's enormous power for overcoming life's opposing forces? What changes might you consider making as you face your current challenges? Will you dare give what little you have to God, trusting that He will take your small offering and make something amazing out of it?

JANUARY 14
(Y7, D2)

Listen More, Babble Less

But avoid irreverent babble, for it will lead people into more and more ungodliness.

—2 Timothy 2:16 (ESV)

Joan was one of those persons who seemingly knew something about everything, and she would be the first to tell you. People who knew her well would sarcastically say that "what Joan doesn't know isn't worth knowing." Of course, with her supposed infinite amount of knowledge came the opinions. Although she was frequently labeled as a gossip, I'm not really convinced that was her true intention. She just didn't have much of a skill for listening. Some would say she just loved to hear herself talk. Joan could talk incessantly about trivial matters that in the whole scheme of things didn't matter all that much. I personally found her rather exhausting to be around and would quickly find an excuse to take my leave if I was scheduled to be with her for very long. Still, I suppose in some ways, we all find ourselves to be a bit like Joan from time to time. When we become so full of ourselves and our meaningless chatter, we often find that there is little, if any, room for God. If and when this occurs, we are in serious trouble.

Such was the case of the descendants of Noah in Babylonia over 4,000 years ago when the world had "one language and a common speech" (Genesis 11:1 NIV). Those who populated the earth had become skilled in construction and decided to build a city with a tower that would reach to heaven. In doing so, they wanted to make a name for themselves and also prevent their population from being scattered. God came to see their city and the tower they were building. In His infinite wisdom, He knew that the successful completion of their project would only serve to isolate the people from Him. God did not like the pride in their hearts, so He caused them to suddenly speak different languages. In doing so, they became disorderly and could not communicate and work together to finish the tower. This resulted in what they had feared the most—their scattering across the earth. The structure was named the Tower of Babel because the word *babble* means confusion. This story is a powerful reminder of how important it is to obey God's Word and to not think that we can build a life in which we propose to know it all.

Today things have not changed all that much. Useless babble continues to clutter the world around us. From cell phones to social media, from talk shows to the break room at work, it consumes our culture, resulting in a decreasing amount of opportunity for a meaningful exchange of ideas. More and more, if you don't agree with what I am saying, well, then there's just no point in having a conversation. How sad for our society that a healthy debate where people actually listen to one another is in many arenas no longer socially acceptable. The Apostle Paul provided this wise counsel to his student, Timothy: "Turn away from godless chatter and the opposing ideas of what is falsely called knowledge" (1 Timothy 6:20 NIV). If he could talk to us now, he might say that "we look without seeing, listen without hearing, and speak without understanding." Sometimes, even in Christian circles where you would least expect it, a true connection with God often gets shoved aside because of our worthless chatter and arrogance.

The reason many of us speak so many idle words is that we sometimes speak far too many. We talk so much that we have no time to think and no time to listen to each other or to hear the voice of God. The Old Testament identifies this as foolishness: "To answer before listening—that is folly and shame" (Proverbs 18:13 NIV). We live in a time when never before have so many been able to say (and hear) so much in so many ways. The airwaves, cyber waves, print waves, and every other wave of human understanding have bombarded our minds. This has resulted in an information overload, much of which is unhelpful if not downright misleading or false. We must therefore take personal responsibility for the words we digest as well as those that we repeat. Jesus gave us this warning: "You must give an account on judgment day for every idle word you speak. The words you say will either acquit you or condemn you" (Matthew 12:36 NLT). We would do well to listen more and speak less, and when we do speak, learn to follow His lead. As we draw closer in our relationship with the Lord—perhaps, bottom line, we need to take a little more time to listen and spend a lot less time engaging in useless babble.

Reflection

Are there any man-made "stairways to heaven" you are building in your own life? Who are you listening to as you formulate and evaluate your life plans? Have you taken time to listen and consider the thoughts of others as well as the counsel of God's Word as you focus on these goals?

JANUARY 15
(Y1, D3)

A Dose of Humility

Do nothing out of selfish ambition or vain conceit. Rather,
in humility value others above yourselves.

—Philippians 2:3

Sam Rayburn served as the Speaker of the House of Representatives in the United States Congress for seventeen years. As the Speaker, Rayburn wielded incredible power and prestige. He was third in the line of succession to the presidency. On one occasion, he found out that the teenage daughter of a reporter friend had tragically died. Early the next morning, he knocked on the door of his friend. When the door opened, Rayburn asked if there was anything he could do. The reporter stammered and replied, "I don't think there is anything. We are making all the arrangements."

"Well, have you had your coffee this morning?" he asked.

"No. We haven't had time," said the grieving man.

The Speaker of the House replied, "Well, I can at least make the coffee."

As he watched this powerful man make him coffee, the father suddenly remembered something. "Mr. Speaker, I thought you were supposed to be having breakfast at the White House this morning."

His answer was, "I was, but I called the president and told him I had a friend who was in trouble and I couldn't come." Sam Rayburn turned down breakfast with the President of the United States to make coffee for a grieving friend. That was humility in the mid-1900s.

Humility is believing and acting with the attitude of "It's not about me." It can be exercised by anyone and, on occasion, is demonstrated by people of great power. Every four years, a political leader takes the oath of office as President of the United States. We yearn for leaders who not only speak humble words but who also seek to personify acts of humility. Stories about Abraham Lincoln teach us many things about the importance of being humble. One such lesson is embodied in a famous moment on a battlefield of the Civil War in Gettysburg, Pennsylvania. Lincoln asserted that "the world will little note, nor long remember, what we say here." That phrase was not an expression of false modesty nor even a prediction of how he might be remembered. It was, rather, a symbol of deep-seated humility. On another occasion, in December 1859, Lincoln responded to a request for a short sketch of his life by writing: "There is not much of it, for the reason, I suppose, that there is not much of me. If anything be made out of it, I wish to be modest, and not go beyond the material." We need leaders willing to live up to Lincoln's understanding that humility breeds compassion while arrogance can only lead to division.

Many theologians teach that humility is *the* core Christian value, the characteristic that makes us most like Jesus. Humility helps us to realize that even though we may be blessed with gifts and talents, this does not make us better than anyone else. A true sign of humility involves helping others when we will gain absolutely nothing from it. Christ's power strengthens us to love God above all and our neighbors as ourselves. God has promised to give grace to the humble while He opposes the proud. Matthew 23:12 (NIV) says, "For those who exalt themselves will be humbled, and those who humble themselves will be exalted." We must realize that humility is a heart attitude, not merely an outward demeanor. Many of us put on a show of humility but still have a heart full of pride and arrogance. The Bible makes it clear that a humble heart is essential to spiritual growth. "As God's chosen people, holy and dearly loved, clothe yourselves with compassion, kindness, humility, gentleness and patience" (Colossians 3:12 NIV).

The Reverend Billy Graham wrote:

> The greatest act of humility in the history of the universe was when Jesus Christ stooped to die on the cross of Calvary. And before any man can get to heaven, he must kneel at the foot of the cross and acknowledge that he is a sinner, that he has broken the Ten Commandments of God, and that he needs the grace of God in Christ. No man can come proudly to the Savior.

Directed by God's love, people who are humble in spirit invest themselves in what the world often considers to be weakness; they move to finding delight when others are in the spotlight. "So humble yourselves under the mighty power of God, and at the right time he will lift you up in honor" (1 Peter 5:6 NLT). While it may be a hard pill to swallow, a dose of humility could do many of us some good each and every day.

Reflection

Do you find yourself seeking recognition for the things you do? Or do you work to try to demonstrate acts of kindness to others with a sense of humility? Can you think of specific ways you might humbly serve others in order to point them to Jesus? If asked, would you be able to explain that your actions are a mere representation of the one who gave of Himself on our behalf? How would you encourage another who is showing ambition and arrogance to consider being a humbler person?

JANUARY 16
(Y2, D3)

On Assignment with a Purpose

Whatever you do, work at it with all your heart, as working
for the Lord, not for human masters."

—Colossians 3:23 (NIV)

At an early age, we make a choice to accept assignments seriously or not. Whether it's homework or doing our chores, the task of finalizing those projects is often carried out with the encouragement of another person. We quickly learn throughout the course of our lives that we gain satisfaction in carrying out our assignments through various means of motivation. For instance, we may receive a reward for every A we achieve or we might get a job promotion if we project better ideas than our colleagues. If we grow to accept our assignments seriously, we will not permit ourself to be diverted from its purpose.

I once heard a story about a young American engineer named Billy who was sent by his company on a two-year assignment to Ireland. He accepted because it would enable him to earn enough to marry his longtime girlfriend, Irene. This was long before easy access to modern communication existed, so they corresponded by letter. As the lonely weeks went by, Irene began expressing doubts that Billy was being faithful to her. He adamantly responded that although the local Irish girls could be tempting, he was paying no attention to them. Not long after, Billy received a package containing a note from Irene and a harmonica. "I'm sending this to you," she wrote, "so you can learn to play it and have something to take your mind off those girls."

Billy replied, "Thanks for the harmonica. I'm practicing on it every night and thinking of you." At the end of his two-year stint, Billy was transferred back home to company headquarters and would be reunited with Irene.

When he first went to embrace her, Irene held up a hand and said sternly, "Just hold on there a minute, Billy. Before any serious affection gets started here, let me hear you play that harmonica." Had he taken his assignment seriously or had he been diverted?

There were many persons in the Bible who were given serious assignments. Of course, there was Noah who took on the duty of building an ark. Moses had the huge task of leading millions of the Israelites out of Egypt, followed by Joshua who assumed the torch to bring them into the promised land. Even though King David was engaged in collecting materials for building a temple in Jerusalem, it was his son, Solomon, who would be charged with the assignment of having it constructed. When Jesus called his first disciples, he gave them a clear task and set them on a destined path. "And he said to them, 'Follow me, and I will make you fishers of men'" (Matthew 4:19 KJV). Later, He provided His followers with their greatest assignment in carrying out the Great Commission: "Therefore go and make disciples of all nations, baptizing them in the name of the Father and of the Son and of the Holy Spirit, and teaching them to obey everything I have commanded you" (Matthew 28:19–20 NIV). Today, those who are called to be missionaries set aside personal ambitions in order to be witnesses of the Gospel. While a Christian missionary is specifically called by God and sent out by a local church, every Christian has their own mission to make disciples. All followers of Christ are on assignment to bring glory to God by sharing the Word of His righteous life, sacrificial death, and absolute authority over all of creation.

God has called and assigned an amazing purpose for your life. It can only be unlocked through your response to His assignments and developed over the course of your faith journey. If your story was documented as a book, your calling would be its title. Your spiritual gifts would shine in the unique writing style and illustrations. The individual chapters would highlight the various assignments throughout your walk with Him. Those assignments would likely unfold in big and small packages. Your job is to unwrap them, accept them, and have faith that our Lord will help you carry them out. As you accept the challenge by stating, "Here I am. Send me" (Isaiah 6:8 NIV), some assignments may seem like side roads to your destination. But all will lead to His purposes as you trust Him with the ultimate wisdom of knowing how to prepare and equip you. At the same time, He will increase the measure of grace in your life to ultimately fulfill your call. One day, each of us will stand before Jesus and give an account on how well we did in accomplishing His mission. He won't need to ask us to audition by playing the harmonica. He'll already know if we seriously accepted our assignment and whether or not we completed it with purpose.

Reflection

What is the primary assignment God has given to you to share with others? Do you sometimes consider your position in life to be too simple to see yourself as an ambassador for the kingdom? How can you work in refocusing your daily assignments to reflect an increased understanding of the heart of God?

JANUARY 17
(Y3, D3)

Out of Routine

But seek first his kingdom and his righteousness, and all these things will be given to you as well."

—Matthew 6:33 (NIV)

"Break routine and add adventure to your life." I think that is close to the words I saw in an advertisement. This time of year, a break in routine is sometimes helpful for those of us who live in certain sections of the country. For many, winter can be a depressing time, and it is not unusual to come down with a good dose of "cabin fever," provoking a strong desire for some type of getaway vacation. For others, however, the basic establishment and maintenance of a good daily routine can enhance their quality of life. This includes children who require structure in their lives, but it can also apply to the elderly who sometimes have poor nutrition habits and are frequently too immobile. It is common knowledge that coffee drinkers often notice that their bodies feel sluggish if they miss their morning brew. When your body requires a certain amount of physical resilience, you might lose your ability to properly function if you do not sustain at least some form of routine exercise.

We have all had the best of intentions with maintaining a sense of routine in our relationship habits as well. We graduate from college and plan to stay in close contact with our friends with whom we experienced four close years of comradery. We are about to change jobs, and on the last day, as we say goodbye to our soon-to-be former colleagues, we promise to keep in touch. Frequent phone calls or texts become less numerous. An occasional email can quickly become an annual birthday or Christmas card. Before you know it, there is less in common, and the out-of-routine becomes the out-of-touch forever. One must wonder if our journey with Christ isn't in jeopardy of becoming disconnected as well. I know, for myself, that when my day starts later than usual and I skip my morning devotions or if I become extremely tired and fall asleep before or during my bedtime prayers, I will feel out of sync.

So if we miss doing our daily Bible reading or fail to come to God in prayer with a concern, does that inhibit our relationship with Him? In the short term, probably not. After all, God created us and understands that we are human. However, He desires that we fellowship with Him.

Getting out of routine can obstruct that relationship, not because God is no longer there but rather because we aren't. It's important for us to understand that we don't pray for God's sake but rather for our own. If we don't practice good Christian habits when we are busy and our journey is going well, then where do we turn when we find ourselves in the valley rather than on the mountaintop? Martin Luther King stated it this way: "The ultimate measure of a man is not where he stands in the moments of comfort and convenience, but where he stands at times of challenge and controversy." If we have not maintained close contact with God, it is likely that our lack of routine will remind us to reach out to Him in those trying times.

Working God into our schedule requires discipline, especially for stressed individuals. But when we allow His Word to fill our minds as we begin and end our day, we stand a much better chance of our thoughts turning to Him during those times of persisting difficulty. In doing so, we give ourselves an opening to rely on His wisdom rather than our own inclinations. "My child, pay attention to what I say. Listen carefully to my words. Don't lose sight of them. Let them penetrate deep into your heart, for they bring life to those who find them, and healing to their whole body" (Proverbs 4:20–22 NLT). Our society spends a lot of time and dollars sponsoring healthy diets and exercise, but we lack consideration for any effort to promote good spiritual habits. The Apostle Paul would warn us: "For physical training is of some value, but godliness has value for all things, holding promise for both the present life and the life to come" (1 Timothy 4:8 NIV). Author Herbert Lockyer says, "A good, healthy, natural or spiritual appetite is a gift of God, and something for which to be grateful." Are you hungry? Our heavenly Father waits patiently for us to resume our routine and make Him first in our life. In doing so, we will be empowered to deal with those valley experiences, but it will also prepare us for eternal fellowship with Him.

Reflection

What are the habits you practice on a regular basis to maintain a close connection with God? How do you become aware when you are spending too much time on the things of this world? What kind of routine might you put in place this week to assure that you are upholding a proper spiritual discipline and working toward a deeper relationship with your Creator?

JANUARY 18
(Y4, D3)

First, Do No Harm

We put no stumbling block in anyone's path, so that our ministry will not be discredited.

—2 Corinthians 6:3 (NIV)

If you were a health care student, one of the general principles you would learn is to "do no harm." It is a reminder to all who practice that before they do an intervention or a procedure. They should first consider any possible harm that might occur to the person whom they are treating. Regarded as an historic rite of passage for those who are about to become physicians, the Hippocratic Oath contains the phrase "Also I will, according to my ability and judgment, prescribe a regimen for the health of the sick; but I will utterly reject harm and mischief." These days, it seems quite apparent that political candidates practice the opposite of this philosophy. Theirs is more about surfacing any past negative history in their opponent's life so that their credibility will be questioned, and an advantageous position would be gained. To be sure, political adversaries do not follow the counsel to "make every effort to do what leads to peace and to mutual edification" (Romans 14:19 NIV).

Most likely, there has been a time in your life when you have stumbled and hurt your toe. Sometimes this can be quite painful, and the nail will turn black as a lasting reminder of the incident. Eventually, it heals and returns to normal. But in a few cases, your toe may become broken or the nail damaged to such an extent that it needs special attention. In fact, for a long time, the injury can serve as a lasting reminder of the hurt that was caused. Life can be like that as well. There are times in our lives when we recover quite quickly after we falter. On other occasions, it can affect us dramatically. Likewise, there may be situations when we stumble, and in our act of doing so, it can have a profound effect on those around us. The Bible makes many references to stumbling, particularly as it relates to others. It goes so far as to even caution how we act with those who oppose us. "Do not gloat when your enemy falls; when he stumbles, do not let your heart rejoice" (Proverbs 24:17 NIV).

We must scrutinize our interactions with all persons and, in particular, the witness we bear as we connect with others. As we mature in our faith, there will be experiences when our practices, however nonthreatening to us, may expose a vulnerability in another. For instance, our view might be that having a glass of wine with dinner is entirely acceptable. However, if among our guests there are those whose discipline does not condone the consumption of alcohol, then we would be wrong to serve it. After all, how might you feel if in the group there was an individual who, by no knowledge of your own, was a recovered alcoholic? Indeed, we have all been faced with situations where it might be better to do nothing rather than to risk doing more harm than good. Paul would tell us, "Take care that this right of yours does not somehow become a stumbling block to the weak" (1 Corinthians 8:9 ESV).

These days, our society condones doing what feels right and to exercise our right to speak out. The greatest freedom we have is to consider others' welfare over our own. The Apostle Paul said:

> So then each of us will give an account of ourselves to God. Therefore let us stop passing judgment on one another. Instead, make up your mind not to put any stumbling block or obstacle in the way of a brother or sister... So whatever you believe about these things keep between yourself and God. Blessed is the one who does not condemn himself by what he approves. (Romans 14:12–13, 22 NIV)

While hitting one's toe can cause a person to physically trip, we never want to give ourselves permission to become a spiritual stumbling block, causing damage to or weakening the faith of another. As we come into contact or fellowship with others, we might take heed from the Latin phrase *Primum non nocere*. It is translated to mean "First, do no harm." Lord, help us to examine our interactions with those in the world around us in order that we do not cause them to stumble and bring harm to their relationship with you.

Reflection

Have there been occasions when you set a poor example for nonbelievers so that being a Christian is the last thing they would want to do? Are there times when you might have said or done something that has caused another person's relationship with Christ to be compromised? How might we implement the philosophy "First, do no harm" when asked for an opinion while in the company of others?

JANUARY 19
(Y5, D3)

Forsake the Foolish

For the fool speaks folly, and his heart is busy with iniquity, to practice ungodliness, to utter error concerning the LORD, to leave the craving of the hungry unsatisfied, and to deprive the thirsty of drink.

—Isaiah 32:6 (ESV)

He suffered from depression throughout much of his life. At the age of twelve, distraught at the news of his grandmother's death, he jumped from a second-story window of the family home, allegedly attempting suicide. Although his family was deeply involved in the church, the young man questioned religion throughout his adolescence, much to the dismay of his father who was an American Baptist minister. However, in his junior year, he took a Bible class, renewed his faith, began to envision a career in the ministry, and later graduated from seminary. He was a very high-energy man requiring only minimal hours of nightly sleep. But he was repeatedly hospitalized for periods of exhaustion when he could no longer function. He would rebound to travel all over the country and the world, sometimes giving multiple speeches and sermons daily. This was his pace for most of his short adult working life. Increasingly, he turned to tobacco and alcohol for support, and his extramarital affairs have been well-documented. Like most of us, he was a flawed individual.

Years after his death by assassination, Martin Luther King Jr. is the most widely known African-American leader of his era. His life and work have been honored with a national holiday celebrated annually on the third Monday in January near his birthday. As with many historical figures, he is remembered for his ability to lead and influence others. His deep commitment for civil rights through nonviolent means brought him distinction. His well-known and frequently quoted "I Have a Dream" speech has served to be a prominent part of his legacy. Because of his activism and his campaigns for social equality, we sometimes forget that King was a Christian minister. He once made the following observation about himself: "In the quiet recesses of my heart, I am fundamentally a clergyman, a Baptist preacher." Some of his lesser-known speeches came in the form of sermons spoken from church pulpits. One of those entitled "Why Jesus Called a Man a Fool" was delivered less than a year before he died.

King used the Parable of the Rich Fool as the basis for this sermon. Taken from the Gospel of Luke is the story of someone in a crowd who asks Jesus to intervene in a request to divide an inheritance. Jesus responds to the person in a manner which probably today would be stated, "Who made me your judge and jury?" He goes on to say that life is not about building up possessions. Then He recites this story:

> The ground of a certain rich man yielded an abundant harvest. He thought to himself, "What shall I do? I have no place to store my crops." Then he said, "This is what I'll do. I will tear down my barns and build bigger ones, and there I will store my surplus grain." And I'll say to myself, "You have plenty of grain laid up for many years. Take life easy; eat, drink and be merry." But God said to him, "You fool! This very night your life will be demanded from you. Then who will get what you have prepared for yourself?" This is how it will be with whoever stores up things for themselves but is not rich toward God. (Luke 12:16–21 NIV)

You might ask why Jesus would refer to the man as a fool. Simply, it was because he did not recognize his dependence on God. His plan was to build up earthly riches, never considering the fact that today, his life could be over. Then he would have died materially wealthy but spiritually deprived.

Somewhere along the line, I remember learning as a child that it was inappropriate to call another man a fool. Now that I have the wisdom of some years behind me, I have come to realize that if we are fortunate to spend many years on this earth, we each take our turns being one from time to time. Jesus said, "But I tell you that everyone who is angry with his brother or sister will be subject to judgment… Whoever says, 'You fool!' will be subject to hellfire" (Matthew 5:22 CSB). Here, Jesus is talking about anger that results in judgment. As Christians, we must preserve love and seek peace with others without delay. In doing so, we are reconciled to God through Christ. Perhaps the King James version states it best: "Forsake the foolish, and live; and go in the way of understanding" (Proverbs 9:6 KJV). I think King would like that, and without a doubt, I am most certain Jesus would.

Reflection

The Apostle Paul said that as we mature, we should discontinue our foolish ways (1 Corinthians 13:11). What are your foolish things? How might you seek God's guidance to overcome them in the days and weeks ahead?

JANUARY 20
(Y6, D3)

Greatness

Yours, O Lᴏʀᴅ, is the greatness, the power, the glory, the victory, and the
majesty. Everything in the heavens and on earth is yours, O Lᴏʀᴅ, and this
is your kingdom. We adore you as the one who is over all things.

—1 Chronicles 29:11 (NLT)

As the orderly and peaceful transfer of power takes place in America at least once every eight years, we are reminded that greatness is defined not by the person who ascends to the presidency but rather by the leadership of a nation founded on the principle of freedom. In 2016, the man who would become president ran on the theme "Make America Great Again," frequently emphasizing what he personally would be able to do for our nation. He did this at the same time as the sitting president of the opposing party campaigned that not voting for his candidate would be a "personal insult" to his legacy. Author of inspiration William Arthur Ward once said, "Greatness is not found in possessions, power, position, or prestige. It is discovered in goodness, humility, service, and character." Unfortunately, most persons who rise to this position claim that they understand with absolute clarity what ails the nation and how to go about repairing it. In politics, however, humility and well-intended acts of service are often superseded by arrogance and divisiveness in order that "a means to an end" is established.

It's a mistake to allow the world to define greatness. It is not about rank and status. It's not about how powerful we become, how rich we are, or whether we have some notable achievement in politics or sports. "I'm the greatest" was a famous line of the late world heavyweight boxing champ, Muhammad Ali. His biographer, Thomas Hauser, author of *Muhammad Ali: His Life and Times*, reflected on the champ following his death:

> We attended a tribute to Muhammad at the Smithsonian Institution in
> Washington DC. I made some opening remarks and referred to an incident that
> had occurred years earlier when Ali took a flight from Washington to New York.

As the flight crew readied for take-off, an attendant instructed, "Mr. Ali, please buckle your seat belt."

"Superman don't need no seat belt," Ali informed her.

"Mr. Ali," the flight attendant said sweetly, "Superman don't need no plane."

Ali fastened his seat belt.

Following a miracle where Jesus healed a boy possessed by an evil spirit, the crowd marveled at all He had done. The disciples told Him that they tried to stop a man driving out demons in His name because he was not one of "the chosen," meanwhile arguing who would be the greatest among them. "Jesus, knowing their thoughts, took a little child and had him stand beside him. Then he said to them, 'Whoever welcomes this little child in my name welcomes me; and whoever welcomes me welcomes the one who sent me. For it is the one who is least among you all who is the greatest" (Luke 9:48 NIV). Jesus seemed to be telling the disciples that our authority comes from God, not because we are a member of a select group. Luke shares another dispute about greatness among the disciples at the Last Supper. Jesus responds, "For who is greater, the one who is at the table or the one who serves? Is it not the one who is at the table? But I am among you as one who serves" (Luke 22:27 NIV). Christ's message to the disciples and to us was that if we want to be great in God's kingdom, we must learn to be the servant of all.

Martin Luther King once stated, "Everybody can be great…because anybody can serve. You don't have to have a college degree to serve. You don't have to make your subject and verb agree to serve. You only need a heart full of grace. A soul generated by love." It is unfortunate that jockeying for position and establishing our legacy in a desire for greatness often diminishes servanthood.

In his inaugural address on January 20, 2017, President Donald J. Trump uttered these words: "At the center of this movement is a crucial conviction that a nation exists to serve its citizens." In that regard, those who strive for greatness should stand up less to demonstrate their power and learn to fall on their knees more as they seek God's direction. When we begin to do that as a nation, then we will have attained a true understanding of what greatness truly is.

Reflection

What is the biggest obstacle you face as you seek to be a faithful servant of Christ? Where do you draw the line between a healthy self-esteem and pride? When it comes to greatness or recognition, how do you face the struggle over the forces of this world and give in to the Spirit who lives within you (see 1 John 4:4)?

JANUARY 21
(Y7, D3)

Offended? Permission Denied

Make allowance for each other's faults, and forgive anyone who offends you.

—Colossians 3:13 (NLT)

A fast-speaking TV weatherman with several decades of experience was talking over a visual of a local park named after Martin Luther King Jr. While presenting the then-current weather conditions, he rushed over the named location of the outdoor scene. In doing so, he inserted what sounded like an all-too-familiar racial slur. Not pausing to acknowledge his on-air flub, he proceeded to give his forecast. Following a backlash on social media, station management acted to discharge the veteran broadcaster in what many deemed as a rush to judgment. The unemployed weatherman insisted that he had always tried to maintain high professional standards. He stated that he accidentally jumbled his words with no intent of malice in any form. The apology was met with skepticism from those who reasoned that he only apologized because he got caught. In response at the time, Dr. Bernice King, daughter of the famous Civil Rights leader, said that it was difficult for her to question someone's intent and insisted the broadcaster should be given a chance to redeem himself. As the nation celebrates the holiday that bears the King name, one might wonder how the late Nobel Peace Prize recipient would have himself responded.

I am reminded of another story about a man who constantly harassed and insulted Buddha, throwing all sorts of verbal abuse at him. He did everything he could to offend Buddha. Unmoved, he simply turned to the man and said, "May I ask you a question?"

The man responded, "Well, what?"

Buddha said, "If someone offers you a gift and you decline to accept it, to whom then does it belong?"

The man said, "Then it belongs to the person who offered it."

Buddha smiled, stating, "That is correct. So if I decline to accept your abuse, does it not then still belong to you?"

The man was speechless and walked away. Friend, when you encounter someone who offends you, consider that it might not have been their intent at all. Even if it was, know that you don't have to make their insensitivities your own. It's what Christ would have you do.

Perhaps, then, we need to learn to become unoffendable. We can allow an assumed offense to be an opportunity to become more Christlike by showing that we value joy, peace, and inner freedom more than clinging to our perceived rights. Being unoffendable is not about being victimized or even being weak. It is about taking the high ground, having self-restraint, and not letting someone else's behavior, however intentional it may seem, to determine ours. Jesus warned that as we near the end of the age, a majority of people will be offended to such a degree that they fall away from the faith. Listen carefully to His warning: "At that time many will turn away from the faith and will betray and hate each other. And many false prophets will appear and will deceive many people. Sin will be rampant everywhere, and the love of many will grow cold" (Matthew 24:10–12 NIV). When we become easily offended, it is contrary to basic Christian teachings. We allow ourselves to be judgmental (Matthew 7:1), we stand at risk of suppressing truth (1 John 3:18), we block opportunities for forgiveness (Matthew 6:14–15), and we fail to allow for a path to redemption (Ephesians 1:7). The God of second chances would remind us that His very own Son said, "Let the one who has never sinned throw the first stone" (John 8:7 NLT).

Members of our society need to grow to be less reactionary and work toward consideration and reasonableness. Most people aren't aiming to insult or offend you; they are likely unaware of the fact that what they said may have hurt or disrespected you. When you consider how many times you have unintentionally said things that may have offended others and were not rebuked, you can certainly extend that same grace and forgiveness to another. James put it this way:

> Understand this, my dear brothers and sisters: You must all be quick to listen, slow to speak, and slow to get angry. Human anger does not produce the righteousness God desires. But if you look carefully into the perfect law that sets you free, and if you do what it says and don't forget what you heard, then God will bless you for doing it. If you claim to be religious but don't control your tongue, you are fooling yourself, and your religion is worthless. (James 1:19-20, 25–26 NLT)

What it really comes down to is a personal choice. Nobody can offend you without your permission. So next time you feel offended, just think "Permission denied."

Reflection

Have you become offended by someone recently? How did you handle the situation? Were you able to brush it off? What is one area of your life where you are likely to take offense? How can you use the concept of denying permission to be offended to become a less-offendable person?

JANUARY 22
(Y1, D4)

Unfinished Business

Do not judge, and you will not be judged. Do not condemn, and you
will not be condemned. Forgive, and you will be forgiven.

—Luke 6:37 (NIV)

After working an overtime shift on September 26, 2018, a thirty-year-old Dallas police officer of four years entered her apartment building, proceeding to what she believed was her residence. When the tenant put her key into the lock that night, she noticed the door seem to be ajar, revealing a mostly darkened apartment. When she went in, she encountered a man there whom she assumed to be an intruder. Following his failure to obey her verbal commands, she used her service weapon to deliver a fatal shot to a twenty-six-year-old financial accountant who had simply been watching TV and eating ice cream in his own home. The officer made a series of mistakes, including parking her vehicle on the wrong floor after her long shift. She then erroneously entered an apartment, believing it was her own, which was located exactly one floor below. As a result of her unclear thinking, a little over one year later, the former police officer was sentenced to serve ten years in prison for the killing of an innocent man.

The sentence appeared to initially disappoint the family of the victim who broke down in tears, shaking their heads as if in disbelief of the jury's decision. But then in an extraordinary turn of events, the victim's eighteen-year-old brother took the witness stand, demonstrating to the world that there was unfinished business that needed attention. He spoke to the defendant, saying, "I know if you go to God and ask Him, He will forgive you." He continued, "I love you just like anyone else, and I'm not going to hope you rot and die. I personally want the best for you. I wasn't going to say this in front of my family. I don't even want you to go to jail. I want the best for you because I know that's exactly what (my brother) would want for you. Give your life to Christ. I think giving your life to Christ is the best thing he would want for you." He then asked the judge if he could give the defendant a hug, a request the judge granted. Moments later, the judge also offered a hug, words of hope, and a Bible. The Dallas District Attorney described the scene as "an amazing act of healing and forgiveness that's rare in today's society."

Jesus sets the ultimate example of forgiveness that we should follow. He illustrated His expectation in "The Parable of the Unforgiving Servant" (Matthew 18:21–35), implying that it is difficult to understand the depth of forgiveness on our behalf if we are holding others accountable for their debts owed to us. Jesus was extremely kind and merciful in the way that He forgave those who sinned against others. He told a paralytic, "My child, your sins are forgiven" (Mark 2:5 NLT), and when a sinful woman bathed His feet with her tears and wiped them with her hair, "Jesus said to her, 'Your sins are forgiven'" (Luke 7:48 NIV). When a woman caught in adultery was brought before Him, He said, "Then neither do I condemn you" (John 8:11 NIV); and as Jesus hung on the cross, He told the repentant criminal, "Today you will be with me in paradise" (Luke 23:43 NIV). Even more compelling is the way that Jesus forgave those who sinned against him directly. After the Roman soldiers had scourged and nailed him, Jesus prayed, "Father, forgive them, for they do not know what they are doing" (Luke 23:34 NIV). For Jesus, forgiveness was not an automatic. Instead, it was an intentional, conscious choice.

The ability to forgive doesn't come naturally. Forgiveness is often very difficult to do, especially when the offender doesn't seem to care nor express any sense of remorse. When someone has wronged us, we frequently want to retaliate, hold a grudge, or hate them forever. The Apostle Paul says that we must "make allowance for each other's faults, and forgive anyone who offends you. Remember, the Lord forgave you, so you must forgive others" (Colossians 3:13 NLT). If you are ever in a situation and find it difficult to forgive, consider the gift of God's grace. To not offer the same gift to another would be like saying you are better than God. When we refuse to forgive another, they're not the one who suffers the most. We are! By pardoning others, we're able to release the bitterness, resentment, and anger that we tend to harbor. Whether the receiver accepts our forgiveness or not doesn't matter; we do it because it's what Jesus would have us do. Bottom line, grace cannot be explained; it can only be experienced. Forgiveness is a true example of God's grace in action. Otherwise, it's simply unfinished business.

Reflection

Are you presently struggling with an issue of forgiveness? In consideration of an offer of granting forgiveness, is it possible for you to focus on it as a gift of letting go? How might you provide counsel to someone who says, "I can forgive them, but I won't forget."

JANUARY 23
(Y2, D4)

Double Standard

The LORD detests double standards; he is not pleased by dishonest scales.

—Proverbs 20:23 (NLT)

When it comes to easily identifying the hypocrites of our society, we don't need to look far. Exercising the use of double standards can be found everywhere, even in places we might not consider. Interestingly enough, the number one reason people give for not going to church is that "there are too many hypocrites there." No doubt there have been times when you have been disappointed by the insincerity or hypocrisy of other believers, but one should not conclude that most people who attend church are hypocrites. In the same regard, naïve churchgoers may look around and sometimes conclude that all those seated around them are filled with persons who are holy and spiritually wise. It might be easy to assume that they most likely never use bad language, overindulge at a party, get really mad at their spouse, yell at their kids, complain about their jobs, or watch trashy TV programs. Well, if they were able to take a closer look, they might be surprised to find that each and every person sitting in those seats is human and has many temptations, weaknesses, and personality flaws. If you come to church with an illusion like this, take the blinders off. If you go to church and try to create this misconception about yourself, don't bother trying. While the church may sometimes disappoint us, we must remember that we do not always see the whole picture. God alone knows those who are truly His (2 Timothy 2:19).

Decades ago, *Reader's Digest* shared the story about a pastor who had been preaching on the importance of daily Bible reading. He and his wife were invited for a meal at a parishioner's home. While there, the pastor's wife saw a note that the hostess had written on her kitchen calendar: "Pastor/Mrs. for dinner—dust all Bibles." All of us are hypocrites in the sense that we have said one thing but acted differently. Double standards were as common in biblical times as they are now. Jesus stated such when He said:

> The teachers of religious law and the Pharisees are the official interpreters of the law of Moses. So practice and obey whatever they tell you, but don't follow their example. For they don't practice what they teach. They crush people with unbearable religious demands and never lift a finger to ease the burden. (Matthew 23:2–4 NLT)

He further taught that it is easier to recognize mistakes made by others than to recognize sins in our own lives. We need to practice humility and not be hypocrites. We need to get right with God before criticizing others and "first get rid of the log in your own eye (Matthew 7:5 NLT). A good example can be found in our social media postings where it is not uncommon to emphasize self, display boldness in our responses, and clearly show a lack of humility. Yet we are taught and profess to show the love of Jesus in all that we do. Scripture says, "Don't just pretend to love others. Really love them" (Romans 12:9 NLT). All we do should be genuine and without hypocrisy.

Hypocrisy is a dangerous sin because it's so easy to ignore the contrast between our words and deeds, blissfully unaware of how we live inconsistently with our professed beliefs. Sometimes we are so blind to our misdeeds that we need confrontation in order to see our sin. Every honest Christian struggles with the discrepancies between faith and life. The Apostle Paul acknowledged this when he said, "I want to do what is good, but I don't. I don't want to do what is wrong, but I do it anyway" (Romans 7:19 NLT). It is not unusual for some to fall into the trap of clinging to the "Christians aren't perfect, just forgiven" philosophy as an excuse for their actions. We cannot on the one hand embrace scripture and then, on the other, be dismissive about what it teaches. This type of hypocrisy deceives the hypocrite, damages unbelievers, and dishonors God. Some have suggested that the best comeback to the person who sees the church to be full of hypocrites might be "Well, there's always room for one more." But that's far too easy. History has proven that Christianity is filled with examples of persons who have demonstrated selflessness, courage, moral reform, and many other positive influences on the world. Jesus would say that we must do likewise and constantly be on guard against the double standards in our life.

Reflection

How would you evaluate your ability to maintain integrity between your words and actions? Are there things that you have advised other Christians to do that you don't always do? Have you ever found yourself in a situation where you confronted someone with a sinful action to later realize that you have committed the same act? When you find yourself in some form of "words versus deeds" deception, how do you work to eliminate this conflict? Are there ways you can work toward helping to cultivate genuine humility and avoidance of hypocrisy in organizations to which you belong?

JANUARY 24
(Y3, D4)

Properly Deflated

Behold, his soul is puffed up; it is not upright within him, but the righteous shall live by his faith.

—Habakkuk 2:4 (ESV)

It's that time of year when everything and everyone begins to focus on the "big game." That is, of course, the upcoming Super Bowl. Whether it's the hype of which team is the underdog, the parties and the food, the halftime entertainers, the TV commercials, or the actual gridiron competition predictions, millions of people find a way to get involved. Super Bowl XLIX in 2015 might best be remembered for the controversy which became known as "deflate-gate." In a championship playoff game between the New England Patriots and the Indianapolis Colts, the NFL reported that a majority of the footballs checked at halftime were underinflated below the acceptable range. It is assumed that an underinflated football can be more easily handled, thereby giving an advantage to the team who possesses them. The dilemma forced many to ask whether there was an intention to cheat in order to win. Good luck finding someone who will admit that. Egos in check? Of course not. Lots of money on the line? Certainly. Will we ever know all the facts? Or has this controversy just come and gone? Your guess is as good as mine.

In our culture, we hear about a lot of things being over or underinflated. Economists inform us that neither severe inflation nor recession is favorable because of their effect on purchasing power and price stability. The garage mechanic will tell you that you should regularly check your tires for proper inflation because you will get better gas mileage if you do so. We don't want the airbags in our car to inflate. But if we are unfortunate enough to be in an accident, we may be grateful that they did. When we're having a celebration, we may use helium to inflate balloons for the festivity, but often, we end up popping or deflating them later. Emergency medical service personnel are taught how to give CPR in order to inflate someone's lungs if they stop breathing. And, yes, even in our own day-to-day experience, we may know someone with an inflated ego and wish that we could find a way to shrink it.

The Apostle Paul described this inflated ego as being "puffed up" (Colossians 2:18 NIV), and he is a wonderful example of humility in action. Before he knew Christ as Savior and Lord, he was indeed full of himself. Later, he became one of the greatest advocates for Christ there ever was. At the same time, however, he considered himself "not even worthy to be called an apostle after the way I persecuted God's church" (1 Corinthians 15:9 NLT). He also said that as far as sinners go, "I am the worst of them all" (1 Timothy 1:15 NLT). He always encouraged those who followed Christ to emulate Jesus' humility. "Don't be selfish; don't try to impress others. Be humble, thinking of others as better than yourselves" (Philippians 12:3 NLT). This is the essence of humility and the exact opposite of ego. True believers will ultimately come to understand that they must "die to one's self" in order to fulfill God's will for their life. Otherwise, somewhere along our path, they may find themselves humbled. We have been fairly warned by a wise writer that "pride goes before destruction, a haughty spirit before a fall" (Proverbs 16:18 NIV).

It's apparent that God does not deal well with persons who are ego-centered. Peter wrote that He "opposes the proud but gives grace to the humble" (1 Peter 5:5 NLV). When we are willing to deflate our ego and become like an empty vessel, then He can fill us and direct our path of service. Martin Luther once said, "Until a man is nothing, God can make nothing out of him." In order to provide a worthwhile contribution to the world, it is important that we view ourselves as fearfully and wonderfully made in the image of God. However, in doing so, it can become quite easy to allow an inflated ego to be unchecked. When this occurs, the joy and peace that God intends for us to experience along our journey is sacrificed. Therefore, we should "do nothing out of selfish ambition or vain conceit. Rather, in humility value others above yourselves not looking to your own interests but each of you to the interests of the others" (Philippians 2:3-4 NIV). Someone once said, "Every time your head touches the ground in prayer, remember, it is to teach you to put down your ego." In doing so as a true believer, you will always give yourself the opportunity to be within the projected bounds of being properly deflated.

Reflection

When you accomplish tasks that are worthy of praise, in what manner do you give the credit to God for equipping you as His instrument? How do you demonstrate godly compassion for others who are self-centered? In what ways can we turn our personal successes into triumphs for His kingdom?

JANUARY 25
(Y4, D4)

A Missed Opportunity

So you see, faith by itself isn't enough. Unless it produces good deeds, it is dead and useless.

—James 2:17 (NIV)

If you are old enough, you might remember a time when missing a TV program meant that you would not have a chance to see it again. Then came the era of the video cassette recorder when you could tape a show if you were not home and view it anytime you desired. That led to the advancement of the DVR and the highly marketed TIVO that offered an improved digital recording without the need for those clumsy tapes. Today, there are many opportunities to view programming, including streaming live events on your Smart TV or mobile device. If you are willing to wait, you can even "binge watch" an entire season over a innumerable number of on-demand services or purchased CDs which can be played when you are ready to view them. There once was a time when not being in front of the TV was a missed opportunity that you would never have the chance to recoup. Nowadays, there are multiple ways to view whatever you want to watch at your own convenience because the pace of our existence has become far too hectic. No more missed opportunities, at least in that part of our life journey.

One day, I was at the grocery store and saw a lady having difficulty getting something off a shelf. The reasonable thing to do was to help her, so I did. When I exited the store a few minutes later, I observed her loading her groceries into her car. I went over, assisted her again, and thought how blessed I was to be able to help this lady twice. I share this story as there was another time weeks before when I was not nearly as responsible. I had again been at the grocery store and was about ready to pull out of my parking space when I saw an elderly woman coming across the lot with a cart full of groceries. I wondered if I should get out and help her, but I decided to see how she did. She struggled unloading the bags and started back toward the store to return her cart. I paused again, thinking that I might embarrass her if I offered assistance. As she deposited the cart at the front of the store, she methodically moved across the lot toward her car. She moved slowly, but she managed.

It would have been much easier for her had I gotten out to help. It was a missed opportunity, and I felt guilty for not having done so.

After this last event occurred, I heard a voice inside me saying, "If I can't trust you with the little things, how will I be able to give you bigger ones?" This was actually my own paraphrase from the Parable of the Shrewd Manager, sometimes known as the Parable of the Unjust Steward, found in Luke 16:1–15. On first reading, it would seem that this parable is about two characters: a master and the steward who manages his money. When the steward learns of his imminent discharge, he manipulates the debt owed to his master for his own future benefit. This prompts Jesus to eventually conclude, "If you are faithful in little things, you will be faithful in large ones. But if you are dishonest in little things, you won't be honest with greater responsibilities" (Luke 16:10 NLT). Everything we have is from God. This includes not only our finances and other earthly possessions but also the blessings of our health, physical, and mental capacities and other talents He has provided. We must endeavor to use those wisely, especially in service to others. Otherwise, we risk denying ourselves the "true riches" (Luke 16:11) of the future.

On a different occasion, Jesus cited another parable (Matthew 25:31–46) in which He talks about meeting the needs of others. In it, He concludes by stating, "And the King will say, 'I tell you the truth, when you did it to one of the least of these my brothers and sisters, you were doing it to me!'" (Matthew 25:40 NLT). For our good deeds should not come as a means to an end, simply to gain approval from God. Rather, they evolve out of that which God has already provided for us through the death of His Son. "But someone will say, 'You have faith; I have deeds.' Show me your faith without deeds, and I will show you my faith by my deeds" (James 2:18 NIV). For when our hearts are in tune with Him, He will make us conscious of missed opportunities so that day by day, year after year, as we take that walk, we will be moving down that eternal path of becoming more like Him and missing fewer opportunities to serve.

Reflection

Can you think of a recent time in your life when you did not respond to another's need in an effective Christlike manner? Did you consider your lack of response later? How did your review make you feel? How might you use those feelings as a source of motivation when the next opportunity presents itself?

JANUARY 26
(Y5, D4)

High Fences, Rough Edges, and Unknown Angels

Each of us should please our neighbors for their good, to build them up.

—Romans 15:2 (NIV)

If you grew up in the golden age of television, you will remember Lucy and Ricky. The Ricardos' *I Love Lucy* neighbors were the Mertzes, the friendly ever-present landlords who became so close to the couple that they served as godparents to Little Ricky when he was born. Another slightly less visible Wilson lived adjacent to the Taylor family in the 1990s *Home Improvement* series. The mostly unseen neighbor peered over the fence and frequently became the go-to guy for solving the Taylors' problems with his engaging conversation. Over the years, the concept of being a neighbor has been an important theme in many media presentations. How can we forget *Mister Roger's Neighborhood*? As Mr. Rogers entered the house, he put on his sneakers and cardigan sweater while he sang "Won't You Be My Neighbor?" to many generations of children, making us all feel that neighboring was the right thing to do.

These days, we often don't know or may not even want to know our neighbors. If we are lucky enough to have a yard, a good fence often keeps us from stating the obvious: "Unless we extend an invitation, you stay on your side and we'll remain on ours." In his poem, "Mending Wall," Robert Frost writes of two neighbor farmers who join hands in the spring to rebuild the stone wall between their properties. The one neighbor, who serves as the poem's narrator, contemplates the need for the wall since there are no animals to be restrained by its created barrier. At one point, he questions why it was even put there in the first place. He says, "Before I built a wall, I'd ask to know…what I was walling in or walling out." But his neighbor hung on to his father's words of wisdom which simply stated the obvious, "Good fences make good neighbors."

Jesus was once asked what was His most important teaching. His reply was:

> The most important commandment is this: "Listen, O Israel! The Lord our God is the one and only Lord. And you must love the Lord your God with

all your heart, all your soul, all your mind, and all your strength." The second is equally important: "Love your neighbor as yourself." No other commandment is greater than these. (Mark 12:29–31 NLT)

There are days when the first of these is much easier to fulfill than the other. I have lived in the same house for several decades, and during that period, the ownership of the house next door has turned over many times. The current occupants were once described by another neighbor as "a little rough around the edges." Even though that description sums up their conduct fairly well, I have always tried to be kind and respectful; you know, neighborly. A few months ago, I responded to the doorbell to observe one of them standing there. They wanted to make me aware they would be going away for a few days and asked me to keep an eye on their house. It reaffirmed who we need to be. The Apostle Paul said, "Love does no harm to a neighbor. Therefore love is the fulfillment of the law" (Romans 13:10 NIV).

Jesus told the Parable of the Good Samaritan because He was prompted by the question, "Who is my neighbor?" (Luke 10:29). Merely put, He responded that our neighbor could be anyone who needs us. A good neighborhood watch program might say it is those who live on our block or in our apartment building. The Reverend Bobby Schuller once phrased it this way: "Don't discredit what you have to give to a hurting world. Be aware of the needs of the people in the fifteen feet of space around you. They are there. Have listening ears and meet the needs of people who are hurting. Be the kind of person that is always available to shine the light." You will find that if you practice this technique, the better neighbor you will become and the more blessings you will receive. So even though some with whom you come in regular contact might be a little rough around the edges, "Keep on loving one another as brothers and sisters. Do not forget to show hospitality to strangers, for by so doing some people have shown hospitality to angels without knowing it" (Hebrews 13:1–2 NIV). While building that fence might be a wise idea, we don't want to build it so high that we miss the cry of one who may need us.

Reflection

Consider who you define as your neighbor. Are you attentive to the needs of those around you? How might adopting and extending the "fifteen-foot rule" improve your vision of ministry to those whom you may not otherwise envision to be your neighbor?

JANUARY 27
(Y6, D4)

Direct Line

This is the new covenant I will make with my people on that day, says the LORD:
I will put my laws in their hearts, and I will write them on their minds.

—Hebrews 10:16 (NLT)

Over a century ago on January 25, 1915, Alexander Graham Bell spoke on a telephone call from New York City to his former assistant, Thomas Watson, who at the time was in San Francisco. Bell echoed those now famous words, "Mr. Watson, come here, I need you," which he had similarly stated for the first time in 1876. But now they were hearing each other with much greater clarity and at a much greater distance than almost four decades years before when Watson was able to just run into Bell's room, indicating he could understand the message. Now he just stated, "It would take me a week to get to you this time." It was the first public demonstration of a transcontinental phone call for AT&T who had purchased Bell's company in 1899 and constructed the lines for initiating the new service. The long-distance call of 3,400 miles was being celebrated at the Panama-Pacific International Exposition. Then President Woodrow Wilson, who witnessed the call, remarked, "It appeals to the imagination to speak across the continent."

Less than half a century later, phone calls were being made across the world. John F. Kennedy became the first US president to have a direct phone line to the Kremlin in Moscow, established on August 30, 1963. The "hotline" was designed to facilitate communication between the president and Soviet premier. The establishment of the direct line came in the wake of the October 1962 Cuban Missile Crisis in which the US and USSR had come dangerously close to all-out nuclear war. The technology utilized was considered revolutionary, being much more reliable and less prone to interception than a regular trans-Atlantic phone call which had to be bounced between several countries before reaching the Kremlin. Although a far cry from the instantaneous communication made possible by today's cell phones and texting, it was the first direct linkage of its kind. No call waiting, no busy signals, no answering machines—just an instant hookup designed to avert threat and prevent miscommunication.

While talking by telephone across a vast stretch of geography was possible, the early days of the telephone could be limiting. Throughout much of the 1900s, it was not uncommon for many customers to have a "party line," a local telephone loop shared by more than one customer. There was no privacy on a party line. If you were talking with a friend, anyone on your party line could pick up their telephone and listen to the intimate details of your conversation. If someone on your party line was using their phone, no one else could make a call. I have often wondered if God doesn't feel like He is listening on one big party line with all of us trying to talk to Him at once. Thankfully, His ability to "listen in" defies all mortal explanation, somehow providing a private line and individual access for each believer. In Jesus' time, there was a veil in the inner sanctuary of the temple that separated man from God, who resided in the Holy of Holies. Only priests could go behind that veil once a year. The Bible says that when Jesus died on the cross, God ripped that veil from top to bottom, symbolizing that there was no longer a barrier, thereby opening a more direct line of communication (Matthew 27:51; Mark 15:38).

Through His sacrificial death, Jesus established a new covenant, allowing us to inherit a permanent, unbroken relationship with God. Paul said:

> He came and preached peace to you who were far away and peace to those who were near. For through him we both have access to the Father by one Spirit. Consequently, you are no longer foreigners and strangers, but fellow citizens with God's people and also members of his household. (Ephesians 2:17–19 NIV)

Under this new covenant, our bodies are a temple for God's Holy Spirit who lives in us. We have immediate contact anywhere at any time. When we feel like God is far away and wonder if our prayers are being heard, we must remember that He is not dwelling in some distant place. Author Wesley L. Duewel wrote "God waits for you to communicate with Him. You have instant, direct access to God. God loves mankind so much, and in a very special sense His children, that He has made Himself available to you at all times." So as we journey with the Lord, we will never need to say, "Lord, come here, I need you." We have a direct line. He's already there.

Reflection

How do you take full advantage of your unrestricted access to God? How might we use our direct line to examine and improve our communication through self-expression, body language, and social media?

JANUARY 28
(Y7, D4)

Except When...

Then I heard the voice of the Lord saying, "Whom shall I send? And who will go for us?" And I said, "Here am I. Send me!"

—Isaiah 6:8 (NIV)

I smiled when I read the following "Help Wanted" ad for a local restaurant. It stated: "Scattered hours. Every Monday 4:00–9:30, every Friday and every other Saturday 4:00–9:00 or 11:00, except every fifth Friday and Saturday, 12:00–5:00." My first thought wondered if there was any individual who would be interested in applying for a job with such irregular hours. Then I recalled being on the other end of similar conversations when I would conduct interviews for a former employer. I'd usually tell applicants that we had openings on a certain shift at a facility which operated round-the clock, seven days a week. In response to my questions regarding their availability, I would frequently hear replies beginning with the words, "Except when." It didn't always make them very useful to this employer, and more often than not, they didn't get the job. Our busy lives, which only grow more complex and diverse with time, present a major obstacle to our availability and resulting usefulness. We are so caught up with personal schedules, and our readiness for the important things in life often suffers. As we consider our relationship with Christ, we should give close consideration to His availability to us as well as ours to Him.

God's availability stands at the heart of Scripture. He is present to guide and protect and, when necessary, to correct. But most of all, we expect Him to be our listening ear when we face the adversities of life as we often do. If we base our emotional security on close friends or family members, we become vulnerable in assuming they will always be there for us. On the contrary, God never hides from us; He is never absent nor consumed by something more important. He is available, as contemporary phrasing would state, 24-7. God's ever-present availability challenges us to ask, how accessible are we to Him? What part of our day can God claim? Do we give Him significant time? Or do we struggle to give Him even five minutes? What do we first have to take care of before we can give God our attention? Jesus struggled with the readiness of those who stated they would commit to Him.

As they were walking along the road, a man said to him, "I will follow you wherever you go." Jesus replied, "Foxes have dens and birds have nests, but the Son of Man has no place to lay his head." He said to another man, "Follow me." But he replied, "Lord, first let me go and bury my father." Jesus said to him, "Let the dead bury their own dead, but you go and proclaim the kingdom of God." Still another said, "I will follow you, Lord; but first let me go back and say good-bye to my family." Jesus replied, "No one who puts a hand to the plow and looks back is fit for service in the kingdom of God." (Luke 9:57–62 NIV)

God is looking for humble people who are totally dependent upon Him. He seeks those followers who are willing to make themselves available whenever He calls, and for whatever reason, those who without any form of hesitation would say, "Here I am, Lord. Send me." In the words of the Apostle Paul: "Therefore, my dear brothers and sisters, stand firm. Let nothing move you. Always give yourselves fully to the work of the Lord, because you know that your labor in the Lord is not in vain" (1 Corinthians 15:58 NIV). God does not expect that each of us will be called into full-time ministry or commit our lives to be missionaries in a foreign land. While it is exceptional when one dedicates to oblige in this way, each of us can serve Him if we just look around, sometimes not very far away. There is the widow down the street who is lonely, the colleague at work who is searching for encouragement, the homeless shelter or foodbank who needs a volunteer, or maybe someone in your own family who is being overlooked. The words of the prophet give us clear direction: "Share your food with the hungry, and give shelter to the homeless. Give clothes to those who need them, and do not hide from relatives who need your help" (Isaiah 58:7). In light of the promise we have from God to be always available (John 14:18), it is vital that we reflect that same love to others. His expectation is that those who claim to be His followers will never look back, saying that we are available to Him, except when we're not!

Reflection

Honestly ask the question: Am I paying attention to my call to grow in love, humility, and living for the glory of God? How can you make yourself more available to someone who has a need you may have ignored? In what ways can you reshuffle your priorities in order to consistently (and without excuse) serve God?

JANUARY 29
(Y1, D5)

Larger than Life Itself

Let the one who is wise heed these things and ponder the loving deeds of the LORD.

—Psalm 107:43 (NIV)

As I sat to the left of the lady being honored, it seemed as though I had known her and many members of her family for a long time. We had gathered at a local restaurant in recognition of her one-hundredth birthday which had occurred only a few days before. She was fortunate to have been blessed with good health; in fact, she made the decision just in the past year to give up driving her car. During our time together, someone asked her about the automobiles of her youth. Her response was that there "were not many to be found." Then I got to thinking about the vast array of changes she would have witnessed during her lifetime. These would have included much advancement in the fields of science and technology and a notable transformation in how we as a society have come to value power and fame over common goodness. The old adage came to mind: "Each successive generation gets wiser and weaker."

While I believe that this statement bears a lot of truth, it is not in the Bible as some have claimed. There are scriptural references, however, that could help to support this belief. In the Old Testament, for instance, one can read: "The war between the house of Saul and the house of David lasted a long time. David grew stronger and stronger, while the house of Saul grew weaker and weaker" (2 Samuel 3:1 NIV). One could easily conclude when we read about the Saul/David relationship that here is a case where it was the younger generation who got stronger and wiser while the older became weaker. Perhaps David, a flawed person in many ways, was blessed with wisdom because He developed a strong relationship with God. He was always searching for and permitting Him to rule over his life. Saul, on the other hand, allowed himself to be fueled by suspicion and jealousy, resulting in spiritual and mental deterioration. It is somewhat ironic that at his death, David would become his successor as King of the Israelites.

While each generation possesses the opportunity to gain more knowledge than the previous one, they frequently make unwise choices. For they have evolved to fix their eyes on what immediately lies before them as they display a disregard for that which is lasting (2 Corinthians 4:18). Take, for example, their infatuation with prominent figures who are promoted to become global icons, almost as if they have been anointed as the chosen ones. These persons are often described as being "larger than life itself." Therein lies the problem. Scripture warns that "a discerning person keeps wisdom in view, but a fool's eyes wander to the ends of the earth" (Proverbs 17:24 NIV). This obsession with today's celebrities has become so fanatical and overstated that it is practically worshipful. Some allow themselves to lose sight of the reality that even famous persons are simply people, each having their own flaws. And if, by chance, something happens to one of these whom we uphold with such high reverence, we are devastated.

Someone once said that when you are labeled as "larger than life," you have to run really fast to be able to keep up with your own image. There is, in fact, no one who has ever walked this earth who is larger than life. The only exception in this category is Jesus Christ. Scripture says, "Our days may come to seventy years, or eighty, if our strength endures; yet the best of them are but trouble and sorrow, for they quickly pass, and we fly away" (Psalm 90:10 NIV). God wasn't promising that every person would live to be seventy or eighty; the psalmist was simply describing an average human experience. Our time on this earth is in God's hands, and for some, their journey here seems to be cut short. But no matter who we are, our life is time-limited, and someday, death will overtake us. Death is a reality, and no one evades it—no matter how strong, how famous, or how many years they have been blessed to live. My one-hundred-year-old friend understands that with each new day, life continues to be a delicate balance. We can assume that King David understood this, and so should we. For our earthly days are but a mere testing ground to determine where we will spend all of eternity. Hopefully, for you and me, we will rise to that heavenly destination and in the presence of the one who *is* truly larger than life itself.

Reflection

Are you giving thought to how you are spending the days God is giving you in this life? Do wisdom and knowledge become factors as you make this determination? Why does each generation think they are smarter than the generation that came before them? How can you control your admiration for people who evolve to become notable legends in our culture and avoid elevating them to godlike figures?

JANUARY 30
(Y2, D5)

All Parts Working Together

In fact, some parts of the body that seem weakest and least important are actually the most necessary.

—1 Corinthians 12:22 (NLT)

The question was once asked, "Who is more important? The president of the United States or a garbage collector?" In March of 1981, there was an attempted assassination on the life of President Ronald Reagan. Following the shooting, he was hospitalized for several weeks. Although Reagan was the nation's chief executive, his hospitalization had little impact on the ability of the federal government to function. On the other hand, suppose the garbage collectors in this country went on strike. Our cities and neighborhoods would not only be in a literal mess, but the pile of decaying trash would quickly become a health hazard. A nationwide strike lasting for several weeks could paralyze the country. Too often, we make unfair judgments about those whom we perceive to perform secondary functions to somehow be low in significance. Albert Einstein displayed his intelligence when he said, "I speak to everyone in the same way, whether he is the garbage man or the president of the university."

If performing best under high pressure contributes to one's level of importance, then I suppose leaders who exhibit this ability are a vital part of any team. However, they cannot function alone. The controversy about which quarterback will lead their team to the Super Bowl always creates an excessive amount of hype. While a champion quarterback is almost always lauded for his quick decision-making, they get far too much credit and sometimes too much blame for a player who isn't even on the field half the time. No matter how great the QB is, he must have a good team around him to win. After all, someone needs to protect him from getting sacked. If he is lucky enough to execute a good pass, he has to have an equally talented receiver downfield. Perhaps one of the greatest tests of a quarterback is how their team does without them if, for some reason, they are unable to play. While there are times that this is disastrous for a team who has come to believe that they are unable to function without their "star player," there are other occasions when teams seem to manage quite well in similar situations.

The Apostle Paul explained it this way:

> Even so the body is not made up of one part but of many. Now if the foot should say, "Because I am not a hand, I do not belong to the body," it would not for that reason stop being part of the body. And if the ear should say, "Because I am not an eye, I do not belong to the body," it would not for that reason stop being part of the body. If the whole body were an eye, where would the sense of hearing be? If the whole body were an ear, where would the sense of smell be? But in fact, God has placed the parts in the body, every one of them, just as he wanted them to be. (1 Corinthians 12:14–18 NIV)

Togetherness is an important theme in the New Testament. We are designed to need God and each other. No one has all the skills, gifts, or wisdom necessary for a successful life. We are pressed to use the gifts we receive—the talents and uniqueness of our created nature as well as our spiritual gifts—to serve one another with kindness, respect, and gratefulness.

As we consider the members of the teams to which we belong, we are reminded that each is unique in the contribution they are capable of making. Consider that God has placed us together to complete each other, not compete with each other. David proclaimed, "How good and pleasant it is when God's people live together in unity!" (Psalm 133:1 NIV). He understood the importance of the sum of the parts working together. Christian teamwork will acknowledge God as the established leader and objective third party in every team, adding strength and cohesion to its bond. Our part is to be a good teammate and do as Paul instructed: "For just as each of us has one body with many members, and these members do not all have the same function, so in Christ we, though many, form one body, and each member belongs to all the others" (Romans 12:4–5 NIV). When we do this, we recognize that we must contribute our part toward the ultimate goal of all parts working together in championing the one true Lord of our life.

Reflection

Why do we tend to believe that one individual's function has more worth than another? Consider this challenge: "Don't think you are better than you really are. Be honest in your evaluation of yourselves, measuring yourselves by the faith God has given us" (Romans 12:3 NLT). In applying this, how does your role in organizations to which you belong motivate you to validate value in others?

JANUARY 31
(Y3, D5)

Everlasting

And this is what he promised us—eternal life.

—1 John 2:25 (NIV)

The story is told of a boy who found himself in trouble for a silly childish mistake. Ashamed, he went to the park and began to cry beneath a tree when a good fairy appeared, asking him why he was weeping. When he explained, she offered him a solution in the form of a spool of thread which represented the remainder of his life. If he ever found himself in a similar situation to his current one, he would only have to snip a tiny bit of the thread to bypass the discomfort. The fairy cautioned him, however, that he must use the spool wisely. Overjoyed, the boy returned home with the spool. The next day, his teacher handed back an assignment on which he had received a poor grade. Embarrassed, he took out his spool, snipped off a tiny bit of the thread, and was instantly transported from the classroom to the end of the school day. The boy immediately understood the usefulness of the contraption: skipping the hard moments. As more incidents of childish dilemmas passed, each time the boy snipped away the moment on his spool of life and escaped it. The pattern continued as he passed through adulthood. Soon enough, he found himself to be an old man. Reminiscing on his life, he realized that he had passed too many moments without fully experiencing them and had lost too much time by not living it. Sorrowfully, he returned to the tree where he found himself during childhood, weeping once more over what his life had become. To his surprise, the same GOOD fairy reappeared. Seeing that he was now an old man, she inquired as to why he was crying. As he explained to her his regret, she reminded him that she had warned him against using the spool excessively. Then she waved her magic wand and promised him a chance at a new life. She left and he fell asleep, waking as a boy once more to relive his life.

Wishing away our lives, worried about what comes next, and wondering what will happen when it ends—this is all very typical of the human condition. Recently, I heard the thoughts of two different individuals. The first came in the words of a friend who had recently lost her husband after fifty-plus years of marriage. She summarized his death as "very sad but good." Sad in the fact that she would now face life without him, but "good" because he had now escaped his debilitating illness of many years. She was grateful that when the end came, she was with him as he passed from this life to the next. The second individual was a relative newcomer to Christianity. One day, as he was discussing the concept of death with members of the church he attended, he emphatically stated that he believed that when you die, that was it! It was over, and you ceased to exist. Somewhere along the line, he missed the point of the life of Jesus and the greatest promise He gave us—that of everlasting life. He had failed to understand of the most memorized of all Christian scriptures: "For God so loved the world that he gave his one and only Son, that whoever believes in him shall not perish but have eternal life" (John 3:16 NIV).

Everlasting or eternal life is the gracious promise every believer holds on to with joy and gratitude. Yet we somehow develop the notion that it only represents our future, that we have to first endure our earthly existence and then one day receive eternal life as our ultimate reward. However, God actually desires that we grow into that promise here on earth. Learning to cope with and getting through the difficult moments in our lives validates our faith. The problem is that we get so bogged down with the challenges, problems, and responsibilities of our lives that we miss the incredible truth that we are empowered to live spiritually in the present, even while we come to believe and develop a connection with Christ. "And this is eternal life, that they may know You, the only true God, and Jesus Christ whom You have sent" (John 17:3 NIV). While each of us must face the limitations of our earthly existence, we have access to God's throne of grace and can know the intimacy of a deep relationship with Him each day. When we don't live as if we are displaying the confidence of everlasting life here and now, we limit what He is able to do through us as we interact with others. Jesus taught, "I tell you the truth, anyone who obeys my teaching will never die" (John 8:51 NLT). We don't need to "snip away" at the difficult portions of our life, concerned about that day when we will find ourselves holding the end of an empty spool. Jesus' promise of eternity guarantees that our life thread is indeed everlasting.

Reflection

Do you give more thought to the securities of this life than you do to eternity? How can you position your life differently by realizing that what is everlasting begins this very day? How might you help others recognize when they are fretting away their time and help them find an eternal perspective?

FEBRUARY 1

(Y4, D5)

Forever Springtime Promise

He was fully convinced that God is able to do whatever he promises

—Romans 4:21 (NLT)

Life is full of promises, most of which have been broken. Each year in early February, the famous Punxsutawney Phil predicts either six more weeks of winter or whether spring is right around the corner. Although we don't take Phil's declarations too seriously one way or the other, there are promises that we do buy into which may have a profound effect on our lives. Or sometimes, their result is just as unfulfilled as you originally suspected. You don't have to look any further than the campaigns of political candidates to realize that they often promise much but deliver far less. Commercial advertising is yet another source of promises that can frequently disappoint us as we come to realize that they commonly contain limited guarantees. On a personal level, a broken promise between two friends can hurt deeply. And as Valentine's Day approaches, there will once again be promises made of what one might seemingly label as "loving relationships" which will never be satisfied.

God's promises are very different. He never breaks His Word. This is evidenced throughout scripture. "Not a single one of all the good promises the Lord had given to the family of Israel was left unfulfilled; everything he had spoken came true" (Joshua 21:45 NLT). And later in Kings: "Praise the Lord who has given rest to his people Israel, just as he promised. Not one word has failed of all the wonderful promises he gave through his servant Moses" (1 Kings 8:56 NLT). A very well-known and understood promise of God is found in His vow to Noah:

> I am going to make a solemn promise to you and to everyone who will live after you. This includes the birds and the animals that came out of the boat. I promise every living creature that the earth and those living on it will never again be destroyed by a flood. The rainbow that I have put in the sky will be my sign to you and to every living creature on earth. It will remind you that I will keep this promise forever. (Genesis 9:9–13 CEV)

Do the promises of God found in the Bible continue to have relevance for us today? Of course because God never changes. If you claim to be a true believer, then they may be applicable to you. Examples include: "If we confess our sins, he is faithful and just and will forgive us our sins and purify us from all unrighteousness" (1 John 1:9 NIV). Then there is His promise of eternal life. "My sheep listen to my voice; I know them, and they follow me. I give them eternal life, and they will never perish. No one can snatch them away from me" (John 10:27–28 NLT). Some of His promises are situational. For instance, "God is our refuge and strength, an ever-present help in trouble" (Psalm 46:1 NIV). In some cases, the promises were made to specific persons or groups such as Israel: "'For the mountains may move and the hills disappear, but even then my faithful love for you will remain. My covenant of blessing will never be broken,' says the Lord, who has mercy on you" (Isaiah 54:10 NIV). So of the hundreds of promises, how do we know if they are for us? Can we still take heart in such assurances, even though they were spoken long ago to people in a far different situation than ours?

Sometimes along our personal journey, we struggle with the path ahead of us. When we stay close to God and permit His Word to speak to us, we may find a scripture so profound that it jumps off the page as if it was ours alone. Even though a specific promise may not have been made generally to all believers when it was made, God can still use it to guide or encourage any of His children to submit to His will and trust Him. In any time of darkness or doubt, when we find a promise and hold onto it with conviction, God is pleased and faithful. "Through these he has given us his very great and precious promises, so that through them you may participate in the divine nature, having escaped the corruption in the world caused by evil desires" (2 Peter 1:4 NIV). Be assured that whatever we are facing, we can be certain that He fulfills His promises yesterday, today, and tomorrow. In that regard, six more weeks of winter will always be acceptable, worth the wait. For as Martin Luther once put it: "Our Lord has written the promise of resurrection, not in books alone, but in every leaf in springtime."

Reflection

How do you know which of God's promises are for you? Do you feel that you can trust God to keep His promises? In your opinion, what is the best promise He has given us? Is there a promise in scripture that has once spoken or is now speaking to you in a very personal way? If so, claim it and ask God to make it your own.

FEBRUARY 2
(Y5, D5)

The Shadow Left Behind

The LORD is your keeper; The LORD is your shade on your right hand.

—Psalm 121:5 (NIV)

Every year on February 2 since 1887 in the western Pennsylvania community of Punxsutawney, some devout followers make their pilgrimage to a famous part of town known as Gobbler's Knob. Donning black top hats, officials of the local club oversee the early-morning event as hundreds of public spectators gather. Each asks the question, "Will he or won't he?" The event known as Groundhog Day features Punxsutawney Phil who, for all intents and purposes, is consulted to predict whether winter is nearing an end. According to folklore, the answer comes rather quickly when the small, furry mammal with buck teeth emerges from his burrow. If the beloved groundhog sees his shadow, the country is in for six more weeks of winter; if he doesn't, an early spring will occur. While the tradition remains popular in various parts of the United States and Canada, it's not surprising that studies have found no consistent correlation between a groundhog seeing its shadow and the subsequent arrival time of springlike weather.

At one time or other, images of shadows have no doubt played a part in your life. Remember being afraid of shadows when you were lying in bed as a young child? Or maybe when you got a little older, you learned that you could create animal shadows on the wall with your hands and the beam of a flashlight. Perhaps as young adult, you were compared to an older sibling or a cousin, having to declare that you wanted to be your own person and not be forced to live in anyone else's shadow. If you have ever seen *Peter Pan*, you may remember Peter losing his shadow. As he seeks to retrieve it, he chases it around the room. While trying to get it back, he discovers that it moves more quickly than he does. Of course, it's impossible for our shadow to move faster or slower than we do. We soon realize that unlike Peter Pan, our shadow sticks with and can never be detached from us.

God is like your shadow; He cannot be taken or moved away from you. Everywhere you go, the Lord follows you. He is your protector. Our kind, benevolent God who is attentive to every one of our steps covers us with His presence. We're never alone. In Psalm 57:1 (ESV), we read: "Be merciful to me, O God, be merciful to me, for in you my soul takes refuge; in the shadow of your wings I will take refuge, till the storms of destruction pass by." Any photographer or artist worth his salt realizes that the realism of their work is captured in the beauty of the light contrasted with shadows. Are our lives, too, not more remarkable because of the shadows? Is this not where God teaches us mercy and compassion and where strength of character is formed (Romans 5:3–4)? And is it not in the valley of the shadow of death where we learn that God is with us (Psalm 23:4)?

Shadows are woven throughout the scriptures. To demonstrate compassion in the Old Testament, "The Lord God provided a leafy plant and made it grow up over Jonah to give shade for his head to ease his discomfort, and Jonah was very happy about the plant" (Jonah 4:6 NIV). When the apostles of the New Testament continued Jesus' ministry after His resurrection, they had a huge impact on the world around them. Their impression was so immense that even the sick and the lame desired to be in Peter's shadow (Acts 5:15), for they realized that even the shadow he left behind was greater than a lot of other religious people they encountered. Perhaps you are going through the valley of the shadow right now. It may be the valley of the shadow of conflict, depression, discouragement, debt, or one of life-threatening illness. Here's the good news—when you look at any shadow, you know that its source is nearby. For wherever there's a shadow, there has to be a light. God's light is infinitely brighter than any light on earth, and His shadow casts brilliance upon us. We are told: "The light shines in the darkness, and the darkness has not overcome it" (John 1:5 NIV). When you see how God brings protection, life, comfort, and peace under the shadow of His wings, you can't help but be joyful. For it is there, living in the shadow of the Almighty, that you must never forget His light is never far away.

Reflection

In what situations have you recognized how important it is to abide under the shadow of the Almighty? What are the things that you need to do to ensure you are living under God's shadow? Challenge yourself to be like the Apostle Peter. When everything is said and done, would people whom you have encountered feel the benefit of being witnesses to the shadow you have left behind?

FEBRUARY 3
(Y6, D5)

Self-Image

So God created human beings in his own image. In the image of God he created them.

—Genesis 1:27 (NLT)

He suffered from depression for many years and underwent psychiatric treatment. Married three times, his personal relationships were described by some as troubled. Defined as a nervous man who contemplated suicide at least once, he was believed to have suffered from some dementia at the end of his life. He had deep insecurities about his work and often referred to himself as an illustrator rather than an artist. Despite all of this, his paintings created nostalgic moments and sentimentalized portrayals of American life. During his eighty-four years, he produced over 4,000 original works which were beloved by a broad spectrum of the culture. These included 321 covers for *The Saturday Evening Post.* In 1920, the Boy Scouts of America featured one of his paintings in its calendar, establishing a relationship he enjoyed for over fifty years. One year before his death in 1978, President Gerald Ford awarded him with the Medal of Freedom.

Norman Rockwell was born on February 3, 1894, in New York City. At an early age, he knew he wanted to be an artist. His works were not always embraced by the critics who frequently dismissed him for not having real artistic merit. Rockwell's reasons for painting were grounded in the world he hoped for. He once stated, "Maybe as I grew up and found the world wasn't the perfect place I had thought it to be, I unconsciously decided that if it wasn't an ideal world, it should be, and so painted only the ideal aspects of it." In 1960, Rockwell produced one of the most famous self-portraits in American art. A clearly modest man, he was reluctant to make himself the subject of a cover. The painting is regarded by many as a thoughtful portrait of the artist's three selves: the painter, the subject model of himself as reflected by a mirror, and the image he created on the canvas. It has become known as *The Triple Self-Portrait.* In describing this work, Rockwell explained why his glasses appear opaque. "I had to show that my glasses were fogged, and that I couldn't actually see what I looked like—a homely, lanky fellow—and therefore, I could stretch the truth just a bit and paint myself looking more suave and debonair than I actually am."

Rockwell's comment reminds me of that well-known passage from the Apostle Paul as he writes to the Church at Corinth: "Now we see things imperfectly, like puzzling reflections in a mirror, but then we will see everything with perfect clarity. All that I know now is partial and incomplete, but then I will know everything completely, just as God now knows me completely" (1 Corinthians 13:12 NLT). It is true that God sees and knows us much more clearly than we sometimes know ourselves. In some ways, Rockwell was not so different than many who struggle with their own self-image. When Jesus told His disciples that He would soon be leaving them to be with the Father, they were confused and questioned Him, perhaps suffering a bit of an image crisis of their own. Jesus stated:

> If you had really known me, you would know who my Father is. From now on, you do know him and have seen him!" Philip said, "Lord, show us the Father, and we will be satisfied." Jesus replied, "Have I been with you all this time, Philip, and yet you still don't know who I am? Anyone who has seen me has seen the Father! So why are you asking me to show him to you?" (John 14:7–9 NLT)

Here, Jesus is not speaking of a physical image but rather that He and the Father are of the same substance.

Hebrews 1:3 (NIV) says that "the Son is the radiance of God's glory and the exact representation of His being, sustaining all things by His powerful word." In the beginning, man was made in God's image with the mental capacity to reason and choose, making us unique in His Creation. In that regard, we are a reflection of God's intellect and freedom but unfortunately marred by rebellion. Today, we still bear the image of God, but we are also scarred by the sin of mankind. Rockwell said, "I paint life as I would like it to be." God did the same on His canvas of Creation. We are very much a part of the image He first imagined, only to be made perfect again through the sacrificial gift of grace provided by His Son.

Reflection

Are you able to separate your own self-perception from the sins of your past? How might you help someone who is struggling with their own self-image understand it is only through Christ alone that we can be made right before God and conform to the image that we were originally created to be?

FEBRUARY 4
(Y7, D5)

Old Faithful

Let love and faithfulness never leave you; bind them around
your neck, write them on the tablet of your heart.

—Proverbs 3:3 (NIV)

Nestled in the Rocky Mountain range of Yellowstone National Park, you will find the most famous geyser in the world—Old Faithful. The Wyoming landmark was given its name in 1870 because of its predictability. Since 2000, the geothermal marvel continues to regularly erupt every few hours, up to twenty times each day. I once knew a lady who volunteered at a nursing home several hours each day, at least five days a week for many years. As long as she could find a ride, she unselfishly served during any kind of weather, sometimes without regard for her own well-being. She said that volunteering was what kept her going. She believed that the little things she was able to do for the residents who lived there were significant and felt that because of her age, she related well to them. She viewed what she did as a ministry, and at one point, I simply began to refer to my friend endearingly as Old Faithful.

The motto, "Neither snow nor rain nor heat nor gloom of night stays these couriers from the swift completion of their appointed rounds" was once attributed to the US Postal Service. Even though it can be found inscribed in block letters on the James Farley Post Office near New York City's Penn Station, the postal service claims that it has no official creed. The words give testimony to the prevailing attitude and dedication that our workers once had for their jobs. These days, the concept of faithfulness does not apply to much of our life view. We take marriage vows, but abandoning them has become far too easy. We are loyal to our favorite sports team as long as they are winning; if not, we look elsewhere. We declare support for a political candidate who we think closely reflects our values, but it is easy to be swayed to someone else's perspective. Even our Pledge of Allegiance to the nation has become tarnished.

I suspect that is also true with many of us in our relationship with God. In Luke 16:1–7, Jesus tells The Parable of the Shrewd Manager. In it, a manager mishandles his master's wealth and is informed that he will be discharged. In his final days of employment, he cleverly plots to seek favor from his master's debtors by reducing what they owe (most likely an excessive amount). He does this in the hope that they might later take care of him. Surprisingly, the rich man expresses his admiration for the steward's actions. Jesus states:

> For the people of this world are more shrewd in dealing with their own kind than are the people of the light. Use your worldly resources to benefit others and make friends. Then, when your earthly possessions are gone, they will welcome you to an eternal home. If you are faithful in little things, you will be faithful in large ones. But if you are dishonest in little things, you won't be honest with greater responsibilities. (Luke 16:8–10 NIV)

At first glance, it may appear that the master may be rewarding dishonesty. The greater principle here is that if everything we own is a gift from God, then we come to understand that we are His stewards. So we can understand Jesus' conclusion that: "No one can serve two masters. Either you will hate the one and love the other, or you will be devoted to the one and despise the other. You cannot serve both God and money" (Luke 16:13 NIV). Bottom line, we must direct our faithfulness toward God, not the things of this world.

When it comes right down to it, we will never be as faithful to God as He is to us. The psalmist said, "Your faithfulness extends to every generation, as enduring as the earth you created" (Psalm 119:90 NLT). Thomas Obadiah Chisholm reflected that wisdom when he penned these words to a famous hymn: "Great is Thy faithfulness! Morning by morning new mercies I see. All I have needed Thy hand hath provided. Great is Thy faithfulness, Lord, unto me!" Therefore, we must be faithful in the little things—our prayers, the love we show to those in need, and by our devotion in applying His Word to our lives. How reassuring it is to know that even when we falter, He is there. The Apostle Paul stated, "If we are faithless, he remains faithful—for he cannot deny himself" (2 Timothy 2:13 ESV). He is the "Old Faithful" to each of us. With great predictability, we can be sure that His next blessing is just minutes away.

Reflection

Consider the times in your life when you have experienced unfaithfulness or have been unfaithful to someone else. How did this affect you over the short and long-term? Over the course of your life, how has God shown His faithfulness to you? What are the little things in which you need to focus in order to be more faithful to Him? What steps will you put in place to demonstrate consistency in practice?

FEBRUARY 5
(Y1, D6)

The State of Your Union

How good and pleasant it is when God's people live together in unity!

—Psalm 133:1 (NIV)

Each year in the United States, the president delivers a State of the Union address to a joint session of Congress. The address fulfills a Constitutional requirement, during which the president traditionally outlines the administration's accomplishments over the previous year as well as the agenda for the coming one. It has become customary to use the phrase, "The State of the Union is strong." During most of the country's first century, a written report had primarily been submitted until the twenty-eighth president, Woodrow Wilson, began the regular practice of verbally delivering the address to Congress. With the arrival of radio and later television, the speech became an effective tool for the president to communicate with the people of the United States. In modern times, the speech is seen as one of the most important events in the US political calendar, one of the few instances when all three branches of the government are assembled under one roof, even though its house is often divided. This separation is often defined by the members' response of standing/not standing and applauding, or not, during key moments.

Three years before his presidency, Abraham Lincoln spoke these words: "A house divided against itself cannot stand." While Lincoln was speaking about the nation's divide over slavery, he was likely referencing his knowledge of scripture. In that passage, Jesus was responding to the religious leaders of Jerusalem who were claiming that He was possessed by Satan because of His ability to cast out demons. By saying that "every city or household divided against itself will not stand" (Matthew 12:25 NIV), Jesus illustrated the fact that success relies on a state of harmony rather than that of conflict. Whether it is a worksite, a sports team, a government party, or a place of worship, things have to work together if anything is to be accomplished. Once conflict occurs, cooperation and usefulness inevitably grind to a halt, and the organization becomes vulnerable. Politics aside, sometimes the best we can do is to honestly examine our personal houses, our own unions, so to speak. For if we are unable to be civil in our day-to-day relationships, we have no right to expect that our appointed leaders will act any different.

The challenge before anyone who claims to follow Christ is to be unified around a common understanding, beginning with our own family. Through the difficult and intense moments in our life, the family should be the mutual support system that strengthens and encourages each of its members. The significance of this basic relationship is regularly mentioned in scripture: "Children, obey your parents in the Lord, for this is right" (Ephesians 6:1 NIV) and "Fathers, do not exasperate your children; instead, bring them up in the training and instruction of the Lord" (Ephesians 6:4 NIV). Likewise, in our chosen relationships such as marriage and friendship, we should: "Always be humble and gentle. Be patient with each other, making allowance for each other's faults because of your love" (Ephesians 4:2 NLT). In Christ's own body of the Church, we should always strive for unity over quarreling. In this case, Paul appeals that "there be no divisions in the church. Rather, be of one mind, united in thought and purpose" (1 Corinthians 1:10 NLT).

Throughout history, we have read of nations and families divided, but it sometimes seems that we have never felt the effects of divisiveness quite as much as today. Rather than having fair and open discussion, character assassinations often prevail. Hatred, scorn, and ridicule seem to have become the norm. The state of our personal unions can only be strong if God is at the heart of their foundation. Additionally, our prayers for those with whom we disagree are essential to keeping our relationships solid. Only God can bring peace to the troubled soul, the troubled nation, and a troubled world. We are challenged to "make every effort to keep the unity of the Spirit through the bond of peace" (Ephesians 4:3 NIV). Rather than dig our trenches and plant ourselves firmly in the ground, we must reach out a hand of love and help heal the discord that is so prevalent. When we find common ground, we will come to realize there is far more that unites us than divides us. Then we will be able to say with absolute certainty that the state of your union is strong.

Reflection

When you take a close look at your everyday unions like marriage, family, friendships, your job, and your church, where do you have work to do? In what aspects of your life have you observed truth, decency, civility, and respect to be thrown out the window? What first steps will you take to initiate the healing process for the rebuilding of healthy and cooperative unions?

FEBRUARY 6
(Y2, D6)

An Everlasting Shield

I can do all things through Him who strengthens me.

—Philippians 4:13 (ESV)

In recent years, all of us have had to become increasingly more aware of the term protective shield. You can get it in the form of a screen shield for your tablet device to resist breakage. During periods of health scare crises, we are encouraged to wear masks. Toothpaste makers are marketing enamel-strengthening toothpastes, making your teeth more resistant to attacks from acid erosion found in food and beverages. There are products that can be purchased when you install carpet that will safeguard your new floor covering from dirt and help it to resist stains. And you can also buy protective sleeves for your credit cards and passports in order to guard from identity theft. Likewise, we have also heard about terrorists who have been surrounded by innocent civilians or their own family members acting as human shields in order to shelter themselves from attack. Indeed, protective shields come in varying forms, some of them helpful to our lifestyle and others which may bear negative consequences if not properly followed.

I remember once hearing a story told by a friend of mine about a time she felt intimidated by the need to advocate to local school officials regarding a special need for her child. Another mother whose child had a similar concern came to her aid and offered to attend the meeting with her. When my friend told this mother how apprehensive she was about this appearance, the mother asked her if she had a nice suit jacket or blazer. She indicated that she did and was told by her comrade to wear it during their conference with school administrators. When she asked why she should do so, the lady told her that she should allow the garment to serve as her suit of armor and that God would protect her during her presentation. She wore the blazer and said that when she began to lose confidence, she would think about her blazer, and it gave her the strength to carry on. She felt that she needed to fight for what her child needed, much the same as a soldier goes to war to take a posture for an ideology.

As Christians, we are also called to put on our armor. When we make a decision to be a believer in Jesus, we are more than simply His child and servant. We are also called upon to become like a soldier firmly standing against the evil that has infiltrated the world and eventually finds its way to us. The Apostle Paul told the Church at Ephesus:

> Finally, be strong in the Lord and in his mighty power. Put on the full armor of God, so that you can take your stand against the devil's schemes. For our struggle is not against flesh and blood, but against the rulers, against the authorities, against the powers of this dark world and against the spiritual forces of evil in the heavenly realms. Therefore put on the full armor of God, so that when the day of evil comes, you may be able to stand your ground, and after you have done everything, to stand. Stand firm then, with the belt of truth buckled around your waist, with the breastplate of righteousness in place, and with your feet fitted with the readiness that comes from the gospel of peace. In addition to all this, take up the shield of faith, with which you can extinguish all the flaming arrows of the evil one. Take the helmet of salvation and the sword of the Spirit, which is the word of God. (Ephesians 6:10–17 NIV)

Now that's real protection!

Peter counseled us to "Stay alert! Watch out for your great enemy, the devil. He prowls around like a roaring lion, looking for someone to devour. Stand firm against him, and be strong in your faith" (1 Peter 5:8–9 NIV). We live in a world where we have become so accustomed to sin that it frequently goes unnoticed or doesn't bother us. We find it far too easy to rationalize our desires based upon what the world values, and our beliefs are sometimes challenged with false doctrine and inaccurate information. James said, "Resist the devil and he will flee from you" (James 4:7 NIV). The full armor of God is not something to be put on and taken off occasionally; it should be wisely worn and permanently. When we equip ourselves in full armor, we have alerted Satan that we're armed because we know who we are in Christ. Unlike the safeguard products we buy, we don't owe a penny for the extra protection. For Christ already paid the price at Calvary. Fortunately for believers, what remains is an everlasting shield.

Reflection

In what ways has God guided and protected you in order that you are able to live every day with an unwavering expectation? How could you use the symbol of God's armor to give hope to others who are having a difficult time taking a stand against worldly values?

FEBRUARY 7
(Y3, D6)

Not Even One Who Is Righteous

He leads me in paths of righteousness for his name's sake.

—Psalm 23:3 (ESV)

Years ago, it was reported that none of the five lead runners in a men's NCAA Division II cross-country championship won. In fact, those five were the only ones of 128 total to run the course correctly. A detour taken by the remaining runners shaved about 1,000 meters off of the steepest portion of the course. The misdirection likely started as the runners neared a place on the route, calling for participants to veer left up an embankment. While there were some flags posted to mark the way, was no monitor present at the next turn. One competitor who stayed on the course waved for fellow runners to follow him, but only four correctly did so. When the remaining runners approached, they apparently lost their bearing, and the others followed. The fastest runners who ended up finishing last could have filed a complaint for the remaining runners to be technically disqualified for leaving the course. But to the relief of meet officials, no one challenged the results. This reflection gives new perspective to the words of the Apostle Paul who said, "I have fought the good fight, I have finished the race, I have kept the faith. Now there is in store for me the crown of righteousness" (2 Timothy 4:7–8 NIV).

Righteousness is often defined as the quality or state of being considered upright, morally correct, and justifiable. Christians believe that they have no ability to achieve righteousness themselves. They receive this precious gift from God exclusively through His mercy and grace. This is contrasted with those who are smugly moralistic and intolerant of the opinions and behavior of others. In Luke 18:9–14, Jesus tells a parable that begins with a warning about self-righteousness and finishes with a timeless biblical principle. The story is about a Pharisee and a tax collector who went into the temple to pray. The Pharisee thanked God that he was not like other sinners and boasted about his fasting and tithing. On the other hand, the tax collector beat his chest and proclaimed that he was a sinner, unable to even lift his eyes toward heaven. The interesting thing about this passage is that Jesus wasn't directing this story to the Pharisees. He was speaking to His disciples, the ones who called Him Lord and teacher. He felt it necessary to address those among His followers who trusted in themselves, displayed self-righteousness, and treated others with contempt. As hard as it is to face the fact that we may be among those to whom this parable is aimed, we are not left without hope. For Jesus concludes: "For those who exalt themselves will be humbled, and those who humble themselves will be exalted" (Luke 18:14 NLT).

Internationally renowned pastor, leadership coach, and author, John Maxwell, tells a funny story about a grandpa visiting his grandchildren. In the afternoon, Grandpa would take a nap. One day, the grandkids decided to play a joke on him. They put Limburger cheese in his mustache. When he woke up, he started sniffing, and he said, "This room stinks!" Then he went into the kitchen. "It stinks in here too." Then he went outside for a breath of fresh air, and after a minute, he said, "The whole world stinks!" If you think about it, that's what the self-righteous person is like. They can sniff out the sins and shortcomings of everyone around them, concluding that everything and everyone smells—except for them, of course. The good news is that true righteousness is possible for each of us but only through the cleansing of sin by Jesus Christ and the indwelling of the Holy Spirit.

The gift of righteousness is entirely free. All we need to do is receive it by faith, by casting off any hope of making ourselves right through our own good deeds, and resting on Jesus alone. Paul tells us, "I do not set aside the grace of God, for if righteousness could be gained through the law, Christ died for nothing!" (Galatians 2:21 NIV). Righteousness brings blessing. It offers peace and joy. It is a law of God's kingdom. Therefore, learning righteousness is a huge investment opportunity, both for this life and for all eternity. It affects not just us but the people around us and the society in which we live. Once you realize that perfect righteousness is not possible for any individual person to attain, then you are running the right course. For we are reminded in Romans 3:10 (NLT) that on our own, "No one is righteous—not even one."

Reflection

Is it really possible to humble ourselves when our natural state is prideful? When others observe you, are they seeing self-righteousness displayed? How are you challenged when you read: "The earnest prayer of a righteous person has great power and produces wonderful results" (James 5:16 NLT)?

FEBRUARY 8
(Y4, D6)

Way Too Long

A scoundrel plots evil, and on their lips it is like a scorching fire.

—Proverbs 16:27 (NIV)

A lady writes to one of those "Dear Doctor" columns about a complaint she has had for over forty years. She states that she has what can be described as a "burning tongue." Her personal physician apparently showed little curiosity or concern. Convinced that she'll never know the cause, the lady was asking for ideas from the professionals at the medical advice column. The responding physician replied that the woman likely has what is commonly known as "burning mouth syndrome." He further stated that while specific medical causes for this condition are not always easily identified, there *is* testing that can be done and helpful treatments which *are* available. He seemed a bit perturbed that both the woman and her physician had tolerated the condition for "way too long." As I read about this medical concern, I recall thinking to myself how there are times when each of us could probably be diagnosed with a burning tongue that one might simply classify as a "sinfully social syndrome."

One day, a friend and I were taking a power walk along a path of a local park. We were chatting away when we began reminiscing about several former classmates, one of whom had lost her husband at a rather young age. The conversation turned to the reality that she had been left to finish raising two children. While they were fairly young at the time of their father's passing, the children would be adults now. Then, in the distance, three women approached us. As they came closer, one of them took off her sunglasses and greeted us with a warm smile and hugs. To our surprise, it was the very classmate about whom we were speaking. I looked at her and said, "You're not going to believe this, but we were just talking about you before you walked up to us." We laughed, acknowledging that it had been a respectful conversation. But one can only imagine how we might have felt had we been gossiping about or maligning this individual in any way! I'm not sure which is worse—a burning tongue or egg on your face.

Badmouthing, slander, and defamation of character are all common ills of our society. Many today believe that gossip is a unifying force, the social glue that tends to hold a group together.

That is, of course, unless you are the focused subject of the gossip. James, the half-brother of Jesus, explains why gossip occurs: "no one can tame the tongue. It is restless and evil, full of deadly poison" (James 3:8 NLT). Sadly, it seems that everyone eventually finds himself or herself to be the recipient of gossip or, worse yet, tempted to gossip about others. The inclination to gossip is part of human nature, and taming the tongue requires God's help. James issues a warning to those who profess to be Christians but fail to regulate their mouth. "If you claim to be religious but don't control your tongue, you are fooling yourself, and your religion is worthless" (James 1:26 NLT). The tongue of humans is sometimes compared to that of an energetic horse which needs a bridle to restrain its fierceness. When there are things that should not be said, a bridled tongue will help one refrain from speaking. When there are things that need to be said, a bridled tongue will assist one to say them in a manner in which they would best be stated.

Half-truths and rush to judgment have become pervasive in our world, and they can destroy a reputation through social media or internet postings in minutes. "Spouting off before listening to the facts is both shameful and foolish… Intelligent people are always ready to learn. Their ears are open for knowledge" (Proverbs 18:13, 15 NLT). Today, many seek neither intelligence nor truth. Rather, they come to delight in spreading the spicy details of the latest scandal, having little concern for the wounded left in its path. Jesus put it this way:

> Whatever is in your heart determines what you say. A good person produces good things from the treasury of a good heart, and an evil person produces evil things from the treasury of an evil heart. And I tell you this, you must give an account on judgment day for every idle word you speak. The words you say will either acquit you or condemn you. (Matthew 12:34–37 NLT)

If you think you are in danger of having burning mouth syndrome, know that it is a condition that can be treated if you consult with the Great Physician. Otherwise, when we come face-to-face with Him, we can fully expect He might ask why we have allowed this sinfully social syndrome to go untreated way too long.

Reflection

What factors make it difficult for some to restrain their tongue? Is it always a sin to criticize? When and how might it be proper? How can you become more accountable for your words?

FEBRUARY 9
(Y5, D6)

The Matter of the Heart

For where your treasure is, there your heart will be also.

—Matthew 6:21 (NIV)

No one wants to be told that they have a heart condition. That diagnosis can oftentimes be concerning and may at some point require invasive procedures or at the very least impose restrictions on one's lifestyle. For years, February has been designated as American Heart Month during which we hear stories about eating heart-healthy, exercising and reducing stress, as well as watching for signs and symptoms of various heart conditions. Just as our heart is recognized as the primary source of life, expressions like "the heart of the matter" are used to designate the essence of an issue that keeps it alive. The heart is depicted as the symbol of love, and this time of the year, heart-shaped boxes filled with chocolates are given as tokens of our affection to someone we care about. We often see a likeness of Cupid represented with his bow and arrow while superimposed over a heart in the background.

Who can forget those fictional characters who strolled down the yellow brick road in the land of Oz with Dorothy? Among them is the rusted old Tin Man who frequently needed a shot from his oil can along the journey, but it wasn't long before we realize that what he really wanted was a heart. In the end, when he finally appears before the Wizard in Emerald City, he gets some false guidance: "And remember, my sentimental friend, that a heart is not judged by how much you love but by how much you are loved by others." In fiction, maybe so, but in the real stuff of life, God would tell us otherwise. In fairness to the story, however, the heart that God wants us to be concerned about is not one that has any physical significance but rather a spiritual one. "For as he thinks in his heart, so is he" (Proverbs 23:7).

The scriptures are filled with hundreds of references about our spiritual heart. These passages tell us that our heart should be forgiving (Leviticus 19:17), willing (Deuteronomy.15:10), discerning (1 Kings 3:9), cheerful (Psalm 16:9), trusting (Proverbs 3:5), wise (Ecclesiastes. 8:5), rejoicing (Zephaniah 3:14), gentle and humble (Matthew 11:29), sincere (Ephesians 6:5), and pure (1 Timothy 1:5). In the Old Testament, Samuel was sent on a mission by the Lord to find Jesse of

Bethlehem, one of whose sons was to be the future king of Israel. Jesse had seven sons and had all but one pass in front of Samuel. "But the Lord said to Samuel, 'Do not consider his appearance or his height, for I have rejected him. The Lord does not look at the things people look at. People look at the outward appearance, but the Lord looks at the heart'" (1 Samuel 16:7 NIV). Interestingly enough, it was the seventh and the youngest, a shepherd by the name of David, whom the Lord had chosen. Consequently, it is no coincidence that it was through the lineage of David that Christ was born.

Just as God knew the heart of David, He also knows our own. For the Lord searches every heart (1 Chronicles 28:9 NIV). As with the great wizard in the land of Oz, the world teaches that our lives will be valued by how many friends we have or how many good deeds we've displayed for others to see. But if that's the measure of a man, then, as in the Parable of the Sower (Matthew 13:1–23; Mark 4:1–20; Luke 8:4–15), we are only sowing seed on rocky soil. We become shallow and have no depth to our roots. Like many in Jesus' time, our society has become spiritually hardened. When this occurs, it's time for a change in our thinking, the root of our conscience, better known as the heart. Jesus said: "For this people's heart has become calloused; they hardly hear with their ears, and they have closed their eyes. Otherwise they might see with their eyes, hear with their ears, understand with their hearts and turn, and I would heal them" (Matthew 13:15 NIV). While it's important that we keep our physical heart healthy, we must protect our spiritual one as well. Therefore, "Guard your heart above all else, for it determines the course of your life" (Proverbs 4:23 NLT). When we do so, we will echo the words of Max Lucado: "The heart of the matter is, and always will be, the matter of the heart."

Reflection

Is it possible that God knows our heart even better than we know ourselves? In what ways can you be part of a worldly society and yet love, serve, and obey Him (Deuteronomy 10:12, 11:13, 30:2) with all your heart? In order to experience the true heart of Christ, what do you need to repent?

FEBRUARY 10
(Y6, D6)

Following His Lead

The LORD says, "I will guide you along the best pathway for
your life. I will advise you and watch over you."

—Psalm 32:8 (NLT)

On a cold, rainy morning of February 11, 1861, one day before his fifty-second birthday, President-elect Abraham Lincoln boarded a two-car private train loaded with his family's belongings for Washington DC. Leaving his home in Springfield, Illinois, he knew that his actions upon entering office would likely lead to civil war. Speaking to a crowd before departing, he said, "Here I have lived a quarter of a century, and have passed from a young man to an old man. Here my children have been born, and one is buried. I now leave, not knowing when, or whether ever, I may return, with a task before me greater than that which rested upon Washington. Without the assistance of that Divine Being… I cannot succeed. With that assistance, I cannot fail… To His care commending you, as I hope in your prayers you will commend me, I bid you an affectionate farewell." Lincoln understood who would direct his path. He would indeed return to Springfield just over four years later on a funeral train following his assassination.

Nick Foles, MVP for the Super Bowl Champion Philadelphia Eagles in 2018, wasn't supposed to be seeing much playing time as the backup quarterback. In fact, two years before, he contemplated retiring and walking away from the game. Foles credits prayer with giving him the strength to stay in the NFL. "It took a lot more faith to come back and play than it would've to go in the other direction," he said. "Either way would've been fine. Either way, I would've trusted in God. I would've done something else and glorified God in that instance." Foles decided to return to football and became the backup for the Eagles, a team he used to start for. However, after the team's new starter, Carson Wentz, suffered a season-ending knee injury, Foles took over, leading the team to their first-ever Super Bowl championship. When Wentz, also a devout Christian, was asked about his replacement, he said, "It's crazy how it has all unfolded, but God has had a plan for him through this whole thing, and he knows that." The next time he leaves football, he indicated, his goal is to become a youth pastor.

What do these two men have in common? They both believed they were on a journey in which God was leading them. Not everyone listens for God's direction, but God's plan is still there. Following the death of Elisha in the Old Testament, God chose the Prophet Jonah to go to Nineveh, the capital of a neighboring nation and enemy to Israel. Jonah feared what would happen if he went into that wicked city, so he tried to run from God by boarding a ship which was going in the opposite direction. Jonah's ill-advised attempt to escape from God was doomed to fail. "But the LORD hurled a powerful wind over the sea, causing a violent storm that threatened to break the ship apart" (Jonah 1:4 NLT). Eventually, his shipmates threw him overboard where "the LORD had arranged for a great fish to swallow Jonah. And Jonah was inside the fish for three days and three nights" (Jonah 1:17 NLT). He soon realized God was with him everywhere he went. Even in the stomach of the great fish, God could hear Jonah's prayer (Jonah 2:2). After rescuing him, God again directed Jonah to go to Nineveh. This time, he did.

Although some classify the story of Jonah as a fable, interestingly enough, Jesus referred to him when He spoke to the scribes and Pharisees who had asked Him for a sign. His response: "For as Jonah was in the belly of the great fish for three days and three nights, so will the Son of Man be in the heart of the earth for three days and three nights" (Matthew 12:40 NLT). The plan for Jesus was clear, just as it was for President Lincoln and quarterback Foles. To follow their example, all you have to do is "trust in the LORD with all your heart; do not depend on your own understanding. Seek his will in all you do, and he will show you which path to take" (Proverbs 3:5–6 NLT). You can be sure that God has a plan for each life. We simply have to pray for direction and listen for His voice. Whether it is revealed through His Word, in the course of events, or through interaction with others, we will know when He is prompting us. "My sheep listen to my voice; I know them, and they follow me" (John 10:27 NIV). When we realize that we are here for a bigger purpose than ourselves, we are well on our way to hearing His voice and following His lead.

Reflection

Have you ever found yourself running away from God and His call for your life? What are some things you might implement in order to be more intentional about listening for His voice? The next time you hear it, will you allow Him to lead you in a possibly uncertain direction?

FEBRUARY 11
(Y6, D7)

The Bigger Person

Be kind to one another, tenderhearted, forgiving one another, as God in Christ forgave you.

—Ephesians 4:32 (ESV)

A number of years ago, a young man who worked for me came into my office and sat down. I could see that he was not having a good day, and I became his listening ear. He started to tell me about the house he and his wife were building. Apparently, there was some property variance issue needing to be resolved. It would affect the adjoining property which they had sold to another couple who had once been good friends. In order to resolve the concern, entrance to the property belonging to my colleague would need a right of access through that of the unyielding neighbors. My young coworker was so distraught about the situation that he was having a difficult time focusing on his job duties. Having a few years of experience beyond that of my colleague, I offered some advice for life. Thoughtfully, I paused and reassured him that one way or another, this situation would ultimately be resolved. "But," I reflected, "what are you going to do down the line?"

With a somewhat puzzled look on his face, he asked, "What do you mean?"

I continued, "When this is all concluded, what do you plan to do when the day comes and this neighbor needs you?" He just looked at me with a blank look of uncertainty. Before he had a chance to answer, I told him, "When that day comes, my friend, you need to be the bigger person." I hope that in some small way, I gave my associate a lesson on forgiveness that day.

When they first met, Edwin Stanton described Abraham Lincoln as a "long lank creature from Illinois, wearing a dirty linen duster for a coat, on the back of which the perspiration had splotched wide stains that resembled a map of the continent." The relationship between Stanton and Lincoln got off to a bad start in 1855 when Mr. Lincoln was hired by Stanton, a high-powered Washington DC lawyer, for a case set to be tried in Illinois. Lincoln accepted and worked tirelessly, conducting research for the legal team, but he felt that Stanton had been very rude and discourteous toward him. Five short years later, in 1860, that same man who Stanton once referred to as "giraffe-like" was now the president of the United States. In 1862, Lincoln needed to appoint a new Secretary of

War. The president's choice of Stanton would reveal his ability to transcend personal humiliation and bitterness, allowing forgiveness to occur. Lincoln's trust of Stanton began to change the relationship, and Stanton responded with unfailing loyalty. Disparaging words of Lincoln not only disappeared from his lips, but neither he nor any of his family members would tolerate a scornful remark of their beloved president. It was Stanton who sat by Lincoln's bed throughout the night after the president was shot at Ford's Theater. As Lincoln passed on from this life to the next, Stanton declared, "Now he belongs to the ages." Because Abraham Lincoln was willing to forgive and trust, he gained a friend—a very dear friend.

Peter once asked Jesus how often one should forgive someone who sins against him, anticipating that seven times might be the expectation. "Jesus answered, 'I tell you, not seven times, but seventy-seven times'" (Matthew 18:22 NIV). Then he proceeded to tell the Parable of the Unforgiving Servant (Matthew 18:23–34) about a king who wanted to settle the debts of his servants. One owed a substantial amount and begged the king for patience in repayment. Eventually, his master took pity on him and forgave the debt. This same man then sought revenge on another who owed him, seemingly failing to show the same compassion. This was reported to the king who called him in, stating, "You evil servant! I forgave you that tremendous debt because you pleaded with me. Shouldn't you have mercy on your fellow servant, just as I had mercy on you?" (Matthew 18:32–33 NIV). The man was then jailed until the entire debt was repaid. Jesus concludes, "That's what my heavenly Father will do to you if you refuse to forgive your brothers and sisters from your heart" (Matthew 18:35 NIV). The takeaway from this parable: if you don't practice forgiveness, you might be the one who pays most dearly. When someone becomes involved in doing wrong, they are acting like a flawed human. But when we forgive them, then *we* are acting like God who is always willing to forgive us. In order to demonstrate that kind of witness, we must swallow our pride and learn to forgive. Then and only then will we become the bigger person.

Reflection

How does God's mercy and grace empower us to pursue His help in seeking forgiveness toward others we might otherwise have a difficult time forgiving? In the Bible, the Greek word translated as "forgiveness" literally means "to let go." What are some things you need to consider letting go?

FEBRUARY 12
(Y1, D7)

Love... Regardless

Hatred stirs up conflict, but love covers over all wrongs.

—Proverbs 10:12 (NIV)

A number of years ago, I was having a visit with a friend whom I had known for over three decades. During this get-together, I was sitting bedside next to her in the nursing home where she now resided. I suspected it would be one of my last conversations with her as she was quite ill. The chatter was mostly light as we reflected on the activities we had shared together. We laughed, enjoying each recollection that came to memory. Then she reminded me that there had been a time when she was angry with me over something I had done. Surprised that I didn't remember, she giggled a little because supposedly, she called me "stupid" at the time. Sharing my reaction on that occasion, she stated that before we parted that day, I asked her if she didn't love me anymore. She was amazed that I had no recall of her response, but *she* certainly did. She apparently said, "Yes, I do love you, but then I love a lot of stupid people." That was the blessing of my friend, Sally, because you always knew where you stood with her.

During the month of February, especially as Valentine's Day draws near, we find ourselves celebrating love. When we think about this day, our mind goes to flowers, candy, and other heart-filled expressions of romantic love. However, love comes in many forms. My friend, Sally, loved me, even when she thought I was stupid and told me so. In the 1970 film adaptation of the novel *Love Story*, author Erich Segal brought fame to the oft-repeated catchphrase, "Love means never having to say you're sorry." The line has been criticized and perhaps unfairly mocked for suggesting that apologies are unnecessary in a loving relationship. However, in my opinion, the author got it wrong. There is always room for an apology, especially when one is seeking forgiveness. One of Jesus' disciples put it this way: "Above all, love each other deeply, because love covers over a multitude of sins" (1 Peter 4:8 NIV). We cover sin by acknowledging it and then extending the forgiveness God gives us to others. To "cover" sin is to forgive it, and the absolute best example of a love like that is Jesus' sacrificial death on our behalf.

I was recently involved in a discussion about what God expects of us. Someone said that if we could just follow the Ten Commandments, we would be doing what God expects of us. I replied that Jesus made it even more simple when in an attempt to try to trick Him, one of the Pharisees considered to be an expert in the Law asked Him what was the greatest commandment.

> Jesus replied, "You must love the Lord your God with all your heart, all your soul, and all your mind." This is the first and greatest commandment. A second is equally important: "Love your neighbor as yourself." The entire law and all the demands of the prophets are based on these two commandments. (Matthew 22:37–40 NLT)

If you love God with all your heart and soul, you are especially obeying the first four commandments, and if you love your neighbor as yourself, you will be obeying the last six. Therefore, love is the fulfillment of the entirety of God's law.

When we prayerfully consider Jesus' words and the fact that all the rules and laws in Scripture can actually be summarized by these two commandments, we understand just how challenging it is for us to keep God's directives and how often we fail to do so. This hopefully leads us to a recognition that we can never be righteous before God on our own accord. As Christians, we can only strive to "love because He first loved us" (1 John 4:19 NIV). As we receive the loving gift of His Son, unworthy as we are, we are able to show love to others who might not otherwise be deserving in our eyes. Jesus loves us fully without any limits, conditions, or restrictions. He doesn't expect anything in return, except for our reciprocal love, of course. As we extend it in His direction, He gives us the ability to offer love to people we don't have to or sometimes don't even want to. Jesus said that the loving actions of His followers would be the way to point the world to Him (John 13:35). In doing so, we demonstrate that we are able to love unconditionally to the end. That, my friends, is the true essence of love—regardless.

Reflection

Consider occasions in your life when you were difficult to love because you were rebellious or perhaps downright stupid. Who were the persons who offered their love to you during those times? Did you seek or feel God's love during those periods of struggle? Think of a specific individual or type of person whom you find difficult to love. In what ways might you extend unconditional love to them?

FEBRUARY 13
(Y2, D7)

Heartbroken

He heals the brokenhearted and binds up their wounds.

—Psalm 147:3 (NIV)

You discover that heart-shaped box of Valentine's Day candy you saw in his car wasn't intended for you. If you are a teenage girl who thought the guy really liked you, you probably feel like your world is coming to an end. If you are his fiancé, it could be the beginning of a slippery slope leading to mistrust and the questioning of whether this relationship is really going anywhere. Either way, your heart is broken. Heartbreak comes in many forms. It can surface in the death of a family member. It may present itself in the mishap of a child. Or it might occur when you realize that a person you once considered to be a close friend has turned their back on you. The only thing you can know for certain is that you are not the first person who has gone down this path and, for sure, you won't be the last.

The medical field has grown to recognize a condition known as "broken heart syndrome." It can result from emotional stress so severe that it actually causes physical damage to the heart. Consider an older couple who had a loving marriage for over half a century and centered their lives around each other. When one of them passes, the grief can be so intense that the other one suddenly dies as well. Their heart is broken. In his book, *The Broken Heart,* Dr. James Lynch states:

> We have learned that human beings have varied and at times profound effects on the cardiac systems of other human beings. Loneliness and grief often overwhelm bereaved individuals and the toll taken on the heart can be clearly seen. As the mortality statistics indicate, this is not myth or romantic fairy tale. All available evidence suggests that people do indeed die of broken hearts.

Heartbreak can move from a temporary emotion of anguish and distress to a sustaining condition of hopelessness and despair. It can be crippling if you allow it to be, and it may affect the way you view the world. It can separate you from God or it can bring you nearer. Scripture tells us that

"The LORD is close to the brokenhearted and saves those who are crushed in spirit" (Psalm 34:18 NIV). Since we don't quickly recover from a heartbreak situation, it is important that we place our hope in the one who will help us to return to some form of normalcy one day at a time. In the interim, His "grace is sufficient" (2 Corinthians 12:9 NIV). If we make God our constant when everything around us seems to have changed, then little by little, we will find healing. It might be in the form of new relationships, old hobbies that have found meaning again, or other persons who have a need and give you renewed purpose. We should take heed from the words of Helen Keller: "When one door of happiness closes, another opens, but often we look so long at the closed door that we do not see the one that has opened for us."

No one understands our heartbreak better than God because He experienced decisive heartbreak. Songwriter Dallas Holm expressed it this way: "So you got your heart broke in two, and you hurt so bad you don't know what to do; And you think that you're the only one who's ever felt this way. But there was sure another one another day." Yes, it was God the Father who allowed His Son to suffer for the world in order that we might be saved from our own sinful nature. Shortly before Jesus died, "He took Peter and Zebedee's two sons, James and John, and He became anguished and distressed. He told them, 'My soul is crushed with grief to the point of death. Stay here and keep watch with me'" (Matthew 26:37–38 NLT). We must first notice His suffering before we can truly understand His heartbreak and, ultimately, His great love. Then we come to understand what is meant in the scriptural passage, "We love because he first loved us" (1 John 4:19 NIV). So, yes, there will be times in each of our lives when we feel like our heart is broken beyond repair. We should not minimize the real feelings we have when this occurs. Nothing about this place is ordinary. It is actually sacred ground. It's the place of the heartbroken, and He can help us through it because He has been there.

Reflection

What heartbreak from your past will assist you in sharing God's love and show it to others? On Valentine's Day and as we prepare to enter the season of Lent, are there ways that you might be sensitive to those who have recently experienced heartbreak?

FEBRUARY 14
(Y3, D7)

Near to the Heart of God

As a face is reflected in water, so the heart reflects the real person.

—Proverbs 27:19 (NLT)

No Valentine's Day is complete without a good love story. In his book, *When God Winks through Love*, Squire Rushnell tells the story of Norma and Gordon Yeager who, having been married on her graduation day, were deeply in love for seventy-two years. The Iowa couple were inseparable until one fateful day when they were in an accident and rushed to the hospital, clinging to life. When the family arrived at the hospital, they noticed that the staff had placed their beds side-by-side and that they were holding hands. At 3:38 p.m., Gordon passed away. But the son looked at his father's heart monitor and noticed it was still beating, questioning how this could be. The nurse simply said, "Oh they are still holding hands. Her heart is beating through his" (the same way it did for seventy-two years). Exactly one hour later at 4:48 p.m., Norma passed away, going on to meet Gordon at the gates of heaven.

In February, the symbol of the heart is as common as a box of chocolates or a picture of one pierced by Cupid's arrow. It represents expressions of love and affection with emblematic references as far back as the Middle Ages. In more recent times, one of the most widely distributed and well-known logos, "I (followed by the heart symbol) NY," was first used in 1977 to promote the American city and the state. In biblical references, the heart was thought to be the central organ that controlled all activities and determined one's character. Because we are created by God, it was assumed by those who knew Him that He fully understood who we were by looking at our heart. This led the psalmist to ask the question, "Would not God have discovered it, since he knows the secrets of the heart?" (Psalm 44:21 NIV). Today, there are often commonly understood heart references used to characterize people. These include terms like "halfhearted," "heart of gold," or declarations such as "His heart was in the right place."

There is no better account of God's understanding of one's heart than His calling of David. The Lord said to his father, Samuel: "The LORD doesn't see things the way you see them. People judge by outward appearance, but the LORD looks at the heart" (1 Samuel 16:7 NLT). After his sins of murder and adultery, King David needed a new heart. He knew the only way to find was to pray these words, "Create in me a clean heart, O God. Renew a loyal spirit within me" (Psalm 51:10 NLT). David clarified that only God could restore his spiritual well-being. In Jesus' day, the teachers of the law once criticized the disciples for not following the handwashing tradition of the elders. Jesus called them hypocrites and quoted Isaiah by saying, "These people honor me with their lips, but their hearts are far from me" (Mark 7:6 NIV).

Now more than ever, our hearts allow us to insensitively retreat from God. Striving for success and recognition, open immorality, and downright selfishness are but a few impediments to becoming closer to Him. We should be challenged by these words: "Above all else, guard your heart, for everything you do flows from it" (Proverbs 4:23 NIV). Despite his sinful actions, David knew that if your motives are pure, you will be moving in the direction of God's will for your life. We can develop a heart acceptable to God when we allow ourselves to be humbled, confess our sins, perform acts of service, and trust in Him. Perhaps the lyricist, Cleland B. McAfee, caught this vision when he wrote these words:

> There is a place of comfort sweet, near to the heart of God;
> a place where we our Savior meet, near to the heart of God.
> O Jesus, blest Redeemer, sent from the heart of God,
> hold us who wait before thee near to the heart of God.

He who made us knows us better than we know ourselves. He sees those conflicts within us that no one else will ever notice. Only He searches the thoughts and intents of our heart. And yet He continues to love us just the same. Now that's impressive because that *is* true love, near to the very heart of God!

Reflection

Jesus said, "God blesses those whose hearts are pure, for they will see God" (Matthew 5:8 NLT). What are those impure things that pull your heart away from Jesus? How might you consider revising your daily routine in order to break old habits and draw closer to His will for your life?

FEBRUARY 15
(Y4, D7)

The Helper

My help comes from the LORD, the Maker of heaven and earth.

—Psalm 121:2 (NIV)

On the outskirts of a small town in rural America, Frank and Carol owned a small restaurant a number of years ago. Carol was a wonderful cook, and people would travel from all over the area to visit their establishment and savor her tasty food. Frank would cover the register, sometimes assist in the kitchen, and he would also tend the bar area. This space held not much more than half a dozen stools and several small tables where folks could have a drink before dinner or gather for some fellowship after a local sports event. Like any other bartender of sorts, I am sure that Frank heard his share of tales and woe. He told me one time that over his many years, he served as a listening ear for a lot of customers. But he also knew that there were occasions when they required some help beyond what he was capable of providing. In those situations, he would often call his pastor friend from the neighborhood church to intervene. The great thing about Frank was that he was able to discern when the conversation was out of his element, knowing that it was time to call in a different helper for support.

Many people who are cult followers of the *Star Wars* series are familiar with the phrase "May the force be with you." Used as an expression of goodwill, it would often be stated as a formal farewell by the Jedi when someone was about to face a test of imminent danger. As sojourners here on earth, we do not have to worry about that far, far away galaxy. Our day-to-day lives are filled with enough challenges, having been born into a world where we will encounter plenty of sin and peril of our own. Any parent knows that when a child falls, you pick him up, let him know he'll be okay, and send them on their way. Similarly, when God's children slip and fall, our Helper is always there to pick us up. We are told, "If you then, who are evil, know how to give good gifts to your children, how much more will the heavenly Father give the Holy Spirit to those who ask him!" (Luke 11:13 ESV).

Someone once said that we should not search for God in times of trouble, for He is already right by our side. Those words would bear out in scripture which states: "God is our refuge and strength, a very present help in trouble" (Psalm 46:1 NIV). But we do not have to be experiencing adversity to feel God's presence and contribution along our journey. The reality for the believer is that God helps us not only in times of failure, but He is also present and answerable for all our triumphs. For without His continual existence in our lives, where would we be? We should strive to be ever-mindful of His presence and be eternally grateful for His ongoing sustenance. Max Lucado has written, "The Wizard of Oz says look inside yourself and find self. God says look inside yourself and find the Holy Spirit. The first will get you to Kansas. The latter will get you to heaven. Take your pick."

You may have heard or even subscribe to the old adage "God helps those who help themselves." While it may be a saying, it's not biblical. God died for us because we were unable to save ourselves. As we walk with Christ, we have the assurance from Him that we will be provided with our own spiritual helper. Jesus said, "I will ask the Father, and He will give you another Helper, that He may be with you forever" (John 14:16 ESV). God not only allowed His Son to die a horrible death for you and me, but He also provided His Holy Spirit to guide us through the remainder of our daily challenges here on earth. In doing so, we are told in scripture that His spirit will teach us (1 Corinthians 2:13), speak through us (Matthew 10:20), give us help in times of weakness (Romans 8:26), and will allow us to experience hope (Romans 15:13) and encouragement (Acts 9:31). My friend, Frank, was smart enough to realize that he couldn't do it on his own and that he needed a helper. If Frank understood that, so should we. In those times when it seems we are facing life all alone, remember "God is my help; the Lord is the one who sustains me" (Psalm 54:4 NIV).

Reflection

How do you currently experience the Helper's presence in meeting your everyday needs? Do you ever feel God's Holy Spirit working and prodding you to help someone else in need? In order to prepare to offer that help and direction, what are some ways you might seek God's provision of guidance and comfort as a living example for others to follow?

FEBRUARY 16
(Y5, D7)

Getting Even

Never pay back evil with more evil. Do things in such a way
that everyone can see you are honorable.

—Romans 12:17 (NLT)

It is not uncommon these days for many folks to take umbrage with decisions, statements, or actions which they feel have created a sense of unfairness directed toward them, regardless of intention. We have become a litigious society where "payback time" is frequently used as its main operating principle. Political protests have become common and can surface anywhere. These range from delay tactics in our legislatures to incited acts of violence in the streets of our communities. In our large cities, gang warfare is prevalent and has resulted in widespread loss of life simply over turf issues. And although these types of situations may seem far-reaching for many, it may not be so unusual for us to become involved in social media posts which also attempt payback. In turn, these may end up slandering or destroying another individual's reputation simply to "get even." The Greek philosopher, Epictetus, is credited as having once stated, "We have two ears and one mouth so that we can listen twice as much as we speak." We all might be better off if we would learn to pause longer and think more deliberately before we act.

Recently, I watched a TV program where one of the recurring characters was closing his place of business for the day when a perfect stranger walked in. The stranger was poorly dressed and seemed uneasy. My guard went up, as did that of the fictional proprietor who asked what the individual wanted. The stranger said that he needed a few hundred dollars to buy a suit because he had a job offer and desired to make a good impression. When the owner tells the man to leave, the viewer anticipates that at any time, this situation is going to turn into a robbery. Instead, the man thanked the manager who had refused him money, and he turned to exit. Then, out of compassion, the businessman reached into the cash drawer and pulled out two hundred dollars. Later, after hearing what he had done, his partners in the business relentlessly made fun of their colleague, stating that the supposed loan was "money he would never see again." Nearing the end of the program, the man walks back into the establishment, this time well-dressed, and repays the borrowed money. The moral of the story is to believe in your fellow man. But we know all-too-well that this type of fairy-tale ending often plays out very differently in real life.

The principle of "an eye for an eye" (sometimes referred to as the law of retaliation) is part of the Law of Moses used in the Israelites' justice system. It was intended to be a guide for judges and was never used to settle grievances personally. However, in Jesus' day, the Pharisees and scribes were applying it to everyday relationships, in fact teaching that personal revenge was acceptable. Enter Jesus who says:

> You have heard that it was said, "Eye for eye, and tooth for tooth." But I tell you, do not resist an evil person. If anyone slaps you on the right cheek, turn to them the other cheek also. And if anyone wants to sue you and take your shirt, hand over your coat as well. If anyone forces you to go one mile, go with them two miles. Give to the one who asks you, and do not turn away from the one who wants to borrow from you. (Matthew 5:38–42 NIV)

Jesus' intent was not to void that governments have the right to punish those who have committed crimes but rather to state that we be personally led by the concept of forgiveness. He continued, "You have heard that it was said, 'Love your neighbor and hate your enemy.' But I tell you, love your enemies and pray for those who persecute you" (Matthew 5:43–44 NIV).

We who follow Christ are challenged to be different from those who follow the natural inclination to respond in kind. The world says, "If someone punches you, punch him back." But one of Jesus' chosen stated just the opposite: "Don't repay evil for evil. Don't retaliate with insults when people insult you. Instead, pay them back with a blessing. That is what God has called you to do, and he will bless you for it" (1 Peter 3:9 NLT). There is no "getting even" in instigating harm against one who has caused you harm. "Evenness" will occur only when we allow God's love to take its place. That's a payback for all of eternity.

Reflection

Can you think of a time when you paid back hurt for hurt, evil for evil? How did it make you feel? Were you an effective witness for Christ when you did so? Will you ponder a different response when the next opportunity presents itself? Are you able to pray for others who oppress you this day?

FEBRUARY 17
(Y6, D7)

A True Friend Indeed

As iron sharpens iron, so a friend sharpens a friend.

—Proverbs 27:17 (NLV)

February 13, 1831, was the birthdate of John Aaron Rawlins, a man who could have easily made little of his life. However, he overcame an impoverished family background and limited education. Rawlins became known as a self-made man who went through a period of self-directed study to make up for his lack of formal education. After studying law, Rawlins passed the bar and entered into a law partnership in his hometown of Galena, Illinois, while also becoming a noted public speaker. At the outbreak of the Civil War, he gave a notable pro-Union speech and soon became known to another Galena resident, Ulysses S. Grant. Rawlins joined the Union Army and served primarily as an officer on Grant's staff. His promotions were linked to Grant's success on the battlefields and Grant's advancement in the Union Army under President Abraham Lincoln. Later, when Grant became President, he appointed Rawlins as his Secretary of War. Unfortunately, he died of tuberculosis at the young age of thirty-eight.

Rawlins had an absentee father who was prone to drink. His father's behavior affected his own strong attitudes and fears concerning alcohol. According to one historian, Rawlins' abstention was caused by his belief that if he took even one drink, he would not be able to stop. When the Civil War started, Rawlins became a personal aide to Grant. He was Grant's principal staff officer throughout the war, and Grant said that Rawlins was nearly indispensable. Grant had a reputation of being a heavy drinker when he served on the frontier in the 1850s, and it appears Rawlins was instrumental in keeping the general from excessive alcohol consumption. On one occasion, when Grant was alleged to have been drinking excessively with other officers, Rawlins became aware. Considering himself to be Grant's protector when it came to alcohol, Rawlins wrote him a letter of concern about the matter which was never sent. It was, however, later found by historians. Rawlins became Grant's chief defender against allegations of insobriety, and the two became close personal friends.

The truth is we all need friends. We often hear that many of the tragedies in our society are provoked by individuals who are friendless, otherwise labeled as loners. A wise principle of friendship is found in Ecclesiastes. "Two people are better off than one, for they can help each other succeed. If one person falls, the other can reach out and help. But someone who falls alone is in real trouble" (Ecclesiastes 4:9–10 NLT). The hymn writer, Will L. Thompson, reflected this sentiment in a more spiritual way with the following lyrics:

> Jesus is all the world to me, my life, my joy, my all;
> He is my strength from day to day, without Him I would fall.
> When I am sad, to Him I go, no other one can cheer me so;
> When I am sad, He makes me glad… He's my Friend.

Even though they may sometimes disagree, friends are like-minded. Friendship is a relationship entered into by individuals and is only as good or as close as those individuals choose to make it. A friend is one with whom you can be yourself, someone in whom you can confide with complete trust. Jesus said:

> Greater love has no one than this: to lay down one's life for one's friends. You are my friends if you do what I command. I no longer call you servants, because a servant does not know his master's business. Instead, I have called you friends, for everything that I learned from my Father I have made known to you. You did not choose me, but I chose you and appointed you so that you might go and bear fruit—fruit that will last—and so that whatever you ask in my name the Father will give you. This is my command: Love each other. (John 15:13–17 NIV)

Someone has said that if you can count your true friends on the fingers of one hand, you are blessed. If you do not have a handful of friends in your life, then invite Jesus to walk your journey with you. He is the best friend you will ever have—a true friend indeed.

Reflection

On those occasions when you have felt loneliness and wondered if you had any true friends, have you considered asking Jesus to be by your side? What are some ways that you might reach out to others who appear to be loners, offering them the gift of Christ and your friendship? In those times when you feel isolated, how can you begin to reconnect with others and learn to trust God in the process?

FEBRUARY 18
(Y7, D7)

A Loose Cannon

A person without self-control is like a city with broken-down walls.

—Proverbs 25:28 (NLT)

In any election year, it's interesting to listen to the political candidates debate the issues. If you observe them with any frequency, there will most likely be one or more who will come across as being a "loose cannon." Theodore Roosevelt was once credited with having made the statement, "I don't want to be the old cannon loose on the deck in the storm." The phrase itself originated years before as a nautical term referring to cannons that were once carried on war ships. As one might expect, cannons were very heavy and were secured to the deck of their vessel. During a battle or a storm, these guns would sometimes break loose. Whenever this happened, there was a great chance they would crush anything in their path, including individuals or the ship structure itself. Similarly, a person who becomes labeled as a loose cannon is one who is seen engaging in reckless behavior (saying or doing anything) that may ultimately endanger the reputation or welfare of others, at times in a most undignified manner.

In a position I once held, my responsibilities contained various personnel functions which included the hiring and firing of individuals. There were times when I was faced with the task of having to dismiss a colleague, sometimes one whom I may have once hired. I always proceeded with the foremost principle that regardless of the circumstances, the person should be allowed to leave with dignity. I suppose I did this knowing that is how I would want to be treated. I also understood that the way I would respond to these individuals was deeply engrained in my faith. I knew of supervisors who would literally try to destroy people they were terminating. I thought it was better to make a person believe that just because it did not work out in one place did not mean that they could not go on and live a successful life. Perhaps at one time, I had taken counsel from Timothy who said: "A servant of the Lord must not quarrel but must be kind to everyone, be able to teach, and be patient with difficult people" (2 Timothy 2:24 NLT).

In Jesus' day, it would not be uncommon to stone one who committed adultery. The Pharisees brought such a woman before Jesus, asking, "Now in the Law, Moses commanded us to stone such women. So what do you say?" (John 8:5 ESV). Aware that they were trying to trick Him, Jesus simply wrote on the ground, using his finger.

> And as they continued to ask him, he stood up and said to them, "Let him who is without sin among you be the first to throw a stone at her." Eventually, when they had all gone away, He asked her who now stood in condemnation of her. "No one, sir," she said. "Then neither do I condemn you," Jesus declared. "Go now and leave your life of sin." (John 8:7–11 ESV).

Had Jesus been a "loose cannon," He would not have been nearly as effective. Instead, He paused, prodding the consciences of the accusers. When they departed, it gave Him private time to show forgiveness toward the one who had, in fact, sinned.

It's been said that "people should always be an ends and never a means." Everyone has intrinsic value. To use or tear down someone in order to build yourself up would certainly not be in accord with the teachings of Jesus. We shouldn't treat people as an object or resource in order that our own goals might be accomplished. Instead, the Apostle Paul said, "Do not let any unwholesome talk come out of your mouths, but only what is helpful for building others up according to their needs, that it may benefit those who listen" (Ephesians 4:29 NIV). Sometimes it is far better to say nothing if it may ultimately hurt or destroy another person. It is obvious that we all have cause to do so on occasion. The political pundits will tell you that it's an effective way to gain an advantage in the polls. However, when we talk more than we listen and accuse more than we praise, then we become much less than God would have us be. We end up becoming one of theirs rather than one of His—just another loose cannon.

Reflection

Looking back on your life, are there times that you have been reckless with the lives of others while acting like a loose cannon? Has your faith journey taken you to a different place? Are there situations or persons that you need to avoid to prevent falling back into this pattern? In what ways might you help others, who are reckless in dealing with others, learn from today's scriptures?

FEBRUARY 19
(Y1, D8)

Planting Seeds for the Kingdom

The Kingdom of God is like a farmer who scatters seed on the ground. Night and day, while he's asleep or awake, the seed sprouts and grows, but he does not understand how it happens.

—Mark 4:26–27 (NLT)

A comment made years ago by any politician can be most unhelpful if that individual is now running for a higher office. It can serve to negatively bias the opinion of thousands of perspective voters. An example was a politician who once said that he could teach anyone how to be a farmer. He went on to explain that all you have to do is dig a hole, put a seed in with dirt on top, add water, and up comes the corn. While this recorded remark was likely a minor portion of a larger conversation, it served to isolate and insult the intelligence of many hardworking Americans who spend a huge portion of their day growing the food that eventually ends up on our tables. The comment is an oversimplification of what has become a complex industry in our country. Even the novice who may occasionally start a plant in their backyard realizes that there is more involved in the planting process. For unless you loosen the soil, provide appropriate fertilizer, and do some occasional weeding, your garden isn't going to amount to much.

In many ways, each of us has the opportunity to do our own sowing of seeds. Many times, however, they are not found in a packet but instead evidence themselves in the seed of ideas. Parents and grandparents, educators, government officials, journalists, pastors, and even those of us who philosophize or express our opinions can become influencers in the way others think and act. We need not look any further than the destructive seeds planted by the propaganda of Adolf Hitler which led to the rise of the Nazi party in Germany, the perpetration of the Holocaust, a World War, and the deaths of millions of Jews and other victims. Fortunately, there are many who have had the opportunity to build character and influence lives for good. One such individual was Fred Rogers, a crafted listener who labored over three decades to plant seeds of hope and expression in the lives of children who felt angry, worthless, or unloved. Without a doubt, he demonstrated the positive value of influential seed planting.

The late Oral Roberts coined the "seed-faith" principle. It included three basic components: recognizing that God is your source (Philippians 4:19); giving first so that it may be given back to you (Luke 6:38); and expecting a miracle (Mark 11:24). Roberts once wrote:

> The moment we ask God for something—the moment we do our part and plant our seed of faith—we should believe God that the answer is on its way. It's important to expect our miracle so we can recognize it and reach out to take it when it comes. And it's also important to remember that God controls the time and method He will use to give back to us. We must keep trusting Him and expecting our miracle, no matter how long it takes to reach us.

Out of this philosophy came the highly persuasive concept of "seed faith offerings," which unfortunately was misused to prey upon the desperate and hurting among some of God's people.

The Apostle Paul focused on a different kind of seed faith in his first letter to the early church whose members were totally divided over which of their leaders they should follow. He wrote, "I planted the seed in your hearts, and Apollos watered it, but it was God who made it grow" (1 Corinthians 3:6 NLT). Paul knew that a real understanding of "faith farming" occurs when we realize that it is God who enables its seeds to sprout roots and ultimately provide for a bountiful harvest. It affirms the once-told story of an older man who prided himself on his beautiful, well-tended garden of flowers. One day, while he was on his hands and knees, a neighbor passed by and complimented him on his grand floral display. "Ah," said the neighbor, "how good the Lord is to produce such wonderful growth."

"Yes," said the gardener, "but you should have seen how magnificent the garden was when God had it all to himself." So you see, it's not as simplistic as just digging a hole and planting a seed. The garden only begins to flourish when God becomes involved in ways we don't quite comprehend. It is evidenced in the fact that our faith is a result of the improbable fruit of what many in Jesus' time would have considered a worthless exercise in farming. This should not surprise us, for they hadn't yet come to understand the kingdom of God.

Reflection

Can you recall a time when you have seen seeds of faith yielding a harvest where you would have least expected it? Have there been other times when your faith seeds have not taken root? Consider planting some new seeds and envision what it will be like when the season of dormancy passes.

FEBRUARY 20
(Y2, D8)

Looking for the Good

For the whole law is fulfilled in one word: "You shall love your neighbor as yourself."

—Galatians 5:14 (NLT)

A few years ago, I was having work done at the back of my house. When I stepped outside to see how the workers were doing, one of them asked, "How do you get along with your neighbors?"

Somewhat perplexed at the question, I said, "Well, I think, okay…why?"

They went on to tell me that apparently, a few of them had parked their vehicles across the line of what would be the neighbor's property. Apparently, the neighbor came out of her house and bluntly asked if those trucks belonged to members of the crew doing work for us, to which they responded affirmatively. Her reply, "Well, okay then, no problem, because we like them." These are the same neighbors whom I surprised once when I revealed I prayed for them for no particular reason but just because they were my neighbors. Having once heard that "you will never criticize those for whom you truly pray," I had taken this to be useful counsel.

Recently, a columnist for a national newspaper wrote an article about her neighbors whom she detested because they are not of the same political persuasion. She wasn't upset about neighbors who might have tagged her house with graffiti or neighbors who held an election watch party and perhaps turned up the music too loud. No, she was upset about living next door to people whom she had labeled and stereotyped, those very neighbors who had plowed her driveway of snow and done "a great job without being asked." She continued, "I realize I owe them thanks—and, man, it really looks like the guy back-dragged the driveway like a pro—but how much thanks?" Speculating that these folks must have had an ulterior motive, she cautiously concluded that perhaps she should be nice, but not *that* nice. She may offer a "wave and a thanks," but she is "not ready to knock on the door with a covered dish."

Loving others can be extremely difficult at times, and as a result, it becomes easy to jump to conclusions about individuals and sling words of judgment without a second thought. How often do we judge our neighbors not on the basis of our actual observations but on what we assume to be true

101

because of hearsay? When faced with the possibility that those with whom we disagree might simply be nice and decent people, we are often prone to dismiss that from consideration. No doubt, we all have at one time or other fallen victim to forming a premature opinion about someone without allowing adequate time to get to know that person. The Apostle Paul would advise that we should "Fix your thoughts on what is true, and honorable, and right, and pure, and lovely, and admirable. Think about things that are excellent and worthy of praise" (Philippians 4:8 NLT). By not doing this, we'll be more likely to find attributes in others that annoy or make us critical rather than the good qualities which are present.

To judge is to form an opinion about someone. According to Scripture, Jesus had a great deal to say about that. He warns believers against judging others unfairly, but instead, He commends "right judgment" (John 7:24 ESV). When Jesus stated, "Do not judge, or you too will be judged" (Matthew 7:1 NIV), He was not commanding us to never judge, but rather, He was challenging us to check the motives and intentions of the heart before formulating an opinion. There is a heavy weight in attempting to judge the heart of others, and it is not something that Christians should take lightly. "We must not judge 'the hidden…purposes of the heart'" (1 Corinthians 4:5 ESV) based on another person's decisions, actions, perspectives, words, or personality that may concern us, especially if those things themselves are not explicitly sinful. When our hearts grow cold toward those around us, we must understand that we cannot love apart from God. As we look for the good in others while exercising discernment, we are acting neighborly. When we love them in spite of their lack of lovability, God's Spirit shines through, He is glorified, and the world will see Christ in us.

Reflection

In what ways might you exercise the gift of discernment before making a judgment about another individual? How can we strike a balance between offering a loving response to those with whom we adamantly disagree while maintaining an appropriate social distance? In what ways can a Christian confront another believer's sinful actions in a respectful and loving way without totally destroying their relationship?

FEBRUARY 21
(Y3, D8)

On a Beautiful Music Journey

Sing to him a new song; play skillfully on the strings.

—Psalm 33:3 (ESV)

Over the course of the latter part of the 190's, a major bus line used the slogan "Leave the Driving to Us." The campaign tagline periodically appeared for over four decades in much of the company's advertising from TV commercials to billboards and magazines. The "Sit back and leave the driving to us" philosophy is based on the premise that if you let another trained driver be in charge, you will be able to relax and arrive at your destination without all of the stress. A new source of stress can result from self-driving car technology which seems to be advancing every year. It's only a matter of time until fully driverless vehicles will appear on our public streets and highways. Meanwhile, we are being eased into acceptance with vehicle alerts that warn us about lane departure and provide braking assistance. I must admit, I have been intrigued by some of the commercials which highlight recent car models that offer a seemingly ingenious solution to one of the trickiest driving tasks: parallel parking. In some vehicles, you can actually stand outside your car as it literally parks itself. How cool is that if it does the job correctly?

Relinquishing control is difficult for most of us, especially when it is deeply personal. Most people would prefer to be knocked out entirely during any surgery. However, most people aren't British violinist Dagmar Turner who plays with the Isle of Wight Symphony Orchestra. As I viewed clips of the fifty-three-year-old woman who played the violin during her brain surgery, I was astonished. Diagnosed with a brain tumor after she collapsed on stage in 2013, Turner had been undergoing radiotherapy and other treatments. But as the tumor increased in size, its removal from her right frontal lobe became necessary early in 2020. Because the tumor was located near an area of her brain that controls the fine movement of her left hand, Turner feared she could lose the ability to play the violin. Though unconventional, the exercise of allowing the patient to make music during the surgery was put in place by specialists at King's College Hospital in London. Awakened at midpoint into the procedure, Turner's ability to play assisted physicians in monitoring areas of her brain responsible for delicate hand movement and coordination. A successful outcome allowed her musical passion, which began at the age of ten, to continue.

Most of us are familiar with the terminology "backseat driver." Indeed, you have likely been one, if you have relinquished the driver's seat to someone else but continued to tell them how to drive. Most of us don't normally have much success trying to boss someone and instilling trust in them at the same time. Backseat drivers often show a limited perspective. Due to their imperfect view, they don't have the full scope of all the cars around them and, therefore, aren't able to make the best judgment call for the situation. Attempting to be in control and surrendering control simultaneously just doesn't work. However, that's exactly what many of us do as we live out our lives as Christians. When we become a believer in Christ, we say we will give Him the driver's seat, but then we position ourselves as backseat drivers. Jesus told his disciples, "If any of you wants to be my follower, you must give up your own way, take up your cross, and follow me" (Matthew 16:24 NLT). A modern-day translation of this scripture puts it this way: "Anyone who intends to come with me has to let me lead. You're not in the driver's seat; I am" (The Message). When you and I accept Jesus as our Savior, we must allow Him to control the wheel. We, in effect, step out of that role and become a passenger. The spiritual reference for this is surrendering our life to Christ, and the Apostle Paul called it "a living sacrifice" (Romans 12:1 NIV).

If we have truly surrendered to Christ, one must regularly ask, who is the one doing the driving? That doesn't mean that we no longer make decisions, but rather that we pause, pray, and prepare ourselves for answers that may, in fact, not place us on the route we thought we were taking. The fact is that Jesus will at times navigate us over roads that aren't very appealing, but those are the times when we must trust him to get us where we need to be. We must seize each opportunity to follow the words of His disciple: "Cast all your anxiety on him because he cares for you" (1 Peter 5:7 NIV). Then and only then will we realize that playing skillfully on the strings of our life can only be accomplished when He alone is in charge of the journey.

Reflection

Are you convinced that allowing God to be in the driver's seat is best? What details of your life are most difficult for you to surrender? What difference would it make to give God control of those areas that cause you concern and stress? Establish a plan for letting go, and allow Him to take the wheel.

FEBRUARY 22
(Y4, D8)

Providing a Real ID for Jesus

This Jesus I'm telling you about is the Messiah.

—Acts 17:3 (NLT)

Conceived as part of legislation in the wake of the 9/11 terrorist attacks, the Real ID Law requires people to show security-enhanced identification to pass through airport security checkpoints or to enter certain federal facilities, such as military bases. Once a traditional driver's license would have fulfilled this requirement. But now, one needs to present documents such as a birth certificate, a Social Security card or tax form such as a W-2, and two proofs of address. For some people, getting the proper paperwork can be a difficult process. If you've changed your name through marriage, you'll need a marriage certificate, and if the certificate isn't actually from the state where you are applying, it will not be sufficient. Additionally, your birth certificate has to be state-issued, not the attractive document your parents may have received from the hospital where you were born. You may have to go back to your hometown to get an official copy from city records. It may take some work to prove who you are.

Hearing a friend describe this process and all the hassle she went through to get her ID reminded me of a personal story. My experience occurred before 9/11 when a work colleague and I went to an educational conference in Chicago. On the day of departure, I decided not to bother with my wallet and just take the cards I thought I would need. Previously having made my flight arrangements, I had the documentation to board the plane at a small airport about sixty miles from my town. Everything went smoothly, and we arrived in the windy city a few hours later. There we enjoyed a good conference for several days and prepared to return home via O'Hare, one of the world's busiest airports. When we checked in, I was asked for an ID, such as my driver's license, which, of course, I had not brought with me. The personnel there could not believe that I had boarded a flight a few days earlier without being properly identified. Fortunately, my colleague could vouch for who I was, and I was permitted to board.

Like I said, that was before the world changed on 9/11. But more than ever, being able to verify who you are is extremely important in today's society. As Jesus neared His remaining days on earth, it was significant that people close to Him could rightly identify who He was. To verify their understanding, He asked a question:

> "Who do people say the Son of Man is?"
> "Well," they replied, "some say John the Baptist, some say Elijah, and others say Jeremiah or one of the other prophets."
> Then he asked them, "But who do you say I am?"
> Simon Peter answered, "You are the Messiah, the Son of the living God."
> Jesus replied, "You are blessed, Simon son of John, because my Father in heaven has revealed this to you. You did not learn this from any human being." (Matthew 16:13–17 NLT)

Jesus went on to explain the events which would soon come to pass. "He then began to teach them that the Son of Man must suffer many things and be rejected by the elders, the chief priests and the teachers of the law, and that he must be killed and after three days rise again" (Mark 8:31 NIV). There was a state of dismay at what He was telling them.

A dreaded childhood experience often occurs when a teacher calls on us, particularly if we are not confident about the answer. Likewise, when we give consideration as to who Jesus is, it will often depend on where we are in life. Our response to this question may differ at various stages of our spiritual development. So Jesus' delay in introducing the subject of His death and resurrection suggests that the disciples' faith needed to mature to the point that they could hear and understand. How the disciples handled the additional information of Jesus' death would depend on who they believed Him to be. Knowing that He was the Son of God, they would be able to trust Him, even to the point of accepting His death (and eventual resurrection) without being shaken. As believers, we are also called to grow in our faith. Paul instructed, "Therefore let us move beyond the elementary teachings about Christ and be taken forward to maturity" (Hebrews 6:1 NIV). As we continue to press ahead and form a solid foundation of our principles, we will become progressively able to speak with conviction about who Jesus truly is and provide a "real ID" each and every time someone asks.

Reflection

If you were asked by Christ the very question that He posed to His disciples, how would you respond? Why do you think there are so many believers unprepared for the world's inquiries and about who Christ is? What additional steps do you need to take to "always be prepared to give an answer to everyone who asks you to give the reason for the hope that you have" (1 Peter 3:15 NIV).

FEBRUARY 23
(Y5, D8)

Getting a Grip on Life

For we live by faith, not by sight.

—2 Corinthians 5:7 (NIV)

From the kitchen window of my house, I can often see the two dogs next door playing together on the hill of the neighboring property. The bigger of the two is very quiet and mild-mannered. The smaller one is much more wired, barking at everything and everyone he sees. Together, they run up and down the hill, at times chasing each other, sometimes just making their presence known to other animals or people in sight. You would think that this time of year, when the yard is covered with a crusty snow or ice, they would proceed with more caution. But they romp with the same enthusiasm and that they would during the summer months. I often laugh at their lack of hesitation and their will to get where they want to go, regardless of the conditions around them. They always seem to be able to get a grip on the situation.

There is a lesson here for us onlookers who struggle at times with being able to keep our own grip on life. We sometimes feel that our personal circumstances have literally gone to the dogs, and our coping mechanisms are much less confident than my canine friends next door. Whenever we experience difficulties with our finances, our jobs, our marriages, and who knows what else, there may have been a time when we might have referred to such a period of life as being "on the skids." It is on these occasions when our faith gets tested and our psyches become filled with emotions such as self-doubt, worry, guilt, and fear. I don't know who said these words, but they are certainly good ones to remember: "Fear knocked at my door. Faith answered. And lo, no one was there."

Facing a nation of people who were suffering from the effects of the Great Depression, President Franklin Delano Roosevelt spoke eloquently as he declared, "Let me assert my firm belief that the only thing we have to fear is fear itself." There are times that we just need to respond to fear with faith, and in doing so, we are no longer afraid. Scripture tells the story of the varying reactions of Jesus and His disciples on one of their journeys.

When He got into the boat, His disciples followed Him. And behold, there arose a great storm on the sea, so that the boat was being covered with the waves; but Jesus Himself was asleep. And they came to Him and woke Him, saying, "Save us, Lord; we are perishing!" He said to them, "Why are you afraid, you men of little faith?" Then He got up and rebuked the winds and the sea, and it became perfectly calm. The men were amazed, and said, "What kind of a man is this, that even the winds and the sea obey Him?" (Matthew 8:23–27 ESV)

In 2015, a pair of American men in their thirties completed what had long been considered the world's most difficult rock climb at Yosemite National Park. Using only their hands and feet to scale a 3,000-foot vertical wall, the unfriendly granite pedestal was considered to be a feat many had thought to be impossible. Using only ropes and safety harnesses to catch themselves in case of a fall, the climbers relied entirely on their own strength. It took nineteen days to complete the effort and realize their year-long dream that has been described by some as an obsession. As they look back on their achievement in years to come, hopefully one of the lessons learned will be that the journey is sometimes just as important, if not more, than the destination.

Lucky for we who believe that we don't have to rely solely on our own strength when we face life's slippery slopes. Nor do we have to become obsessed with the challenges that we encounter. While God always expects that we do our part, He also understands that our reliance on Him is a demonstration of our unwavering belief and faith. "But when you ask, you must believe and not doubt, because the one who doubts is like a wave of the sea, blown and tossed by the wind. That person should not expect to receive anything from the Lord" (James 1:6–7 NIV). It is during those stormy times when we realize that faith develops our realization that God is who He said He is and will do what He has promised; that is, giving us a firm grip on life when we might otherwise find ourself on the skids.

Reflection

When your life is on a slippery slope, how do you respond? Would you describe your faith as faltering or unwavering when you are confronted by the difficulties of life? How can the posturing of your response not only affirm your reliance on God but also function as a witness to others as to how persons of faith should respond in troubled times?

FEBRUARY 24
(Y6, D8)

Change of Address

Yes, we are fully confident, and we would rather be away from these
earthly bodies, for then we will be at home with the Lord.

—2 Corinthians 5:8 (NLT)

February 21, 2018, was the date that William Franklin Graham Jr. entered his eternal home. Known simply as Billy Graham, the man who came to be referred to as "America's Pastor" was born in Charlotte, North Carolina. Graham has been credited with preaching to more individuals than anyone else in history. His live preaching as well as through radio, television, and the written word resulted in leading uncountable millions to Christ. Graham's preaching ministry first gained national prominence in 1949 when he held a crusade in downtown Los Angeles under a large white tent, termed a "canvas cathedral." He was the most prominent evangelist of the twentieth century, providing spiritual counsel for twelve consecutive presidents from Harry Truman to Barack Obama. He has been rated by the Gallup organization fifty-one times as "One of the Ten Most Admired Men in the World," more than any other individual in history. Billy Graham finished his journey on earth the same way he started—under a large white tent in front of thousands of people with given funeral remembrances by family and friends.

On the day that he died, his death was unnoticed by some due to the other prominent news stories of the day. While many famous individuals acknowledged his passing, the opportunity for criticism was not unrestrained. One national headline read "Divorce, Drugs, Drinking: Billy Graham's Children and Their Absent Father." Graham recognized the imperfections of himself and his loved ones, acknowledging in later life that he wished he would have been able to spend more time with his family. He was strongly led by his conviction to evangelism. As people came forward during his crusades to the customary singing of "Just as I Am," he made it abundantly clear that they were not doing it for Billy Graham but that they were giving their life to Christ. He once said, "Being a Christian is more than just an instantaneous conversion—it is a daily process whereby you grow to be more and more like Christ." He was never surprised by the words of his critics. He just kept his eye on the "heavenly prize" (Philippians 3:14 NLT).

Jesus said that those who followed Him would subject themselves to criticism, even persecution. In the Sermon on the Mount, He proclaimed: "Blessed are you when people insult you, persecute you and falsely say all kinds of evil against you because of me. Rejoice and be glad, because great is your reward in heaven" (Matthew 5:11–12 NIV). He told His disciples, "I am sending you out like sheep among wolves. Therefore be as shrewd as snakes and as innocent as doves… You will be hated by everyone because of me, but the one who stands firm to the end will be saved" (Matthew 10:16, 22 NIV). If we choose to allow Jesus to direct our life, then we will no doubt face some type of persecution during our time on this earth. Social exclusion and insult from other individuals, however, will not turn off the growing Christian. For when we come to understand God's reasons for allowing persecution, we not only expect it but are also willing to suffer, for we understand who holds our future. Reverend Graham put it this way: "The will of God will not take us where the grace of God cannot sustain us."

Upon hearing about Billy Graham's passing, former Governor Mike Huckabee stated: "While the critics came and went, Billy Graham never turned to the right or left, but kept his eye on the Cross." Huckabee said, "His influence was bigger than any of the people who temporarily held an office or had a fortune. His power was never his, but that of Christ, and his fortune was massive, but not on earth, but stored in the incorruptible vaults of heaven." Graham once adapted and personalized a line from another well-respected evangelist from the nineteenth century, D. L. Moody. That thought, "Someday you will read or hear that Billy Graham is dead. Don't you believe a word of it. I shall be more alive than I am now. I will just have changed my address. I will have gone into the presence of God." If we follow his lead, we too will be blessed to share that same address when our time here on earth has ended.

Reflection

Have there been times in your life when you have faced criticism because of your Christian beliefs? How did you respond? And how might you respond differently in the future? In light of the promise of eternity, what type of persecution are you willing to bear in this lifetime?

FEBRUARY 25
(Y7, D8)

Friend or Fan?

Take delight in the LORD, and he will give you the desires of your heart.

—Psalm 37:4 (NIV)

I look forward to this time of year. When I hear that pitchers and catchers are reporting for spring training, I know that the start of baseball season is only weeks away. Over the last few years, though, it's been unclear as to who will be on your favorite team. Last-minute trades and unsigned player hold-outs have produced quite a bit of anxiety for devout baseball fans. If they land on your team, standout players in the prime of their career give fans renewed hope and create excitement for the best possible season. They are represented by agents who hammer out the details of mega-million-dollar contracts with interested teams before anyone is signed. A lot of gamesmanship goes on behind the scenes to attract a talented player to a certain franchise as fans become frustrated with the rumors that sometimes go on for months. There are a lot of back-and-forth conversations to negotiate the best possible deal, and it comes down to which team will offer the most money over a proposed contract term. And, ultimately, greed without any guarantee of happiness can influence the final decision.

I was uplifted while watching an episode of the popular series, *This Is Us*, containing a flashback scene into the childhood of one of the main characters. A young Kevin Pearson stood in line for a long time, waiting to get the autograph of one of his favorite baseball players who was rumored might be traded to the Minnesota Twins. His mother watched in the distance as Kevin appeared to have a very cordial conversation with the player who is in the process of autographing his baseball card. When the signing ends and Kevin walks away, the mother approaches the player, inquiring what he and her son discussed. He says that Kevin studied a travel guide from his school library to match the "best places to go" in Minneapolis with the hobbies listed on this rookie's baseball card. He told Kevin's mother that "he just wanted to make sure I was happy." Kevin wanted to be more than a fan with a cherished autograph. He desired to extend the rare gift of friendship to guarantee his favorite player might find true happiness.

Offering happiness is not often the objective of fans with their own selfish motives. If we are fortunate to have any form of success in life, we could acquire fans of some sort. While those persons might never want our autograph, they may use us to satisfy their own agenda. It might come in the form of a request for a job reference or the influence that might be gained by being able to say they are acquainted with you. They may want to pick your brain or, on occasion, they may want to pick your pockets. Who knows what lurks in the minds of those who seemingly wish to befriend us? Jesus said:

> You are my friends if you do what I command… I have called you friends, for everything that I learned from my Father I have made known to you. You did not choose me, but I chose you and appointed you so that you might go and bear fruit—fruit that will last—and so that whatever you ask in my name the Father will give you. (John 15:14–16 NIV)

Jesus wants us to have a relationship with Him. When we do so, the thought process that will follow is not based on what will make us happy but rather what will please God. As a result, the blessings will flow, and our net worth will be evidenced by the fruit that we bear.

Christians and non-Christians do not disagree that happiness should be a human goal, but they should disagree with how this goal is best achieved. If we set to position ourselves to make decisions from a personal perspective of greed, it will never guarantee our long-term happiness. Jesus warned: "Watch out! Be on your guard against all kinds of greed; life does not consist in an abundance of possessions" (Luke 12:15 NIV). When a sports team examines the cost/benefit analysis of signing a new player, there is a point that they simply have to be willing to walk away. The same is true with any Christian who is assessing an accumulation of wealth decision. When a situation like that challenges you, you have to scrutinize the motives of who or what you will allow to control your life. Then you will be able to easily respond to anyone who might ask: Is Jesus really your friend? Or are you merely a fan?

Reflection

Which makes you more happy? To be humbled or exalted? How serious are you about a relationship with Jesus? Would you say you are more of a fan or a friend? What sacrifices would you have to make if you were to move into a closer relationship with Him? Are you willing to make these sacrifices, preparing for the fact that your decision might not result in short-term happiness?

FEBRUARY 26
(Y1, D9)

Just One More

The thief comes only to steal and kill and destroy. I came that
they may have life and have it abundantly.

—John 10:10 (NIV)

Nominated for six Academy Awards, including Best Picture, the 2016 film *Hacksaw Ridge* tells the true-life story of Desmond Thomas Doss who became the first conscientious objector to be awarded the Medal of Honor. A youthful Doss decided that he could not sit by and watch others go off to World War II, so he enlisted with the intention of becoming a medic while refusing to carry a firearm. He excels physically in basic training, but because of his strong belief in the Ten Commandments (including "Thou Shalt Not Kill"—Exodus 20:13), he becomes an outcast among his fellow soldiers. As the story progresses, his unit engages in the Battle of Okinawa and is assigned to secure an area labeled as Hacksaw Ridge. Here the Japanese launch a massive counterattack and drive the Americans to retreat. Doss hears the cries of the injured and decides that he cannot abandon them, so one-by-one, he rescues and lowers them by rope over the cliff's edge to safety. Driven by his faith, he prays "just one more" after each rescue, eventually saving the lives of seventy-five while placing his own at risk with each attempt.

In a dramatic scene, the Captain of Doss' unit makes the following confession: "All I saw was a skinny kid. I didn't know who you were. You've done more than any other man could have done in the service of his country. I've never been more wrong about someone in my life, and I hope someday you can forgive me." How many times have we found this to be true in our own life? We judge others by what we see or sometimes, even worse, by what we hear or think we know about them. Because a person has a certain name runs with a particular crowd or is otherwise known to be "from the wrong side of the tracks," we have all been guilty of making judgments that are sometimes questionable at best. I know there have been times I have heard wonderful things about someone after they have died, causing me to wonder how I ever formed the conflicting opinion I had held about them when they were alive. To Desmond Doss, it didn't matter, for all he saw was a life worth saving.

In the Gospels of Matthew and Mark, Jesus asks His disciples, "Who do people say that I am?" (Mark 8:27 NIV). They respond with various answers, naming John the Baptist, Elijah, Jeremiah, or one of the prophets. Then He asks an even more profound question: "But what about you? Who do you say that I am? Simon Peter replied, 'You are the Christ, the Son of the living God'" (Matthew 16:15–16 ESV). Then Jesus says something very interesting: "You are blessed, Simon son of John, because my Father in heaven has revealed this to you. You did not learn this from any human being" (Matthew 16:17 NLT). Afterward, He affirms that Peter is the rock upon which He will build His church. He also sternly warns the disciples not to tell anyone that He is the Messiah as He foreshadows His own death.

What do we learn from Desmond Doss and Jesus about finding meaning in our life? Doss clearly demonstrated that there was a way to serve his fellow man without breaking the laws of God. His selfless acts of fearlessness were rewarded with a long life. Although he was just a "skinny kid" when he entered WWII, his determination and faith in God more than compensated for any lack in physical size. He was a modern-day David as he faced his own Goliath treating and rescuing his comrades in close proximity to enemy forces. While Doss was in the business of saving men physically, Jesus understood that He would have to sacrifice His own life in order to spiritually save ours. He revealed who He truly was to only a close few, knowing that through his ultimate death and resurrection, He would become the Savior for all humankind. He reaches out on a personal level, setting a challenge for each of us to be nonjudgmentally involved with others daily. For both Doss and Jesus, all they ever saw was a life worth saving. So we, like the young soldier, must dare to look heavenward and say, "Just one more."

Reflection

Are there ways that you can impact your world and help in healing the wounds of a hurting friend or even a stranger who needs a word of encouragement? Do you see others around you whom you may be misjudging because of their own physical or emotional wounds? How might you ask for spiritual guidance in order to provide a more abundant life for someone in need?

FEBRUARY 27
(Y2, D9)

Words

Do not be quick with your mouth, do not be hasty in your heart to utter anything before God. God is in heaven and you are on earth, so let your words be few.

—Ecclesiastes 5:2 (NIV)

One year after watching the Academy Awards, I decided that there are just too many useless words. It's not so much about the length of the acceptance speeches during which winners want to thank numerous individuals. But it's more about the testimonials, the inside stories, or the far too many inappropriate references, sometimes needing to be bleeped, making us wonder if it was all so necessary. The use and number of words is a curious thing. Most State of the Union messages are remembered not for the power of their words but rather for the length of time it took to speak them. Conversely, Lincoln's Gettysburg Address is frequently memorized and recalled not only for its brevity but for the inspiration and effectiveness of its 270-word choices. Someone once prayed these thoughts: "Please, God, make my words today sweet and tender, for tomorrow I may have to eat them." How profound!

A former public relations director at Lake Superior State University came up with the idea that certain words and phrases should just be eliminated from use. W. T. Rabe and fellow LSSU faculty and staff initiated such a list at a New Year's Eve party in 1975, printing it on January 1, 1976. Every year since, the annual "List of Words Banished from the Queen's English for Misuse, Overuse, and General Uselessness" receives contributions from all over the world. If these word-watchers are able to target their pet peeves from everyday speech, then we should certainly be able to censor our own verbosity. The problem is that most of us have no desire to do so. In most cases, our society embraces people who speak their mind. However, bluntness in the wrong situation can be harmful. Once the words are out there, you can't take them back. In this day of social media, far too many have learned the hard way that what goes out into cyberspace lives out there forever and may just come back to haunt you.

There is much contained in the Word of God about what flows from our lips. As we walk our journey, we have each fallen to listening to or perpetrating gossip. "The discerning heart seeks knowledge, but the mouth of a fool feeds on folly" (Proverbs 15:14 NIV). We have perhaps passed on a confidence that really wasn't ours to tell. We must understand that this only cheapens who we are. "Those who consider themselves religious and yet do not keep a tight rein on their tongues deceive themselves, and their religion to be worthless" (James 1:26 NIV). We find ourselves in the wrong situation, our emotions to get out of control, and we let a few choice words fly. "With the tongue we praise our Lord and Father, and with it we curse human beings, who have been made in God's likeness. Out of the same mouth come praise and cursing. My brothers and sisters, this should not be" (James 3:9–10 NIV). Maybe as we think about what we might give up for Lent, we might consider editing some of our words.

Our mouth can often get us into hot water and has caused many to consider if the words they spoke would have been best left unsaid. We have all made empty statements, taken cheap shots at the expense of another, or spoken harshly when someone just needed to know they were loved. Therefore, the Apostle Paul would tell us: "Do not let any unwholesome talk come out of your mouths, but only what is helpful for building others up according to their needs, that it may benefit those who listen" (Ephesians 4:29 NIV). There have been times when I knew that I would be with a person who was hurting. I mistakenly prayed that God might bless me with the right words to say. On many of those occasions, I walked away feeling that I was the one who had been blessed because the other person didn't need my words. They simply needed me to be a good listener. I came to understand just how accurate Martin Luther King was when he said, "In the end, we will remember not the words of our enemies but the silence of our friends." Next time, before speaking, I'll simply pause and say, "Set a guard over my mouth, Lord; keep watch over the door of my lips" (Psalm 141:3 NIV). Now those are words worth speaking.

Reflection

As a follower of Jesus, what are the questions you should be asking about the use of words in your life? Does your choice of words represent who you claim to be? How might you be a stronger encourager to others through the use of fewer words and better listening?

FEBRUARY 28
(Y3, D9)

Accepting the Invitation

If you hear my voice and open the door, I will come in,
and we will share a meal together as friends.

—Revelation 3:20 (NLT)

There was a time when I would invite a house full of people to gather for a holiday dinner and social at my home. It was not unusual to have upward to thirty people. It was a lot of work, but I really enjoyed doing it. The most frustrating part was figuring out how many folks would be in attendance. While there is not a significant difference in feeding twelve or fifteen people, there is a huge variance between preparing for twelve as compared to twenty-five. Therefore, each year, when I would send out invitations, I would ask my guests for their reply by a specific date, usually about a week before the event. Every year following the due date, I would need to contact a number of the invitees for an answer. One couple would inevitably show up, regardless of whether I had received their reply or not. So I learned over time to just include them in my final tally. While this always appeared to be a get-together everyone enjoyed, there were a number of years that I threatened to not plan it because of my exasperation in getting an accurate count.

Invitations, whether to something as casual as a weekday lunch or as special as a wedding, are an expression of thoughtfulness and inclusion. According to those who give proper etiquette advice, invitations always deserve a gracious response. A speedy reply ensures the host can plan accordingly, plus it demonstrates appreciation for being included. If your schedule won't allow you to respond right away, you should call or text the host to let them know you'll be in touch with your RSVP as soon as you can establish your schedule. When the invitation arrives and doesn't say anything about a response, you should still reach out to the hosting party and let them know whether or not you will be able to attend. There once was a time when it would have been unnecessary to list an RSVP because people would have been considerate of the invitation and would have replied without any prompting. Not so these days!

Jesus told an entire parable about responding to an invitation. It followed a statement made by one who was dining with Jesus who said:

> "Blessed is the one who will eat at the feast in the kingdom of God." Jesus replied, "A certain man was preparing a great banquet and invited many guests. At the time of the banquet, he sent his servant to tell those who had been invited, 'Come, for everything is now ready.' But they all alike began to make excuses… The servant came back and reported this to his master. Then the owner of the house became angry and ordered his servant, 'Go out quickly into the streets and alleys of the town and bring in the poor, the crippled, the blind and the lame.'
> 'Sir,' the servant said, 'what you ordered has been done, but there is still room.' Then the master told his servant, 'Go out to the roads and country lanes and compel them to come in, so that my house will be full. I tell you, not one of those who were invited will get a taste of my banquet.'" (Luke 14:15–18, 21–24 NIV)

Here, Jesus makes reference as to how each of us are invited into the kingdom of God, and yet our excuses, however reasonable they may seem, may prevent us from entering that very kingdom.

One of the main themes of the Parable of the Great Banquet is the open invitation to any and all, not just to the perfect, popular, or powerful. When we first hear His invitation extended to us, we think it must be a mistake. Certainly, *we must be* unworthy. Then we learn that coming to Jesus isn't about deserving, denying our sins, being good enough, or trying hard enough. It's about accepting His invitation as well as His unmerited forgiveness and favor. He offered the most personal invitation to humanity—Himself. He died on the cross so that our stains could be washed clean, whiter than snow. And because of His grace, we find ourselves at the same crossroads as Matthew when Jesus spoke these words to the fisherman. "Come, follow me, and I will send you out to fish for people" (Matthew 4:19 NIV). That was just the beginning, but the same is true today. Jesus has made room for you to sit at the table, no matter who you are, no matter how religious you strive for, no matter how broken you might be. You are already invited, and He has saved you a seat. All that remains for you to do is accept the invitation.

Reflection

In your busy life, what do you need to do to become more intentional about accepting Jesus' invitation to spend more time with Him? How can you be more effective in handling your personal evangelism to better enable others to express their commitment to Christ's invitation for their life?

FEBRUARY 29
(Leap Year)

Leap of Faith

Now faith is confidence in what we hope for and assurance about what we do not see.

—Hebrews 11:1 (NIV)

Every four years, our calendar grows by an extra day, adding February 29 to make a total of 366 days. We call it a leap year. Since the earth revolves around the sun every 365.25 days, a corrective measure is made every fourth year to enable the calendar to catch up with itself. This synchronizes the seasons with the true solar year. In a common year, all dates on the calendar move up one day of the week. If Christmas was Wednesday last year, it will be on Thursday in the current year. It all flows along very nicely until we have an extra day in February. In those years, your birthday, which last year occurred on Friday, will leap over Saturday and be celebrated on Sunday this year. It has become rather logical to most persons, and unless you were born on February 29, most of us really don't think much about it.

In the 1992 movie, *Leap of Faith*, a touring Christian evangelist played by Steve Martin takes his faith-healing revivals from city to city. The donations flow freely, but the healings are bogus. When the evangelist and company find themselves stuck in a remote nook of Kansas, they decide to perform for the locals and take them for all they are worth. Each of the shows go off without a hitch until one man recognizes the acts for the scam that they are and sets out to expose them. A real-life leap occurred thirty years before this movie in 1962, when Neil Armstrong joined the NASA Astronaut Corp. In 1969, on his second and final spaceflight, he exited his Apollo 11 spacecraft and became the first man to ever walk on the moon. On that day, no one thought he was a fraud as he spoke those words which have since become immortalized: "This is one small step for a man, one giant leap for mankind."

The act of leaping takes on many meanings as we go through life. When we are young, we learn to play leap frog in which, with our legs parted, we master hopping over others who are bent down. As we get older, we may hear the expression "leap of faith" being used. I am not sure that I completely understood what that meant until I bought my first home. I remember saying to a relative of mine that I was a little apprehensive about the whole thing. What if for some reason I would lose my job, become ill, or otherwise not be able to make my payments.

He said, "So what do you have now?"

"Nothing," I said.

"What would you have then?" he prodded.

I again responded, "Nothing." It was his way of saying to me that unless we make a change from where we are now to where we want to be, nothing really gets done. He didn't exactly use the words, but I understood what he meant. It was a leap of faith.

Jesus loved it when persons with whom he came in contact took a spiritual leap of faith. In one situation, a centurion came to Jesus and asked him to heal his servant who was paralyzed and suffering. Jesus asked to be taken to the servant, but the centurion said that he was not worthy to have Jesus under his roof. He then expressed great confidence that if Jesus would just will it to be so, the servant would be healed. "When Jesus heard this, he was amazed and said to those following him, 'Truly I tell you, I have not found anyone in Israel with such great faith'" (Matthew 8:10 NIV). As a man with power, the centurion understood that authority transcends distance. On another occasion, He found himself in the midst of a large crowd. "Jesus realized at once that healing power had gone out from him, so he turned to the crowd and asked, 'Who touched my robe?'" (Mark 5:30 NLT). A woman who had suffered with bleeding for twelve years was certain that if she could simply touch His clothes, she would be healed. As she came forward, falling at His feet, and trembling with fear, "He said to her, 'Daughter, your faith has healed you. Go in peace and be freed from your suffering'" (Mark 5:34 NIV).

As we pass down the road of life, like the centurion and the sick woman, we will undoubtedly face many obstacles along the way. Unlike the cartoon characters of our youth, we cannot simply confront each new challenge by jumping off the edge of a cliff. We must pray for discernment. If it's a risk God has blessed, then we will find the courage and the strength to embrace the journey. It will be more than a leap year to remember. It will be a leap of faith worth taking, and it will no doubt enable us to fulfill one of God's purposes for our life.

Reflection

When God calls you to step out and take a risk, how do you respond? In what ways might you pray for direction when God seems to be leading you to demonstrate an act of faith? How can you use what God has already done in your life to give you the strength and courage to follow His lead?

MARCH 1
(Y4, D9)

Who Are You Wearing?

For I have given you an example, that you also should do just as I have done to you.

—John 13:15 (ESV)

Did you ever notice as you pass through the clothing section of a department store how all the name brand labels are placed near the walkways where they are readily noticed? Sometimes they are given display areas of their own so that if you are looking for a certain brand, it is easy for you to find. Frequently, you will discover that these popular trademarks carry the highest price tags and are often excluded from store markdowns. I once worked with a lady who would occasionally find one of these items to be on sale and affordable to buy. When she would wear it for the first time, she would always make a habit of allowing the label to show so that her colleagues would know that she was wearing the more expensive brand. She did this in a joking manner because when someone would point out that the label was out, she would simply smile and say, "Oh my goodness, how did that happen?" Anyone who was her friend knew with all certainty that she would never have paid full price for that item.

Annually, the various award shows tout a red-carpet pre-show where celebrities do interviews and flaunt the latest styles. Depending on the venue, the dresses can range from outlandish and distasteful to classy and glamourous. The most popular of these pre-ceremony rituals occurs at the Academy Awards, known as The Oscars. Until recently, interviewers always found a way to ask the ladies, "Who Are You Wearing?" Designers would covet the opportunity to have their names dropped as the stars would mention Jovani, Marc Jacobs, Valentino, Prada, Dior, Chanel, or Versace. In recent years, some have asserted that probing the ladies in this way is inappropriate as their male counterparts seldom, if ever, are asked to respond to similar questions. I have found the phrasing to be interesting since the question is never posed in the format "Who designed your dress?" The inquiry has simply become "Who are you wearing?" The latter implies that the dress itself has taken on the unique persona of the one who made it.

It's a question Christians might want to ponder as we take our walk down the runway of life and are forced to consider whom it is that we are portraying. "For we are His workmanship, created in Christ Jesus for good works, which God prepared beforehand so that we would walk in them" (Ephesians 2:10 ESV). While we do not dress like Jesus, we are challenged to be like Him by becoming His hands and feet. We bear the responsibility of demonstrating to the world what Jesus might appear through his acts were He to walk the earth today. It's been said that "we're the only Jesus some may ever see." Whenever things are going well for us, in what ways do we show appreciation for God's guidance in our lives? When we are facing adversity, do we rely on His strength to carry us? Or do we become angry and distance ourselves from Him? When we find ourselves in conflict with others, how do we act then? Jesus said, "You did not choose me, but I chose you and appointed you so that you might go and bear fruit—fruit that will last—and so that whatever you ask in my name the Father will give you. This is my command: Love each other" (John 15:16–17 NIV).

The Apostle Paul challenges each of us do useful work with our hands to "share with those in need" (Ephesians 4:28 NIV). Our talk must be wholesome, ridding ourselves of "bitterness, rage and anger, brawling and slander, along with every form of malice. Be kind and compassionate to one another, forgiving each other, just as in Christ God forgave you" (Ephesians 4:31–32 NIV). Paul would advise that we garb ourselves in an entirely new way of life with renewed conduct as God accurately refashions His character within us. When we do so, our hearts and minds will be made completely new, designed in God's likeness, and showcased by a true life which is upright and holy (Ephesians 4:22–24 NIV). Our award for doing so will not be an earthly one from which we will earn recognition and fame. It is, rather, one which can only be provided to us through God's grace. Therefore, each of us must ask if we are working toward becoming more like Christ as we relate to others in our stroll down life's walkway. Or is the name "Christian" just a label we pretend to wear simply in a display for others to see?

Reflection

What impression do you make on nonbelievers who may be observing you as you go about your day-to-day life? How might you challenge others who claim to wear the "Christian label" to be genuine and not simply a mere imitation of the real thing?

MARCH 2
(Y5, D9)

Good News... Bad News

But my life is worth nothing to me unless I use it for finishing the work assigned me by the Lord Jesus; the work of telling others the Good News about the wonderful grace of God.

—Acts 20:24 (NLT)

Having been there before, I was telling my colleague about the many sights and sounds of New Orleans. One of the best among them is the wide variety of great food to be found there, including homemade beignets and a freshly brewed cup of chicory coffee in the French Quarter's Café Du Monde. I had her anticipating the experience long before we ever landed at the airport. Due to our different roles in the organization for which we were employed, we did not participate in all of the same presentations at the conference we were attending. On one of our first days there, my afternoon session adjourned early. I decided to walk a few blocks down the street and enjoy one of those delicious beignets that I had been so fondly recalling to my friend. I ordered a coffee and two beignets, one for me and the other to take back to the hotel for my coworker. When I later knocked on the door to her room, I had a big smile on my face and greeted her by saying, "I have good news and bad news. The good news is that I went for beignets, and I bought one for each of us."

She looked at me and said, "Okay, then, so what's the bad news?"

I lowered my eyes as well as my voice and said, "I ate both of them!"

Isn't that quite typical of most of us as we blunder through our lives? On many typical days, we start off with the absolute best of intentions. While we run errands, we plan to stop by the nursing home to check on our elderly neighbor who is confined there after a nasty fall. We aim to have lunch with a fellow employee who recently lost his wife but then allow the piles of paper and the need to return calls get in the way of doing so. We sit down after our evening meal with purpose to address a card or check in by phone on an out-of-state friend, but instead, we justify needing to take some time for ourselves to relax. It's neglecting those things that God would want us to do. No one understood this better than the Apostle Paul who said:

> I don't really understand myself, for I want to do what is right, but I don't do it. Instead, I do what I hate. But if I know that what I am doing is wrong, this shows that I agree that the law is good. So I am not the one doing wrong; it is sin living in me that does it. And I know that nothing good lives in me, that is, in my sinful nature. I want to do what is right, but I can't. I want to do what is good, but I don't. I don't want to do what is wrong, but I do it anyway. (Romans 7:15–19 NLT)

In his 1970s variety show, comedian Flip Wilson became famous for creating the character, Geraldine, who coined the phrase "The devil made me do it." Too often, we excuse our circumstances or our temptations for not doing what is acceptable in God's eyes by finding someone or something to blame. Jesus made it clear that we must be responsible for our own actions.

> For I was hungry, and you didn't feed me. I was thirsty, and you didn't give me a drink. I was a stranger, and you didn't invite me into your home. I was naked, and you didn't give me clothing. I was sick and in prison, and you didn't visit me… And he will answer, "I tell you the truth, when you refused to help the least of these my brothers and sisters, you were refusing to help me." (Matthew 25:42–43, 45 NLT)

During the season of Lent, we are challenged to get right with God in some way in order to exercise His will for our life. We seek to find answers to those things that keep us from being in full communion with Him. The traditional thought is that by giving up something we enjoy or rely on, we make a sacrifice and thereby identify with Christ's suffering experience. In reality, any self-imposed denial we might make would fail in comparison with the price He paid and the ensuing grace He provides. Therefore, we should use the Lenten season as a time to reexamine our relationship with Him. While we will inevitably fall short, we should be repentant, conceding that confession truly is good for the soul. We don't ever want to be face-to-face with the Lord and have Him say, "I have good news and bad news. In this house, there are many mansions (John 14:2), but unfortunately…there is no reservation in your name."

Reflection

Consider a few recent good intentions that you neglected to fulfill. How did your lack of action in this regard miss the mark of becoming an effective witness for Christ? What can you "give up" this Lenten season that has until now served as a barrier between you and Him?

MARCH 3
(Y6, D9)

Only One Miracle Worker

If I were you, I would go to God and present my case to him. He does great
things too marvelous to understand. He performs countless miracles.

—Job 5:8–9 (NLT)

On March 3, 1887, two ladies met and changed each other's lives forever. The older of the two, Johanna Mansfield Sullivan, was born to illiterate and impoverished immigrants who migrated to the United States from Ireland during the Great Famine. At a very young age, she contracted a bacterial eye disease which, over time, made her nearly blind. Through a course of events, she was enrolled in the Perkins Institution for the Blind where she learned the manual alphabet in order to communicate with a classmate who was deaf and blind. Eventually, several operations improved her weakened eyesight. She graduated at age twenty as the valedictorian of her class and became known simply as Anne Sullivan. Then she was introduced to a seven-year-old blind and deaf girl by the name of Helen Keller. Challenged to socialize her wild, stubborn student, she began to teach her using the manual alphabet she had learned at Perkins. One day, a breakthrough occurred, and Sullivan stated, "My heart is singing for joy this morning. A miracle has happened. The light of understanding has shown upon my little pupil's mind, and behold, all things are changed!" It was the beginning of a forty-nine-year relationship during which Sullivan evolved from teacher to governess and finally to companion and friend. Literary references and performance productions labeled her "the miracle worker" because of significant contributions to Helen Keller's most accomplished life.

Believers in Christ know that there is only one true miracle worker; that is, if we define miracle as a wonder or marvel that defies rational explanation surpassing all known human or natural powers. The biblical accounts of Jesus miracles here on earth are evidenced in the healing of the ten lepers (Luke 17:11–19), a blind man named Bartimaeus (Mark 10:46–52), and a woman who had been afflicted for twelve years who reached out and touched His garment (Matthew 9:20–22). Everyone whom Jesus willed to be healed was healed. Sometimes He healed those who expressed their faith in Him, and He clearly stated it to be so. Other times, in His great mercy, He healed those who had no faith and later drew them to Himself. We come to understand then that it is only by the power of Christ that miracles occur, not through the influence of our faith. Faith is only the instrument, not the power itself. St. Augustine concluded, "Miracles were necessary before the world believed, in order that it might believe." Some say that miracles no longer exist since the message of Jesus and His apostles has already been confirmed in the Scriptures. The logical question which follows then is, does God still perform miracles today?

To answer that, you just have to give attention to the March 2015 story of twenty-five-year-old Lynn Jennifer Groesbeck who lost control of her car and landed in the icy Spanish Fork River in Utah. Fourteen hours later, first-responders found her eighteen-month-old daughter, Lily, in her car seat, hanging upside down just above frigid river water. Prior to finding Lily, both police officers and firefighters report that they heard an adult voice yell, "Help me!" All were emphatic it came from the vehicle. It looked as though no one could have survived, but the voice prompted three officers and firemen to lift the car. They determined that the plea for help could not have come from the young mother, who likely died from the impact. Authorities had no explanation as to how the girl survived hanging upside-down for many hours in freezing temperatures with meager clothing and no food or water. Coincidence, some might say? Little Lily made a full recovery, and her survival could only be clarified by three words: "It's a miracle."

As long as people have faith in God, miracles are certainly possible since it's faith that ushers miracles into the world. After all, "Jesus Christ is the same yesterday, today, and forever" (Hebrews 13:8 NLT) and God is still on the throne. Likewise, we should not necessarily expect miracles to occur in the same way they did in biblical accounts. There will be occasions in which He will use His Holy Spirit to work through us. The Apostle Paul stated so: "Now to him who is able to do immeasurably more than all we ask or imagine, according to his power that is at work within us" (Ephesians 3:20 NIV). And yet the greatest miracle of all continues to occur each time there is a spiritual transformation of a sinful heart through faith in Christ Jesus.

Reflection

Are you able to give an example of a modern-day miracle? How would you argue the fact that something which happens at exactly the right time is more of a divine alignment than a true miracle?

MARCH 4
(Y7, D9)

Till We Meet Again

For the wages of sin is death, but the gift of God is eternal life in Christ Jesus our Lord.

—Romans 6:23 (NIV)

One Sunday afternoon in late winter, I decided to go for a walk to get some fresh air. Several blocks from my home, I passed a small church and happened to notice the billboard. In addition to listing the times of the services, I was drawn to a quote which also appeared. It read "Christians Never Meet for the Last Time." I remember considering the powerful thought expressed in that statement, and I began to recall a church massacre that had occurred years before. It was on the evening of June 18, 2015, that a twenty-one-year-old White male entered an historic Black church in Charleston, South Carolina, where some of its members gathered for a weekly prayer meeting. He was one of thirteen people in attendance and was seated next to the pastor. Initially listening to others during the service, he reportedly began to disagree when they started to discuss scripture. After waiting for the other participants to begin praying, he pulled out a gun, began shooting, and ended up murdering nine of those present, including the senior pastor. At that time, it was considered to be the deadliest mass shooting at an American place of worship.

The relatives of the victims directed comments to the accused gunman at his first court appearance. One by one, those who chose to speak did not turn to anger. Instead, they offered him forgiveness and said they were praying for his soul, even in the pain of their losses. One grandchild stated, "Although my grandfather and the other victims died at the hands of hate, everyone's plea for your soul is proof that they lived in love, and their legacies will live in love…so hate won't win." The irony of the event was that a soon-to-be slayer was welcomed by those he murdered and forgiven by those who would feel their loss. The killer most likely chose the famous church because he undoubtedly wanted a symbol. Against all his intentions, however, the symbol became different than the one he had intended. While the executioner set out to defile a sacred place, he ended up showing why it was a place of living faith. What he no doubt thought would be the last time these people would ever meet together, he did not understand that they would gather again in a new location that would become their eternal home.

Jesus put it this way:

> Do not let your hearts be troubled. You believe in God; believe also in me. My Father's house has many rooms; if that were not so, would I have told you that I am going there to prepare a place for you? And if I go and prepare a place for you, I will come back and take you to be with me that you also may be where I am. (John 14:1–3 NIV)

This promise applies to all believers, even those whose earthly life has been cut short. We need not be concerned for our loved ones or ourselves as to where we will be when we leave this life; that is, if we know and follow the teachings of Jesus. John puts it quite simply: "God has given us eternal life, and this life is in his Son. Whoever has the Son has life; whoever does not have the Son of God does not have life" (1 John 5:11–12 NIV). These divine traits we see from the Emmanuel AME Christians in Charleston—hospitality to the stranger and then forgiveness to the murderer—are truly incredible examples of following Jesus Christ's witness of love and mercy. They reflect some of the greatest virtues we are called to live by in our Christian lives. What an amazing example of Paul's words to "overcome evil with good" (Romans 12:21 NIV) while exceeding dark hatred with a force that is even greater than the greatest evil. That, my friends, *is* divine love.

In the heart of the horrible event at Charleston, we can also see beauty and goodness from Christians who were able to forgive in the midst of their deep pain and utter sorrow. They were able to ask for God's mercy and grace to come upon a lost soul. This story is a great example that we can choose what we take away from a tragedy. Will we only see the crazed and forsaken man filled with racism and hatred that led to violence? Or will we witness a unique opportunity to respond to hatred with love and find violence conquered by mercy? Perhaps it helps to remember those heartfelt words—expressing again and again the lovely sentiment from an old hymn, "God be with you till we meet again."

Reflection

Consider hate-filled or otherwise tragic events in your own life experience. Were you quick to reciprocate with anger and blame? How can you position yourself or help others prepare to practice love and forgiveness in the face of similar circumstances when they occur?

MARCH 5
(Y1, D10)

Making a Deal with the Devil

"Get out of here, Satan," Jesus told him. "For the Scriptures say, 'You
must worship the Lord your God and serve only him.'"

—Matthew 4:10 (NLT)

When wars become prolonged and thousands of lives have been sacrificed, it seems as though there is no rational conclusion to an otherwise endless conflict over ideologies. There are those who would claim that sometimes a deal with the devil is better than no deal at all. When you make those kinds of deals, you'd better be certain the expectations are clear and you have the upper hand. Personally, I have heard it said that when it comes to selecting the lesser of two evils that "it's better to deal with the devil you know than the one you don't know." This phrase is often utilized when it seems wiser to side with someone you dislike but with whom you are familiar over someone you don't know at all who could be far worse. This might apply along the entire gamut of tough decision-making from considering between job offers to concluding who to vote for in an upcoming election. We must recognize that logical determinations do not always occur when emotions are high or a sense-of-urgency comes into play.

Take the case of Aunt Freda who found herself on the wrong end of what appeared to be a concerning situation. One day, when she answered the phone, she was told by a man that he was a law enforcement officer in Canada. He went on to relate that he had her nephew, Bill, in custody who could be released and returned to the United States if he could find payment for a $5,000 fine. In the background, she could hear someone who sounded like Bill, pleading, "Please send the money, Aunt Freda, and I will pay you back just as soon as I can." Sickened by the thought of her nephew being held in a jail cell, she wrote down the details and agreed to wire the money within the next few hours. Shortly thereafter, she found herself at a Western Union money transfer location. Appearing somewhat distraught, she shared her nephew's situation with the clerk who asked her one very important question. "Have you attempted to call your nephew today?" Freda indicated she had not, and the clerk urged her to do so. When she dialed the number, Bill answered the phone and assured

Aunt Freda that he was okay. She was about to make a deal with the devil by becoming a victim of a well-rehearsed scam on a lady who was up in years.

The idea of "bargaining with the devil" is much more cultural than it is biblical. There are times in scripture, however, when Satan attempts to strike a deal with God. In the book of Job, for instance, Satan proposes that if God would allow him to bring great suffering to Job, whom God had described as "the finest man in all the earth" (Job 1:8 NLT), that Job would surely curse God to His face (Job 1:9–11). Satan argues that Job was only faithful because he was blessed with a family and wealth, and later that he only served Him because he had good health. God allows this to play out through conversations Job has with three friends who offer him false comfort. Job's response: "Though he slay me, yet will I hope in him; I will surely defend my ways to his face" (Job 13:15 NIV). God finally rebukes Job's friends who accuse him of having sinned. In the end, He has considerably more than when he began his suffering. In the New Testament, the devil proposes bargaining with Jesus at the end of His forty days of fasting in the wilderness: "If you are the Son of God, command this stone to become bread" (Luke 4:3 ESV). In other words, "Why are you hungry if you are God's Son?" After showing Jesus "all the kingdoms of the world and their splendor" (Matthew 4:8), Satan offers them to Jesus if He will merely bow down and worship him. Jesus sends Satan away with His own rebuke from God's Holy Word.

Someone has said that most of us don't have to make a deal with the devil because he's already got us. Satan pretends that he's far away, but he is a lot closer than you might think. The story is told of a hunter who went out into the forest to shoot a bear, out of which he planned to make a warm coat. Eventually, he saw a bear coming toward him, raised his gun, and took aim. "Wait," said the bear, "why do you want to shoot me?"

"Because I am cold," said the hunter.

"But I am hungry," the bear replied, "so maybe we can strike up a deal." Ultimately, the hunter was well-wrapped in the bear's fur, and the bear had a good dinner. We always lose out when we compromise with the devil. He will consume us in the end. Revise your course of action, and be prepared to simply say, "Get away from me, Satan."

Reflection

Think of specific ways that the world is currently tempting others you know to make a deal with the devil. In what kinds of situations have you found yourself where you have or been tempted to compromise your faith in God? How can you learn to trust Him more, even in suffering and death?

MARCH 6
(Y2, D10)

On Loan from God

Each of you should use whatever gift you have received to serve others,
as faithful stewards of God's grace in its various forms.

—1 Peter 4.10 (NIV)

When a well-known conservative talk show host died in February 2021, many remembered his thirty-plus years on radio during which he pioneered a new era of talk show history. Marking the occasion of his passing, the *New York Post* recalled one of his famous lines: "With 'talent on loan from God,' Rush Limbaugh used to mock-brag on his show. Now the loan's been called, as the man who remade talk radio went off to meet his maker after a long battle with lung cancer." Having the opportunity to influence twenty million listeners a week for three hours a day on over 600 stations, his opinions were classified anywhere from radical to insightful at times. He knew he was an entertainer first and only then a political commentator. His fake egotism led many to believe he was arrogant, but those who knew him best said he was actually a somewhat shy person. When his persona declared "with talent on loan from God," he showed recognition that his gift came from elsewhere and would ultimately end one day.

Jesus once shared the Parable of the Talents (Matthew 25:14–30). Differing from the concept of a "talent" as a gift or natural ability, here it refers to a unit of measurement, often used to weigh out silver or gold. Jesus describes a man who goes on a journey, entrusting his servants in his absence with his wealth and possessions proportionate to each of their abilities. When the master eventually returns, the servants who were faithful were praised and allocated with more of the master's wealth. The servant who was fearful and negligent, however, was swiftly reprimanded by his master. Jesus has assigned His followers with His greatest treasures, making them caretakers of his ministry. A wise steward will be faithful with what the master has provided, taking care of that which he's been given. Knowing that the master will eventually return, there is understanding that those talents are only borrowed for a time, and they should be used to further God's work.

I once heard a pastor share a story he had heard about those things which we claim to be ours. It involves a man who was overlooking a plot of land that just days before had held his family's home. There, with a friend next to him, he observed his house had been completely leveled by fire. As the two of them examined the devastation, it was apparent that everything within sight had been completely destroyed. Feeling a great sense of empathy for his friend and his family for their significant loss, he didn't quite know what to say or do. Then he simply put his arm around the friend and somehow verbalized how very sorry he was. The man gazed out over the space of ashes in front of them, took a deep calming breath, and spoke these simple words: "Oh, well, there was nothing here I was planning to take with me to heaven." He understood that the possessions that we spend so much time chasing, collecting, and caring for will all break, rust, be stolen, or eventually burn up. Absolutely none of our physical possessions will be making the journey into eternity with us, even if we are buried with them.

Our culture supports one's efforts to establish a personal legacy. On the other hand, scripture tells us that we should "store your treasures in heaven, where moths and rust cannot destroy, and thieves do not break in and steal. Wherever your treasure is, there the desires of your heart will also be" (Matthew 6:20–21 NLT). A lasting legacy, one that continues for eternity, should be written on our hearts and the hearts of our loved ones. Leaving a legacy involves far more than handing down a monetary inheritance or passing on a good family name. For those things will surely pass away and forever be forgotten. The belief in Jesus Christ as the Son of the Living God and Savior of the world is the one legacy that will last. It is therefore not *my* glory, but *His* glory reflected through me; it is not *my* legacy, but *His* legacy continuing through me. There is no greater legacy than this. So whether talents and abilities or actual physical possessions, our practical obedience is demonstrated in how we manage everything under our control. It is the dedication of one's self and possessions to God's service that will live on in the lives of those we touch. All the other stuff is simply on loan from God.

Reflection

What are the foundations of your legacy? Are they superficial things of earth or everlasting things of heaven? How can you be a better steward of the talents and gifts which God has given you? In what ways might you give consideration in applying this scripture to the story to your life: "A person is a fool to store up earthly wealth but not have a rich relationship with God" (Luke 12:21 NLT)?

MARCH 7
(Y3, D10)

Perfect Timing

Be still before the Lord and wait patiently for him.

—Psalm 37:7 (NIV)

We snap the photo just as the key play is made or as the colors of the sunset are most vibrant. We submit the application as a vacancy occurs for a job requiring the exact credentials we possess. Or when we're on vacation, we pull off the highway minutes before a nasty storm and register for the last room the hotel has available that night. Some would call it luck; others might say it was just perfect timing. Whatever it was, we're just glad it happened that way. But what about when it doesn't? What happens if we have to wait or if our plans are altered? I remember once checking into the gate at an airport to be told that my flight had been overbooked and that I was on standby. Even though I tried to be courteous, I insisted that I needed to get home. I am sure that I appeared frustrated, impatient, and perhaps less than gracious while efforts were being made to acknowledge my reservation and get me home in a timely manner. In the hustle and bustle of our hectic lives, we often find it difficult to wait for anything or anyone. We want what we want, and we want it now.

It's always an uplifting occasion as the weekend arrives when we set the clocks ahead to begin Daylight Savings Time. No matter what's happening outside with the weather, the days will now seem to be longer, and we know that spring is just around the corner. Most of the clocks in my house are electric, but I do have one that instead can be erratic. It is a battery-powered atomic clock that resets itself. When I wake up the morning after a time change, it will have successfully gained or lost an hour, depending whether it's spring or fall. But just as I think it's up and running the way it should, it will suddenly adjust itself again, and the timing will be totally off. Precise timing is hard to achieve with most things in life. I am so glad that we have a God whose timing is always perfect, even though we might not always think so. Charles Stanley says: "When we surrender to His timing, He does mighty things in and for us, according to His will and His timing. God acts on behalf of those who wait for Him."

Three friends of Jesus were caught up in a timing issue. They were sisters Mary and Martha as well as their brother, Lazarus, all known to Jesus. Lazarus became ill, and the sisters sent word to Jesus about their brother's failing condition. When Jesus received the news, He intentionally waited where He was for several more days (John 11:5–6). By the time Jesus arrived, scripture tells us that Lazarus had died and was already in the grave for four days (John 11:17). A grieving Mary said to Jesus that she knew if He had been there that her brother would not have died (John 11:32), and Martha states that even so, she is confident that God will do whatever Jesus asks of Him (John 11:22). The event provides opportunity for Jesus to demonstrate that He was who He claimed to be as He indeed raises Lazarus from the dead. He also sends a clear message that God will be glorified for all those who have faith and wait on Him

We can rest assured that our heavenly Father knows exactly where we are in our lives and what we need at every moment. He allows us to sometimes walk down a difficult path in order to develop patience (Galatians 5:22) and draw us closer to Him.

> But do not forget this one thing, dear friends: With the Lord a day is like a thousand years, and a thousand years are like a day. The Lord is not slow in his keeping his promise, as some understand slowness. Instead he is patient with you, not wanting anyone to perish, but everyone to come to repentance. (2 Peter 3:8–9 NIV)

God knows the big picture, not the one where the timing of events makes no sense and seems impossible for us. It's our job to cross the finish line, trusting Him with each step. We need to stop trying to figure out all of the details and simply let God be God. And if, by chance, we are someday able to look back and reflect on the journey, we will affirm with all certainty, "That was perfect timing. It was exactly the way it was supposed to be."

Reflection

Do you become frustrated when it seems like your prayers have not been answered? Are there times that you have found that waiting for an answer turns out to be the best direction for where you are in your journey? Can you remember a time when a period of waiting provided spiritual growth as you found yourself drawing closer to Him?

MARCH 8
(Y4, D10)

That's Where I'll Be

But now I am going to him who sent me, and none of you asks me, "Where are you going?"

—John 16:5 (ESV)

When we are young, we can sometimes become quite insecure if we do not feel that someone who loves and cares about us is nearby. It's calming to know that during a thunderstorm in the middle of the night, we can jump into bed with our parents. When we are at the playground, we want to be sure that Mom is right there to catch us when we go down the slide for the first time. When the training wheels are removed from our bike and we begin to solo on our own, it's comforting to know that Dad is running alongside of us in case we lose our balance. As we take our first strokes in the pool when we are learning to swim, it's reassuring when our instructor gives us the confidence to know that they will not let us go under the water. In each case, the person encourages us by stating they will be right there to protect us from falling or sinking into dangerous territory.

My friend once related a story to me about her parents many years ago. They were having a rather vivid disagreement about a family issue, and the wife thought her husband was not being very Christian-like regarding the matter. So she decided to write him a note, telling him that she needed some space for a while and thought that he needed to reexamine his values. The note ended with these words: "I'm not telling you where I'm going, but if you need me, I'll be at Aunt Sue's." How interesting a commitment when you feel strong enough to recognize the necessity to take your leave but loving enough to want the person to know where you will be, just in case they need you. It reminds me of a line I once heard from Diane Sawyer at former First Lady Nancy Reagan's funeral. She attributed the quote to President Ronald Reagan and said it went something like this: "If you must leave, could you just take me with you?"

Jesus' disciples must have felt that way also whenever He told them that He needed to leave them. How conflicted they must have been, knowing that they had walked away from their lives to follow someone who is now saying He was parting. Jesus said to them:

> "Do not let your heart be troubled; believe in God, believe also in Me. In My Father's house are many dwelling places; if it were not so, I would have told you; for I go to prepare a place for you. If I go and prepare a place for you, I will come again and receive you to Myself, that where I am, there you may be also. And you know the way where I am going." One of the twelve, Thomas, said to Him, "Lord, we do not know where You are going, how do we know the way?" Jesus said to him, "I am the way, and the truth, and the life; no one comes to the Father but through Me." (John 14:1–6 NIV)

Even though Jesus told those who loved Him exactly where He would be, it must have confused them to some degree. He further explained, stating, "I have told you these things before they happen so that when they do happen, you will believe" (John 14:29 NLT). And over time, their faith increased in understanding and ministry. Jesus understood that in order for the salvation of mankind to be accomplished, He would have to suffer a brutal death. The plan was that His followers might continue to be comforted. Jesus set the record straight when He said, "I tell you the truth: it is to your advantage that I go away, for if I do not go away, the Helper will not come to you. But if I go, I will send him to you" (John 16:7 ESV). Following His resurrection, He made good on His promise, for "After the Lord Jesus had spoken to them, he was taken up into heaven and he sat at the right hand of God" (Mark 16:19 NIV). There He sits as our intercessor before the throne. For like all those who have reassured us with their love by comforting, catching, or keeping us balanced and afloat, He too reassured us. As an encouragement to those who loved Him, you can almost hear Him saying, "That's where I'll be."

Reflection

Why is it important that the Son of God serves as our mediator with God the Father? In what ways have you experienced the reassuring love of God's presence through His Holy Spirit? What would you say to someone who rejects Jesus' gift of salvation? How might you use the security of a caring person to explain God's great love for us?

MARCH 9
(Y5, D10)

Riding the Ups and Downs of Life

Be strong and of good courage; do not be afraid, nor be dismayed,
for the LORD your God is with you wherever you go.

—Joshua 1:9 (NKJB)

I was confused recently when I read two different devotional books back-to-back on the same day. The first one was titled *The Way Up is Down*. The subject matter related to the topic of humility. It concluded with the following statement: "You'll find that the best way to go up is to reach down to others." The second focused on prejudice and proclaimed, "Looking up to Jesus prevents us from looking down on others." Without much thought, I laughed at the perceived inconsistency and asked the easy question: "So is it up or is it down?" It appeared as though these two devotions offered a contradiction. On closer examination, I became convinced that the messages actually supported each other.

Our lives, likewise, are full of ups and downs. We often describe our current status as being on an upswing or a downswing. This has come to be reinforced by the way that our culture defines the ebbs and tides of everything about us. If we are an investor, we are happy when the market is up and tend to find it worrisome when it is on a downtrend. It's not unusual to base our purchases or entertainment selections on whether others have specified a thumb up or down rating for the product. Additionally, we become obsessed with the lifestyle of the upscale of society and pay little, if any, attention to the downtrodden. There's an old story about a man who jumped out of an airplane only to discover that his parachute was jammed. As the wind rushed by him, he took it off and desperately tried to untangle it. Suddenly, a man shot past him, flying upward at a tremendous rate of speed. The man with the chute looked up and yelled, "Hey, do you know anything about parachutes?"

The other man called down, "No. Do you know anything about gas stoves?" I guess it's all in our perspective.

When we stop to think about the totality of our existence to it, we spend more of our life in the valley or going up and down the mountain than we actually do on the mountaintop itself. Whenever

137

we fail to accept that "downtimes" are a natural part of life, some will attempt to correct their station in life by creating a world of excess. This can range anywhere from substance abuse to buying sprees, searching for anything or any way to make them feel better. The absence of a spiritual connection can result in attempting to climb the mountain with an accumulation of material wealth, feeling overwhelmed with emptiness, dissatisfaction, and a need for change. Evangelist and author Rick Warren has stated it this way: "Transformation is a process, and as life happens, there are tons of ups and downs. It's a journey of discovery—there are moments on mountaintops and moments in deep valleys of despair." Therefore, it is important to acknowledge Jesus told us, "In this world you will have trouble. But take heart! I have overcome the world" (John 16:33 NIV). The psalmist likewise reassures us that "God is our refuge and strength, an ever-present help in trouble" (Psalm 46:1 NIV).

I suspect that the most powerful parts of our lives are lived in the valley rather than on the mountaintop. The valleys are where we do our struggling. In the twenty-third Psalm, David showed his understanding that every valley had a shepherd who would go before the flock leading the sheep to safe passage. Whether we're in the depths of the valley, sinking into it, or trying to climb up the slopes, each season should motivate us to trust the Lord, our Good Shepherd, and seek His direction in all that we do. Being in the valleys of life is never easy, but the challenges in those valleys strengthen who we are and give us hope for a future. Paul said:

> For our present troubles are small and won't last very long. Yet they produce for us a glory that vastly outweighs them and will last forever. So we don't look at the troubles we can see now; rather, we fix our gaze on things that cannot be seen. For the things we see now will soon be gone, but the things we cannot see will last forever. (2 Corinthians 4:17–18 NLT).

We will do a disservice to ourselves and others if we portray the Christian life only as a mountaintop experience. It's much more like the ups and downs of a roller coaster. However, we can be sure the Lord is in the seat beside us and that we are never taking the ride alone.

Reflection

Where do you spend most of your life? On the mountain or in the valley? In what ways has God sustained you and help you to be a stronger person through your "valley" times? What would you say to a new believer who is having difficulty facing and handling the difficulties of life?

MARCH 10
(Y6, D10)

Rich Toward God

Yet true godliness with contentment is itself great wealth. After all, we brought nothing with us when we came into the world, and we can't take anything with us when we leave it.

—1 Timothy 6:6–7 (NLT)

Conceiving a life full of money, wealth, and power in the midst of the Great Depression, an unemployed electrical engineer by the name of Charles B. Darrow developed his version of a board game involving the buying and selling of land and the expansion of that land. Using playing pieces named after locations around his home in Atlantic City, New Jersey, Darrow introduced Monopoly® on March 7, 1933. After showing a draft to Parker Brothers who rejected his design, Darrow decided to release the game on his own, but he was unable to keep up with production due to increasing demand for its popularity. He once again contacted representatives of Parker Brothers who turned Monopoly into a household name as it soon became the best-selling game in America. It has been distributed to countries all over the world and has been translated into dozens of languages. Over the years, the most expensive version was made from eighteen-karat gold estimated to be worth roughly $2 million, and the world's largest permanent outdoor Monopoly board is thirty-foot square, made from granite, and located in San Jose, California. How fascinating that a game about living the high life as a financier would be introduced at a time when the country was trying to rebound from its worst economic depression continues to have relevance today.

As we develop the skill set of playing games as children, we sometimes learn valuable life lessons as well. Author and Pastor John Ortberg tells the story of playing Monopoly with his grandmother at an early age. He described the manner with which she maneuvered through the game as "totally ruthless." As a little kid, his approach was always to hold on to his money. Inevitably, his grandmother would buy everything she could, take his assets, and win the game. Without reservation, she would always say, "One day, you'll learn to play the game." After many hours of practice with a friend, he was determined to beat his grandmother at her own game. When he finally did so, he thought it was a great moment. But Grandma had a final word, one remaining lesson. She simply

139

said, "None of it was really yours. You got all heated up about it for a while, but it was around a long time before you sat down at the board, and it will be here after you're gone. Players come and players go. But it all goes back in the box." Ortberg has written a book logically entitled *When the Game Is Over… It All Goes Back in the Box*. It's a profound lesson he learned from his grandmother.

Our society often fosters the attitude that aggressive achievement is necessary to win in life and that you have to relentlessly get everything you can, while you can. So it's important to accumulate wealth, grow that résumé, build up power. Those who live out that philosophy can quickly succumb to feelings of great emptiness. Ortberg says, "You have to ask yourself: When you finally get the ultimate possession, when you've made the ultimate purchase, when you buy the ultimate home, when you have stored up financial security and climbed the ladder of success to the highest rung you can possibly climb it, and the thrill wears off—and it will wear off—then what?" Jesus said, "Don't store up treasures here on earth, where moths eat them and rust destroys them, and where thieves break in and steal. Store your treasures in heaven, where moths and rust cannot destroy, and thieves do not break in and steal. Wherever your treasure is, there the desires of your heart will also be" (Matthew 6:19–21 NLT). The most valuable success for any Christian is to learn how to play the game in light of this one great truth: to consider what will significantly matter and what's not important in light of eternity. When we make sure that our heart is right with God, all else will follow. "Do not love this world nor the things it offers you, for when you love the world, you do not have the love of the Father in you" (1 John 2:15 NLT). We can expend a lot of energy and time gathering things that merely go back in the box when the game of this earthly journey is over. As true believers, we must realize that our ultimate goal is to become rich toward God and that accumulation of stuff is only an exercise in futility.

Reflection

Have there been times when you wished that your accomplishments could remain as a permanent memorial of your greatness? What might a life that is rich toward God look like? As you consider your life—where you have been, where you are today, where you'd like to be, and what you'd like to do tomorrow—what is it you are trying to achieve? How are you setting a strategy to make that successful conclusion a quest which will glorify your heavenly Father?

MARCH 11
(Y7, D10)

Each Life Matters

Did not he who made me in the womb make them? Did not
the same one form us both within our mothers?

—Job 31:15 (NIV)

On the occasion that you pick up the daily newspaper and look at the obituaries, most of us pay little if any attention to the names whom we do not recognize. However, when it happens to be someone you do know, you feel a different feeling. Depending on the relationship you had with that person or their loved ones, you might also have a deep sense of sadness. One day, I read that two people, a mother and daughter, were murdered. Their names didn't register with me, but subsequently, when I saw their pictures, I realized that I had met the mother years before. I also recognized the daughter from being a customer in a store where she had worked. I was surprised to learn how they had died, and I felt empathy for the shock that those who had known them well must have experienced.

On March 11, 2005, Ashley Smith was a twenty-six-year-old waitress in Atlanta, simply trying to get her life in order. She was a struggling mother and widow dealing with substance abuse as well as attempting to regain custody of her five-year-old daughter. That evening, after she had finished work, Brian Nichols, an escapee from a rape trial, forced his way into her apartment where he held her hostage for seven hours. Earlier, he had stolen a gun from a sheriff's deputy and shot a judge and court reporter before fleeing. As Smith was held by her captive, she appealed to his humanity while telling him about her daughter and asking him about his own infant son. She read passages to him from Rick Warren's bestselling book, *The Purpose Driven Life*. She later said that both of their lives were changed that night. Nichols' heart was softened, and she came to terms with her drug use. Because of the incident, she was confronted with the question "Do you want to do this or do you want to have a different life?" In the ensuing years, she wrote a book, *Unlikely Angel*, telling her story. She married, gained custody of her daughter, and states that by the grace of God, she hasn't used illegal drugs since the day before that event. Additionally, in 2015, a faith-based film was released called *Captive* in which she shared her true-to-life revelation.

We live in a time when human life is no longer regarded as special, let alone sacred. Unless with have developed a connection with another individual, it becomes quite easy to write them off or simply "unfriend" them on our social media page. God values each life. It is indeed sacred to Him, for we are created in His image. We are His most prized possession. Jesus said, "Are not five sparrows sold for two pennies? And not one of them is forgotten before God. Why, even the hairs of your head are all numbered. Fear not; you are of more value than many sparrows" (Luke 12:6–7 NIV). God's interest in the smallest details of human beings isn't limited to the disciples or a chosen few; He is that intimately aware of and interested in each of us. Jesus enlightens us that "the thief's purpose is to steal and kill and destroy. My purpose is to give them a rich and satisfying life" (John 10:10 NLT). The abundant life that He promised has nothing to do with collecting more earthly treasures. It has everything to do with developing the right relationship with God through faith in Christ and accordingly spending eternity in His company.

Paul reminds us that all human beings live, breathe, and everything else because of God (Acts 17:25). God surrounds His children with His presence. There is no place we can go, no word we can say, no action too insignificant for God not to notice. The relationship we build with our Creator will enable us to exhibit more genuine love toward our fellow man, just as He has for us. Pastor and author Chuck Swindoll once said: "Words can never adequately convey the incredible impact of our attitudes toward life. The longer I live the more convinced I become that life is ten percent what happens to us and 90 percent how we respond to it." The sanctity of life must always be respected. The unborn child, the person with a disability, older and infirm individuals, those with diverse or ethnic backgrounds different than our own—He cares for every one of us, and so should we. God says that you are valuable regardless of who you are, for through His very own eyes, He sees His creation and knows for certain that each life matters.

Reflection

Do you sometimes feel inferior or superior to others around you? What is it about that person that makes you think he or she is better or lesser than you? Do you really think that God loves you any differently than they? Is it enough for you to know that God considers your life to be sacred? In what ways might you reflect and share your understanding of His deep love for each individual?

MARCH 12
(Y1, D11)

True Generosity

A generous person will prosper; whoever refreshes others will be refreshed.

—Proverbs 11:25 (NIV)

In the midst of the Great Depression, a mother of seven becomes frustrated that no one in the family seems to be pulling their weight in completing their assigned chores. So she stages what she calls her "own personal sit-down strike." Probably the most self-sacrificing member of the TV-family known as *The Waltons*, mother Olivia Walton appears to be frustrated that her kindness and generosity is being taken for granted. If you were a fan of this 1970s family drama, you know that in this episode, like all the others, everything turns out just fine, including a lesson to be remembered. That was then, and it appears that these days, not much has changed. Not long ago, a lady writes to an advice columnist that "while she likes doing kind things for people," she believes that her "kind acts should be appreciated but not to be expected." She goes on to express that her generosity has begun to turn to resentment. She must feel some guilt from this because she asks the advice-giver what she is doing wrong.

The words of wisdom shared from the columnist are no doubt intended to get the writer to examine her own actions. At one point, she states, "If your self-worth is tied up in the idea that you're a generous person, you should disengage it." While that advice might be adequate for many in today's society, it should also be compared with biblical teachings when considered by modern-day Christians. Scripture is filled with many examples of kindness and self-sacrifice. In the New Testament, we read about a person named Tabitha from Joppa who was always doing good. Dorcas, as she was also called, was known for her compassion for the poor in her community and investing in those who were needy. In Acts 9:36–40, we learn about her at the time of her death. Friends search for Peter to see if there was something he could do. Widows showed him all the clothing Dorcas had made for them—gifts that reminded them of her love. Dorcas is described as a disciple and was one who imitated the generosity of God.

From the beginning of Creation, God has been generous toward us. He created us in His image, provides for us, and wants us to be in a relationship with Him. Above all, God demonstrated His generosity when He offered His Son as a sacrifice to atone for our wickedness. The gift of Jesus to sinful mankind was the ultimate validation of His love. He is always seeking people who will reflect His character and model His generosity through self-sacrifice, evidenced by their attitude and actions toward others. While at times we might feel that our generosity is unappreciated, we are not to expect repayment in kind or from any worldly praise. Our reward will come from the Lord in His way and in His time. In fact, we are challenged to show generosity even to our enemies: "If someone takes your coat, do not withhold your shirt from them… But love your enemies, do good to them, and lend to them without expecting to get anything back. Then your reward will be great, and you will be children of the Most High, because he is kind to the ungrateful and wicked" (Luke 6:29, 35 NIV).

Lent begins with Ash Wednesday and runs for six weeks leading into Holy Week and Easter Sunday. It marks a period of time when some Christians reflect on the biblical account of Jesus' time in the desert where he fasted and prayed before his eventual death and resurrection. During the Lenten season, we are expected to make sacrifices as children of God and followers of Christ. The sacrifices should remind us of the one made by Jesus through which He saved us from sin and won salvation of our souls. While the historical intent behind the season of Lent is purposeful, it has often lost meaning in our culture. It has become fashionable to "give up something" for Lent, so why not consider allowing it to be a period of generosity through self-sacrifice? Wouldn't it be wonderful if someone could benefit from the sacrificial offerings of your acts of service? Mother Teresa reminds us that "you have never really lived until you have done something for someone who can never repay you." True generosity begins with a heart of sacrificial service ending with God's grace and the knowledge that He alone has been exalted.

Reflection

If you rely on your generosity to be based on the acceptance and praise from others, how does your attitude and obedience change on a daily basis? How can you combat the falsehood that what God can do through you is limited to what others expect from you? Consider ways you might display God's generous heart to someone in need through an unexpected act of service?

MARCH 13
(Y2, D11)

Living a Life of Excess

Then he said to them, "Watch out! Be on your guard against all kinds of greed; life does not consist in an abundance of possessions."

—Luke 12:15 (NIV)

Years ago, I went to a birthday party for a young child. In attendance were several neighborhood children and some adult relatives. So there were lots of presents. Midway through opening his gifts, the guest of honor looked up and said, "No more." On what would normally be a festive occasion, the child had become so overwhelmed with all the attention directed at him, and no doubt the massive amount of stuff he received, that he just had to quit. Over the years we have resided on this earth, most of us have accumulated such a material abundance that we, too, would have every right to feel overcome. Forget those who could be labeled as hoarders or pack rats. We simply have attained far too many possessions. Indeed, if you have duplicates of certain items, more than one junk drawer, or regularly contemplated renting a storage unit, you should consider that you just might be living a life of excess.

Society tries to sell us on the idea that having more in our lives should be our goal. Restaurants serve "all you can eat" buffets. Advertisements constantly push things we absolutely need to buy because, of course, what we now have just isn't good enough. We live in a culture where each of us is viewed as a consumer and what we buy impacts our social status as well as our self-image. Professionals have stated that generations of overindulged American kids are growing up seriously lacking in discipline, direction, and conviction. The common denominator here is excess. Without a doubt, we are out of control and will most likely never recover from an agenda that promotes every opportunity to binge. It's hard to keep your eye on heavenly treasures when so much value is placed on earthly ones. We have greatly distanced ourselves from the philosophy of Socrates who once stated, "The secret of happiness, you see, is not found in seeking more but in developing the capacity to enjoy less."

The wise King Solomon once stated:

> Anything I wanted, I would take. I denied myself no pleasure. I even found great pleasure in hard work, a reward for all my labors. But as I looked at everything I had worked so hard to accomplish, it was all so meaningless—like chasing the wind. There was nothing really worthwhile anywhere." (Ecclesiastes 2:10–11 NIV)

Jesus knew that worldly stuff could be enticing and that living with excess can take over your life. When He called His disciples into ministry, He said to them, "Do not get any gold or silver or copper to take with you in your belts—no bag for the journey or extra shirt or sandals or a staff, for the worker is worth his keep" (Matthew 10:9–10 NIV). You see, Jesus didn't want them to be anxious about stuff. God would provide what they needed and just enough of it. This was later echoed by the Apostle Paul as he wrote, "Don't love money; be satisfied with what you have. For God has said, 'I will never fail you. I will never abandon you'" (Hebrews 13:5 NLT).

When accumulating stuff becomes our norm, attempting to live a life of moderation is an uphill battle. At times, it can feel like our stuff owns us rather than the other way around. Eventually, it robs us of the joy we can find when we are able to spend more time focusing on heavenly things. Likewise, it erodes our faith when we trust more in our stuff than we do in God, thus leaving us still desiring what our hearts really need—Him. The only area in which we don't need to be concerned about moderation is in our relationship with God. We are to love Him without limits with all our heart, soul, and mind (Luke 10:27). The more we ask Him to fill us and occupy our lives with His Holy Spirit, the easier it becomes to live in moderation in all earthly things. God's Holy Word tells us, "Don't store up treasures here on earth, where moths eat them and rust destroys them, and where thieves break in and steal" (Matthew 6:19 NLT). The Lenten season is a wonderful time to experience a spiritual journey of uncluttering. Be like my young friend those many years ago. Give yourself permission to let go of some of the things you are holding right there in front of you. You will find that your hands are now free to do some wonderful life-changing activities as you suddenly move from saying "no more stuff" to "more of you, Lord."

Reflection

What is your definition of enough? How has holding on to all the stuff of this life been keeping God at a distance? What is stopping you from trying to find your own path to less while getting rid of the mindset that more is better? Are there some initial steps you can take in the days ahead to make this happen? How will you hold yourself accountable for doing so?

MARCH 14
(Y3, D11)

Blessings

Taste and see that the Lord is good; blessed is the one who takes refuge in him.

—Psalm 34:8 (NIV)

I had finished all I needed to say. The phone call was about to conclude, and the person at the other end simply said, "God bless you." Without any hesitation, I replied, "God bless you as well." It was rather inspiring, especially since the last time I may have been the receiver of those words was after I had sneezed. I never did quite understand how the discharge of a full-hearted sneeze could result in the offering of another's well wishes. However, through the ages, several explanations have been documented. One justification is that sneezing was the body's attempt to expel an evil presence. Another account dates far back to the time of Pope Gregory I in AD 590 when the blessing became common practice in an effort to halt the spread of the bubonic plague. In my previously mentioned phone call, it was just a refreshing way of saying thank you for what I hoped had been a helpful conversation in providing an honest reference for someone I had known for many years.

Each March 17, our Irish friends remind us on Saint Patrick's Day that through all that may happen to us in our journey, we should pause along the way to greet each other with statements of warmth, happiness, and goodwill. So old Irish blessings reflect sentiments, such as "May the roads rise to meet you. May the wind be at your back. May the sun shine warm upon your face, the rain fall soft upon your fields. And, until we meet again, may God hold you in the palm of His hand." We could perhaps learn a bit from the Irish as we struggle through the uncertainties of life, especially when we are forced to echo the words "There's no way I can see this as a blessing." When we're dealing with an injury that might halt our career, receive the news of an unplanned pregnancy at the absolute worst time, or are confronted with the possibility that we may be facing financial ruin, it is true that most of us might fail to see the blessing on any of these occasions. As the passing of time so preciously offers an opportunity to reflect and heal, there are many who will later tell you that what once appeared to be a life-threatening disaster turned out to be nothing more than a real blessing in disguise.

For those who follow Christ, there are many opportunities to experience blessings. One does not have to look any further than the beginning of the Sermon on the Mount, commonly known as the Beatitudes (Matthew 5:1–12). Here we learn that the poor in spirit, those who mourn, the meek, the merciful, and others will be blessed spiritually. You might ask how one can be in any one of these conditions and feel blessed. It's because when this is our situation, we hopefully realize just how dependent we are on Him. Anytime we are drawn closer to God, there in and of itself is the blessing. Along our path, we are prompted as well to be a blessing to others. It can indeed be a blessing to all concerned when the recipient is one with whom we might not be on good terms. "Do not repay evil with evil or insult with insult. On the contrary, repay evil with blessing, because to this you were called so that you may inherit a blessing" (1 Peter 3:9 NIV). In other words, blessings sometimes create blessings.

Our greatest blessing in this life is without a doubt the grace that has been bestowed upon us through Jesus' death on the cross. In that regard, we conclude that there are even more blessings awaiting believers when we pass from our human form into eternity. "Blessed be the God and Father of our Lord Jesus Christ, who has blessed us in Christ with every spiritual blessing in the heavenly places" (Ephesians 1:3 ESV). For now, remember the blessing of the Old Testament which we often hear passed on as a benediction: "The Lord bless you and keep you; the Lord make his face to shine upon you and be gracious to you; the Lord lift up his countenance upon you and give you peace" (Numbers 6:24–26 NIV). So God bless you, my friend. May you find a way to work it into a conversation with your favorite Irishman. Or maybe just stop trying to hold back that sneeze, and you just may hear it a little more often.

Reflection

Can you think of a time that on the backside of what appeared to be a crisis made you feel blessed? Will you be able to apply that knowledge in your life the next time you feel like you are on a sinking ship? What might you offer someone who would say to you, "There's no way that I can see this as a blessing"?

MARCH 15
(Y4, D11)

Present

This is my command—be strong and courageous! Do not be afraid or discouraged. For the Lord your God is with you wherever you go.

—Joshua 1:9 (NLT)

There are more times than not when I have become easily disturbed in an attempt to resolve a problem through a phone call to a utility company or an appliance help line. With increased frequency, it seems as though I have to call back more than once to get a matter resolved. Habitually, there is not a good record of my prior conversations. Sometimes I get placed on hold and must then speak with a person who exhibits a superior attitude or I end up being transferred to an individual with whom I struggle to understand. Recently, in anticipation of a call about a situation that I felt might not be easily resolved, I found myself doing a lot of "self-talk" in preparation for the exchange. I took on the attitude that I would not have one; an attitude, that is. I simply gave the person on the other end credit for being there to help me. I decided to be less aloof and more present during the dialogue. In doing so, I found that I was more polite and was able to choose my responses more carefully.

Our present culture has made it challenging to effectively engage with others. With the growing dependence on electronic communication and the advent of social media, communication on a personal level often takes a back seat. So when we do need to talk with another person, we sometimes do not know how to apply respectable social graces. Even a casual "Hello, how are you?" to a passerby on the street or a simple "Thanks for your help" to the clerk at the store who has provided assistance are common rarities. I sometimes hear others express that they don't know what to say to someone who is sick or has had a death in the family. Sometimes what they need most are not your words but your caring presence. I know from my experience that what I most remember from the tough times in my life are not so much what people said but rather who was there for me in those vulnerable periods.

Far more than anyone of us ever will, Jesus understood the importance of the human connection. He said, "I am the vine; you are the branches. If you remain in me and I in you, you will bear much fruit; apart from me you can do nothing" (John 15:5 NLT). Yet we, His children, find ourselves distracted and overwhelmed by the countless number of diversions life throws at us each and every day. Jesus demonstrated the importance of being present. He scolded His followers on occasion for missing the point. Prior to feeding the five thousand, scripture tells us that Jesus showed compassion on them.

> As evening approached, the disciples came to him and said, "This is a remote place, and it's already getting late. Send the crowds away, so they can go to the villages and buy themselves some food." Jesus replied, "They do not need to go away. You give them something to eat." (Matthew 14:15–16 NIV).

And at the home of Mary and Martha, Mary sat at the feet of Jesus while her sister was distracted. "But the Lord answered and said to her, 'Martha, Martha, you are worried and bothered about so many things; but only one thing is necessary, for Mary has chosen the good part, which shall not be taken away from her'" (Luke 10:41–42 NLT). Mary understood what it meant to be truly present.

The Apostle Paul counseled that we must rise above these life distractions and be led by the Spirit. "But the fruit of the Spirit is love, joy, peace, forbearance, kindness, goodness, faithfulness, gentleness, and self-control. There is no law against these things" (Galatians 5:22–23 NIV). How can we begin to implement these virtues in our life's journey unless we allow ourselves to be truly in the here and now for those who cross our path? We start by finding strength from He who created us. The Psalmist said: "I know the Lord is always with me. I will not be shaken, for he is right beside me" (Psalm 16:8 NLT). Once we finally understand that God is always there, waiting to be our guide, we will understand that when we find ourselves in His presence—nothing else matters. Wouldn't it be nice if we could do the same for others who need to feel that from us?

Reflection

What are some of the distractions that you need to be more aware of in your life in order that you might be more appropriately present in your daily social interactions? How might you find collective strength in the words of Matthew 18:20 NIV ("For where two or three gather in my name, there am I with them") to increase your touching the lives of others?

MARCH 16
(Y5, D11)

Rules for Winning

Listen, my son, to your father's instruction and do not forsake your mother's teaching.

—Proverbs 1:8 (NIV)

After a late-winter snowfall one March, I became very aware of the rules of living in small town America. Being very conscious of an article I had seen published in the local newspaper, I knew that it was a requirement that sidewalks must be shoveled within twenty-four hours following a snowfall. That one made sense to me. I had also heard that when removing snow from the walks, you were supposed to throw it on your property instead of the street. I guess I could understand that one also since it would only make additional work for someone else or could create a slippery area on an already-treated road. Then I thought, *Gee, I wonder if there's a rule that the snowplows cannot throw snow onto my sidewalk? There ought to be a law about that one.* I laughed as I recalled that had been the name of an old cartoon strip years ago.

Rules…rules…rules. Some say they are only made for breaking. Not so if you wanted to be a member of Saint Anthony's in New Jersey where Bob Hurley coached for over fifty years. His presence was a godsend to hundreds of inner-city kids. A thousand victories and several dozen state championships later, Hurley explained their success in one word: rules. Each player (and their parents) were expected to sign a "Student/Athlete Contract" containing a list of twenty expectations the team members must do to succeed. The list included maintaining a clean-cut appearance (no facial hair, tattoos, or mohawks), refraining from all forms of substance abuse (alcohol, drug, and tobacco use), as well as no cell phone use while in school. The coach concluded with this challenge "So at the end of four years, we've taken you to a place where you can go to college." They were obviously doing something right because the entire student body had 100 percent college acceptance for a twenty-five-year period.

Since the creation of mankind, God gave us a choice to follow His rules or to break them. In the beginning, it was simple. "And the LORD God commanded the man, 'You are free to eat from any tree in the garden; but you must not eat from the tree of the knowledge of good and evil, for when you eat from it you will certainly die'" (Genesis 2:16–17 NIV). That one didn't work out so well. In the Old Testament, one discovers that God handed down many rules, some of which man obeyed and died in disobedience of others. Not only did God speak through Moses in the provision of the Ten Commandments (Exodus 20:1–21), He also directed:

> Give the following instructions to the people of Israel: Throughout the generations to come you must make tassels for the hems of your clothing and attach them with a blue cord. When you see the tassels, you will remember and obey all the commands of the LORD instead of following your own desires and defiling yourselves, as you are prone to do. The tassels will help you remember that you must obey all my commands and be holy to your God. (Numbers 15:38–40 NLT)

Throughout the many centuries, civilizations have established rules for their citizens to follow for the creation of societal living. Jesus found Himself in the middle of such a society where the teachers of the law were often more concerned about the ritualistic details than they were about the heart of its instruction. They frequently planted spies in Jesus' public gatherings, asking questions where He might improperly speak against the authorities. In one case, He was quite aware of their attempt and simply responded with the line, "Give to Caesar what belongs to Caesar, and give to God what belongs to God" (Luke 20:25 NLT). Once, one of the Pharisees, an expert in religious law, tried to trick Jesus by asking: "Teacher, which is the most important commandment in the law of Moses?"

Jesus replied, "'You must love the LORD your God with all your heart, all your soul, and all your mind.' This is the first and greatest commandment. A second is equally important: 'Love your neighbor as yourself.' The entire law and all the demands of the prophets are based on these two commandments" (Matthew 22:36–40 NLT). Herein are the most important rules for each of us now and always. Whether we find ourselves on the basketball court or shoveling snow on the sidewalks of our hometown, they guarantee we will have a winning season.

Reflection

Are you more in conflict with breaking the rules of man or God? Consider some ways you can better practice His greatest commandments? What personal rules might you establish for yourself in order to fulfill them?

MARCH 17
(Y6, D11)

May God Bless

We may throw the dice, but the Lord determines how they fall.

—Proverbs 16:33 (NLT)

Images of tiny green men, rainbows with pots of gold, and lucky shamrocks are all symbolic of St. Patrick's Day celebrated internationally each March 17. Although he was not Irish, he was one of the most successful missionaries in history. Saint Patrick was born into a Christian family in the late fourth century at a time when the Roman Empire, of which Britain was a part, was on the verge of collapse and vulnerable to attack. When Patrick was sixteen years old, a group of Irish raiders invaded his village and took him captive. They transported Patrick to Ireland where he spent six years in slavery. In those Irish hills where he worked as a shepherd, he was exposed to a harsh climate and nearly starved to death. Often completely alone, he turned to God for comfort and companionship. He discovered a way to escape finding passage on a ship to Britain, and he was eventually reunited with his family.

Believing he had been called by God to Christianize Ireland, Patrick joined the Catholic Church and studied for fifteen years before being consecrated as the church's second missionary to Ireland in 432. While spreading and preaching the Gospel, he faced frequent opposition and was in constant danger of being killed for his bold faith. By the time of his death, believed to be on March 17 in AD 461, the island was almost entirely Christian. Patrick used his sturdy resolve and ambition to advance God's kingdom in a mighty way, making him one of the great saints of the church. Early Irish settlers to the American colonies, many of whom were indentured servants, brought the Irish tradition of St. Patrick's feast day to America. For thousands of years, the Irish have observed the holiday of Saint Patrick's death by attending church services in the morning and celebrating with food and drink later in the day. Today, Americans of Irish descent rejoice on St. Patrick's Day by participating in parades and engaging in raucous partying. As millions around the globe put on their best green clothing and toast the luck of the Irish, it's a day when many claim that along their ancestral line, there is just a "bit of Irish in their blood."

St. Patrick lived his years as a great example for us today. Whether or not one believes his life held the "luck of the Irish" doesn't much matter. For it's easy to see that God's presence and sovereignty were powerful throughout his years. The life experiences of St. Patrick are reminiscent of a different story that happened many centuries before. In the book of Genesis (37:1–50:26), Joseph, a son of Jacob, was sold into bondage as a young man at the very hands of his jealous brothers. As a slave in Egypt, he lived many years under the rule of another and suffered in prison. He was unjustly accused of wrongs he did not do, and he was forgotten by those whom he had tried to help. Yet even in his loneliness, weariness, and confusion, God comforted him. Just as He provided a way of escape for St. Patrick, God also paved a path of freedom for Joseph. Slavery and imprisonment could not keep either of them contained because the Lord had a greater purpose in mind. While some might describe their fate as luck, it is clear that both men recognized who had been in control of their lives. In speaking to his brothers years later, Joseph said, "You intended to harm me, but God intended it all for good. He brought me to this position so I could save the lives of many people" (Genesis 50:20 NLT).

St. Patrick would want us to remember him not for the secular revelry which has become so much a part of the day that bears his name but more as a reason to follow Christ. He stated this prayer: "Christ with me, Christ before me, Christ behind me, Christ in me, Christ beneath me, Christ above me, Christ on my right, Christ on my left, Christ when I lie down, Christ when I sit down, Christ when I arise, Christ in the heart of every man who thinks of me." The word *luck* does not appear in the Bible or much adapt to the Christian faith. While the phrase "good luck" is often spoken by those who certainly have kind intentions, it's important to understand that luck is a way of trying to explain things without including God in the discussion. Paul wrote "In him we were also chosen, having been predestined according to the plan of him who works out everything in conformity with the purpose of his will" (Ephesians 1:11 NIV). Let's honor Him with the sentiment of the Irish: "May God be with you and bless you, as He holds you in the palm of His hand." Or just simply, "May God bless."

Reflection

When you look back on your life, what outcomes have you attributed to "dumb luck?" Are you able to rethink those events (good or bad) and attribute the navigation of your life to a Higher Power?

MARCH 18
(Y7, D11)

Praying for You

So we have not stopped praying for you since we first heard about you.

—Colossians 1:9 (NLT)

"I guess people take me seriously because they keep giving me names." The statement was made by a friend of mine making reference to the fact that she is frequently requested to pray for folks she doesn't even know. This came about because she maintains a prayer list and often tells others she will put them on it when they express a need. Recently, I had a text from a friend, asking me to remember a couple whom we mutually know in my prayers. I responded that I certainly would and said that they had actually been on my prayer list for some time. She answered back by stating, "I would have never thought of prayer lists if I didn't know you." Quite frankly, the idea of maintaining a prayer list is not a novel idea. I started keeping one years ago when I was told it was sinful to tell someone you would be praying for them and then not do so. Scripture says, "Just say a simple, 'Yes, I will,' or 'No, I won't.' Anything beyond this is from the evil one" (Matthew 5:37 NLT). While my offer of prayer is always expressed with the best of intentions, I also know that my memory is, at times, short-lived. Hence my list.

There are times when folks make prayer far more complex than it needs to be. There is a story of a man who learned how easy it could become. The man's daughter had asked the local pastor to come and pray with her father who was bedfast. Assuming the old fellow had been informed of his visit, the pastor introduced himself. Pointing to an empty chair beside the bed, he said, "I figured you were expecting me."

"Oh yeah, the chair," said the bedridden man. "I've never told anyone this, not even my daughter, but all of my life I never knew how to pray. At church, I used to hear the pastor talk about prayer, but it always went right over my head. One day about four years ago, my best friend said to me, 'Joe, prayer is just a simple matter of having a conversation with Jesus. Here's what I suggest. Sit down, place an empty chair beside you, and in faith see Jesus on the chair. Then just speak to Him and listen in the same way you're doing with me right now.' So I tried it and I've liked it so much that I do it a couple of hours every day. I'm careful, though. If my daughter saw me talking to an empty chair, she'd think I had gone crazy." The pastor was deeply moved by the story and encouraged man to continue on the journey. Then he prayed with him and returned to the church. Two nights later, the daughter called to tell the pastor that her father had died that afternoon.

"Did he pass peacefully?" the pastor asked.

"Yes, when I left the house around two o'clock, he called me over to his bedside, told me one of his corny jokes, and kissed me on the cheek. When I got back from the store an hour later, he was gone. But there *was* something strange. Apparently, just before Daddy died, he leaned over and rested his head on a chair beside the bed." Joe had come to appreciate who it was sitting in the chair next to him.

Spending time alone with God in prayer is a great privilege that not only allows us to touch the lives of others but also seek personal help in our own struggles and weaknesses. If you have ever been on the receiving end of prayer, you know how effective prayer can be. I can't tell you how many times I didn't know someone was lifting me in prayer to later be told by them, "Hey, I've been praying for you." It's always been a moment of revelation for me, for I knew when I was walking in that dark valley, I felt close to God. To be certain, "The earnest prayer of a righteous person has great power and produces wonderful results" (James 5:16 NLT). It's become far too easy to acknowledge someone's pain and suffering with a simple "thinking of you" in passing. Social media posts are only one example of dismissive comments such as "Praying for you." Let's hope that all those who flippantly use that expression are really doing so. The difference between saying you're praying for someone and actually praying for them is one simple action—talking to our Father. Those who take prayer seriously will pray continually and trust that God answers each prayer, according to His perfect will and in His perfect timing. A Christian who prays repeatedly and effectively for others in the manner taught in scripture will pray to God the Father (Matthew 6:9), in the power of the Holy Spirit (Romans 8:26–27), and in the name of Jesus (John 14:13). When we do so, it gives a whole new life to the phrase "Praying for you."

Reflection

In addition to asking God to "move" as you pray about specific names or situations, consider listening for your own self-reflective thoughts. Carefully reflect on what God's Spirit is prompting you to do in light of your request (make a call, send a card, share a scripture, schedule a visit). During those times when you are feeling inadequate or worthless, why not begin a personal prayer list ministry?

MARCH 19
(Y1, D12)

Social Distancing

The LORD sustains them on their sickbed and restores them from their bed of illness.

—Psalm 41:3 (NIV)

It's interesting to see how people react when life as they knew it yesterday is suddenly different today. When we have to experience confinement due to a recent surgery because we are infectious, facing an unsafe weather emergency, or responding to imposed restrictions intended to reduce the spread of a deadly disease like the coronavirus, many of us become frazzled. The mantra from children and others who need some form of direction in their lives is, "So what do I do now?" When our daily routine becomes interrupted, oftentimes, our coping skills do as well. The disruption of the security of a familiar schedule makes us anxious for a norm that *was* but no longer *is*, at least for a while. It becomes worse when we are told to restrict our interpersonal contact with those outside of our immediate household. This practice has come to be known as "social distancing."

You may recall times when you were young that you weren't allowed to play with friends who were contagious with certain childhood diseases. If you are one of the millions of older Americans, you will remember a period when doctors made house calls and, if a quarantine needed to be imposed, visitation restriction signs were posted on the front doors of infected homes. The Bible contains many references to uncleanliness. Worshippers had to comply with the laws of the day, and if they were considered to be unclean, they could not approach God with reverence. A good case in point were persons who had become afflicted with leprosy. Those who had the disease were required to remain apart from others until they were healed. Their clothes would be torn, and they had to cover their head and face and cry out, "Unclean! Unclean!" (Leviticus 13:45 NIV). Also, as long as the serious disease lasted, they were considered ceremonially unclean and had to live in isolation outside of the camp (Leviticus 13:46).

In God's Holy Word, Luke writes about ten lepers who collectively approached Jesus while remaining at a distance as required by the law. They called out to Him, "Jesus, Master, have mercy on us" (Luke 17:13 NLT). Without seemingly doing anything to heal them, "He looked at them and said, 'Go show yourselves to the priests'" (Luke 17:14 NLT). At the moment of His direction, no physical change took place, but they did as Jesus had instructed. As they began their walk, it was then that they were cured. However, only one returned to thank Jesus for the healing. Even though He had not withheld healing from the other nine, He made a point of remarking about their lack of gratitude (Luke 17:18). Note Jesus' final words to the thankful Samaritan: "Stand up and go. Your faith has healed you" (Luke 17:19 NLT). This man received the blessing of a spiritual healing, in addition to the cleansing of his skin.

It is important that we don't become like the nine lepers who failed to give glory to God for the provision of His blessings. Having to socially distance by temporarily sheltering in place is not the end of the world. We have the luxury of maintaining contact with others by phone. In these situations, many persons are able to continue interaction by video applications such as Skype and Facetime. If possible, we should be using these to reach out to those who may be isolated and have basic needs for which we can offer support. If we are on the receiving end, we need to be grateful. Those of us who are fortunate to share a home should value this time of renewed fellowship. Also in this day and age, we have no reason to feel separated from a spiritual connection. There are twenty-four-hour broadcast TV and radio programs available, and worship services are streaming from various churches and spiritual leaders. Periods of isolation are a great opportunity to count your many blessings. Worry is counterproductive and indeed a sin against hope with no reason to be fearful. I once heard that "be not afraid" is mentioned 365 times in scripture. Why not begin to search and reflect on one of those references each day? You will find encouragement and affirmation that you are, indeed, never socially distanced from God.

Reflection

In what ways does learning about the laws of physical uncleanliness contained in scripture help you understand more about Jesus' ministry and His purpose to make us spiritually clean? How can these lessons relate to us, especially during periods of confinement and social isolation? As you relate to those who need to socially distance, how might you apply the words contained in 3 John 1:2 (NLT): "Friend, I hope all is well with you and that you are as healthy in body as you are strong in spirit."

MARCH 20
(Y2, D12)

Time for Pruning

I am the true vine, and my Father is the gardener. He cuts off every branch in me
that bears no fruit, while every branch that does bear fruit he prunes so that it will
be even more fruitful. You are already clean because of the word I have spoken to
you. Remain in me, and I will remain in you. No branch can bear fruit by itself; it
must remain in the vine. Neither can you bear fruit unless you remain in me.

—John 15:1–4 (NIV)

Spring will soon be here. Given a few pleasant days in mid-to-late March, it can be a wonderful
opportunity to do some pruning of bushes, hedge plants, and decorative landscaping trees before
budding begins. Pruning is done for various reasons. These include providing for restoration and
rejuvenation, promoting overall health, or to direct growth. A gardener who is experienced in pruning does it selectively and knows exactly how and where to trim. Pruning properly will enhance
the beauty of a shrub or tree. But pruning that is not done correctly can ruin the desired outcome.
Pruning is one of the most important processes in the wine vineyard. If the wine dresser is a knowledgeable pruner, his work will enable the vines to yield a better harvest. I have a wonderful neighbor
across the street who has a beautiful yard filled with colorful flowers. Not only does she fertilize and
water them faithfully, but during the summer months, she spends many hours each week deadhead-
ing her plants. Removing the spent flowers on a regular basis promotes blossoms throughout the
season. In her own way of pruning throughout the growing months, she helps create a front yard that
commands attention as you pass by.

As believers in Christ, we have a periodic need for pruning in our lives because like the flowers,
we too can become spent. Sometimes we are able to deadhead the undesired habits that have crept
into our life and self-improve. At other times, we, the branches, find ourselves becoming so detached
from the vine (Christ) that only the Master Gardener (God) can restore us. In doing so, we find
ourselves in good spiritual health and are once again able to produce fruit. We can allow the prospect
of pruning to be easily dismissed at times, especially if we're still attached to the things that we know

God is telling us to separate from. But the act of pruning is done out of love in order to stimulate growth. Understanding the purpose of pruning is key if we're to appreciate it as a positive exercise when we're called to do it in our lives. No one is a better pruner than God.

In relation to the early Christian church, Paul described it this way:

> Do not consider yourself to be superior to those other branches. If you do, consider this: You do not support the root, but the root supports you. You will say then, "Branches were broken off so that I could be grafted in." Granted. But they were broken off because of unbelief, and you stand by faith. (Romans 11:18–20 NIV)

The promise of pruning applies to all fruit-bearing believers abiding in the vine of Christ. No matter how fruitful we may already be, as His children, our heavenly Father will prune our lives to abundantly increase our spiritual fruitfulness by making us more like His Son. When we allow distractions in our lives that channel our time and resources into worldly activities and detract from our spiritual fruitfulness, God will prune us. God will cut off those unfruitful distractions to focus us on more fruitful activities.

We most likely can find ourselves in one of three places: in the process of being pruned, healing from being pruned, or if you are fortunate, you may be in full bloom. As Christians, we are all subject to times of pruning. Pruning is not only necessary when our lives are a mess. Sometimes we are in need just because there is untapped potential. During these times of reshaping, we may be subject to difficulty, disappointment, and discouragement. Just like the gardener, we should see God's pruning as a sign that He is taking an active role in our lives, is concerned about our growth, and wants us to reap the best potential harvest for His kingdom. The process of pruning is rarely easy. But we must remind ourselves of the point of it, the fact that it frees us up to fulfill God's purpose for us as well as helps us adjust to the changes we're called to make. In need of a good pruning? If not now, you soon will be.

Reflection

Are you able to understand that God sometimes allows us to suffer not as an act of punishment but because He wants to see us be more productive fruit bearers? Looking back on your life, can you identify times when pruning has occurred? As you look ahead, will you be better prepared to view God's pruning as an act of encouragement?

MARCH 21
(Y3, D12)

He Knows My Name

When I look at your heavens, the work of your fingers, the moon
and the stars, which you have set in place. What is man that you are
mindful of him, and the son of man that you care for him?

—Psalm 8:3–4 (ESV)

I hate when it happens. Someone comes up to you and says, "Do you remember who I am?" Sometimes I do; at other times, I don't have a clue. If the names Sam, Diane, Woody, Carla, Cliff, and Norm sound familiar, then you were probably a fan of the sitcom *Cheers* which aired for eleven seasons from 1982 to 1993. You'll recall the Boston Cheers Bar as the place "where everybody knows your name." As the theme song asked, "Wouldn't you like to get away…where they're always glad you came?" Whether that place is work, school, church, or just in the loving arms of your family and friends, we each long for that familiarity. Maybe you have appreciated and been impressed by that individual who remembered your name. It's a skill we should all work on because when we do recollect someone's name, they feel valued. W. C. Fields said, "It ain't what they call you, it's what you answer to." His thought begs the question—to what or whom do you answer?

On March 7, 2015, God knew the name Lily Groesbeck, an eighteen-month-old child from Utah who was trapped and suspended in an upside-down vehicle for some fourteen hours. It was determined that Lily, who had been traveling alone with her mother, had survived an accident with their car ending up in a river. Days after the rescue, responders agreed that they heard an adult voice coming from inside the car. They admitted that the mysterious sound had prompted them toward a more rapid recovery effort. A fisherman spotted the vehicle and summoned emergency personnel who revived the child and led to her astounding recovery as the only survivor. One of the officers who heard the voice was quoted as saying that "it was plain as day." Lily, who became known as "the miracle baby," needed help, and it's apparent that God provided it. "The voice of the LORD is over the waters; the God of glory thunders, the LORD thunders over the mighty waters" (Psalm 29:3 NIV).

Names are important. Jesus gave Simon the name of Peter, further stating "on this rock I will build my church" (Matthew 16:18 NIV). God renamed Jacob to be Israel (Genesis 35:10) because he had struggled with the Lord by demanding a blessing. In Genesis 17:5, we learn that God changed the name of Abram ("exalted father") to Abraham ("father of a multitude'). It's as though He set each one of these individuals on a fresh path of life when they received their new names. God knows our names in a very personal and intimate way as well. If He cares enough to know the name of every star (Psalm 147:4) and the numbering of each of the hairs on our head (Matthew 10:30), we can be sure He comprehends everything about us and our life journey. I am fond of the words of a chorus by Tommy Walker:

> I have a Maker, He formed my heart;
> Before even time began, My life was in his hands.
> I have a Father, He calls me His own;
> He'll never leave me, No matter where I go.
> He knows my name. He knows my every thought;
> He sees each tear that falls, And He hears me when I call.

Long before Jesus said, "I am the good shepherd. I know my own and my own know me" (John 10:14 ESV), a young shepherd by the name of David reflected on the awesomeness of God's knowledge about us. Might we somehow be like David. For when it comes right down to it, He whose "name that is above every name" (Philippians 2:9 NIV) is the most important one who also knows our very own.

Reflection

Can you recall specific events in your life when it was very clear that God not only knew your name but everything about you? How do we handle those times when we are ashamed for God to remember us by name? Take time to read Psalm 139 and meditate on the wisdom of this chapter.

MARCH 22
(Y4, D12)

The Ultimate Lesson in Humility

All of you, clothe yourselves with humility toward one another, because,
"God opposes the proud but shows favor to the humble."

—1 Peter 5:5 (NIV)

Did you hear the one about the inspirational speaker who said he had a wonderful presentation on humility but was waiting for a large crowd before he delivered the speech? Although there is humor in that statement, the theme is no joke, for it could easily serve to represent a realistic portrayal of anyone in today's society. There's another story about a humbler man named Lincoln who got caught up in a situation where he wanted to please a politician, so he issued a command to transfer certain regiments. When the secretary of war, Edwin Stanton, received the order, he refused to carry it out. He said that the president was a fool. Lincoln was told what Stanton had said, and he replied, "If Stanton said I'm a fool, then I must be, for he is nearly always right. I'll see for myself." As the two men talked, the president quickly realized that his decision was a serious mistake, and without hesitation, he modestly withdrew it.

When it comes to the topic of humility, we might be wise to remember that oft-quoted passage from the Old Testament: "If my people who are called by my name humble themselves, and pray and seek my face and turn from their wicked ways, then I will hear from heaven and will forgive their sin and heal their land" (2 Chronicles 7:14 ESV). Once Jesus went to eat in the home of a prominent Pharisee and was aware that He was being carefully observed.

> When he noticed how the guests picked the places of honor at the table, he told them this parable: "When someone invites you to a wedding feast, do not take the place of honor, for a person more distinguished than you may have been invited. If so, the host who invited both of you will come and say to you, Give this person your seat. Then, humiliated, you will have to take the least important place. But when you are invited, take the lowest place, so that when

your host comes, he will say to you, Friend, move up to a better place. Then you will be honored in the presence of all the other guests. For all those who exalt themselves will be humbled, and those who humble themselves will be exalted." (Luke 14:7–11 NIV)

No one understood and could teach what it means to be humble like Jesus was able to do.

Once upon a time, a rider came across a few soldiers who were trying to move a heavy log of wood without success. The corporal was standing by, just watching as the men struggled. The rider couldn't believe it. He finally asked the corporal why he wasn't helping. The corporal replied, "I am the corporal. I give orders." The rider said nothing in response. Instead, he dismounted his horse and went up and stood by the soldiers. As they tried to lift the wood, he assisted them. With his help, the task was finally able to be carried out. Who was this kind rider? It was George Washington, the commander-in-chief. He quietly mounted his horse and went to the corporal and said, "The next time your men need help, send for the commander-in-chief." Likewise, God sent Jesus to serve as our Commander-in-Chief.

The events of Passover in that last week of Jesus' life on earth are a true lesson in humility. As He entered Jerusalem, He did so on the back of a donkey. "Go into the village over there," he said. "As soon as you enter it, you will see a donkey tied there, with its colt beside it. Untie them and bring them to me" (Matthew 21:2 NLT). Any earthly king would have never presented himself in this manner, but in doing so, He fulfilled a prophecy (Zechariah 9:9) and demonstrated humility rather than arrogance. In the midst of His betrayal as He was arrested, he reached out to restore the man who had his ear cut off by one of His disciples. "But Jesus answered, 'No more of this!' And he touched the man's ear and healed him" (Luke 22:51 NIV). This last recorded miracle before the cross flowed out of His humility. Only hours later, He was shamed and beaten. "Being found in appearance as a man, He humbled Himself by becoming obedient to the point of death, even death on a cross" (Philippians 2:8 NIV). At Easter, we should fall on our knees with a humble spirit of gratitude and the assurance that because He lives, we can face tomorrow. To be sure, Holy Week and the celebration of the risen Christ is indeed a lesson in humility for all of humankind. Each new day, as we fail to pass the test, we live with hope and promise that He will keep on loving us just the same. Thanks to Him, our debt has been fully paid.

Reflection

How can we use the events of Christ's final week on earth to serve as the ultimate test of humility? Consider ways that you might be a living example to others by showing an act of humility. In what manner might you be able to help an arrogant Christian learn to become a humbler person?

MARCH 23
(Y5, D12)

Eye on the Prize

I press on to reach the end of the race and receive the heavenly prize
for which God, through Christ Jesus, is calling us.

—Philippians 3:14 (NLT)

The story is told of a well-known major league baseball player who was seventy-eight hits shy of breaking Ty Cobb's all-time hit record. In an interview during that year's spring training, the player was asked how many at-bats he would need to get those seventy-eight hits. Without hesitation, his matter-of-fact response was, "Seventy-eight." A reporter questioned his philosophy. The player simply answered with this claim: "Every time I step up to the plate, I expect to get a hit! If I don't expect to get a hit, I have no right to step in the batter's box in the first place! If I go up hoping to get a hit," he continued, "then I probably don't have a prayer to get a hit. It is a positive expectation that has gotten me all of the hits in the first place." It is not unusual for athletes who have a success story to attribute their success to keeping an eye on the prize.

If you have ever learned to play a musical instrument, you soon became aware that maintaining the proper beat is just as important as playing the correct notes. For that reason, it is not unusual for music teachers to make use of a metronome, a device that produces an audible sound set to an established tempo, assisting the beginner to internalize a clear sense of timing. As they advance and these student musicians take their place in bands and orchestras, the role of the metronome is replaced by the conductor. Here, combined instrumentation with changes in rhythm and tone force the musician to pay close attention to the conductor's baton. They learn to position themselves and their music in such a way that they are equally aware of both. When successful, the melodies to which they contribute result in a powerful performance, in part because they have become very aware of the conductor.

It is for that reason that I reminded an old friend of mine who was having a health crisis that he needed to recollect our times together in high school band. I urged him to recall that when we focused too much on the music, we could easily become out-of-sync with the director, resulting in a failed performance. Similarly, I cautioned that with his illness, he needed to focus on the one who could lead him through the music he was facing rather than on his disease. The Apostle Paul said:

> When I am with those who are weak, I share their weakness, for I want to bring the weak to Christ. Yes, I try to find common ground with everyone, doing everything I can to save some. I do everything to spread the Good News and share in its blessings. Don't you realize that in a race everyone runs, but only one person gets the prize? So run to win! All athletes are disciplined in their training. They do it to win a prize that will fade away, but we do it for an eternal prize. (1 Corinthians 9:22–25 NLT)

When runners learn to compete in the hundred-meter race, they learn never to look to their right or left but only to keep their eyes fixated on the finish line because in ten seconds or less, the race can be over. Paul is saying don't waste your time over the past. Don't worry about the circumstances nor obsess about the detractions that might come your way. He is telling us not to get caught up in the moment but to stay centered on what truly matters. He would agree with the hymnist, Helen H. Lemmel, who must have been aware of Hebrews 12:2 as she wrote: "Turn your eyes upon Jesus; Look full in His wonderful face. And the things of earth will grow strangely dim, In the light of His glory and grace." I personally like the thoughts of pastor and author Dr. David Jeremiah who wrote, "We should be holy people eager to greet our Lord when He returns, ready at any moment for the trumpet's call, people of optimism, busy in evangelism, hands to the plow, eyes on the prize." So, my fellow sojourners, do not take your eyes off the conductor and risk losing your place with the music of your life. Fix your eyes on the only prize that matters—in both life and death—and you will always be in tempo.

Reflection

What is one of your most memorable prizes or awards that you have received? What effort or sacrifices did you have to make in order to stay focused on the task at hand? How can you keep your eye on God's prize when there are so many worldly ones that seem to be more easily within your grasp?

MARCH 24
(Y6, D12)

An Escape Artist Like No Other

So give the order for the tomb to be made secure until the third day. Otherwise,
his disciples may come and steal the body and tell the people that he has been
raised from the dead. This last deception will be worse than the first.

—Matthew 27:64 (NIV)

Erik Weisz was born in Budapest on April 24, 1874, to a Jewish family. Weisz arrived in the United States just over four years later with his parents and brothers. The family changed their name to the German spelling Weiss, and Erik became Ehrich. They settled in Appleton, Wisconsin, where his father served as a Rabbi and later moved to New York City in 1887. As a child, Weiss took several jobs, making his public début as a nine-year-old trapeze artist, "Ehrich, the Prince of the Air." Later, he became a professional magician, soon to be known as Harry Houdini. Initially, he had little success, so he began trying out escape acts and was performing with great achievement by the early 1900s. He would free himself from handcuffs, chains, canvas bags, coffins, and straitjackets, sometimes hanging from a rope or suspended in water. The greatest and most sensational of all Houdini's escapes was without doubt his Chinese Water Torture Cell. In this trick, Houdini was to escape from an extraordinary contraption resembling a fish tank filled with water, while he was placed head down in full view of the audience.

Houdini reappeared from many a desperate situation and anticipated he could also do so from the grave. But then on October 31, 1926, death laid its hands on Harry Houdini, never to escape. Before dying, Houdini told his wife, Beth, that if there was any way out, he would find her and make contact on the anniversary of his death. He said he would communicate the message "Rosabelle believe," a secret code which they agreed to use as it referenced their favorite song. For ten years on his birthday, she kept a vigil before a candle-lit portrait of Houdini, believing and waiting for a signal from him. On the Halloween of 1936, Bess and a group of Houdini's friends gathered in Hollywood for what would later become known as the "final Houdini séance." After trying to reach the late magician's spirit for over an hour, Bess finally addressed a worldwide radio audience, stating these words: "Houdini did not come through. My last hope is gone. I do not believe that Houdini can come back to me, or to anyone… The Houdini shrine has burned for ten years. I now, reverently, turn out the light. It is finished. Good night, Harry!"

The expression of loss of hope that Houdini's wife so profoundly expressed is often the sentiment articulated by far too many of us. As the followers of Jesus celebrated His arrival in Jerusalem on what we now refer to as Palm Sunday, their hope for a Messiah was soon shattered when He died on a cross by week's end. While drawing his last breath, Jesus declared, "It is finished" (John 19:30 NIV). However, the difference between Houdini's wife giving up all hope and uttering those same words was that for her, it was indeed an end. For Jesus, it was only the beginning of hope for humankind. When He said, "It is finished," He did *not* say, "I am finished." As Jesus died, His Spirit was released, removing the debt owed by each of us—the debt of sin. Three days later, His empty tomb was more than mere deception. Had Jesus Christ not died and risen again, we would have been lost and doomed to everlasting separation from God. But because of His suffering, each of us has been extended hope and the offer of eternal life.

What do we do when things fall apart and we've lost all meaning for whatever comes next? This is exactly where the disciples found themselves when Jesus was crucified. They did not understand the hope of His pending resurrection, even though Jesus had told them (Matthew 17:23). The lesson for all of His followers is that God can bring wonderful things out of the darkest moments of our lives. He surrendered His Son to death so we could have life, and He will not abandon us. While many of us enjoy a good magic trick from time to time, we appreciate that distraction is the key to a trick's success. Houdini once said, "What the eyes see and the ears hear, the mind believes." The Apostle Paul stated it differently: "When the perishable has been clothed with the imperishable, and the mortal with immortality, then the saying that is written will come true: 'Death has been swallowed up in victory'" (1 Corinthians 15:54 NIV). The risen Christ will always seek to draw us away from the illusion that there is no hope. You can count on it!

Reflection

Why do you think it is easier for us to believe in escape artistry than it is to have faith in Christ? Can you think of a time when God brought you peace and newness when you thought it was too late? How does Easter and the rebirth of the earth through spring offer new hope in Jesus?

MARCH 25
(Y7, D12)

Never Very Far Away

And this same God who takes care of me will supply all your needs from
his glorious riches, which have been given to us in Christ Jesus.

—Philippians 4:19 (NLT)

In 1895, a former slave by the name of Booker T. Washington gave what later came to be known as the Atlanta Compromise speech. He used the following illustration:

> A ship lost at sea for many days suddenly sighted a friendly vessel. From the mast of the unfortunate vessel was seen a signal, "Water, water. We die of thirst!" The answer from the friendly vessel at once came back, "Cast down your bucket where you are." A second time the signal, "Water, water! Send us water!" ran up from the distressed vessel and was answered, "Cast down your bucket where you are" The captain of the distressed vessel, at last heeding the injunction, cast down his bucket, and it came up full of fresh, sparkling water from the mouth of the Amazon River.

Using this story, Washington encouraged his audience to take what they had in front of them and make "friends in every manly way of the people of all races by whom we are surrounded." His words stressed cooperation and helped to establish him the leading black spokesmen of his time, eventually giving him credibility to be an adviser to several presidents.

Washington's story reminds us of another boat at sea. Its inhabitants were also struggling but not because they needed water. They were located on the Sea of Galilee in a small craft filled with experienced fisherman who spent the entire night with no catching success (John 21:3). These inhabitants were already in a depressed mood because of the horrific events leading to and culminating in the recent death of their friend, Jesus. Several of His closest disciples were in that boat, doing what they knew best—fishing. Early the next morning, they were headed to land as a voice called to them from the shore, asking if they had any fish. It was difficult to see who was calling to them, and they reluctantly admitted that they had not caught a single fish all night long. The voice called back that they should throw their net on the right side of the boat. What possible difference could it make to put the net in on the right side instead of the left where they have been? But for some unknown reason, they unquestioningly took out the nets and threw them into the water on the other side of their boat. Scripture tells us that "When they did, they were unable to haul the net in because of the large number of fish" (John 21:6 NIV). They are stunned by what has happened when it suddenly became evident who had been calling to them: "Then the disciple whom Jesus loved said to Peter, 'It is the Lord'" (John 21:7 NIV).

Years ago during the Super Bowl, FedEx ran a commercial that spoofed the movie *Castaway*. In it, actor Tom Hanks played a FedEx worker whose company plane went down, stranding him on a desert island for years. Looking like the disheveled Hanks in the movie, the FedEx employee approaches the front of a suburban home, package in hand. When the lady of the house comes to the door, he explains that he survived five years on a deserted island. During that whole time, he safeguarded the package in order to deliver it to her. She gives a simple thank-you, but he is curious about its contents. Therefore, he poses this question: "If I may ask, what was in that package after all?" She opens it, and they check out what's inside.

Her comments: "Oh, nothing really. Just a satellite telephone, a global positioning device, a compass, a water purifier, and some seeds." Like the contents in this package, the resources for growth and strength are accessible to every Christian who will take advantage of them.

While most of us expend a lot of time and energy looking around for the next best thing, we often miss that precious gem which is available to us right now. For you see, it is when we come to the "end of us" that we will find the "beginning of God." There He will meet us, right when we seemingly have exhausted all of our resources. "For the LORD God is our sun and our shield. He gives us grace and glory. The LORD will withhold no good thing from those who do what is right" (Psalm 84:11 NLT). So the next time you find yourself in desperate need, just lower your bucket or cast your net. You may be delightfully surprised to realize that the very thing you required was never very far away.

Reflection

How often do you find yourself seeking some other place or circumstance to make everything better? Is your lack of faith preventing God from showing His power through your storm? Consider a time when your personal success was followed only after an act of submission to God. Or if you can't recall such a time, how might you be more receptive to a future submission?

MARCH 26
(Y1, D13)

Leaning and Coping in Anxious Times

Anxiety weighs down the heart, but a kind word cheers it up.

—Proverbs 12:25 (NIV)

It takes something rather dramatic to bring a society together. Most certain, events like the Great Depression, the attacks of Pearl Harbor and 9/11, as well as the coronavirus pandemic of 2020 are good examples where there was, for the most part, an effort toward a spirit of unity. During the latter, a group of residents in an apartment building in Dallas, Texas, stuck their heads out their windows, joining in a chorus of quarantined voices led by one soulful tenor who began singing the Bill Withers' lyrics: "Sometimes in our lives we all have pain; We all have sorrow. But if we are wise, We know that there's always tomorrow." Little by little, other residents began to join in the refrain, "Lean on me, when you're not strong. And I'll be your friend. I'll help you carry on." While some added harmonies, others simply peered outside or recorded the impromptu sing-along on their phones. This display affirmed that when we feel anxiety in uncertain times, "we all need somebody to lean on."

Some authorities state that anxiety has overtaken depression as the leading mental health problem in the United States. To be sure, life is not without uncertainties. Whether they come in the form of a major life transition, family issues, health scares, or financial trouble, anxiety usually results. Anxiety has three main elements. The first is *insecurity*, the feeling that something bad is going to happen. The truth is that bad things do happen, but seldom does the worst-case scenario we imagine ever play out. Then there is *helplessness*, the idea that there is nothing I can do to change this. The reality is that there is almost always something you can do, even if it just is a small step in making a positive difference in your life today. Add to that *isolation*, there is no one to help me. While anxiety for most folks is temporary and can be brought under control with some self-talk and intentional reaching out, it must be recognized that there are indeed those who suffer from true anxiety disorder. There are professionals and organizations who can help, some of which are able to be accessed directly from one's home.

In his book, *Anxious for Nothing*, Max Lucado presents an acronym for helping those of us who subscribe to faith in God and feel anxious at any given time. The abbreviated letters are remembered by the word *calm*, the opposite of anxious, and just what we are seeking. Here is his advice:

> *Celebrate* God's goodness. 'Rejoice in the Lord always'" (Philippians 4:4 NIV). How will you express your joy for God's goodness today? *Ask* God for help. "Let your requests be made known to God' (Philippians 4:6 ESV). If you don't already keep a prayer journal, start one. Begin with today's requests. *Leave* your concerns with Him. "Thank him for all he has done" (Philippians 4:6 NLT). At bedtime, review the concerns you left with God this morning. Thank him for relieving you of your anxious thoughts. *Meditate* on good things. "Think about things that are excellent and worthy of praise" (Philippians 4:8 NLT). Plan your day to include time alone with God.

Do you have anxieties? The results may be costly, since anxiety drives our attention away from spiritual matters and drains our energy away from the important things of daily living. Scripture does not state specifically what causes anxiety, but in every case, it evidences itself as a crisis of faith. Throughout the Bible, almost all of the major players had the opportunity to experience anxiety. Each were confronted with a choice to be consumed by it or to relinquish it to God and recognize it to be part of His plan. Jesus asked His followers, "which of you by being anxious can add a single hour to his span of life?" (Matthew 6:27 ESV). We must turn over whatever burdens us in exchange for the peace that only He can give. It takes humility to admit we can't handle things ourselves, and it requires trust to allow God to work the situation according to His will. So "cast all your anxiety on him because he cares for you" (1 Peter 5:7 NIV). If you will surrender your burdens to Him, there is only thing you have to lose is—you guessed it, your anxiety.

Reflection

What situations are causing you to be anxious at this time? How might you make a conscious shift to focus on the blessings of today rather than on the worst-case scenario? Are there ways that you might be that "somebody to lean on" for someone you know going through an anxious time?

MARCH 27
(Y2, D13)

Impersonators and Impostors

We serve God whether people honor us or despise us, whether they slander us or praise us. We are honest, but they call us impostors.

—2 Corinthians 6:8 (NLT)

Our world is full of impersonators and imposters, many of whom manifest themselves as scam artists in today's culture. They often prey upon the most vulnerable in our society, like older folks who may tend to be more trusting. Unfortunately, anyone can fall victim to a scam artist. As incredibly busy as most folks are these days, we don't have the time to scrutinize every email, text, or phone call. In years past, a con man would have to face his victim. Now scammers are people who are often far away, targeting anonymous people with whom they have no personal connection. As a result, scam artists are confronting us from every conceivable angle. One of the most famous impostors in recent history was Frank Abagnale, who served as inspiration for the Spielberg/DiCaprio film, *Catch Me If You Can*. His schemes included falsifying checks, masquerading as a Pan Am pilot, impersonating a pediatrician in a Georgia hospital, and forging a Harvard University Law diploma, then later passing the bar exam.

Each of us may have at one time or another been fascinated with a particular impostor because of the incredible style with which they performed. There are no doubt times we have enjoyed certain impersonators as they imitated the appearances, sounds, and mannerisms of many famous people we love and others…well, maybe not so much. Some of the best political impressionists have appeared on *Saturday Night Live*. You might remember Dana Carvey as George H. W. Bush, Chevy Chase as Gerald Ford, Darrell Hammond as Bill Clinton, Tina Fey as Sarah Palin, or Amy Poehler as Hillary Clinton. Rich Little was so effective at his impersonations that he was nicknamed "the Man of a Thousand Voices." One individual who has been impersonated the most is Elvis Presley. His imitators work all over the world as entertainers, and their tribute acts remain in great demand due to the unique persona of Elvis. While most impressions are usually done for entertainment value, we have to be aware that there are persons out there who are simply up to no good when they engage in deceptive efforts to present as someone they are not.

Jesus addressed the concept of deception with those who were closest to Him. Not completely understanding that He would someday return, the disciples privately approached Him at the Mount of Olives. "'Tell us,' they said, 'when will this happen, and what will be the sign of your coming and of the end of the age?' Jesus answered: 'Watch out that no one deceives you. For many will come in my name, claiming, 'I am the Messiah,' and will deceive many'" (Matthew 24:3–5 NIV). When Jesus was brought before Pilate to be punished, Pilate asked Jesus whether he was the king of Jews, to which Jesus answered, "You have said so" (Mark 15:2 NIV). Pilate's question implies that the Jewish leaders accused Jesus of claiming to be an impostor, king of the Jews, which is how they perceived their awaited Messiah. Matthew 27:64 (NIV) tells us that the Pharisees and chief priests went to Pilate, asking him to place guards at the tomb where Jesus' was placed. "Otherwise, his disciples may come and steal the body and tell the people that he has been raised from the dead. This last deception will be worse than the first."

Regarding the concept of impersonating, the Apostle Paul gave instruction to the Church at Corinth: "And you should imitate me, just as I imitate Christ" (1 Corinthians 11:1 NLT). Paul challenges us to not be fake Christians but to otherwise be true to our faith and follow the example of Christ. Many centuries later, Charles H. Spurgeon put it this way:

> If Jesus is precious to you, you will not be able to keep your good news to yourself; you will be whispering it into your child's ear; you will be telling it to your husband; you will be earnestly imparting it to your friend; without the charms of eloquence, you will be more than eloquent; your heart will speak, and your eyes will flash as you talk of his sweet love. Every Christian here is either a missionary or an impostor.

Bottom line, if you call yourself a Christian and are not an imitator of Christ, you have two choices—you either change your name or your conduct.

Reflection

Has your character and conduct changed as your faith has deepened? How are you challenged in today's world to be an imitator of Christ rather than a religious impostor? In what ways are all Christians challenged to heed the words found in 2 Timothy 3:13 (NLT): "But evil people and impostors will flourish. They will deceive others and will themselves be deceived?"

MARCH 28
(Y3, D13)

Paid in Full

When he had received the drink, Jesus said, "It is finished." With
that, he bowed his head and gave up his spirit.

—John 19:30 (NIV)

I heard recently on several media outlets that a young entertainer who has been notorious for not-so-pleasant run-ins with the law picked up the tab for a group of police officers at a diner in mid-town Manhattan. After posing for a picture with the officers, the performer later stated that he was committed to being a better person and restoring his image. In contrast, a friend related a story to me years ago about a group of residents from a nursing home who had been transported to a local restaurant where they were scheduled to have a luncheon outing. A nice gentleman who had also been dining there came over to their table, asked where they were from and, after a brief conversation, wished them a wonderful day. Later, when the nursing home residents requested their bill, the waitress told them it had been taken care of. It was obvious who had most likely paid their debt, but the waitress was not allowed to say. Now, if these two stories were a modern-day parable as they easily could be, Jesus would have us answer this question: Even though both balances were paid by a generous individual, which one received the greatest blessing from God?

Jesus went to the cross to pay our debt in full. On either side of Him hung a convicted criminal who had been sentenced to die (Matthew 27:38). One of them mocked Jesus, but the other seemed to appreciate who He was. The latter had his debt forgiven and received the gift of eternal life (Luke 23:40–43). While it is not clear how this thief may have come to have such a clear understanding of Jesus, he received far more than he deserved—just like us. We all awaken in the morning with what some would label as a fresh start. In reality, our new day is anything but a clean slate. However, our life failures do not condemn us in God's eyes because of what His Son did for us on the cross. The blood of Jesus provided a new covenant in that Jesus came to do for us what we were incapable of doing for ourselves

Paul says that "we always carry around in our body the death of Jesus, so that the life of Jesus may also be revealed in our body" (2 Corinthians 4:10 NIV). Our role is that as we progress through our journey, we must position ourselves as a living example of His teachings, fully demonstrating that we are a true child of God. Unfortunately, we spend a lot of time making our own rules and hoping for the free gift of the "last-minute save" similar to that which was given to the thief on the cross. Our culture perpetuates this idea by promoting deals on last-minute flights and vacations and portraying contestants on reality shows being scooped up in a "save" by another team. I don't know about you, but I don't want to treat my promise of the hereafter in the same way that some might portray their view of the here and now. Warren Wiersbe has interestingly stated, "Most Christians are being crucified on a cross between two thieves: yesterday's regret and tomorrow's worries." Paul professed a different perspective when he said, "I have been crucified with Christ and I no longer live, but Christ lives in me. The life I now live in the body, I live by faith in the Son of God, who loved me and gave himself for me" (Galatians 2:20 NIV).

A group of artists were once asked how they knew when their painting was done. The one who spoke first stated that before he begins, he has a clear vision of what it is that he wants to paint. That vision inspires his work, and he knows whenever it has been satisfied on the canvas. Another, who was a man of fewer words, declared that his work is completed only when he signs his name on the piece. When he does so, it is finished. Likewise, Jesus knew when His mission had been fulfilled when he said, "I have brought you glory on earth by finishing the work you gave me to do" (John 17:4 NIV). He had paid in full the debt of sin for all mankind. Just as He was triumphant at Calvary, He will ultimately win the victory in our lives when we surrender ourselves to Him. While the painting may be completed, the rest of the story has not yet been written for the sinner whose work will eventually be signed off and paid in full with the blood of Christ.

Reflection

In what ways do you sometimes ignore the simple commands of Christ and make up our own rules? As such, do you assume that the free gift of salvation is always there for the taking? How can you improve on walking that fine line between knowing your debts have been paid in full while displaying a better life and witness for the one who paid the ultimate price?

MARCH 29
(Y4, D13)

Politically Correct

My dear brothers and sisters, how can you claim to have faith in our
glorious Lord Jesus Christ if you favor some people over others?

—James 2:1 (NLT)

As I entered the checkout line at the local supermarket, I looked behind me to see a lady with whom I had worked a number of years before. As we chatted while waiting for the line to move, I asked about her nephew who had also worked with us at one point. Remembering that he had studied the culture of Indian tribes, collected memorabilia, and at one time lived on a reservation, I inquired how he was doing. I thought I had posed a very logical question by asking, "Is he still living with the Indians?"

She looked at me hesitantly and said, "You mean Native Americans, don't you?"

I replied, "Well, I guess I do." The interesting thing about this conversation is that I don't recall this individual being a particularly sensitive person. However, it was now a different point in time in the realm of political correctness.

More and more, our culture provides us with what the appropriate references should be toward others so that they do not take offense. Much of the time, most of us fall in line in order that respectful communications and positive relations can be maintained. It has come to the point, however, that any mention of God or love of country can force us to be thrown off a team, ostracized by the neighbors, or lose our livelihood. It's infiltrated our society and is forcing young people to be raised with a new set of values and self-expression. Examples include a high school track team disqualified because one of the runners made a gesture, appearing to thank God once he had crossed the finish line. At one California school, five students were sent home for wearing shirts that displayed the American flag on the Mexican holiday of Cinco de Mayo. A student at a western state university was ordered to take off a cross that she was wearing because someone could be offended. For those of us who grew up freely wishing folks a "Merry Christmas," we are surprised when seldom offered a reply more than "Happy Holidays."

From its beginning, the concept of Christianity was offensive to those who followed the old law of Jewish custom and tradition. Jesus was frequently politically incorrect. When He dined with Levi, many tax collectors and sinners of that day were also gathered there. The teachers of the law criticized Him for doing so. "When Jesus heard this, he told them, 'Healthy people don't need a doctor—sick people do. I have come to call not those who think they are righteous, but those who know they are sinners'" (Mark 2:17 NLT). He was questioned about fasting and also healing on the Sabbath. "Then Jesus said to them, 'The Sabbath was made to meet the needs of people, and not people to meet the requirements of the Sabbath. So the Son of Man is Lord, even over the Sabbath!'" (Mark 2:27–28 NLT). The result is that the notion of being visibly offended can enable support for others to judge the motives of one's heart.

Political correctness in and of itself is not a bad thing. If we reduce it to mean that we treat people of different backgrounds with respect and do not use gender stereotypes, racial slurs, or other derogatory references, then we are practicing what is, in fact, very biblical. After all, we are each part of God's creation. However, as believers in Christ, we must not allow our sensitivity for political correctness to diminish our expression of faith to that of second-class citizenship. The Apostle Paul warned his young friend, Timothy, to not be ashamed to preach the Gospel, saying:

> Preach the word of God. Be prepared, whether the time is favorable or not. Patiently correct, rebuke, and encourage your people with good teaching. For a time is coming when people will no longer listen to sound and wholesome teaching. They will follow their own desires and will look for teachers who will tell them whatever their itching ears want to hear. They will reject the truth and chase after myths. (2 Timothy 4:2–4 NLT)

Christians should boldly focus on being biblically correct. We must not allow correctness in the secular or political arena to be our primary concern, for our ultimate citizenship is not of this world but rather in heaven. It is there where we will eventually reside with our Creator who is correct in every possible way.

Reflection

Have there been times in your life during which you have been so concerned about being politically correct that you failed to consider what Jesus would have you do? What criteria do you use to assure that you speak with biblical correctness while at the same time being sensitive to not hurt others? How would you explain to another that you are primarily focused on what God would have you say?

MARCH 30
(Y5, D13)

Learn How to Listen

Anyone with ears to hear should listen and understand!

—Matthew 11:15 (NLT)

Remember when you were a child, you were no doubt told with great frequency that you needed to listen? The concept of listening at that age meant obeying. As one grows older, it's more about paying attention. And, yes, there is a difference. Who or what are you listening to these days? Could it be a nagging spouse or a demanding boss? When you turn on the TV or play music, who are you listening to then? Have you shut out the world with your earbuds? Or are there times you just need to be silent and turn down the volume? A. A. Milne's character, Winnie the Pooh, stated, "If the person you are talking to doesn't appear to be listening, be patient. It may simply be that he has a small piece of fluff in his ear." I can completely understand that claim. Once, while present at a concert of a rock band I had come to enjoy in my youth, the person with whom I was attending leaned over, attempting to say something to me. I pointed to my ears which I had plugged with rolled up tissues following the group's performance of several songs. While the music was much the same as I had remembered, the person running the soundboard was providing a nearly deafening experience for those of us in the audience. That's the way it frequently is in life as well when we decide to allow one loud voice to dominate and ruin our existence.

As we mature in our faith, we come to understand that it is important to listen with discernment. When we permit other things to get in the way of proper listening, we lack understanding. When the Lord tried to speak through Moses to the Israelites whose spirits had been broken, "They did not listen to him because of their discouragement and harsh labor" (Exodus 6:9 NIV). Later, in Psalm 81:11–12 (NIV), we read: "But my people would not listen to me; Israel would not submit to me. So I gave them over to their stubborn hearts to follow their own devices." When Jesus took Peter, James, and John with him to the mountain to pray, their lack of listening and focus denied them vital insight into the events that would soon occur in the life of Jesus. One translation of scripture indicates that Peter had no idea what he was saying, and "while he was speaking, a cloud appeared and covered them, and they were afraid as they entered the cloud. A voice came from the cloud, saying, 'This is my Son, whom I have chosen; listen to him' (Luke 9:34–35 NIV). While Peter was jabbering away, God told him He just needed to listen.

There are other times when we do not listen simply because we lack faith and are afraid. This is illustrated in the story of a little girl who was in bed and scared of the dark. She went into her parent's room, telling them she was afraid. Her mother said, "It's okay, sweetheart. There is nothing to be afraid of. God is in there with you." The little girl retreated to her room. As she climbed into bed, she said, "God, if you're in here, don't you say a word. You will scare me to death." It is important to appreciate that God often speaks in the quietest of moments as He whispers, "Be still and know that I am God" (Psalm 46:10 NIV). It is when we fail to listen to Him that fear will open the door and we give place to the devil to do his destructive work. Sin can deafen the ears of any child of God, however young or old. When on your journey and not listening to God, you are setting yourself up for one tumultuous ride.

Fear has a voice and faith has a voice. We must choose to listen to the right one. If you are seeking God and trying to walk with Him but are not experiencing His peace, you might be listening to the wrong voice. Scripture reminds us: "Dear friends, do not believe everyone who claims to speak by the Spirit. You must test them to see if the spirit they have comes from God. For there are many false prophets in the world" (1 John 4:1 NLT). Remember, our ears are tuned to whatever holds our hearts and minds. When we ignore the nudging of the Holy Spirit or allow the world to drown out God's Holy Word, earthly things will become more dominant in our thinking and in our feelings. After a while, we will cease to pay attention to what God is saying because we are no longer listening to the One who cares the most (Hebrews 2:1). When we turn a deaf ear to God, we are going down a path we do not want to travel. Remember, "faith comes from hearing the message, and the message is heard through the word about Christ" (Romans 10:17 NIV). But first and foremost, we must learn how to listen.

Reflection

Are you interested in what God has to say to you on any given day? What's the first voice you hear in the morning? Do you set aside time each day to listen to God? When you hear God telling you do something that is in conflict with your plans, how do you proceed? In what ways might you consider refining both your listening and obeying skills when it comes to God's voice?

MARCH 31
(Y6, D13)

To the Glory of God Alone

It's not important who does the planting, or who does the watering.
What's important is that God makes the seed grow.

—1 Corinthians 3:7 (NLT)

Born on March 31, 1685, in the small German town of Eisenach, he is widely regarded as one of the greatest musical composers of all time. Johann Sebastian Bach was orphaned when he was ten, so he went to live and study with his older brother. By his mid-teens, he was ready to establish himself in the musical world, showing immense talent in a variety of areas and getting his first job as a church organist at age seventeen. His Lutheran family was pleased to see him carry on the family tradition in music. Besides being one of the most productive geniuses in the history of western music, Bach was also a theologian who just happened to work with a keyboard. Through personal losses within the family and professional frustrations, Bach maintained a loyalty to perfection that never quit. During one of the unhappiest periods of his life, he wrote a cantata each week of which several hundred survive. Worship for Bach was not an end in itself but rather a collective response made by God's people to His redeeming grace in Jesus Christ. Nearly three-fourths of his 1,000 compositions were written for use in worship. Today, his music is played and studied around the world as well as used in nearly every Christian denomination.

It is generally accepted that Bach is one of the most brilliant composers ever. However, most of his works received little notice until the mid-nineteenth century. Bach had profound talent and eventually became a respected icon in the music world. His enduring legacy is that in his life and work, he gave the glory to God. The story has been told that on one occasion, he was scheduled to debut a new arrangement. He arrived at the church, expecting it to be full, but instead, no one showed on that wintry night. Bach told his musicians that they would still perform as planned. Taking their places, Bach raised his baton, and soon the empty church was filled with magnificent music. Bach often wrote *INJ* for the Latin phrase *In Nomine Jesu* on his manuscripts. It is translated in English as "In the name of Jesus." He also initialed *SDG* for the Latin phrase *Soli Deo Gloria* on at least one of his works. It is a translation from Romans 16:27 (NLT): "All glory to the only wise God, through Jesus Christ, forever. Amen."

When Johann played music, he felt his soul praising God. In fact, he once said, "I play the notes as they are written, but it is God who makes the music." He undoubtedly understood Jesus' words:

> The Kingdom of God is like a farmer who scatters seed on the ground. Night and day, while he's asleep or awake, the seed sprouts and grows, but he does not understand how it happens. The earth produces the crops on its own. First a leaf blade pushes through, then the heads of wheat are formed, and finally the grain ripens. And as soon as the grain is ready, the farmer comes and harvests it with a sickle, for the harvest time has come. (Mark 4:26–29 NLT)

God invites us to know, serve, and praise the Grower as He reaps the benefits of the spiritual gifts He has created within us. There are times, however, when God will cultivate us for His greater purpose, using the gifts He provides to further His kingdom long after we are gone.

One of God's most faithful servants, King David, wanted to build a temple to honor God (1 Chronicles 17:1). But God spoke through a prophet and said, "Go and tell my servant David, 'This is what the LORD has declared: You are not the one to build a house for me to live in'" (1 Chronicles 17:4 NLT). David's desire to build a house for the Lord was noble, but God had other plans for David's son to build the temple (1 Chronicles 17:11–12). David accepted God's promise that it would be so. He contributed to the cause by gathering materials and making preparation for its construction before he died (1 Chronicles 22:5). We may find ourselves like King David, not always being able to see the fruits of our labor in this lifetime. As we work to further God's kingdom, it is important that we do not allow ourselves to become discouraged. We are merely seed-planters. We should do what we can with the abilities God gives us, accepting that the fruits of our labor will be harvested only when He is ready. In the meantime, we serve, deferring appreciation for any triumph to the glory of God alone.

Reflection

What abilities and talents has God given you? And how are you developing those? Do you invest your abilities in order to secure public gratification? Would you be upset if the fruits of your labor were not somehow acknowledged during your lifetime? How can you follow Bach's example and do all you can, simply for the glory of God?

APRIL 1
(Y7, D13)

No Joke

But the story sounded like nonsense to the men, so they didn't believe it.

—Luke 24:11 (NLT)

On April 1, 1957, the BBC reported that Swiss farmers were experiencing a record spaghetti crop and showed footage of people harvesting noodles from trees; numerous viewers were fooled. If you were around on the first day of April in the 1990s, you may have attempted to buy a "left-handed Whopper" at Burger King, the fake sandwich of the day promoted by the food chain. If not, you may have been caught up in the falsehood that Taco Bell was going to purchase Philadelphia's Liberty Bell and retitle it using their restaurant's name. Although the exact origin remains a mystery, it is believed that the practice of playing practical jokes on April 1 has existed in many cultures for several centuries. English pranksters began popularizing the annual tradition of April Fools' Day as early as 1700. In some places, it is known as All Fools' Day, which makes sense since the goal is to get as many people to buy into the fake story as possible and as a result be fooled. And when you fall for it, of course, the joke is on you.

It's one thing to play harmless practical jokes on others during an expectant day of frivolousness. But when you're vulnerable and misunderstood, being the target of a joke can be hurtful. The story has been told of a terminally ill boy by the name of Jeremy who, at the age of twelve, was still in second grade, seemingly unable to learn and frustrating to his teacher. Jeremy sometimes drooled and made unusual noises, making it easy for his fellow students to poke fun at him. Nearing Easter, the teacher gave each of the students an empty plastic egg with the assignment to place something in it that represented new life and bring it back the next day. Her intention was to contact Jeremy's parents that evening to explain the project so that he would be successful, but several interruptions prevented her from doing so. The next day, the teacher began to open each egg of her nineteen students. The first one contained a flower, and the teacher affirmed that it indeed represented new life. The second had a butterfly in it, and everyone agreed it accomplished the goal. A third egg was a stretch, but the teacher found a way to explain how a moss-covered rock demonstrated new life as well. But when she opened the fourth egg, it was empty. So she laid it down without comment. Jeremy spoke up and asked why she didn't say anything about this egg which happened to be his. Flustered, she said, "Jeremy, your egg is empty."

Looking up at the teacher, he simply replied, "Yes, but Jesus' tomb was empty too." Three months later, when Jeremy died, his theology was represented by nineteen plastic eggs on his casket, all of which were empty.

After Jesus' crucifixion, the religious leaders of the day went to Pilate, concerned that someone might take His body. Not wanting any kind of foolishness, they told him:

> "Sir, we remember what that deceiver once said while he was still alive: 'After three days I will rise from the dead.' We request that you seal the tomb until the third day. This will prevent his disciples from coming and stealing his body and then telling everyone he was raised from the dead! If that happens, we'll be worse off than we were at first." Pilate replied, "Take guards and secure it the best you can." So they sealed the tomb and posted guards to protect it." (Matthew 27:63–66 NLT)

The Jewish leaders remembered well that when they had demanded miraculous signs to prove His authority, He had responded in this manner: "'Destroy this temple, and I will raise it again in three days.' They replied, 'It has taken forty-six years to build this temple, and you are going to raise it in three days?' But the temple he had spoken of was his body" (John 2:19–21 NIV).

Early on the first day of the week, several women who loved Jesus visited His tomb to find it empty. In their fright, they were reminded of His words. "They rushed back to tell the others, but no one believed them" (Mark 16:13 NLT). Generally, most of them did not believe until they saw and met the resurrected Christ. Suddenly appearing to them behind locked doors in the midst of their fear (John 20:19–20), there had to be someone in the group who dared to think, "Is this a joke?" Instead, it was the fulfillment of a promise. For it is His resurrection which completed the story that He was who He had proclaimed to be—the very Son of God. And that, my friends, is very good news for each one of us. No joke!

Reflection

How does the concept of a "risen Christ" satisfy some and raise doubt in others? How is everything changed by the empty tomb? Why is the Resurrection the greatest of Christ's miracles? Are there ways you could use Jeremy's story to help others find new meaning in the risen Christ?

APRIL 2
(Y1, D14)

How Easily They Forget

This means that anyone who belongs to Christ has become a new person. The old life is gone; a new life has begun.

—2 Corinthians 5:17 (NLT)

It's always enlightening to me that whenever there is something novel, unique, or otherwise trending, people will be drawn toward it. When this occurs, we may be prompted to begin a new project or venture. For instance, you might start a diet after hearing that others have lost a lot of weight on it. But if your willpower is different than theirs or the food choices are unappealing, your level of interest might quickly regress. When the project or goal starts to wane in significance, becomes unappealing, or cannot stir enough motivation, it can be quite easy to move on with diminished enthusiasm. We humans are easily swayed when we allow ourselves to be sidetracked by current whims or popular opinion. There are times, however, when we encounter life-altering events that have the capability to hold our attention for a lifetime. But if we do not keep the memory alive, practice what we have learned, or strive to maintain an intense level of focus, it will not take long for our passion to fade.

The expression "Lest we forget" is commonly used in war remembrance services and commemorative occasions. It was first created in an 1897 Christian poem written by Rudyard Kipling called "Recessional." The phrase occurs eight times and is repeated at the end of the first four stanzas in order to add particular emphasis regarding the dangers of failing to remember. As Moses spoke to the nation of Israel before they entered the promised land, he said: "But watch out! Be careful never to forget what you yourself have seen. Do not let these memories escape from your mind as long as you live! And be sure to pass them on to your children and grandchildren" (Deuteronomy 4:9 NLT). He reminded them that there had been a time when he had to issue a reprimand. On that occasion, he descended after forty days from Mount Sanai where God had provided the Ten Commandments: "There below me I could see that you had sinned against the LORD your God. You had melted gold and made a calf idol for yourselves. How quickly you had turned away from the path the LORD had commanded you to follow" (Deuteronomy 9:16 NLT).

We are a fickle lot when it comes to the following of religious practices. There is no better example than the event commonly referred to as Palm Sunday. As Jesus rode a donkey into the town of Jerusalem during the annual Passover, a large crowd gathered and laid palm branches and their cloaks across the road, giving Him royal treatment. Hundreds of people shouted, "Hosanna to the Son of David! Blessed is he who comes in the name of the Lord! Hosanna in the highest heaven!" (Matthew 21:9 NIV). But even as the multitudes waved the palm branches and shouted for joy, they missed the true reason for Jesus' presence. They could neither see nor comprehend the salvation gift He would provide through His sacrificial death on a cross in just a few days. The masses quickly turned on Him when he did not lead a revolt against Rome. In fact, one must wonder how many who were in the crowds shouting "Hosanna" on Palm Sunday would be crying out, "Crucify Him!" later that week (Matthew 27:22–23). Palm Sunday was the beginning of the end of Jesus' work on earth, the final seven days of His earthly ministry known to us as Passion Week. This day has grown to become a significant event to Christians throughout history.

When the crowds in Jerusalem used the word *Hosanna*, it served as an expression of joy and praise for deliverance granted or anticipated. We have the advantage of understanding what those who shouted that greeting during Jesus' triumphal entry did not. As Paul so aptly later wrote, "We know that our old sinful selves were crucified with Christ so that sin might lose its power in our lives. We are no longer slaves to sin" (Romans 6:6 NLT). Slaves, hopefully not, but at times, we certainly do regress, don't we? On the other side of a life-altering crisis, we often fail to learn from its lessons, thereby becoming our old selves again. By moving closer to Jesus during and after the experience, these events can become life-affirming. When that happens, no one would dare look at us and say, "How easily they forget!"

Reflection

Consider a time when you offered a great deal of yourself to another, and then it appeared that they no longer remembered. How did this make you feel? If you were to see yourself through the eyes of Jesus, what kind of life-altering event would affirm your relationship with Him? Are there ways you might consider using the events of Holy Week to create a lasting impression for others?

APRIL 3
(Y2, D14)

Being an Encourager Like Jesus

Therefore encourage one another and build each other up, just as in fact you are doing.

—1 Thessalonians 5:11 (NIV)

The story has been told of two men who were seriously ill and occupied the same room in the hospital. One of them was lying in the bed near the only window in their room. Every day, he was allowed to spend some time sitting up in his bed, and the other man was forced to spend all his days lying flat on his back. They talked a lot about their lives. When the first man was sitting by the window, he described details of an amazing view and all wonderful things that he saw outside. His roommate always appreciated those moments as he would close his eyes, imagining all the beautiful scenes that were told to him. One night, the man whose bed was near the window died peacefully during sleep. The roommate was very sad, and after some time, he asked if he could be moved next to the window. The nurse agreed and kindly made the switch. When she left, the man slowly and painfully propped himself up on one elbow and took the first look at the world outside. He was stunned. The window faced a blank wall. When the nurse later returned, he told her about the beautiful outside view that his roommate had described to him. The nurse replied that his roommate was blind, stating, "Most likely, he was just trying to encourage you."

In the book of John, we find one of the very last conversations that Jesus had with His disciples. He said:

> I have spoken of these matters in figures of speech, but soon I will stop speaking figuratively and will tell you plainly all about the Father. Then you will ask in my name. I'm not saying I will ask the Father on your behalf, for the Father himself loves you dearly because you love me and believe that I came from God. Yes, I came from the Father into the world, and now I will leave the world and return to the Father… But the time is coming—indeed it's here now—when you will be scattered, each one going his own way, leaving me alone. Yet I am not

alone because the Father is with me. I have told you all this so that you may have peace in me. Here on earth you will have many trials and sorrows. But take heart, because I have overcome the world. (John 16:25–28, 32–33 NLT).

These are Jesus' final words of encouragement to His disciples as He leaves them to soon go to the cross. Jesus' grim forecast was tempered with cheer; He followed His prediction of trouble with a dazzling word of encouragement. He will overcome the world. When they see Him again, their sorrow would be turned to joy.

Throughout the Bible, we read scriptures to encourage one another and others which are meant to encourage us. A man in the early church by the name of Joseph was actually given the nickname Barnabas because it means "son of encouragement." As the apostles worked to spread the good news and grow the church, Barnabas played a large role in inspiring and connecting people. "He encouraged the believers to stay true to the Lord. Barnabas was a good man, full of the Holy Spirit and strong in faith. And many people were brought to the Lord" (Acts 11:23–24 NLT). He put his reputation on the line to encourage the acceptance of Paul after his conversion. "Barnabas brought him to the apostles and told them how Saul had seen the Lord on the way to Damascus and how the Lord had spoken to Saul. He also told them that Saul had preached boldly in the name of Jesus in Damascus" (Acts 9:27 NLT). Barnabas also mentored the young John Mark when others didn't want to give him a second chance (Acts 15:39).

One day some time ago, I was speaking with a lady whom I knew had been diagnosed with a terminal illness. She was rather downhearted, and I was struggling to find some helpful words. As we closed our conversation, she said, "Thank you for encouraging me." I was pleased that I had taken the time because it would be the last interaction I ever had with her. It's not always simple, but it is what the Lord would have us do. He will help us find the right words. The Apostle Paul put it this way: "We should help others do what is right and build them up in the Lord" (Romans 15:2 NLT). Without encouragement, life would soon feel pointless and burdensome. Without encouragement, we can become overwhelmed and feel unloved. Without encouragement, we can begin to think that God is a distant figure rather than one near to our very being. Therefore, scripture tells us to encourage one another, to remind each other of the truth that God loves, equips, and cares for us and that our struggles are always worth it in the end.

Reflection

Why is encouragement emphasized in scripture? How have you been encouraged by fellow believers in your time of need? In what ways can we use the hope of the resurrection to encourage others who are currently experiencing a difficult time in their lives?

APRIL 4
(Y3, D14)

Risen Indeed!

My nourishment comes from doing the will of God, who
sent me, and from finishing his work.

—John 4:34 (NLT)

An older friend of mine told me a story a while back about the time she went to her bank to execute some business. Please understand that my friend worked most of her life at this bank where she continued to maintain her finances. However, she had now been retired for many years. On one of her bank visits, she took some coinage that needed to be run through a sorter and wrapped. When she told the teller what she wanted, the teller stated that it wasn't something she was able to do for her. My spunky friend, Dorothy, stated that was all it took. She looked at the young lady and said, "Oh yes you will. Please close your window, and I will show you where and how to do it." What the teller did not know was that during her employment at this institution, Dorothy had at one time been the supervisor for all tellers. Dorothy told me that while she had been kind, she had also made up her mind that she expected the same customer service she would have once provided. Dorothy chuckled and indicated that when the transaction had been completed, she found the bank manager and self-reported.

More and more, I hear people using the phrase, "That's not my job." Our society has become so specialized that people are either afraid or incapable of stepping beyond the boundaries. I have frequently phoned one company or another for some kind of assistance, worked my way through a successive series of prompts, been placed on hold, and was later told by the "live" representative that they would have to transfer my call to another department. It can be very frustrating to finally get to a real person who may or may not be able to address your concern. One would like to think that along our journey, we should be able to demonstrate and receive gracious acts of service in all walks of life. However, in many situations, we are discouraged from doing so while the concept of public service becomes rejected rather than embraced. I wonder where we would be if on the way to Calvary, Jesus had said, "You know, I'm not sure this whole dying thing is really in my job description."

It is very clear that Jesus came to serve and not to be served. Ultimately, He came to sacrifice His life and said that those who chose to follow Him must "count the cost" of doing so. He once stated, "Any one of you who does not renounce all that he has cannot be my disciple" (Luke 14:33 ESV). Jesus' words should resonate with us, for there will be times we'll wonder what we signed up for as we seek the will of God for our own life. Jesus himself struggled to bring His will in complete submission to His Father's. In fact, "During the days of Jesus' life on earth, he offered up prayers and petitions with fervent cries and tears to the one who could save him from death, and he was heard because of his reverent submission" (Hebrews 5:7 NIV). Robert Law is quoted to have said: "Prayer is a mighty instrument, not for getting man's will done in heaven, but for getting God's will done in earth."

When we hear Jesus foretelling His death prior to Good Friday (Mark 8:31), we can understand why His followers were puzzled. He said to them, "Whoever wants to be my disciple must deny themselves and take up their cross daily and follow me" (Luke 9:23 NIV). After all, who of us would want to see that on a list of job description duties? But as followers of Jesus, we will be asked over and over again to self-sacrifice, serve others, rather than wait to be served, and to realize His will for our life until that day when He calls us home. As we celebrate the risen Christ on Easter Sunday, we are reminded of the joyous news that the death of Jesus was not in vain. As the hymn says, "Because He lives, I can face tomorrow." It is only when we stand with Peter and John at the empty tomb that we come to realize Jesus was called to do far more than we would have ever imagined. And when we hear the words "He has risen," we can give full response with our own proclamation, "He has risen, indeed!"

Reflection

Can you think of ways that you might better deny yourself in His service? Do you have a clear understanding that following the will of God is the only key to victory in your own struggles of life? Are you able to respond, filled with the assurance that He has risen indeed?

APRIL 5
(Y4, D14)

Implosion: A Path to Self-Destruction

He sent out his word and healed them, and delivered them from their destruction.

—Psalm 107:20 (ESV)

It has happened on most main streets of small-town America. The old storefronts have disappeared and are now replaced with more progressive buildings in an effort to revitalize what was at one time a thriving downtown business area. In our town, buildings that once contained clothing shops, five and ten department stores, as well as banks and other places of local commerce have now been demolished. Structures which have housed the local mercantile for many generations have been leveled in the name of progress. An all-in-one service center will soon provide groceries, health and beauty supplies, as well as a full-pharmacy. Many wish it could be like it once was, but those who have seen it decline live in hope of something better. And with it, the memories of yesterday will be preserved only in photos.

Sometimes things get destroyed that were never intended to be so. One day, homeowners in a small Texas town had their house reduced to rubble when a demolition company mixed up addresses and bulldozed the wrong house. The families who lived there were waiting on their insurance to cover costs for damages to the home caused months before by a tornado. Part of the confusion resulted from a twisted sign that directed the crew down the wrong street, leading to an improper identification of the duplex scheduled for demolition. In much the same way, it should not surprise us when our personal lives can also head for destruction when the paths we choose to take become somewhat misguided. When this occurs and our lives become twisted, the Apostle Paul gave good advice when he sent out this warning: "They are headed for destruction. Their god is their appetite, they brag about shameful things, and they think only about this life here on earth" (Philippians 3:19 NLT).

There's an interesting form of structure demolition called an implosion in which blasting material is strategically placed so that when it is exploded, the structure will cave inward onto itself. Sometimes large parking garages or sports complexes are destroyed in this manner. I have also heard references made about organizations that have imploded. Not so long ago, I observed the use of the term by a baseball manager whose team was in the lead until the latter few innings of a game. When bullpen pitchers took the mound in relief, they blew the lead and were appropriately described by this phrase. It is not unusual for similar destruction to occur within churches, families, or within our own journey. The psalmist writes: "Unless the LORD builds the house, the builders labor in vain. Unless the LORD watches over the city, the guards stand watch in vain" (Psalm 127:1 NIV). Implosion is always possible when we fail to honor God's fundamental principles and instead allow the selfish purposes of what is right in our eyes to rule. Sometimes it may not even be intentional. Like Paul, we may find ourselves conflicted and cry out: "I don't really understand myself, for I want to do what is right, but I don't do it. Instead, I do what I hate" (Romans 7:15 NLT).

Years ago, the television show *Mission Impossible* began every episode with a scene in which the team leader would receive a tape describing his next mission. The tape always began, "Your mission, should you choose to accept it" and ended with, "This message will self-destruct in five seconds." Lucky for us, we have a Creator who makes our mission a possible one. "I have swept away your sins like a cloud. I have scattered your offenses like the morning mist. Oh, return to me, for I have paid the price to set you free" (Isaiah 44:22 NLT). Just as the suffering of Israel paved the way for forgiveness and the rebuilding of the nation, we, too, can be restored. We have a Savior in the name of Jesus who gives us this direction: "Enter through the narrow gate. For wide is the gate and broad is the road that leads to destruction, and many enter through it" (Matthew 7:13 NIV). He gives us plenty of time and opportunity to choose a path that is always heartened, never confusing, and one that we should always consider a desirable mission, unless our goal is to somehow implode.

Reflection

What are those twisted signs in your life that have misdirected you from a true fellowship with Jesus? What faith practices do you need to put in place in your daily journey to assure that you are being constructive? How can you apply these in your network of family, friends, and organizations?

APRIL 6
(Y5, D14)

Free for the Taking

He gave his life to purchase freedom for everyone.

—1 Timothy 2:6 (NLT)

Several years ago, a survey was taken involving people in line for free tattoos at a New York City nightclub. When asked if they would get a tattoo if they had to pay for it, 68 percent stated they would not. However, here they were, having something done to their bodies that was practically permanent, simply because it was free. I used to find it amusing when I would attend trade shows where companies would display their products or services utilized in my profession. Vendors would give away anything imaginable from pencils and mugs to drawing entries for a larger prize, just to get you to visit their booth. The smart ones learned to engage you in conversation to obtain your contact information before they would give you the free stuff. I was surprised how many of my colleagues would participate in this monotonous chitchat for hours, simply to get their gift bags filled with these giveaways.

It's true for most of us at one time or other that the opportunity of getting something for nothing was enticing. I used to appreciate the garage where I would take my car to be serviced because inevitably, when I went there, they would give it a courtesy wash. It kept me going back for many years until the manager changed, as did the service. An observant restaurant owner will admit that a complimentary glass of wine provided to a frequent patron will promote loyalty and recurring business. I well remember when I bought my first car that the manufacturer was endeavoring to increase their sales by offering two free domestic airline tickets with the buying of a new model. Even though I perceived those tickets to be free, I am sure the cost was hidden somewhere in my purchase price. But because I had never flown, I took advantage of the offer by traveling from one coast to the other.

Sadly, marketers have stripped much of the meaning away from "free." Our society has convinced us, for instance, that when we buy bottled water, we obtain a superior product, even though most communities offer excellent tap water. Spiritually, we get an even better deal. When John had his vision of a "new heaven and a new earth" (Revelation 21:1), he spoke of a different water. "He who was seated on the throne said, 'I am making everything new… I am the Alpha and the Omega, the Beginning and the End. To the thirsty I will give water without cost from the spring of the water of life" (Revelation 21:5–6 NIV). How did this water without cost come to be? It's called grace, and Jesus paid the price in full when He died on the cross at Calvary. He accomplished what Adam began when the original sin created distance between God and man. This "fall of man" resulted in an inherited death sentence for all humans thereafter. "Consequently, just as one trespass resulted in condemnation for all people, so also one righteous act resulted in justification and life for all people" (Romans 5:18 NIV)—a price so high we could never pay. Christ did for us on the cross what we were incapable of doing for ourselves.

What's the catch, you ask? As much as we love the idea of anything being free, we have learned to be suspicious of anything classified as such. There's an old story about a man who purchased a new refrigerator for his home and wanted to easily dispose of the old one. He placed it outside on the curb and taped a sign on it: "Free for the Taking." It sat there for days, and he wondered what he might do differently to get rid of it. So he put another sign on it which read "Refrigerator for Sale: Just $50." He looked out his window the next morning, and it was gone. One can only assume it was taken because it was now perceived to have value. Likewise, some struggle to accept salvation as a free gift. "Truly no man can ransom another, or give to God the price of his life, for the ransom of their life is costly and can never suffice" (Psalm 49:7–8 ESV). Fortunately for us, because we are of God's own creation, He placed a great value on our lives. He gave His Son to pay the price so that we might have eternal life. All He wants in return is to steal your heart. There is no hidden agenda. It truly *is* free for the taking.

Reflection

Have there been times in your life that you have been offered something labeled as being "free" and you have refrained from taking it because you were sure that there had to be a catch? Does that recollection make it a little easier to understand other's skepticism as you speak to them about the free gift of salvation? How can knowing and reflecting upon what Jesus went through to pay for your freedom change how you personally embrace that freedom and present it to others?

APRIL 7
(Y6, D14)

Missing the Mark

Since they did not know the righteousness of God and sought to establish
their own, they did not submit to God's righteousness.

—Romans 10:3 (NIV)

On April 6, 1909, American explorer Robert Peary, assistant Matthew Henson, and four Eskimos reached what they determined to be the North Pole. Peary, a US Navy civil engineer, made his first trip to the interior of Greenland in 1886. In 1891, Henson, a young African-American sailor, joined him on his second arctic expedition. In 1893, the explorers began working toward the North Pole, and in 1906, during their second attempt, they came within 150 miles of their objective. So now in 1909, they crossed hundreds of miles of ice to reach what they calculated as latitude ninety degrees north, believing they had reached the long elusive dream. Although their achievement was widely praised, Dr. Frederick A. Cook (a former associate of Peary) challenged their distinction of being the first to reach the North Pole, claiming he had arrived there by dogsled the previous year. A major controversy followed, and in 1911, the US Congress formally recognized Peary's entitlement. Decades after Peary's death, however, navigational errors in his travel log surfaced, placing the expedition in all probability thirty miles short of its goal. In 1997, Robert M. Bryce released a book entitled *The Polar Controversy, Resolved*, in which he used newly uncovered documentation from diary entries, ship logs, and newspaper transcripts. He believed that these were further evidence to settle the epic debate about the claim by Frederick A. Cook that he was the first to reach the North Pole in 1908, a year ahead of rival explorer Robert E. Peary.

Peary's destiny is not all that different from our own as we diligently try but somehow miss the mark in our personal trek. And like his, there is frequently someone in the wings who is quick to point out our blunder. For those who walk with Christ, we realize that it is impossible to be perfectly on target and sinless in the case of our spiritual journey. We are fortunate, however, to worship a God who is filled with grace which He extends to each of us. He is indeed the "God of second chances" (and more). Some criticize this phrase, saying that it deceives folks into believing that they just need to try harder, trusting in their own works as being necessary to achieve righteousness and thus missing the point of His grace entirely. In reality, we find that scripture is full of second chances. After he had disobeyed God once, "Then the LORD spoke to Jonah a second time: 'Get up and go to the great city of Nineveh and deliver the message I have given you'" (Jonah 3:1–2 NIV). As Jesus healed the invalid by the pool of Bethesda (John 5:1–15) as well as when He refused to condemn a woman who was caught up in adultery (John 8:3–11), He told them both to "go and sin no more." In saying this, Jesus was not speaking of sinless perfection. He was warning against returning to sinful lifestyle choices. His words both extended mercy and demanded holiness. Jesus was always the perfect balance of "grace and truth" (John 1:14 NIV).

With God's forgiveness comes the expectation that we will not continue along the same path of rebelliousness. If you ever had the opportunity to experience parental discipline either through a child's eyes or as a parent yourself, you know that it is not uncommon to repeat the phrase, "How many times do I have to tell you?" That same is true in our relationship with God. In the acceptance of His grace, we are expected to make a heartfelt change, try harder, and do better. The Apostle Paul stated it this way: "Since we respected our earthly fathers who disciplined us, shouldn't we submit even more to the discipline of the Father of our spirits and live forever? For our earthly fathers disciplined us for a few years, doing the best they knew how. But God's discipline is always good for us so that we might share in his holiness" (Hebrews 12:9–10 NLT). We quickly learn in life that we can offer second chances to others until a healthy relationship is no longer realistic. So it is with God. He does everything possible to draw us into becoming more like Him, offering forgiveness and second chances. "The Lord is not slow in keeping his promise as some understand slowness. Instead, he is patient with you, not wanting anyone to perish, but everyone to come to repentance" (2 Peter 3:9 NIV). At some point, however, if sin becomes our god, we find that we have not only missed the mark but instead may lose our way for all of eternity.

Reflection

When you examine your own life, in what ways do you fall short of becoming more like Jesus? How can you avoid falling into the trap of thinking that because you have received God's grace, you can do as you please? In what ways might you help others see both His grace and His truth and define it for their own lives?

APRIL 8
(Y7, D14)

Like-Minded

Two people are better off than one, for they can help each other succeed. If one person falls, the other can reach out and help. But someone who falls alone is in real trouble.

—Ecclesiastes 4:9–10 (NLT)

Woven in and out of the fabric of one's life are many persons, some of whom become quite special to us over time. Brandon Lane Phillips was born with a congenital heart defect. Due to his health situation, he was granted a gifted-wish at the age of eleven. Having less than a great home life, he prayed that God would show that he cared about him. He used his wish to meet actor Jeremy Miller who portrayed Ben Seaver on the popular 1980s sitcom, *Growing Pains*. Both Jeremy and Kirk Cameron, who played the older brother in the show, began to assure Brandon that God had a plan for his life. That day, they formed a friendship with Brandon who began to develop a new level of self-confidence. As the years passed, he went to medical school and became a cardiologist. As God's providence would have it, a day came when Jeremy needed Brandon. Jeremy had become addicted to alcohol, and Brandon was able to help him enter into a very exclusive recovery program. Together, they have written a book, *When I Wished Upon a Star,* affirming that "God placed us in each other's lives when we needed it the most."

The Bible is filled with instances when God brought people together for a farsighted purpose. King Saul hated and pursued to kill David, but Saul's son, Jonathan, loved (1 Samuel 20:17) and protected him. "Jonathan said to David, 'Go in peace, for we have sworn friendship with each other in the name of the LORD, saying, 'The LORD is witness between you and me, and between your descendants and my descendants forever'" (1 Samuel 20:42 NIV). When Naomi's son dies, his widow elects to stay with Ruth rather than return to her own family. She tells Naomi: "Your people will be my people, and your God will be my God" (Ruth 1:16 NLT) and she is, in turn, blessed for her loyalty. The Apostle Paul praises his student, Timothy, for his deep faith (2 Timothy 1:5). Later, he tells the Church at Philippi, "I have no one else like Timothy who genuinely cares about your welfare" (Philippians 2:20 NLT). Scripture references people who are brought together in this way as being "like-minded." When believers are challenged to be of one mind and voice, they are known for their acceptance of one another by their display of the spirit of God's love. We are, therefore, inspired by the words of the great apostle: "Finally, all of you, be like-minded, be sympathetic, love one another, be compassionate and humble" (1 Peter 3:8 NIV).

As we mature, we quickly learn that many of the people who we refer to as friends come and go as if they are only with us for a season of our lives. We are fortunate if we find just a few persons with whom we can develop a deep, lasting relationship. When we enter into a true Spirit-filled, fully surrendered walk with the Lord, one of the first things to occur is that God will create an awareness of individuals who may not be good for us. God's Holy Word states that he who keeps company with fools will suffer harm (Proverbs 13:20). The Bible also warns that we are not to team up with those who are unbelievers (2 Corinthians 6:14), that we are to stay away from people who cause divisions and obstacles (Romans 16:17), and even pull back from those believers who are disruptive and do not live according to our faith teachings (2 Thessalonians 3:6).

Some of these teachings may sound very harsh. While we never want to pass up an opportunity to witness or help meet the basic needs of those who do not know Christ, God also knows who is best suited for us spiritually at any point in time. So we must let Him guide us toward those who will have a positive impact on sharpening our character. "As iron sharpens iron, so one person sharpens another" (Proverbs 27:17 NIV). Such individuals will help to keep us spiritually in line when we are getting off-track, assist to get us through and make sense of some of the downswings that can occur in our daily walk, as well as provide affirmation that we are heading in the right direction. In that way, we serve each other and continue to stay on the path where God seems to be leading us. While we are sometimes misled to think that there are many who can do this for us, the end-result will be that if it is to be true and lasting, it will come from God who connects us with special persons who are like-minded.

Reflection

With whom are you sharing the important parts of your life? How can you help others understand that being like-minded doesn't mean we unite around a specific set of doctrines, political issues of the day, or a certain theology? What are some concrete ways that you can encourage others to earnestly seek the mind of Christ while building up one another in faith?

APRIL 9
(Y1, D15)

Gathering and Scattering

A time to scatter stones and a time to gather stones. A
time to embrace and a time to turn away.

—Ecclesiastes 3:5 (NLT)

Years ago, I bumped into a lady I had gotten to know through a local business which I frequented. She no longer worked there, and it had been a while since I had seen her. Through our over-the-counter chats, she had shared that her father was up in years and had developed some health problems. It was natural then when I greeted her to ask how he was doing. She looked down and sadly said, "Oh he passed away last week due to influenza." I moved toward her, thinking maybe I should perhaps give her a hug in expression of sympathy, when she proceeded to say, "And now I think I have it too." "It," of course, referenced the flu. I found myself smiling and slowly backing away, continuing to say how sorry I was for her loss while, strategizing how I might make a respectfully quick exit. As I reflect on this encounter, I believe how normal my response would have been for many others as well. We attempt to gather in order to do the right thing but find ourselves scattering whenever things don't seem to be so good.

Gathering and scattering are fairly commonplace. Throughout the history of cultures, we come together to assemble and then return again to our various scattered places. Families and friends gather to recognize holidays, birthdays, anniversaries, and other special events. Classmates gather for reunions, and those who have a common interest such as hunting or football often gather to share in rivalry of these activities. I once worked with a lady who frequently talked about her monthly card club with a group of ladies. One day, out of curiosity, I asked her what kind of cards they played. She snickered and said, "Oh my, we don't play cards. We just get together to eat and enjoy each other's company." Contained in God's Word are regular references to gathering and scattering. We read in the Old Testament that there are times to gather and scatter stones. When the Israelites crossed the Jordan, Joshua had them gather stones, stating,—"We will use these stones to build a memorial. In the future your children will ask you, 'What do these stones mean?'" (Joshua 4:6 NLT). On another occasion, however, Isaiah spoke of the need to scatter stones: "He dug it up and cleared it of stones and planted it with the choicest vines" (Isaiah 5:2 NIV).

Evidence of gathering and scattering is prominent in that holiest of weeks before Jesus suffered and died a horrible death on the cross. As Jesus gathered with His disciples in the Upper Room on the occasion of what Christian tradition has come to refer to as Maundy or Holy Thursday, it was the last time the chosen disciples would be together as the twelve. "Jesus said, 'I have been very eager to eat this Passover meal with you before my suffering begins. For I tell you now that I won't eat this meal again until its meaning is fulfilled in the Kingdom of God'" (Luke 22:15–16 NLT). Then Jesus told them, "This very night you will all fall away on account of me, for it is written: 'I will strike the shepherd, and the sheep of the flock will be scattered'" (Matthew 26:31 NIV). As He broke bread with them, it was then that Jesus predicted one of His own would betray Him. It came to pass, for "as soon as Judas took the bread, Satan entered into him. So Jesus told him, 'What you are about to do, do quickly'" (John 13:27 NIV). And Judas left at once.

Even though many of Jesus' disciples were scattered at the time of His death and resurrection, Jesus gathered the remaining eleven at Galilee. There He commissioned them to scatter "and make disciples of all nations, baptizing them in the name of the Father and of the Son and of the Holy Spirit" (Matthew 28:19 NIV). Having gathered once more, those who followed Christ would now be equipped to do the other half of what they were called to achieve; that is, to scatter. The Church is, therefore, tasked with this mission: to gather for worship, instruction, and fellowship, but also to find ways to effectively scatter as demonstrated by the early followers. "But the believers who were scattered preached the Good News about Jesus wherever they went" (Acts 8:4 NLT). For you see, being part of a Christ-centered community not only means knowing about Jesus, but it also means sharing Him as a living presence and personal Savior. It is only when we do this that we will have captured the true meaning of Easter.

Reflection

The women who gathered at Jesus' tomb were asked, "Why are you looking among the dead for someone who is alive?" (Luke 24:5 NLT). How should Jesus' resurrection prompt us to not only worship Him at our Easter gatherings but also prepare us as we scatter to serve Him in the days that follow?

APRIL 10
(Y2, D15)

The Sting Left in an Empty Tomb

The last enemy to be destroyed is death.

—1 Corinthians 15:26 (NIV)

Consider the following scenario: a father and his seven-year-old daughter were on a journey in the family car on a very busy interstate highway. It was a hot summer day, and a big yellow bee emerged from somewhere in the car, most likely having found its way in there at their last stop. The bee began to fly up to the front window and then to the back window, buzzing past their heads. The young daughter was very frightened, and she began to swat at the bee. Her dad warned her not to do that, but now the little girl was becoming hysterical while the father was shouting at her to just sit still and not be afraid. About that time, the bee, which he recognized as a honeybee, landed right on the father's neck and stung him. Now the child became absolutely petrified and hysterically began to weep. The father tried to calm her down and finally said to her: "Dear, you don't need to be afraid anymore. The bee has lost its sting. Look here, the stinger is right here in my neck. See, the bee has lost its sting."

It is true that a honeybee's stinger is structured in such a way that once it punctures human skin, the stinger will become imbedded there, leaving the bee incapacitated to sting again. When I heard this story, it reminded me that I used to have a product in my medicine cabinet that reduces the effects of a sting. I immediately looked to see if it was there, and it was. It is classified as a "topical analgesic" and relieves the pain and itching from bee and wasp stings. With the arrival of spring and the emergence of green branches and flowers in my yard, it was a good reminder that I may need this remedy for those unpleasantries out there. It also triggered that familiar scripture to be recalled: "Where, O death, is your victory? Where, O death, is your sting?" (1 Corinthians 15:55 NIV). It's one of those that if we don't hear it at any other time, we are sure to hear it at Easter. For Easter holds a wonderful promise! It is the day in which God reaffirms the resurrection of His Son and challenges any skepticism that might lie in the corner of any human heart. It gives us confidence to sing aloud that familiar church hymn, "Up from the Grave He Arose," as we rejoice on one of the most important days in the entire Christian calendar.

The story of Easter is one which is steeped in the most troubling part of the human experience, that of death itself. It's the one thing that unites people across historical and cultural barriers—for everyone, no matter who they are, eventually dies. The sting of death is sin, and it is culminated as we stand before God under the penalty of His law which we have broken. But because of Christ's resurrection, we no longer need to live in the darkness of despair. Paul lifts up his own exclamation, reminding us that "then, when our dying bodies have been transformed into bodies that will never die, this Scripture will be fulfilled: 'Death is swallowed up in victory'" (1 Corinthians 15:54 NLT). Centuries before that first Easter morning, the Lord promised the Prophet Hosea: "I will deliver this people from the power of the grave; I will redeem them from death" (Hosea 13:14 NIV). As it turns out, God's chosen form of deliverance was Himself. It was God who came to conquer over that which would defeat us.

Max Lucado wrote:

> Jesus saw people enslaved by their fear of a cheap power. He explained that the river of death was nothing to fear. The people wouldn't believe him. He touched a boy and called him back to life. The followers were still unconvinced. He whispered life into the dead body of a girl. The people were still cynical. He let a dead man spend four days in a grave and then called him out. Is that enough? Apparently not. For it was necessary for him to enter the river, to submerge himself in the water of death before people would believe that death had been conquered. But after he did, after he came out on the other side of death's river, it was time to sing…it was time to celebrate.

For the believer, death will not consume us because Jesus Christ has won the conquest. He has absorbed the pain of the stinger meant for us. The sentence which we all deserve has been overcome by Christ. Like He, we, too, will one day share in this victory over the grave. Not because of our efforts or due to anything we can ever achieve on our own but because of the sting that was left in an empty tomb.

Reflection

Recall a time when you were with suffering with the sting of loss and grief. Who or what helped you to move through it? How have those experiences prepared you to help others who are going through similar situations? In what ways will you allow the celebration of Easter to affirm your belief in a risen Savior and share His gift in the lives of those around you?

APRIL 11
(Y3, D15)

Holier than Thou... And Yet Last

So the last will be first, and the first will be last.

—Matthew 20:16 (NIV)

As we witness the earth coming to new life, baseball fans are thrilled to see the arrival of a different season. They sometimes pay less attention to the arrival of spring than they will to their favorite team taking the field. Right now, all of the teams are equal in the standings which will ultimately determine who makes the division playoffs and perhaps get a chance to go on to the World Series. At the start of the new baseball year, the win-loss record doesn't mean all that much, at least for a while. A team that wins a few and loses a few can easily end up near the top of the heap if other teams in the same division are losing more than they are winning. However, it doesn't take long until a disproportionate number of losses will propel any team in first place to descend to last place rather quickly.

It's interesting how often we refer to rankings or placement. For years, the Nielsen ratings have measured audience share for TV programs, helping to determine where advertisers might get the biggest bang for their buck. The famous Gallup Poll samples public opinion, one of the most well-known being the approval rating of the current president. These days, as we make purchases online, we can often limit our decision by reviewing the ratings a product has received from others who have already registered their level of satisfaction. This can be true even in our personal interactions. A month or so ago, I saw a lady who I heard had been having health problems and told her that she was on my prayer list. She replied, "Well, I'm still having a few issues, so would you mind moving me to the top of that list?"

Jesus' disciples once got into a disagreement about who was the greatest of the twelve. "But Jesus, knowing the reasoning of their hearts, took a child and put him by his side and said to them, 'Whoever receives this child in my name receives me, and whoever receives me receives him who sent me. For he who is least among you all is the one who is great'" (Luke 9:47–48 ESV). Later, He shares the Parable of the Workers in the Vineyard (Matthew 20) whose owner pays the same amount to all of his workers, regardless of when they were hired. Jesus essentially responds that all who toil the field for the master are treated alike, regardless of how long they serve. The point of the lesson was that no matter how long or how hard a believer might work for God's purposes during their lifetime, the reward of eternal life will be the same for all.

We must, therefore, ask the question if there are not times when we tend to see ourselves better than others. Perhaps we view ourselves to be just a little higher on the scale because we believe we have worked harder and performed better. We can see that there are issues in our family, but we are confident that ours is nothing like the neighbors down the street. We casually slip into the pew at church, look across the aisle, and assure ourselves that while we are a sinner for sure, our sins aren't nearly as bad as theirs. I once saw a sign that read "Jesus loves you, but I'm His favorite." That "holier than thou" attitude can get us into trouble, and we can very quickly get pulled down on our knees in the realization that we shouldn't judge someone just because their sin is different than ours. Jesus asked, "Why do you look at the speck of sawdust in your brother's eye and pay no attention to the plank in your own eye?" (Matthew 7:3 NIV).

Spiritual teacher and writer, Anthony de Mello, is credited with this thought: "Said the self-righteous preacher, 'What, in your judgment, is the greatest sin in the world?' 'That of the person who sees other human beings as sinners,' said the Master." Bottom line, there is no first or last in the eyes of God. There are only we sinners who are far worse off than we think we are and get treated far better than we deserve through His saving grace. By the way, I saw that person again for whom I was praying, the one with the health problem. I asked how she was doing and told her I had moved her up on the prayer list as she had requested. She looked at me, smiled, and said, "You know, I bet that's why I have been feeling a whole lot better." I smiled back and assured her I was most certain that where she had been placed on my list had nothing to do with it whatsoever.

Reflection

Do you sometimes see yourself higher on God's list than others? Have you been guilty of comparing your personal sins against those of others? How can we improve our focus on the fact that every sin is destructive and could separate us from God were it not for his amazing grace?

APRIL 12
(Y4, D15)

Way: The Place that the Lord Will Provide

Teach me your way, O Lord and I will walk in your truth.

—Psalm 86:11 (NIV)

It's become a culturally accepted response that when you prompt the statement "No way," the person to whom you are speaking will respond by saying, "Way." In other words, if something is unbelievable and you become excited, you may evoke the sentiment that there is no way this could be. Someone tells you that of course, this is so that, in fact, there is a way. The term *way* can be understood by several definitions. For instance, it can mean the manner in which someone acts ("It's just his way"). It can be used to describe a distance, such as "He was raised a long way from here." Or it can reference a system or a method of doing things, as in "We'll try it your way first." It can also mean a road or a path as evidenced in this scriptural passage when Jesus responds to His disciple. Thomas asks, "Lord, we don't know where you are going, so how can we know the way. Jesus answered, 'I am the way and the truth and the life. No one comes to the Father except through me'" (John 14:5–6 NIV)

I love the scene that is set in one of my favorite commercials crafted by State Farm Insurance. A young man tells his buddies he is never getting married, while the next scene shows him with a jeweler who is giving praise for his selection of a beautiful ring. On an airplane with his wife at his side, overhearing a baby crying, he states that they are never having kids, flashing, of course, to the next shot with the wife in labor. In their city apartment, they vow to never move to the suburbs. The next scene shows them in the front yard of—you guessed it. Then, "We are never getting one of those," pointing to the car that they will soon own. This followed by him saying, "We are never having another kid" and then her response, "I'm pregnant." At every corner of life, it's as if he is yelling out, "No way," and someone or something pops up and says, "Oh yes—way!" The best part of the ad, however, occurs at the very end, while sitting on the couch surrounded by his family, echoing the words, "I am never letting go." Fade to the voiceover which states, "For all the 'nevers' in life—God is there." Well, actually, the voice says State Farm, but this is my rendition, not theirs.

There are many great examples in scripture of God providing a way for the faithful. There is no better illustration than when God tested the faithfulness of Abraham (Genesis 22:1–13). God asked him to take his only son, Isaac, to a mountain and sacrifice him as a burnt offering. Abraham did as God requested, and when asked by Isaac where the lamb was for the burnt offering, Abraham responded that God would supply. Just as Abraham draws his knife to slay his son whom he had laid on the altar, God provides the way—a solution in the form of a ram. "So Abraham called that place the LORD will provide. And to this day, it is said, 'On the mountain of the LORD it will be provided'" (Genesis 22:14 NIV). Songwriter Don Moen penned these lyrics to a contemporary chorus: "God will make a way when there seems to be no way. He works in ways we cannot see. He will make a way for me. He will be my guide, hold me closely to His side. With love and strength for each new day. He will make a way for me."

For many of us, this can be a difficult exercise. We are much more familiar with the lyrics of the Frank Sinatra song, "My Way," than we are with those in the previously mentioned chorus. In our journey, we choose to rely on our own life experience, and we do not allow our faith to move beyond our own comprehension. If we are patient, we will come to understand that the Lord often acts in ways which transcend human reasoning. "For my thoughts are not your thoughts, neither are your ways my ways, declares the Lord. As the heavens are higher than the earth, so are my ways higher than your ways and my thoughts than your thoughts" (Isaiah 55:8–9 NIV). So in ways that often will not make sense at the time, we must learn to put the faith that we say we have into practice. In doing so, the word *never* disappears from our personal vocabulary. When someone says, "No way," we will instead cry out, "Way!" And we will be in full agreement with Abraham, certain that our LORD will indeed provide.

Reflection

Try to remember a time in your life when in the face of hopelessness and despair, you were able to discover God's truth and promise. Have you been able to recall His provision in a later personal experience or in the course of offering help to another who is struggling in their own journey?

APRIL 13
(Y5, D15)

Spoiler Alert

Trust in the Lord with all your heart; do not depend on your own understanding.

—Proverbs 3:5 (NLT)

Since the advent of the digital video recorder, commonly referred to as the DVR, it has become possible to "binge watch" multiple episodes of your favorite show at one time. With the explosion of online streaming services, you can start a series from the beginning and catch up at your leisure. The only problem is if you hang out with other fans of the show who assume you are at the same place, they may ruin it for you by revealing one or more key turns of events. That's why movie previews or appearances of stars promoting newly released movies never discuss critical scenes. Their desire is to entice you into wanting to see more but never to tell you too much. They want to be teasers but at no time spoilers.

Have you ever given a book to someone to later find out that before deciding to devote their time to reading it, they looked at the last chapter? Most people cannot understand why someone would want to do that. However, there are folks out there who have to know the ending before they will dare to invest in the beginning. Often, those individuals do not grow very deep in their relationships. They will only commit so far because they lack the ability to feel secure in their decisions without knowing how things will eventually turn out. In some ways, our society has also moved in this direction. Unless there is definitive scientific evidence of how something came to be, it encourages skepticism. There are times that sort of doubt is true for each of us in our faith as well if we try to define God in human terms. The Old Testament prophet cautions us, "'My thoughts are nothing like your thoughts,' says the Lord. 'And my ways are far beyond anything you could imagine'" (Isaiah 55:8 NLT).

I am always amazed at the rebirth of our earth each spring. Martin Luther said, "Our Lord has written the promise of resurrection, not in books alone but in every leaf of springtime." The fact that plants become dormant and then revitalize in the warmer seasons of the year is nothing short of a miracle. Botanists can clarify the growth, biochemistry, and development of plants. But if we keep asking the basic question, how, they will eventually reach a point where any explanation defies logic and can only be attributed to something beyond normal reasoning. Jesus affirmed this:

> The Kingdom of God is like a farmer who scatters seed on the ground. Night and day, while he's asleep or awake, the seed sprouts and grows, but he does not understand how it happens. The earth produces the crops on its own. First a leaf blade pushes through, then the heads of wheat are formed, and finally the grain ripens. And as soon as the grain is ready, the farmer comes and harvests it with a sickle, for the harvest time has come. (Mark 4:26–29 NLT)

The storyline is somehow incomplete without the provision of a higher power.

It is easy to appreciate how the disciples became confused when Jesus began to talk about leaving them to be with the Father. He said, "'You know the way to the place where I am going.' Thomas said to him, 'Lord, we don't know where you are going, so how can we know the way?'" (John 14:4–5 NIV.) It was as though they had started a novel, were told about the ending, but were missing the intervening chapters for further understanding. Jesus said, "Just believe that I am in the Father and the Father is in me. Or at least believe because of the work you have seen me do" (John 14:11 NLT). And therein lies the foundation of our faith: Jesus' assertion that He was the Son of God, who was crucified, and three days later would rise from the dead, thereby confirming He was who He claimed to be. If Christ is not risen, everything we proclaim to believe would be worthless. Paul stated it frankly: "And if Christ has not been raised, then all our preaching is useless, and your faith is useless" (1 Corinthians 15:14 NIV). For the Christian, what might otherwise be our final chapter is good news. When we die and someone arbitrarily says, "They're gone," the answer to the obvious question as to "where" has already been promised. For "He is not here. He has risen" (Luke 24:6 NIV). It's a spoiler alert worth sharing but indeed not the end of His story nor ours.

Reflection

How would you explain to a new Christian that the existence of their faith is grounded in the resurrection? What are some things about God that you just have to accept as being beyond human comprehension? Why is it not necessary to understand all the details as long as you learn to trust and have faith in God?

APRIL 14

(Y6, D15)

False Hopes and Tragic Endings

God is our refuge and strength, always ready to help in times of trouble. So we will
not fear when earthquakes come and the mountains crumble into the sea.

—Psalm 46:1–2 (NLT)

April 14 was a tragic day in history. Five days after General Robert E. Lee's surrender at Appomattox in 1865, the sixteenth president of the United States, Abraham Lincoln, was shot at Ford's Theatre in Washington DC by Confederate sympathizer John Wilkes Booth. Many years later, Ward Hill Lamon—Lincoln's former law partner, friend, and sometimes bodyguard—related a story about the president's premonition of his own death. According to the tale, just a few days before his assassination, Lincoln shared a recent dream. In it, he walked into the East Room of the White House to find a covered corpse guarded by soldiers and surrounded by a crowd of mourners. When Lincoln asked one of the soldiers who had died, the soldier replied, "The president. He was killed by an assassin." Lincoln told Lamon that the dream had "strangely annoyed" him. However, on the afternoon before his death, he accompanied his wife, Mary, on her daily carriage ride. It was a pleasant spring day, and the Lincolns discussed their plans for life after his presidency. He was said to have been quite blissful on this final day of his life. Following the shooting, the president would live throughout the night but passed at 7:22 a.m. on April 15, 1865.

Forty-seven years later in 1912, just before midnight in the North Atlantic on April 14, the RMS *Titanic* failed to divert its course from an iceberg, ruptured its hull, and began to sink. One of the largest and most luxurious ocean liners ever built, the *Titanic* was considered unsinkable. On its maiden voyage, the ship carried some 2,200 passengers and crew. Because of a shortage of lifeboats and the lack of satisfactory emergency procedures, more than 1,500 people went down in the ship or froze to death in the icy North Atlantic waters. A number of notable American and British citizens died in the tragedy, including the ship's architect and captain. Some survivors later reported that the ship's string ensemble played the hymn "Nearer My God to Thee" as the vessel sank. At 2:20 a.m. on April 15, 1912, she slipped beneath the waters of ocean, leaving only 710 survivors. The wreckage itself was never discovered until 1985, and her memory was kept alive by numerous works of popular culture.

These two events give credence to the statement that we should live and have our best possible today. Jesus said, "Therefore do not worry about tomorrow, for tomorrow will worry about itself. Each day has enough trouble of its own" (Matthew 6:34 NIV). The song "A Lot of Livin' to Do" tells only part of the story. While full of hope about the future, it might be more realistically titled "A Lot of Livin' to Do… Maybe!" These days, we often act as if we are going to live forever but, on the other hand, we expect to be protected from everything. A good example is the offer of travel insurance. Normally included is coverage for trip cancellations and interruptions, baggage loss or damage, medical expenses, emergency evacuations, as well as accidental death and dismemberment. Some plans protect travelers from their driveway to their destination and then back home, including exposure to terrorist activities. One wonders if *Titanic* survivor Eva Hart's parents would have made such an insurance purchase had it been available in 1912. Hart once stated, "My mother had a premonition from the very word *go*. She knew there was something to be afraid of and the only thing that she felt strongly about was that to say a ship was unsinkable was flying in the face of God. Those were her words."

For the Christian, the only insurance policy we have as we journey through life is the "assurance" that our forever has been signed with the blood of Jesus. This is the wonderful gift of Easter. Lincoln seemed to agree when he said, "Surely God would not have created such a being as man, with an ability to grasp the infinite, to exist only for a day! No, no. Man was made for immortality." Whatever you are facing this day, my friend, you can be certain that if you look toward the heavens, "You will be rewarded for this; your hope will not be disappointed. My child, listen and be wise: Keep your heart on the right course" (Proverbs 23:18–19 NLT). For if our hope is based only on holding tight to the things of this earth, then we will never know the things of God, and that would indeed be quite a tragic ending.

Reflection

As you reflect on the tragedies you have faced in your lifetime, could there be anything worse than an existence without God? When you think of hope for your future, what considerations do you have? How can you help yourself and others free themselves about obsessing over earthly matters?

APRIL 15
(Y7, D15)

Bargaining with God

You would have no power over me if it were not given to you from above.

—John 19:11 (NIV)

The practice of bartering has been going on for thousands of years. Each of us most likely did this when we were young, sometimes trading lunch items at school. Even today, we occasionally engage in swapping things, such as providing childcare for your family if you prepare dinner for mine. In each situation, the offer is successful only if both parties have something the other needs and considers what they are giving to be a fair exchange for what they receive. More often than not, people prefer dickering where there is disagreement over the value of the exchange. Our family once had an older couple as neighbors. Years ago, when they went to buy a car, the wife haggled over the purchase price until the salesperson agreed to "Eighteen thousand and not a cent more." When the couple went to pick up their new car, the franchise presented an invoice for $18,000 plus taxes and transfer costs. The wife argued that this was "not the bargain." Guess who won as her husband just smiled and shook his head?

Can you imagine being bold enough to bargain with God? When you're dickering with a merchant, you possess the money, and they hold the merchandise. You each have something the other person wants, so you have some bargaining power. But when it comes to God, He holds everything. The good news is that if we try to bargain with God, He is gracious to deal with us right where we are. The story is told that Martin Luther's father, who worked as a miner, wanted his son to become a lawyer, so Martin studied law. He was almost done with his preparation when one day, at the age of twenty-one, he was caught outside during a violent thunderstorm. In the midst of his fear, Luther cried out to St. Anna, the patron saint of miners, "Save me, Saint Anna, and I shall become a monk!" God spared Luther, and he kept his vow to the great disappointment of his father and his mother. In our limited understanding of who He is and because He is sovereign over all, God can even use our feeble attempts at bargaining to accomplish a more glorious purpose as He did with Luther.

In the Old Testament, we can read about Jacob leaving his home on a journey to find a wife from among his people. "Then Jacob made a vow, saying, 'If God will be with me and will watch over me on this journey I am taking and will give me food to eat and clothes to wear so that I return safely to my father's house, then the LORD will be my God, and this stone that I have set up as a pillar will be God's house, and of all that you give me I will give you a tenth'" (Genesis 28:20–22 NIV). Later in 1 Samuel, we discover Hannah who has been unable to conceive and bear a child while her husband's other wife had many children. "And she made a vow, saying, 'O LORD Almighty, if you will only look upon your servant's misery and remember me, and not forget your servant but give her a son, then I will give him to the LORD for all the days of his life'" (1 Samuel 1:11 NIV). We come to understand that it is not possible to make deals with God, except perhaps in special cases where deal-making is part of God's teaching process. Both Jacob and Hannah had lessons to learn along the way, so it appeared that God bargained.

God is not a master who passes along favors to His servants who strike bargains with Him. If one thinks that they can manipulate God into doing things their way, they are deceived. Making promises to God in order to gain favor shouldn't serve as a basis for our relationship. Rather, we must live our lives according to His will. Remember Jesus in the Garden of Gethsemane when He cried out "Father, if you are willing, please take this cup of suffering away from me" (Luke 22:42 NLT). And the Father said no. That no was a turning point, replacing the old covenant of works with the new covenant of grace (Ephesians 2:8–9). It made the way for those who follow Jesus to live for all of eternity in God's holy presence. We receive the grace of God because He loves us and not because we talked Him into it by promising to do things we should have been doing all along. While God will sometimes allow us to be in difficult situations so that He can connect with us, the good news is that He is sovereign and gracious. We are simply called to trust and submit to Him—absolutely no bargaining needed.

Reflection

Recall a time in which you found yourself in a difficult situation and tried to bargain with God. If that worked out favorably, did you consider that the result may have been what God desired for you all along? How does bargaining with God reveal a low image of Him?

APRIL 16
(Y1, D16)

New Normal, New You

Therefore, if anyone is in Christ, the new creation has
come: The old has gone, the new is here!

—2 Corinthians 5:17 (NIV)

How dramatic does an event have to be to bring about permanent change? It is a question often asked following a human tragedy or otherwise catastrophic occurrence which is accompanied by some form of imposed sacrifice. After such happenings, life as we know it is often altered for a while. In the midst of the coronavirus pandemic, experts told us that on the other side, there would be what many referred to as a "new normal." No one was able to tell us exactly what that would look like or how long it would last. After a hurricane, for example, people frequently join to help their neighbors. They cut up one another's fallen trees, drag waterlogged furniture to the curb, and grill food from powerless freezers. Sometimes the bonds that form last forever; most times, however, they are fleeting. Life often returns to what it had previously been, and over time, the memory of the shared experience begins to fade. In the end, as we emerge on the other side of a life-altering event, we will likely struggle to define a new normal based upon what had once been mixed with the need to adapt as a result of what happened.

Experiencing new life and implementing a new normal are inherent in the Christian faith. Following the death of Jesus, Paul told the early Christians they were a new creation (2 Corinthians 5:17) and that those who believed in Christ died with Him and would no longer live for themselves. Their lives would no longer be worldly; they were now more spiritual. The same is true for us as our old sin nature was also nailed to the cross with Christ. It was buried with Him. As He was raised by the Father, so are we raised to "walk in newness of life" (Romans 6:4 ESV). Because of the new life that we have been given, there is an expectation that we will live a "new normal." Paul continues, "You were taught, with regard to your former way of life, to put off your old self, which is being corrupted by its deceitful desires; to be made new in the attitude of your minds; and to put on the new self, created to be like God in true righteousness and holiness" (Ephesians 4:22–24 NIV). It is

213

then that our purposes, desires, and understandings are made fresh. We hopefully see the world differently with new feelings toward all people—a new love for family and friends, a new compassion never before felt for enemies, and a new respect for the world.

A new normal can be experienced as either positive or negative, depending on the way we react to the change. New norms encourage one to deal with current conditions, rather than lamenting about what could have been or what was. It is often dependent on our ability to exercise some degree of control over the situation in which we find ourselves. In those circumstances where social distancing is essential, perhaps a silver lining will occur, awakening a better appreciation for the simple things. Maybe we will never again take for granted a hug from our grandparents, the roar of a crowd at a sports event, coffee with a neighbor, a walk with a friend, a taste of communion, a potluck supper, a packed concert hall, or a handshake with a stranger. Possibly it's our turn to answer the question many of us have asked of the older generation: "What did you do during such times, and how did you change?" When the pause from our old normal ends, we will hopefully find that we have become more like the person we were called to be. And it just might be that we will change for the better because of the worst we have seen.

A new creation can be an amazing thing. But if it is imposed by an outside force like a pandemic, it may not lead to any permanent change. If it is a conscious choice, such as a decision to follow Christ, it is given opportunity to result in a transformation and a true new normal. When we decide to walk with God, He will be by our side and not abandon us. His Word tells us, "Because of the LORD's great love, we are not consumed, for his compassions never fail. They are new every morning; great is your faithfulness" (Lamentations 3:22–23 NIV). If you're on the cusp of a new normal, you won't always know what to do, but those first fumbling steps can be a sweet training ground. As you follow Jesus, you'll learn how to trust and lean on your faith. So be faithful, my friend, and allow that new normal to form a new you.

Reflection

As you walk into a season of life challenged with uncertainty, how can you prepare yourself for acceptance of that new reality, if only for a time? The Apostle Paul wrote, "Forgetting the past and looking forward to what lies ahead, I press on" (Philippians 3:13–14 NIV). When you are faced with a sudden change in your life, in what ways can you positively press on in order to embrace what lies ahead?

APRIL 17
(Y2, D16)

Leaving It All at the Cross

He canceled the record of the charges against us and took it away by nailing it to the cross.

—Colossians 2:14 (NLT)

One day, a man went to visit a church. He arrived early, parked his car, and got out. Another car pulled up near him, and the driver told him, "I always park there. You took my place!" The visitor went inside for Sunday School, found an empty seat, and sat down. A young lady from the church approached him and stated, "That's my seat! You took my place!" The visitor was somewhat distressed by this rude welcome but said nothing. After Sunday School, the visitor went into the church sanctuary and sat down. Another member walked up to him and said, "That's where I always sit. You took my place!" The visitor was even more troubled by this treatment, but he still said nothing. Later, as the congregation was praying for Christ to dwell among them, the visitor stood, and his appearance began to change. Horrible scars became visible on his hands and on his sandaled feet. Someone from the congregation noticed him and called out, "What happened to you?"

The visitor replied, "I took your place."

What if you had not only been present at the crucifixion of Jesus, but you were also directly responsible for executing the order to carry out His death sentence? In the 1953 movie, *The Robe,* we witness a Roman officer by the name of Marcellus Gallio who is charged with overseeing the execution of two criminals and Jesus. The focal point of the story is a red robe Jesus wore which remains at the cross following His crucifixion. A drunken Marcellus wins it by rolling dice with his detachment officers. The robe is eventually stolen by his slave, Demetrius, who escapes from the young tribune. Marcellus later experiences disturbing visions, is haunted for his actions, and found repeatedly asking the question, "Were you there?" of others whom he encounters along the way. Convinced that destroying the robe will lift the curse and cure him, Marcellus sets out to find Demetrius. His pursuit results in his personal redemption and conversion, leading to martyrdom when he comes to recognize Jesus as the true Messiah.

While some of the characters and narratives of this movie are fictional, it is somewhat based on biblical accounts. For instance, one scripture which certainly applies is:

> When the soldiers had crucified Jesus, they divided his clothes among the four of them. They also took his robe, but it was seamless, woven in one piece from top to bottom. So they said, "Rather than tearing it apart, let's throw dice for it." This fulfilled the scripture that says, "They divided my garments among themselves and threw dice for my clothing." So that is what they did. (John 19:23–24 NLT)

I am reminded of an online picture of a sign in front of a church that I once viewed during Holy Week. It said "1 Cross Plus 3 Nails Equals 4 Given." Think about it, but don't think too long. Jesus took the path to Calvary so that He could take us home. He wore our garment so that He could give us His own.

All of this begs the question, what will you bring to the cross? Until we walk up the hill and leave something behind, we haven't embraced what happened there. Maybe it's our bad habits we should take. Possibly it's the list of things we dislike about some challenging people in our lives. Consider that He inspired one servant to write "Love does not keep a record of wrongs" (1 Corinthians 13:5), so we are challenged to place this list at the cross. Maybe we should consider leaving our anxious moments there. Or how about our failures and the many feelings which linger from those experiences? God wants that list also. Don't be cautious and think you're leaving too much behind. There is nothing too great that will cause God to reject your burdens. Knowing all that He shed on that cross, you have no reason to think that He won't handle these things as well. Paul stated it this way: "Since he did not spare even his own Son but gave him up for us all, won't he also give us everything else?" (Romans 8:32 NLT). Just place all those things that are troubling you at the feet of Jesus by simply leaving them at the cross.

Reflection

Are there things which you have never considered turning over to Jesus? What would be your reasons (embarrassment, guilt, afraid to admit, too trivial for God, etc.)? Why is it easy to ponder what Christ left at the cross but much more difficult to wonder what we should leave there?

APRIL 18
(Y3, D16)

Because I Said So

Then Jesus said, "Did I not tell you that if you believe, you will see the glory of God?"

—John 11:40 (NIV)

A young boy looks at his father and asks the usual series of "why" questions. Finally running out of answers, the dad becomes somewhat exasperated by trying to satisfy his son with a response. So he simply bends down, gives the child a hug to let him know he cares, and then looks at him firmly and says, "Because I said so. That's why." As we mature, it does not become any easier. We continue to question the decisions of our parents, the authority of our teachers, the thinking of our bosses, and the trust of our spouse. And when it comes to matters of faith, we try to apply the same logic to God that we learn in our science and math classes. We suddenly realize that two plus two doesn't always equal four.

The question becomes, if one of Jesus' very own disciples doubted, can we expect to be any different? "So the other disciples told him, 'We have seen the Lord!' But he said to them, 'Unless I see the nail marks in his hands and put my finger where the nails were, and put my hand into his side, I will not believe'" (John 20:25 NIV). This follower became known as the "doubting Thomas disciple," and there is at least a little bit of him in each of us. We believe in Jesus, but we're not sure about all those Bible stories. You know the ones—Jonah and the whale, David and Goliath, the parting of the Red Sea, and the raising of Lazarus after he had been dead for three days. The list could likely go on and on. But God has given us the gift of faith so that we can take what's unseen and make it part of who we are. In response to His Thomas: "Jesus told him, 'Because you have seen me, you have believed; blessed are those who have not seen and yet have believed'" (John 20:29 NIV). That, my friends, is you and me.

I remember at one point in my life listening to a pastor speak about the miracle of the loaves and the fishes (Matthew 14:15–21; Mark 6:41; Luke 9:16–17). All of the scripture accounts indicate that the thousands of followers ate from a small number of fish and a few loaves of bread and were satisfied. This pastor gave several explanations as to how the hunger of the multitudes may have been fulfilled, giving little if any credence to the fact that the food may have been sufficiently multiplied to actually feed those present. What bothered me about his rationalizations was that they left very little room for God to be God. The problem with mankind is that we have come to expect methodical proof for everything we deem to be real. We try to define God in terms of our own human understanding. We get lost in being able to do so because He cannot be defined in ways that we are able to comprehend. "'For my thoughts are not your thoughts, neither are your ways my ways,' declares the Lord" (Isaiah 55:8 NIV).

We come to realize somewhere along our journey that we don't have to obtain the answer to all the questions we might ask, at least not in this lifetime. Meanwhile, as our heavenly Father deals with our insecurities, doubts, and fears, He remains patient, telling us, "Do not let your heart be troubled; believe in God, believe also in Me. In My Father's house are many dwelling places; if it were not so, I would have told you; for I go to prepare a place for you" (John 14:1–2 NIV). Personally, as I think of the vastness of our universe and my understanding of who God is, I am reminded of the words of a song popularized in the 1960s by Mahalia Jackson and Elvis Presley:

> Who made the flowers to bloom in the spring?
> Who made the song for the robins to sing?
> And who hung the moon and the stars in the sky?
> Somebody bigger than you and I.

If that "somebody bigger" is the God I have grown to love, then He can speak to me with those words: "Because I said so." I can accept this answer with a childlike faith (Mark 10:14–15). C. S. Lewis put it this way: "I believe in Christianity as I believe that the sun has risen: not only because I see it, but because by it I see everything else." And if perhaps there are times you struggle to see it now, it will one day become quite clear when "we will see everything with perfect clarity" (1 Corinthians 13:12 NLT).

Reflection

How prepared are you to defend your belief in God? Can you positively respond to others who are expressing doubts about their faith? What are some changes you need to make in your own life so that you can be less of a doubting Thomas?

APRIL 19
(Y4, D16)

More than Enough

> But when they measured it out, everyone had just enough. Those
> who gathered a lot had nothing left over, and those who gathered only
> a little had enough. Each family had just what it needed.

> —Exodus 16:18 (NLT)

I don't know about you, but when I invite guests for dinner, I like to have what I believe to be an acceptable menu. I try to get an idea ahead of time what their preferences are, and then I plan the meal accordingly. In doing so, I feel that the basic entrée with a starch, vegetable, salad, and dessert will be adequate, and I anticipate a generous portion size for each person. Beyond that, I don't worry about the meal other than what to serve for dessert. I am pleased when my guests eat all that I have prepared, and I don't become overly concerned that they had enough to eat. I know others, however, who subscribe to the belief that their company was not satisfied if they consumed everything. In other words, if there is no food left over, they will conjecture that their guests must not have had enough to eat. I'm not sure who has the most gracious philosophy. I tend to think if they enjoyed the meal, there was plenty.

When Jesus was faced with the feeding of a very large crowd, His disciples expressed concern that they were not adequately prepared to feed them and that the masses should be sent away.

> Jesus replied, "They do not need to go away. You give them something to eat."
> "We have here only five loaves of bread and two fish," they answered.
> "Bring them here to me," he said. And he directed the people to sit down on the grass. Taking the five loaves and the two fish and looking up to heaven, he gave thanks and broke the loaves. Then he gave them to the disciples, and the disciples gave them to the people. They all ate and were satisfied, and the disciples picked up twelve basketfuls of broken pieces that were left over. The number

of those who ate was about five thousand men, besides women and children. (Matthew 14:16–21 NIV)

This miracle was recorded by Matthew, Mark, and John, and in each case, it is stressed that after all had been fed and satisfied, there was food remaining. John states it this way: "When they had all had enough to eat, he said to his disciples, 'Gather the pieces that are left over. Let nothing be wasted.' So they gathered them and filled twelve baskets with the pieces of the five barley loaves left over by those who had eaten" (John 6:12–13 NIV). Not only did Jesus perform a miracle here, He was also attempting to teach a lesson to His followers. It's as if He was saying, "Can you not see that you don't have to concern yourself with how much you have? I can supply all that you need and more." The fact that there is an abundance left over demonstrates that God is a gracious provider. Just as He delivered bread for the five-thousand and manna for the Israelites of the Old Testament who were in exile (Exodus 16), He will meet our needs as well if we trust Him to do so.

We live in a society of excess, and seldom are we grateful for all we have. We overextend ourselves financially and sometimes become so deep in debt that we will never see the light of day. We embrace our politicians who promise us the world and fail to realize that somewhere along the line, we will end up paying for all that "free stuff." We say what we want is enough to get by and keep us comfortable, but what we have is never sufficient. If our neighbor has it, we want one which is bigger and faster. We need to come to terms with the fact that the God who loves and cares for us is, in fact, a God of abundance who fulfills our daily needs. However, through the worry and anxiety that we most often bring on ourselves, we can miss out on the true bread of life. St. Augustine put it this way: "He who has God has everything; he who has everything but God has nothing." Embrace Him as your absolute *everything*. He is indeed all you'll ever need. "And this same God who takes care of me will supply all your needs from his glorious riches, which have been given to us in Christ Jesus" (Philippians 4:19 NLT). What He provides is more than enough. We just have to trust and believe it to be so.

Reflection

Do you ever find yourself sometimes becoming indifferent with all the blessings God pours on you each day? What is that thing that you may need to reconsider being a necessity? As you reassess what God has already made available to you, what would it take for you to realize that it is more than adequate? How might you help others understand that sufficiency is not based on material possessions?

APRIL 20
(Y5, D16)

Watching from the Clouds

Do you know how the clouds hang poised, those wonders
of him who has perfect knowledge?

—Job 37:16 (NIV)

A friend of mine told me recently that she had contacted a lawn care service because she had concerns about the increased number of weeds in her lawn. The phone representative asked for her email and home address so that additional information could be sent out to her. During the conversation, he said, "I can see that you have a really nice home" as he described her house and its surroundings with detailed accuracy. She stated that at one point, she was a bit "creeped out" with the fact that he could see her home so clearly. She discontinued the conversation and told the representative that she would call back later if there was further interest. I informed her that it's easy to see your house from space using Internet software that grabs imagery from thousands of earth observation satellites. While the pictures displayed on the many available tools rely on historically captured images, we are quickly moving into an era where "real-time" viewing from space will be the norm.

I can understand that it is somewhat disconcerting to think that someone has the ability to look down on us. It gives a whole new meaning to the phrase "Big Brother is watching." As technology is developed, just imagine satellites able to check out our neighborhoods for what kind of car we drive, whether packages have been delivered to our front porch, or zoom in with high resolution to see what kind of food we are having for the weekend picnic on our deck. New terminology like "cloud storage" only adds to the wonderment, causing some to question just where our personal information is being stored and who has access to it. But as a society, we like the expediency of being able to access our files from anywhere or have the ability to start watching a movie on one device and finish it on another without missing a scene. In many ways, we appear willing to sacrifice some of our privacy in order to gain optimal performance and immediate discovery to whatever we desire.

The reality is that "the cloud" (as it has come to be known) is far from some mist floating overhead. It's a very sophisticated network of information storage, enabling quick retrieval for our convenience. Just for fun one day, I pulled out my iPhone and asked Siri where she lived. The response: "Wherever you are, that's where I am."

I thought to myself, "Why, that's rather scriptural." God spoke to Jacob in a dream, stating "I am with you and will watch over you wherever you go, and I will bring you back to this land. I will not leave you until I have done what I have promised you" (Genesis 28:15 NIV). After the death of Moses, the Lord spoke to Joshua: "This is my command—be strong and courageous! Do not be afraid or discouraged. For the LORD your God is with you wherever you go" (Joshua 1:9 NLT). Therefore, it should not surprise us that Jesus affirmed this same message after His death and triumphal resurrection. In what has come to be known as the Great Commission, He reassured those closest to Him, stating, "Teach these new disciples to obey all the commands I have given you. And be sure of this: I am with you always, even to the end of the age" (Matthew 28:20 NLT).

Isn't it inspiring to know that we have a God who loves us so much that He is always watching over us and can reach us from anywhere? That means that even in the most turbulent times and in the most unpredictable places, He can protect us. He is not trapped somewhere in the cloud. Our God is all-knowing; He is omniscient. The psalmist David understood that God's omniscience is personal and relational. "You know when I sit down or stand up. You know my thoughts even when I'm far away. You see me when I travel and when I rest at home… Such knowledge is too wonderful for me, too great for me to understand" (Psalm 139:2–3, 6 NLT). God knows where you are and what you are thinking about this very moment. He is able to view us in real-time. That should give us great comfort in an age when we consider what the motives for others who are looking down on us might be.

Reflection

Have you ever thought about the immediate access we have to God? Why do you think we sometimes become overwhelmed with the volume of information available to us today and somehow forget that God never becomes burdened with His watchful care for each one of us? How can you explain the omniscience of God to another who needs to have a deeper understanding?

APRIL 21
(Y6, D16)

Fake News

You were running a good race. Who cut in on you to keep you from obeying the truth?

—Galatians 5:7 (NIV)

On the third Monday in April, the state of Massachusetts commemorates Patriots' Day, the anniversary of the Battles of Lexington and Concord. These were the first of the Revolutionary War. On that day, mounted reenactors retrace the midnight rides of Paul Revere and William Dawes. The festivities also include the Boston Marathon, an annual race which began in 1897. It is the world's oldest annual marathon and ranks as one of the best-known road racing events. The event attracts half a million spectators each year with over 30,000 registered participants from many nations. On April 21, 1980, the Eighty-Fourth Boston Marathon, twenty-six-year-old Cuban-born Rosie Ruiz finished first in the women's division with a time of 2:31:56. It represented the third fastest marathon time in history for a woman and was a twenty-five-minute improvement over her New York City Marathon time the former year. Ruiz was unknown in the running world, and her victory raised suspicion with some. When interviews were conducted, it was discovered that neither the monitors at the various checkpoints nor any of the marathon runners remembered seeing her during the race. After studying photographs, it was noted that Ruiz didn't appear in any of them until the very end. Eight days later, Ruiz was stripped of her victory after race officials learned she entered the race about a mile before the finish line. Her New York time from the prior year was also later invalidated when officials discovered she had taken the subway during part of that race.

The Greek philosopher, Plato, once wrote, "Things are not always what they seem; the first appearance deceives many; the intelligence of a few perceives what has been carefully hidden." A further lesson we might take from the incident at the Boston Marathon is that we cannot always be certain that the world's way of ranking things represents truth. Jesus was once asked by a young rich man what he had to do to inherit eternal life. Jesus responded by saying, "Why do you ask me about what is good? There is only One who is good. If you want to enter life, keep the commandments" (Matthew 19:17 NIV). The man replied that he felt he had been doing all those things and wondered what he still lacked. "Jesus answered, 'If you want to be perfect, go, sell your possessions and give to the poor, and you will have treasure in heaven. Then come, follow me.' When the young man heard this, he went away sad, because he had great wealth" (Matthew 19:21–22 NIV). Jesus teaches us that there will be many surprises in heaven where the value system is far different than that of the world we know. Those who are esteemed and respected in this world (like the rich young ruler or deceptive persons whom we know) may be frowned upon by God. The opposite is also true, for those who are despised and rejected in this world (like the disciples) may be rewarded by God. In fact, Jesus concludes this passage by saying: "But many who are first will be last, and many who are last will be first" (Matthew 19:30 NIV).

So what is the takeaway here? It is simply this. The world's way of making judgments is often far too prone to error. In the twenty-first century, the impact of "fake news" has become widespread with instant access to social media. The usage of the term has also increased in the midst of heavily fought political campaigns. And while it wasn't always a favorite subject of politicians and news media—misinformation, spin, lies, and deceit have been around forever. It is up to each of us to speak for God. In opening the holiest week of the Christian calendar in 2018, Pope Francis delivered a Palm Sunday homily suggesting Jesus was the original target of "false public spin" as he urged young people not to keep quiet about their faith. That's good advice for all believers, regardless of our age. In the words of Jesus: "The time promised by God has come at last! The Kingdom of God is near! Repent of your sins and believe the Good News!" (Mark 1:15 NLT). If we want to be persons of fact, then we must steep ourselves in the ultimate truth of Christ and share it with others. Unfortunately, good news of any kind is not always what our society values or wants to hear. And that's too bad because there will undoubtedly be a time ahead when the Good News about Jesus may represent the only real news of the day that is not fake.

Reflection

How do you weigh the news you see and hear in published, broadcast, and social media against what you know to be true? In what ways can you do this without becoming judgmental? How might you apply the words of Peter: "Always be prepared to give an answer to everyone who asks you to give the reason for the hope that you have. But do this with gentleness and respect" (1 Peter 3:15 NIV).

APRIL 22
(Y7, D16)

Then Came Morning

In the morning, Lord, you hear my voice; in the morning I
lay my requests before you and wait expectantly.

—Psalm 5:3 (NIV)

If a tree falls in the woods and there is no one there to hear it, is there still a sound? Remember that question you were probably asked and pondered as a child? It was learned about the same time as young people were told, "It will be okay—things will look better in the morning." I had a chance to recall both of these old sayings not so long ago on a late winter evening with high wind gusts. As the heavy winds picked up, I heard a thump outside. I was suspicious that a tree had fallen close to our home, and I assumed it was the dead one belonging to my neighbor that I had been concerned about for some time. A late evening peek outside verified that a tree had indeed come down next to the house, but it appeared to have caused little if any damage. When I walked out onto the front lawn the next morning to get a better look, I was surprised to find that it was a live tree from my own yard that had toppled and took down two others, including the dead one belonging to the neighbor. It was then that I revised the old adage to now say, 'Wait till morning when things may indeed look different.'

After Jesus had been crucified, He was placed in a tomb sealed with a big stone and guarded by soldiers. In scripture, there are four accounts of what occurred on the morning we now refer to as Easter. Mark tells us that on

> Saturday evening, when the Sabbath ended, Mary Magdalene, Mary the mother of James, and Salome went out and purchased burial spices so they could anoint Jesus' body. Very early on Sunday morning, just at sunrise, they went to the tomb. On the way they were asking each other, 'Who will roll away the stone for us from the entrance to the tomb?'" (Mark 16:1–3 NLT).

These women were the first to witness that the world they thought they knew was about to be far different than they ever could have expected. Then they experienced the first indication that the darkness of grief, despair, and broken dreams was conquered. As another disciple picked up the account, we see that a new day has dawned:

> Suddenly there was a great earthquake! For an angel of the Lord came down from heaven, rolled aside the stone, and sat on it. His face shone like lightning, and his clothing was as white as snow. The guards shook with fear when they saw him, and they fell into a dead faint. Then the angel spoke to the women. "Don't be afraid!" he said. "I know you are looking for Jesus, who was crucified. He isn't here! He is risen from the dead, just as he said would happen. Come, see where his body was lying. And now, go quickly and tell his disciples that he has risen from the dead, and he is going ahead of you to Galilee. You will see him there. Remember what I have told you." (Matthew 28:2–7 NLT)

There is just something about the morning that God holds dear. He dwells in perpetual light, and He appears to love the dawning of each new day. On that first Easter morning, Jesus triumphed over death and darkness and brought life and immortality to light. The fact that He was raised from death guaranteed that all evil and sorrow is only temporary and that good and joy are eternal. Easter is about conquering all obstacles that get in the way of achieving the purpose of Christ. The stone was rolled away, not for Jesus to come out of the tomb but instead for others to see its emptiness. Prior to that, there was a world of darkness. Then came the morning with a light that could never be extinguished. Before, there was a world of hate. Then came the morning, and love triumphed over hate. Previously, there had been a feeling of despair. Then came the morning, and hope was born anew. On Easter Sunday, we celebrate how the dawn of that new day changed everything. For those of us who love Christ, we come to understand that because of His resurrection, there is no end to our personal stones that need to be rolled away to fulfill God's purpose for our life. We are therefore comforted by these words: "The faithful love of the Lord never ends! His mercies never cease. Great is his faithfulness; his mercies begin afresh each morning" (Lamentations 3:22–23 NLT). Jesus came to live and die for each of us. And just when many thought all hope was lost, then came morning, and the world was never the same again.

Reflection

Consider a time in your life when you felt all hope was lost. Did you face that occasion with or without Christ by your side? As you think about your huge personal obstacles that need to be "rolled away," will you run away trembling, fearful, and bewildered? Or will you face the dawn, knowing that the resurrected Jesus will provide hope and everlasting peace for each and every day that follows?

APRIL 23
(Y1, D17)

A Simple Trust

If you are faithful in little things, you will be faithful in large ones.

—Luke 16:10 (NLT)

Let your mind wander back to the day you first learned how to ride a bike. You are nervous as you hop onto the seat of your shiny new Schwinn, but you trust the adult who stands at your side and, of course, the training wheels which are in place as part of the purchase package. One day, those wobbly wheels are finally removed, and you are confident that you are now prepared to ride a bike. With that adult figure running beside you, holding onto the seat, they finally let go. You are either off and running or ready to face a few scrapes and bruises. Learning to ride a bike is a rite of passage for any kid, but the days when we first learned to rely on training wheels are fading as a part of the past. Enter the balance bike, sized so that a child can comfortably put both feet on the ground but high enough so that they can lift their feet and glide. Child experts say that it's a more efficient way to learn the technique of bike balance, therefore providing the opportunity for riding more safely at a younger age. Who knew?

One might think that teaching a child to ride a traditional bike might be a bonding experience that some parents might not want to miss. For the child, it is one of those occasions where they learn to appreciate the value of placing trust in another individual. Assured that even if he or she fell off the bike, that faithful adult would be there to pick them up and provide the necessary care. Perhaps that's why Jesus identified so readily with children. Children are characteristically humble, trusting, and therefore teachable. Jesus promoted unpretentious faith in God, and He used the innocence of a child to demonstrate His point. When He wanted to bless the children, Jesus said, "Let the little children come to me, and do not hinder them, for the kingdom of God belongs to such as these" (Mark 10:14 NIV). While simple childlike faith is perhaps a good place to start, it is important for us to grow into a deeper faith, hopefully leading us to a personal relationship with our heavenly Father. This only comes from an assured confidence when we know with certainty who the object of our faith is. For "it is impossible to please God without faith. Anyone who wants to come to him must believe that God exists and that he rewards those who sincerely seek him" (Hebrews 11:6 NLT).

Mature faith is characterized by conviction, not by blind belief. We are sometimes surprised by those who display this type of faith.

> When Jesus returned to Capernaum, a Roman officer came and pleaded with him, "Lord, my young servant lies in bed, paralyzed and in terrible pain."
> Jesus said, "I will come and heal him."
> But the officer said, "Lord, I am not worthy to have you come into my home. Just say the word from where you are, and my servant will be healed." When Jesus heard this, he was amazed. Turning to those who were following him, he said, "I tell you the truth, I haven't seen faith like this in all Israel! And I tell you this, that many Gentiles will come from all over the world—from east and west—and sit down with Abraham, Isaac, and Jacob at the feast in the Kingdom of Heaven. But many Israelites—those for whom the Kingdom was prepared—will be thrown into outer darkness, where there will be weeping and gnashing of teeth." Then Jesus said to the Roman officer, "Go back home. Because you believed, it has happened." And the young servant was healed that same hour. (Matthew 8:5–13 NLT)

Identifying oneself as a member of "the faithful" can easily create circumstances where individuals are included or excluded by the self-righteous. In *The Message* translation of verse 12 (above), a profound statement is made: "Then those who grew up 'in the faith' but had no faith will find themselves out in the cold, outsiders to grace and wondering what happened." Of course, Jesus was speaking here of the religious elite who would have classified themselves as dutifully practicing their faith. Consider the possibility of how many persons might have been raised in the faith but show no conviction. Just remember, "People may be right in their own eyes, but the LORD examines their heart" (Proverbs 21:2 NLT). When we are tested by circumstances that to us seem out of control, God will acknowledge those who are truly faithful. With just a little faith, great things can happen. For whenever you give your faith to Jesus, it's like riding a bike—you never forget. All it takes is a simple trust in Him.

Reflection

Can you think of examples where you have been surprised by individuals whom you thought were strong in their faith but did not demonstrate it in times of crisis? In what specific ways might you serve as a positive example by exercising a simple trust in God today? How can you help those who might be doubtful in understanding that faith begins with small steps that become affirmed over one's lifetime?

APRIL 24

(Y2, D17)

An Investment in Caring

Love each other with genuine affection, and take delight in honoring each other.

—Romans 12:10 (NLT)

While watching a major league baseball game, I was pleased to observe an interaction between two young fans. A well-known player and reigning National League MVP for the home team hit a fly ball out to right field which was pursued by a visiting fan. With glove in hand, he missed catching the ball by inches—causing it to fall into the bullpen. However, after several tries, he finally caught the ball thrown to him from the ground. But then the cameras caught him doing the unexpected. Instead of keeping the souvenir for himself, he gave the ball to a fan of the opposing team who was wearing a jersey bearing the name of the player who hit it. Just minutes later, the boy to whom the ball was gifted was observed walking back over to express his appreciation to the young man and his father. This exchange was picked up on social media and viewed by the MVP who later surprised the father/son duo with a baseball signed by him and their favorite player from the visiting team. It's real proof that when you do something nice for another without expecting anything in return, you can demonstrate true caring and even generosity.

The positive affirmation I felt when I made this observation is contrasted with what I feel when I read the local daily newspaper. I am baffled at times by the recurring letters to the editor which surface from a few personalities who babble on with their political opinions in back-and-forth commentaries. These characters attempt to influence the readers' beliefs by impressing the opposition with their wealth of contradictory knowledge. Typically, their arguments are reduced to a "gotcha" mentality. Bottom line, if you don't support their opinion, then you are not worthy of one. I am reminded of that oft-quoted statement attributed to Teddy Roosevelt: "Nobody cares how much you know until they know how much you care." Unfortunately, the cancel culture will never give way to a sense of caring. Perhaps they need to consider this wise counsel: "Don't have anything to do with foolish and stupid arguments because you know they produce quarrels. A servant of the Lord must not quarrel but must be kind to everyone, be able to teach, and be patient with difficult people" (2 Timothy 2:23–24 NIV).

An encounter with a loving, caring individual can change a person's life. Such were the experiences of those who encountered Jesus Christ when he walked on earth. Consider some of these: Mary Magdalene, a woman who seemed intent on self-destruction, driven by demons. Zacchaeus, who became willing to return fourfold what he had extorted from people. Finally, Matthew, who was willing to walk away from a lucrative position to follow the Master. Each of these stopped making themselves their primary focus of existence and actually learned to care deeply about others. Their encounter with Jesus Christ changed the focus of their lives from solely pleasure-seeking to showing care and compassion. The Apostle Paul reminds us, "Don't be selfish; don't try to impress others. Be humble, thinking of others as better than yourselves. Don't look out only for your own interests, but take an interest in others, too" (Philippians 2:3–4 NLT). This is affirmed over and over again in God's Word.

Demonstrations of compassion are highly contagious, but they can be caught only by direct contact with someone who has them. Too often, proclaimed believers and the Christian Church give lip service to acts of caring. They are not unlike the story of an eleven-year-old girl and her eight-year-old brother who bickered and fought over the slightest thing. Their parents were surprised when the girl made an artistic card for her brother's birthday. Inside, she wrote the following message: "Happy Birthday to my nine-year-old brother. I am so glad to have a brother to love. So God gave me you. P.S. Don't read this out loud or I will twist your head off." We find the message of caring for others central to the very fabric of the Christian faith, laced throughout scriptures such as "share each other's burdens" (Galatians 6:2 NIV). For the Christian, how well we endure in sacrificially serving others is one of the greatest indicators of how deeply we understand what Christ did for us on the cross. While there may be times when social distancing is necessary, relational distancing will never give witness to an investment in caring.

Reflection

Think about someone who has made an indelible impact on you. Does this person still resonate with you because they were smart or because they emitted a genuine sense of caring? How would you feel if you heard that you claim to be a Christian but certainly don't demonstrate a very caring attitude toward others? How can you make a personal investment in another person who needs a genuine expression of compassion?

APRIL 25
(Y3, D17)

Not My Day

This is the day the Lord has made. We will rejoice and be glad in it.

—Psalm 118:24 (NLT)

We've all had them. Days, that is, when nothing seems to be going right. Things aren't working the way they are supposed to. Times when we feel we should go back to bed because we certainly must have crawled out on the wrong side this morning. When this occurs, it's not unusual to hear the phrase "Today's just not my day." In stating so, we often muddle through what remains of it, just hoping that tomorrow will be better and run a little smoother. If we're fortunate enough to pick up our Bible on a day like that, we would be very blessed to receive comfort from the words of Paul which he spoke to the church at Corinth. "So we do not lose heart. Though our outer self is wasting away, our inner self is being renewed day by day" (2 Corinthians 4:16 ESV).

Corrie ten Boom, a survivor of a Nazi concentration camp, came to understand the value of each day as she learned to trust and serve God. She became a well-known author of faith who said, "This is what the past is for! Every experience God gives us, every person He puts in our lives is the perfect preparation for the future that only He can see." Her wisdom can be applied in many situations. On April 19, 1995, 168 people died when a bomb was set off at the Alfred P. Murrah building in Oklahoma City. Decades later, a mother of one of the victims stated that she has since learned to make the most of each new day because you never know what tomorrow might bring. At times like this, when we hear of a tragedy that others must endure, we would do well to pause and simply thank our heavenly Father for whatever kind of day we might be having. It's actually rather scriptural when you think about it. "Do not boast about tomorrow, for you do not know what a day may bring" (Proverbs 27:1 NIV)

On April 15, 2015, it was just a normal day for twenty-nine-year-old Jason Warnock of Idaho. He was doing what he did most days, driving to work, when he saw debris near the road. He looked up to see an SUV suspended on the edge of a cliff. The vehicle was being held in place only by a chain-link fence. It most certainly hadn't been a very good day for twenty-three-year-old Michael

Sitko who crashed this vehicle, at least not until Warnock parked his car and pulled Sitko out to safety. Warnock, unidentified at the time, chatted briefly with the victim, waited for the arrival of emergency personnel, and casually left the scene to go to work. Police later stated that the SUV may have been intentionally crashed, and the only thing that saved the driver was the fence and the unknown hero. Warnock, who later came forward, thought differently as he stated, "I think maybe God put me here at the right time."

Years ago, I heard the late Robert H. Schuller say these words at the end of one of his *Hour of Power* services: "Lord, lead me to the person you wish to touch through my life as I serve you this day." I try to remember to close my devotions each morning with that thought. For I have come to realize that "the steadfast love of the Lord never ceases; his mercies never come to an end; they are new every morning; great is your faithfulness" (Lamentations 3:22–23 ESV). Our life is by no means an accident. We are here for God's intended purpose, and we have a limited amount of time. A voice from the Old Testament echoed this sentiment: "You have decided the length of our lives. You know how many months we will live, and we are not given a minute longer" (Job 14:5 NLT).

So the next time you find yourself saying, "Today is not my day," you are absolutely correct. Instead, we learn to understand that every day is His, a gift from God. On those days when it might seem like you don't have a purpose, recognize that you are allowing life circumstances to define you rather than trusting God to lead. When our priorities become smothered by the stuff of life, we will not be open to God's prodding spirit. As the psalmist said, "Teach us to number our days that we may gain a heart of wisdom" (Psalm 90:12 NIV). Even though we will likely become busy with our imposed challenges, each day also provides a chance for us to serve and love Him more. We simply have to listen for His call.

Reflection

In what ways are you presently living for God? How is God glorified when you are following the purpose He intends for your life? How can you make time each morning to ask the question, "Lord, what are you leading me to do this day?"

APRIL 26
(Y4, D17)

What Is It that You Want?

Do not be anxious about anything, but in everything, by prayer and
petition, with thanksgiving, resent your requests to God.

—Philippians 4:6 (NIV)

Two talk show cohosts find themselves at odds over a botched communication that one of them is planning to leave his current job for a bigger role on another network program. Hearing the news at almost the same time as it was released to the public, his female counterpart then fails to appear on their program for several days, stating that she feels hurt and betrayed. After a lot of media drama and behind-the-scene conversations, the two reunite on-the-air. While they apparently have an agreement to "play nice," he transitions off of the show sooner than expected. Much speculation persists that if she doesn't get a new co-host of her choosing, she will also walk away when her contact expires. Then the labeling, from him being classified as "inconsiderate" for not giving the cohost a heads-up to her being called a "diva" for the way she reacted. If you refused to take sides and didn't allow your emotions to be affected, you might have simply wanted to yell out, "Just what is it that you want?" While there were more important things to be concerned about, the world continued to watch with great anticipation.

A relative of mine related a story about a friend of hers who some time ago had been diagnosed with cancer. After several series of chemotherapy treatments, it would soon be time for an imaging test to scan for the presence of the disease. The friend told my relative that she was asking God to be healed, stating, "I know I am expecting a miracle, but that's what I want." In a desire to not discourage the friend, her reply was that certainly if that was God's will, He could make it so. She was concerned that if the scan continued to show presence of the cancer that her friend, who had been doing somewhat better, would lose heart and not continue to positively move forward. By helping the friend to recognize her progress and giving thanks for what God has already done, she helped to create an atmosphere for continued healing rather than defeat. She also encouraged her friend to ask for God's revelation about what it is that she might be able to learn while her faith journey takes her though this current situation.

Is it acceptable to be very specific with God about our needs? Jesus was often direct with those who were seeking His help.

> Then they came to Jericho. As Jesus and his disciples, together with a large crowd, were leaving the city, a blind man, Bartimaeus was sitting by the road-side begging. When he heard that it was Jesus of Nazareth, he began to shout, "Jesus, Son of David, have mercy on me!" Many rebuked him and told him to be quiet, but he shouted all the more, "Son of David, have mercy on me!" Jesus stopped and said, "Call him." So they called to the blind man, "Cheer up! On your feet! He's calling you." Throwing his cloak aside, he jumped to his feet and came to Jesus. "What do you want me to do for you?" Jesus asked him. The blind man said, "Rabbi, I want to see." "Go," said Jesus, "your faith has healed you." Immediately he received his sight and followed Jesus along the road. (Mark 10:46–52 NIV)

When someone whom we care about is in crisis, the first question most of us normally ask is, "What can I do to help?" We ask for specifics because when we have something concrete, we can focus on meeting that need. Should we think that the God who created us cares any less than we? Of course not. It is important that we not only be specific but also be persistent. Jesus said, "And so I tell you, keep on asking, and you will receive what you ask for. Keep on seeking, and you will find. Keep on knocking, and the door will be opened to you" (Luke 11:9 NLT). His timing might not meet our expectations, and His answer may come in a different form that we expect. But be assured, God hears our requests and answers our prayers according to his merciful will and purpose in our lives. He never gives up on you, so don't give up on Him. When we keep praying and don't lose heart in spite of our frustration and disappointment, we affirm our relationship with Him, and He realizes just how much we are trusting Him. In the end, we recognize that our answer to "What do you really want?" should always be a part of our prayer petition.

Reflection

Are there times that you have wondered why you have to keep asking God for what He knows you need? Have you been specific, persistent, and accepting of God's timing in your prayers? How do you determine when you need to recognize that your relationship with God is more important than that for which you are asking?

APRIL 27
(Y5, D17)

Love to Tell the Story

We will not hide these truths from our children; we will tell the next generation about the glorious deeds of the Lord, about his power and his mighty wonders.

—Psalm 78:4 (NLT)

"Once upon a time in a land very far, far away." They were the opening words to some of our favorite childhood stories. Sometimes they were told at bedtime or another special time of day, and our eyes would open wide with a deep gaze of anticipation. Whether it was a fairy tale like *Alice in Wonderland* or *Green Eggs and Ham* by Dr. Seuss, the art of storytelling has been passed down through the generations. These stories stimulated our imagination and pretty much ensured that as we grew slightly older, we would be making up our own tales as we dared to outdo our friends with a ghost story at our first sleepover. I can still recall short stories and poems recited by my grandmother which somehow also became etched into my memory. The stories told to us by parents and grandparents help us to understand their history and our heritage, developing strong and loving bonds. Dating back to a simpler time before technology took over, they were one way in which our ancestors lived on long after they were gone.

As he looked out at the congregation, he prompted them by saying just two words: "It's Friday."

Everyone shouted in reply, "But Sunday's comin'!" The speaker was Rev. Tony Campolo who is one of the best Christian storytellers there is. He recalls preaching in his home church in Philadelphia, Pennsylvania, decades before. On that particular Sunday, when several ministers would speak in this African American Church, he was really preaching his heart out to an urging congregation. After he finished, he sat down by his pastor and said something like "Bet you can't top that" to which the elderly Black minister said, "Son, sit back 'cause the old man is gonna do you in." Campolo said for the next hour and a half, his pastor preached one of the best sermons he has ever heard using the recurring phrase "It's Friday, but Sunday's comin'." The theme of the message illustrated how dark and gloomy things appeared for the followers of Jesus at Calvary. But the good news is that it did not end there, for it was only Friday. The motivational message goes on to reinforce that when Sunday arrived, everything changed.

If we are lucky, we too have memories of special times when we were inspired by a Bible story after bedtime prayers or as we gathered with our friends during the children's message at church or during a summer Bible School. One of the best storytellers was Jesus Himself who would frequently use parables to illustrate a truth or moral lesson. He was once asked by His disciples why He spoke in parables to which He replied, "To those who listen to my teaching, more understanding will be given, and they will have an abundance of knowledge. But for those who are not listening, even what little understanding they have will be taken away from them" (Matthew 13:12 NLT). The Lord's parables are rich in imagery and not easily forgotten. It's been said that the parables of Jesus are earthly stories with a heavenly meaning. They are a blessing to those with willing ears. But for those who were unwilling to hear His message, they did not understand and were declared to be spiritually deaf.

A good storyteller may at some point publish a novel. But just as well, they could become a songwriter or capture the hearts of children at a Saturday morning public library reading hour. Or just for a moment, they might rekindle the fractured memory of a nursing care resident as they share the reading of a once familiar scripture or the verse of a frequently sung hymn somehow retained in the cobwebs from Sunday School decades before. Good stories invite us to experience make-believe life through their fictional characters, but God's story invites us to experience truth through Christ's Word. Paul pleaded, "But how can they call on him to save them unless they believe in him? And how can they believe in him if they have never heard about him? And how can they hear about him unless someone tells them?" (Romans 10:14 NLT). We should not become complacent in assuming that Bible stories and old hymns are such a precious part of our heritage that they will always be remembered. God has chosen people to be the primary communicators of His gospel. He has entrusted us to be His storytellers. Take time to share His great story so it becomes part of theirs. For if not you, then who?

Reflection

In what specific ways has storytelling been included in your family traditions? How have you made an effort to keep it alive and, in particular, share those personal and biblical reflections of faith? In what ways will you endeavor to preserve the personal stories that were such an important part of your heritage for future generations?

APRIL 28
(Y6, D17)

See What God Has Done

Our help is from the LORD, who made heaven and earth.

—Psalm 124:8 (NLT)

On April 27, 1791, Samuel Finley Breese Morse was born in Charlestown, Massachusetts, the eldest of three sons of clergyman, Dr. Jedediah Morse. The Morse boys were educated at a Christian boarding school and later at Yale College. As part of his studies at Yale, Samuel saw demonstrations of electricity, which had not yet been put to any useful purpose. His real interest was drawing, but his father believed that being an artist was not a suitable occupation for a gentleman. When his talent began to be recognized, the father finally agreed to send him to England to study art where he gained public acclaim. During his lifetime, Morse observed firsthand the problems that delays in communication could cause. While on a ship traveling back to the United States from Europe in 1832, he conceived the idea of a single-circuit electromagnetic telegraph. His ideas included the use of a code containing a series of dots and dashes representing letters of the alphabet, later known as Morse Code. In 1837, he applied for a patent for the telegraph. After many setbacks and disappointments, his projects eventually received funding. He demonstrated the telegraph for the first time on May 24, 1844, by transmitting a Bible verse, "What hath God wrought?" (Numbers 23:23), translated in modern versions as "See what God has done!"

On May 23, 1939, the submarine USS *Squalus* sank during a test dive off of the coast of Portsmouth, New Hampshire in 243 feet of water. A valve failure caused flooding of the torpedo room, both engine rooms, and the crew's quarters, drowning twenty-six men. Quick action by the remaining thirty-three crewmen prevented the other compartments from filling. It had only been a decade earlier when sailors in a similar situation tapped on the hull of their vessel a Morse Code message to their would-be rescuers, asking, "Is there any hope?" They eventually died from a depleted supply of oxygen. This time, for the USS *Squalus*, there *was* hope in what became the greatest submarine rescue in US history. Navy and Coast Guard vessels rushed to the scene and picked up some of the Morse Code messages hammered on the side of the *Squalus*. They knew thirty-three men were alive in the forward compartments. Having prepared for such an occasion, a rescue ship arrived carrying and attaching a never-before-tried device to the hatch, enabling the remaining sailors to be rescued after a thirty-nine-hour ordeal. The invention of Morse Code nearly a century before and the transmission of SOS alerts became an internationally recognized distress signal. In popular usage, SOS became associated with such phrases as "Save Our Ship" and "Save Our Souls."

Hope for rescue becomes a customary life reaction when any of us are in distress. Stories of hope and searching for help from God affirm our faith. In the Old Testament, we read about a widow whose husband, a man who respected the Lord, had died and left her in debt. If the debt was not paid, the creditor would come back and take her two sons as slaves. In her distress, she looked to God for help by turning to His servant, Elisha. When Elisha asked her what she had in her house, she said that she only had a little olive oil. He told her to ask her neighbors for as many empty jars as she could gather and then to go to her home and close the door. He further instructed her that she and her sons should fill each of the jars with oil, setting each one aside. When there were no more jars remaining, the oil stopped flowing. "When she told the man of God what had happened, he said to her, 'Now sell the olive oil and pay your debts, and you and your sons can live on what is left over'" (2 Kings 4:1–7 NLT). This needy widow had hope that God could do something about her situation. And He most certainly did!

Four years before his death, Samuel Morse wrote "The nearer I approach to the end of my pilgrimage, the clearer is the evidence of the divine origin of the Bible, the grandeur and sublimity of God's remedy for fallen man are more appreciated, and the future is illumined with hope and joy." Unfortunately, hope is what people often seek when it appears no one else will answer their cause. Some people live their lives trapped in a hull of emptiness and despair, wondering if there is any hope for escape. It is when we fully turn over our lives to God and trust that our help will come through Him alone that we will be able to rejoice in the blessings that follow. It is only then that we will say to all who will listen, "Come and see what God has done."

Reflection

How can you become more reliant on God's help in our daily walk rather than turning to Him as a last resort? Are there ways that you can affirm the words of the Apostle Paul as He speaks of God's Son, "This hope is a strong and trustworthy anchor for our souls" (Hebrews 6:19 NLT)?

APRIL 29
(Y7, D17)

Faith Tested by Fire

When you walk through the fire, you will not be burned; the flames will not set you ablaze.

—Isaiah 43:2 (NIV)

The famous Notre Dame Cathedral in Paris is a spiritual pilgrimage for many. For others, its fame grew because of Victor Hugo's classic novel, *The Hunchback of Notre Dame*, cementing its place in literary history. When a massive fire broke out on April 15, 2019, it destroyed the wood lattice-work roof of the 850-year-old building and caused the spire to collapse. Before the blaze, the church had been undergoing an extensive multimillion-dollar renovation. Notre Dame Cathedral housed some of Christendom's most sacred religious relics, including the preserved crown of thorns said to contain fragments of the original circle worn by Jesus Christ. Only a week before, sixteen bronze statues from the twelfth and thirteenth century were removed from the spire. A trio of round stained-glass rose windows from the thirteenth century, a single Holy Nail and a fragment of wood believed to be from the True Cross on which Christ was crucified, and the great organ dated to the Middle Ages all survived amid significant overall damage to the structure itself. It's indeed a blessing that there were no lives lost, and through time, the cathedral will be restored.

Restoration comes in many forms. While man can never fully restore something which has been consumed by fire, God can! In His Holy Word, the book of Daniel tells the story of three Hebrew teenagers—Shadrach, Meshach, and Abednego—who refused to worship the golden idols of their king. He had the young men brought before him and said to them, "I will give you one more chance to bow down and worship the statue I have made when you hear the sound of the musical instruments. But if you refuse, you will be thrown immediately into the blazing furnace" (Daniel 3:15). Their response: "If we are thrown into the blazing furnace, the God whom we serve is able to save us. He will rescue us from your power, Your Majesty" (Daniel 3:17 NLT). The ruler was enraged and had them thrown into a fiery furnace where they should have died. But while they were in there, the king saw something he did not expect. "Look! I see four men walking around in the fire, unbound and unharmed, and the fourth looks like a son of the gods" (Daniel 3:25 NIV). The passage says that when they were released from the furnace, "Not a hair on their heads was singed, and their clothing was not scorched. They didn't even smell of smoke!" (Daniel 3:27 NLT). They came out with no sign they had been in the fire, and their faith passed the ultimate test.

There are applications here for all who love the Lord. The first of these is that when you are in the fire, you can be assured that you are not there alone. God shows up in fiery places. The second lesson is that when we have an attitude of faith, God works with us through the difficult times. In doing so, we experience the third lesson: It's part of God's plan to get us to where we need to be. There is purpose in His allowing us to go through the fire. The psalmist spoke these words: "Though you have made me see troubles, many and bitter, you will restore my life again; from the depths of the earth you will again bring me up. You will increase my honor and comfort me once more" (Psalm 71:20–21 NIV). You may be facing a fire in your own life. However, you need to convince yourself that this fire is not going to burn you. I used to hear some older folks use the expression, "I feel like I've been pulled through a knot hole backwards" when they were having a really bad day. As I grew in years, there came a time when I understood what they meant. Facing times of trouble and tribulation is not unusual as evidenced by examples of godly men and women throughout the scriptures. Their stories can serve as inspiration to us because the same God who was faithful to them will also be faithful to us. Peter tells us that we are grieved by various situations that "have come so that the proven genuineness of your faith—of greater worth than gold, which perishes even though refined by fire—may result in praise, glory and honor when Jesus Christ is revealed" (1 Peter 1:7 NIV). When gold is refined by fire, it becomes even more valuable. When God sees one of His children worthy of refining, they, too, should be prepared to be tested by fire.

Reflection

Consider a time when you were tested by the fires of life. How genuine was your faith? Was it built upon the underlying character of God or fixated upon the changing circumstances you were facing at the time? How does the way we handle our trials and tribulations serve as a witness for others who are not grounded in the faith?

APRIL 30
(Y1, D18)

Before It's Too Late

Here I am! I stand at the door and knock. If anyone hears my voice and opens
the door, I will come in and eat with that person, and they with me.

—Revelation 3:20 (NIV)

In the storyline of an old *Little House on the Prairie* episode titled "If I should Wake Before I Die,"
an eighty-year-old widow feels lonely for her children and grandchildren who never visit her. At the
funeral of another widowed friend whose family members failed to show up for her last birthday
party, one of the main, young characters declares that it is not fair for loved ones to ignore a birthday
but show up for a funeral. This prompts the surviving widow to make a decision to have her funeral
wake before she dies. Accordingly, she enlists the help of the town doctor and her neighbors to
secretly plan the event. On the day of the reception, she attends incognito at first with a veil hiding
her face. It is not long until she surprises those present, including a young priest and her son whom
she had not known was still alive. The event provides an occasion for reuniting the lady's family and
hopefully serves as a "wake-up" call for all the participants to love each other here and now while
there's still time.

Consider this question: If you could share a meal with anyone, past or present, who would that
be? It's an interesting inquiry which was regularly posed on a food segment of a weekly variety program. The answers varied, depending on the role of the person being asked. Some of the responses
included the desire to share that meal with famous persons in history as well as individuals who had
mentored those being asked. Interestingly enough, the replies frequently listed loved ones who had
passed on. Occasionally, it crossed my mind if some of these folks perhaps had regrets for not spending enough time together in days gone by which were now lost. For when we lose someone to whom
we should have paid more attention, we don't get any second chances to fulfill those "should've,
would've, could'ves." When we permit our lifestyle to disrupt maintaining contact with those about
whom we say we care, then we are potentially allowing ourselves to one day be floundering in a sea
of regret.

In providing a similar warning, Jesus told this parable:

> A man prepared a great feast and sent out many invitations. When the banquet was ready, he sent his servant to tell the guests, "Come, the banquet is ready." But they all began making excuses. One said, "I have just bought a field and must inspect it. Please excuse me." Another said, "I have just bought five pairs of oxen, and I want to try them out. Please excuse me." Another said, "I just got married, so I can't come." The servant returned and told his master what they had said. His master was furious and said, "Go quickly into the streets and alleys of the town and invite the poor, the crippled, the blind, and the lame." After the servant had done this, he reported, "There is still room for more." So his master said, "Go out into the country lanes and behind the hedges and urge anyone you find to come, so that the house will be full. For none of those I first invited will get even the smallest taste of my banquet." (Luke 14:16–24 NLT)

The Parable of the Banquet reflects the relationship many of us have developed with others who care about us. Our response is to say we have something "better" to do with our time. However, in all actuality, we are simply giving way to bad excuses, thereby taking the place of what we know is the appropriate thing to do. In many cases, we are forfeiting fellowship with one who deeply cares and longs to spend time with us. Those who ignore the invitation miss out on a special gift and will ultimately choose their own destiny. This can occur in our families, with our friends, as well as in our other social circles. It can also transpire in our relationship with God. He wants His table to be full, and there will always be an open invitation for a seat. The anticipation is that we will come and share in His fellowship. This puts a responsibility on us to accept the offer and likewise participate in the banquet. Jesus extends an invitation to all who will listen and are willing to accept it. Consequently, if we decide to delay until that day when the funeral plans are in process, we will have missed out. So take your place at the table today and enjoy the feast of a lifetime. And please, do so now before it's too late.

Reflection

Are you making mistakes in your own life similar to those portrayed in this devotion? Whose invitation are you neglecting? Jesus has invited you to spend time in his presence, to spend time in his Word, and to spend time in fellowship with Him. Have you exchanged the good things God has planned for you at His banquet table for some worldly thing that seems better or more important in the moment?

MAY 1
(Y2, D18)

Truth: The Foundation of Our Faith

Do not let any unwholesome talk come out of your mouths, but only what is helpful for
building others up according to their needs, that it may benefit those who listen.

—Ephesians 4:29 (NIV)

It had been a while since I had seen this old friend. We were meeting at a local restaurant to have lunch and simply catch up. After exchanging information about family and other pleasantries, the discussion takes a turn, and voices are lowered from rowdy laughter to quiet whispers. Sentences begin with phrases like "Did you ever find out what really happened there?" And if you're not cautious, the conversation can take on new life and quickly become a gossip session where both parties shift from facts to their own versions of the truth. No doubt each of us has become engaged in a similar scenario where speaking "our truth" moves from good intentions to negative implications about others who are not there to defend themselves. Even though we may weigh our words and are careful not to exaggerate, as a participant in these situations, we recognize that our communication is not always as precise as it should be. In those instances, I am thankful for the grace others give me, grateful when those with whom I am sharing look at the whole of my message instead of focusing on a few biased phrases here and there.

A gossiper can be defined as one who has privileged information about people and reveals such to those who have no business knowing it. Gossip is an easy sin to commit and comes in many forms from idle talk to spreading rumors on social media. How thrilling it may be to hear a tidbit about someone that the rest of the world may not know! Gossipers love to secretly reveal embarrassing and shameful information about associates and sometimes even friends. Furthermore, their desire to share is so great that they feel compelled to spread the details. Scripture speaks plainly about a gossiper: "Scoundrels create trouble; their words are a destructive blaze" (Proverbs 16:27 NLT). Gossip divides relationships, destroys trust, and the pain associated with it can be felt long after the words are spoken. It would do us well to recognize that someone who gossips to you will gossip about you, and it will undo a friendship (Proverbs 16:28). A person who gossips often falls into the category of many in our society who justify what they think they know or understand to be classified as their personal truth.

You have likely heard "This is my truth" or "Know your truth." You may have to catch yourself since it is one of the phrases that people use without even knowing why they are using it. Just because I insist something is true for me does not mean it is the truth. The phrase "their truth" simplifies one person's interpretation of a given event, and that person's understanding may not provide an actual portrayal of reality. It gives way to a philosophy that there is no actual truth, that truth is something purely subjective and personal. It serves to validate an individual who insists that what they would like to be true is substantiated simply because they wish it to be so. There have been many times in my life when I have believed something was true for me, but it was not actually true. No matter how much I believed as a child that the tooth fairy was the one putting a few bucks under my pillow, my truth was not the truth. My insistence that the tooth fairy was true did not change the reality that if I would lose a tooth and place it under my pillow now as a grown adult, I would not find money there in the morning.

When we lack seriousness about controlling untruths and other falsehoods and in our lives, then we are in danger of becoming what the Apostle Paul predicted: "They will learn to be lazy and will spend their time gossiping from house to house, meddling in other people's business and talking about things they shouldn't" (1 Timothy 5:13 NLT). The Christian faith is liberating because we don't have to build our lives on "our truth." We follow the one who called Himself "the truth." Jesus said, "I am the way and the truth and the life. No one comes to the Father except through me" (John 14:6 NIV). If we know Him and hold to His truth, we are free. We are free from the pressure of constructing our lives on limited knowledge and understanding. It is when we come to trust His truth alone that we will have shaped the foundation of our faith.

Reflection

Do you or persons you know think of gossip as a lesser sin or not a sin at all? How can you distance yourself from those who regularly engage in destructive and slanted communication by asking the question, "Are my thoughts going to lead to gossip or to God?" Consider incorporating the following thought into your daily prayers: help me to not dishonor anyone with my words today.

MAY 2
(Y3, D18)

Fearfully and Wonderfully Made

He who did not spare his own Son, but gave him up for us all; how will
he not also, along with him, graciously give us all things?

—Romans 8:32 (NIV)

I recall being astounded many years ago in my high school chemistry class when my teacher quoted the minuscule amount that the human body would be worth; that is, if you could break down all the chemicals it contains. A study conducted in April 2011 summarized this value to be about $160, more than when I was in high school but still not a lot. Try telling baseball's Giancarlo Stanton that's all he was worth in 2014. Then the twenty-five-year-old outfielder for the Miami Marlins signed a thirteen-year contract extension for $325 million. It was cited to be the most lucrative contract in sport's history but has since been surpassed. There was no doubt that Stanton had the capability of being a great power hitter, although the very next year, in 2015, he experienced an injury-shortened season. In 2017, he became an MVP but, in the off season, was traded to the New York Yankees. There he had a good first year, followed by several successive ones plagued with injuries. It's always a gamble with high paid sports figures, and it is highly doubtful that few professional athletes can yield a profitable harvest for as many years as their contracts often specify. Then the once-hero of the team becomes valueless and at risk of being thrown overboard.

We have indeed become a throwaway society, not only with our natural resources but with our human ones as well. The trend in some companies is to use their workers until they no longer successfully contribute or begin to raise too many questions. Then they can quickly become an expendable item. I find it's always interesting to read *Parade Magazine*'s annual survey of what people earn in various positions. Those who by title have an opportunity to make a positive difference in society are oftentimes far underpaid for what they contribute. I recall reading one year about a CEO of a firm which he founded took a 90 percent pay cut over the subsequent three years in order to increase the annual minimum wage of his workers to $70,000. In doing so, he hoped that the employees would be less distracted about fulfilling their basic needs and that this move would enable many of them to pay off existing debt or establish new beginnings. He described the raises as a "moral imperative" that could prompt leadership to do the right thing for those whom they were leading.

Although our society may model different values, the worth of a person cannot be measured in terms of how much money one has, the amount of power they possess, or what kind of standing they maintain in society. Sit back sometime and watch how a person treats those whom the culture would deem to be inferior. This will help you to determine the worth of that individual. Jesus was criticized for spending time with those who would have been labeled as outcasts in His day.

> When the scribes of the Pharisees saw that He was eating with the sinners and tax collectors, they said to His disciples, "Why is He eating and drinking with tax collectors and sinners?" And hearing this, Jesus said to them, "It is not those who are healthy who need a physician, but those who are sick; I did not come to call the righteous, but sinners." (Mark 2:16–17 NIV)

Jesus made it perfectly clear that He came for those who are lost (Luke 15:3–7), that they might repent (1 John 1:9) and believe in Him (John 1:12).

In the end, our worth cannot really be defined by others at all. It is given to us by God, for He alone is worthy. Because we are created in His image, we are of immeasurable value to Him. "But God showed his great love for us by sending Christ to die for us while we were still sinners" (Romans 5:8 NLT). All we have to do is believe. This should be more precious to us than any million-dollar deal we might create. Even more significant, the length of the contract is for all of eternity—no extensions will ever be needed. So, my friend, when society has used us to our fullest and is ready to chew us up and spit us out, we simply need to recall the sentiments of the psalmist of old who wrote "I praise you because I am fearfully and wonderfully made; your works are wonderful, I know that full well" (Psalm 139:14 NIV). Now that's the real value of a life, to be sure.

Reflection

If Jesus were to walk among us today, where do you think we would find Him? Would He find you obsessing over your self-worth or worrying about what others think of you? Would He observe you treating others as part of His creation as true children of God? How can you find ways to intervene when you face situations where others are treated as worthless?

MAY 3
(Y4, D18)

And You Looked after Me

Share each other's burdens, and in this way obey the law of Christ.

—Galatians 6:2 (NLT)

Several years ago, two eight-month-old stray puppies from Philadelphia received their fifteen minutes of fame. Given the names Jeffrey and Jermaine, it was instantly noticed when they were rescued that the two were inseparable. The dogs were brothers, but the perfectly seeing Jermaine served as a guide dog for Jeffrey who was noted to be blind in both eyes. Thanks to his brother, he was able to get around safely. When they were discovered wandering around the streets of the city, they were frightened, but Jermaine did everything possible to stay close to Jeffrey to let him know that he was there. The story of the devoted canine and his dependent sibling remind us that even animals are capable of expressing comfort and support for someone who is less fortunate and in need.

A friend recently recalled two instances where showing support proved to be most appreciated. In both cases, it was just a simple "thinking of you" that seemed to mean so much to the recipients. In the first situation, she was unsure how to reach out to a former colleague whose husband she had heard had been diagnosed with cancer. As Easter neared, it seemed like an appropriate time to just send a note. Days later, she received a phone call from the wife, indicating how much her expression of thoughts and prayers had meant. In the second case, she sent a card to an old neighbor who had just entered a personal care facility. Again an unassuming expression of concern and the words, "If you would like a visit, please give me a call." Days later, she was contacted by a third party that her friend had been admitted to a hospital and was asking that she respond with a visit. Two insignificant acts which required little time and effort on her part were each received with deep gratitude.

In the Old Testament, it is written that Job became afflicted by Satan "with painful sores from the soles of his feet to the top of his head" (Job 2:7 NIV) because he would not sin and curse God. When Job's three friends

> [H]eard about all the troubles that had come upon him, they set out from their homes and met together by agreement to go and sympathize with him and comfort him. When they saw him from a distance, they could hardly recognize him; they began to weep aloud, and they tore their robes and sprinkled dust on their heads. Then they sat on the ground with him for seven days and seven nights. No one said a word to him, because they saw how great his suffering was. (Job 2:11–13 NIV)

Likewise, when Jesus told His Parable of the Sheep and the Goats, He used an analogy to describe how His heavenly Father will separate those who are His (the sheep) from the unfaithful (the goats). Jesus said that one of the ways the righteous would be known was on the occasion when "I was sick and you looked after me" (Matthew 25:36 NIV).

The Apostle Paul counseled that we might have empathy to enter into another's sorrow and comfort them. To the church at Corinth, he wrote:

> Blessed be the God and Father of our Lord Jesus Christ, the Father of mercies and God of all comfort, who comforts us in all our affliction, so that we may be able to comfort those who are in any affliction, with the comfort with which we ourselves are comforted by God. For as we share abundantly in Christ's sufferings, so through Christ we share abundantly in comfort too. (2 Corinthians 1:3–5 ESV)

The requirement is that we take action with the same love and mercy for others that God has shown us. I know a gentleman who visited a friend of his in a nursing home nearly every day for six months. When asked about the dedication he had shown to his friend, he frankly replied that when he was once in the same situation (again for months), that very friend only missed coming to see him two days. In his book, *When the Darkness Will Not Lift*, author and theologian John Piper writes: "For most people who are passing through the dark night of the soul, the turnaround will come because God brings unwavering lovers of Christ into their lives who do not give up on them." Thanks be to God and to all those whom He sends in our direction to look after us.

Reflection

Romans 12:13 (NLT) says, "When God's people are in need, be ready to help them. Always be eager to practice hospitality." How have you demonstrated your willingness to look after others? In what ways might you be able to search for opportunities to share the same comfort you have once received from another?

MAY 4

(Y5, D18)

Powerful and Persistent Prayer

One day Jesus told his disciples a story to show that
they should always pray and never give up.

—Luke 18:1 (NLT)

I looked out the window and saw the mailman across the street, so I decided to meet him on my porch. Watching him work his way from house to house, I heard him talking to himself. As he came onto my front walk, I realized that he had a hands-free device and was engaged in a phone conversation. He thrust a handful of mail in my direction without any form of greeting, turned, and walked away. My response was similar then to the way I feel whenever I am at the grocery store and the cashier is having a personal conversation with another store employee. I want to say, "Hey, I am here. Pay attention to me." I think that is also a good indicator as to how some people pray, at times viewing themselves as God's faithful customer. Although they may not have had a good conversation with Him for a while, when they do have a need, they expect His close attention and immediate results.

Evangelist D. L. Moody told the story of two Christian women who were burdened for their unsaved husbands. They agreed on a fundamental plan that they would each spend an hour every day praying for the salvation of their men. After seven years, they could see no progress. They were discouraged and debated giving up. But the women committed themselves to lifelong perseverance and rededicated themselves to the task. Three years later, one of the women was awakened in the night by her husband who was in great distress about his soul. As soon as the sun rose, she hurried off toward her friend's house to tell her that God was about to answer her prayers. She was astonished to meet her friend coming from the opposite direction with the same news. Ten years of unyielding prayer was crowned with the conversion of both husbands on the same day.

In teaching His disciples about prayer, Jesus told the Parable of the Persistent Friend. He said:

Suppose you went to a friend's house at midnight, wanting to borrow three
loaves of bread. You say to him, "A friend of mine has just arrived for a visit,

and I have nothing for him to eat." And suppose he calls out from his bedroom, "Don't bother me. The door is locked for the night, and my family and I are all in bed. I can't help you." But I tell you this—though he won't do it for friendship's sake, if you keep knocking long enough, he will get up and give you whatever you need because of your shameless persistence. And so I tell you, keep on asking, and you will receive what you ask for. Keep on seeking, and you will find. Keep on knocking, and the door will be opened to you. For everyone who asks, receives. Everyone who seeks, finds. And to everyone who knocks, the door will be opened. (Luke 11:5–10 NLT)

This is not the only time that Jesus encouraged persistence in prayer. He wants us to keep praying for what we need, even if it seems to be taking a long time for our prayer to be answered.

In the United States, a National Day of Prayer is held annually on the first Thursday of May when citizens are asked "to turn to God in prayer and meditation." While observances such as these cannot be minimized, God's expectation is that we personally pray a bit more regularly. The Apostle Paul said that we should "pray without ceasing" (1 Thessalonians 5:17 ESV). Can we become too bothersome as we repetitively petition God for answers to prayer? I don't think so. In the Lord's Prayer (Matthew 6:9–13 NIV), Jesus modeled that we should pray for "our daily bread" to fulfill our basic needs. Included in those are nutrition, warmth, security, and physical well-being. When you are praying for the needs of others, be assured that God does not get bored with your recurring requests. If you maintain a prayer list, know that it's not about needing to remind God, but it's more about the continued connection you are maintaining with Him. He wants to have an ongoing relationship with you, not just a "when all else fails, then pray" association. Nothing is more pleasing to our Father in heaven than direct, unrelenting, and persevering prayer. It keeps us humble and demonstrates our total dependence on Him.

Reflection

What kinds of things can happen in our lives that can cause us to lose hope and fail to maintain consistent prayers? Can you think of an example where you prayed for a very long time and eventually got an answer to that prayer in a different way that you expected? How would you reassure others who have become discouraged because they feel their prayers have gone without a response?

MAY 5
(Y6, D18)

A Bending Willow of the Wilderness

The Spirit then compelled Jesus to go into the wilderness.

—Mark 1:12 (NLT)

On May 5, 1864, the forces of Union General Ulysses S. Grant and Confederate General Robert E. Lee clashed in the tangled wilderness west of Chancellorsville, Virginia, in one of the largest campaigns of the Civil War. On what had been the site of his brilliant victory the year before, Lee hoped that confronting the Federalists in the dense woods would mitigate the nearly two-to-one advantage Grant possessed. The fighting was intense and complicated by the fact that the combatants rarely saw each other through the thick undergrowth. Whole brigades were lost as muzzle flashes set the forest on fire, and hundreds of wounded men died in the inferno. On May 6, the second day of battle in the wilderness, the Federalists were on the verge of breaking through the troops of James Longstreet, a lieutenant general of the Confederates and one of Robert E. Lee's most trusted subordinates. Becoming disoriented as they drove back the Union troops, Longstreet was wounded by his own men and suffered an injury that paralyzed his right arm. Following two days of intense fighting in which neither side would gain a clear victory, the Union lost 17,000 men to the Confederates' 11,000, nearly one-fifth of each army.

It is not unusual to become lost in a wilderness situation. Indeed, just the opposite is also true at times when those who are already lost enter into a type of wilderness experience to find themselves again. These can include troubled or disadvantaged youth who are closely supervised while they are being taught skills of interdependence and self-reliance. It can also be useful instruction for leadership training in corporations where the basics of team-building need improvement. The wilderness experience is relevant, too, for believers who are enduring a tough time of trial or discomfort. In such a period, the pleasant things of life are unable to be enjoyed, may be absent altogether, and are often coupled with forceful temptation or spiritual attack. Some argue that periods like these are a time of God-ordained testing when one may struggle to simply exist day to day. During these occasions which may contain financial, material, physical, or emotional burdens, the believer is forced to wait on the Lord and hopefully finds God's peace and joy. Many claim their "wilderness experience" ends up being a turning point in their life because their surrender to Christ results in a more mature walk with Him.

Words translated as wildernesses occur nearly 300 times in the Bible. Wilderness in the context of scripture refers to a desert situation, rather than the forests we might imagine today. God liberated the Israelites from slavery, with Moses leading them out of Egypt and into a barren wilderness. They became hungry and complained. In faith, Moses prayed for God to sustain them, and He responded with the provision of manna and quail (Exodus 16:1–16:21). God appeared to the Israelites through a cloud (Exodus 16:10), tested their faith, and established commandments for serving Him (Exodus 20:1–17). Through forty years there, they were transformed to be God's chosen people. In the New Testament, we find John the Baptist preaching in his wilderness of many years (Matthew 3:1). And although Jesus performed much of his ministry in populated settings, many of his most transformative moments occurred in the outdoors including bodies of water, mountaintops, and, yes, the wilderness. It was where He spent forty days and was tempted by Satan three times (Matthew 4:1–11).

The wilderness of the Bible is an isolating place where ordinary life is suspended, identity shifts, and new possibilities emerge. Through the experiences of the Israelites in exile, we learn that while the wilderness can be a place of danger and uncertainty. It is also where solitude, nourishment, and revelation from God can be found. Ralph Waldo Emerson said, "I am a willow of the wilderness; loving the wind that bent me." God often uses wilderness situations to mold people and prepare them for His purposes. If you have never had such an experience, you will most likely find yourself there at least once in your lifetime. God puts you in the wilderness to set you apart so that nothing else matters, except hearing His voice and growing closer to Him. Ultimately, the experience of the wilderness can positively fashion and mature every believer in a unique way. The alternative is to wallow in self-pity, allow temptation to rule over you, or become so lost that you simply lose sight of who you are. You choose!

Reflection

Have you ever had the chance to observe someone in a wilderness experience? Can you learn to become that "willow in the wilderness" without allowing the emotions of fear and resentment to enter into your state of mind? How can you counsel someone who may be in such a situation?

MAY 6
(Y7, D18)

The Whole Nine Yards

A greedy man stirs up strife, but the one who trusts in the LORD will be enriched.

—Proverbs 28:25 (ESV)

As I was conversing with my neighbor, he was telling me about all the outdoor improvement projects he had planned for the warm weather months. He concluded by stating, "We're going for the whole nine yards." It was an expression I had not heard for some time, and it got me to reflecting about what that phrase meant years ago, contrasted with what some might interpret it to mean today. Back when those who said it basically meant they wanted everything that was coming to them, and they were willing to work hard to get it. Compare that with today's prevailing attitude that we want it all, and we expect it for little or no effort. Back then, we wanted everything that went with the meal which we had undoubtedly paid for. Nowadays, the expectation is that the meal will be provided for little or no cost. This boldness is pervasive throughout our society, and it is only heightened by the rhetoric of our politicians who promise all kinds of free stuff. But those of us who have been around for a little while remember and believe in the once popularized phrase "There is no such thing as a free lunch."

More often than not, the more we get, the more we want. We have become a culture of gluttony that refuses to be satisfied. The topics of money and greed are discussed throughout God's Holy Word. In fact, Jesus talked about this issue more than any other, except for the kingdom of God. Greed is a strong and selfish desire to have more of something. Jesus warned, "Watch out! Be on your guard against all kinds of greed; life does not consist in an abundance of possessions" (Luke 12:15 NIV) in his illustration of the Parable of the Rich Fool (Luke 12:13–21). Money or wealth is of itself not a problem, but rather it is our attitude toward it. When we place our confidence in wealth or are consumed by an insatiable desire for more, it is usually accompanied by failing to give God the glory for all of His provisions. Jesus rebuked the religious leaders of His day when He stated, "What sorrow awaits you teachers of religious law and you Pharisees. Hypocrites! For you are so careful to clean the outside of the cup and the dish, but inside you are filthy—full of greed and self-indulgence!"

(Matthew 23:25 NLT). Jesus also mentioned a long list of sins, including "deeds of coveting," which He says come from our hearts (Mark 7:21–22). So greed is not necessarily defined by amount but rather by our attitude and motives. This would imply that even those who are poor can become subject to greed, just like those who have great wealth.

The story is told of a financier who was visited by an angel who said he would grant him one wish. The businessman asked for a copy of the financial news one year in advance. As he was greedily scanning the stock prices and drooling over the profit he would make on his investments, his eye glanced across the page to the obituaries where he saw his own name. Suddenly, his earthly wealth didn't matter quite so much. This example begs the question, if you knew that you were to die in one year, would you do anything different in the management of your resources? Greed places a false value on temporal things, treating them as though we will be here forever. But we could die today or all of our "stuff" could instantly be taken from us as a result of some tragic event. One of the wise writers in the Old Testament wrote that "some people are always greedy for more, but the godly love to give" (Proverbs 21:26 NLT).

In his day, John D. Rockefeller Sr. became one of the richest persons in the world. Rockefeller also had a deep sense of God-given responsibility for the generous use of his wealth to improve life for others. But according to legend, when asked the question, "How much is enough?" he replied, "Just a little more." Each of us will at times make greedy choices, but it can be far too easy to become complacent with our own lack of effort to personally define what is truly "enough" in our own lives. When we become fixated on storing up treasures on earth instead of in heaven, when we shrug off our own greed by comparing ourselves with those who are richer than us, we might want to take a step back and ask how eternally happy we would be, even if we are fortunate to somehow achieve those whole nine yards.

Reflection

How much do you mourn the loss of money and things? What can you begin to accumulate less of today? In what areas of your life do you have to work especially hard at controlling your appetite for material possessions? In light of eternity and the brevity and uncertainty of this life, dare to ask the question, am I managing what God has entrusted to me so as to be rich toward God?

MAY 7
(Y1, D19)

Fight, Flight, or Faith?

The Lord will fight for you; you need only to be still.

—Exodus 14:14 (NIV)

It was during the first spring mowing of my lawn that I made an unexpected discovery. As I was mowing next to a rather large evergreen bush, I was startled by a bird which flew out very close to me. Later, I found a small blue egg on the ground and realized that the bird had apparently built a nest in the bush. So I wondered whether I had spooked my feathered friend or had it gone into a protective mode and flown out of the bush in an attempt to protect the nest? It is well understood that birds may be territorial about a particular feeding area, nesting location, or other types of personal habitat, and they may demonstrate anger to protect it. Scents in the air, vibrations on the ground, other sounds, sights, or tastes can carry messages that allow wildlife to react and respond. Once a threat or opportunity has been addressed, they return to a natural, calm, relaxed state, allowing them to conserve their energy.

When human beings are confronted with threatening or even challenging situations, their bodies also react with a personal fight and flight response. The response helps them decide whether they should stay and fight, run, or remain still during a threatening situation. Unlike other life-forms, we often linger in a high stress state long after an initial trigger has passed. Doing so requires enormous energy, eventually overloading our body and keeping us on edge as we prepare for the next shoe to drop. This can lead to serious anxiety issues, preventing an otherwise peaceful and happy life. For the believer, however, there is a very simple way to turn off the fight or flight response which, if followed, will help to guide them through a less conflicted and more joyful life. It is found in Deuteronomy 20:4: "For the LORD your God is the one who goes with you to fight for you against your enemies to give you victory."

In Exodus 14:14 (NIV), we're reminded that God sees all that we're going through and acts on our behalf. The verse reads, "The Lord will fight for you; you need only to be still." Some translations replace the word *still* with *calm* (NLT) or *silent* (ESV). Whichever way you read it, the words and concept are powerful for weary hearts in need of assurance. After letting the Israelites go out into the wilderness, Pharaoh pursued them with the might of his army and his own hardened heart. The Israelites were spiritually and emotionally weak and cried out to Moses, complaining that perhaps they should have stayed in Egypt where they were enslaved but at least safe and well-fed. With the Egyptian army bearing down, and the Red Sea at their backs, the Israelites needed God to find hope. Moses spoke these confident words just before parting the sea: "Do not be afraid. Stand firm and you will see the deliverance the LORD will bring you today" (Exodus 14:13 NIV). Christians would live a powerful life if they could trust in this amazing truth, but it seems to be difficult to believe it. Nonetheless, it is as true for us as it was for the Israelites.

There may be many occasions when we feel just like these Israelites, cornered with absolutely no way to see a way through our problem. The way God chooses to work in our situation may look very different from the way He provided for them. There may be times He certainly wants us to pick up our spiritual armor and fight. Or it could be that He simply wants us to wait where we are until He prompts us to move through a path He has cleared just for us. Whether He wants to fight through you or for you, He will come and help you when you rely on Him alone. As with Israel, we must never lose sight of the previous battles He has fought for us along the way. Whatever God's direction is for us, it has a purpose. When it comes to our spiritual well-being, it is always right to take flight in the midst of danger. But we should do so right into the sheltering arms of our loving God. Through His Son, Jesus Christ, we are promised freedom from the fears of an uncertain future. Although our circumstances may feel overwhelming, we need to let Him have control to fight the battle we are facing. While other options may sound like a good idea in the heat of the moment, always decide that you won't take flight from but only into the Lord's protection. We must stand firm in the faith that only He alone can provide.

Reflection

Has there been a time when you've felt attacked? How did you respond (with fight or flight)? With what are you currently struggling? Spend some time in prayer to see whether God wants you to fight, lay down your weapons, or simply exercise your faith by giving the battle over to Him? How can we prepare to find strength and provide wise counsel to others as we read these words from the Apostle Paul: "A final word: Be strong in the Lord and in his mighty power" (Ephesians 6:10 NLT)?

MAY 8
(Y2, D19)

Mother, May I?

When she speaks, her words are wise, and she gives instructions with kindness.

—Proverbs 31:26 (NLT)

It's hard to escape childhood without participating in at least one game of "Mother, May I?" More gender-neutral variations on the theme have included "Father" or "Captain" as the leader. The goal of the "Mother, May I?" game is for one of the players to be the first to reach the mother on the other side of the room or lawn. The mother faces away from a line of participants and distances far enough to make the game interesting but close enough that everyone can hear each other. Each participant asks a question, starting with the phrase, "Mother, may I?" followed with a statement of request for a suggested movement, such as, "Mother, may I take three steps forward?" The mother must reply "Yes, you may" or "No, you may not" by providing another directive. If a child forgets to say, "Mother, may I" before their question, they must return to the starting line. The participant who reaches the mother first wins the game and is then designated as the leader for the next game. The child must do what the mother says with the intention of leading them closer or farther away from the ultimate goal.

The premise of the game is fairly typical to what most of us experience in our growing up years. When we are determined to do something, it is often our mother who gives the go-ahead, makes an alternate suggestion, or shuts down our request entirely. Eventually, we learn to ask permission, and she responds based on family values or out of consideration for what is socially acceptable and appropriately safe. While we do not always like her answer, we learn that mothers most often base their decisions on what they consider to be right for us at the time. While the role of motherhood evolves over the life of a child, the love, care, and encouragement she gives never ceases. We know that mothers generally have our best interest at heart. Even when we are fully grown and she lends her unsolicited advice, we accept that fact that it comes from a good place. That is why a special occasion called Mother's Day is set aside to honor, remember, and, if possible, to spend some time with her. It's an opportunity to let her know just how much we appreciate all she has done and continues to do for us.

When it comes right down to it, our mothers are one of those persons whom we take pride in pleasing. We all like to be recipients of caring, and for most of us, our moms are one of its best sources. There are all kinds of mothers: those who have given birth, those who have adopted, and those who have loved and supported the children of others. The gift of motherhood, therefore, isn't necessarily a biological function; it comes from the heart and is placed there by God. God even described Himself as having a mother-like attribute. In Isaiah 66:13 (NIV), we read: "As a mother comforts her child, so will I comfort you; and you will be comforted over Jerusalem." Likewise, Jesus told those who loved him that He would not leave them as orphans (John 14:18), but the Father would send a Helper in His name (John 14:26). When we affirm this relationship with His Holy Spirit, we can be like David who said, "I have calmed and quieted myself, I am like a weaned child with its mother; like a weaned child I am content" (Psalm 131:2 NLT).

British novelist William Makepeace Thackeray once wrote: "Mother is the name for God in the lips and hearts of little children." Following Jesus' example, mothers often display an attitude of self-sacrifice in order that their children might everything they need. With incredible patience, they give of themselves in such a way that those whom they nurture are pointed toward God. Recognizing that there will be a time when she will be separated from us, Mother trusts that our access to His Holy Comforter will always be without restraint. An effective mother understands that she must "start children off on the way they should go, and even when they are old, they will not turn from it" (Proverbs 22:6 NIV). In doing so, they will never need to seek answers from any "Mother, May I?" game. Their children will always be inherently guided, and each step they take will place them on the right path.

Reflection

Consider those persons who played important "mother-like" roles in your life. How can you extend gratefulness to you mother when she appears to interfere with your wishes? In what ways do you learn to find great comfort from the Holy Spirit, knowing that separation from your mother is imminent?

MAY 9
(Y3, D19)

Lessons from Mom

Her children stand and bless her. Her husband praises her.

—Proverbs 31:28 (NLT)

When I was a young child, I used to pick bouquets of dandelions and give them to my mom. Years later, I went to college, and I would send my mother roses because I thought she deserved them. I had no way to pay for those roses, so days later, the florist would send her the bill. In present times, I enjoy the opportunity to buy her flowering plants that can be placed outside the window of her home where she can enjoy them for the entire growing season. It never seemed to matter whether they were taken off of the front lawn or who paid the bill; she always seemed to appreciate the thought. "No one loves you like your mom," she would say. And, you know, I believe that to be true. There is a special bond between a mother and her child to which only she can attest.

A woman who delivered a child in 1952 when she was a teenager kept the secret for fifty years. She spent most of that time, however, trying to find him, knowing that he was in her thoughts every day and wondering if she was ever in his. Born in an era when teen pregnancies were not spoken about, the son she had out of wedlock was given up for adoption against her will. The true story became a book, *The Lost Child of Philomena Lee.* Later in 2013, it was released as a movie simply entitled *Philomena.* One of the prevailing themes of the narrative is that a mother never forgets her child. How could she? For scripture tells us, "You made all the delicate, inner parts of my body and knit me together in my mother's womb" (Psalm 139:13 NLT), the place where God's unique creation begins.

If you take the time to study various women in the Bible, there is much to learn about motherhood. Sarah, the wife of Abraham, teaches us that it's important to have a sense of humor. When she was in her nineties, she became aware that she would have a child. "So she laughed silently to herself and said, 'How could a worn-out woman like me enjoy such pleasure, especially when my master—my husband—is also so old?'" (Genesis 18:12 NLT). By her experience, mothers should understand that through faith and trust, God will keep His promises. Abraham and Sarah's son,

Isaac, married Rebekah from whom we can learn much about conflict. "And the LORD told her, 'The sons in your womb will become two nations. From the very beginning, the two nations will be rivals. One nation will be stronger than the other; and your older son will serve your younger son'" (Genesis 25:23 NLT). And then there was Jochebed, the mother of Moses, through whom we come to appreciate that there are times when children need to be protected. After Pharaoh ordered the killing of all Israelite male babies, she hid Moses for a time but later made a small boat for him and placed him in the reeds along the bank of the Nile River. There he was found by Pharoah's daughter and eventually reunited with his very own mother to care for him (Exodus 1:22–2:10). You know how that one turned out.

As the New Testament unfolds, we find Jesus' mother, Mary, providing the gift of encouragement at the wedding feast in Cana. "When the wine was gone, Jesus' mother said to him, 'They have no more wine.' 'Woman, why do you involve me?' Jesus replied. 'My hour has not yet come'" (John 2:3–4 NIV). Here, Mary simply makes Jesus aware of a need, and He performs His first miracle. Moms are the first important teachers in our lives, and early childhood training is frequently passed from one generation to another. The Apostle Paul writes "I am reminded of your sincere faith, which first lived in your grandmother Lois and in your mother Eunice and, I am persuaded, now lives in you also" (2 Timothy 1:5 NIV). Moms play with and read to us, make our favorite dessert, kiss away the pain from a tumble or a fall, and teach us our first words which often include bedtime prayers. There are still times when my day is done and I have finished my nighttime devotions that I conclude with "Now I lay me down to sleep, I pray the Lord my soul to keep. If I die before I wake; I pray the Lord my soul to take." It's perhaps one of the best lessons my mom ever taught me.

Reflection

If you are a young mother, how can you use the examples above to inspire you? If you are fortunate that your mother is living, how might you honor her (Ephesians 6:2–3)? If you no longer have your mother, are there ways you might serve someone else's, respecting Jesus' very own words from the cross, "Woman, here is your son" and to the disciple "Here is your mother" (John 19:26–27 NIV)?

MAY 10
(Y4, D19)

Mom and the Kitchen Table

And let us consider how to stir up one another to love and good works,
not neglecting to meet together, as is the habit of some, but encouraging
one another, and all the more as you see the Day drawing near.

—Hebrews 10:24–25 (ESV)

When I invite a group of friends for dinner, I usually give them an arrival time that is about thirty minutes ahead of the planned meal serving. This often sets me up for a second invitation: "Please get out of my kitchen." I usually say it more diplomatically, but on occasion, I'm sure those were my exact words. What happens is that when my guests arrive, they inevitably end up gathering there as I am trying to put the final touches on the meal. Maybe it's the smell of the food or possibly because they just want to chat with the host, but there is something about that kitchen which tends to attract people. In fact, one of my usual invitees insists that after dinner, we need to stay gathered around the table for good conversation. That dining table has ended up being so much more than a flat surface for serving food.

An inviting place, to be sure, the old kitchen table has provided an area where families often gather to connect for many activities. It's a welcoming space because it's a great place to simply be with Mom. It is where younger children gather to play games and older ones congregate to do their homework under her watchful eye. When warm cookies come out of the oven, you may be lucky enough to get a sampling with a glass of cold milk. If one of the ladies from the neighborhood stops by, undoubtedly, it is there where she will serve a cup of steeped tea or fresh brewed coffee. Mom did a lot of informal counseling around that kitchen table. With her heart, love of family, and faith in God, it was better than a psychiatrist's couch to dissect the lessons of life.

Credited with the founding of the evangelical movement known as Methodism, John Wesley confirmed that his mother was the person who had influenced him the most. Spending time with a different one of her young children each evening of the week, Wesley is said to have once written to her as an adult, "Oh, Mother, what I'd give for a Thursday evening." He obviously would have embraced the Old Testament writing, "My son, keep your father's command and do not forsake your mother's teaching. Bind them always on your heart; fasten them around your neck. When you walk, they will guide you; when you sleep, they will watch over you; when you awake, they will speak to you" (Proverbs 6:20–22). A true mother hangs with us through thick and thin as did Mary, the mother of Jesus, who stood at the base of the cross to be a witness of His crucifixion (John 19:25). American author and historian, Washington Irving, once wrote:

> A mother is the truest friend we have, when trials, heavy and sudden, fall upon us; when adversity takes the place of prosperity; when friends who rejoice with us in our sunshine, desert us when troubles thicken around us, still will she cling to us, and endeavor by her kind precepts and counsels to dissipate the clouds of darkness, and cause peace to return to our hearts.

If you were fortunate to have a good mom, you will undoubtedly count her as one of the greatest treasures of your life. Growing up, I remember my own listening to Paul Harvey on the radio each day. He was talking about her and others like her when he spoke these words: "And on the sixth day, God looked down on Adam in his planned paradise and said, 'I need a nurturer.' So God made a mother. God said, 'I need someone who feels deeply and loves fiercely, whose tears flow just as abundantly as their laughter, whose heart is as warm as their ability to guide and set limits is strong. I need someone whose influence on those that they nurture is eternal.' So God made a mother." My mother would have never asked me to leave her kitchen. She was always happiest when I played at her feet and created clutter on her table which she could help sort out while she kept an eye on me. The table might not always have been set perfectly, but the loving embrace which surrounded it was always served with perfection.

Reflection

In what way has your mother influenced your life and, through you, the lives of future generations? If you are not a mother or were not blessed with a mother as described above, are there ways in which you might be able to create this sort of loving persona for those younger persons whom you encounter along your life's journey?

MAY 11
(Y5, D19)

Somebody's Mother

Charm is deceptive, and beauty is fleeting; but a woman who fears the LORD is to be praised.

—Proverbs 31:30 (NIV)

Whether it was her homemade apple pie, freshly baked chocolate chip cookies, or even that store-bought dessert, she knew that it was your favorite. And it would be there to top off a meal or brighten your day just when you needed a special treat. As a little kid, when you fell on the playground, no one could kiss away your "boo-boos" like your mom. She knew exactly how to read you to sleep each night and could scare away monsters from under the bed when you woke up later from a bad dream. And as you grew older and thought there were times that you didn't need her input or advice, it only took a disconcerting event in your life to realize that she was a great source of comfort. The contribution of mothers has not dwindled in importance over time and is never needed more than today. A good mother sets the standard for the lives she touches. The wisdom that she shares is often beyond her years and no doubt enriched by generations of mothers before her.

While distance sometimes separates mothers and her offspring, children are often grateful for substitutes who pick up the slack for their inability to attentively be present. I was recently hugged by the out-of-town daughter of a lady whom I have assisted on various occasions. I have been blessed to be able to do small acts of kindness for her, recognizing that if it was my own mother, I would be appreciative. Over a century ago, a poet by the name of Mary Dow Brine wrote several verses about a young boy who was going home from school on a wintry day while having a good time with his buddies. They passed a woman "old and gray" who seemed a bit timid about crossing the busy street. When one of the boys paused and offered to assist, "her aged hand on his strong young arm she placed" as he guided her safely to the other side with a happy feeling of satisfaction about having done so. He reflects:

> She's somebody's mother, boys, you know,
> for all she's aged, and poor and slow;
> And someone, some time, may lend a hand

to help my mother—you understand?
If ever she's old and poor and gray,
And her own dear boy so far away.

Although I first heard this entire poem recited from memory by my grandmother in my child-hood, its words continue to have relevance even today.

Jesus offered us an example of providing for His mother while He was dying on the cross. "When Jesus saw his mother there, and the disciple whom he loved standing nearby, he said to her, 'Woman, here is your son,' and to the disciple, 'Here is your mother.' From that time on, this disciple took her into his home" (John 19:26–27 NIV). His mother was likely so consumed with His suffer-ing that she hadn't even considered what would become of her. But one of His last earthly concerns was to ask His beloved friend John to take care of her and regard her as his own. John must have felt privileged by this request. No different was the honor paid to Naomi by her daughter-in-law, Ruth, centuries before. When Ruth's husband died, Naomi encouraged her to return to the home of her own mother. Feeling an obligation to remain with and provide for Naomi, "Ruth replied, 'Don't ask me to leave you and turn back. Wherever you go, I will go; wherever you live, I will live. Your peo-ple will be my people, and your God will be my God'" (Ruth 1:16 NLT). As a result, Ruth's loyalty enabled her to remarry and give birth to a son who became grandfather to King David. Likewise, Naomi had a direct hand in the raising of the child, imparting her faith and good character into the lineage into which Jesus would be born.

Abraham Lincoln said, "All that I am or hope to be, I owe to my angel mother." Our mother is that female presence who has nurtured us and has been there to comfort us through the difficult times of life. While her role will evolve over time, the love, care, and encouragement that she shares will never cease. Even when she physically departs from this life, her influence continues to be part of who you are and always will be. Jesus would ask that we serve those have made such an impact on our world. For when we see a lady who seems to be struggling, our arm should be extended to assist. For, in all likelihood, she may have been blessed by God to be "somebody's mother."

Reflection

How can you encourage better respect for mothers of all generations? In what ways might you draw from the examples of Jesus and Ruth with regard to their loyalty to the mother figures? Is there a mother you know whose child is not near to whom you might be helpful? How might you be a listening ear and counsel someone you know who is struggling to have a positive relationship with their mother?

MAY 12
(Y6, D19)

Do Not Give Up

But the one who endures to the end will be saved.

—Matthew 24:13 (NLT)

At the beginning of World War II, Hitler invaded Holland, Belgium, and the Netherlands. Winston Churchill, known for his military leadership ability, was appointed British Prime Minister on that very occasion—May 10, 1940. He formed an all-party coalition and quickly won popular support. In the first year of his administration, Britain stood alone against Nazi Germany, but Churchill told his country and the world, "We shall never surrender." In their book, *God and Churchill*, Jonathan Sandys (Churchill's great-grandson) and journalist Wallace Henley conclude that despite his early years as an agnostic, he came to personally believe in God. They relate a story in which he narrowly escaped a bomb while on a walk with his bodyguard in St. James Park in London during the 1940 blitz. Churchill is said to have told his companion not to worry, that there was someone else who was looking after him. He went on to lead Britain to victory and grew to become one of the twentieth century's most significant figures. He later made a statement (frequently misquoted), "Never give in, never give in, never, never, never, never—in nothing, great or small, large or petty—never give in except to convictions of honor and good sense." His glowing courage, clarity of purpose, and perseverance made him an admired leader who lived to be ninety.

Fifty-four years to the day when Churchill became Prime Minister, it was on May 10, 1994, that Nelson Rolihlahla Mandela was sworn in as the first Black president of South Africa. Similar to Churchill, Mandela said, "A winner is a dreamer who never gives up." He spent twenty-seven years of his life as a political prisoner of the South African government, the first eighteen of which were under brutal conditions. However, Mandela's resolve remained unbroken. When his release was ordered in 1990, he promoted reconciliation efforts between the races. This led to negotiations with the minority in power, an end to apartheid, and the establishment of a multiracial government, resulting in the country's first free election. Mandela's message as President four years later was one of forgiveness. While he didn't say much publicly about his personal beliefs, ministers who knew him say he was a man of deep faith. The ideals for which he is most remembered are indeed contained in scripture. An example is found in this statement: "As I walked out the door toward the gate that would lead to my freedom, I knew if I didn't leave my bitterness and hatred behind, I'd still be in prison." It is amazing that after a lifetime of hardship and persecution, he was around for ninety-five years and remained a global advocate for peace and social justice until his death.

While at times each of these men could be a controversial figure, both had moments that concealed everything else and made the world a better place. Their lives challenge us to persevere, regardless of the odds we may be facing. Jesus shares the Parable of the Persistent Widow (Luke 18:1–8) who is poor and powerless but who nevertheless persists in nagging a corrupt, powerful person to grant justice for her. Jesus focuses the parable on the fact that we are to "always pray and never give up" (Luke 18:1 NLT). One can conclude from His teaching that if persistence pays off with a corrupt human of limited power, how much more will it pay off with a just God of infinite power? It serves as an encouragement for Christians to persevere in their faith in spite of the odds. It provides hope that even in the midst of what may appear to be injustice, justice may be done. We must never give up hope and never stop working for the greater good. God can heal wounds, even in an unethical world. Suddenly, an apartheid regime crumbles or peace triumphs over war. This parable suggests that God is the unseen actor as Jesus asks, "Will not God bring about justice for his chosen ones, who cry out to him day and night?" (Luke 18:7 NIV).

Applying perseverance in a positive way is not an easy task for most of us. In a world where instant gratification is the prevailing expectation, it is difficult to be patient and accept that resolution may not be immediate. The Christian must continue to walk with God by our side while unyielding in the journey of serving him with whatever talents and abilities He has gifted us. "And let us not grow weary of doing good, for in due season we will reap, if we do not give up" (Galatians 6:9 ESV). If our motives are pure and our convictions are honorable, then God will indeed hear and answer the cry of those who love Him.

Reflection

Can you recall a situation in your life when you had to persevere for a long time before you found resolution? Were there emotions or hardships you had to endure? How can you use your experience in helping others who are struggling for a solution while growing impatient or discouraged in their wait?

MAY 13
(Y7, D19)

Becoming a Complete Person

May you experience the love of Christ, though it is too great to understand fully. Then you will be made complete with all the fullness of life and power that comes from God.

—Ephesians 3:19 (NLT)

In modern society, the concepts of self-image, self-esteem, and self-love have become hot topics and the subjects of much discussion. It is not unusual to find expressions of low self-worth. An example is the following that once appeared in an advice column posted by a woman who stated that she had won various academic awards and held three degrees. She wrote:

> I am now 48, the mother of two children with special needs. I have spent most of my life being their caregiver and a full-time homemaker. I feel disappointed somehow, as though I wasted my talent. I don't know how to describe it. I feel as though I was given this talent and I didn't use it to the fullest. Do I have a responsibility to use my gifts?

It was signed "Really Not Conceited." The response:

> You haven't let anyone down. You've raised two kids and made a loving home. So please stop beating yourself up for not having pursued all of your dreams yet… It's about honoring the part of yourself that wants to shine more light onto the world… You won't be satisfied until you do.

My first reaction to this letter was that the lady who penned it was very selfish. A woman who has been given the gift of two children, even if they do have special needs, should be grateful for the blessing of motherhood. I am not sure the columnist helps her, as she concludes that she really needs to continue to find herself and be all she can be.

Someone once wrote:

> My mother gave me life and never asked for anything in return. That is her secret you know, always giving without any expectations. She is as constant as the sunrise, the moon, the stars, and I count on her. She helps me find my way through the years and makes me laugh while doing it. There are some things only a mother can do.

I wish I knew that "someone" because I agree with her. When it comes to being a good mother, degrees and academic awards don't matter. One of Jesus' chosen understood this when he wrote: "Each of you should use whatever gift you have received to serve others, as faithful stewards of God's grace in its various forms" (1 Peter 4:10 NIV). This passage certainly encourages us to use our God-given gifts for His glory, not our own. Anyone who feels that they have existed as "just a mother and a housewife" is simply missing the point. The Apostle Paul encouraged us to "Be devoted to one another in love. Honor one another above yourselves" (Romans 12:10 NIV). For him, that was the "be all and end all" of finding true happiness while serving God.

The problem is that we are living in a day in which we have become lovers of self. Our society has grown to be fixated on terminology such as self-actualization and self-fulfillment. When we do this, we are practicing self-centeredness. As we strive to lift ourselves up, we fail to exalt God and His plan regarding who we are. While it is always important to utilize our abilities and talents, we must keep in mind who provided those in the first place. We must affirm: "It is not that we think we are qualified to do anything on our own. Our qualification comes from God" (2 Corinthians 3:5 NLT). Mature believers in Christ know who they are, why they are here, where their strength lies, where they are going, and look forward to their ultimate destiny and reward. When they achieve this level of understanding, they will no longer be dependent on man's standards for success, the response of others for their happiness, or the need to satisfy any craving for a personal sense of identity. When we comprehend and accept by faith the value God places on our lives, we will find fulfillment like never before. Therefore, my friends, "Don't think you are better than you really are. Be honest in your evaluation of yourselves, measuring yourselves by the faith God has given us" (Romans 12:3 NLT). Then and only then will we even come close to following what He had in mind for us all along—that of becoming a complete person.

Reflection

Describe in your own words the biblical concept of self-image. How does this differ from your actual self-image? In what areas of your life do you use incorrect standards as a measurement of your effectiveness and success? Do you live daily with an ongoing confidence of God's love for you? Do you demonstrate it to those around you with an attitude of hopefulness? How might you apply the words of the psalmist who said, "You will show me the way of life, granting me the joy of your presence and the pleasures of living with you forever" (Psalm 16:11 NLT) to help another who is struggling?

MAY 14
(Y1, D20)

Having Truly Seen and Heard

My ears had heard of you but now my eyes have seen you.

—Job 42:5 (NIV)

No doubt you have at one time or another been criticized for not listening. When you were a teenager, you were probably told when asked to look for something that you failed to see what was right in front of you. Even as adults, we will sometimes overlook things because we are preoccupied and not focused. Our brain meshes with our vision and hearing to create a conscious understanding, and when we lack regard for one or the other, we set ourselves up to be labeled as unthoughtful or inconsiderate. Along with the influence of the other senses, seeing and hearing combine to assist us in navigating through the world. Our personal history, however, shows that we are often led by misperceptions. Add to that the increasingly prevailing attitude that we are often expected to conform to what others believe, we are afforded little tolerance when we attempt to develop our own sense of individuality. "Blessed are those who don't feel guilty for doing something they have decided is right" (Romans 14:22 NLT).

The religious leaders in Jesus' time often acted with contempt. To contest their doctrines, Jesus gave indication that many of them were both spiritually deaf and blind. When asked by His disciples why He spoke to the people in parables, His answer was simply this:

> To those who listen to my teaching, more understanding will be given, and they will have an abundance of knowledge. But for those who are not listening, even what little understanding they have will be taken away from them. That is why I use these parables. For they look, but they don't really see. They hear, but they don't really listen or understand. (Matthew 13:12–13 NLT)

It's as if He was saying, "Those who reject me are spiritually blind because they automatically cast off any understanding of who I am. The truth sounds foolish to them, and if they hear it, they do not comprehend that it is God's truth and therefore fail to take it to heart."

A good case in point is the relationship between King David and the Prophet Nathan, who challenged his self-awareness. Having been sent by God, Nathan tells David the story of a rich man who took a prize possession from a poor man and used it for his own purposes (2 Samuel 12:2–4). Upon hearing the story, "David burned with anger against the man and said to Nathan, 'As surely as the LORD lives, the man who did this must die!'" (2 Samuel 12:5 NIV). Although he heard the words of the prophet, he failed to hear the truth of those words. That is until Nathan confronted him.

> You are that man! The LORD, the God of Israel, says: I anointed you king of Israel and saved you from the power of Saul. I gave you your master's house and his wives and the kingdoms of Israel and Judah. And if that had not been enough, I would have given you much, much more. Why, then, have you despised the word of the LORD and done this horrible deed? For you have murdered Uriah the Hittite with the sword of the Ammonites and stolen his wife. (2 Samuel 12:7–9 NIV)

"Then David confessed to Nathan, 'I have sinned against the LORD.' Nathan replied, 'Yes, but the LORD has forgiven you, and you won't die for this sin'" (2 Samuel 12:13 NLT).

Each of us have times in our life when we are blinded by and deafened to God's truth because we have become subject to the deception that is in the world. The goal of the Great Deceiver (Satan) is to devour the weak who fall prey to temptation, fear, loneliness, worry, and depression. Jesus said: "Your eye is like a lamp that provides light for your body. When your eye is healthy, your whole body is filled with light. But when your eye is unhealthy, your whole body is filled with darkness. And if the light you think you have is actually darkness, how deep that darkness is!" (Matthew 6:22–23 NLT). Every day, our thoughts and concentrations are bombarded with rather dark ideas from print, electronic, and social media as well as those around us. It's easy to be deceived, unless we take the opportunity to renew our mind. God wants us to listen more intently for His voice and also to see with greater clarity the blessings He has placed right in front of us, including His Word. When we do this, our light will shine for the world (Matthew 5:16), and those around us will know, without a doubt, that we have truly seen and heard.

Reflection

Are there ways you might consider changing some of the sources of what you daily see and hear to better reflect God's Word and consistency with His character? How can we be challenged by one of Jesus' apostles who said: "Resist him, standing firm in the faith, because you know that the family of believers throughout the world is undergoing the same kind of sufferings" (1 Peter 5:9 NIV)? How might you help another who are not thinking objectively based upon the sources for what they see and hear?

MAY 15
(Y2, D20)

Retaliation

Do not be overcome by evil, but overcome evil with good.

—Romans 12:21 (NIV)

Late one summer evening in a hill county of Texas, a weary truck driver pulled his rig into an all-night truck stop. He was tired and hungry. The waitress had just served him when three tough-looking, leather-jacketed motorcyclists decided to give him a hard time. Not only did they verbally abuse him, one of them grabbed the hamburger off his plate, another took a handful of his French fries, and the third picked up his coffee and began to drink it. This trucker did not respond as one might expect. Instead, he calmly rose, picked up his check, walked to the front, put the check and his money on the cash register, and exited the establishment. The waitress followed him to put the money in the drawer and watched out the door as the big truck drove away into the night. When she returned, one of the cyclists said to her, "Well, he's not much of a man, is he?"

She replied, "I don't know about that, but he sure isn't much of a truck driver. He just ran over three motorcycles on his way out of the parking lot."

While some say that "revenge is sweet," others will tell you that in certain circumstances, retaliation is most certain.

Retaliation is just what was expected from the Philadelphia Phillies when their high-paid outfielder Bryce Harper got hit in the face by a 97 mph fastball in April 2021. Cardinals' pitcher Génesis Cabrera drilled Harper and another Phillies teammate, showing total lack of command on his first two pitches. After Harper was removed from the game, the play-by-play announcers deliberated in a lengthy discussion about how and when retaliation would occur, convinced that there would be. When Harper's mom heard that her son would be okay, she told Bryce, "You must have angels with you tonight." The morning after, Harper went through a battery of tests confirming that, but he did not have a concussion and was left without any bruises on his face. But rather than promoting some form of retaliation, Harper made sure to check in on the well-being of the Cardinals' reliever. He did so by sending a message in which he stated that he knew the twenty-four-year-old lefty didn't try to hit him intentionally. The Cardinals' manager told reporters, "Whoever's a fan of Bryce Harper, whoever has children that are fans of Bryce Harper, support that guy because what he sent over in a message today was completely a class act."

Retaliation is when we take matters out of God's hands and insist on fixing things ourselves. All of us have been wronged and have had a desire to get back at the one responsible, but two wrongs never make a right. When anyone threatens our rights or takes what we think belongs to us, we are inclined to become revengeful. When we feel hurt, it can seem like retaliation will make us feel better. We believe we are entitled to the last word, subscribing to the old adage, "Don't get mad, get even!" But an older saying from Jesus tells us, "You have heard that it was said, 'Eye for eye, and tooth for tooth.' But I tell you, do not resist an evil person. If anyone slaps you on the right cheek, turn to them the other cheek also" (Matthew 5:38–39 NIV). While it is highly doubtful that Bryce Harper would have desired to have his other cheek hit, he was willing to extend an act of reconciliation rather than retaliation. And, bottom line, isn't that what we are challenged to do when we sign up to be followers of Christ?

Getting even is a natural response to being wronged, but what then? God calls us to live above our natural responses. We do not win people to Jesus by beating them up on them. We were not won that way, so neither do we become more like Christ by retaliating. The Apostle Paul said:

> Never pay back evil with more evil. Do things in such a way that everyone can see you are honorable. Do all that you can to live in peace with everyone. Dear friends, never take revenge. Leave that to the righteous anger of God. For the Scriptures say, "I will take revenge; I will pay them back," says the LORD. (Romans 12:17–19 NLT)

God's purpose is to show His grace through His people. His purpose is to touch people's hearts by His mercy and to develop our character by conforming us to the nature of His Son. Just as He demonstrated holiness through Him, He offers to empower us through His Holy Spirit, thereby enabling us to rise above our selfish instincts. As disciples of Christ, we must look for ways to love our perceived enemies rather than retaliate. In doing so, we can be certain that God will find a way to bless us.

Reflection

Are you sometimes tempted to take matters into your own hands? What is one specific instance where you felt you had been wronged? Did you wish that you could retaliate? How would God desire to work through you in sharing His Good News with the person who hurt you? Are there ways you can demonstrate to others that retaliation isn't the only available option, especially for believers?

MAY 16
(Y3, D20)

911, What's Your Emergency?

This poor man called, and the Lord heard him; He saved him out of all his troubles.

—Psalm 34:6 (NIV)

The story has been passed down through the years in our family that there was a time when those who needed a meal would show up at the home of my ancestors and others like them. In those days, there was not a lot of homelessness in our town. But there were those who roamed from place to place, often getting there by hopping aboard the freight trains. When they would get to the towns, they would locate markings positioned in front of the homes by others who had passed before them and had been given a free meal simply for the asking. It was a different time then when you were pretty sure that those who showed up on your front porch for food was all they wanted. In that era, you didn't have to fear for your safety, and you knew that the motives of those who asked for the handout were most likely pure. That day has, unfortunately, long since passed.

Unable to show up anywhere asking for food, an eighty-one-year-old North Carolina man recently returned home from the hospital after spending the past few months there, receiving cancer treatments. When he found himself in a weakened state with nothing to eat and no one to help, he simply dialed 911. He could have been told that his call was not an emergency. However, on the other end of the phone was an empathetic operator who knew what it was like to be hungry, took pity on the man, and promised to bring him some groceries. Together with some police officers, she personally dropped off the food and said she never thought twice about doing so. The recipient later indicated that he had felt blessed, stating, "I thought, Jesus, you answered those prayers." Perhaps the 911 operator had heard the story of the sheep and the goats.

Shortly before Jesus was killed, He told a parable. He stated that at the time of judgment, the people will be gathered and separated in a similar manner which a shepherd would do with his sheep and goats. In this case, those persons who are righteous will inherit eternal life. He illustrates in this way: "For I was hungry and you gave me something to eat, I was thirsty and you gave me something to drink, I was a stranger and you invited me in, I needed clothes and you clothed me, I was sick and you looked after me, I was in prison and you came to visit me" (Matthew 25:35–36 NIV). To those who did not do these things, the unrighteous, "he will answer, 'I tell you the truth, when you refused to help the least of these my brothers and sisters, you were refusing to help me'" (Matthew 25:45 NLT). This latter group would receive "eternal punishment."

We may have found ourselves on either side of the 911 call. We may not have responded to a request because of the current state of the world. We may have been skeptical that someone may be using us or even felt threatened for our own well-being. In such cases, it can become easy to look the other way. Jesus would say to us, "Give to the one who asks you, and do not turn away from the one who would who wants to borrow from you" (Matthew 5:42 NIV). Having this knowledge, we should make every effort to find a way to help those in need. "From everyone who has been given much, much will be demanded; and from the one who has been entrusted with much, much more will be asked" (Luke 12:48 NIV).

Just as realistically, there are those moments in life when *we* are the needy ones who are distressed, discouraged, and hopeless. In these situations when we feel we have run out of options, know that God is waiting for our 911 call. He's available 24-7-365, and He never gets tired of our pleas for help or comfort. He does not need a street address or a GPS to find us, and He is there with us, even when we can't feel His presence. So, my friend, "Don't worry about anything; instead, pray about everything. Tell God what you need, and thank him for all he has done" (Philippians 4:6 NLT). Connecting with God is more than just a safety net or an intervention at a time of crisis. It is an open line and an assurance that wherever our journey takes us, there is someone on the other end with our very best interests at heart.

Reflection

Are there times that you have felt uneasy, reaching out to others in time of need? Is it possible to partner with others or an organization to help address those needs? If you have found yourself to be that person in need, in what ways do you seek God's direction for your life?

MAY 17
(Y4, D20)

One Who Prayed Us Through

I urge you, brothers and sisters, by our Lord Jesus Christ and by the love of
the Spirit, to join me in my struggle by praying to God for me.

—Romans 15:30 (NIV)

I had prayed for her many months before I ever met her. Julie had seen more serious moments in her life than most of her peers in their early teens. Over the past year, she had recovered from the removal of her pancreas at a major medical center for children. Her aunt had told me about the procedure and asked me to pray for her niece. Knowing at the time that this surgical procedure was uncommon, I was honored to be introduced to her when she came to my town to visit her grandparents. While she was there, I was astounded to hear her play several classical piano pieces. Now quite a number of years later, I found myself in attendance at her grandfather's funeral. I had continued the entire time to keep Julie on my prayer list, knowing that complications could have easily developed. I asked her aunt how she was doing. As it turned out, Julie was well, still playing the piano, and in college. While she was unable to be present at the funeral, the aunt introduced me to her sister (Julie's mom), reminding her that I had been "one of those who prayed us through" that touch-and-go period that just seemed like yesterday.

The act of praying for others is known as intercessory prayer. Both the Old and New Testaments contain wonderful examples. Daniel petitioned God on behalf of his people in a lengthy prayer found in the ninth chapter of the book he authored. Acknowledging their sinfulness, he stated: "We do not make requests of you because we are righteous, but because of your great mercy" (Daniel 9:18 NIV). The Apostle Paul prayed for the people he served. To the church at Ephesus, he wrote that he remembers them in his prayers, asking that God "may give you the Spirit of wisdom and revelation, so that you may know him better" (Ephesians 1:17 NIV). In the midst of His greatest trial, Jesus prayed passionately for His disciples and for us. "I do not pray for these alone, but also for those who will believe in Me through their word; that they all may be one, as You, Father, are in Me, and I in

You; that they also may be one in Us, that the world may believe that You sent Me" (John 17:20–21 NKJV). True intercessory prayer pursues God and results in His glorification, not our own.

One must question that if even those who claim to be Christians would engage themselves in prayer more often, what a better place this world might become. Instead, we grow to be self-absorbed in our digital communications and realize that the simple answers we may find there are not the life-affirming substance that soothes the soul. If you have an iPhone, you have no doubt been introduced to Siri. More than just a mechanical response common to some computer programs, it is derived from actual human voice recordings in many languages, both male and female. Siri will retrieve the latest game score for you or show you the best route home. Want tomorrow's weather forecast or curious where the stock market closed today? Just ask Siri. A promotion of the personal assistant says, "Talk to Siri as you would to a friend." There are times, however, when you discover that there are times your newfound friend in unable to answer your request. Then you receive the response, "I don't understand what you are asking." Conversely, our one true friend, God, always hears and understands our heartfelt petitions.

Mother Teresa once said, "Prayer is not asking. Prayer is putting oneself in the hands of God, at His disposition, and listening to His voice in the depth of our hearts." Just as the Holy Spirit enters our hearts and intercedes for us in accordance with God's will, we are to intercede for one another. Intercessory prayer reflects God's own character of outgoing love and mercy. Praying for others helps us to think beyond ourselves and to mature in compassion. Paul exhorts us "that petitions, prayers, intercession and thanksgiving be made for all people—for kings and all those in authority, that we may live peaceful and quiet lives in all godliness and holiness" (1 Timothy 2:1–2 NIV). What a wonderful privilege we have in being able to come boldly before the throne of the Almighty with our prayers and requests and be so humbled when someone says that we are "one of those who prayed us through."

Reflection

Can you recall a time that you prayed for someone to find out later that your prayers helped to make a real difference in their life? Has anyone ever thanked you for prayers on their behalf? If those prayers were answered, did you consider it a privilege and remember to give the credit to God? For what individuals are you being prompted to be in need your prayers today?

MAY 18
(Y5, D20)

The Solid Foundation of Doers

Now that you know these things, you will be blessed if you do them.

—John 13:17 (NIV)

As he stood up to speak at his friend's funeral, he enthusiastically said these words: "Jim always showed up." He went on to explain that his buddy predictably followed up on things he had heard about. If he went to a service club meeting and they had a community event scheduled on that upcoming Saturday, Jim would be there rain or shine. If he became aware that a neighbor was having a difficult time completing a project, he would stop by to offer assistance. When leaders of his church would ask for volunteers, he'd always lend a hand. In those troublesome times when a friend or family member was hurting and needed to feel someone's presence, Jim would always be on hand even if he didn't quite know what to say. He always showed up, and those who had been the benefactors of his presence knew just how much he would be missed. For you see, Jim was a "doer."

The story is told of a pastor who was holding a Bible study at his church. He was teaching about the principles and promises of the scripture. As part of his instruction, he spoke with the participants how to affirm these lessons by personally applying them in their daily lives. He felt like the group had been listening intently, so as the end of the hour was nearing, he decided to review. He asked the question, "Now what do we do with these commands we have been discussing?" The attendees were quiet as one older lady lifted her voice and stated, "Well, I highlighted them all in yellow." Not quite the application the pastor had in mind. James put it this way: "But don't just listen to God's word. You must do what it says. Otherwise, you are only fooling yourselves" (James 1:22 NLT). Some translations imply that if hearing the word is all we do, we are leading a life of deception and our religion will lack worth and significance. James goes on to say, "For if you listen to the word and don't obey, it is like glancing at your face in a mirror. You see yourself, walk away, and forget what you look like" (James 1:23–24 NLT).

Only those who look at the Word and submit to it will be blessed. Those who take only a passing glance and lack concern for how they act are not embracing the opportunity to change and serve.

By using a parable, Jesus illustrates that God's blessing comes from obeying the truth in addition to knowing it.

> Therefore, everyone who hears these words of mine and puts them into practice is like a wise man who built his house on the rock. The rain came down, the streams rose, and the winds blew and beat against that house; yet it did not fall, because it had its foundation on the rock. But everyone who hears these words of mine and does not put them into practice is like a foolish man who built his house on sand. The rain came down, the streams rose, and the winds blew and beat against that house, and it fell with a great crash. (Matthew 7:24–27 NIV)

Being a carpenter, Jesus understood the difference between a well-constructed house and an inferior one. His parable demonstrates the understanding that building a house without a stable foundation is no different than making a life without lasting substance.

As a result, we must choose how we are going to live out our days. Will we identify the principles of a Christian life by filling our Bible with yellow highlights? Or will we take action, be a doer, and demonstrate God's Word in how we act and do for others? Regardless of the storms we face, we will show our trust in Him when we decide to build on a strong foundation. As in the words penned by the hymn lyricist Edward Mote, we will then be able to recite that old familiar refrain, "On Christ, the solid Rock, I stand; All other ground is sinking sand." Decide now to make a conscious effort to become a doer. Don't be a "do as I say" parent; set an example your child will want to emulate. Count your many blessings as you reach out to others who are less fortunate. When you say you will pray for someone, be intentional about doing so. Treat others as you would want to be treated. Speak with kindness, and show forgiveness. Proverbs 24:3 (NIV) reminds us, "By wisdom a house is built, and by understanding it is established." For if you truly are a doer, it will uphold the strength of your foundation.

Reflection

If you were asked to describe your spiritual foundation, would you be more apt to use the words solid rock or sinking sand? Can you recall a time when you personalized and followed God's command and, as a result, received a blessing? How can you begin to apply something God already told you to do through His Word but that you haven't yet implemented?

MAY 19
(Y6, D20)

An Angel on the Battlefield of Life

I myself will tend my sheep and give them a place to lie down in peace, says the Sovereign LORD. I will search for my lost ones who strayed away, and I will bring them safely home again. I will bandage the injured and strengthen the weak.

—Ezekiel 34:15–16 (NLT)

When she was young, Clara Barton was an extremely shy person. The youngest of five children, it was recommended that she become a teacher to overcome her profound inhibitions. She did so in her home state of Massachusetts, later moving to Washington DC where she became the first female clerk at the US Patent Office. Clara wanted to assist with the American Civil War effort as much as she could, initially collecting and dispersing supplies and eventually nursing the wounded. In accord with her own deep desire to help others in need, Clara Barton sacrificed personal well-being to bring healing and comfort to others. Working close to the battlefields, she narrowly escaped death herself many times. It is said that once while tending to a wounded soldier during the Battle of Antietam, she felt her sleeve move as a bullet went through it and killed the man she was treating. In 1865, Clara was appointed by President Abraham Lincoln to "search for missing prisoners of war," helping soldiers separated from the units reunite with those units while also informing families of the fate of missing soldiers. While in Europe in 1870, she worked for the International Red Cross. Upon returning to the United States, she later gathered support for an American branch of the organization which was established on May 21, 1881. Clara Barton was a woman ahead of her time, always prepared for the calls for help that followed disasters. No one could have predicted that God would have created this once shy little girl to become a woman who, years later, would be referred to as the "Angel of the Battlefield."

The American Red Cross received its first US federal charter in 1900. Barton headed the organization into her eighties and died in 1912. These days, a red cross is widely used to designate first aid and medical supplies. Commonly used at the sites of medical and humanitarian relief workers in war zones as well as natural disasters, their service under this symbol of protection has grown to become unquestioned. The Son of God ministered to emotionally wounded and unhealthy sinners and was frequently questioned by those of His day before He would bear His own cross.

> As Jesus was walking along, he saw a man named Matthew sitting at his tax collector's booth. "Follow me and be my disciple," Jesus said to him. So Matthew got up and followed him. Later, Matthew invited Jesus and his disciples to his home as dinner guests, along with many tax collectors and other disreputable sinners. But when the Pharisees saw this, they asked his disciples, "Why does your teacher eat with such scum?" When Jesus heard this, he said, "Healthy people don't need a doctor—sick people do." Then he added, "Now go and learn the meaning of this Scripture: 'I want you to show mercy, not offer sacrifices.' For I have come to call not those who think they are righteous, but those who know they are sinners." (Matthew 9:9–13 NIV)

Jesus is known as the Great Physician offering ultimate healing to a broken world. A doctor cannot help you if you claim to be well, and Jesus cannot help you if you claim to be righteous. The Apostle Paul said that we should "do nothing out of selfish ambition or vain conceit. Rather, in humility value others above yourselves, not looking to your own interests but each of you to the interests of the others" (Philippians 2:3–4 NIV). Jesus is clear that no one is actually righteous. Yet, tragically, there are millions who cover up their bruised souls and act as if they are. Jesus would want you to know that "the doctor is in" for all who acknowledge that they need to see Him. Those who seek His loving care have the privilege of leading others who are spiritually sick to a place of healing and hope. We get to carry the bandages and crutches as we, the walking wounded, continually pursue healing from the one who can truly make us whole. Just as the red cross became the symbol for a humanitarian organization providing aid to those in need, the rugged cross of Calvary represents a Godly sacrifice of salvation for all. He continues to comfort us through His Holy Spirit, a true angel for whatever battles we are facing.

Reflection

Have you found there are times when you need to recognize your own feelings of righteousness and realize that you are, in fact, a sinner? Are you part of any informal groups or organizations that are quick to notice "sick people" around you but who fail to acknowledge your own woundedness? What are some specific ways that you might you challenge others to examine their own self-righteousness?

MAY 20
(Y7, D20)

Making Your Intentions a Reality

Do not withhold good from those who deserve it when it's in your power to help them.

—Proverbs 3:27 (NLT)

My mother often told the story of her mother's way of reaching out to others. When my grandmother heard about someone at the other end of the street who was going through a tough time, she would reach out to these neighbors who, in some cases, she barely knew. If someone lost their job or if the family was struggling in some way, she might make an extra kettle of soup and see that it was delivered to them. It was not untypical in those days that when you heard of someone who had a need, you would just show up. Unfortunately, that principle escapes us today as it would not be expected to do so. In fact, it probably wouldn't even cross our minds. Feeling a sense of commitment is not valued or stressed like it once was. There was a time one would be recognized for perfect attendance at school or work. Now any level of expectation for the same behavior would be unusual. I cannot tell you how many times I have scheduled job interviews for applicants who were a "no show." Persons who decide to just "wing it" regarding employment have little chance of being sensitive in reaching out to others who are in need.

For twenty-one seasons, baseball legend Cal Ripken Jr. took the field day in and day out through all kinds of weather to play in more than 3,000 games for the Baltimore Orioles. The revered shortstop helped to lead his team to victory in the 1983 World Series. On September 6, 1995, Ripken broke Lou Gehrig's formerly unsurpassed fifty-six-year-old record, setting a new mark of 2,131 consecutive games. He then went on to play an additional 501 without a break. Throughout his career, Ripken was admired for his consistency, hard work, and loyalty. In his inspirational book, *Just Show Up*, he claims that simply being there builds good character not only in sports but also establishes an important life practice. He says that "winging it does not sustain success." Instead, he has always subscribed to an old-fashioned sense of doing what was right every single day. No doubt he would agree with the biblical principle, "If anyone, then, knows the good they ought to do and doesn't do it, it is sin for them" (James 4:17 NIV).

Famous people like Ripken may have an impact on our thinking, but we must put this mental motivation into personal practice. If we are Christian, we need to model our actions to imitate what Jesus would do. Consider the emotional state of His followers after His death and how they must have felt when He showed up following His resurrection.

> On the evening of that first day of the week, when the disciples were together, with the doors locked for fear of the Jewish leaders, Jesus came and stood among them and said, "Peace be with you!" After he said this, he showed them his hands and side. The disciples were overjoyed when they saw the Lord. Again Jesus said, "Peace be with you! As the Father has sent me, I am sending you." (John 20:21 NIV)

When Jesus shows up, everything is different. Jesus shows up when things seem hopeless. Secondly, He shows up because he understands the struggles we are facing. Third, but certainly not last in significance, Jesus shows up because he cares, and He wants us to demonstrate that sense of caring to others. The Apostle Paul stated it this way: "Carry each other's burdens, and in this way, you will fulfill the law of Christ" (Galatians 6:2 NIV). "And don't forget to do good and to share with those in need. These are the sacrifices that please God" (Hebrews 13:16 NLT).

So do that thing you know to be right. Make the call, bake that casserole, send that card, ring that doorbell, or put some cash in an envelope and send it anonymously. Reach out in a way that will be practical for you as the giver but also able to be delivered in a spirit that will be comfortable for the receiver as well. If you know someone is hurting and they need to experience the love of Jesus, don't sit back and do nothing because you are uncomfortable or think someone else will. Get over it, my friend. It's what Christ would have you do. By all means, when you feel that nudge, you can be certain He is prompting you that it's time to move forward, show up, and make your intentions a reality.

Reflection

When is the last time someone showed up to help you through a difficult time? Can you recall knowing of a need and later feeling guilty for not helping to fulfill it? Consider someone who you know could benefit from your reaching out to them. Develop a plan to act on this prompting. Consider if there a way that you could effectively involve others or if it would be best to be done alone.

MAY 21
(Y1, D21)

Music to God's Ears

For before he was taken, he was commended as one who pleased God.

—Hebrews 11:5 (NIV)

A friend of mine once told a story about her teenage son who years ago was planning a graduation party at their home for his high school classmates. In addition to the food and pool games, there would most likely be the presence of noise from the raucous crowd and loud music. In consideration for their elderly neighbor, the parents insisted that the teen drop by a few days prior to alert her as to what she might expect. In a half-hearted attempt to apologize for the anticipated would-be-commotion, there was a pause in the conversation. The usually congenial neighbor looked directly at the boy and said, "Just when did you say this party is going to be?"

Slightly hesitant, the youth politely responded, "Saturday evening, starting around eight." The lady, then into her nineties, got a twinkle in her eye and responded, "Oh good. I'll want to be sure to open the windows so I can hear the music."

Relieved, the soon-to-be graduate learned a life-lesson that day and captured a beautiful memory of an older friend and neighbor. Having now passed, her epitaph might well read "Enjoyed the music of life through her many years."

Each year, during the Memorial Day holiday, many will visit cemeteries. As they place flowers on the graves of remembered loved ones, they may notice an epitaph or two. For those who have developed an interest in tracing their ancestry, they too may find themselves led to the gravestones of their descendants in order to collect information. There they will find two dates: one for the date of birth and the other indicating a date of death. These are commonly separated by a dash. Regardless of how long the person lived, one has to wonder about the totality of the life represented by that simple dash. The beginning date and the ending date are not as important as how the years were spent in between. On older tombstones, the "in-between" is occasionally underscored by a short phrase honoring the deceased person. While it has to be difficult to capture the essence of a person life in a one-line statement, sometimes, a few words like "Gardening in Heaven" or "Safely Home" is all that really needs to be said.

Epitaph inscriptions have evolved over the years. Sometimes they are comical, like that of legendary talk show host Merv Griffin which reads "Stay tuned. I will not be right back." At times, they signify something from the person's life. For instance, the epitaph on the tombstone of famous singer and film actor Frank Sinatra reads "The Best Is Yet to Come," taken from the title of one of his greatest hits. One should not find it surprising that on the marker of the celebrated preacher and activist Martin Luther King Jr., there is a quote from his famous "I Have a Dream" speech. The words reflect lines from a chorus to a classic spiritual, "Free at last, free at last, Thank God Almighty, I'm free at last." At times, epitaphs have a religious connotation containing frequently used passages of scripture. Examples include "Well done, my good and faithful servant" (Matthew 25:21 NLT), "Whoever believes in him should not perish but have eternal life" (John 3:16 ESV), and "To live is Christ and to die is gain" (Philippians 1:21 NIV).

The once shepherd boy who was called to be King David became known as a man after God's own heart. God testified as such (Acts 13:22). What a wonderful way to be remembered. Did you ever consider how your life might be summed up in just a few words? When someone dies, it often becomes apparent where their life priorities were. There are times when I read an obituary that I find out far more about a person than I really wanted to know. For the Christian, what a tribute it would be if serving Jesus had a place in those conversations. Like David, we must realize that we are placed here for a limited time in His service, not for personal pleasure. For "when David had served God's purpose in his own generation, he fell asleep" (Acts 13:36 NIV). There is nothing more inspirational than what is spoken about those who followed Jesus during their days here on earth. For those of us who remain, we have assurance that they are now celebrating eternal life with Him. And in the end, that has to simply be music to God's ears.

Reflection

What do you think those who survive you would write as an epitaph representing your life? What kind of impact are you having on your generation? When you leave this walk of life, what kind of personal and permanent inspiration would you like to leave as a trail for others to follow? If you would be honest enough to examine your life and admit that you haven't had the kind of positive influence that you would like to have, what steps might you start making to motivate you in that direction?

MAY 22

(Y2, D21)

Pretense, Popularity, and Passion

For God is working in you, giving you the desire and the power to do what pleases him.

—Philippians 2:13 (NLT)

I don't know about you, but I have a difficult time keeping up with fashion trends. Denim is a great example. You may recall baggy jeans or, in contrast, those labeled as tight or low-rise. I personally favor just regular old blue jeans. Patched jeans, frayed cuffs, and lightweight jeans were popular for a time, and faded, acid, and stone-washed eventually disappeared. Straight legs are common, but may remember a time when denim was flared and embellished. Past promotors of jean brands would testify over the years that "nothing will come between me and my Calvin's," at least until Jordache and Tommy Hilfiger came along. Button-fly jeans instead of a zipper closure were introduced in the 1950s, and they trended once again in the 1990s, courtesy of Levi's. Trying to stay in touch with jean styles is enough to make you a little distressed, but then that's a type as well; you know, the ripped ones. Fashion trends come and go, but denim jeans are one item of clothing that are likely to remain a staple in our wardrobe. While wearing them might not be acceptable in every situation, they have become much more mainstream.

King David got in trouble with his wife for wearing the wrong kind of garment. It was on the occasion of the return of the Ark of the Covenant to Jerusalem that he found himself to be in a state of ecstatic joy. David's wife, Michal (daughter of his predecessor King Saul), condemned his celebratory leaping and dancing. She was embarrassed at his lack of proper etiquette, feeling that his actions and attire were beneath his dignity as King. In a sarcastic rebuke of her husband, she said: "How the king of Israel has distinguished himself today, going around half-naked in full view of the slave girls of his servants as any vulgar fellow would!" (2 Samuel 6:20 NIV). In actuality, David wore a linen garment (2 Samuel 6:14) usually reserved for priests and those ministering before the Lord.

As David led the procession of the ark into the city, he had humbly laid aside his royal fashions. He was undeterred by Michal's criticism. In fact, he doubled down, telling her:

> I was dancing before the LORD, who chose me above your father and all his family! He appointed me as the leader of Israel, the people of the LORD, so I celebrate before the LORD! Yes, and I am willing to look even more foolish than this, even to be humiliated in my own eyes. But those servant girls you mentioned will indeed think I am distinguished! (2 Samuel 6:21–22 NLT)

When we, like David, give our all to God, there is always going to be someone criticizing us for our passion. They might say we take our love for God too far. Our actions or words might be contrary to the popular fashion, but we should not be attentive to what the world thinks. If God is pleased with us, that's all that matters, for He will bless us for our passion. If one never gets persecuted for their faith, they might consider how strong their Christian witness actually is. The challenge is to stay authentic in the face of persecution and to remain steadfast, even when it's not popular to do so. For Jesus said, "God blesses you when people mock you and persecute you and lie about you and say all sorts of evil things against you because you are my followers" (Matthew 5:11 NLT). When we choose to allow God to define our value rather than other people, we free ourselves to follow everything He calls us to do.

When we focus on popularity, we become self-absorbed. Pride will inflate our view of our own importance and blind us to our sins and failings (Proverbs 16:18). As long as we pursue popularity as a means to happiness, we flirt with idolatry. To be popular, we choose to concern ourselves with things such as how many social media followers we have. In doing so, it becomes increasingly difficult for Jesus to be Lord of our life. We must be prepared to answer the question, "Am I now trying to win the approval of human beings or of God?" (Galatians 1:10 NIV). If we try to please people, we will not be an effective servant of Christ. Bottom line, what we say and do is always on display for others, but it must serve as an effective witness for Christ. We must be careful that we are listening to the voice and the Spirit of God. David recognized that he was part of a royal priesthood and one of God's chosen people. That's true for us as well. That is if we're willing to give up pretense and popularity and serve Him with passion.

Reflection

Do we evaluate success by our audience's size and applause? What can we learn from our Lord's own life and death about the shallowness and peril of popularity? How can you apply the following scriptural passage in your life as you consider your own degree of popularity: "Woe to you when everyone speaks well of you, for that is how their ancestors treated the false prophets" (Luke 6:26 NIV)?

MAY 23
(Y3, D21)

Failure to Thrive

The living at least know that they will die: but the dead know nothing.
They have no further reward, nor are they remembered.

—Ecclesiastes 9:5 (NLT)

I have a friend who likes to take a daily walk. On her walks, she sometimes passes by a neighborhood cemetery. Recently, she began to notice an older lady going by in a car heading to or from that cemetery. Since these occurrences have increased in frequency, she began to acknowledge the lady with a smile or a wave. One day, the lady stopped, rolled down the window of her car, and the two began to talk. My friend found out that the lady's son had passed away many months before, and yet she continued to visit the cemetery twice a day. The mother did not live particularly close and would have to travel some distance in order to sustain this grieving practice. I told my friend that it was nice that their paths had crossed because it sounded as though the lady was in need of an empathetic ear. We began to refer to the woman as the "Rose Lawn Lady" in reference to the name of the cemetery she visited. We decided we would pray for her as such, knowing full well that God would know her by name.

At the end of each May, our nation celebrates Memorial Day, a time to remember those who died in a branch of the armed forces while serving our country. At one point in time, it was introduced as Decoration Day after the Civil War. While designated as a patriotic and federal holiday, it is often recognized as the unofficial beginning of summer. The last Monday of May celebration not only stands witness to a display of American flags but also serves as an occasion for gatherings and picnics. It is not uncommon for family members to visit a cemetery and place flowers near the tombstones where perhaps many of their ancestors have been laid to rest. Unlike the "Rose Lawn Lady," this graveside visitation may only occur once each year for these individuals.

Some time ago, I was baffled by the cause of death which I saw written on a death certificate. The primary contribution to the person's demise had been listed as "failure to thrive." I came to learn that the term was associated with infant deaths where there had been insufficient weight gain or inappropriate weight loss. But in the case of the document which I had viewed, it had been used in reference to an older adult whose nonspecific health decline had caused normal life functions to cease. I have thought about it over the years and have rationalized that this diagnosis could at times be appropriately stated for many individuals who have been unable to overcome loss of many kinds. We may have called it by a different name such as heartbreak, but we should recognize it as the inability to let go of what we no longer have. Perhaps the "Rose Lawn Lady" is one such person.

At the time of the death of Jesus, several women went to His tomb days later to find that the stone had been rolled away. "While they were wondering about this, suddenly two men in clothes that gleamed like lightning stood beside them. In their fright the women bowed down with their faces to the ground, but the men said to them, 'Why do you look for the living among the dead? He is not here; he has risen!'" (Luke 24:4–6 NIV). Likewise, it's can serve as a wonderful tribute to remember our loved ones with graveside visits at certain times of the year. As we do so, it is important that we hold on to the promise that when we depart from our "earthy tent," we have a "heavenly dwelling" which awaits us (2 Corinthians 5:1 NIV). Although sometimes misinterpreted, I appreciate the adage "Absent from the body; present with the Lord." I like this interpretation: "For we walk by faith, not by sight. Yes, we are of good courage, and we would rather be away from the body and at home with the Lord" (2 Corinthians 5:7–8 ESV). Here, the Apostle Paul seems to be encouraging us that during this lifetime, we should not fail to thrive but rather be about our Father's business. When our earthly journey comes to an end, we can shed the burdens of this life and be at home with the Lord where we will thrive for all of eternity.

Reflection

Have you known someone who has had difficulty recovering from the grieving process? How does faith in Christ and His promise of eternity help to sustain those who suffer loss? Are there ways that you might appropriately focus on God's purpose for your life today, knowing that in doing so, He is preparing you for a restored life tomorrow?

MAY 24
(Y4, D21)

One Peaceful Filling

You will keep in perfect peace those whose minds are steadfast, because they trust in you.

—Isaiah 26:3 (NLT)

There is a law of physics which states that two things cannot occupy the same space at the same time. I once heard someone say that if you are preoccupied with a certain thought while you are engaged in prayer, your conversation with God would most likely be more meaningful if you would just stop and pray about the thing that is affecting your concentration. Our culture challenges our minds to be filled with many things, and we seem unable to shut off the flow. Recently, I heard a sleep expert say that we should be able to fall asleep within seven minutes after retiring for the night. If we can't do that, our brain is too cluttered and we need to respond by "vacuuming" it. Concentration overload, some of which results from fear and worry from misinformation, permeates society. Once the details are in our subconscious, however inaccurate they might be, it's often difficult to put the genie back in the bottle.

You no doubt have seen the acronym TMI representing the phrase "too much information." The COVID-19 pandemic underscored more than any previous crisis how our minds can become overwhelmed with way too much information, much of it conflicting. The worldwide event gave urgency to the debate over lockdowns and social distancing, which vaccine to consider, and when or when not to wear a mask. Frequent news updates and the lack of a clear spokesperson made us question what part science should play in driving government decisions. This sometimes-unclear guidance resulted in significant disruption to our economy and spread confusion, fear, and mistrust through a hyped social media. Growing paranoia from those around us and within our communities weakened established unity as a result of not being able to maintain open and comfortable communication with one another. Our minds were boggled.

The mind is a tricky thing, not unlike an empty jug displacing air while being filled with water. The more we fill it with godly thoughts, the less room there will be for ungodly ones. Likewise, there will be no room for worry and anxiety. The Apostle Paul provided a list of things on which we should meditate. He said:

> Fix your thoughts on what is true, and honorable, and right, and pure, and lovely, and admirable. Think about things that are excellent and worthy of praise. Keep putting into practice all you learned and received from me—everything you heard from me and saw me doing. Then the God of peace will be with you. (Philippians 4:8–9)

If we drift from God and those things which Paul encourages us to follow, we can allow various forms of temptation to creep into our lives. Unlike any worldwide pandemic which is often misguided by outside forces, we must take personal responsibility for making the necessary steps to rid ourselves of whatever evil virus has penetrated our mind, body, and soul.

Fortunately for Christians, we can be spared by a unique filling, first experienced on the day of Pentecost. On that occasion, the Holy Spirit descended on and filled the followers of Jesus who were meeting together (Acts 2:4). The Spirit of God came down from heaven to indwell in every believer, just as He had promised. Jesus said that by asking God the Father, "He will give you another Advocate, who will never leave you" (John 14:16 NLT). Christians recognize that only through the filling of His Holy Spirit will we be able to accomplish God's work.

Just as it is possible for our physical body to be compromised by disease processes, it is also possible that we can bring grieving or sorrow to the Holy Spirit when we ignore, disobey, or reject what the Spirit is telling us (Ephesians 4:30). If we habitually show disregard and do not repent, our hearts will grow hardened to God's Word. Then a time will come when the Spirit's voice will be muted or quenched in our lives (1 Thessalonians 5:19). The moment we became a follower and believer of Jesus, the Holy Spirit took up residence in our life. We must be acutely aware of His presence and become keenly sensitive to those areas of our life that offend Him. The heart of God can only be recognized by living in daily and deliberate submission. Ask Him to fill you with His presence and power that you might renew His delight in you today. As we do so, we will come to realize that it's one peaceful filling.

Reflection

Are you grieving the Spirit by your sharp tongue and your unkind words? Does your impatience quench the Spirit of God when experiencing everyday things such as waiting for your turn in a long line? Do you grieve and quench the Holy Spirit by being argumentative, pouting when you don't get your way, or by holding a grudge? Pray that your mind will be ever-filled with godly thoughts.

MAY 25
(Y5, D21)

Are We There Yet?

We do not want you to become lazy, but to imitate those who through
faith and patience inherit what has been promised.

—Hebrews 6:12 (NIV)

As I pulled up the article about my favorite major league baseball team, I was intrigued by its title. The team has not contended in the post-season for many years, and the fan base is starting to get restless. Those in management must soon provide answers to some important questions. They include: Do we have any players currently on the team whom we can build around? Who do we have in our minor league system that might be able to give some spark and provide some energy to a team who is frequently inconsistent? Or is it time to just sell off and buy some pieces who will give this franchise the impetus it so badly needs? The title of the article was "Are We There Yet?" I laughed, thinking to myself that these are the same whining words that will soon resonate from the back seat of many a minivan loaded with families about to embark on vacation destinations all across America.

A number of years ago, Chrysler provided a positive application on its Pacifica's rear seat Uconnect theater system. The name of the app? You guess it: "Are We There Yet?" Similar to data one is able to retrieve from a GPS, restless children are now furnished with the information they need without resorting to the traditional annoyance of nagging. According to marketing reports, "The app displays the distance remaining to the destination and estimated arrival times, all presented in fun, colorful, child-friendly graphics." Now if only a similar app could be invented for the new graduate who is ready to change the world in their first job. Or for the rest of us, for that matter, when our patience is dwindling thin as we wait for an answer to a medical test guidance from our company about possible downsizing or whether or not the loan will come through to finance that new home we have been planning for years. While generations of children have echoed the accustomed refrain "Are we there yet?" they grow into adults who continue the all-too-familiar question with varying degrees of impatience and uncertainty.

How many times Moses must have heard that question from the Israelites! Before rescuing them from slavery and leading them out of Egypt, Moses provided information that the Lord would lead them to "a land flowing with milk and honey" (Exodus 3:8 NIV). However, they first spent forty years wandering in the wilderness because they became convinced that they could not banish the current inhabitants of the land (even though God told them they could). Failing to trust and obey, their lack of patience and belief in God's Word brought forth His wrath. This resulted in their curse as nomads and eventual demise as an unbelieving generation who never stepped foot into the promised land. Only a few faithful survived. Centuries later, Paul wrote:

> Today when you hear his voice, don't harden your hearts as Israel did when they rebelled. And who was it who rebelled against God, even though they heard his voice? Wasn't it the people Moses led out of Egypt? And who made God angry for forty years? Wasn't it the people who sinned, whose corpses lay in the wilderness? And to whom was God speaking when he took an oath that they would never enter his rest? Wasn't it the people who disobeyed him? So we see that because of their unbelief they were not able to enter his rest. (Hebrews 3:15–19 NLT)

This truth is no different for us today. He will never lead us where His grace cannot provide for us or His power cannot protect us. God wants us to come out of the wilderness and find rest. Therefore, be patient, for "the Lord isn't really being slow about his promise, as some people think. No, he is being patient for your sake. He does not want anyone to be destroyed, but wants everyone to repent" (2 Peter 3:9 NLT). Put away the regrets of yesterday and learn to live more in the moment, looking forward to what lies ahead. In life, it will sometimes seem as if we are wandering in circles. We want to ask God, "Are we there yet? How much longer?" At such times, it helps to remember that the journey, not just the destination, is important to God. He uses it to humble us, test us, and show us what is in our hearts.

Reflection

Is there something in your life that you know God is asking you to do but upon which you have not acted due to fear or lack of faith? What action steps might you put in place to get from here to there? How might you explain to another person of faith that what sometimes appears to be a nonanswer is God was of taking us on a journey where He draws us to a place of total dependence on Him?

MAY 26
(Y6, D21)

All Good Things

And be sure of this: I am with you always, even to the end of the age.

—Matthew 28:20 (NLT)

If you were to ask who the best baseball player of all time is, most persons would reply that it was Babe Ruth. George Herman Ruth Jr. acquired the nickname "Babe" while playing for the Baltimore Orioles minor league team when he was referred to by a team scout as one of manager Jack Dunn's babes. Not only did Ruth become the premier slugger of his era, he did what no one had done before. Many of his records took years to be broken, and some of them still stand today. When he joined the majors in 1914, the all-time record for home runs in a season was twenty-seven. Within seven years, he had more than doubled it with fifty-nine, and he eventually produced a personal high of sixty. Playing for the Yankees in 1929, he hit his 500th career home run while the player with the next most homers had only 237. On May 25, 1935, in Pittsburgh, Pennsylvania, he hit number 714 out of the park over the right field upper deck. It was the first time anyone had hit a fair ball completely out of Forbes Field. This was one of Ruth's last games, going four for four on the day, hitting three home runs and driving in six runs. His record of 714 for career home runs would stand for another thirty-nine years until Hank Aaron broke it. Ruth retired only a few days later with his worst full-time yearly average fulfilling the old adage "All good things must come to an end."

Ruth's legendary power and charismatic personality made him a larger-than-life figure. During his career, he was the target of intense press and public attention for his baseball exploits and off-field proclivities for drinking and womanizing. His often irresponsible lifestyle was tempered by his willingness to do good by visiting children at hospitals and orphanages, no doubt recalling his own reckless youth labeling him as incorrigible. He said he had no faith in God before he was sent to a Catholic school and that the biggest lesson he got from the experience there was learning that "God was Boss." With the help of some friends, these final documented words were published in 1948 by *Guidepost Magazine*:

> I doubt if any appeal could have straightened me out except a Power over and above man—the appeal of God. Iron-rod discipline couldn't have done it. Nor all the punishment and reward systems that could have been devised. God had an eye out for me, just as He has for you, and He was pulling for me to make the grade.

It sounds like in the end, the Babe recognized what was truly important in life.

Recently, I overheard a group of retirees talking about the years they had worked together. One of them said, "Those were good times, weren't they?"

The others nodded in agreement, uttering "But nothing lasts forever." The Apostle Paul would dare to argue with that statement, for he wrote "Three things will last forever—faith, hope, and love—and the greatest of these is love" (1 Corinthians 13:13 NLT). Our time on earth is very short, but what we do here will have a lasting effect on those with whom we share our lives. The things of this world will pass away (1 John 2:17), and the only effects we will be able to take to eternity are our relationships with God and the people we hopefully reached. As we affirm God's Word in our own lives, we can't help but witness to those around us. In scripture, we read:

> You yourselves are our letter of recommendation, written on our hearts, to be known and read by all. And you show that you are a letter from Christ delivered by us, written not with ink but with the Spirit of the living God, not on tablets of stone but on tablets of human hearts. (2 Corinthians 3:2–3 ESV)

We spend many hours every day trying to improve systems, knowledge, relationships, and situations. In our preoccupation with these worldly concerns, we often become consumed with our efforts toward wealth, fame, and accomplishment, failing to realize that in the end, it will all simply fade away. In the process of doing so, we may lose touch with God, the one true constant in our life. If your relationship with Him has changed or your faith seems more distant than it once was, dare to ask the question, "Who moved?" The King of Eternity always has His hand extended to be your soul mate. For when all else passes, He will be our shepherd to a world without end. What a peaceful reassurance it is to know that He alone is the essence of all good things.

Reflection

What parts of your life contain heavenly value? Consider ways to apply these words of Paul in your personal journey: "So we fix our eyes not on what is seen, but on what is unseen, since what is seen is temporary, but what is unseen is eternal" (2 Corinthians 4:18 NIV). How can you serve to set an example for others as you demonstrate through your actions the essence of what is good?

MAY 27
(Y7, D21)

Ultimate Sacrifices

This day shall be for you a memorial day, and you shall keep it as
a feast to the LORD; throughout your generations.

—Exodus 12:14 (ESV)

The word *sacrifice* can be defined in many ways. When a major league baseball player gets called out but is able to advance a base runner from his own team, the play is called a sacrifice. Parents who give up their personal desires in order that their children receive what they need in life are sacrificing as well. And, yes, men and women who join the armed services do so with the knowledge that someday they might be placed in danger, and the ultimate sacrifice of their life may become a reality. Those who do so deserve to be remembered, and that is the essence of the Memorial Day celebration. For far too many of us, the annual holiday is merely the beginning of summer and perhaps the first outdoor swim, picnic, or camping retreat. However, to the war veteran and the families of fallen soldiers, Memorial Day carries a significance so deep that words cannot express their emotions.

Part of our struggle to understand the fallen soldier comes with our difficulty in accepting sacrifice, especially when those sacrifices seem so final and appear to hold no obvious reward. In this land of opportunity, we spend so much of our time trying to acquire or win. Contemplating that someone might personally give their life for something greater than themselves can be confusing if not unfathomable for many who have grown to become self-centered. It would not be surprising if the spirit of Memorial Day could soon be forgotten. These days, attempts to erase the significance of historical events has become far too easy as we deem the sacrifices and the manner in which they were attained to be no longer politically correct. Perhaps Franklin D. Roosevelt's sentiment was insightful when he stated, "Those who have long enjoyed such privileges as we enjoy forget in time that men have died to win them."

Through the years, Memorial Day has held a tradition for decorating the graves of our veterans with flags or taking flowers to be placed near the tombstones of family members as an act of remembrance. If you have spent any time visiting a cemetery, you may have found it curious to look there for the oldest markers or to pause and read the epitaphs inscribed on them. In the book of Acts, these words have come to be regarded as an epitaph to David: "Now when David had served God's purpose in his own generation, he fell asleep" (Acts 13:36 NIV). The essence of a servant is that they do the will of another, and David was one of the most devout servants ever. His lifelong choice to be within the will of God was why God rewarded him so highly. We can almost hear the words, "Well done, good and faithful servant" (Matthew 25:23) when we think of David.

Throughout history, memorials have been important to every nation. They not only help us remember the past, but they also encourage us to look with hope toward the future. In the Old Testament after Israel crossed the Jordan River, Almighty God told Joshua to take twelve stones from the riverbed and set up a memorial so no one would ever forget God's miraculous deliverance. Joshua said, "We will use these stones to build a memorial. In the future your children will ask you, 'What do these stones mean?'... 'These stones will stand as a memorial among the people of Israel forever'" (Joshua 4:6–7 NLT). As Christians, we remember Jesus' ultimate sacrifice each time we celebrate the Lord's Supper. Through the symbols of the bread and wine, we personalize what He did for our salvation. His very words remind us that "Greater love has no one than this: to lay down one's life for one's friends" (John 15:13 NIV). The Apostle Paul wanted us to appreciate the love of Christ and the meaning of His great gift when he stated, "May you experience the love of Christ, though it is too great to understand fully" (Ephesians 3:19 NLT). Though it might be difficult at times to grasp, we should allow the Memorial Day remembrance and the sacrament of Holy Communion to profoundly demonstrate the ultimate sacrifices made for you and me. They should be received by each of us with great appreciation and deep humility.

Reflection

When people reminisce about your life in years to come, what would you like them to remember? Would those remembrances include any sacrifices you made to benefit others? If God sent down an order to write out an inscription to the company creating your tombstone, would His words include anything about your being a faithful servant or living a life of sacrifice? How can you encourage others to more deeply remember the sacrifices others made for them to create a better way of life?

MAY 28
(Y1, D22)

Looking for the Real You

Then the LORD God called to the man, "Where are you?"

—Genesis 3:9 (NLT)

I made an appointment for my car at a local dealership to have some work done, just as the restrictions of COVID-19 were beginning. Not knowing how long I would be, I decided to take my laptop along to help pass the time. After checking in, I proceeded to the waiting area where I inquired about the guest login password to access their Wi-Fi network. Finding a comfortable seat, I turned on my device which uses facial recognition software. As the system attempted to sign in, the following words appeared on the screen: "Looking for you" followed by "Trying to find you." This went on for about a minute with my concluding that I must have been given incorrect password information. Then I suddenly realized that the camera on my laptop was not recognizing me because I was wearing a face mask. Glancing around to see if there was anyone watching, I gently pulled the mask loop off my one ear to reveal my face. And, just like magic, I entered cyberspace. I chuckled and mumbled to myself, "How stupid!"

Historically, masks have been used for many purposes, and they are commonly worn by healthcare professionals. I am not sure I would recognize my dental hygienist without one. They are a familiar and vivid element in many traditional pageants, rituals, ceremonies, and festivals such as Halloween. In order that people wouldn't recognize him, the legendary Zorro wore one over the upper half of his face. Theatrical masks play two roles—one for the wearer and one for the viewer. In *Phantom of the Opera,* the main character is forced to hide his face because of physical disfigurement while also symbolizing his vulnerability and the injustice from which he suffers. On the TV reality competition, *The Masked Singer,* celebrities performed while wearing head-to-toe costumes, including face masks that conceal their identity from other contestants, panelists, and the viewing audience.

During health crises, people wear a facial covering because they are motivated by ethics or fear, having been told it symbolizes concern for others as well as a guard for their own well-being. In ancient cultures, masks were worn by those who wanted to disguise themselves from participation in acts of hedonism. There are those who cover their face with a mask of happiness so that others do not see their loneliness. In current times, it is not unusual for us to become remarkably accustomed to wearing a mask of pretense. Even for those who know God, the "Good Christian Mask" can play a prominent role in one's life at times. Whatever the reason, God always knows and understands the person behind it. God sees through your mask, right down to the real you. He sees all the flaws, mistakes, and failures, yet He loves you completely and unconditionally. David understood this when he said, "I can never escape from your Spirit! I can never get away from your presence!" (Psalm 139:7 NLT). When it comes to our relationship with God, there is nowhere to escape His love, and no mask will hide us from Him.

Wearing a mask all the time can be harmful by preventing us from developing genuine relationships. Instead of building one another up and encouraging each other in the faith, we pretend that we are just fine as we hide behind our masks. It's important to also understand that those flaws we attempt to cover also prevent us from experiencing intimacy with God. Rather than spending time trying to impress others as we mask our true self, we must try to pursue an honest relationship with Him and rely on His strength. By doing so, it becomes the work of the Spirit to remove the veil. The Apostle Paul stated it this way: "So all of us who have had that veil removed can see and reflect the glory of the Lord. And the Lord—who is the Spirit—makes us more and more like him as we are changed into his glorious image" (2 Corinthians 3:18 NLT). Instead of striving for other people's approval and praise, live to please God alone, no matter what others think of you. Remove that mask you are wearing and adapt to the world around you. Establish your identity on earth by shifting your focus on becoming a disciple of Jesus. Don't hide behind a mask. Jesus would tell you He's been looking to see the real you for some time!

Reflection

Do you ever try to make yourself look better than you sometimes are? What masks do you find yourself wearing in order to face the world? How does growing in Christ change us by allowing freedom to remove those masks that hinder an intimate, spiritual relationship with Him? In what ways can you help others come to the realization that what they are masking will be loved by God?

MAY 29
(Y2, D22)

Unexpected, Super, and Everyday Heroes

Commit everything you do to the LORD. Trust him, and he will help you.

—Psalm 37:5 (NLT)

Memorial Day is a day of remembrance for those who have died in our nation's service. It is a time when we honor many of our nation's heroes. During one of the bloodiest battles of World War II in the Pacific, an unexpected hero surfaced without ever carrying a weapon. A quiet, skinny kid from Lynchburg, Virginia, Desmond Doss, enlisted in the army as a combat medic. Doss believed in the cause but had vowed as a Seventh-day Adventist not to kill. His fellow soldiers threw shoes at him while he prayed, viewing him as someone who shouldn't be allowed to serve. Hard as they tried, the army couldn't force Doss to use a weapon, so he and his company found themselves at Okinawa in the spring of 1945. There they faced a grueling task: climb a steep, jagged cliff, sometimes called Hacksaw Ridge, to a plateau where thousands of heavily armed Japanese soldiers were waiting for them. Under a barrage of gunfire and explosions, Doss crawled on the ground from one wounded soldier to another. He dragged severely injured men to the edge of the ridge, tied a rope around their bodies, and lowered them down to other medics below. He saved seventy-five men, including his captain, over a twelve-hour period. The same soldiers who had shamed him now praised him. One might wonder if he had been motivated by these words from Paul: "We who are strong have an obligation to bear with the failings of the weak, and not to please ourselves" (Romans 15:1). Sometimes we find our heroes in unexpected places; at other times, we just fictionalize them.

Since the debut of *Superman* in 1938, many stories of superheroes have been published. The genre mainly began through American comic books, though it has expanded to other media forms, especially movies. Superhero fiction includes a broad spectrum of characters and storylines. There are often positive lessons to be gleaned from superheroes, such as right and wrong or good and evil. Batman shows that you don't have to be born with superpowers to be a hero. Power Rangers demonstrate teamwork. The Hulk can teach the importance of controlling your temper, so as not to be out of control when angry. Spider-Man imparts that with great power comes great responsibility.

Superman, Iron Man, and other superheroes show us that, while no one is perfect, you can still make a difference in this world. Even with these positives, we should be cautious that becoming a fan of superhero fiction to the point of obsession can contribute to the detriment of one's spiritual walk. There are those who have tried to portray Jesus as the ultimate superhero. But unlike superheroes, Jesus had no faults, He wore no costume and had no need for special gadgets. Superheroes have enemies who might defeat them. Jesus does not, for as we have witnessed by His Life, God was and is in control of all things. No, Jesus is not a superhero; He is our Savior.

Many have treated athletes, movie stars, and musicians as the heroes of their time because they appear to be capable of doings things we cannot. When we consider the concept of heroes, it's easy to think of the big names. We envision a hero looking a certain way, brave and strong (maybe even with a cape flapping behind them). But often, the real heroes are the people we've forgotten about, taken for granted, or never even heard of. If we look around carefully, we can identify heroes such as health care workers, delivery persons, and grocery store stockers who report for work and just do their job during pandemics. They might simply be your friend, parent, mentor, or others who have sacrificed for your happiness. God's heroes, the heroes of the Bible, were not men and women of unusual ability or talent but rather persons of extraordinary faith. Humble acts of dedication are what God values most, even more than dramatic demonstrations of bravery and heroics. Christian heroes are individuals who are willing to believe God's Word and commit themselves to His will and work. They subscribe to the philosophy that "we are God's handiwork, created in Christ Jesus to do good works, which God prepared in advance for us to do" (Ephesians 2:10 NIV). Their heroism results from faith transformed into action as they reach within themselves. To be an everyday hero, you must believe in what God says about you. And as the song lyrics state, "You'll finally see the truth…that a hero lies in you." Everyday heroes don't need to do anything extraordinary; they just need to be extraordinarily dedicated in all that they do.

Reflection

Think about those you have considered to be heroes within your lifetime. Were they famous persons? Over time, with how many of those have you become disillusioned? Who were the persons who sacrificed for you? Did you ever consider that they might just be your everyday heroes?

MAY 30
(Y3, D22)

Fighting the Good Fight

But if you are careful to obey him, following all my instructions, then I will be
an enemy to your enemies, and I will oppose those who oppose you.

—Exodus 23:22 (NLT)

You may have once watched the National Spelling Bee which is held annually in Washington DC, near Memorial Day weekend. The event is for those who are younger than fourteen and have not yet completed the eighth grade. What is interesting about the competition is that many of the contestants know each other because they may have participated in a prior year or have a sibling who did so. Due to their familiarity, they often find themselves cheering each other on. In an interview with one of the finalists, she explained that they don't view the challenge as a threat coming from the other participants but, instead, from the word they are given to spell. In this way, it is "the dictionary who becomes the enemy." Ultimately, they learn a valuable lesson that enemies are sometimes of our own making, embracing: "When people's lives please the LORD, even their enemies are at peace with them" (Proverbs 16:7 NLT).

In warfare, we often find that yesterday's enemies are today's allies. Nearly seventy-one years after an atomic bomb fell from the skies onto the city of Hiroshima, bringing an end to World War II, an American President placed a wreath at the Peace Memorial of that city. President Obama credited the United States and Japan for forging "not only an alliance but a friendship." Relationships are formed in the strangest ways between people whose countries were once adversaries. I recently heard a story of an American man whose mother delivered him in a German bomb shelter while aircraft from the allied forces flew overhead, targeting his homeland. Many decades later, he became friends with a local businessman in small town America who flew in one of those bombers. On the occasion that he introduced this friend, he shared the story of his birth and concluded with the tagline, "Thanks for missing." He was no doubt protected by a Higher Power. God's Holy Word says: "Though I am surrounded by troubles, you will protect me from the anger of my enemies. You reach out your hand, and the power of your right hand saves me" (Psalm 138:7 NLT).

As we celebrate another Memorial Day weekend, it's easy for the meaning of the holiday to lose the significance. As we open the backyard pool and invite friends and relatives over to share a meal prepared on the grill, we must recognize that this unofficial beginning of summer is more than just a three-day weekend. Memorial Day is a solemn pause for the remembrance for all those who have given their lives serving in the American armed forces. The holiday, originally known as Decoration Day, started after the Civil War to honor the Union and Confederate dead. Even in that war, opposing ideologies positioned friend against friend and sometimes brother against brother. In memory of all those who have sacrificed for our country, Henry Ward Beecher wrote, "They hover as a cloud of witnesses above this nation."

For we who choose to journey with Christ, we must also be aware of the enemy at work in our own lives. Most biblical scholars agree that there are three. The first of these is the world itself. The Apostle John has written: "Do not love this world nor the things it offers you, for when you love the world, you do not have the love of the Father in you" (1 John 2:15 NLT). The world is our outer enemy, but we have an inward one as well which evolves from our own sinful nature. Paul said:

> I find then the principle that evil is present in me, the one who wants to do good. For I joyfully concur with the law of God in the inner man, but I see a different law in the members of my body, waging war against the law of my mind and making me a prisoner of the law of sin which is in my members. (Romans 7:21–23 NASB)

The third and last of these is the shrewd devil himself, perhaps our greatest foe. "So humble yourselves before God. Resist the devil, and he will flee from you" (James 4:7 NLT). In this way, it is clear that we are challenged in our own war, just like those who marched onto the field of battle. Therefore, my friends, we must "fight the good fight for the true faith. Hold tightly to the eternal life to which God has called you, which you have confessed so well before many witnesses" (1 Timothy 6:12 NLT). Who among us can argue that this is not a battle indeed worth fighting?

Reflection

In what ways do you need to equip yourself to fight your personal spiritual battles? How do you feel about the statement once made by General George S. Patton: "It is foolish and wrong to mourn the men who died. Rather we should thank God that such men lived." Are there persons within your social circles whom you need to encourage to become more aware of their own spiritual enemies?

MAY 31
(Y4, D22)

Roses Will Bloom Again

In their hearts humans plan their course, but the LORD establishes their steps.

—Proverbs 16:9 (NIV)

It had been a difficult time that year, and there had been those weeks when her heart was aching almost more than she could bear. She was not hurting for herself but for her child who was going through a very painful time. One day, as she sat at her window, she looked out and saw a rosebud on a bush that she was sure had died. Knowing how much she loved roses, the rosebush was there in the first place because it had been planted by her late husband. When she related this story to her child, he stated, "Don't you know, Mom, only God knows when something no longer has a purpose?" She was convinced that the rose had to have been sent by her husband through God. Now in a new year of growth, the rose bush has three buds on it this time, one for each of them.

In the opening lyrics of a song composed by Jeff and Sherri Easter, there is sadness about a rosebush when "the petals drooped and fell to the ground" as winter arrived. But then the uplifting realization, "I'd forgotten who had made it." This is followed by the refrain:

> Roses will bloom again,
> Just wait and see
> Don't mourn what might have been
> Only God knows how and when that
> Roses will bloom again.

While it may be true that rose blossoms can only be found in one season of the year, there is the realization that the love of God's Word endures for all seasons. Scripture tells us that "the grass withers, the flower fades, but the word of our God will stand forever" (Isaiah 40:8 ESV).

Holding on to the hope of God's Word, a twenty-three-year-old once accomplished something many thought he would never do. With the help of his fiancé, He walked across an Iowa college stage to receive his diploma. Four years before, Chris Norton suffered a spinal cord injury from a football accident and was given a 3 percent chance of walking again. In an interview on *Good Morning America*, he stated, "I just had a feeling that God had a bigger plan for me." He understood that without faith, family, and friends, he would not have been able to make it through. "I would not change a thing. It has given me such a purpose in life to help others—I feel so blessed." So in the midst of what many would have termed a tragedy, Norton echoed the words of Paul, "In every thing give thanks: for this is the will of God in Christ Jesus concerning you" (1 Thessalonians 5:18 KJB). The new graduate was encouraged to tell his story in a book entitled *The Power of Faith When Tragedy Strikes.*

Jesus challenged His disciples with these words: "I tell you the truth, if you had faith even as small as a mustard seed, you could say to this mountain, 'Move from here to there,' and it would move. Nothing would be impossible" (Matthew 17:20 NLT). So make your plan as though God will bless it and then implement it. He will reveal to you what He wants for your life. Don't be so caught up in pruning the thorny bush that you fail to step back, enjoy its beauty, and smell the roses. If we believe that our God has a design for a world that creates order out of disorder, then surely we must also believe that He has a plan intricate enough for those who love Him. Maria von Trapp once said

> It will be very interesting one day to follow the pattern of our life as it is spread out like a beautiful tapestry. As long as we live here we see only the reverse side of the weaving, and very often the pattern, with its threads running wildly, doesn't seem to make sense. Someday, however, we shall understand. In looking back over the years we can discover how a red thread goes through the pattern of our life: the Will of God.

For when God allows us to journey to the top of the mountain to see the sunrise after we have spent time in the shadows of the valley, we must always remember who guided us there in the first place.

Reflection

In what area of your life have you lost hope? How can you use God's Word to carry you and others with whom you share? When difficult times come your way (and they will), are you able to find sustaining faith in His promises? How might you strive to implement Paul's words in Ephesians 5:17 (NIV), "Therefore do not be foolish, but understand what the will of the Lord is"?

JUNE 1

(Y5, D22)

Old Dogs, Rising Creeks, and Faulty Plans

We can make our plans, but the LORD determines our steps.

—Proverbs 16:9 (NLT)

I walk in a local park most weekdays with a close friend. Because we nearly always walk about the same time each day, we have gotten to know other folks who do likewise. One older gentleman by the name of Harry maintains a regular presence with his dog. We frequently engage in conversation with Harry who is in his late seventies. Sometimes we have wondered if Harry doesn't become a bit too adventuresome for his age. This became apparent on one occasion when we observed him walking on the top of a barrier wall located between the walking path and a creek on the other side. When we asked Harry if he wasn't concerned about falling, he indicated that he had to follow where the dog decided to take him. When he disappeared from our routine some months afterward, we were anxious that he might be having health problems or perhaps suffered a fall. Later, when we did run into him, he told us that when he and his dog leave the house, he allows the pet to direct their walk. If he heads for the car, they come to the park. Otherwise, the dog takes him on a different adventure through the neighborhood. I considered how many of us would tolerate our pet setting the agenda for the path we would follow that day. I'm sure I wouldn't.

The month of June is one of those months when many plans are laid. Families strategize about upcoming summer vacations. The weather forecast will often dictate whether one can pack lightly or if preparations for varying climate changes must be made. Depending on the ages of the persons who will be traveling, the balance between relaxing and entertainment options must be taken into account for each participant. If the event being finalized happens to be our wedding, confirming that all the last-minute details are executed assures the special day will come off without a hitch. Or if one happens to be sitting on a chair at an outdoor commencement, they just might be dreaming of plans to change the world, even before they receive that diploma or move their tassel from one side of the cap to the other. Plans can be exciting, but we can also find ourselves drowning in the concern for the many details.

While I haven't been able to discover exactly who said it, I find that I can personally identify with the expression "If the Lord is willing and creeks don't rise." I think we would all be better off if we subscribed to this old adage. It acknowledges the fact that we can plan all we want, but there is no guarantee that the path we lay out today will ever come to fruition tomorrow. James stated it this way in the New Testament:

> Look here, you who say, "Today or tomorrow we are going to a certain town and will stay there a year. We will do business there and make a profit." How do you know what your life will be like tomorrow? Your life is like the morning fog—it's here a little while, then it's gone. What you ought to say is, "If the Lord wants us to, we will live and do this or that." Otherwise you are boasting about your own plans, and all such boasting is evil. (James 4:13–16 NLT)

While there is nothing inherently negative and often necessary that we make preparations for our ensuing days, it is probably not a bad idea to sometimes pose the question, "What's my Plan B?" What if God takes hold of this idea I have, this relationship I have developed, or this recognition I have received and nudges me in a direction I have never even considered? What if the plan you have been formulating over time is not within His will for your life? Those who seek maturity in the faith come to realize that making plans without seeking God's will is a little bit like a quarterback who finds himself in the middle of a game without a playbook. If you are making decisions based primarily on what brings happiness, then your priorities may very well be out of focus with what He desires for you. Accordingly, you are in danger of stumbling at every turn. While we don't always realize it, God often calls us from a place of vulnerability at the most unexpected time. So be ready to "commit your work to the Lord, and your plans will be established" (Proverbs 16:3 ESV). After all, if we don't consider God's will as part of our planning, we might just as well be following the whim of an old dog.

Reflection

How could you live your life in such a way that it would bring the most glory to God? Consider the challenge offered in Matthew 6:33 (NLT): "Seek the Kingdom of God above all else, and live righteously, and he will give you everything you need." What are some ways you need to consider placing His will first in your life? How will you defend your decision if others endeavor to change your direction?

JUNE 2
(Y6, D22)

Truth that Will Ultimately Matter

With their mouths the godless destroy their neighbors, but
through knowledge the righteous escape.

—Proverbs 11:9 (NIV)

Corruption in the government at the highest level. Spies implanted in political campaigns of candidates by the FBI. Collusion with foreign governments in order to influence elections. These insinuations are all too familiar for those who have lived in America in the twenty-first century. However, if you go back several generations to the early 1950s, you will find a man by the name of Joseph McCarthy, a senator from the state of Wisconsin. Senator McCarthy spent almost five years trying in vain to expose Communists and other left-wing loyalty risks in the US government. In the hyper-suspicious atmosphere of the Cold War, suggestions of disloyalty were enough to convince many Americans that their government was packed with traitors and spies. On June 2, 1954, he charged that communists had infiltrated the Central Intelligence Agency and the atomic weapons industry. Just weeks before, thirty-six days of televised investigative "McCarthy Hearings" were led by the senator in which he displayed his bullying style and hysterical behavior. The character assassinations he imposed quickly turned off the audience. McCarthy was thoroughly disgraced when an attorney asked him whether he had any sense of decency at all.

Over time, McCarthyism has been used in modern political discussions as a reference to defamation of character by means of widely publicized indiscriminate allegations frequented with unsubstantiated charges. In today's society, it is common to observe daily examples of executed attempts to tarnish a person's reputation. It may involve exaggeration, misleading half-truths, or manipulation of facts to present an untrue picture of the targeted person. Such conspiracy theory plotting is not new; in fact, it's been around for centuries. People throughout history have speculated on hidden meanings and dared to jump at the potential of juicy secrets. Our society's nonstop use of social media and obsession with round-the-clock news outlets has created an outflow of instantaneous information from which it is difficult to escape. Unfortunately, when these things are unfounded, false narratives are unstoppable, and the reputations of innocent people are irreparably damaged. Frequently, Christians have been the focus of these attacks, and even worse, they are sometimes the ones perpetuating them. This directly violates Scripture's prohibition from bearing false witness against our neighbors (Exodus 20:16). It devalues the name of Christ, who is the essence of truth, and it inflicts pain upon the people involved.

The Bible tells us that the relationship between Jesus and the Pharisees was frequently marked by the practice of character assassination with Jesus as the main target. This group of religious intellectuals witnessed His works with envy and heard his instruction with resentment because they recognized He threatened their position and prestige. Jesus responded by saying: "The teachers of religious law and the Pharisees are the official interpreters of the law of Moses. So practice and obey whatever they tell you, but don't follow their example. For they don't practice what they teach" (Matthew 23:2–3 NLT). In fear and hatred, they did all they could to falsify the point of his lessons, attempted to negatively paint His personal character, and began a plot to kill Him (Mark 3:6). David also felt the persecution of false witnesses, but fortunately, he knew how to respond. As he prayed to his God, he said, "Arrogant people smear me with lies, but in truth I obey your commandments with all my heart" (Psalm 119:69 NLT).

The question must be asked how we separate ourselves from the character assassinations of this world. First and foremost, don't repeat what you do not know to be true. If there appears to be a degree of accuracy, do as David did—listen to your heart and pray for those involved. Don't become part of the rumor mill, and do not seek to discredit the accused. If you are the target of such allegations, follow this advice: "But do this in a gentle and respectful way. Keep your conscience clear. Then if people speak against you, they will be ashamed when they see what a good life you live because you belong to Christ" (1 Peter 3:16 NLT). Consider yourself blessed by the one who knows the truth that will ultimately matter.

Reflection

Is this an appropriate time to reexamine your social media interactions and sources for news and information? What habits do you need to consider changing in light of your relationship with Jesus? How can you set an example to not get caught up in hearsay about others that has no foundation of fact? Are there ways you might reach out to another whose reputation has been damaged by rumors?

JUNE 3
(Y7, D22)

One of a Kind

I praise you because I am fearfully and wonderfully made;
your works are wonderful, I know that full well.

—Psalm 139:14 (NIV)

At the Indianapolis Motor Speedway where the famous "Indy 500" is held each May, there is permanent seating for more than 257,000 people and additional infield seating that raises capacity to approximately 400,000. When you think about this venue being filled, consider that there are no two persons who have ever attended there who are exactly alike. Indeed, there are no two people in history who have been precisely the same. Our Creator has made us to be one of kind. We're the crowning beauty, the highest of everything God made; the first and the best of His creatures (James 1:18). That alone should make us feel really special. When Oliver Wendell Holmes was in his eightieth year, a friend greeted him and asked, "How are you?" "I'm fine," said Holmes. "The house I live in is tottering and crumbling, but Oliver Wendell Holmes is fine, thank you." In this materialistic age when most of us spend a great deal of time trying to be like everyone else, we often forget that the real, enduring part of us that makes us unique is fixed more on our spirit than it ever was on our physicality.

Throughout the Bible, we learn the stories of very unique individuals. We discover people such as King David, a man of great spiritual depth and understanding, yet also one of fiery human passion and imperfection. He was one of a kind who came to be remembered as a man after God's own heart (Acts 13:22). In God's Holy Word, you can also meet Saul of Tarsus who was dedicated to persecuting the early supporters of Jesus. Ironically, Paul (as He is later known) becomes one of the faithful after an encounter with Jesus on the road to Damascus following His resurrection. The Lord chose Paul to proclaim His name to both Gentiles and the children of Israel (Acts 9:15) and to speak against the conformity of this world (Romans 12:2). The New Testament would be significantly shorter if it was not for his transformation to become one of a kind. The scriptures also tell of other very distinctive persons who are lesser known. There you will find a woman who anointed Jesus by pouring expensive perfume over His head (Matthew 26:7). After a disciple chastened her for wasting it, Jesus said, "Wherever this gospel is preached throughout the world, what she has done will also be told, in memory of her" (Matthew 26:13 NIV). She was one of a kind, and Jesus said she would never be forgotten.

It's that time of year when graduates will be hearing all kinds of speeches from famous and accomplished persons. While most graduates may have some in hearing an inspirational message, many speakers will fail to deliver and focus on their own agenda. The best of them will challenge them to grow into their own uniqueness and exercise their God-given abilities to make the world a better place. Perhaps someone will quote Charles Spurgeon who said, "Character is always lost when a high ideal is sacrificed on the altar of conformity and popularity." Maybe a few will dare to cite references of faith by stating: "In his grace, God has given us different gifts for doing certain things well" (Romans 12:6 NLT) and "Each of you should use whatever gift you have received to serve others, as faithful stewards of God's grace in its various forms" (1 Peter 4:10 NIV). While these words specify spiritual gifts, they can also provide wise counsel that we should sensibly utilize all the talents with which we have been blessed.

So many exceptional individuals will come and go during the course of one's lifetime: sports figures, actors, politicians and explorers, some of whom went to the moon and back. The ones who gained notoriety did so because of their uniqueness. Someone said that in life, we become either an imitator or an innovator. Persons who stand out are not those who cater to conformity, but rather, it is the person who allows their distinctiveness to shine who will be remembered. Followers of the Christian faith come to understand that we will truly be happy only when we give ourselves the freedom to express our uniqueness as a contribution to God's plan. "For we are God's handiwork, created in Christ Jesus to do good works, which God prepared in advance for us to do" (Ephesians 2:10 NIV). God made you for glory and excellence so He could manifest His beauty, grace, and righteousness through you. Go forth then and celebrate that you are His most unique creation. In fact, you will be just what He intended you to be when you allow yourself to truly become one of a kind.

Reflection

Do you remember certain periods of your life that you felt a sense of enforced conformity? In what ways can you challenge yourself and those you love to practice your uniqueness for God?

JUNE 4
(Y1, D23)

The Here and Now of God's Presence

He said to his disciples, "Why are you so afraid? Do you still have no faith?"

—Mark 4:40 (NIV)

A siren-like alarm was sounding in a nearby room of our home. I wasn't exactly sure what it was, and then it occurred to me that it might be the NOAA weather radio which had not activated for some time. The alarm stopped and was followed by the message that there would be a severe thunderstorm warning for the county in which we live to be in effect for the upcoming hour. The alert continued to caution of heavy downpours and lightning, including wind gusts up to sixty mph with quarter size hail capable of causing damage to trees, vehicles, roofing, and siding. I remember thinking to myself that I was glad I was at home with a basement to go to if necessary. Imagine being outside in this kind of storm with nowhere to take cover! But I knew by the bulletin that there would be an approximate beginning and ending time, giving assurance that this storm would soon pass.

When the disciples went out on a lake with Jesus, they no doubt had a very different feeling. "A furious squall came up, and the waves broke over the boat, so that it was nearly swamped" (Mark 4:37 NIV). Scripture tells us that Jesus was sleeping. So "the disciples went and woke him up, shouting, 'Lord, save us! We're going to drown!' Jesus responded, 'Why are you afraid? You have so little faith!' Then he got up and rebuked the wind and waves, and suddenly there was a great calm" (Matthew 8:25–26 NLT). Although the text doesn't say which apostles were with Christ on the boat, it's probable that seasoned fishermen were aboard who would have been quite familiar with the ways of the sea. Yet they were frightened and apparently thought He would be able to do something. Even when Jesus calmed the storm, the disciples gave every indication that they still weren't yet convinced He was God in the flesh. For they asked each other, "Who is this? He commands even the winds and the water, and they obey him" (Luke 8:25 NIV).

Based on the 1997 nonfiction book by the same name, the film *Perfect Storm* tells the story of the *Andrea Gail*, a commercial fishing vessel with six crew members that was lost at sea after being caught in the storm of the century. Boasting waves over one hundred feet high, the converging combination of clashing weather systems was so rare that meteorologists deemed the October 1991 marvel "the perfect storm." This terminology, which has since been devised for common usage, has come to refer to a very unpleasant situation in which several bad things happen at once. This certainly was the case in 2020 when the worldwide pandemic prompted government officials to issue stay-at-home orders for millions of Americans. Following months of business and manufacturing closures, an unbelievably high level of unemployment witnessed results that had not been seen since 1934. Just as restrictions were starting to lift, an incident of police brutality caused the death of an African-American male followed by protests sparked deadly looting and riots throughout the nation. One perfect storm indeed!

The imagery behind the story of Jesus calming the storm should bring great encouragement and hope for anyone facing any storm in life. But first, one must take stock of who they have in the boat with them. Frequently, we will find names like despair, hopelessness, worry, uncertainty, depression, stressfulness, discontent, exhaustion, and disillusionment to be among those who take these troublesome journeys with us. We know of God and may, like the disciples, have a relationship with His Son, Jesus. But just like those followers who were caught with Him in the storm, we cannot rely on the emotions of doubt. We must come to trust not only in the power but also in the presence of the one who can bring true peace to the unsettled circumstances around us. If Jesus was able to save the disciples, He will also rescue us from the unsettling disorders of life. For He is with us and will never leave us (Hebrews 13:5). If He can still the turbulence of the sea with one word, He can calm our everyday upheavals as well. It is when we understand the "here and now of God's presence" that our storms will be perfected.

Reflection

What are the emotional factors that keep you from fully trusting God when you are facing various trials? Are you able to see Him as not only the God of power but also the God of presence? If you are unable to constantly sense His presence, what do you need to change in your life for this to happen?

JUNE 5
(Y2, D23)

Identity—Crisis or Creation?

So God created human beings in his own image.

—Genesis 1:27 NLT

As family and friends gather around a newborn, one of the first topics of conversation is often, "Who does this child look like?" Sometimes family resemblances are immediately obvious. In other cases, they appear over time and may be based more on personality or temperament than appearance. Identity is something that everyone strives to discover during their lifetime, and it can be influenced and formed by many factors. Being able to identify who you are holds significant value for many. For instance, if we are scheduled to have surgery, we want the medical personnel to know exactly who we are in order that the correct procedure is performed. If we are applying for a benefit to which we are entitled, such as Social Security, we want to be certain that there is precise verification so that we do not make claim on someone else's account or they on ours. Likewise, if we are traveling internationally, we are required to establish our identity to border officials by means of a passport before entering another country.

According to a decades-old *Our Daily Bread* devotion, the renowned nineteenth-century French artist, Paul Gustave Dore, once lost his passport while traveling in Europe. When he came to a border crossing, he explained his predicament to one of the guards. Giving his name to the official, Dore hoped he would be recognized and allowed to pass. The guard, however, said that many people attempted to cross the border by claiming to be persons they were not. Dore insisted that he was the man he claimed to be. "All right," said the official, "we'll give you a test, and if you pass it, we'll allow you to go through." Handing him a pencil and a sheet of paper, he told the artist to sketch several peasants standing nearby. Dore did it so quickly and skillfully that the guard was convinced he was indeed who he claimed to be. Almost finding himself in the midst of an identity crisis, his work ultimately confirmed his word.

In modern society, the need to establish an identity becomes increasingly important over the course of our life. However, the exploration to find it is as old as humankind itself. The theme of identity can become very complicated as individuals discover themselves on various journeys. While most persons are able to accept and feel confident about who they are from childhood, others are unable to do so even after investigating over a long period of time. More than ever, there are an increasing number of persons searching for their ancestral connections so that they have a more complete understanding of their cultural heritage. Some who have been raised in an adopted family have a burning desire to make a connection with their birth parents to better comprehend their true background. Ultimately, when you aren't certain about your roots, you will inherit the identity others declare you to be.

For believers in Christ, claiming one's spiritual identity is life-changing. Discovering this characterization involves continually searching the Scriptures for lessons on how to be more like Christ. It means praying that the Holy Spirit will reveal the mysteries of godly living by affirming our need to spend time with mature Christians who are deeply rooted in Jesus. "Being in Christ" requires that we let go of those past, more worldly identities. In doing so, we sustain the belief that we belong to Jesus rather than to ourselves. "Therefore, if anyone is in Christ, the new creation has come: The old has gone, the new is here" (2 Corinthians 5:17 NIV). It is an ongoing process that takes deliberate practice, constant thinking, and many attitude adjustments. One of the richest scriptural lessons about identity is found in Ephesians 1:4–14. In this passage, Paul addresses the church in Ephesus, explaining the new identity given to a person when they are in Christ. As we focus on his words, we will read that we have been chosen, adopted, redeemed, forgiven, covered with grace, and unconditionally loved and accepted. We learn that we are pure, righteous, and forgiven. As we increase this understanding, we realize there is something worthwhile to be considered in the motto of a well-known identity theft prevention company known as LifeLock: "You only have one identity… protect it with the best." And as that once-famous artist discovered many years ago, our work will be confirmed by our word when we find our best in Him.

Reflection

Do you define your identity in the knowledge that you're a child of God or in the things you do or don't do? How could affirming the truth about your identity in Christ change the way you live? Does maintaining your Christian identity as foremost in your life help you confront modern-day subjects such as politics or gender issues in which others attempt to weaponize their identity?

JUNE 6
(Y3, D23)

Finding Perfect Peace

Turn from evil and do good; seek peace and pursue it.

—Psalm 34:14 (NIV)

As I took my daily walk around the local park, it suddenly occurred to me that something was not quite right. Then I realized that the normally tranquil path which is usually populated with squirrels, chipmunks, and ducks by the creek had, on this day, been occupied with noise all around me. There was power equipment from the conservation corps who were clearing brush and sawing up dead tree limbs. Somewhere in the distance was a mower, and there were numerous sirens from emergency service personnel rushing by on the upper road responding to their latest crisis. Their alarms had caused dogs from houses across the creek to bark and make their presence known. It was not a time for a peaceful walk, at least not on this day in this area of town.

Then I paused and felt a little guilty, realizing that there are those who seldom have the opportunity to find an escape to any form of tranquility. It was just a day or so later that I appreciated that fact that lasting peace is often relevant to our world situation. It happened to be June 6, and across the globe, many were remembering the Allied invasion of Normandy, France, often referred to as D-Day. In 1944, much of Europe had been occupied by the German Nazi forces of Adolf Hitler. It took months for the largest seaborne invasion in history to once again free these nations. The Normandy invasion began to turn the tide, and the war was formally ended the following spring after millions had lost their lives. In the aftermath of the deadliest military conflict ever witnessed, nations regained their sovereignty, and peace was restored. It raises the question, if peace is the absence of war, then what is true peace? The Old Testament prophet put it this way, "You will keep in perfect peace those whose minds are steadfast, because they trust in you" (Isaiah 26:3 NIV).

While peace hopefully returns to nations following years of conflict and great human sacrifice, most boroughs and municipalities find it necessary to hire folks who maintain continual peace. These include any person who works in the public sector with the responsibility of upholding the laws of the land. Examples are customs officials, police officers, sheriffs, constables, deputies, and correction officers who enforce the regulations that support peace in our towns, neighborhoods, and occasionally, even within our own households. There are those who go through life, never finding peace in their personal lives, and they sometimes create less than peaceful situations for their families. They could learn from the wisdom shared in God's Word: "Better a dry crust eaten in peace than a house filled with feasting—and conflict" (Proverbs 17:1 NLT). Many individuals spend much time and energy searching to find fulfillment. Far too often, they never come to understand that the real way to happiness and a good life is only through finding one's own personal peace.

True peace can only come from God who grants His children a peace that passes all understanding (Philippians 4:7). This peace doesn't affect our surroundings; rather, it touches our inner souls. Paul affirmed that it will go deep into our hearts and minds and that it will unite all parties as one. Referring specifically to the Gentiles and Jews, he stated, "For he himself is our peace, who has made the two groups one and has destroyed the barrier, the dividing wall of hostility" (Ephesians 2:14 NIV). If you have His peace, then you can start solving the conflict around you. As followers of Jesus, we should be the ones others look to not necessarily because our surroundings are peaceful but because our hearts and minds are at peace with God. Jesus said, "I am leaving you with a gift— peace of mind and heart. And the peace I give is a gift the world cannot give. So don't be troubled or afraid" (John 14:27 NLT). It is possible for anyone to experience God's peace. For when we learn to cast our cares on Him, faith will replace fear and discontent. Living a peace-filled life comes down to a choice to follow Him or not. For, you see, He alone is the only official who can maintain a perfect peace. All others will fail in comparison.

Reflection

Where does your peace come from? What is the inevitable result of peace based on external conditions? How would you encourage others who always seem to have a stressed life, resulting in personal difficulty to find an inner peace?

JUNE 7
(Y4, D23)

Blurring, Blind Spots, and a Better Focus

For we live by faith, not by sight.

—2 Corinthians 5:7 (NIV)

I have a friend who recently had cataracts removed from each of her eyes. Months before, when she last visited her optometrist, she was informed that nothing more could done to improve her vision until she had this surgery. Over a course of the last several years, she had come to realize if she was driving in a strange area, it was easy to miss a street sign due to blurred vision. She had difficulty engaging in some of her hobbies, and routine chores such as cooking and cleaning were more complicated because of her inability to focus. Trees and grass looked green, but she could no longer distinguished individual leaves or blades which were distorted. Now weeks after the procedure, she barely needed glasses. Many objects had taken on a new appearance, and colors of many things appeared different and more vivid than she had remembered. Her visual perspective had changed over time, and she hadn't even realized it. Her view of life had become compromised.

Unless we stay focused on the right things, we can lose perspective in our spiritual life as well. Much of our faith is dedicated to the unseen. In this day and age, we live in a world with a "show me" mentality. If we do not keep grounded in God's Word and stay connected with Him in our prayer life, our faith can become blurred. For the skeptic, it will be easier to doubt than it is to believe. I remember the first time I saw someone walking down the aisle of a food store, presumably talking to themselves. I caught myself smiling when I realized that they were actually talking on their phone. But unless we truly see the smartphone or the Bluetooth connection device, one can easily jump to a different conclusion. It creates a blind spot in our judgment. We can identify with how the nonbeliever must react when they observe us worshipping or praying to a God they cannot see or begin to understand. Scripture tells us: "Now we see things imperfectly, like puzzling reflections in a mirror, but then we will see everything with perfect clarity. All that I know now is partial and incomplete, but then I will know everything completely, just as God now knows me completely" (1 Corinthians 13:12 NLT).

Most of us are familiar with the term "blind spot" as it applies to driving. It is usually defined as those perceived lines of sight where we are unable to see things around us. If someone is passing your car, you can see them in your rear or side view mirror, but there is a certain spot where they temporarily disappear. Yet they are still there. If we become insensitive to this blind spot, we can place ourselves in an unsafe situation. The human eye also has a blind spot—a small area on the retina which escapes our awareness. This is because our brain fills in this blank area with the surrounded images, making our field of vision appear to be seamless. We not only have blind spots in driving and with our eyes, we have them in life as well. These include gaps in our perception that keep us from seeing the truth about others and ourselves. Too many of us live without proper observation controlled by our own mistakes or the faults of others. In doing so, we stumble around with blind spots blocking the work God wants us to do.

When the Pharisees investigated Jesus' healing of a blind man, they asked Him if they too were blind. "Jesus said to them, 'If you were blind, you would have no guilt; but now that you say, 'We see,' your guilt remains'" (John 9:41 ESV). The Apostle Paul put it another way: "So we fix our eyes not on what is seen but on what is unseen since what is seen is temporary, but what is unseen is eternal" (2 Corinthians 4:18 NIV). Not unlike my friend who lived with her cataracts and imperfect vision for many years, we are often blind to what we think we can see. That is until the Great Physician reveals to us that our world has in fact been one big blur for a very long time.

Reflection

Have there been times when you have lost perspective and had blind spots in certain areas of your life? Are there persons whom you can trust to make you aware when you are developing blind spots? Helen Keller once said: "The best and most beautiful things in the world cannot be seen or even touched—they must be felt with the heart." Can you apply her wisdom to correcting some of the blind spots in your journey? How could you use her quote to assist others in understanding theirs as well?

JUNE 8
(Y5, D23)

One Joyful Reunion

After that, we who are still alive and are left will be caught up together with them in
the clouds to meet the Lord in the air. And so we will be with the Lord forever.

—1 Thessalonians 4:17 (NIV)

At the age of five, a boy from India by the name of Saroo got separated from his older brother. Searching for his sibling, the young lad boarded a train, fell asleep, and traveled for days before he was able to get off. Now alone in the large city of Calcutta, he finds himself hungry, afraid, and unable to speak the language. He ends up in a state-sponsored orphanage from where he is blessed to be adopted by an Australian couple. He grew up in Tasmania with nurturing parents and a somewhat troubled brother, who was also adopted. As he progresses into his twenties, he is bothered by the fact that even many years later, his family might still be wondering what happened to him. He embarks on an all-consuming journey to find his way back to them with only a few vague memories of his past for assistance. Utilizing online digital mapping software, he eventually identifies his birthplace and travels back to find his biological mother and younger sister still living in the same village. There he has an emotional reunion as he learns that his brother was killed on the same night in which they were separated decades before. His mother never gave up hope and believed that one day, her missing son would return. The wonderful reunion story can be found in the nonfiction book *A Long Way Home* or viewed in the Oscar-nominated 2016 film *Lion*.

Not all reunions are quite so dramatic. A friend of mine told me about an experience she had at a retirement luncheon. The event was in conjunction with an anniversary celebration of the company for whom she had been employed. While the gathering was very nice, there were a number of people who had been inadvertently omitted from the list of invitees. This evoked some emotional upset, ranging from hurt feelings to anger. While the employer made a good faith last-minute effort to correct the situation, there were those who felt slighted or assumed that they were intentionally missed. Perhaps you have had a similar experience as part of a large family or high school reunion committee. You may remember that attempting to find those folks who have not been in the fold for a while can sometimes be difficult. Or you may have been one who was missed, knowing exactly how it felt to be excluded.

Perhaps the best reunion story ever told came from Jesus in the Parable of the Son found in Luke 15:11–32. It is the well-known tale of a man with two sons, the younger of whom asks his father for his portion of the estate. Upon its receipt, he departed to another country, lived a wild life, and squandered his wealth. Finding himself poor and destitute in the midst of a famine, he "came to his senses" (v. 17 NLT), realizing that returning home as a hired servant would be better than the circumstances in which he found himself. As he goes home, he throws himself at the mercy of his father, surprised that he is greeted by a loving and compassionate parent. The reunion is a bit clouded when a jealous brother appears, discovering that the "red carpet" has been rolled out for his vanished brother. After being confronted with rage by the son who has been faithful, "His father said to him, 'Look, dear son, you have always stayed by me, and everything I have is yours. We had to celebrate this happy day. For your brother was dead and has come back to life! He was lost, but now he is found!'" (vv. 31, 32 NLT).

This reunion story reflects the amazing patience that God demonstrates for us. Even when we act selfishly, He indulges us. He yields out of the respect for the freedom He Has given us, desiring that we will hopefully learn our lesson and come back to Him. God's children never have to experience permanent separation if they repent their misdoings and obey His laws. When we do so, we realize that our place is secure and our heavenly reward is salvaged. One day, you and I will participate in a great reunion with our friends and loved ones who shared a belief in Jesus, the Son of God. It was He who said that, "Just as you can identify a tree by its fruit, so you can identify people by their actions" (Matthew 7:20 NLT). We should, therefore, establish activities and relationships He would desire. For when it's time for the reunion, we'll assure our place on the list and hear Him say, "I never knew you" (Matthew 7:23 NLT).

Reflection

Why is the concept of reunions so important to Christians? How would you speak with a new believer who is concerned about reuniting with other loved ones in Christ? In what ways can we find comfort in associating and forming relationships with other believers?

JUNE 9
(Y6, D23)

One Day at a Time

How do you know what your life will be like tomorrow? Your life is
like the morning fog—it's here a little while, then it's gone.

—James 4:14 (NLT)

What happens when you bring together a New York City stockbroker and an Ohio physician with a common personal concern? You end up with a solution. At least that's what happened on June 10, 1935, when Bill Wilson and Dr. Bob Smith, two recovering alcoholics, came together to institute Alcoholics Anonymous. The cofounders had a chance meeting, and with each other's help, they both achieved lasting sobriety. With other early members, they developed AA's 12-Step program of spiritual and character development. The first step for a new member is to admit that they have a problem and are "powerless over alcohol." Making this acknowledgment in the presence of others who share their addiction allows the individuals to draw strength from one another. Members of the strictly anonymous organization control their addictions through guided group discussion and confession, reliance on a "higher power," and a gradual return to sobriety. While the program of treatment references God, members define that higher power in their own way. In that regard, both persons of faith and nonbelievers as well are welcomed. The only requirement for membership is a desire to stop drinking. There is an estimated membership of nearly two million people who work the 12-Step program. It requires commitment, and many people benefit from the use of a sponsor to help them through the process.

I once heard a story of a man who asked a pastor to pray over him so that he would be freed from his drinking problem. Recognizing that the motivation of the man was only to achieve a quick and easy fix, he told the individual that he really needed to go to an Alcoholics Anonymous meeting, follow the outlined program, and become grounded in biblical teaching. He reduced his advice to a few words—"Do the hard work." In this day and age, it has become far too easy for many individuals to expect an immediate fix to their problems. One might think that finding the right app, paying a fee for a service, or receiving a drive-through prayer should do the trick and allow one to move on.

In Scripture, we find Paul counseling his student to establish his life so that he could be a model for other believers. "But you, Timothy, are a man of God; so run from all these evil things. Pursue righteousness and a godly life, along with faith, love, perseverance, and gentleness. Fight the good fight for the true faith. Hold tightly to the eternal life to which God has called you, which you have confessed so well before many witnesses" (1 Timothy 6:11–12 NLT). If we would paraphrase Paul's directive, it might sound something like this: "Timothy, pursue, fight, and hold tightly; in other words, work the program as you have been instructed."

As one takes a closer look at the basics of the Alcoholics Anonymous program, you will find one remaining principle of importance. Each member refrains from the use of alcohol using the slogan "One day at a time." In doing so, their abstinence can be achieved successfully using a daily goal rather than becoming overwhelmed with all of the tomorrows which lie ahead. That philosophy is in line with the teachings of Jesus who said, "So don't worry about tomorrow, for tomorrow will bring its own worries. Today's trouble is enough for today" (Matthew 6:34 NLT). It's good advice for any believer. We should seize the opportunities and be grateful for the many blessings that God gives us each and every day. Lyricist Cristy Lane reflects on this in the words of her modern chorus:

> One day at a time sweet Jesus; That's all I'm asking from you.
> Just give me the strength, to do every day what I have to do.
> Yesterday's gone sweet Jesus, and tomorrow may never be mine.
> Lord help me today, show me the way… One day at a time.

For anyone with an addiction, the key to success is to trust in a higher power for the strength to say no to today's temptation. For we who believe in God as that higher power, He reminds us to look to Him. When the prospect of tomorrow seems too difficult to endure, instead, just do so one day at a time.

Reflection

What compulsions and obsessions do you face in your life that prevent you from making the most of each day? How might you apply these words from Billy Graham in your daily faith walk: "Take one day at a time. Today, after all, is the tomorrow you worried about yesterday"?

JUNE 10
(Y7, D23)

One Move from Center

The Lord is near to all who call upon him, to all who call on him in truth.

—Psalm 145:18 (NIV)

What matters most is the attitude we have about change. This is the overarching theme of the 1998 book, *Who Moved My Cheese?* Its author, Spencer Johnson, tells a story, a fable of sorts, which captures the empty and sometimes devastating feelings we emote when we experience loss such as a job or a relationship. When all seemed to be right with the world as it previously existed, now the unsettling of "what was" produces uncertainty and sometimes downright fear. Johnson's message can be summarized as follows: instead of viewing change as the end of something, we must learn to see it as a beginning. For years, his tale was used by leaders in business who were implementing change, but his narrative also reveals personal applications as well. While sometimes disconcerting, change is not always bad. Our days should not be wasted; life demands a level of risk and adventure.

In the past year, our family has been affected by the relocation of a dear friend to another town as well as the move of a neighborhood family to a different area of the community. The friend had become part of our daily routine, and the neighbors were simply a source of comfort. For most of us, whether at work or personally, we learn to feel secure with that which is familiar. Whenever change occurs, our world becomes a little shaken. Years ago, I had a good friend who would often express a need to become "centered." For her, she seemed to always be searching for that state of being grounded where she would find peace, feel emotionally healthy, and become purposefully focused. Although she tragically died at a young age, I think she found that for which she had been searching. It evidenced itself through her eventual marriage and manifested itself as she became anchored in her relationship with God.

What my friend had to learn was what we all need to come to terms with in our own journey. And that is this: when we base our faith on feelings, it will fluctuate with every emotional high and low we experience. On the contrary, when we find ourselves in the midst of change, we need to remember a brief verse of scripture from the Old Testament: "I am the LORD, and I do not change"

(Malachi 3:6 NLT). He is the one constant on whom we can always depend, no matter how far away He might feel at the time. Someone once made a statement that parallels the title of Spencer Johnson's book: "If you feel distant from God, guess who moved?" He is always by our side if we choose to trust and believe in Him. "Instead, each person is tempted by his own desire, being lured and trapped by it" (James 1:14 ISV). As a result, we are challenged to make a decision as to whom we will follow. "Come close to God, and God will come close to you. Wash your hands, you sinners; purify your hearts, for your loyalty is divided between God and the world" (James 4:8 NLT).

As Jesus' time on earth was coming to an end, He spoke of a move that confused His disciples and filled them with grief and many questions. "But the time is coming—indeed it's here now—when you will be scattered, each one going his own way, leaving me alone. Yet I am not alone because the Father is with me" (John 16:32 NLT). Through these very words of Jesus, we are assured of God's nearness and faithfulness. We are reminded and reassured by the lyrics of the great hymn:

> Great is Thy faithfulness, O God my Father,
> There is no shadow of turning with Thee;
> Thou changest not, Thy compassions, they fail not
> As Thou hast been Thou forever wilt be. (David Chisholm)

We come to realize that moves, both in the form of big and small changes, will persist throughout this lifetime. Nothing lasts forever, except the God of all the ages. So hold on to Him as you journey. For, in doing so, you will find that you are only one move from center. Keep Him in the midst of all you do—having the peace, joy, and confidence that He will most assuredly sustain you wherever you go.

Reflection

What changes or temptations are currently prompting an uneasiness within your spirit? Have you moved closer to or distanced yourself from God as a result? As you recognize that you know a God who is unchanging in His love and concern for you, are there ways that you might consider improving your expressions of faithfulness and devotion to Him?

JUNE 11
(Y1, D24)

My Eyes Are Upon You

He guides the humble in what is right and teaches them his way.

—Psalm 25:9 (NIV)

Why can't men ask for directions when they are lost? Why can't they read an instructional manual when they don't know how to do something? These are questions that have been asked by women for some time. However, as women have gained prominence in the workplace and power in positions of leadership, they are often guilty of not asking for help as well. Many of us who have become accustomed to appearing strong and in control are fearful that asking for help will exhibit signs of weakness or incompetence. Asking for directions is like admitting defeat. For if we assume that when all else fails, we should ask for or read the directions, does that then make us the failure for needing to do so? James, the half-brother of Jesus, gave us a powerful promise when he wrote, "If any of you lacks wisdom, you should ask God, who gives generously to all without finding fault, and it will be given to you" (James 1:5 NIV). James would tell us that it's perfectly okay to acknowledge that in those times when we don't know what to do, we should ask God for wisdom and direction while believing that we will receive an answer.

I remember once reading that many years ago, an Irish evangelist was speaking about how we should learn to test God in every trial and difficulty. To emphasize his point, he told those present that when they found themselves challenged by circumstances where they needed direction, they were to prompt themselves to say, "For this, I have Jesus." During his message, one young lady in attendance received word that her mother was quite ill and that she should take the train home immediately. She was challenged by her uneasiness and the lack of direction ahead. She had never experienced taking such a long journey alone. Then she remembered the words of the evangelist as a feeling of peace and strength came over her. Weeks later, the evangelist received a letter from her, thanking him for his humble yet practical message. She had come to realize that no matter what difficulties she would face in life, there was understanding that finding direction would lie within one certain phrase—"For this, I have Jesus."

God's Word gives us one example after another of persons who lacked direction. In one case, Joshua was deceived when he relied on his own judgment but neglected to ask God for help. Joshua 9:14 (NIV) admits that "The Israelites sampled their provisions but did not inquire of the Lord." Someone once said that he who knows not and knows that he knows not is a wise man, but he who knows not and knows not that he knows not is a fool. Perhaps then, Jehoshaphat, king of Judah, was no fool. When a vast army had gathered against Jerusalem, and the king realized what he was up against, he knew where to turn for guidance. He uttered this prayer: "Our God, will you not judge them? For we have no power to face this vast army that is attacking us. We do not know what to do, but our eyes are on you" (2 Chronicles 20:12 NIV). Even Peter, one of Jesus' very own disciples, confessed the need for direction when he stated, "Lord, to whom would we go? You have the words that give eternal life" (John 6:68 NLT).

There is certainly nothing wrong in admitting that the course we have been seeking is beyond our limited understanding. However, God knows what we should do, and He is always close by and available to us. We can't expect that He will knock us over the head to get our attention, but He will respond to our simple cry of, "Lord, I need your help." We can come to Him in prayer to seek wisdom and direction for both big and small decisions. Billy Graham once said, "Heaven is full of answers to prayers for which no one ever bothered to ask." The psalmist would tell us that we simply need to know where to look: "Joyful are those who obey his laws and search for him with all their hearts" (Psalm 119:2 NLT). God is loving and powerful, and He wants us to come to Him instead of trying to do things our own way. We must seek His will, even when it appears to be contrary to the path we had in mind. So when you find yourself fumbling through life, remember the phrase, "For this, I have Jesus." As you look heavenward for your answer, do so with patience by simply letting God know, "My eyes are upon you."

Reflection

When you ask God for help, are you truly looking for His direction or are you seeking confirmation of what you already believe to be true? Are you in need of an answer to a prayer that you have not yet prayed? What is holding you back from asking for His direction? Might you be fearful that the answer you will receive might be in conflict with your present beliefs and understanding?

JUNE 12
(Y2, D24)

Sufficiency: When Enough Is Enough

My grace is sufficient for you, for my power is made perfect in weakness.

—2 Corinthians 12:9 (NIV)

If you had a regular seat at our family table, you might hear the phrase "I've had sufficient." It's our way of saying that we have been satisfied when the serving bowls are passed around one final time. You would not find us to be customers at the local fast-food chain who select the "supersize" option. A profit will likely be made on us when we patronize the "all-you-can-eat" buffet. While we occasionally go back for more, we most often find that we are satisfied and grateful for that which we have been provided. Satisfaction seems to be a rare condition in our world today. We find ourselves immersed in a culture where our gluttonous behavior has extended into all aspects of our lives. We expect our employer to provide health care, guaranteed retirement income, educational opportunities, and paid time away from work. And if for some reason we are not employable, we assume that our government will take care of these things. We live in a state of expectation for free stuff, begging the question, "Just when is enough, enough?" As long as we pursue our own idea of what will satisfy, we may never quite find it.

Christian author and pastor Max Lucado tells the story of a small group of folks who are flying across the country in a chartered plane. All of a sudden, the engine bursts into flames, and the pilot rushes out of the cockpit. "We're going to crash!" he yells. "We've got to bail out!" He passes out a parachute to each person, giving them a few pointers while he throws open the door.

The first passenger steps up and shouts over the wind, "Could I make a request?"

"Sure, what is it?"

"Any way I could get a pink parachute?"

The pilot shakes his head in disbelief. "Isn't it enough that I gave you a parachute at all?" And so the first passenger jumps. The second steps to the door.

"I'm wondering if there is any way you could ensure that I won't get nauseated during the fall?"

"No, but I can ensure that you will have a parachute for the fall." Each of the passengers comes with their unique request as they receive a parachute.

"Please, Captain," says one, "I am afraid of heights. Would you remove my fear?"

"No," he replies, "but I'll give you a parachute."

Another pleads for a different strategy. "Couldn't you change the plans? Let's crash with the plane. We might survive."

The pilot smiles and says, "You don't know what you are asking" and gently shoves the fellow out the door. One passenger wants some goggles, another wants boots, another wants to wait until the plane is closer to the ground. "You people don't understand!" the pilot shouts as he helps, one by one. "I've given you a parachute! That is enough."

The purpose of the story, of course, is to highlight our customary state of discontent. The pilot makes available the one thing that will most likely ensure survival. Instead of accepting the only provision necessary for the jump, the passengers are restless, anxious, even demanding. As we work through life's journey, we hopefully come to understand that God is our pilot who provides all that we need. A genuine Christian is absolutely satisfied, but this satisfaction is very different from the contentment that people commonly talk about. Bottom line, contentment is not having all that you want; true contentment is wanting only what you have. When we are in right relationship with God, our souls are satisfied. Jesus clearly stated, "I am the bread of life. Whoever comes to me will never go hungry, and whoever believes in me will never be thirsty" (John 6:35 NIV). Jesus Christ gives what the world cannot—contentment.

Through His conversion and apostleship, Paul was taught that worldly circumstances are elusive. They do not minister to the deep needs of the heart, whether in want or abundance. He wrote, "I have learned how to be content with whatever I have. I know how to live on almost nothing or with everything. I have learned the secret of living in every situation, whether it is with a full stomach or empty, with plenty or little" (Philippians 4:11–12 NLT). When we make it our goal to live for Christ, the result is a satisfaction that carries us into eternity. The moment one gives into Him is when they will begin to understand contentment. Even when earthly needs or wants clamor for attention, our souls know this state is temporary. It's easy to find contentment when we realize enough is enough and that our forever satisfaction lies just ahead. This, my friend, should be sufficient for our happiness.

Reflection

If God's only gift to you was His grace to save you, would that be enough for you to be content? How can you disclaim commercial ads which appeal to our essential desire to claim happiness as a right? What wisdom do you find in the words of this scriptural passage: "Better what the eye sees than the roving of the appetite. This too is meaningless, a chasing after the wind" (Ecclesiastes 6:9 NIV)?

JUNE 13
(Y3, D24)

A Road Worth Taking

But small is the gate and narrow the road that leads to life, and only a few find it.

—Matthew 7:14 (NIV)

This time of the year, many families will be taking off on road trips to various parts of the country. I remember some of my best vacations while growing up would not have occurred had it not been for the many hours spent in the car on our nation's highways. While we are on these family outings, who among us has not asked the question, "How much longer till we get there?" Over time, we come to realize that frequently, we remember more about the journey than the destination. The late CBS news journalist, Charles Kuralt, became renowned for his *On the Road* segments about Americana which ended up lasting for a quarter of century. Who can forget the Griswold family's cross-country drive to Walley World with a cast of characters headed by Chevy Chase? Much earlier in the last century, Bob Hope, Bing Crosby, and Dorothy Lamour made a series of seven movies that came to be known as the Road Pictures.

The imagery of roads has been popularized in music over the years. In his song "Blowing in the Wind," Bob Dylan asked the question, "How many roads must a man walk down before you call him a man?" Recently, newcomer Chris Mann introduced these words with his melodic voice in his song "Roads:"

> There are roads in this life that we all travel,
> There are scars and there are battles where we roam.
> When we are lost, Oh, wherever we may go
> They will always lead you home!

In the 1980s, country singer Willie Nelson released one of his most famous songs, *On the Road Again*, and three decades later boyband, One Direction, made their multicontinent tour using the same title.

Indeed, the concept of roads plays a significant role in scripture as well. In the Old Testament, we read these words: "A voice is calling, 'Clear the way for the LORD in the wilderness; Make smooth in the desert a highway for our God'" (Isaiah 40:3 NASB). Jesus used a familiar road from Jerusalem to Jericho to illustrate His parable of the Good Samaritan (Luke 10:25–37). It was also on a road approaching Jericho that Jesus encountered a blind man sitting by the side, begging (Luke 18:35–42). The man called out for mercy, and when Jesus asked the man what it was that He needed, he received his sight because of his demonstration of faith. On the road to Emmaus (Luke 24:13–35), Jesus appeared and walked with two of His followers after His death. At the time, they did not recognize Him. Later, when He broke bread with them, they realized who He was and that He had in fact risen. "They said to each other, "Didn't our hearts burn within us as he talked with us on the road and explained the Scriptures to us?" (Luke 24:32 NLT). It was a journey that had begun in sadness and disbelief but ended with joy and affirmation.

The great poet, Robert Frost, is oft-remembered for his celebrated line, "Two roads diverged in a wood, and I—I took the one less traveled by, And that has made all the difference." In current times, we are able and tempted to follow almost anyone we want if we have the most relevant information-sharing account. I have never felt I had the need to know every little detail that was happening with a person, especially those who think their very lives are so important that we should know everything about them. Following someone on social media has very little relevance to who I am or who I might wish to imitate. But there was a day "As they were walking along the road, a man said to him, 'I will follow you wherever you go'" (Luke 9:57 NIV). Now that man understood the meaning of the road less traveled and had a clear direction as to who he should follow while he journeyed his way through life.

Reflection

Under what circumstances is it sometimes easier to travel down the easy roads of life? Are there lessons to be learned from "the road scriptures" above, such as making sure we are traveling with God, going out of our way for others, making a leap of faith, and not taking for granted those who share your journey? What obstacles along the road might stand in your way of following God?

JUNE 14
(Y4, D24)

Life Hanging in the Balance

A false balance is an abomination to the LORD, but a just weight is his delight.

—Proverbs 11:1 (ESV)

When twenty-four Republican congressmen gathered in Alexandria, Virginia, around 6:30 a.m. on June 14, 2017, to practice for their annual Congressional Charity Baseball Game, little did they know that their lives were hanging in the balance. The team had been practicing for about a half-hour that day when a man who had posted online about his hate of conservatives began shooting at his directed targets. The injured included a congressional aide, a lobbyist, a police officer, and Representative Steve Scalise. Several witnesses said their lives were saved by the presence of the Capitol Police who were there because of Scalise's position as the House Majority Whip. They were able to immediately engage the shooter, keep him pinned down, and prevent him from continuing to fire on the unarmed baseball players. When the shooting began, Scalise said he simply started to pray. "It was amazing how that removed so much of the anxiety and all of a sudden I was calm, and I knew that God was taking care of me, and boy did he ever." The attack drew a bipartisan response, and the game was played as scheduled the following day.

The phrase "hanging in the balance" is often used to describe situations where those involved are about to experience an uncertain future. It can be applied to groups of persons who are facing potential life-threatening situations, such as the thirty-three Chilean men who were trapped underground in a collapsed mine in 2010 before they were rescued sixty-nine days later. It can certainly apply to any individual who is about to escape the fate of certain death. On December 18, 1867, twenty-eight-year-old John D. Rockefeller, an entrepreneur widely known in Cleveland and the oil refining industry, was about to make a quick business trip to New York City to check on his East Coast operations. He got an unusually delayed start that morning, so he sent his bags ahead of him. Hours later, Rockefeller pulled into Cleveland's Union Station just a few minutes too late. His bags made the train, but he didn't—and it saved his life. By missing the Lake Shore Express that morning, Rockefeller escaped one of the worst railroad accidents in nineteenth-century America. As a latecomer to the Cleveland station, he would have sat in the end car which jumped the track and fell into an icy gorge while crossing over a high railroad bridge in the western New York. Rockefeller came across the scene himself when the later train he had taken was forced to stop because of the wreck. He immediately telegraphed his wife, stating, "Thank God I am unharmed. The six-forty train I missed had bad accident." In fact, nearly fifty persons died in the incident that fateful day.

We hear about situations like this all the time. But it never happens to us until it does! So what do we do then? How are we to face that potentially perilous situation lurking right around the corner? The Christian's perspective to having a balanced life begins by examining our relationship with God. The closer you walk with God, the more faith you have that He will help you through the toughest times. Moses warned of the curses that would fall upon those who distanced themselves from God's laws: "Your life will constantly hang in the balance. You will live night and day in fear, unsure if you will survive" (Deuteronomy 28:66 NLT). For those who are making their life journey with Jesus by their side, the answer for balancing life's uncertainties doesn't have to be worrisome or overwhelming. Jesus said, "I came that they may have life and have it abundantly" (John 10:10 ESV). Knowing someone is always there and who understands what we are going through is a major component in the process of getting one's life in balance. As you become more in sync with God, you will realize that even in times of struggle, you will remain in balance when your focus remains on Him. We learn that our first instinct should be to call on God, just as Representative Scalise did when he was shot. We come to understand that our Lord and Savior has not only promised an abundant life but also an everlasting one. Far too often, we allow ourselves to become so distraught that our story progresses like a cliff-hanger in the season-ending finale of our favorite TV drama. We end up wondering if we will survive long enough to continue playing our role. If you are right with God, no matter what happens in this lifetime, you can be assured that you will not be written out of the script. You will never have to feel that your life is simply hanging in the balance—that's security only He alone can provide.

Reflection

Do you seek find yourself seeking God's wisdom or are you trying to go through life on your own strength? What specific steps do you need to take to know that your life is not hanging in the balance? In what ways can you reassure others who are struggling that they can find renewed life with Jesus?

JUNE 15
(Y5, D24)

Faith Insurance

I tell you the truth, if you had faith even as small as a mustard seed, you could say to this mountain, "Move from here to there," and it would move. Nothing would be impossible.

—Matthew 17:20 (NLT)

We crawl into our car to conduct one last visual check, making sure we haven't missed anything. The tires have been checked, the oil has been changed, the navigation system has been loaded with each of the estimated destinations, and all of the emergency likelihoods have been anticipated. Having done everything possible to assure a successful trip, we back out of the garage and begin to make our way toward a long-awaited getaway. We are as secure as we can possibly be, but we have no guarantee we will ever get there. Maybe our trip is a costlier once-in-a-lifetime venture by plane to a far-off destination or a cruise aboard a luxurious passenger ship offering amazing ports of call. As we finalize the details of our journey, we are given the opportunity to purchase travel insurance. We weigh the possibilities such as illness, family emergency, or other possible reasons for cancellation, and we wonder if the extra cost is worth it. The truth is that most days, the deliberate acts we take are based on our experience that we have done them before, and everything has been okay so far. But when it comes to heading off for parts unknown, things are a little different for many of us. There's a lot more to consider.

Our faith-walk is a lot like that as well. Jesus often spoke about how faith, or the lack of it, will directly affect our ability to be an effective follower. At Jesus' prompting, His disciple, Peter, walked on water. "But when he saw the wind, he was afraid and, beginning to sink, cried out, 'Lord, save me!'" (Matthew 14:30 NIV). On another occasion, a man approached Jesus with his son who was afflicted with seizures, kneeling before Him, saying, "I brought him to your disciples, but they could not heal him" (Matthew 17:16 NIV). In both instances, He scolded them for their lack of faith. There were times, however, when He was amazed at the faith others showed. Once He was approached by a Roman soldier who was grieved by the suffering condition of his ailing servant. "Jesus said, 'I will come and heal him.' But the officer said, 'Lord, I am not worthy to have you come into my home. Just say the word from where you are, and my servant will be healed'" (Matthew 8:7–8 NLT). "When Jesus heard this, He marveled and said to those who followed Him, 'Truly, I tell you, with no one in Israel have I found such faith'" (Matthew 8:10 ESV).

God's Word is filled with stories of faith, frequently demonstrated by a surprising cast of characters. One of those featured in the Old Testament is the story of Rahab, a prostitute woman in ancient Jericho who saved two spies who had been sent by Joshua to measure the defenses of the city. People had told her how God helped the Israelites during their journey to Canaan. She stated to the men: "For the LORD your God is the supreme God of the heavens above and the earth below" (Joshua 2:11 NLT). Knowing that her city would be attacked and destroyed for its wickedness and idol worship, she protected the men and helped them escape with the promise that they would provide safe passage for her and her family, even if they slaughtered everyone else in Jericho. When it was time, "The men who had been spies went in and brought out Rahab, her father, mother, brothers, and all the other relatives who were with her. They moved her whole family to a safe place near the camp of Israel" (Joshua 6:23 NLT).

Rahab trusted God to save her, and she wanted to join His people. So God gifted these things to her because of her faith. Having special significance for Christians, she is among four women listed in Matthew's gospel as ancestors to Jesus of Nazareth (Matthew 1:5). We find in Rahab's life the inspiring story of each of us who have failed through sin but been saved by grace. It's not an insurance package that we can purchase, for Jesus has already paid our premium with His death. What an awesome gift we inherit when we finally realize that the faith which is tough enough to withstand difficult times is not created by our feelings or even what we perceive with our physical senses. It must be based first and foremost on what we know about God. It's an insurance package worth having and holding on to.

Reflection

As you look back over your life, can you see times that you were like Peter, sinking in the water for a lack of faith? How do Rahab and the Roman soldier provide direction for your faith walk? Can you think of other biblical or personal examples when faith ensured a positive outcome? How might these examples be shared with others who are presently struggling in their faith?

JUNE 16
(Y6, D24)

Commander-in-Chief

My child, don't make light of the LORD's discipline, and don't give up when he corrects you.

—Proverbs 3:11 (NLT)

There would have been a day not so long ago when any grade school student would have been able to tell you, without hesitation, that the "father of our country" was George Washington. Today, there are those who would find that title to not be politically correct or who would seek to undermine the credibility of the man himself. It was on June 15, 1775, that Washington accepted an appointment to lead the Continental Army as its commander-in-chief. Washington's determination, leadership, and refusal to give up made the difference between victory and defeat on more than one occasion. Indeed, so powerful was Washington's character and reputation that the organizers of the Constitutional Convention believed that the Convention would not succeed unless Washington attended it. Due to his military fame and humble personality, Americans overwhelmingly elected Washington to be their first president in 1789. Just as a good father can provide leadership for his family, Washington provided unquestionable direction for a new country. Historian Joseph Ellis has stated that "Washington was the glue that held the nation together." He seemed to understand the "big picture" more than many of his day, and he was at the forefront of every major event in American history from 1754 to 1799. The respect for Washington was a direct result of his personal virtue which was cultivated over his lifetime. He was keenly aware of his faults from an early age, and he worked at controlling his shortcomings. In his book, *Our Sacred Honor*, William Bennett states, "Washington wasn't born good. Only practice and habit made him so." It certainly sounds as if his own self-discipline made him worthy of the label as the father of his country.

As we celebrate another Father's Day, it could be useful for any of us to apply some of the examples that Washington displayed. He would have been the first to tell you he was an imperfect man but was trying to do better. Recently, an older friend of mine told the story of her own father. She, along with her two older brothers, always seemed to find themselves in trouble at a young age. They frequently heard the oft-used threat from their mother: "Just wait till your father gets home." My friend said that on those occasions, as their father appeared after a hard day's work, he would remove his dirty work shoes, put on his slippers, and motion the three of them to the cellar. When they arrived there, they each understood the drill. As their father removed his slipper, he began to slap it loudly against his own hand. He then proceeded to tell each of the children to yell out, one by one, as if they were being disciplined. The story of their punishment remained a secret into adulthood with their father undoubtedly recognizing that his demonstration of love yielded better results than a sore bottom may have accomplished. The Lord is very merciful as well, and He normally gives us ample time to repent. His discipline usually comes after our recurring acts of disobedience and His repeated warnings. After all, when we show obedience to our heavenly Father, it will only strengthen our relationship with Him. The Apostle Paul put it this way: "Nevertheless, when we are judged in this way by the Lord, we are being disciplined so that we will not be finally condemned with the world" (1 Corinthians 11:32 NIV).

The great news is that like my friend's father, God is gracious. If we haven't been living for Him, if we haven't been following His commandments, if we've been living in and for the world, we can be transformed by the blood of Jesus Christ. We can ask God for forgiveness, and He will give it. And He will choose to forget our sin, just like it never happened. "Since we respected our earthly fathers who disciplined us, shouldn't we submit even more to the discipline of the Father of our spirits and live forever? For our earthly fathers disciplined us for a few years, doing the best they knew how. But God's discipline is always good for us so that we might share in his holiness" (Hebrews 12:9–11 NLT). If we have ever experienced the love of an earthly father who showed discipline in his life, we have indeed been fortunate. But what is even more precious is that all of God's children can know a heavenly Father who they will learn to embrace more and more each day. All who do so will come to recognize and regard Him as their true Commander-in-Chief, now and for all of eternity.

Reflection

Reflect on some examples of ways you practice self-discipline each day. In pursuit of your own spiritual and faith development, what aspects of your life do you consider in need of tougher discipline? What is your plan for making this happen? How will you be sure to include God in the process?

JUNE 17
(Y7, D24)

Forgive and Forget

I, even I, am he who blots out your transgressions, for my
own sake, and remembers your sins no more.

—Isaiah 43:25 (NIV)

When asked to be forgiven, she received this response: "Well, through the help of God's love, I can forgive you. But I don't know that I am strong enough to continue to be your friend, because I will always remember how deeply you have hurt me." I wasn't quite sure I agreed, but I certainly understood. There are many of us who have probably felt this way at one time or other. None of us go through life without experiencing some level of betrayal. Although we may find that eventually we may be able to verbalize an expression of forgiveness, letting go and forgetting what happened may be an entirely different matter. When trust has been broken, the whole concept of "forgive and forget" may be something we need to pray about in order for true healing to begin or for the relationship to have any hope of a future.

On what appeared to be a normal Wednesday night at the Emanuel AME Church in Charleston, South Carolina, the senior pastor began the weekly prayer meeting and Bible study on June 17, 2015. A twenty-one-year-old man and stranger to the group sat next to the pastor who led the discussion for nearly an hour. Then in an apparent racially motivated hate crime, the young man pulled out a handgun and fatally wounded nine of those who were in attendance, including the pastor. Less than two days later, the alleged shooter appeared before a judge where family members of the victims were present. A lady whose mother had died in the shooting spoke to the accused, stating, "I will never be able to hold her again, but I forgive you. And have mercy on your soul. You hurt me. You hurt a lot of people, but God forgives you, and I forgive you." How does one find the courage to forgive in circumstances like this, knowing that the magnitude of the atrocity will most likely never be forgotten? We come to realize that it is when we are in the deepest part of our pain that forgiveness has its greatest impact. It is then that our witness to others may just help to initiate change in the world around us.

It is clear in scripture that God's forgiveness is based upon the repentance of our own sin in harmony with our forgiveness of those who have sinned against us. In Jesus' example of how we should pray, He says, "And forgive us our sins, as we have forgiven those who sin against us" (Matthew 6:12 NLT). The one who has committed wrongdoing may not desire forgiveness and may never change, but that doesn't negate God's desire that we would possess a forgiving spirit by loving our enemies and pray for those who persecute us (Matthew 5:44). The Apostle Paul tell us:

> Do not repay anyone evil for evil. Be careful to do what is right in the eyes of everyone. If it is possible, as far as it depends on you, live at peace with everyone. Do not take revenge, my dear friends, but leave room for God's wrath, for it is written: "'It is mine to avenge; I will repay,' says the Lord." (Romans 12:17–19 NIV)

When Peter asked Jesus about forgiveness, He told the Parable of the Unmerciful Servant (Matthew 18:23–34). It is wise for us to focus on the concluding words of His story: "This is how my heavenly Father will treat each of you unless you forgive your brother or sister from your heart" (Matthew 18:35 NIV). And therein lies our answer. While forgiving and forgetting may not be compatible from our viewpoint, it's more a matter of the heart. It's our job to not allow a root of bitterness to take hold (Hebrews 12:15) as we let God go and work to transform a heart that will make a difference. We must move forward in our journey for the sake of Christ and strive toward what lies ahead. God's Holy Word tells us, "For I will forgive their wickedness and will remember their sins no more" (Hebrews 8:12 NIV). So as we take stock of our own lives, we can each be thankful that "God does not wish to remember what He is willing to forget" (George A. Buttrick). We can rest assured in knowing that whenever our heart is right with God, we can move beyond forgiveness and become prepared to simply let go.

Reflection

How do you react when hurt or offense occurs in your life? Do you sometimes feel that getting revenge or wounding the one who hurt you would resolve your problem? What characteristics in your life might indicate that you haven't fully forgotten past hurts, even if you may have verbalized forgiveness? How do you bring lasting peace and release to a spirit that feels wounded?

JUNE 18
(Y1, D25)

I Just Wanted to Hear It Again

"And I will be a Father to you, and you will be my sons and daughters," says the Lord Almighty.

—2 Corinthians 6:18 (NIV)

We have an ongoing joke in our family. When someone says, "I love you," the other person replies "What?" It's an imitation of the commercial. You know the one. An older gentleman and his adult son appear to be doing woodworking. The son looks over at his father and affectionately says, "I love you, Dad." To which the father replies, "What?" This happens a second time. The camera moves to the father who tells his story about how he has pulled away from others due to his hearing problem. But he refuses to spend what he considers to be a ridiculous amount of money for a hearing aid. Then he introduces an alternative at a much lower price. Eventually, we see the two of them back in the shop, assuming the father has his new hearing device in place. The scene repeats itself with the son saying to his father, "I love you, Dad." To which the father again replies, "What?" Then he smiles, looks up at his son, and says, "I heard you the first time. I just wanted to hear it again."

As we celebrate another Father's Day, we should take that opportunity to tell our earthly fathers that we love them. We can think it, gift it, feel it, demonstrate it, and talk our way around it. But, bottom line, we need to say the words out loud. We shouldn't wait another day because we don't know how long he might be around. Many have already lost their fathers, perhaps never knew them, or simply didn't have a healthy connection with one. However, each of us has the opportunity to grow into a relationship with our heavenly Father. You were created as an object of God's love, and even those who turn from Him come to recognize that connection. "Yet you, LORD, are our Father. We are the clay, you are the potter; we are all the work of your hand" (Isaiah 64:8 NIV). That means that you were created for the purpose of having a relationship with Him and, as a result, the most important thing you can recognize in life is the assurance of His steadfast love. Pastor Rick Warren says, "Everything else will change during your lifetime, but God's love for you is constant, steady, and continuous. It's the foundation for unshakable confidence." Accordingly, you can add great significance in your walk with your heavenly Father by just demonstrating your love for Him. That should include telling Him so.

It is God's wish for you to lean into Him just as a child was once able to lean into a loving father's arms. And even if you missed out on that, He is the perfect example of what a Father should be. He wants to be one in every aspect of our lives if we will only let Him. God will never abandon us nor leave us as orphans (John 14:18). He will be with us to guide, help, and protect us through whatever life brings our way. Jesus was once asked which was the greatest commandment in the law. This was His answer: "You must love the Lord your God with all your heart, all your soul, and all your mind." He said that this is the first and greatest commandment but that a second is equally important: "Love your neighbor as yourself" (Matthew 22:37–39 NLT). There's a reason why Jesus said that the second greatest commandment was like the first: if we love God with all our heart, loving our neighbor will naturally follow. The scriptures tell us, "We love each other because he loved us first" (1 John 4:19 NLT).

The most loving thing we can do for others is love God more than we love them. For if we love God most, we will love others best. So what does a relationship with Him look like? Well, that is going to be different for each person. Just as our associations with people differ, each of us will have our own unique relationship with God because of our varied personalities. Remember that every relationship is based on trust, and that same principal applies to God (Psalm 84:12). The more you know Him and trust Him, the more intimate your relationship will be. He adores you. It would be a meaningful act of personal worship if you would simply tell Him that you love Him. If you do this, you can almost see His arms outstretched and a voice from heaven with those words of affirmation stating, "I just wanted to hear it again."

Reflection

If you tell God that you love Him and desire to keep His commands but fail to spend time with Him, how might you expect Hm to feel? What do you know about God that makes Him the perfect father? How does knowing this affect your choices and your actions? In what ways do you think a daily verbal expression telling God that you love Him might begin to change your day?

JUNE 19

(Y2, D25)

Decisions, Decisions!

"I have the right to do anything," you say—but not everything is beneficial. "I have the right to do anything"—but not everything is constructive.

—1 Corinthians 10:23 (NIV)

An old legend tells of a farmer with a beautiful daughter who was courted by a variety of young men, all wanting to marry her. So the farmer promised the hand of his daughter in marriage to the one who could walk through his field of corn, never backtracking, and select the largest, most perfect ear of corn in the entire field. The beautiful daughter ended up unmarried. So goes the myth. Here's why. The most promising suitor ended up walking through the field, looking, waiting, uncertain. As he approached the end of the field, in desperation, he selected an ear of corn having passed up many which were superior to what he ended up with. But other young men walked through the field, unable to backtrack, ending up with nothing because they couldn't decide which ear of corn was the most perfectly formed. Sometimes it's difficult to make a decision, commonly referred to as analysis paralysis. I once knew a gentleman who went through his entire life unable to make significant decisions. He was raised in an orphanage where he was told what to do. When he turned eighteen, he enlisted in the armed services, constantly following orders. After his discharge, he married a domineering lady who bossed him all her life. Following her passing, he procured the services of a trustee to execute his decision-making.

Indeed, most of our life can be summed up by the decisions we've made or perhaps didn't make. The process of decision-making includes making a judgment about an attitude or action. Decisions are a willful act, and they are always influenced by the mind, the emotions, or both. Many of our decisions never reach our conscious level because they are simply made out of habit. On the other hand, there are some decisions that require thoughtful consideration. Woven together, they form the tapestry of our daily lives. Additionally, there are times we must face life-altering decisions that cause us to struggle. For instance, there is a big difference between the thought process for a having elective surgery compared to contemplating a decision to discontinue treatments for a terminal illness.

The latter requires wisdom and clarity of thought based upon the facts at hand, counsel from other devout believers who care about you, and an understanding of God's will. The key question before making a decision is "Do I choose to please myself, or the Lord?" Joshua set the standard: "If serving the Lord seems undesirable to you, then choose for yourselves this day whom you will serve… But as for me and my household, we will serve the Lord" (Joshua 24:15 NIV).

We are shaped by the choices we make. God gives us the freedom to make our own decisions. He allowed men and women of the Bible to think, reason, and make their own choices. He gave Adam and Eve a choice to eat from all the trees in the Garden of Eden, except the tree of the knowledge of good and evil (Genesis 2:16–17). Ruth had a choice to stay in Moab or go to Judah with Naomi (Ruth 1:11–14). David had a choice to either kill Saul or to allow him to live (1 Samuel 24:6–7). Samson didn't think about the repercussions of his decision to confide in Delilah (Judges 16:16–23). Peter made three different decisions to deny Christ, even after being warned that he would do so (Matthew 26:69–75). We are given a choice to make good or bad decisions. If we choose good, then we must seek God's promise through prayer that He would give His children wisdom. "If any of you lacks wisdom, you should ask God, who gives generously to all without finding fault, and it will be given to you" (James 1:5 NIV). You might not get a heavenly revelation, but God just might give you all the wisdom you need to make the best choice. Pour your heart out to Him in prayer, and commit to honor Jesus through it all. For Jesus opens doors in your life that no one can close, and He closes doors in your life that no one else can open. When you passionately walk with God daily, the power of Christ will see you through every decision you make.

Reflection

Are there aspects of your life that are preventing you from making a decision to fully follow Christ? How often do you pray about the decisions of life? Do you include prayers for others such as employers and legislators who make decisions which affect you? How can you make personal application and encourage others to consider Proverbs 3:5–7 (NLT) in the decision-making process? It reads, "Trust in the Lord with all your heart; do not depend on your own understanding. Seek his will in all you do, and he will show you which path to take. Don't be impressed with your own wisdom."

JUNE 20
(Y3, D25)

My Father's Smile

May the Lord smile on you.

—Numbers 6:25 (NLT)

There are certain things that remind us of the special people in our lives, especially if they have passed on. For me, the smell of sawdust will almost instantly bring back memories of my father because he was an avid carpenter. American author and international speaker Squire Rushnell tells a delightful story. It was about the experience of a daughter of one of the country's most famous clowns, Emmett Kelly, at the time of his passing. After receiving word that her father had died, Stasia Kelly boarded a plane to fly home. The man seated beside her asked her why she was so low. She explained that she was traveling back to be with family and attend her father's funeral. She showed him a newspaper picture announcing his demise. The man beside her was quite taken back. He revealed that on the day she was born, he was the photographer who snapped this picture of the well-known clown recognized for his normal sad expression. In the photo, however, his face projected a beautiful smile as he received word of Stasia's birth. In his book, *Divine Alignment,* Rushnell labels these moments in life to be called "God Winks."

Through his sober expression, Kelly's job was to make others smile by his sad appearance. On this occasion, the birth of a daughter instantly brought an uncommon smile to his clown face. As we mature, we come to realize that fathers are one of the most important people in our lives. Dad will get you to stretch out in his arms in the swimming pool for the first time. And when he tells you that he is going to let go and that you are to paddle, you are confident he will be there to keep you from sinking if you start to sink. When your friends or siblings convince you to climb that old oak tree in the backyard, Dad is the one waiting for you to jump into his loving arms when you freeze after you realize just how high you have climbed. News commentator Paul Harvey once said that "a father never feels entirely worthy of the worship in his child's eyes. He never is quite the hero his daughter thinks, never quite the man his son believes him to be. This worries him, sometimes. So he works too hard to try and smooth the rough places in the road for those of his own who will follow him."

Fathers teach us about life in a way that no one else can. When we break the rules, Mom says, "Just wait till your father gets home." When we run to him to shield us from the monsters, we are confident that he will protect us. When he teaches us to ride a bike or drive a car, we might become frustrated with all the cautionary instructions but will one day be grateful that he taught us the right way. When we move away and are welcomed home again at any time, it somehow becomes easier to tell him how much we love him. All of these things make Dad smile. It's somewhat remarkable that the same obedient heart, absolute trust, use of his gifts and instruction, and expression for continual love are the identical things that make our heavenly Father smile as well.

As we move forward in our life journey, not yet complete, we might find ourselves echoing this prayer from *The Message*: "Smile on me, your servant; teach me the right way to live" (Psalm 119:135). For as we traverse along the path, we hopefully become humbled to understand that "The LORD makes firm the steps of the one who delights in him; though he may stumble, he will not fall, for the LORD upholds him with his hand" (Psalm 37:23 NIV). As the path becomes rocky and we falter along its way, we think of Dad and remember his example. As we develop a new relationship with our Heavenly Father, it's vital that our faith and trust in Him deepens. "But without faith, it is impossible to please Him, for he who comes to God must believe that He is, and that He is a rewarder of those who diligently seek Him" (Hebrews 11:6 NKJB). Therefore, grant us unwavering day-by-day faith, Lord, that we would be attentive to the tasks you have placed before us, knowing that when our day is done, you will be able to smile and say to us, "Well done" (Matthew 25:21).

Reflection

Think back on those things that made your earthly father smile. Or if you are a dad, on what occasions do your children make you smile? Can you see similarities with what makes your heavenly Father smile? If you are not already doing so, what changes will you make to bring a smile to Him?

JUNE 21
(Y4, D25)

Hiding Old Shoes and Newfound Faith

You are my hiding place and my shield; I hope in your word.

—Psalm 119:114 (ESV)

Some time ago, I ran into a lady I had not seen in a long time. She was sitting in a car, waiting on her daughter who was doing some shopping. She rolled down the window and told me how happy she was to see me. On her last birthday, she had turned ninety-five. To see and speak with her, you would have no idea she was that age. I had heard, however, that she had fallen, and I told her I was glad to see that she was doing all right. She proceeded to inform me her children were blaming the fall on the fact that she was wearing her favorite old pair of shoes. "Now," she stated, "they are looking for them because they want to throw them away." Bound and determined that was not going to happen, she just smiled and told me that she had hidden them in a place they would never find. She lived to be over a hundred years of age.

Hiding places meet different needs and depend on varying situations which confront us. Tragically, intended victims of several shootings in our nation have sought refuge. Anything from classrooms with barricaded doors to restrooms in secluded places have been used as sanctuary areas. The concept of hiding is often utilized in circumstances created by man in which we become fearful. In the early 1970s, a biographical book was released about the life of Corrie ten Boom. Her amazing narrative is centered in 1940s Netherlands when that country was invaded by the Nazis. Having strong Christian values, the ten Boom family, who made its living by running a watchmaker's shop, began to secretly shelter Jews in their home. Their mission was eventually discovered, and they were imprisoned, eventually leaving Corrie to share their story many years later in *The Hiding Place*.

God's Word is filled with passages about hiding beginning with Adam and Eve who hid from God (Genesis 3:8). Many of the prophets found themselves in hiding, including Elijah from Jezebel (1 Kings 19:1–3). David was known to be one of the bravest men who ever lived, yet he is often noted in scripture to be hiding from someone, including Saul. But his friend, Jonathan, Saul's son, told him to "stay in a secret place and hide" himself (1 Samuel 19:1–2 NKJV). Jesus, however, said that there is a time when we can no longer hide. The parable of the lamp under a bushel is reflected in three of the four gospels. In Matthew 5:14–16 (NASB), Jesus says:

> You are the light of the world. A city set on a hill cannot be hidden; nor does anyone light a lamp and put it under a basket, but on the lampstand, and it gives light to all who are in the house. Let your light shine before men in such a way that they may see your good works, and glorify your Father who is in heaven.

There will be always evil in the world from which we will sometimes want to hide. Some have guns; others just threaten to snuff out the light of our nation's Christian heritage and the practice of displaying our faith in public places. And yet even in our hiding from unjust men, we will find comfort in the loving arms of God who knows and holds our future. In *The Hiding Place*, Corrie ten Boom says: "There are no 'ifs' in God's Kingdom. His timing is perfect. His will is our hiding place. Lord Jesus, keep me in Your will! Don't let me go mad by poking about outside it." As followers of Jesus, we will frequently find our journey conflicted. It's difficult to let our light shine before others when we are often told that it is not acceptable for us to do so. While our light may still shine brightly in our homes and other private places, we find comfort in the words of the psalmist: "You hide them in the shelter of your presence, safe from those who conspire against them. You shelter them in your presence, far from accusing tongues" (Psalm 31:20 NLV). For one Dutch watchmaker and his family, what once could be lived openly now had to go into hiding. It's indeed humiliating when our old ways have to be hidden from those who say they must be thrown away, especially when they're our favorite pair of shoes.

Reflection

Have there been periods in your life when you have felt a need to go into hiding? Has this sometimes applied to your faith practices as well? Can you envision a time when Christianity will not be publicly tolerated and confined completely to our homes and underground churches? In what ways do those who walk with Christ have to make sure that the light which we shine before men does not get hidden or completely snuffed out?

JUNE 22
(Y5, D25)

The Lost Art of Hospitality

Share with the Lord's people who are in need. Practice hospitality.

—Romans 12:13 (NIV)

One of the best compliments I can ever receive is after someone has been to my home, they express appreciation for my hospitality. On one occasion, I had a group of friends over for a dinner. I furnished a few items, but the other attendees also brought various side dishes to share. It worked out really well, and there was a lot of great food. Prior to the occasion, there had been a lot of discussion about whether we should meet at a restaurant or gather at a home. Then one of the friends made the statement that it is "more intimate" when we get together at someone's home. She meant that it was more heartfelt and easier to have conversation in that setting than it would be at an eatery. In some ways, the practice of hospitality has grown to be a lost art. It has somehow become less bothersome to go out to a restaurant than invite people over, clean up the house, and cook for them. For me, it is pleasing to have others visit in my home. Even if it does require an effort of preparation, there is a feeling of contentment in being able to provide a place of comfort for others. God's Word tells us: "Do not neglect to do good and to share what you have, for such sacrifices are pleasing to God" (Hebrews 13:16 ESV).

Someone shared the story of an employee at an entertainment venue where parents invite the friends of their children for birthday parties or other special occasions. One of the mothers complimented a young man who worked at the establishment on how hospitable he was with the guests. He indicated that he was just doing his job while earning money for school. He went on to state that he appreciated her comments because very few people ever said much to him. To encourage him, she said, "But just think, here you are being so gracious in this job you probably don't like all that much. Can you imagine how well you are going to do if you apply the same enthusiasm someday to a job you really like?" It definitely made the young man's day. Contrast that with the attitude of an acquaintance of mine who invited a former coworker to stay with their family anytime she was passing through the area for her new traveling job. After she took them up on the offer twice within the same year, they complained that the former coworker had taken advantage of their generosity. I couldn't help but remember the scriptural passage, "Show hospitality to one another without grumbling" (1 Peter 4:9 ESV).

Part of the challenge of hospitality is to extend your graciousness to strangers. Jesus stated it this way:

> When you give a luncheon or dinner, do not invite your friends, your brothers or sisters, your relatives, or your rich neighbors; if you do, they may invite you back and so you will be repaid. But when you give a banquet, invite the poor, the crippled, the lame, the blind, and you will be blessed. Although they cannot repay you, you will be repaid at the resurrection of the righteous. (Luke 14:12–14 NIV)

I am reminded of the Parable of the Good Samaritan (Luke 10:25–37). While most of us concentrate on the example set by the passerby in assisting someone in distress, we forget the lesson that we can also learn from the innkeeper who served as the host after the Samaritan departed. While he was given a stipend to take care of the injured man, he took on the greatest responsibility, having no assurance whether he would ever be fully reimbursed (even though the Samaritan gave indication he would do so).

The Greek word *hospitality* is translated to mean "love of strangers." In the Old Testament, the Prophet Elisha was shown hospitality by a wealthy woman who provided food and lodging for him whenever he passed through (2 Kings 4:8–17). And in the New Testament, we learn that Jesus and His disciples depended entirely on the hospitality of others as they ministered from town to town. The essence of hospitality is showing kindness and compassion. It is a symptom of the joy that is found within our heart and resides deep within one's soul. When we realize that God constantly shows grace toward us, we also come to understand that receiving God's generosity deteriorates and dies over time if it doesn't have the opportunity to flourish through our own hospitality to others. It's an intimacy we can comprehend only when we truly recognize Him in the real-life expressions of our faith.

Reflection

Can you reflect on a time when a complete stranger displayed graciousness on your behalf? Have there been times when you have extended hospitality to someone but then grumbled about it? How can we maintain a constant positive attitude through the practice of hospitality for others? Are there ways you might demonstrate a readiness to welcome persons who aren't normally a part of your life?

JUNE 23
(Y6, D25)

Walk of Faith

[S]o that your faith might not rest on human wisdom, but on God's power.

—1 Corinthians 2:5 (NIV)

Holding a forty-three-pound balancing pole, he prayed out loud as he walked untethered across a 1,400-foot-long, 8.5-ton two-inch-thick steel cable suspended 1,500 feet above the Little Colorado River. It was June 23, 2013, and thirty-four-year-old aerialist, Nik Wallenda, became the first person to walk a high wire across this river gorge near Grand Canyon National Park in Arizona. Just one year before, he became the first to negotiate a tightrope over Niagara Falls. On that occasion, broadcast officials required that he wear a safety tether in case he fell. This time, however, he wasn't wearing a harness as he traversed a quarter mile across the ravine. Nik Wallenda, a member of the famous Flying Wallendas family of circus performers, learned to walk on a wire as a young boy making his professional debut as an aerialist at the age of thirteen. The Grand Canyon trek was the highest walk of his career, and he completed it in just less than twenty-three minutes. I remember thinking as I watched this event on TV, *Is this man fearless, faith-filled, or just foolish?* Before beginning his journey, Wallenda prayed with Lakewood Church Pastor Joel Osteen, asking God for strength and endurance. It was certainly uplifting to hear this daredevil calling out to heaven and saying, "Thank you, Jesus" dozens of times during his walk. Indeed, much has been made of Wallenda's deep faith, and He should be admired for his openness. But I wasn't quite sure at the time whether I saw this act as a walk of faith or whether I just couldn't help but wonder if deep down he was simply crazy.

Maybe that's how the other disciples felt when Peter walked on the water toward Jesus. After He had ministered to a huge crowd of followers, Jesus instructed His disciples to get back in the boat while he sent the people home. He then went to be alone so that He could pray, and nightfall came. Meanwhile, the disciples found themselves in a boat:

[A] considerable distance from land, buffeted by the waves because the wind was against it. Shortly before dawn Jesus went out to them, walking on the

349

lake. When the disciples saw him walking on the lake, they were terrified. "It's a ghost," they said, and cried out in fear.

But Jesus immediately said to them: "Take courage! It is I. Don't be afraid."

"Lord, if it's you," Peter replied, "tell me to come to you on the water."

"Come," he said. Then Peter got down out of the boat, walked on the water, and came toward Jesus. But when he saw the wind, he was afraid and, beginning to sink, cried out, "Lord, save me!" Immediately, Jesus reached out his hand and caught him. "You of little faith," he said, "why did you doubt?" And when they climbed into the boat, the wind died down. Then those who were in the boat worshiped him, saying, "Truly you are the Son of God." (Matthew 14:24–33 NIV)

It's important to consider that Peter and the other disciples embarked upon this journey in response to a request from their master. Like the disciples on that boat who would have been aware of the dangers of traveling on the Sea of Galilee with its sudden storms, we should begin our journey with an understanding that there will be risks along the way. We find that there are forces capable of upsetting our most carefully improvised plans. But we, like Peter, can discover that our Savior stands nearby, ready to help us if we will simply reach out to Him and accept his divine assistance.

Nik Wallenda and Peter provide a common lesson for us: it's important that we have a strong foothold and know who provides that strength. The Apostle Paul said, "Do not give the devil a foothold" (Ephesians 4:27 NIV). While Wallenda's assurance may have been somewhat grounded in his years of training, Peter's was at least for a short while based on His faith in His Lord. Peter's attention was drawn from Jesus, the object of his faith, to the vigorous wind and waves around him. In a moment of confusion, fear overpowered his faith, and he started to fall. We should not be critical of Peter because that has been our issue as well. Each of us has stepped out on faith many times and have taken our eyes off Him. The waves around us are as real as Peter's waves were to him, and we, too, might slip as we feel the awful descent toward a dangerous outcome. I can't claim to be free of fears or doubts, and I would suppose you can't either. We are all humans on a shaky wire, walking to our own self-destruction unless God, by His grace, gets us to the other side. Each and every time, it becomes a true walk of faith.

Reflection

Are there times when the storms of life have influenced your faith walk? How has the concept of free will affected your faith and the ability to make wise decisions? In what ways can you know if you are exercising your faith or simply using it to further a worldly agenda?

JUNE 24
(Y7, D25)

If You Must, Use Soap

Take control of what I say, O Lord, and guard my lips.

—Psalm 141:3 (NLT)

There was a day when many will remember that the use of a cuss word would immediately invoke the image of one's mother holding a bar of soap. Claiming that she would wash out your mouth if she ever heard it again, it was more of a threat than actual practice. Today, it would likely be viewed as old-fashioned, an infringement of free speech, or at the very least, an improper way to raise one's child. It has become increasingly difficult to monitor the use of offensive words when, in reality, their common usage is pervasive. Social media has gone so far as to give profane expressions code abbreviations so that users can apply the language without having to spell it out. Whenever profanity is spoken around children or vocalized in the midst of those who might become offended, there occasionally will be someone who will voice a warning with the exclamation, "Language!" Perhaps then, those who are speaking will tone it down a bit. But what can one do when you walk by someone in the grocery store who, while on their cellphone, is using curse words that are obviously part of their everyday conversation?

Recently, I had the experience of subscribing to a streaming app because I wanted to view new episodes of a cancelled drama I had previously enjoyed on network TV. Partway into the third episode, I decided I just couldn't watch anymore. I don't consider myself to be prudish, but the abundant use of vulgarities was just too over-the-top. If this is how the dramatic series was going to survive, then they would have to do so without my viewership. I wondered if there had been script concerns expressed by any of the actors who'd been involved in both productions. It most likely didn't matter since, either way, it was money in their pocket. Writers will contend that use of crude language makes their creation more realistic, arguing that the portrayal reflects how people normally express themselves. For those of us who don't want to share in such a reality, they maintain that we have been fairly given content warnings in order to make an informed decision to watch or not. My answer would be not.

Who among us has not articulated a few choice words after we have stubbed our toe or perhaps bitten our lip to prevent what might now days be interpreted as road rage after someone cuts us off in traffic? Cursing another person may take many forms. While it can be as demonstrative as using vulgar and unmistakable hand gestures out of a car window, it can be as harmless as mumbling what might be considered an inappropriate reference under our breath. Cursing is so commonplace that it shouldn't surprise us that it seems to be built right into the emotional part of our brain. This is a cautionary challenge for we who are followers of Christ. If we rein in those emotions, then perhaps we'll no longer need to use the colorful metaphors. Paul would warn us, "But now is the time to get rid of anger, rage, malicious behavior, slander, and dirty language" (Colossians 3:8 NLT). God's Word further tells us, "Do not let any unwholesome talk come out of your mouths, but only what is helpful for building others up according to their needs, that it may benefit those who listen" (Ephesians 4:29 NIV).

There are varied arguments that have been raised about cursing. Some say that people who do so have a limited vocabulary and just don't know any better. That argument doesn't always hold water since many individuals who utilize expletives as part of their everyday language are very well-educated. Others claim that it's all based on one's perception. The Christian, then, is left to answer the question, is cursing or swearing a sin? James had a lot to say on the issue: "If you claim to be religious but don't control your tongue, you are fooling yourself, and your religion is worthless" (James 1:26 NLT). He continues, "With the tongue we praise our Lord and Father, and with it we curse men, who have been made in God's likeness. Out of the same mouth come praise and cursing. My brothers, this should not be" (James 3:9–10). When all is said and done, Jesus makes it quite clear: "It's not what goes into your mouth that defiles you; you are defiled by the words that come out of your mouth" (Matthew 15:11 NLT). When we endanger that the very light we shine in the world might be extinguished, then we also risk that no one will ever see Jesus in us. A word to the wise, then: clean up your act. And if you must, use soap.

Reflection

Does your everyday speech show proper respect and reflect your true relationship with Christ? Before you find yourself in a situation where you might expose others to cursing, ask what kind of example will be made for those who might overhear. Are there appropriate ways you might express disapproval when children in your company are in a position to overhear someone who is cursing?

JUNE 25
(Y1, D26)

Pass/Fail

God blesses those who patiently endure testing and temptation. Afterward they
will receive the crown of life that God has promised to those who love him.

—James 1:12 (NLT)

A friend of mine once told me that during the final semester of her senior year of college, she took a course, pass/fail. What this essentially meant for her was that if she got anything except an "F" for the course, she would get academic credit. This is advantageous in some cases because the grade you achieve does not affect your overall grade point average (GPA). About halfway through the semester, my friend came to the conclusion that there was a distinct possibility she might not pass the class. If she failed, she would not have enough academic credits to graduate. She decided to make an appointment to speak with the professor during his office hours. While presenting her dilemma to her instructor, she disclosed that she was taking the course, pass/fail. The professor admitted that educators were not normally aware of students who elected to do so. However, he promised her that if she came to all of the classes and showed an honest effort to learn, he would make sure that she would not fail.

My friend's story somewhat reminds me of a company with which I was once employed. Throughout the year, each business unit was required to rate their performance in several key categories as either adequate or inadequate. The basis for the rating was that each key category had defining factors which, when evaluated, helped to assess whether the various units were performing as they should. Many of us who used the system were frequently frustrated because the process was not always objective and often laborious. Additionally, it repeatedly did not bring about the desired performance results because the organization was either unwilling or unable to pledge the human and/or financial resources which might have improved the end-result. I sometimes wonder if our faith journey isn't all that different; we know that we are not always achieving the desired standard, and we aren't always ready or willing to commit.

When it comes to evaluating our relationship with God, we can sometimes find ourselves making a comparison with others. Unfortunately, it can become far too easy to relate our sins to those around us, justifying that ours most likely is not as bad as theirs. Seeing sin on a sliding scale is not much different than an educator who grades on a curve. Grading on a curve essentially allows the other test takers to set the standard rather than the instructor who developed the test. It's different in our spiritual journey. Jesus took the test on the cross and got a perfect score. The rest of us pale in comparison and pass only because of His grace. Paul provides this counsel: "Don't copy the behavior and customs of this world, but let God transform you into a new person by changing the way you think. Then you will learn to know God's will for you, which is good and pleasing and perfect" (Romans 12:2 NLT).

So you must "choose this day whom you will serve" (Joshua 24:15 ESV): a perfect God or a failing world. The apostle knew that Jesus was the only one who could ever score a 100 percent on God's test. It was perfectly clear to him that on his own he could never receive the passing score required for eternal life. He knew his entrance into heaven would only come through having total confidence in the ultimate teacher. "We are made right with God by placing our faith in Jesus Christ. And this is true for everyone who believes, no matter who we are. For everyone has sinned; we all fall short of God's glorious standard. Yet God, with undeserved kindness, declares that we are righteous. He did this through Christ Jesus when he freed us from the penalty for our sins" (Romans 3:22–24 NLT). My friend had to be sincere about her course so that she would be able and free to graduate. When we trust in Christ, looking to him as our example, we, too, will find victory. Then and only then will we pass the test.

Reflection

When it comes to your walk with Christ, have you ever paused to wonder if you are making the grade? In doing so, what is the basis of your source for comparison? How can you work on letting go of the things of this world and move more toward those that count for eternity? Are there ways in which you might be helpful in also engaging others to follow by your example? How would you help them to understand that life is a test and that we either pass or we fail?

JUNE 26
(Y2, D26)

Game Not Over

The LORD will withhold no good thing from those who do what is right.

—Psalm 84:11 (NLT)

A story has been told by Christian speakers as far back as 1955 when Billy Graham told a variation of it early in his ministry. Two men were wandering through a museum, gazing at all the works of art when they came upon a depiction of two individuals locked up in a game of chess. One of the persons looked like an ordinary man, but the other character appeared to be the devil himself. The title of the painting was *Checkmate*. The impression of the man in the picture was that he was in a hopeless situation, that all was lost. One of the two observers, a chess champion, studied this painting at great length while his companion became impatient and asked what he was looking at. The chess champion told his friend to go on ahead as he wanted to study the painting a bit more because something was bothering him. A little later, his friend returned, and the chess master said, "I need to contact the artist who painted this piece. He either needs to change the painting or change the title." When his friend asked why, he replied, "It is not checkmate. If you look closely at the painting, it becomes clear the king still has one more move."

In his use of this story, Billy Graham concluded, "I believe there is one looking down from above who looks upon the board and says to you and me: There is a move, there is one move that you can make, and you can win! That move is toward Jesus Christ." This concept is mirrored throughout the Bible. There you will find the story of a lame man who had to break through several barriers to overcome the apparent checkmate which had been placed in his life (Luke 5:18–26). First, there was the physical barrier of paralysis (Mark 2:3), and secondly, there was the inability to access Jesus because of the large crowds. So "they made an opening in the roof above Jesus by digging through it and then lowered the mat the man was lying on" (Mark 2:4 NIV). Jesus healed the man spiritually by forgiving his sins (Mark 2:5) and also restored him physically (Mark 2:11). Whatever it took, this man was determined to get into the presence of the true King and not allow himself to be placed into any discouraging circumstance.

Caleb was facing the checkmate of advanced age. Every one of his generation had died, except for his friend, Joshua. For many long years, he had held onto the dream of the promised land, remembering the mountain that Moses had professed would belong to him. He declared, "Now, as you can see, the LORD has kept me alive and well as he promised for all these forty-five years since Moses made this promise—even while Israel wandered in the wilderness. Today, I am eighty-five years old... So give me the hill country that the LORD promised me" (Joshua 14:10, 12 NLT). What if Caleb had given up his dream? There seemed to be no end to his wilderness journey. He could have become hopeless and abandoned his vision, right on the brink of his miracle. Caleb serves to remind us that there will be times when we find ourselves in a spiritual desert, wandering around in circles in the wilderness. When this is the case, it is important that we keep our focus on the vision of our mountain. For the promises that God makes have no expiration date; He will not force us into checkmate.

If you are like most people, you will repeatedly come up against situations where it seems like all is lost and the enemy has won. There are many barriers in life that will appear to create a checkmate condition, preventing you from experiencing God's intention for a full life. If you are to advance these possibilities, then you must press beyond the limitations hindering your next move. As we search God's Word, we will glean wisdom, strength, and encouragement. We can see that no matter what obstructions were confronting God's people, He always showed them that they still had one more move. If the King is present in your life, there is a miracle in the making for you. If you open your heart, He will meet you right where you are. The game is not over, my friend. There is yet another move to be made.

Reflection

What are the negative circumstances that have you trapped and make you feel as though you are in a checkmate situation? Recall a time when you felt like you were a failure or were out of options. Would you be able to share a story with others as to how the King has stirred your life at a time when you felt like you were defeated and had no more moves to make?

JUNE 27
(Y3, D26)

Heart Integrity, No Matter What

May integrity and uprightness protect me, because my hope, Lord, is in you.

—Psalm 25:21

As contractors and engineers implement projects such as high-rise buildings and bridges, they must consider the integrity of the steel to be used. It is possible to have two pieces of steel that both look great on the outside with no apparent difference between them. Yet one of them may be compromised. When it is put under stress, it may not support the weight. The reason the other piece of steel holds up under stress is because it has integrity. The same terminology can be used to describe people as we measure and observe them for who they claim to be. There's an oft-told story of a man who sent a letter to the Internal Revenue Service. He wrote, "I cheated on my income taxes and felt so bad that I couldn't sleep. Enclosed find a check for $150. And if I still can't sleep, I'll send the rest of what I owe." Many of us can relate to that guy. We know it is right to be honest, but sometimes we simply try to find a way to compromise our values so that our conscience is not bothered. In doing so, we discover that we're lacking any absolute values for right and wrong. It becomes relative, and it certainly lacks integrity.

The Bible is full of references to integrity, character, and moral purity. David says in 1 Chronicles 29:17 (NLT), "I know, my God, that you examine our hearts and rejoice when you find integrity there." And in Psalm 78:72 (NIV), we read that "David shepherded them with integrity of heart; with skillful hands he led them." In 1 Kings 9:4 (NIV), God instructs Solomon to walk with "integrity of heart and uprightness" as his father did. The book of Proverbs provides an abundance of verses on integrity. Proverbs 11:3 (NIV) states, "The integrity of the upright guides them, but the unfaithful are destroyed by their duplicity." Proverbs 20:7 (NLT) says, "The godly walk with integrity; blessed are their children who follow them." A righteous person who walks in integrity, therefore, provides a legacy for his or her descendants. Finally, when the Apostle Paul wrote to Timothy, he told him to show integrity in belief and actions. "Be an example to all believers in what you say, in the way you

SPIRITUAL UPLIFTS FOR A RAPIDLY CHANGING WORLD

live, in your love, your faith, and your purity" (1 Timothy 4:12 NLT). Paul wanted Timothy to hold fast to the truth of God and not be compromised.

Years ago, there was a newspaper article about a man in Long Beach who went into a KFC to get some food for himself and the young lady who was with him. She waited in the car while he went in to pick up the chicken. Inadvertently, the manager confused the customer's order with a box he had disguised as a fried chicken box containing the daily financial proceeds he was planning to deposit. When the man and his lady friend got to the park for their picnic, they opened the box and discovered it was full of money. Realizing the mistake, he got back into the car and returned to the establishment giving the money back to the manager. The manager was so pleased that he told the young man, "Stick around. I want to call the newspaper and have them take your picture. You're the most honest guy in town."

"Oh, no, don't do that!" said the fellow.

"Why not?" asked the manager.

"Well," he said, "you see, I'm married, and the woman I'm with is not my wife." A person of integrity is authentic with no deception of attitudes and actions. Proverbs 10:9 (NIV) says that, "Whoever walks in integrity walks securely, but whoever takes crooked paths will be found out." Bottom line, a person of integrity will have a good reputation and not have to fear that he or she will be exposed.

Living with integrity in a world where the corrupt seem to be favored is challenging for all of us. At times, even those who claim to be devout followers of Christ seem to miss the mark. Rather than sitting in judgment of them, step up and be the kind of Christian you want to see in the world. For "who is going to harm you if you are eager to do good? But even if you should suffer for what is right, you are blessed. 'Do not fear their threats; do not be frightened.' But in your hearts revere Christ as Lord" (1 Peter 3:13–15). Integrity is the unwavering determination in the heart to do right, no matter the cost of doing so. If it is not in the heart, integrity is up for grabs. If it is not in your heart, then the mind will begin to rationalize and figure out a way to get around it. If your integrity is only in your hands, somebody will be able to buy it from you. If your integrity is only in your mind, somebody will talk you out of it. But if integrity is in your heart, then with God's help, you can keep it, no matter what.

Reflection

Do you pass the test when unbelievers look at your life and wonder if the gospel is true? Consider those things you would do or say if you had absolute assurance that no one would ever find out. How would you caringly confront a person lacking integrity about a situation that affects you?

JUNE 28
(Y4, D26)

What's in Your Pocket?

I have told you these things so that you will be filled with my joy. Yes, your joy will overflow!

—John 15:11 (NLT)

If you purchase one of his books, you will also get his personal cell number located at the back of the book. Bob Goff, author of *Love Does, Everybody Always*, and *Dream Big* believes it is his responsibility to act like Jesus; that is, to be available and to love your neighbor. Jesus identifies with those who are hungry, thirsty, in need of clothing and shelter, sick, or in prison (Matthew 25:35–36). Goff does as well, so much that he spends part of his time teaching at San Quentin Penitentiary. One day, he received a phone call from a man who had been imprisoned there and was standing outside, looking at the facility from which he had just been released. When Goff asked him what he was thinking, his thoughtful response was, "I've got pockets." Fully aware that you can't wear anything with pockets when you are incarcerated, Goff's reply was simply, "Well, be careful what you put in them."

I don't know about you, but I would have a difficult time functioning without pockets. I love my cargo pants, particularly when I travel. Each pocket is methodically equipped with things that I need to have at my immediate disposal. The word *pocket* has taken on various references over the years. If you or the organization you represent are known for having "deep pockets," then you are credited for having substantial financial resources. Then there are others who are known for "lining their pockets," meaning to accumulate money using dishonest or illegal methods. God had a message about pockets as well. When He spoke through His prophet Haggai to the nation of Israel, the people were justifying that the time had not yet come and for them to re-build the temple. Therefore, God rebuked them by saying:

> Why are you living in luxurious houses while my house lies in ruins? This is what the LORD of Heaven's Armies says: Look at what's happening to you! You have planted much but harvest little. You eat but are not satisfied. You drink but

are still thirsty. You put on clothes but cannot keep warm. Your wages disappear as though you were putting them in pockets filled with holes! (Haggai 1:4–6 NLT)

A current-day lesson might be lifted out of this situation. When we concentrate on ourselves too much and continue to remain dissatisfied, we might do well to refocus on getting in tune with God. The way to repair a pocket with holes in it is to invest in your future by doing His work. That's the way a leading financial institution promotes the benefit of using their credit card by asking the question, "So what's in your wallet?" A similar inquiry could be made about what might be found in our pockets. Most of us put things in our pockets that we want to hold on to, oftentimes having little if any value except to us. You may remember well the days of your childhood when your pockets might have been filled with random scraps of plastic, a pebble or seashell, some coins, a scrunchie, a marble, pieces of melted candy, or gummy bears. As we grew older, we became more strategic about our contents. However, none were more joyful than the "pocket stuff" of our childhood.

Perhaps we need to consider returning to an earlier time and load up our imaginary pockets with things that will bring us the simple joys of life again. If something makes you smile, tuck it away. Then, when you are having one of those difficult days, pull it back out. When someone brings happiness into your life, enjoy the moment fully, slip it away into that flap pocket, and remember where you stashed it when the world looks bleak. When you feel blessed, loved, and valued, zip it up in that special pocket where it can't fall out, for you might just need the reminder very soon. Those special pockets are blessings that get us through, little "God winks" that He sends our way just at the right time. When life can be all-consuming and it feels like the valleys outnumber the hills, those pockets of joy will refresh you. As you are revived, make yourself available to do work for the pleasure and honor of God. "Give, and you will receive. Your gift will return to you in full—pressed down, shaken together to make room for more, running over, and poured into your lap" (Luke 6:38 NLT). It's a recipe for true happiness. So answer me, my friend, just what is in your pocket?

Reflection

How many resources has God given you that you are merely holding in your pocket or perhaps wasting as you allow them to carelessly slip through the holes? If you were to ask each day, "What can I give away from my pocketful of treasures?" how much more fulfilled would your life be? Consider taking an inventory of your many blessings and how you might actively share them through God's work.

JUNE 29
(Y5, D26)

Boundaries

The Lord is my chosen portion and my cup; you hold my lot. The lines have
fallen for me in pleasant places; indeed, I have a beautiful inheritance.

—Psalm 16:5–6 (ESV)

As I was riding with my friend in her car, she remarked that when we stopped, she would have to make an adjustment to the mirror on the passenger side of the vehicle. She explained that she had hours before moved it inward, close to the side of the car because it was being attacked by a male cardinal. I had never heard of this before, but when I got home, I did a little research. Sure enough, while a male cardinal may accept a different bird species in the area where he has staked his territory, it will not tolerate another male cardinal nearby. This is because too many of one species in that zone may deplete the desired food sources and nesting locations, thus presenting as a threat. When a cardinal observed its reflection as in my friend's car mirror; for instance, its perception was that there's another like bird in his territory. It will attack until the other retreats. In nature, the one attacked will just go away, but in a reflection, of course, he remains. Therefore, the cardinal continued to pursue his own image.

Animals are very territorial; however, staking out one's territory is very common to humans as well. If you ever shared a bedroom with a sibling when you were young, it would not be unusual to establish an imaginary line down the middle of the room. The premise to this exercise was most often followed by the affirmation, "You stay on your side, and I'll stay on mine." That works very well until it becomes necessary to cross the other's space to go to the kitchen for a snack or to use the bathroom. We're not always good at sharing what we perceive to be ours. As we grow into adulthood, we sometimes find ourselves proclaiming our territory even more than ever. When we buy our first house, we put up a fence to make it perfectly clear where the property lines are located. At work, we sometimes establish turf issues around projects or responsibilities which we deem to be our own. One must wonder how the God we worship feels about the boundaries we establish and the territories we protect.

A person with healthy boundaries takes responsibility for his own life and allows others to live theirs. Learning limitations at a young age is important. If as children we do not learn to follow those set for us in the home, it will be difficult to respect God's as we become adults. In our spiritual journey, we hopefully learn to establish boundaries according to God's law and the teachings of Christ. Paul tells us that we are to exercise self-control (Galatians 5:23). Boundaries come with submitting to God's will, and He will enable us to make godly choices. Establishing proper boundaries assist believers in separating themselves from the dark worldly influences to which we are frequently exposed. Instead, as His followers, we find ourselves led "as captives in Christ's triumphal procession" (2 Corinthians 2:14 NIV).

Healthy boundaries define expectations, but it is important that they also show respect for others. It's difficult for us to see others who are not within our boundaries in the same way that God would. It isn't easy to not feel anger or even a sense of injustice when we think that God loves someone who stands outside of what we believe to be His established borders. We have to be careful that we do not become self-righteous and allow ourselves to be defined by pride. For just as God shows grace to you and me does not mean that there should be less grace available to my neighbor. Scripture tells us that "The Lord tears down the house of the proud but maintains the widow's boundaries" (Proverbs 15:25 ESV). So sometimes those who have less-defined boundaries than our own but who remain humble may have God's blessing and protection more than the self-reliant sinner. We must let God be the one to judge these circumstances. If we are setting healthy and spiritually led boundaries, then God will bless us. However, if we are maintaining distance simply because we desire to exclude someone, that is sinful. For if we find ourselves like the cardinal looking into the mirror of life and see anything but God's reflection, then it may be time to take a closer look at the boundaries we have defined for ourselves.

Reflection

Think about the boundaries you have set in your life? Do they raise you up or do they honor God? How can we break free from those boundaries which have been defined for us if we feel a conviction that they are not of God? What should we do if we are part of organizations or other established groups whose core values are different than those within our own boundaries?

JUNE 30
(Y6, D26)

Simply Gone with the Wind

The wind blows, and we are gone—as though we had never been here.

—Psalm 103:16 (NLT)

When Margaret Mitchell selected *Gone with the Wind* as the title for her epic tale, she was referring to a remembered past. The main characters in the story find themselves trying to survive in a world which had considerably changed. One of the best-selling novels of all time, it was published on June 30, 1936, and served as the basis for a blockbuster movie just three years later. The expression "gone with the wind" itself comes from a poem by Ernest Dowson. In Mitchell's novel, protagonist Scarlett O'Hara also uses the phrase from a line of dialogue in the book. When her hometown is overtaken by the Yankees during the Civil War, she wonders if her home plantation is still standing or if it was "also gone with the wind which had swept through Georgia." The reference here, of course, is to the prewar South's elite culture with its expansive plantations and elegant society which so easily contrasted with the oppression of slavery. The romanticized view of passion and loss captivated readers far and wide and was ranked by a 2008 Harris Poll as the second favorite book of American readers, just behind the Bible.

Whether you saw the movie or read the book, you'll remember the first views of Scarlett as innocent, charming, and flirtatious when the most important thing on her mind was which dress to wear to a barbecue. She would never have imagined herself three years later, scavenging for food with no shoes or change of clothes. We identify with her character because in our lifetime, many of us also find ourselves in or having gone through humbling situations. The Apostle Paul gave this warning: "Look here, you who say, 'Today or tomorrow we are going to a certain town and will stay there a year. We will do business there and make a profit.' How do you know what your life will be like tomorrow? Your life is like the morning fog—it's here a little while, then it's gone" (James 4:13–14 NLT). Once, when I visited a few local cemeteries, I observed two massively engraved monuments placed by persons in an effort to memorialize themselves and their family. I found no humility in those grave markers. Those who are so desperate to be remembered could benefit from the wise words found in the Old Testament: "Let someone else praise you, and not your own mouth; an outsider, and not your own lips" (Proverbs 27:2 NIV).

If we are realistic, we can easily conclude that life as we know it can change in an instant. If we become too self-absorbed, we risk being able to appreciate the things around us and learning to know God at His fullest. No one can attest to that better than Joni Eareckson Tada. Born in Baltimore, Maryland, in 1949, she was the youngest of four daughters. Experiencing a very active life all through her growing up years, Joni enjoyed riding horses, hiking, tennis, and swimming. On July 30, 1967, she dove into the Chesapeake Bay after misjudging the shallowness of the water. She suffered a cervical fracture, and her earthly life drastically changed. Now as a quadriplegic, she has experienced anger, depression, suicidal thoughts, and religious doubts. Following years of rehabilitation, she emerged with new skills and a fresh determination to help others. Today, she is married, has written over forty books, recorded several musical albums, starred in an autobiographical, and is an advocate for people with disabilities. In 2017, fifty years after her accident, she wrote, "Grace softens the edges of past pains, helping to highlight the eternal. What you are left with is peace that's profound, joy that's unshakable, faith that's ironclad."

Jesus told a brief parable in which He said, "The kingdom of heaven is like treasure hidden in a field. When a man found it, he hid it again, and then in his joy went and sold all he had and bought that field" (Matthew 13:44 NIV). Bottom line, the kingdom of heaven is more precious than anything we possess, and it is worth all we have. Once we have found the prize, we are willing to give up everything to possess this spiritual truth missed by many. It cannot be gained by possession of power, worldly wisdom, or earthly shrines that list the great things we have done. We need to secure our future through a higher power and come to realize that life, as we now know it, will one day be simply gone with the wind.

Reflection

How should the fleeting nature of life humble us? What parts of your daily life do you take for granted that could easily change in an instant? How might you refocus your view of normalcy as being boring or monotonous? In light of scriptural teachings about the temporary nature of satisfaction and recognition, what changes in your earthly life would better prepare you for an eternity with God?

JULY 1
(Y7, D26)

Living Upright in an Upside Down World

Blessed is the nation whose God is the Lord, the people he chose for his inheritance.

—Psalm 33:12 (NIV)

When I visited the bird store in the spring, I told my "bird man" that I wished to decrease the bird population in my yard over the summer since there is an abundance of natural food in supply for my feathered friends. He recommended that a specialized goldfinch thistle feeder might create the desired effect. These are designed so that the perches are above the small ports to accommodate the tiny seed. Since the birds who gather there literally have to hang upside down when they eat, the only ones that can easily manage are little birds like goldfinches and chickadees. The larger birds become discouraged and go elsewhere. I must admit I was a little skeptical at first but nonetheless purchased one at a reasonable price with a gift certificate I had received. To my amazement, it has made a big difference, and we continue to be able to enjoy the beauty of a few species who gather upside down while feasting.

It is vividly clear that the world of these birds is not the only one presently upside down as evidenced by the everyday news headlines. Many persons hate when they should love, quarrel when they should be welcoming, fight when they should be peaceful, gossip when they should be silent, wound when they should heal, steal when they should share, and do wrong when they should do right. Our nation has an increasingly diminished vision of the godly principles on which it was founded. Society says that what might normally be considered right is often not defined the same for everyone. Therefore, individuals can decide for themselves what is right and wrong while intimidation toward others who believe differently than you is gradually becoming more tolerated. An increasing number believe that it's okay to remove or destroy historical statues and art when someone considers them to be politically incorrect. In many parts of the world, it is considered appropriate to condemn, restrict, and even eliminate displays of faith in public places. To a sinner, a righteous person is an oddity. To those who have no recognition of a higher power, a Christian's values are eccentric and based on wishful thinking.

Jesus calls us to live principles not of our own making but rather those of a world in which God has provided for the betterment of all persons. He had His own upside down way of thinking. He told His followers that in His kingdom, the last would be first (Matthew 19:30), the least would be the greatest (Luke 9:48), and the lost would be found (Luke 15:6, 24). The unusual lot that He called to be His apostles—a group made up of fishermen, a hated and outcast tax collector, a zealot, and a bunch of other "no name" guys from Galilee—were to be His chosen and would reflect his commitment to building a new kingdom. Jesus provided a whole new definition of what a King should be. He said, "For even the Son of Man came not to be served but to serve others and to give his life as a ransom for many" (Mark 10:45 NLV). Jesus tells us to love our neighbor, even the ones who hate us. He tells us to forgive those who have hurt us, to pray for our enemies, and to turn the other cheek when someone strikes us. He tells us not to worry about the day-to-day needs of life for which God will provide. He tells us to not depend on ourselves but instead to depend on God. He tells us that we should give those who sue us even more than they are asking and give our lives and our treasures away for others, even if they don't appreciate it. He turned the world upside down on its head, and He challenged us to do the same.

As we celebrate another anniversary of our nation's independence, we must realistically ask how long the blessings and protection God has bestowed on this country will continue. We should take time to reexamine our values and the symbols for which we once stood. The US Flag Code states: "The flag should never be displayed with the union down, except as a signal of dire distress in instances of extreme danger to life or property." Perhaps it's time for us to acknowledge that the very condition of nationwide "dire distress" does exist from sea to shining sea. While we must always strive to live in obedience to the laws of man, we must do so only when we are not violating the Laws of God (Acts 5:29). As followers of Jesus, we must realize that being respectful doesn't mean we must accept whatever society demands of us. When we apply this, only then will we be prepared to live upright in an upside-down world.

Reflection

In what ways might you reexamine the contrasts of Jesus while living in a contradictory society? Are there changes you should make in the way you think and act? How might you do a better job of encouraging others in the faith to not always listen to what the world is telling them?

JULY 2
(Y1, D27)

Perfection: Yesterday, Today, and Tomorrow

But he said to me, "My grace is sufficient for you, for my power is made perfect in weakness."

—2 Corinthians 12:9 (NIV)

As we anticipate the celebration of another Independence Day weekend, we find ourselves at a time when there is a movement to fundamentally rewrite our history. Not long ago, America's Founding Fathers were respected for who they were. Today, their imperfections are likely to be under attack from educators, politicians, and the media. An outcry has developed to remove many statues and monuments around the country that glorify Confederate generals, advocates for slavery, defenders of segregation, and others whose racial views or conduct are now widely detested. It's not only Confederate tributes that have come under attack but also those of Washington, Lincoln, and Jefferson, to name a few. It has long been established that at least half of the fifty-six signers of the Declaration of Independence were slave owners. Yet, through the years, buildings and memorials have been dedicated to honor those who performed extraordinary feats, even though their character was less than perfect. The more we focus on the flaws, the less likely we are to recognize the virtues that can be learned from these lives.

It is interesting to note that on July 9, 1776, the Declaration of Independence was read for the first time in New York City. Washington and many others had been waiting for a such a declaration for some time while efforts at reconciliation were made by others who were reluctant to rebel against the crown. Only days after its passage, Washington had the Declaration presented to his troops and onlookers from the citizenry. Sparking a celebration through the streets in reaction to what had been read, soldiers and citizens alike went to Bowling Green, a park in the Southern tip of Manhattan, where a statue of King George III on horseback stood. The 4,000-pound lead statue was torn down, and the head was cut off. Writing in his diary the next day, Washington expressed displeasure at this destruction of property by stating he hoped in the future, people would leave this sort of thing "to the proper authorities." In the George Orwell novel, *1984*, one of his characters warned that "every book has been rewritten, every picture has been repainted, every statue and street and building has been renamed, every date has been altered. And that process is continuing day by day and minute by minute. History has stopped."

These "cancel culture revisionists" seek to eliminate any remembrance of any person in history who was not perfect as defined by today's standards. Absolute perfection is a quality that belongs to God alone. No matter how hard we try, we sin by our very nature and will always miss the mark. We commit sins of commission, doing that which we shouldn't, as well as sins of omission, not doing that which we should. Except for Jesus Christ, every other person who has walked the face of the earth is flawed. God sees and knows our shortcomings, and that is why we need His undeserved gift of grace each day. Our relationship to God, therefore, is not based on our perfection but rather in that of His Son's. Sinners need a Savior, and that's why Jesus came. "For by one sacrifice he has made perfect forever those who are being made holy" (Hebrews 10:14 NIV). When we trust in Him, He will forgive our imperfections and iniquities. We can stop striving for an arbitrary, worldly perfection, and rest in the one who is.

Followers of Christ should be encouraged to pursue perfection by maturing in their faith. "So let it grow, for when your endurance is fully developed, you will be perfect and complete, needing nothing" (James 1:4 NLT). The concept of tearing down and building up is repeatedly demonstrated in the scriptures as a model for personal repentance. But when we seek to erase history, be it personal or that of our nation, we risk losing any remembrance of the foundation on which we were built, placing us in danger of repeating the same mistakes over and over again. So regardless of how flawed our past may be, we do not want to lose sight of how far we have come. If it is perfection that we seek, better to hold on to the one who was perfect yesterday, is perfect today, and who will also be perfect tomorrow.

Reflection

What does our nation's history mean to you? Why is it important that we continue to honor those who were flawed but rose to represent equal rights and justice? How do you show concern for actions that seek to erase biblical history and destroy Christian values? How would you serve as a witness to others that it is God's perfect love that continues to set you free?

JULY 3
(Y2, D27)

Living the Dream

And it shall come to pass afterward, that I will pour out my Spirit on
all flesh; your sons and your daughters shall prophesy, your old men
shall dream dreams, and your young men shall see visions.

—Joel 2:28 (ESV)

In talking with a friend of mine, she mentioned that she had run into a former work colleague of ours. While we could not remember this individual's full name, we did recall one thing about him. Whenever you would ask this guy how he was doing, he would always look at you, smile, and say, "Living the dream." I used to think to myself, *What dream?* I figured it was some form of sarcasm, but I wasn't completely sure I understood and, at the time, I truly didn't care enough to ask. But for sure, it was always an expected part of any conversation with him. I have since realized that this expression is frequently associated with an individual's cynical remark in reference to their current monotonous existence. But it can also imply that a person is realizing something they have planned for a long time, such as a dream vacation. Bottom line, the dream is whatever someone who holds it defines it to be.

For many years, advertisers have tantalized us with the ideal of the American dream. If you lived through the peak of idealized commercials in the latter part of the twentieth century, you will remember Coca Cola's jingle, "I want to teach the world to sing in perfect harmony." Or better yet, who didn't want a Chevy after you heard the mantra, "Baseball, hotdogs, apple pie, and Chevrolet." What could be more American than that? In 1935, President Roosevelt signed legislation to enable the Treasury Department to sell savings bond to support the war efforts. After the attack on Pearl Harbor, they became known as war bonds, and American citizens felt proud to buy them, knowing that they were partnering with their country. Not so these days. Bonds are no longer popularized, and this once-touted American dream has become somewhat of an enigma.

Serious coin collectors know that on the 1926 Peace Silver Dollar, the word *God* in the motto "In God We Trust" is notably bolder than the other letters. Some say that this reflects the nation's sentiment at a time when Darwin's Theory of Evolution was squaring off against biblical creationism. One wonders if such a position favoring the Creator could occur today when there are many in our culture who advocate for the removal of this religious reference from all currency entirely. In a released conducted by the Public Religion Research Institute, only 69 percent of those surveyed think that believing in God is "truly American" while 58 percent considered it being born in American, and 53 equated it with being a Christian. This gives indication that there is a huge gap in affirming that belief in God or birthright has much to do with what has traditionally been considered as American. One might reflect on the Scripture: "Blessed is the nation whose God is the LORD, the people he chose for his inheritance" (Psalm 33:12 NIV).

As we celebrate another Independence Day, we cannot help but wonder what has happened to the religious values on which our nation was founded. The great orator and statesman, Patrick Henry, said, "It cannot be emphasized too strongly or too often that this great nation was founded not by religionists, but by Christians; not on religions, but on the Gospel of Jesus Christ." Whether or not the American Dream ever existed or still exists could be relentlessly debated, but it is clear that the nation who moves forward without the one true God is headed down an ill-fated path. The Word of God is clear:

> If a prophet or a dreamer of dreams arises among you and gives you a sign or a wonder, and the sign or wonder that he tells you comes to pass, and if he says, "Let us go after other gods," which you have not known, "and let us serve them," you shall not listen to the words of that prophet or that dreamer of dreams. For the LORD your God is testing you, to know whether you love the LORD your God with all your heart and with all your soul. (Deuteronomy 13:1–3 ESV)

So the next time someone tells you that they are "living the dream," it might do you well to ask the question as to where exactly they think that dream might be taking them.

Reflection

In your journey, how might you move away from dreams focused on earthly things and more toward visions of heavenly things? How would you respond to someone who tells you that they would feel more liberated living in a nation which displays less emphasis on God?

JULY 4
(Y3, D27)

Free to Believe

Live as people who are free, not using your freedom as a
cover-up for evil, but living as servants of God.

—1 Peter 2:16 (ESV)

I once had a neighbor who liked to stay busy doing projects. He had a problem, though, because he frequently did not see them through to completion. One day, while his wife was ranting about how he never finished what he started, he leaned over the backyard fence and said, "I have a philosophy."

"What's that?" I inquired.

He shrugged his shoulders and replied, stating, "If it doesn't get done by the Fourth of July, it doesn't get done." I guess he felt that after that date, there was not enough of summer remaining to bother, thereby hoping to get an earlier start next year. Or, on the other hand, maybe he realized there was just enough summer remaining to enjoy himself, and he wanted to be free from being tied down. It's interesting how we express our desire for a sense of entitlement regarding free time, especially when we are consumed with a lot of responsibilities such as work and family.

The Fourth of July is a time to pause and think about the freedoms we have in America. Freedom means different things to many people. We can view freedom politically, as having the opportunity to vote for particular ideas, people, or parties which best represent our views. Closely tied to this is the notion of freedom of speech, where one has the liberty to voice their personal opinion or perspective. In recent years, there are those who have expressed concerns that our basic freedoms are being challenged by the culture. The framers of the Constitution, known to be God-fearing men, made a sincere effort to establish a new nation on biblical principles. One of the liberties they recognized was freedom of religion. Thomas Jefferson called religious freedom "the most inalienable and sacred of all human rights." The First Amendment of the US Constitution includes the following words: "Congress shall make no law respecting an establishment of religion or prohibiting the free exercise thereof." Religious liberty includes the right to freely practice any religion or no religion without government coercion or control.

Freedom is also expressed clearly in God's Word. In the creation story, God gave Adam and Eve freedom to make decisions. "But the LORD God warned him, 'You may freely eat the fruit of every tree in the garden—except the tree of the knowledge of good and evil. If you eat its fruit, you are sure to die'" (Genesis 2:16–17 NLT). God created Adam and Eve to be free beings able to make choices. Giving them the ability to follow Him of their own accord was the only way for them to be truly free. In Matthew 19:16–20, a rich young ruler comes to Jesus. After a brief conversation about what he must do to obtain eternal life, Jesus states that he must "keep the commandments" (v. 17). He states that he has done this and asks Jesus what he is still lacking. "Jesus said to him, 'If you wish to be complete, go and sell your possessions and give to the poor, and you will have treasure in heaven; and come, follow Me.' But when the young man heard this statement, he went away grieving; for he was one who owned much property (Matthew 19:21–22 NASB). The striking point here is that Jesus let him go. God does not force us to believe in Him. Faith is commanded but never coerced.

True freedom occurs only when the heart is changed and made new. This is accomplished by His Holy Spirit whenever we make a conscious decision to follow Him. The Apostle Paul said, "Now the Lord is the Spirit, and where the Spirit of the Lord is, there is freedom" (2 Corinthians 3:17 NIV). If you are one of those who is looking for freedom in the various corners of society, you may struggle to find it. If you do encounter it somewhere along your journey, you may discover it to be short-lived. That is, of course, unless you have connected with the Holy One who provides that real sense of freedom for which you have been searching all along. "So if the Son sets you free, you will be free indeed" (John 8:36 NIV). For all who are searching for something more, you don't have to be concerned that you need to complete that project by the Fourth or July or else. There is One who will always welcome you with open arms. All you have to do is make the choice. This is true freedom. This is grace. It is yours simply for the asking.

Reflection

Do you find a sense of freedom in serving God? Are there ways in which you feel that society is beginning to create a challenge to your basic right to freely worship? How would you counsel someone who is struggling with the concept that belief in God feels more like enslavement to a set of rules than it does to experiencing real freedom?

JULY 5
(Y4, D27)

God's Greatness Revisited

Great is the LORD! He is most worthy of praise! No one can measure his greatness.

—Psalm 145:3 (NLT)

Every Fourth of July, the firework spectaculars are broadcast from different areas of our nation. These include Boston, New York City, and Washington DC. The musical performances always seem to be finely synchronized with the light shows in these network TV broadcasts. However, there is nothing quite like the "oohs and aahs" of the crowd when you experience an event like this in person. I well remember my first music concert, my first Broadway show, and my first major league sports event. Your favorite performers, musicians, and players take on a whole new persona when they are right there in front of you. Early in his career, I was privileged to see an up-and-coming singer in a very small venue with just a hundred or so others. After he became famous, I saw him again in a large arena. But the closeness of that first concert will always be a fond memory. I will also never forget taking my mother to see Barbra Streisand at Madison Square Garden. Looking down at the crowd from our high arena seating, we saw several well-known personalities who had also come out that night to take in what was undoubtedly a presentation of a lifetime. I remember the excitement on my mom's face as she said, "I have never quite seen anything like this." It remains a cherished memory with one of the all-time great vocalists.

Sadly, large venues have become a target for those who wish to do harm. For them, the opportunity to make a statement is often more pronounced when it can be achieved where large numbers of people can potentially be affected. Yet, many continue to pay huge sums of money to see their favorite team in the Super Bowl or World Series. It makes one wonder if the Lord Himself would appear today, would the masses accumulate as they did during Jesus' time? Scripture tells us that then "crowds gathered around Him again, and, according to His custom, He once more began to teach them" (Mark 10:1 NASB). "And all the crowd sought to touch him, for power came out from him and healed them all" (Luke 6:19 ESV). Would we be so bold today to express a desire to see Jesus? Or would we be embarrassed? While we gather to cheer for our favorite sports team, would we dare lift our hands in a rally to praise God? We know the song lyrics of our favorite music performers. But would we take the time to learn and recite the words of scripture that have provided comfort for us in times of need? We cannot help but wonder, "With whom, then, will you compare God? To what image will you liken him?" (Isaiah 40:18 NIV).

David understood the greatness of God and was unapologetic to reveal his emotion: "When I consider your heavens, the work of your fingers, the moon and the stars, which you have set in place, what is mankind that you are mindful of them, human beings that you care for them? Lord, our Lord, how majestic is your name in all the earth" (Psalm 8:3–4, 9 NIV). Perhaps if we, like David, would dare to search for the greatness of God, we wouldn't get so discouraged with the godlessness of our culture and the state of this world. For just as He has created a universe that continues to mystify and astound us, so too has He fashioned a plan that far exceeds any threat we might need to face. Maybe we will simply wait as in the story of a gravely wounded soldier who kept inquiring over and over, "Where is He? Where is He?" Thinking that he was asking for his superior, his caretakers brought his captain to him. But that wasn't who he wanted to see. In a moment of coherence, the nurse said to him, "All day long you've been asking for someone. Whom did you want to see?" The soldier said that he was waiting for the one who was greater than any earthly master. Moments later, he saw Jesus and passed.

One day, those who reign and reside on earth will also see Jesus. When He appears, it will be more remarkable than any fireworks display. It will be more dramatic than any concert or half-time extravaganza. "For as the lightning flashes in the east and shines to the west, so it will be when the Son of Man comes" (Matthew 24:27 NLT). Until then, our country must continue to remember what made us great in the first place. In the words of our fortieth president: "If we ever forget that we are One Nation Under God, then we will be a nation gone under" (Ronald Reagan). Great is He who has kept us free!

Reflection

Who are those persons whom you idolize for having achieved a status of greatness? How do they equal or fail in comparison with the great things God has done for you and those you hold dear? In what ways can you serve as an effective witness who idolize earthly superstars and don't know Jesus?

JULY 6
(Y5, D27)

Have I Told You Lately?

See what great love the Father has lavished on us, that we should be called children of God!
And that is what we are!

—1 John 3:1 (NIV)

I was preparing to mow the yard when I saw something white in color a distance away. As I got closer, it just looked like a plain sheet of paper. When I picked it up and turned it over, I discovered that it was a laminated homemade poster that had apparently been thumbtacked onto something. On it were the following words: "Lost: Sky Rover Remote Control Helicopter. Last seen flying toward First Church on North Main Street. May be stuck in trees, shrubs, etc. If found"—followed by a contact number. As I read the printed message, I thought to myself, *Hmmm…now they are both lost, the helicopter and the poster.* How true that sometimes is in our lives as well. We lose our way, and in doing so, we also lose contact with the personal sky rover—our heavenly Father.

Squire Rushnell tells the story of inspirational novelist, Karen Kingsbury, who had just received news that her book sales were though the roof. As she, her daughter, and son-in-law were leaving the offices of her New York publisher, they decided to take a stroll through a park in Lower Manhattan. She wished she could share the news of her recent success with her late father. On a similar occasion such as this, she would hear the song "Have I Told You Lately that I Love You?" by Rod Stewart playing. Years before her father had told them he was fond of that song, but it was unlikely that she would hear it today. Pausing along their walk to snap a remembrance selfie, a passerby offered to take the picture. As he walked away, Kingsbury's daughter said, "Mom, do you know who that is? It's Rod Stewart." They called out to him. As he verified his identity, they related the story of their special song. Stewart lifted his hands in the air, telling them that they had made his day. He referred to the chance meeting as a "divine intervention." Rushnell just calls it one of the many "God winks" people have shared with him.

On July 5, 1908, a church in West Virginia sponsored our country's first event in honor of fathers. It was in the form of a Sunday sermon in memory of several hundred fathers who had died in a local mine explosion the previous year. Just a few years later in 1910, the State of Washington celebrated the nation's first Father's Day. The idea came from Sonora Dodd whose father, a Civil War veteran, had raised she and her five siblings alone after her mother died. Slowly, the holiday caught on. In 1924, President Calvin Coolidge supported the idea of such an observance. In 1972, Richard Nixon signed a proclamation finally making Father's Day a federal holiday. The annual event is a nice remembrance of our dads, but it can also be a sad day for those who no longer have or never had an earthly father.

All of Scripture serves to remind us that we have a heavenly Father: "One God and Father of all, who is over all and through all and in all" (Ephesians 4:6 NIV). The personality of God the Father is evidenced in two parables told by Jesus. In the first (Luke 15:11–32), He speaks of a lost son who humbly returns to a home he chose to leave behind. "And he arose and came to his father. But while he was still a long way off, his father saw him and felt compassion and ran and embraced him and kissed him" (Luke 15:20 ESV). In the second parable, Jesus shares His story of the man who rejoiced when he found the one lost sheep who strayed from the other ninety-nine. "In the same way, your Father in heaven is not willing that any of these little ones should perish" (Matthew 18:14 NIV). As we journey through life, we hopefully grown to have an understanding of who our heavenly Father is and the kind of relationship He so desires to have with each one of us. We realize that we are loved and valued far more than we know. Have you told Him lately that you love Him? God will always wink in affirmation!

Reflection

Do you know with all certainty that you are a child of God? How can we further appreciate the Father's love for us knowing that He is forgiving (Matthew 6:14), merciful (Luke 6:36), our provider (Matthew 6:26), never changes (James 1:17), and holds our future (John 14:2)? In what ways might you set an example for others who do not know God as their heavenly Father as referenced in Matthew 5:16?

JULY 7
(Y6, D27)

Still Being Called

For the time is coming when people will not endure sound teaching, but having itching ears they will accumulate for themselves teachers to suit their own passions.

—2 Timothy 4:3 (ESV)

John Adams and Thomas Jefferson, the second and third presidents of the United States respectively, both passed away on the fiftieth anniversary of the adoption of the Declaration of Independence. Both men had been central in the drafting of the historic document in 1776. Twenty years later, Adams defeated Jefferson in the presidential election, but Jefferson became vice president because, at that time, the office was filled by the candidate who finished second. In 1800, Jefferson's Democratic-Republicans defeated the Federalist party of Adams and Hamilton, and Adams retired to his estate. Their contrasting political views caused them to develop an intense rivalry, and the two did not speak for well over a decade. By 1812, they started corresponding and eventually mailed more than 185 letters, now regarded as masterpieces of American enlightenment. Over the next few years, a tenderness crept back into the founders' relationship. As he grew older, Jefferson wrote "Crippled wrists and fingers make writing slow and laborious. But while writing to you, I lose the sense of these things, in the recollection of ancient times, when youth and health made happiness out of everything." By remarkable coincidence, Jefferson and Adams died on the same day, July 4, 1826, the semicentennial celebration of the Declaration of Independence. Adams' last words were, "Thomas Jefferson still survives," though his old friend and political adversary had actually died a few hours before. When they passed, Jefferson was eighty-three while Adams had turned ninety. Though both were not well, their deaths came as a surprise to many.

In those days, men like Adams and Jefferson were viewed as true patriots. Noted members of the clergy as well as prominent politicians felt that their same-day passing was more than a coincidence. Then there was a spirit that America and its people were exceptionally blessed by God. Gifts like theirs, according to Daniel Webster, were "proofs that our country and its benefactors are objects of His care." While eulogizing these men, he said: "Adams and Jefferson are no more. On our fiftieth anniversary, the great day of national jubilee, in the very hour of public rejoicing, in the midst of echoing and re-echoing voices of thanksgiving, while their own names were on all tongues, they took their flight together to the world of spirits." In those young days of a new nation, there was a lot of pride in the country. Today, not so much. A Gallup Poll taken in 2018 indicated a record low percentage of Americans identifying as "extremely proud" of their nationality, lower than at any other time in the prior eighteen years that the group had conducted the poll. This significant decline in the poll numbers is anything but inspiring news about the country's patriotism and thereby paints a dismal picture of our nation.

The same can be said for Christianity and the commitment of believers to their faith. Jesus said, "You are the salt of the earth. But what good is salt if it has lost its flavor? Can you make it salty again? It will be thrown out and trampled underfoot as worthless" (Matthew 5:13 NLT). The message is similar in the prophecy of John where Jesus provides this revelation: "I know your deeds, that you are neither cold nor hot. I wish you were either one or the other! So, because you are lukewarm—neither hot nor cold—I am about to spit you out of my mouth" (Revelation 3:15–16 NIV). Through our own selfish interests, we often lose perspective that we were meant to serve Him. It's okay to be free to be who you are, but at the same time, we must never forget where we came from. There is a trend these days to ignore or erase history in order to somehow satisfy our own passions. For when we decide to follow the lessons of false teachers, we often do so merely to validate the hollowness of our own existence. Jesus is calling us to be hot or to be cold. When we permit ourselves to just sit on the fence, we neither quench the thirst of those who are lost nor soothe the souls of a hurting world. Our founding fathers would remind us, as did the great apostle, that we should "live as people who are free, not using your freedom as a cover-up for evil, but living as servants of God" (1 Peter 2:16 ESV). Instead, we are neither good patriots nor model Christians. Yet we are still being called to be both.

Reflection

Have you lost your saltiness as a follower of Jesus? What steps do you need to take to revitalize your zest? In what ways do you value the lessons of scripture and of history and apply them in your life? How might you mentor others who have become self-centered to develop a better appreciation for historical perspectives?

JULY 8
(Y7, D27)

No Service

God is our refuge and strength, always ready to help in times of trouble.

—Psalm 46:1 (NLT)

Author and former President of the Moody Bible Institute, Dr. Joseph Stowell, once wrote for the *Our Daily Bread* devotional:

> An acquaintance of mine was hunting with friends near Balmoral, the country estate of the queen of England. As they walked, he twisted his ankle so badly that he couldn't go on, so he told his friends to continue and he would wait by the side of the road. As he sat there, a car came down the road, slowed, and stopped. The woman driving rolled the window down and asked if he was okay. He explained and said he was waiting for his friends to return. She said, "Get in; I'll take you back to where you are staying." He limped to the car and opened the door only to realize that it was Queen Elizabeth!

If, in fact, this event truly happened, the queen may have put her own safety in peril in order to risk helping someone else who appeared to be more vulnerable than she.

These days, there are not many people who feel comfortable stopping to serve someone in distress. I can attest to that because it happened to me not long ago. As our family was traveling by car to visit a friend on what would normally be about a forty-minute drive, we needed to pass over a mountain range. As we did so on a beautiful Sunday morning, our vehicle suddenly had no acceleration. As I pulled off onto the narrow brim of the four-lane highway, I suddenly realized that we were situated in the valley of two tall mountains with no cellphone service to get help. Pausing to rethink the situation, we remembered an older phone in the car. Placed in a compartment, it had not been charged for a while. For whatever reason, which we attribute to a higher power, we were able to make the necessary connections we needed in order to get home. In the meantime, a call to 911 brought a state policeman our way who remained with our car until the tow truck arrived.

While we were not assisted by the queen, the King of all kings kept us safe and guided us through the stressful details of our journey that day. We can rejoice in knowing that His faithfulness to us isn't determined by our actions or level of commitment at any given time. We have a direct line to Him, and it is never out of service. David is a great example of someone who struggled through many life-threatening situations but who, even so, pursued God as his shield. David said, "Trust in him at all times, you people; pour out your hearts to him, for God is our refuge" (Psalm 62:8 NIV). David unswervingly asked God to intervene on his behalf. He knew he had nothing to fear because in Him he found a fortress stronger than any opposition he might face. When we turn to God for help and protection, we begin to recognize Him as our protector. If you are in relationship with Him, knowing He is your King and you are His child, then no matter what life may bring your way, you will be eternally safe.

It is important for us to understand that just because God is our refuge does not mean He will never allow us to experience difficult or threatening situations. You will remember that Jesus Himself led the disciples into a boat, knowing full well that a violent storm was brewing. The disciples were terrified, but Jesus calmed the storm and became their safe harbor (Matthew 8:23–27). When we are in God's loving care and feel His presence, we can face even the most treacherous situations with confidence. No matter what our circumstance, the safest place to be is always in the center of God's will. I love the imagery that the psalmist provides with these words: "This I declare about the LORD: He alone is my refuge, my place of safety; he is my God, and I trust him… He will cover you with his feathers. He will shelter you with his wings. His faithful promises are your armor and protection" (Psalm 91:2, 4 NLT). This most certainly gives us the assurance we need when we find ourselves stranded in an unsettling situation along the sideline of one of life's busy highways with no service except what He alone can provide.

Reflection

Can you think of times when the scriptural words "I will never leave you nor forsake you" (Hebrews 13:5 ESV) were evident in your life? How does knowing that God is our refuge provide a sense of peace even though nations may be in uproar and earthly kingdoms are falling? Are there ways you might help others to increase their appreciation for the shelter you can find in God alone?

JULY 9
(Y1, D28)

Blowing Your Own Horn

Let someone else praise you, and not your own mouth; an outsider, and not your own lips.

—Proverbs 27:2 (NIV)

I recall a story about a man being tailgated by a stressed-out woman on a busy boulevard. As the traffic light turned yellow just in front of him, he did the right thing by stopping at the crosswalk, even though he could have beaten the red light. The tailgating woman hit the horn, screaming in frustration as she missed her chance to get through the intersection. While she was still in mid-rant, she heard a tap on her window and looked up into the face of a very serious police officer. The officer ordered her to exit the car. After he ran her license information, he returned and stated, "I'm very sorry for this mistake. You see, I pulled up behind your car while you were blowing your horn, flipping off the guy in front of you, and cussing a blue streak at him. I noticed the 'Choose Life' license plate holder as well as the 'What Would Jesus Do' and the 'Follow Me to Sunday School' bumper stickers. Since these things did not match the person I observed in the car, I assumed you had stolen it. Just call it a case of mistaken identity."

These days, acting in a manner such as this can evoke road rage. It also speaks poorly of you if, in fact, you do claim to be a follower of Christ. When it comes to your connection to Jesus, have you ever paused to ask if others observe you to be the person you claim to be? If we're wise, we accept the God-given task of promoting honorable living and formulating a right relationship with Him while all along expecting the same from others. In the Old Testament, a few individuals were called to be prophets with the mandate to bring God's Word home to his people. This was the case of Ezekiel who said, "But if the watchman sees the enemy coming and doesn't sound the alarm to warn the people, he is responsible for their captivity. They will die in their sins, but I will hold the watchman responsible for their deaths" (Ezekiel 33:6 NLT). All who claim to be Christian are called to the prophet's job. We are to be lookouts not only to hold ourselves upright but to likewise be answerable for the people around us.

During Jesus' day, many people were going through the motions of religion so that they would receive accolades from others. Jesus had no quarrel with the traditional forms of religious practice, but He called His followers to be truly God-centered in their performance and not oriented toward self-righteousness. He warned them, "So when you give to the needy, do not announce it with trumpets, as the hypocrites do in the synagogues and on the streets, to be honored by others. Truly I tell you, they have received their reward in full" (Matthew 6:2 NIV). He went on to say:

> When you pray, don't be like the hypocrites who love to pray publicly on street corners and in the synagogues where everyone can see them. I tell you the truth, that is all the reward they will ever get. But when you pray, go away by yourself, shut the door behind you, and pray to your Father in private. Then your Father, who sees everything, will reward you. (Matthew 6:5–6 NLT)

Things have not changed much over the last two-thousand years. Religious leaders of Jesus' day struggled with these issues, and many people continue to wrestle with them today.

If you are old enough, you will remember following a marriage ceremony the bridal couple and their wedding party would get into their cars often draped with ribbons, cans, and a sign that said "Just Married." Blowing their horns, they would drive around the town eventually stopping at the place of where the wedding reception would be held. Everybody knew that this behavior had nothing relevant to do with the actual marriage ritual. It was simply a public display to show someone had "tied the knot." The marriage itself grows and develops privately through good and bad days that will follow. After years of being together, hopefully with Christ at the center, the union gives silent affirmation to the fulfillment of those once-spoken vows. It doesn't have to be expressed with horn blowing or another public exhibition. The commitment is obvious to all who observe the relationship. Someone once said, "Make sure it is God's trumpet you are blowing. If it's only yours, it won't waken the dead; it will simply disturb the neighbors." May it be so as we carefully witness to the world around us.

Reflection

Are there times your actions do not display Christian values? How does it make you feel when you hear others bragging about or announcing the amount of their financial support for a cause? In what ways can you modify your life to be more of a positive example rather than a public declaration?

JULY 10
(Y2, D28)

No Better Time to Let Go

A time to keep and a time to throw away.

—Ecclesiastes 3:6 (NLT)

I don't know about you, but I tend to hold on to a lot of stuff. Over the years, this has been reinforced in my personal as well as my professional life. Those receipts, old bank statements, and tax-filing papers don't get purged nearly as frequently as they should. At work my custom has always been to make a paper copy as a backup, even with the recognition that many documents can be found online or saved to my computer. But I have always had a distrust that they could be lost by some software glitch or a virus that might cause my computer to crash. Therefore, I hold on to a hard copy, just in case! This attitude often spills over to my possessions. Even though I have been blessed to be able to buy new, updated, or in-fashion items, my inclination is often to hold on to the old—also just in case. Just in case I need an extra, the new one goes on the blink or that clothing item comes back in style. As I prepared recently to let go of some of my "old stuff" for a yard sale, I found myself weighing the value of keeping certain items versus simply letting go. If we subscribe to being a follower of Christ, we must be certain that we exercise caution to not treat our relationship with Him in the same way.

Jesus once told a parable about a rich young man who asked what good thing he must do to inherit eternal life? Jesus responded that the man must follow the commandments, including "You shall not murder, you shall not commit adultery, you shall not steal, you shall not give false testimony, honor your father and mother, and love your neighbor as yourself" (Matthew 19:18–19 NIV). The young man said that he had done these things, asking if there was anything further that he must do. Jesus responded, "'If you want to be perfect, go, sell your possessions and give to the poor, and you will have treasure in heaven. Then come, follow me.' But when the young man heard this, he went away sad, for he had many possessions" (Matthew 19:21–22 NLT). Jesus teaches that affluence and faithfulness are difficult to separate. He affirmed that one's life is not about the abundance of possessions and that there is nothing greater than being rich toward God. There is nothing wrong with having possessions, but we must make sure those possessions don't have us. The real test is what would happen in your relationship with Him if all of your "stuff" went away.

We must consider that the concept of letting go is not limited to our possessions alone but is also displayed through our emotions. Letting go of anger, hurt, bitterness, resentment, as well as pain and hate from offenses long ago can keep one from moving forward with a full life. The Apostle Paul counseled that we must "get rid of all bitterness, rage, anger, harsh words, and slander, as well as all types of evil behavior. Instead, be kind to each other, tenderhearted, forgiving one another, just as God through Christ has forgiven you" (Ephesians 4:31–32 NLT). When Paul wrote this, he was clear that we must make the first move. We must be intentional in ridding ourselves of these sinful behaviors while taking the initiative to be kind to others, display tender hearts, and by showing forgiveness. After all, the degree to which we exercise forgiveness to others is infinitely less than how much God has forgiven us.

Travel experts tell us that before we take a trip, we need to give careful consideration to what we are going to need for our journey. Often, we tend to overpack with things we don't really need. When we get home, we realize they were only taking up space and may have actually been a burden. We need to give some serious consideration in downsizing our life clutter. The key is to trust God, focus on the right priorities, and live a Christ-centered existence. As we do this, it will keep our heart in the right place. If our life journey leads to wealth or riches, just don't make them your sole pursuit. Don't define your blessing by how much stuff you have; rather, define it by how much of God you have in your life. Doing so will allow you to share in the joy of the relationships He intended for your journey, including a special one with Him. Downsizing much? There is no better time to let go than the present.

Reflection

Are you sometimes overwhelmed with the task of burdening yourself with stuff? What things in your life are you committed to more than God? Take stock of your emotions and consider if you are holding on to any emotional baggage. What steps must you take to move your full allegiance back to Him? Make a commitment to doing this and set goals and a timeline for following through.

JULY 11
(Y3, D28)

Old Shade Trees

"For I know the plans I have for you," says the LORD. "They are plans
for good and not for disaster, to give you a future and a hope."

—Jeremiah 29:11 (NLT)

One day, I visited with a lady from my church. She was in her mid-nineties, and her body was simply playing out. She had become weary with this life and was spiritually prepared to move on to the next. Several times, those caring for her felt that she was dying, but she always managed to bounce back. I had no reason to believe that this time would be any different. However, as I knelt at her bedside on this occasion, there seemed to be a change. She looked up at me, squeezed my hand, and said, "Pray that the Lord will take me." I smiled, held onto her hand, and replied, "You're still here, so God must continue to have a purpose for you." Without hesitation and a bit of a twinkle in her eye, she reacted, "Now just what would that be?" I didn't know how to respond, and even though everyone had been encouraging her to live on, God soon provided an answer to her prayer. I used to love to read devotions published in *Our Daily Bread* by the late Julie Ackerman Link. One of her writings spoke to me as my friend passed. Julie wrote: "If we stand where others have fallen, it's to raise our hands to heaven in praise and to spread our arms as shade for the weary. The Lord enables us to be a tree of rest for others."

On another occasion, I looked out the window of my office. It was evident that a nasty storm was brewing in the distance. The sky was getting quite dark, and lightning was flashing over the mountains beyond. Immediately in front of the building, there was a worker mowing the grassy area that contained a few shade trees. Several people had gathered there to converse on a nearby bench. I felt very uneasy and promptly went outside to encourage everyone to take shelter due to the impending storm. They respected my concern, came into the office waiting area, and within minutes, a very loud clash of thunder and a sharp bolt of lightning struck the ground outside damaging one of the trees. Not only did the building shake, but I did also, realizing that just a few minutes before those folks had been out on the front lawn. I think we all learned an important lesson that day: theirs, to come inside when the skies look threatening, and mine a bit more philosophical. Life is not done as long as God has a purpose. I was sure that tree would die. Now, many years later, it remains quite beautiful in all seasons.

In each of our lives, we can sometimes feel as though our life is over, especially after tragedy strikes. But sometimes it's just a bend in the road, and God allows us to walk down a new path as part of our journey. It is during those stretches that we draw close to Him and come to realize that "I can do all things through him who strengthens me" (Philippians 4:13 ESV). Like my older friend who felt she had no more to give, we can, on occasion, feel like we are a mirror image of our former self. It is then that God steps in and restores our worth through grace. In his letter to the church at Rome, Paul echoed this sentiment: "So, too, at the present time there is a remnant chosen by grace" (Romans 11:5 NIV). We would be wise, therefore, to understand that in God's eyes we always have worth, and His hope for us never dies. In our darkest hours, in the worst of storms, and even in our utmost frailties, we hold on to these words: "For the sake of Christ, then, I am content with weaknesses, insults, hardships, persecutions, and calamities. For when I am weak, then I am strong" (2 Corinthians 12:10 ESV). In doing so, you will be able to raise your arms and provide shade for the weary, thereby offering a witness to others who may follow by your example. For according to the Greek Proverb, "A society grows great when old men plant trees whose shade they know they will never sit in." Time to do some planting?

Reflection

How do you define significance in your own Journey? Is your personal worth cluttered by wealth, status, or recognition for good works? What is your mission for the next season of life? In what ways will you leave a legacy that affirms God's purpose?

JULY 12
(Y4, D28)

Broken But Still Useful

My sacrifice, O God, is a broken spirit; a broken and contrite heart you, God, will not despise.

—Psalm 51:17 (NIV)

I walked into the den, and there on the floor, I was surprised to see a broken collector's plate. It had apparently fallen from the plate rail on my wall and hit a piece of furniture on the way down before it broke into four pieces. Having a display of many such plates, I had never had this happen before. I surmised that over time the plate must have shifted from vibrations in the house. As I picked up the fragments, I was reminded of the nursery rhyme we sometimes learn as children, something about not being able to be put back together again. Then I recalled it was *Humpty Dumpty*. Upon further examination, however, it appeared as though these breaks were fairly clean. After a few brushings of the edges with some good glue and the application of a little pressure, the plate is now back on the plate rack in one piece. Unless one would know better, you could never tell it had been broken. I think our lives are also that way at times. Through a course of events, we become broken. But rather than "all the kings horses and all the king's men," it only takes the King of kings to restore our life.

Over the past year, I have been listening to some wonderful sermons preached by the head pastor of one of America's mega churches. After delivering the message this past Easter, he disappeared. I became concerned that maybe he was seriously ill. Recently, I heard that through a course of events, there had been infidelity in his marriage. Consequently, this pastor resigned his pulpit. Interestingly enough, I found two lines that he had posted on social media quite a while before these happenings had occurred. The first: "Your brokenness is fertile ground for a forgiving God to make something new and make something beautiful." The second, "Brokenness precedes usefulness." I believe both of his statements to be true, and I look forward to seeing the evidence of how they will be fulfilled in his life.

I guess when it comes right down to it, we are all broken, each in our own unique way. The Bible is full of stories about broken people who provided great service to God. Just like they, we find that when we become broken, we suffer a variety of emotions ranging from shame to guilt and fear.

We feel useless, sometimes lose hope, and just want to withdraw from society. We would be wise during these times to reflect on the words of Vance Havner: "God uses broken things. It takes broken soil to produce a crop, broken clouds to give rain, broken grain to give bread, broken bread to give strength. It is the broken alabaster box that gives forth perfume. It is Peter, weeping bitterly, who returns to greater power than ever." We come to realize that where brokenness exists, it is hugely a state of mind. The body and soul can remain whole. It is important that we sustain them with what they need, including these words: "Have I not commanded you? Be strong and courageous. Do not be afraid; do not be discouraged, for the LORD your God will be with you wherever you go" (Joshua 1:9 NIV).

When we traverse through our journey as persons of faith, we have a lot more going for us than the average Humpty Dumpty.

> We can rejoice, too, when we run into problems and trials, for we know that they help us develop endurance. And endurance develops strength of character, and character strengthens our confident hope of salvation. And this hope will not lead to disappointment. For we know how dearly God loves us, because he has given us the Holy Spirit to fill our hearts with his love. (Romans 5:3–5 NLT)

Therefore, we do not have to be ashamed of our brokenness when it occurs. We must simply understand that it is through these periods that God is humbling and preparing us to be better servants for His kingdom here on earth. Henri Nouwen once said, "The main question is not, how can we hide our wounds…but how can we put our woundedness in service to others." I have often wondered what it might be like to worship in a body of brethren known as "The Sinner's Church." It would be curious to see who might attend as well as to take stock of who would not want to be seen there. To be sure, eligibility for membership there would not be an issue for any one of us.

Reflection

Can you recall a time in your life when your sinful nature took over and you felt broken? Do you remember those who ministered to or otherwise stood next to you? Are there ways you been able to use the grace you were given as an opportunity for service to others?

JULY 13
(Y5, D28)

Up to Something Good

God alone, who gave the law, is the Judge. He alone has the power to save
or to destroy. So what right do you have to judge your neighbor?

—James 4:12 (NLT)

All around us, there are now monitoring and security cameras. They are at your ATM machine, in your favorite department store, attached to traffic lights, stationed around public areas, and secured to law enforcement officers and their vehicles. In each of these cases, the installation of these cameras was done with the intention of catching someone doing something they should not be. Many a theft or traffic violation can be substantiated through their use, and playback footage is often all the proof that is needed to show that an individual was breaking the law. There is no longer a reasonable escape from cameras as one can now go online and pull up a satellite view of your home. In addition, anyone who has a cell phone now has a camera at their disposal and will immediately activate it for their own purposes without regard for another person's right of privacy. Through all the benefits of these devices, I wonder how often they are used to prove that someone was actually up to something good.

American humorist and entertainer Will Rogers is credited with having said, "I never met a man I didn't like." Whether he actually meant it or otherwise made this remark tongue-in-cheek, it is a statement to which I cannot personally attribute in my own life. For there are many a man (and woman) for whom I have not cared, and in some cases, I have misjudged those individuals. Maria happens to be one of those. She used to visit her mother at a long-term health care facility which I also frequented. My impressions of her were mostly derived from her demeanor. She barely smiled and, to me came across as being a really nasty lady. I formed opinions about her which were incorrect. Years later, I found out through several mutual friends that she is a very giving individual. It is not unusual for her to show up at the hospital to sit with the family members of an ill person or extend an invitation to her home for special holiday meals to persons who might otherwise be alone. One day, she was behind me in line at the grocery store. Feeling guilty for the judgments I had made about her, I said, "Maria I have been hearing such wonderful stories about all the kind things you do for people." She simply replied by saying that she is just doing what we are supposed to do. Yes, she was, and by prejudging her, I certainly was not.

How and when are we supposed to judge, if at all? Jesus said, "Do not judge or you too will be judged" (Matthew 7:1 NIV). Is it a contradiction that He also said, "Stop judging by mere appearances, and make a right judgment" (John 7:24 NIV)? So often when we make a judgment about someone else, we might find that if we look closely at our own life, we may be guilty of doing the same thing. That is perhaps why Jesus said, "Why do you look at the speck of sawdust in your brother's eye and pay no attention to the plank in your own eye?" (Matthew 7:3 NIV). We quickly learn in life that if there are no standards, there is nothing by which to measure behavior. A personnel director has to make certain judgments about an employee's work. A teacher must make a judgment about a student's performance before issuing a grade. A parent must judge a child's behavior prior to handing out a punishment. Some may even argue that in our day and age, we need more—not less—judgment. If, therefore, we subscribe to certain standards about "proper living," how often do we allow those to be applied to something good?

Long before Jesus walked the face of the earth, Joseph (son of Jacob) was sold into slavery by his older brothers because they were jealous of him. God proved his presence and protection for Joseph, providing him with the divine ability to interpret dreams including that of a great famine. The pharaoh rewarded Joseph with overseeing the land of Egypt. During prosperous times, he stored up an abundant harvest which he was later able to share with his brothers and save a nation from starvation. Although at first his brothers did not recognize him, he revealed his identity and forgave them. He said to them, "You intended to harm me, but God intended it all for good" (Genesis 50:20 NIV). If God can make good out of circumstances such as these, then we certainly should try to search for the same in others.

Reflection

Has there been a time when someone has falsely accused you of wrongdoing? Have you been guilty of making a negative judgment about others with no real reason to do so? Are there ways you might be more purposeful to look for the good in people before you form any opinion of them?

JULY 14
(Y6, D28)

The Old Book

The grass withers and the flowers fade, but the word of our God stands forever.

—Isaiah 40:8 (NLT)

Several decades before the fictional Dr. Spock of *Star Trek* fame became a household word, another Dr. Spock was making a name for himself providing child-rearing advice for millions of Americans. On July 14, 1946, Dr. Benjamin Spock released his book, *The Common Sense Book of Baby and Child Care*, which would become one of the best-selling books of the twentieth century. Unlike other leading child care experts prior to the 1940s as well as his own mother's fairly stern parenting style, Spock encouraged a gentler approach to bringing up children, telling parents to trust their own instincts and common sense. Mothers heavily relied on Spock's advice and appreciated his friendly, reassuring tone as he offered practical tips on everything from toilet-training to calming a colicky baby. Later in his life, he was motivated by politics, explaining, "It isn't enough to bring up children happy and secure, you need to provide a decent world for them. And this is why I have expanded my horizon." While much of his advice continues to be appropriate today, some of it has been replaced and even discredited. Spock suspected that he was being punished for his liberal politics. Many came to refer to him as the overly permissive child-rearing expert, even labeling him as the corruptor of an entire generation.

While the effectiveness of most advice books wanes with the evolving of each successive generation, there is one such book which has stood the test of time—the Holy Bible. While many dismiss it because it references people and events from long ago, this has never caused it to be outdated or irrelevant. It tells us about an unchanging God and His eternal presence. Just as pertinent is the aspect of human nature revealed through God's very own creation. While our culture has developed over time, we need our Creator no less than those who walked the earth thousands of years ago when the first texts were written. The Apostle Paul would have us know that the child-rearing advice within its writings and lessons for life we obtain in the scriptures are the best we will ever receive. He says:

> You have been taught the holy Scriptures from childhood, and they have given you the wisdom to receive the salvation that comes by trusting in Christ Jesus. All Scripture is inspired by God and is useful to teach us what is true and to make us realize what is wrong in our lives. It corrects us when we are wrong and teaches us to do what is right. God uses it to prepare and equip his people to do every good work. (2 Timothy 3:15–17 NLT)

Over eight decades before Dr. Spock published his book, George Washington Carver was born in 1864 near the end of the Civil War. He was the son of a slave, orphaned as a baby, and raised after the abolishment of slavery by his former owners, Moses and Susan Carver. Carver became a prominent African-American scientist and inventor, and he is best known for the many uses he devised for the peanut. In 1920, Carver spoke at the United Peanut Association of America's convention. His success gained him an invitation to speak before Congress about peanuts and the need for a tariff. Carver captivated their interest by drawing them into his testimony about the many products he had made from peanuts. The story is told that when he was asked how it came to be that he knew so much about peanuts, he said he had learned it from an "old book." This prompted the question as to the name of the book. He replied that it was the Bible. Then someone asked if all the things he had learned about peanuts had come from reading it. He replied that was not the case but that old book taught him much about the one who had created peanuts. "Then," he said, "I asked Him what to do with them, and He showed me."

God's Word, as found in the Holy Scriptures, shows us the way to lead a blessed life. As he praised his Maker, the psalmist said, "Your word is a lamp to guide my feet and a light for my path" (Psalm 119:105 NLT). In those days, a lamp would only illuminate, at best, a few feet ahead of one's steps at night. Sometimes in life, all we need is enough light to take the next step as "we walk by faith, not by sight" (2 Corinthians 5:7 ESV). As we make our journey, we can take advice on that faith from lots of sources. This might include the reading of an old book. As you read it, pay attention to the one who guided its words. Be assured that any advice you find there worth remembering will stand the test of time for all generations. It's one old book that becomes new again, each and every time we read it.

Reflection

Do you view God's Word as an old book full of stories about how to live a good life? Or do you see it as a living, breathing document that has relevance until the end of time? How would you provide sound rebuttal to someone who says that the truth of the Bible is that it seeks to justify itself?

JULY 15
(Y7, D28)

There by the Grace of God

Hypocrite! First get rid of the log in your own eye; then you will see
well enough to deal with the speck in your friend's eye.

—Matthew 7:5 (NLT)

What is one thing you find to be intimidating? For me, going through a metal detector is one of the worst. No matter what I do, I always seem to fail at this effort. "Metal," I think to myself. "Anything metal." I take off any jewelry, empty the change from my pockets, and place my car keys into the provided container. But anytime I go through a metal detector at an airport or other location, I always miss something. Sometimes it's my belt. At other times, it's my glasses. Inevitably, I set the darn thing off, am asked to step back, and think about what I might have overlooked. There is no forgiveness with those devices, and I usually end up feeling frustrated if not just downright stupid. There is no mercy. I am so thankful that when it comes to grace that God is much more merciful.

For many years, I have heard the expression, "There but for the grace of God go I." I have used it myself, and I would suppose there are times I have quoted it improperly. On one such occasion, I was standing in line at a bargain store waiting, perhaps impatiently, for the lady ahead of me to pay for her purchases. She pulled out a few folded dollar bills and began to count out coinage, mostly pennies. I began to feel a degree of compassion for this individual, thinking that if she didn't have enough, I would make up the difference. But I remained hesitant to jump in, not wanting to create any embarrassment and thereby granting her the dignity to pay her way. I remember thinking to myself, *That could be me.* Then the phrase came to mind, *There by the grace of God go I.*

Often when we hear this expression, it is stated as an acknowledgment that another's misfortune could be our own if it wasn't for the blessing of the Almighty. While I believe it is true that God does bless us in different ways, I also feel it is incorrect to conclude that some are eligible for His grace while others are not. Grace is not some kind of dumb luck we receive, like the guy who gets through the metal detector easier than me. Grace is a gift we don't deserve. Even so, it is available to all and our good works cannot earn it. The Apostle Paul stated it this way: "For I am the least of the apostles and do not even deserve to be called an apostle because I persecuted the church of God. But by the grace of God I am what I am, and his grace to me was not without effect. No, I worked harder than all of them—yet not I but the grace of God that was with me" (1 Corinthians 15:9–10 NIV). Paul fully understood that grace was related to sin and that, out of our sinful nature, God does for us what we are incapable of doing for ourselves. That is, He sets us free from condemnation.

If we look around our world, it is easy to see that we have become much more inclined to be accusing than forgiving. Our government officials are a great example of being quick to point a finger at each other. More times than not, the issues raised by one side are the same that the opposition has already committed. "It's just politics," they say. Jesus called it something else: hypocrisy. Yet even on a personal level, we look at what someone else has done and often label their sin far worse than our own. I don't know about you, but I have never been convinced it's either wise or helpful to get into the business of starting to compare whose sin is greater. "You, therefore, have no excuse, you who pass judgment on someone else, for at whatever point you judge another, you are condemning yourself, because you who pass judgment do the same things" (Romans 2:1 NIV). I sometimes listen to a radio talk show personality reply to his callers as they cordially ask how he is doing with the statement, "Better than I deserve." That should be the response from each of us who have grown to know Jesus as our Lord and Savior. For when it comes right down to it, we are all sinful. Fortunately, we are also equally loved and forgiven, thanks to God's gift of grace. There you go, and gratefully, there go I as well.

Reflection

How might your discussion of God's grace be different for a Christian than a non-Christian? Do you sometimes find it difficult to rationalize that God's grace is available to all, even when they seem to be undeserving? How would you provide counsel to someone who questions the difference between a Christian motivated by grace and someone who performs good works to gain a right standing with God?

JULY 16
(Y1, D29)

Things Aren't Always What They Seem

Don't jump to conclusions—there may be a perfectly good explanation for what you just saw.

—Proverbs 25:8 (The Message)

Two traveling angels stopped to spend the night in the home of a wealthy family. The family was rude, offering the angels a small space in the cold basement instead of the guest room. As they made their bed on the hard floor, the older angel saw a hole in the wall and repaired it. When the younger angel asked why, the older angel replied, "Things aren't always what they seem." The next night, the pair came to rest at the house of a very poor but hospitable farmer and his wife. After sharing what little food they had, the couple let the angels sleep in their bed where they could have a good night's rest. The next morning, the angels found the farmer and his wife in tears. Their only cow, whose milk had been their sole income, lay dead in the field. The younger angel was infuriated and asked the older angel, "How could you have allowed this to happen? The first man had everything, yet you helped him. The second family had little but was willing to share everything, and you let their cow die." The older angel replied, "When we stayed in the basement of the mansion, I noticed there was gold stored in that hole in the wall. Since the owner was so obsessed with greed and unwilling to share his good fortune, I sealed the wall so he wouldn't be able to find it. Then last night, as we slept in the farmer's bed, the angel of death came for his wife. I gave him the cow instead. Please understand, things aren't always what they seem."

When Jesus was in Jerusalem, He pointed out this type of contradiction to those whom He had called. "Some of his disciples were remarking about how the temple was adorned with beautiful stones and with gifts dedicated to God" (Luke 21:5 NIV). On the surface, they saw its external beauty, but He told them, "As for what you see here, the time will come when not one stone will be left on another; every one of them will be thrown down" (Luke 21:6 NIV). The disciples failed to see what was really behind it: spiritual bankruptcy, hypocrisy, oppression, rejection of Christ and the Gospel, and Christ's impending death at the hands of the religious authorities. That's why Jesus warned them to beware of the false teachers who would come and proclaim that they were the promised Messiah. "Watch out that you are not deceived. For many will come in my name, claiming, 'I am he,' and, 'The time is near.' Do not follow them" (Luke 21:8 NIV). He knew that just like the temple's beauty hid its ugly secrets, the false teachers with their appearances, methods, and teachings would hide their true motives as well.

When we judge situations by the world's standards, we often miss the hidden beauty of what lies right before us. In 2009, a lady took the stage of the competition show *Britain's Got Talent*. In comparison to the other participants, she was quite plain-looking. Judging by her appearance, no one expected much when she raised the microphone to sing "I Dreamed a Dream." As she began her performance, the judges were spellbound, taken with the loveliness and power of the voice that filled the auditorium. Jumping to their feet, those in the audience were surprised that such a riveting voice came from such an unlikely source. The performer, Susan Boyle, rose to fame and soon recorded the UK's best-selling debut album of all-time. Scotland's daily newspaper, *The Herald*, described Boyle's story as "a modern parable and a rebuke to people's tendency to judge others based on their physical appearance." Jesus Himself said that we must "stop judging by mere appearances but instead judge correctly" (John 7:24 NIV).

The best television shows and movies are usually ones that have a plot with an unexpected twist. When this happens in real life, we must evaluate the circumstances. With today's instantaneous sound bites and edited video clips, it has become far too easy to twist the truth, often prompting us to jump to a conclusion without knowing all of the facts. Sometimes what appears to be correct on the surface emerges from an attempt to bias or enrage some people against others. We would be wise if we followed this advice: "You must all be quick to listen, slow to speak, and slow to get angry" (James 1:19 NLT). A faithful Christian is discerning of what he hears and is careful in finding judgment. We must be ever-vigilant that we are not being deceived by a wolf in sheep's clothing (Matthew 7:15). There are plenty of them out there. For a wise angel once said, "Things aren't always what they seem."

Reflection

In what situations do you find it easy to jump to conclusions? How do you weigh theoretical factual information when it comes to hearsay about people or situations? Are there ways you can gain increased spiritual maturity be exercising the ability to discern between good and evil (Hebrews 5:14)?

JULY 17
(Y2, D29)

Your Forever Friend

There is a friend who sticks closer than a brother.

—Proverbs 18:24 (NIV)

I was "the best friend a guy could have." That's what the inscription said in my yearbook. It was written at the time of my high school graduation, and I truly have no idea what happened to the person who penned it. Bottom line, we went our separate ways and simply failed to stay in touch. Realistically, our friendship, like many other things in life, was significant for only a few fleeting moments in time. That yearbook entry was not dissimilar to what many others had written. I can't tell you how many individuals used acronyms such as AVGFA (A Very Good Friend Always) as they signed their senior pictures. Yet, there are only a handful of those who have remained friends at all, let alone "very good" ones. When we are young, our definition of friendship is quite loosely defined. Hopefully, as we grow older, we become less naïve while we develop a more mature definition of what true friendship really is.

Recently, as I visited in the home of a friend, I knew it would most likely be the last time I would see him in this lifetime. He had been dealing with a life-threatening illness for over a year. Having been denied several surgeries and declining any further treatments, he was out of options. He was now receiving palliative care through a local hospice organization. He had been one of those individuals who had written that he would be "a friend always" in my high school yearbook. Although our lives had taken various twists and turns, it also intersected at several significant points. One of those happened to be a church connection. As we talked on this day, I knew that our time together was most likely goodbye for now. However, I was able to leave, knowing that there would be a "later reunion." My parting words, "I'll see you when I see you," was both an understanding and also an affirmation that we both knew the Lord.

On one occasion Jesus had a conversation with his disciples about friendship. He said, "I no longer call you servants, because a servant does not know his master's business. Instead, I have called you friends, for everything that I learned from my Father I have made known to you" (John 15:15

NIV). Jesus gave everything to His friends, including a knowledge of God and His own life. By demonstrating love without limits, He made it possible for us to experience lifelong friendships as well. For, "It was just before the Passover Festival. Jesus knew that the hour had come for him to leave this world and go to the Father. Having loved his own who were in the world, he loved them to the end" (John 13:1 NIV). Here "to the end" means to the fullest extent as well as to the last and to the highest degree. Jesus had joy in knowing that through His death, it would allow those who loved Him to be His friends forever in eternal glory. Just imagine the infinite, all-powerful, holy God of the universe wanting to be your friend!

Sometimes we form friendships which have only been significant in our life for a season. Even though that friendship may no longer exist, we should treasure that time and rejoice in the fact that God brought this person into our life. Perhaps the greatest privilege we inherit by forming a lasting friendship with Jesus is that He begins to prepare us in this world for our life eternal. That's what scripture tells us: "This is eternal life, that they may know You, the only true God, and Jesus Christ whom You have sent" (John 17:3 NIV). Eternal life begins here on earth through Jesus and is perfected in the afterlife when our physical bodies die. If, as Christians, we can accept this view of eternity, it would make it easier to cope with the frailties of this earthly life. While we are assured that all of our infirmities will be restored after physical death, we can continue to learn, grow, and enjoy a measure of eternal life right here and now. For when we come to know Jesus, He will write AGFA ("A Good Friend Always") in our book of life. We will come to understand that eternal life is liberty from all things of the flesh so that we can live in the everlasting things of God. For He is now and will always be your forever friend.

Reflection

Most often, we think about Jesus as being our Savior, but have you also considered that He wants to be the best friend you could ever have? What do you think would be your favorite thing about having a friendship with Jesus? How should we respond to the difficulties here on earth, knowing that we have already begun our eternal life? How might you help someone who is facing physical death understand that their passing is more than just leaving earth and moving to the uncertainty of an eternal home?

JULY 18
(Y3, D29)

The Voice

Your word is a lamp to guide my feet and a light for my path.

—Psalm 119:105 (NLT)

While I generally display little interest in any type of reality TV (including competition programs), I occasionally pay attention to how some of the contestants are advancing on NBC's *The Voice*. What is somewhat interesting about the show is that celebrity judges initially select vocalists during "blind auditions" in which they hear the performance but do not see the competitors. At times, they are quite surprised by the bodies that contain some of the voices. Over a course of successive weeks, participants are mentored. Then through public voting the number of contestants is narrowed and a winner eventually declared. Voices, whether set to music or in our minds ready to be penned or spoken, are important. Mahatma Gandhi once said, "Everyone who wills can hear the inner voice. It is within everyone."

A friend of mine told me recently about another type of voice she heard. While attending the funeral of her neighbor's husband, she heard a faint voice during the service. While relating the story, she smiled and said that for a moment, she wondered if it might be the voice of the recently departed. As she listened more closely, she discerned the words "low battery." It was then that she realized that her hearing aid was just telling her that the charge in her device was weakening. For many years, the trademark of RCA Victor consisted of the image of a dog sitting in front of an old wind-up gramophone. The symbol evolved from a painting by English artist Francis Barraud. The picture titled *His Master's Voice* depicted a terrier named Nipper sitting in front of the trumpet-like speaker. The idea came to Barraud when he observed the dog of his late brother taking a peculiar interest in his former master's recorded voice coming from a cylinder phonograph, an image which went on to gain worldwide fame.

As we go about our journey and draw closer to God, we can hear His voice as well. Although we come to sense His presence in many ways, it is when we begin to hear the Master's voice that we are assured that we are one of His. In scripture, Jesus spoke of the Shepherd and the Flock:

The gatekeeper opens the gate for him, and the sheep recognize his voice and come to him. He calls his own sheep by name and leads them out. After he has gathered his own flock, he walks ahead of them, and they follow him because they know his voice. They won't follow a stranger; they will run from him because they don't know his voice. (John 10:3–5 NLT)

Jesus could not be any clearer, stating, "Whoever is of God hears the words of God. The reason why you do not hear them is that you are not of God" (John 8:47 ESV).

So how does God speak to us? In the Old Testament, we are told to "Listen carefully to the thunder of God's voice as it rolls from his mouth" (Job 37:2 NLT). But more frequently, I have found that God speaks with a still, small voice. At times, I hear Him through the promptings in my conscience. Frequently, I recognize His voice in the counsel of trusted friends or family, the lyrics and melody of a song, or when I hear the birds of the air, the sound of a distant rain, or in the gentle rustling of the leaves in the trees during a summer breeze. And when I am alone, quiet, and make time to meditate on scripture, God speaks through His Word. It is as relevant today as it was when it was written those many years ago. "For the word of God is living and active, sharper than any two-edged sword, piercing to the division of soul and of spirit, of joints and of marrow, and discerning the thoughts and intentions of the heart" (Hebrews 4:12 ESV). By comparing what we perceive to be factual in our lives to the truth of His written word, we can learn to recognize the voice we hear as that of The Master. And we come to realize that it's not so much about how He speaks but what we do with what He says that truly matters.

Reflection

How have you heard God's voice? Rick Warren says that "God's truth is consistent. He is not going to tell you one thing in the Bible and then tell you something different in an impression." How could you use his quote to encourage others who might say that some scripture is not relevant today?

JULY 19
(Y4, D29)

H.E.L.P.

I lift up my eyes to the hills. From where does my help come?

—Psalm 121:1 (ESV)

When I go shopping with a friend of mine, we have two different philosophies. Mine is to get what I want and get out. Hers is more patient and relaxed. In my way of thinking, I will spend a minimal amount of time looking for the items on my list. However, if I can't find what I want, and it's something I need or think the store has, I will find someone and ask for help. She will occasionally get upset with me if in the course of her searching, I simply turn to a clerk to inquire further. When the store employee isn't able to assist us, she will say, "See, they don't know any more than we do." Sometimes, however, they are able to lead me to the item, provide additional information, or suggest an alternate solution. I guess I am never hesitant about asking because I simply view it as part of their role.

Today, help is available to us in so many forms. There are food pantries and shelters for persons who struggle meeting their basic needs. If you are looking for a job or are an employer searching for help, there are recruiters who offer services. Out of work or disabled? There is government assistance for you. If you are in an emergency situation, you can call 911. Or if you are elderly and have the right equipment, you can use your "Help, I've fallen and I can't get up" device. There are medical clinics for those who have chronic health concerns. Many community organizations and churches sponsor helplines for people who need counseling services or are in crisis. In need of directions? Then your GPS can provide them. Educational scholarships are accessible to qualifying individuals. There are financial institutions to help you borrow money for a new home or another project. Some would and have, in fact, argued that there is so much help available that in many ways, we have created a dependent society.

There is an expression that has been around for decades which states "God helps those who help themselves." It is probably one of those frequently quoted phrases that most persons think is sacred. However, it is not found in the Bible. Whatever the original source of this saying, the teachings we find in scripture are quite the contrary. When Jesus told his disciples that He would be leaving them, they asked Him to show them the way where He would be going (John 14:5). He explained that He was "the way" and that He would be with the Father (John 14:6–7). He stated:

> Whatever you ask in my name, this I will do, that the Father may be glorified in the Son. If you ask me anything in my name, I will do it. If you love me, you will keep my commandments. And I will ask the Father, and he will give you another Helper to be with you forever—the Spirit of truth, whom the world cannot receive, because it neither sees him nor knows him. You know him, for he dwells with you and will be in you. (John 14:13–17 ESV)

God knew that we would be incapable of helping ourselves, so He provided a spiritual Helper. In the Old Testament, we find that the psalmist also understood where to find relief from the distress of life. "God is our refuge and strength, a very present help in trouble" (Psalm 46:1 ESV). Those of us who seek the refuge He provides will realize all the help we will ever need. For help which is God-given can be defined as His Eternal Liberating Promise. It is *H*is and His alone. It is *E*ternal because it is everlasting. It is *L*iberating because it frees us from the worry and burdens which somehow find us. Finally, it is also a *P*romise that He made and will provide to all those who love Him. So if you are struggling this day to find the right kind of help, look beyond the hills of this world. Instead, look to the One who created them. For not only did the psalmist ask the question, "I lift up my eyes to the mountains—where does my help come from?" (Psalm 121:1 NIV). He also knew the answer as he replied, "My help comes from the LORD, the Maker of heaven and earth" (Psalm 121:2 NIV). Likewise, we too should know where our best source of help is found and never be reluctant to seek it.

Reflection

To what sources have your turned in the past year to find the help you have needed? Which ones did you find to be true and lasting? On what do you rely on for a sense of assurance, peace, security, and comfort? How would you explain to a nonbeliever that the sources of help in this world are never long-lasting but that they can know the one who can provide help that is life-sustaining?

JULY 20
(Y5, D29)

Loyalty: A Two-Way Street

Never let loyalty and kindness leave you! Tie them around your
neck as a reminder. Write them deep within your heart.

—Proverbs 3:3 (NLT)

Customer loyalty programs have now been around for decades. Beginning in the 1980s with frequent flyer miles, they evolved into almost every facet of our lives. Included are hotel booking incentives, car rental programs, online point earnings, money back credit cards, and store savings via family and friends. Convenience stores that you frequent will at times offer their own card, specifically tailored to offer rewards with free or discounted items identical to those you have purchased. One research study noted that an average consumer belongs to over a dozen loyalty programs but only actively utilizes just half of those in which they are enrolled. Another study highlighted noted that participation in most programs does not really drive any real sense of loyalty and that program engagement is actually declining.

We are trained to become wasteful consumers based on the messages we encounter on a daily basis. It is not hard to understand why we have become labeled as a "throwaway society." It's practically guaranteed customers will in time replace products with newer models but not necessarily from the same company. Even more bothersome is our evolving proclivity for throwing away people. We easily tire of relationships and frequently do not invest the time to develop them. In his book, *Loyalty: The Vexing Virtue*, author Eric Felten writes:

> We come and go so relentlessly that our friendships can't but come and go too. What sort of loyalty is there in the age of Facebook, when friendship is a costless transaction, a business of flip reciprocity? Friendship held together by nothing more permanent than hyperlinks is hardly the stuff of selfless fidelity... How much is the anxiety we feel these days a function of the disheartening suspicion that, in a real jam, there might not be anyone we can count on?

In our relationships with one another, biblical principles call us to steadfast loyalty. There is no stronger evidence of this than the relationship between David and his friend, Jonathan. While Jonathan's father, King Saul, sought to kill David, the two struck a lasting covenant between them. "At last Jonathan said to David, 'Go in peace, for we have sworn loyalty to each other in the LORD's name. The LORD is the witness of a bond between us and our children forever'" (1 Samuel 20:42 NLT). In the New Testament, Paul speaks of a "true companion" (Philippians 4:3 NIV). Jesus reminds us that such loyalty is to be expressed in both our relationships with the heavenly Father as well as our fellow man. This is evidenced in first two commandments: "Love the Lord your God with all your heart and with all your soul and with all your mind and with all your strength" and "Love your neighbor as yourself" (Mark 12:30–31 NIV). If we follow this, we can be assured that His loyalty to us will be reciprocated: "Know therefore that the LORD your God is God, the faithful God who maintains covenant loyalty with those who love Him and keep His commandments, to a thousand generations" (Deuteronomy 7:9 NIV).

The problem with most of us is that our loyalty is divided at times. We are caught between the things of God and the things of the world. James called it "double minded" and went on to state, "Their loyalty is divided between God and the world, and they are unstable in everything they do" (James 1:8 NLT). That instability certainly hinders a deep relationship with God, but it likewise interferes with the loyalty in our human associations as well. It is safe to assume then that loyalty requires some work on our part. Woodrow Wilson is quoted as saying, "Loyalty means nothing unless it has at its heart the absolute principle of self-sacrifice." Unlike the loyalty programs being promoted in our product world, we come to realize our relationships are not a commodity but rather a two-way street. As we consider our relationship with the Creator, it is built on trust. Therefore, "Let us hold tightly without wavering to the hope we affirm, for God can be trusted to keep his promise" (Hebrews 10:23 NLT). Can we?

Reflection

Looking back on aspects of your life, can you think of situations where you believed relationships you thought to be based on loyalty were discovered otherwise? Why do we not need to be concerned about such unfaithfulness in our relationship with God? What steps can you take to foster more loyal relationships with others as well as with God? What degrees of sacrifice are you willing to make?

JULY 21
(Y6, D29)

The Walk

For we walk by faith, not by sight.

—2 Corinthians 5:7 (NIV)

Stepping off the lunar landing module *Eagle*, American astronaut Neil Armstrong became the first human to walk on the surface of the moon, 240,000 miles from Earth. As he made his way down the ladder, a television camera attached to the craft recorded his progress and beamed the signal back to Earth where hundreds of millions watched in great anticipation. At 10:56 p.m. on July 20, 1969, Armstrong spoke his famous quote, which he later contended was slightly garbled by his microphone and meant to be "That's one small step for *a* man, one giant leap for mankind." He then planted his left foot on the gray, powdery surface, took a cautious step forward, and humanity had walked on the moon. "Buzz" Aldrin joined him on the moon's surface at 11:11 p.m. as they took photographs and planted a US flag. Knowing that they were doing something unprecedented in human history, Aldrin felt he should mark the occasion. So he made the following statement: "This is the LM pilot. I'd like to take this opportunity to ask every person listening in, whoever and wherever they may be, to pause for a moment and contemplate the events of the past few hours and to give thanks in his or her own way." In a not-often-told story, he then ended radio communication and there, on the silent surface of the moon, read a verse from the Gospel of John and followed with communion. He later reflected, "It was interesting for me to think the very first liquid ever poured on the moon, and the very first food eaten there, were the communion elements."

Among the items the astronauts left on the moon's surface was a plaque that read: "Here men from the planet Earth first set foot on the moon, July 1969 AD—We came in peace for all mankind." In doing so, these men left their mark in the history of space exploration. If you were asked who you feel made the greatest mark on the history of mankind, who would you name? It might depend on what has influenced your life to this point. Scientists might cite Newton, physicists possibly Einstein, or others could consider Edison as the greatest inventor. Churchill or Julius Caesar might be named as the greatest of all politicians, while Mozart and Beethoven would undoubtedly be at the top of the list of composers. Humanitarians might look to Nelson Mandela or Mother Teresa. However, those who have fallen in step with Jesus as their Lord and Savior would not have to think about their answer. In fact, *Time* once had Jesus Christ at the top of its list as the Most Significant Figures in History. Dr. James Allan Francis reminded us that Jesus "never traveled more than two hundred miles from the place where he was born. He did none of the things usually associated with greatness. He had no credentials but himself." Yet no individual has "affected the life of mankind on earth as powerfully as that one solitary life."

Consider a walk you may decide to take at some future time with another individual. When you walk with that person, you won't be going in opposite directions. If you decide, for whatever reason, to do that, you won't be able to effectively listen. You can't enjoy them, you can't share things with them, and you won't be able to understand them. The same is true in your walk with the Lord. Referencing a journey with Christ, the Apostle Paul said, "For we are his workmanship, created in Christ Jesus for good works, which God prepared beforehand, that we should walk in them" (Ephesians 2:10 NIV). When you walk with the Lord, your will is going to align with His will. When you fall in step, walking side by side with Him, your focus will be on Him, and you will not falter. The Old Testament prophet put it this way: "Whether you turn to the right or to the left, your ears will hear a voice behind you, saying, 'This is the way; walk in it'" (Isaiah 30:21 NIV). We have all heard someone say how much easier it is to talk the talk than it is to walk the walk. If you are unable to effectively walk your talk, the worth of your words will be lost. When you are true to God's Word, your walk will reflect His talk. Someone once spoke this truth: "In the end, it's not the talk but the walk that matters." The Bible puts it this way: "Therefore, as you received Christ Jesus the Lord, so walk in him" (Colossians 2:6 ESV). Think of someone whom you could honor at their funeral by saying, "This world was a better place because they walked here." Wouldn't it be great if someday the same could be said about you? It can if you simply walk the walk.

Reflection

As you examine your journey with Christ, what areas of your walk with Him do you need to improve? How might you use others to truthfully advise you when your walk is not matching your talk? How will you commit to setting an example for those who are drifting in a direction apart from God?

JULY 22
(Y7, D29)

Hitting the Pause Button

Understand this, my dear brothers and sisters: You must all be
quick to listen, slow to speak, and slow to get angry.

—James 1:19 (NLT)

A friend informs you that your neighbor has just been nominated to receive recognition as a generous community servant. Over the course of the last few months, this neighbor has been uncompro-
misingly nasty about a comment you had made concerning pet boundaries. Your friend has no idea
that an issue has recently developed with this neighbor who is a mutual acquaintance. You clear your
throat about to make a few choice remarks. And then you hesitate, wondering if your comments
would really serve any useful purpose. Or perhaps you are at work when your boss asks if he might
see you for a few minutes. As you go into his office, a new work opportunity is laid out before you.
Over the course of the next year, the company has identified you to be part of a special work project
that will offer you bonus pay. If you consent, you will be agreeing to work many extra hours. The
recently established hobby time during which you have been able to bond with your teenager will
ultimately suffer. Also, that weekly Bible study that you have committed to teach will have to be put
on hold for now. Your boss would like an answer. With all things considered, you might be sacrificing a lot more than you would gain. So you decide to hit the pause button. More often than not,
our tendency to give deliberate reflection to the choices directly in front of us frequently gives way to
flaw-filled impulsivity. We are quick to criticize, hasty in our decision-making, and often thoughtless
about how the choices we make might ultimately affect not only ourselves but those around us as
well. While there are occasions in which it is imperative that we act quickly, an impulsive person is
habitually quick in the wrong way. They jump too soon and have a tendency to look before they
leap. They repeatedly lack vigilance, failing to give proper attention to the potential consequences of
their thoughts and actions.

Impulsive behavior is now new. A good example of an impetuous person was one of Jesus' chosen, Peter. When the Lord told His disciples that He must suffer and die, "Peter took him aside and

began to rebuke him. 'Never, Lord!' he said. 'This shall never happen to you!'" (Matthew 16:22–23 NIV). When Jesus told his disciples that those closest to Him would scatter and deny Him, "Peter declared, 'Even if everyone else deserts you, I will never desert you'" (Matthew 26:33 NLT). At times, Peter's hastiness placed him in danger. When a band of soldiers came after Jesus as He was betrayed, "Peter drew a sword and slashed off the right ear of Malchus, the high priest's slave" (John 18:10 NLT). We see that Peter's impulsiveness often demonstrated a lack of understanding. As he said to Jesus: "'You will never ever wash my feet!' Jesus replied, 'Unless I wash you, you won't belong to me'" (John 13:8 NLT). Many people in Scripture made poor choices because they became impatient. The Lord used Peter's thoughtless statements to teach some very important lessons about the Christian life and how the believer should deal with sin. Even though Peter made many missteps and blunders in his life, Jesus understood his passion. God needs followers like this apostle who are ready to step up and prepared to obey His will. This prompted Jesus to say: "You are Peter (which means 'rock'), and upon this rock I will build my church" (Matthew 16:18 NLT). Peter became one of the greatest preachers the church ever had.

Colossians 1:11 (NIV) says that we are strengthened by the Lord to "great endurance and patience." Reducing impulsivity and developing patience does not occur overnight, yet we will not have a meaningful Christian journey without it. "So let it grow, for when your endurance is fully developed, you will be perfect and complete, needing nothing" (James 1:4 NLT). As we seek God's power and goodness for our maturation, at times, it is necessary to just stop what you are doing, catch your breath, and take a moment to turn to the Lord. Consider what He wants you to say; simply imagine what He might tell you about what you are experiencing. In order to have a vigilant heart, one must rely on a check valve rather than a heart valve. Peter came to understand that while we "prepare our minds for action," we must also "exercise self-control" (1 Peter 1:13 NLT). Learning to hit the pause button from time to time will make you a more effective witness for Jesus, and there is where you will find your just reward.

Reflection

Describe situations in which you find it difficult to persevere and have a tendency toward impulsiveness? Can you think of occasions when it may be right to act hastily or be quick to speak? How will you work toward developing a greater reaction time when asked for an opinion or decision?

JULY 23
(Y1, D30)

Cool Down and Leave No Scars

A hot-tempered person stirs up conflict, but the one who is patient calms a quarrel.

—Proverbs 15:18 (NIV)

While engaged in the task of sweeping the carpet in the family downstairs game room, the vacuum I was using suddenly shut off. I thought maybe the dirt bin needed emptying, so I did that. Perhaps I had tripped a breaker; I checked that as well. Neither of these enabled the sweeper to restart. Then I took the next best step. I searched for the owner's manual for this product, now less than three years old. The manual gave me several things to try, including allowing the appliance to be unplugged for at least forty-five minutes in case it had become overheated. The vacuum did feel a little warm, so I did something else for a while. An hour or so later, I pushed the on/off button, and it started like a charm. I chuckled to myself, recalling that earlier that day I became a bit overheated at a local chain store where management was not enforcing a policy they had promoted. Fortunately, I had not allowed my frustration to shut down the shopping trip. I simply focused on my list and allowed myself to cool down before it became an issue.

In Matthew 5:22–24 (NLT), Jesus teaches us about the unhealthiness of two different types of anger: being angry oneself or causing anger in another. Both are unhealthy because our anger is not from God. It is written:

> If you are even angry with someone, you are subject to judgment! If you call someone an idiot, you are in danger of being brought before the court. And if you curse someone, you are in danger of the fires of hell. So if you are presenting a sacrifice at the altar in the Temple and you suddenly remember that someone has something against you, leave your sacrifice there at the altar. Go and be reconciled to that person. Then come and offer your sacrifice to God.

Even though it is possible that anger may serve us positively in certain instances, it has been proven that excessive or habitual anger will result in negative, self-destructive consequences, both to the one who is angry and to those who are around them. It is therefore true that managing one's anger as well as reconciling with those with whom one is angry or may have angered are two fundamental aspects of spiritual growth.

A story was told of young boy with a very bad temper. The boy's father wanted to teach him a lesson, so he gave him a bag of nails and told him that every time he lost his temper, he must hammer a nail into their wooden fence. On the first day of this lesson, the little boy had driven thirty-seven nails into the fence. Over the course of the next few weeks, the boy began to control his anger, so the number of nails that were hammered into the fence dramatically decreased. It wasn't long before he discovered it was easier to hold his temper than to drive those nails into the fence. The day finally came when the boy didn't lose his temper even once. He was so proud of himself and couldn't wait to tell his father. Pleased, his father suggested that he now pull out one nail for each day that he could hold his temper. Many weeks went by, and the day finally came when the young boy was able to tell his father that all the nails were gone. Very gently, the father took his son by the hand and led him to the fence. "You have done very well, my son." He smiled. "But look at the holes in the fence. The fence will never be the same." The little boy listened carefully as his father continued to speak, "When you say things in anger, they leave permanent scars just like these. And no matter how many times you say you're sorry, the wounds will still be there."

We are not able to easily track those occasions where we might have done irreparable harm by not acting appropriately in "the heat of the moment." It seems as though it has become quite easy to irritate others and provoke anger in today's world. Consider how social justice declarations at a sporting event can upset and alienate fans who are there purely for the love of the game. Entering into a political discussion at a high school reunion can cause division that takes away from the fellowship of the affair itself. Dredging up an old conflict at a family holiday get-together can evoke an intense argument, thereby isolating relatives. Believers in Christ are called upon to be peacemakers, finding a solution before an incident or conflict escalates. "Human anger does not produce the righteousness God desires" (James 1:20 NLT). We must practice how we might respond to potential opportunities for conflict. For God is glorified when we ignore it, walk away, let it go, or at least allow forty-five minutes to cool down.

Reflection

Have you had events of anger occur that have resulted in or caused permanent marks? Are there ways you have applied Christian values in an attempt to resolve them? How can you contribute to preventing heated situations from getting out-of-hand in organizations of which you are a part?

JULY 24
(Y2, D30)

Who Do You Trust?

Commit everything you do to the LORD. Trust him, and he will help you.

—Psalm 37:5 (NLT)

According to Amazon founder Jeff Bezos, one of the most important things you need to do to have success in your career is to build trust. On July 20, 2021, Jeff Bezos and his three fellow passengers went on a costly flight in a spacecraft over which they had no operational control. They placed their trust and their lives in the technological design of a rocket which had been extensively tested over a six-year period by a space company. The company, known as Blue Origin, was founded by Bezos in 2000 and served to make the world's richest man also an astronaut. After the rocket's capsule separated from its reusable booster, the crew enjoyed a few minutes of weightlessness before parachuting back to the ground. As they became preoccupied with passing floating ping pong balls and catching freely suspended candy in their mouths, the passengers were reminded that perhaps they should look outside at the stunning view from above. However, this seemed to be devoid of any reference to who might have provided that creation below. It made some recall a time when the first crew to orbit the moon on Apollo 8 read from the book of Genesis during a live broadcast which would have certainly been less controversial in 1968. If this new flight had any spiritual effect, the travelers didn't reveal it in their remarks in space or in the press conference after they were back on land. The only rare reference to any divine trust were the announced words "Godspeed, first crew of New Shepard. Let's light this candle" spoken when the rocket launched.

Although our culture promotes that we need to take charge of our personal destiny, life as we know it is anything but predictable. Yet many of us subscribe to the philosophy, "Everything I plan will eventually come to pass." Those who hold onto this belief may one day find themselves facing a rude awakening that none of us are truly in control of our world or our lives. Life was unpredictable for people of the Biblical era as well. Abraham was called to follow God's leadership while "not knowing where he was going" (Hebrews 11:8 ESV). Moses was a fugitive from justice when he was called to confront the Egyptian pharaoh (Exodus 14:3–18). Shadrach, Meshach, and Abednego trusted God no matter what the outcome would be when they were thrown into a blazing furnace (Daniel 3:12–17). Even though Gideon's backup plan was to have a large army before he faced the Midianites, God whittled it down to 300 men to instill trust (Judges 7:7). David faced Goliath with no armor or weapons apart from a slingshot and some stones (1 Samuel 17). Daniel went into the lions' den armed with no protection other than God's presence (Daniel 6). Peter and John showed trust by defying the same religious authorities who arranged for Jesus' execution (Acts 4:19–20). Zechariah and Elizabeth trusted God when their longing for a child was unfulfilled (Luke 1:5–17). Here was the difference in their trust over ours: they put their lives in the hands of a God who knows the future, sustains us in the present, and employs the outcome of our lives.

Trusting is believing in the promises of God in all circumstances, even in those where the evidence seems to be to the contrary. It is a faulty proposition to trust in ourselves because our understanding is temporal and often tainted by our worldly natures. While we frequently have a Plan B for our lives, that's not the way God operates. Sometimes, God will open and close doors while He lead us down one path or another. No matter how many paths in life we take, He will use those paths we have chosen with all their twists and turns in order to bring us closer to Him. David said, "Those who know your name trust in you, for you, O LORD, do not abandon those who search for you" (Psalm 9:10 NLT). God's plan is very simple: to know Him and to glorify Him. No matter what we do in life, if we are growing to know Him more and if we are glorifying Him in all that we do, then God's plan is never thwarted. There's an old hymn, which the lyrics to its chorus are as follows: "Jesus, Jesus, how I trust Him! How I've proved Him o'er and o'er. Jesus, Jesus, precious Jesus. Oh, for grace to trust Him more!" As we submit to trusting Him today, we will recognize He is already in all of our tomorrows. Each of us depends on others and on resources we did not create. We should give careful consideration to placing our trust in the one who did!

Reflection

Look at God's track record in your life. Notice when His hand was on your plans and when you trusted Him for the outcome. How does the thought of God's eternal wisdom help you to deal with your concern for the future? Consider ways that your open demonstration about trust in God might serve as an effective witness to others who burden themselves with controlling all of the details of their lives?

JULY 25
(Y3, D30)

Moving from Hopelessness to Hope

I pray that God, the source of hope, will fill you completely with
joy and peace because you trust in him. Then you will overflow with
confident hope through the power of the Holy Spirit.

—Romans 15:13 (NLT)

Our world is fashioned with fears of economic collapse, pandemics, wars, global warming, extreme rioting, and natural disasters such as earthquakes and hurricanes. There are those who at times just want to crawl into a corner and curl up in the fetal position. Others may not be quite ready to do just that, but they might admit they are less hopeful than they once were. If we add the above to the personal trials of everyday existence—a confrontational divorce, a pending lawsuit, trying to find work because of a job loss, or facing the uncertainty of an illness for ourselves or a loved one. It can be quite overwhelming. It's no wonder so many people struggle with an increasing sense of hopelessness, even to the point of despair. When fear grips us, it disables us from moving forward. When a crisis hits, you have to do the smart things necessary to get through it. You listen to helpful advice from others whom you respect, you make good choices, and you should affirm that this too will pass. Soon enough, you will marvel at all that God did in the midst of this trouble as you are able look at it from the other side.

We can learn much from King David and how he responded to news of the impending death of his illegitimate child. "David begged God to spare the child. He went without food and lay all night on the bare ground. The elders of his household pleaded with him to get up and eat with them, but he refused" (2 Samuel 12:16–17 NLT). Seven days later, the child died, but the attendants were afraid to tell David for they were concerned that he might do something out of desperation. When David was told that the child had passed, he:

[G]ot up from the ground, washed himself, put on lotions, and changed his clothes. He went to the Tabernacle and worshiped the Lord. After that, he

413

returned to the palace and was served food and ate. Then his servants said to him, "What is this thing that you have done? You fasted and wept for the child while he was alive; but when the child died, you arose and ate food." David replied, "I fasted and wept while the child was alive, for I said, Perhaps the LORD will be gracious to me and let the child live. But why should I fast when he is dead? Can I bring him back again? I will go to him one day, but he cannot return to me." (2 Samuel 12:20–23 NLT)

David knew it was time to move forward. Soon he was blessed with another son, and "they named him Solomon. The LORD loved him" (2 Samuel 12:24 NIV).

The Apostle Paul wrote, "We are pressed on every side by troubles, but we are not crushed. We are perplexed, but not driven to despair" (2 Corinthians 4:8 NLT). Paul suffered many hardships yet not hopelessness, because, like David, his hope was not based on earthly circumstances. He held on to the knowledge that God was ultimately in control of it all. As translated in English, the word *hope* often conveys doubt. For instance, "I hope it will not rain tomorrow." Or it could be used as a response one might give when asked if they think that they will go to heaven when they die. They say, "I hope so." For the Christian biblical hope is a reality and not a feeling. It carries no doubt. Biblical hope is a sure foundation upon which we base our lives, believing that God always keeps His promises. Followers of Christ never lose sight of hope because "our light and momentary troubles are achieving for us an eternal glory that far outweighs them all. So we fix our eyes not on what is seen, but on what is unseen, since what is seen is temporary, but what is unseen is eternal" (2 Corinthians 4:17–18 NIV).

At one time or another, we will all find ourselves in a situation that seems to be hopeless. For those who know Jesus as their Savior, it's an opportunity for God to call us closer to Him. We don't have to think all is lost because we cannot control the circumstances. Instead, we can learn to trust the one who controls all things. Therefore, "do not be surprised at the fiery ordeal that has come on you to test you, as though something strange were happening to you" (1 Peter 4:12 NIV). Hope is a confident expectation that God will do what He has promised. Either you can move forward with the rest of your life or allow the world as you know it may come to an end. In either case, Jesus will be there if you believe in Him. Simply wait patiently and be established in hope. Things are going to get better—much better!

Reflection

What feels uncertain in your world today? Have you sometimes felt hopeless during times of crisis? What would it take to restore your hope? How can you implement God's solutions for hopelessness and despair? How will respond to someone in your life who needs encouragement?

JULY 26
(Y4, D30)

No Strings Attached

But if serving the Lord seems undesirable to you, then choose for yourselves this day whom you will serve… But as for me and my household, we will serve the Lord.

—Joshua 24:15 (NIV)

Think back to your childhood, and you will most likely remember the story of a wooden boy named Pinocchio who was attached to strings and magically came to life. He is one of the most famous marionette characters ever created. Originally published as a novel in 1883, *The Adventures of Pinocchio* has been adapted many times, the best known of which is most likely the animated feature created by Walt Disney. Anyone who grew up in the early days of TV will remember another well-known marionette by the name of Howdy Doody. He, along with the show's host, Buffalo Bob, conducted a pioneer children's program that became famous for the line "It's Howdy Doody Time" which ran on NBC from 1947 to 1960. Interestingly enough, there is documented evidence that marionettes, string and wire-controlled puppets, were used throughout history, some say as early as 2000 BC.

In today's culture, we can find strings attached to much of the world around us. These range from physical confinement to the manipulative controls others attempt to exercise over us. It's everywhere. When I take my daily walk, I notice the sign stating, "All dogs must be on a leash" at the entrance to the recreational park where I get my exercise. Whenever I have been in big cities, I have observed professional dog walkers strolling with many canines at one time. I think there has to be an aptitude to accomplish that. Leashing children has been controversial with opinions from those who want to whatever is necessary to keep their child safe to others who say this is simply lazy parenting. And beware of the strings attached to that credit card for which you just enrolled or the mortgage contract you recently signed. What seems like a good deal today may come back to haunt you in a short period of time.

From the beginning of creation, God has always desired a "no strings attached" relationship with mankind. He could have commanded that we love Him, but then we would have been no different than the stringed puppets previously mentioned. Without the ability to choose for ourselves, we would have been less than human; merely a body controlled by a higher power. Theological discussions about "free will" can become very deep and confusing, sometimes to the point that they defy logic. Suffice it to say that each one of us is inherently sinful by nature, but we can freely choose which path we will follow. "Submit yourselves therefore to God. Resist the devil, and he will flee from you" (James 4:7 NIV). Even though God deeply desires to fellowship with us, we are free to accept or reject Him. Jesus said, "Everyone who commits sin is a slave to sin" (John 8:34 NKJV). But He also stated, "For whoever does the will of my Father in heaven is my brother and sister and mother" (Matthew 12:50 NIV).

Free will should be valued as a uniquely human quality. Ultimately, it is a choice between life and death. Charles Spurgeon once said, "Free will carried many a soul to hell, but never a soul to heaven." If we make the decision to follow the teachings of Jesus and align our will with that of God's, we consciously decide to constrain the kinds of things we say and do. True free will isn't freedom to be sinful. It's the desire to receive the undeserving grace of God; that is to move beyond our inherited fallen state and be destined for eternity. That's a journey worth taking, for sure. Jesus said, "Anyone who chooses to do the will of God will find out whether my teaching comes from God or whether I speak on my own" (John 7:17 NIV). So don't ever be mistaken about God's intention. He won't connect us to wires or otherwise manipulate what we do with our lives. He doesn't tie us to a leash to keep us within His grasp. Instead, God pulls at our heartstrings, for love freely given is so much more valuable.

Reflection

Do you sometimes find it frustrating to be in situations where you are not allowed to make your own decisions? How is your relationship with God different as you realize He gives you the freedom to choose the direction of your thoughts, words, and actions? Is there argument for the fact that belief in the concept of free will can equip you to be a better person? How would you react to a statement from another that free will in its truest form cannot coexist with a belief in God?

JULY 27
(Y5, D30)

Fear

For I am the Lord your God who takes hold of your right hand and says
to you, "Do not fear; I will help you." (Isaiah 41:13 NIV)

I heard recently that a pastor stood before his church on a Sunday morning and asked the congregation, "How many of you are scared? If so, raise your hand." Many of those present did so, and we should not be surprised. In the midst of a time when our country and world is experiencing an extreme amount of gun violence, this response is perhaps inevitable. A sense of uncertainty rises, and fear sets in when those who have been hired to protect us become the targets. We question whether it is safe to go shopping at the mall or watch a movie in a public theater. We become concerned whether our children will be protected at school. Complicate that with the turmoil of cultural divisions and atrocities of radical terrorism. It is no wonder that many people are scared. In today's world, fear is a common response, and what we do with it will determine who we are as a person.

Social media, advertising, and even some news outlets each send a persistent message that people should be afraid. We are warned to safeguard our personal identity and our private information. It is being advised that we should stockpile silver and gold in case the financial system collapses. We hear that there are those who purchase dehydrated food packets to feed their families in the event there is a national emergency. Hysteria is pervasive, and it affects the way we view life. Our politicians sometimes capitalize on the concept of a frightening world and pledge that if elected, they will make it safer. Such statements are not new to the political arena. This was the case when Franklin D. Roosevelt took office in 1933 at one of the most troublesome times of our nation. During the depth of the depression and in his first inaugural address, he said, "The only thing we have to fear is fear itself."

The only fear we should have is the fear of the Lord, but it is not a fear that calls us to be afraid. It is rather a recognition of who He is and our appropriate worshipful response to His awesomeness. "The fear of the Lord is the beginning of wisdom" (Psalm 111:10 NIV) and an acknowledgment of His holiness. Having been given the assignment to "explain God," an eight-year-old California boy by the name of Danny Dutton is credited with the following revelation: "If you don't believe in God, besides being an atheist, you will be very lonely because your parents can't go everywhere with you, like to camp, but God can. It is good to know He's around you when you're scared, in the dark, or when you can't swim and you get thrown into real deep water by big kids." Danny not only understood the meaning of fear, but he knew where to place his hope and find assurance. He is able to echo similar words to those of David, "When I am afraid, I put my trust in you" (Psalm 56:3 NIV). Regardless of what is happening in the world around us, we do not ever need to indicate that we are afraid. "So we can say with confidence, 'The LORD is my helper, so I will have no fear. What can mere people do to me?'" (Hebrews 13:6 NLT).

If you remember a time when you were quite fearful, you no doubt experienced feelings of horror, panic, or despair. You might well recall a number of years ago when the captain of an Italian cruise ship, the *Costa Concordia*, abandoned his ship. Thirty-two passengers were lost when the vessel capsized and sank after striking an underwater rock obstruction. Those of us who know God as our Captain will never feel abandoned. He spoke to His chosen people through the Prophet Isaiah who found themselves in exile and captivity hundreds of years before the birth of Christ. "So do not fear, for I am with you; do not be dismayed, for I am your God. I will strengthen you and help you; I will uphold you with my righteous right hand" (Isaiah 41:10 NIV). Likewise, we have no reason to believe that He does not have the same message for we who follow Him today. Those whom He has chosen as His faithful servants are always provided the same promise. Fear only sets in when we lose sight of God and who He is.

Reflection

Can you recall a time in your life when you were afraid? To whom did you call on for help? What are your greatest fears today? Do you handle them differently than you once did? Romans 8:31 (NIV) states: "If God is for us, who can be against us?" How can you apply that message in your journey? Are there ways that you might also share this passage with others who express their fears to you?

JULY 28
(Y6, D30)

For Members Only

But we are citizens of heaven, where the Lord Jesus Christ lives. And
we are eagerly waiting for him to return as our Savior.

—Philippians 3:20 (NLT)

For most of us, there has been a time when we have profited from the application of the motto, "Membership Has Its Privileges." Once the slogan of the American Express Card, the implication was that for the payment of an annual fee to have an AMEX card, there were benefits to be had. This has been extended over the years through the offering of "Members Only" store cards to online ordering memberships where those who pay a periodic fee will receive free expedited shipping and special access to other online services. The concept of somehow being part of an inner circle is not a new one. It certainly has been promoted over time by many fraternal organizations as well as limited memberships to organizations such as country clubs and professional associations. In doing so, the sense of community they create is sometimes criticized as being carried out at the expense of excluding or discriminating against others who might otherwise want to belong.

Following the American Civil War, the question of how to create a sense of belonging for those who had been brought here as slaves became part of the struggle of healing during the Reconstruction Period. Ratification of the Fourteenth Amendment to the Constitution on July 28, 1868, attempted to resolve questions of African-American citizenship by stating that "all persons born or naturalized in the United States…are citizens of the United States and of the state in which they reside." The amendment then reaffirmed the privileges and rights of all citizens and granted these citizens "equal protection of the laws." In the decades which followed, the equal protection clause was cited by many African American activists who argued that evolving racial segregation denied them what they believed the law had intended. Indeed, there have been many Supreme Court cases challenging the concept of due process and equal protection. Subsequently, the "birthright citizenship" of the amendment has raised modern-day controversy regarding the assumed citizenship of those whose parents have immigrated into the country illegally.

It's interesting to reflect on the role that citizenship plays in our faith journey. Recalling the faith shown by Abraham and Sarah, the Apostle Paul spoke these words:

> All these people died still believing what God had promised them. They did not receive what was promised, but they saw it all from a distance and welcomed it. They agreed that they were foreigners and nomads here on earth. Obviously, people who say such things are looking forward to a country they can call their own. If they had longed for the country they came from, they could have gone back. But they were looking for a better place, a heavenly homeland. That is why God is not ashamed to be called their God, for he has prepared a city for them. (Hebrews 11:13–16 NLT)

In some ways, their journey is also ours. We spend much of our life trying to belong, seeking inclusion, and determined to gain some sort of membership for our own earthly satisfaction. But as we give our life to Christ, "So then you are no longer strangers and aliens, but you are fellow citizens with the saints and members of the household of God" (Ephesians 2:19 ESV).

It is important to realize that being a good citizen is complemented by being a good Christian. Our neighborhood, our town, and our state are enhanced when our citizenry membership is exemplified through a demonstration of Christian values. After all, the very same ingredients that make a good Christian should also make a good citizen. It's easy to see obvious examples of contempt and hate for our government officials, deteriorating civic pride, and outright disrespect for the symbols of our nation. As we model God's character here on earth, we are honoring Him. Consider today how your words and actions convey where your citizenship lies. Enjoy the assurance of your eternal citizenship and be grateful for what Jesus did to secure your place as He paid the cost for you and all who love Him.

Reflection

Do you have a membership in any organization that excludes others? Are you able to justify this exclusion? What happens to our relationships with God and community when we refuse or fail to participate in support of good government? How can you remain faithful to God and show your respect to those in authority, even in those times when you do not like them or disagree with their decisions?

JULY 29
(Y7, D30)

The Boss of the Whole World

For God gave us a spirit not of fear but of power and love and self-control.

—2 Timothy 1:7 (ESV)

My friend has often reminded me of the story of her son when he was just a child. One snowy evening as he sat next to her, he begged her to stay home from work the next day. She informed him that would not be possible because she had responsibilities, and her boss would expect her to be there. The youngster looked up and innocently asked if her boss was "the boss of the whole world." Their interaction became a teaching moment about commitment. The mother did the right thing by modeling an image of accountability to her son at such an early age. Furthermore, her sense of loyalty turned the relationship with her manager into a lifelong friendship. I would know because I am "the boss" in the story. We smile together each time she repeats the tale. Over the years, employees like my friend have become more difficult to find. The values of our society have weakened the importance of dedication. Simply having an association with one's employer does not always guarantee any form of devotion to them.

Unfortunately, the same is often true for persons of faith. They frequently live by the example of "one foot in the world and the other in heaven." It is pervasive in our society and is sometimes regrettably displayed by our community leaders. In July 2019, the issue of separation of Church and State placed city officials in a South Carolina town in a "no-win" situation. A monument featuring a prayer for officers had been placed in front of the new police station by a women's group. When a collection of local residents complained, representatives plastered over the word *Lord* so as to appease those in opposition. The community quickly became divided over the modification, and this resulted in city officials making a decision to remove the monument. While some stated that God and government must remain separate from religious references, others noted that the nation was founded by many who believed that America could not expect to be blessed if it failed to acknowledge and honor Almighty God. The latter group would agree with the Apostle Paul who wrote: "If we live, we live for the Lord; and if we die, we die for the Lord. So, whether we live or die, we belong to the Lord" (Romans 14:8 NIV).

In today's world, people readily blame others for their lack of character and self-control. They often fault society, their parents, their boss, the government, or others in positions of authority. Not wanting to accept any personal responsibility for their own shortcomings, they seek to find a scapegoat. Followers of Christ have found a better answer, but they must always be clear for what and who they stand. Jesus said, "I tell you the truth, everyone who acknowledges me publicly here on earth, the Son of Man will also acknowledge in the presence of God's angels. But anyone who denies me here on earth will be denied before God's angels" (Luke 12:8–9 NLT). Public acknowledgment of our Christian values can be difficult in a society where our greatest struggle in exercising self-control might be as simple as saying "no" to another cookie or as difficult as spending an additional half hour on Netflix or Facebook. If we face our Christian walk with a similar approach, we still have a lot to learn.

It is important to understand that self-control is a work of the Holy Spirit, not a work of the individual. After all, Galatians 5:22–23 lists the fruit of the Spirit, not the fruit of the Christian. Because self-control is a gift produced in and through us by God's Spirit, Christians should be hopeful about maturing in the faith. For in Jesus, we have a source for true self-control far beyond that of our personal weaknesses. Similar to an athlete preparing for a higher vision, we have a firm expectation for ourselves. "All athletes are disciplined in their training. They do it to win a prize that will fade away, but we do it for an eternal prize" (1 Corinthians 9:25 NLT). When all is said and done and we decide to journey with Christ, we face two tasks before us. The first of these is to form a relationship with the Lord. The second is just as important: we must decide who will be in control of our lives. When we finally decide to "let go and let God," then we have discovered who is truly the boss of the whole world.

Reflection

Does it comfort or distress you that God can have an influence on the world through you? How does increasing your knowledge of His role in your life help you to trust He is ultimately in control? In a world that often feels out of control, how can you justify to others it is important to trust God?

JULY 30
(Y1, D31)

First Things First

The first of the firstfruits of your land you shall bring into the house of the Lord your God.

—Exodus 23:19 (NKJV)

There's an old story about a lighthouse keeper who was beloved by the people of a small shore town. Frequently, they would stop by to visit him because it seemed that he was always on duty. His responsibilities were many and had to be carried out in all kinds of weather. Some of the most basic included filling the lights with fuel each day, maintaining the wicks, and lighting the lamp at sunset and putting it out each morning. One day, a lady stopped by and said, "My family is cold and we need some oil to keep our house warm. Would you give us some?" Out of compassion for the family, he did so. Over time, others also came making the same request. He thought, *Well, I can't do for one family and not help the others*, so he gave fuel to all. A day came when he depleted his supply. That evening, several ships crashed on the shores, and a number of people died. Thinking he had been doing a good thing, he lost his sense of priority and purpose. As such, the lighthouse keeper is in good company with many of us.

In 2017, the Oakland Raiders made quarterback Derek Carr the highest-paid player in NFL history. Carr, then twenty-six, agreed to a five-year contract worth $125 million. In an interview about his soon-to-be financial success, he stated the following: "The first thing I'll do is pay my tithe like I have since I was in college while getting $700 on a scholarship check. That won't change." Having already been involved in mission efforts, he went on to say, "The exciting thing for me, money-wise, honestly, is this money is going to help a lot of people, not only in this country but in a lot of countries around the world. That's what's exciting to me." He gives modern-day voice to the words of the Apostle Paul who says, "Everything comes from Him and exists by His power and is intended for His glory" (Romans 11:36 NLT).

The situation with many of us is that we rationalize to give God what remains. Yet how many of us would invite a special guest for dinner and serve leftovers? While there is nothing wrong with leftovers per se, they are not exactly what we would provide for a king, let alone the King of kings.

As living sacrifices (Romans 12:1–2), are we free to give God any old thing with the expectation that He must accept it or else? Does He not deserve the best we have? Jesus is very clear about priorities when He said that we must "seek first his kingdom and his righteousness and all these things will be given to you as well" (Matthew 6:33 NIV). On another occasion, He connects the dots between loving and doing when He states, "If you love me, you will keep my commandments" (John 14:15 ESV). If we are serious about keeping first things first, we must pray that the Lord will show us when our priorities are skewed and where we need to make changes.

Ultimately, our purpose for living should be to bring honor and glory to God rather than seeking pleasure for ourselves. Paul speaks of this when he says: "Live your lives in a way that God would consider worthy" (1 Thessalonians 2:12 NLT). With that purpose in mind, we can set our priorities by discovering what will bring the greatest recognition to God. When we do that, we'll be rich in God's eyes. If we further listen to the philosophy of the Raiders quarterback, we will discover the foundation of his belief. Carr continued, "I have a very strong faith in God. He is the reason I play football. He has given me this special talent and I want to use it to glorify Him. I am grateful for the opportunity to further His kingdom by sharing my faith on and off the football field. At any moment, any second, my football career could be taken away, but my faith and relationship with God will never be taken from me." The search for God requires a singleness of purpose. When God's people put Him first, God's blessings begin to flow. First things first, it's what He deserves from us.

Reflection

In what ways have you experienced the blessings of God as a direct result of setting God-honoring priorities and seeking Him first in your life? How does your leisure time reflect your devotion to Jesus Christ? If you were to map out the remaining years of your life, what would they look like? What priorities would you need to change in your finances, interests, relationships, and daily routine to evidence that God is indeed first in life?

JULY 31
(Y2, D31)

Contents Perishable

Do not work for the food that perishes, but for the food that endures
to eternal life, which the Son of Man will give to you.

—John 6:27 (ESV)

I am one of those grocery shoppers who likes to get my perishable items such as meat, milk, and ice cream just before I go to the checkout counter. If it happens to be a warm day, I immediately go home so that these items are not absent from cold temperatures any longer than necessary. I am always amazed when I receive the delivery of an online food purchase which is usually packed in one of those insulated containers with dry ice inside. Since the food is perishable, the skeptic in me cautions that I should carefully check the contents. They always arrive frozen as promised. However, I do wonder if there are people out there who do receive food that has not been well-preserved. I sometimes think about what it must have been like before current day refrigeration when folks bought blocks of ice for cooling or sometimes used salt for preservation. It prompts me to further consider that our lives are much like perishable food. We must either use it or lose it. It would do us well to be reminded that all of our precious gifts as well as many of our golden opportunities should be labeled as "Contents Perishable."

Those who follow Jesus must be careful to recognize just how perishable life is. We should exercise caution to not throw it away in exchange for valueless things. Instead, we must give our life in service, sacrifice, and in selflessness to others. Because those "perishable things" that we frequently rely on simply lack the ability to satisfy our deepest need, what we require is the life that only God can provide. One of the most memorized scriptures is found in John 3:16 (NIV): "For God so loved the world that he gave his one and only Son that whoever believes in him shall not perish but have eternal life." If a person dies without receiving God's free gift of salvation, then they will perish in eternal separation from God. So we should ask this one pertinent question: do I want to enjoy life within the Lord's framework so my life can flourish into eternity or will I devote my life to the temporary values of this world and ultimately perish? If you decide on the latter, prayerfully reconsider by reflecting on these words by one of Jesus' own: "The Lord is not slow to fulfill his promise as some count slowness, but is patient toward you, not wishing that any should perish, but that all should reach repentance" (2 Peter 3:9 ESV).

In the Old Testament, we can read about the challenge of Esther to go before her king unannounced, an unlawful act even for a queen, such as herself. But according to scripture, she first gave this directive: "Go and gather together all the Jews of Susa and fast for me. Do not eat or drink for three days, night or day. My maids and I will do the same. And then, though it is against the law, I will go in to see the king. If I must die, I must die" (Esther 4:16 NLT). In other words, bolstered by three days of fasting by the Jews, she would put her life at risk for an audience with her husband, the king—a huge leap of faith that she was resolved to do. "If I perish, I perish" were the words on her lips as she took each step of the journey, signifying that she readily and cheerfully risked her life for the good of the Jewish people. Esther was fully committed to accomplishing God's purpose for her life, no matter the personal cost.

As Christ's ambassadors, we are called upon to represent Him everywhere, and with that comes great responsibility. While there are many who will demonstrate unfaithfulness, we are called upon to do what is right, regardless of the price. We must prepare for the imperishable world by engaging in a transformation of the perishing world. Consider the immortal words of American missionary Jim Elliot written shortly before he was killed by a South American tribe he was trying to reach with the gospel. "He is no fool who gives up what he cannot keep in order to gain that which he cannot lose." He gave up his own life, which he had surrendered to Jesus. All of the men who participated in killing him eventually received Christ. Today's believers are called upon to show the same resolve for His cause. God expects us to speak up on behalf of those who are troubled and to be bearers of the good news, whatever the sacrifice. For it is not only our own lives which are fragile; they are perishable as well!

Reflection

What is it that you are being called upon to do in furthering the cause of Christ? Are there insignificant perishables in your life which are usurping your time, talent, and treasure? What might you do to divert that energy toward preserving and creating significance in the lives of others?

AUGUST 1
(Y3, D31)

Painting the Picture

Let us hold fast the confession of our hope without wavering, for he who promised is faithful. And let us consider how to stir up one another to love and good works.

—Hebrews 10:23–24 (ESV)

This past week, I received a promotional advertisement in the mail for a collector's plate featuring a Rockwell painting. It prompted me in recalling a story I had heard years ago about this beloved artist. It reveals a stark contrast between the personal rearing of the painter and what is reflected in his art. Rockwell was born and raised for a period of time in New York City, absent of a particularly close relationship with his parents. It is related that at an early age, he went up to the rooftop of the boarding home where his family lived. There he was greatly affected by what was displayed in the realities on the street below. The images ranged from gangs fighting with bicycle chains to a drunken beating of a woman who used an umbrella as her weapon. His work revealed little of his own turmoil or of the nation in which he lived. In fact, over the decades, he came to charm that same nation with an idealism that was esteemed on covers of magazines such as the *Saturday Evening Post*. He is quoted as having stated: "The view of life I communicate in my pictures excludes the sordid and ugly. I paint life as I would like it to be." I suppose that he communicated for all of us a better picture of America than it sometimes is, while at the same time providing us with a sense of optimism and hope we all need.

It is not unusual in our daily walk to find ourselves in a position where we are either creating or exposed to images that may be different than reality. We are bombarded each day with various forms of advertising which, by its very purpose, only presents an exaggerated viewpoint of the product being offered. Likewise, our work situations may require us to convey the most positive image in order to promote ourselves or boost others to conduct themselves in a manner that meets the company's expectation. In our home life, we need to paint a proper picture and model desired behaviors for our children that we want them to develop. Additionally, there are also times it may be necessary to put up a good front and provide a calming effect for someone who may be ill or under distress. Bottom line, for many reasons, things are not always what they seem.

Those who journey with Christ are often faced with a task that is less than ideal. We learn to embrace values such as hope, faith, peace, grace, service, and joy. But it isn't always easy to continually reflect them. I once knew a chaplain in a social ministry setting who was very critical of some of the workers there because he felt that they should display more joy through the nature of their work. Interestingly enough, there were times he could be one of the most joyless persons I ever knew. It becomes vitally important that "we walk the walk as we talk the talk," especially during those periods when we don't feel like it. We do this "to equip his people for works of service, so that the body of Christ may be built up until we all reach unity in the faith and in the knowledge of the Son of God and become mature, attaining to the whole measure of the fullness of Christ" (Ephesians 4:12–13 NIV).

Perhaps, then, we are not so different than Rockwell. We paint our space to be a better place than it sometimes is. Appropriately so because we must demonstrate Jesus to the world around us. As a result, there will be those times when we feel depleted of the energy to positively reflect on the canvas of life. We must remember, however, that we are shaping our souls to automatically do the right thing when challenged. "So prepare your minds for action and exercise self-control. Put all your hope in the gracious salvation that will come to you when Jesus Christ is revealed to the world" (1 Peter 1:13 NLT). For when we do this, we can be certain that we are also painting the picture as He would like it to be.

Reflection

Do you sometimes find it difficult to offer an appropriate display of Christian values when you are just not quite feeling it? Conversely, do you feel less than sincere when you mirror what you should do but don't really mean it? Does it help when you understand that regardless of your feelings, there are times it is important that you simply be the only Jesus some will ever see?

AUGUST 2
(Y4, D31)

A Round Tuit

But be doers of the word, and not hearers only, deceiving yourselves.

—James 1:22 (ESV)

A friend of mine was telling me about her neighbor who never seems to be able to see a project through to completion. It is evidenced by the way the neighbor cares for his yard. In the spring, there is usually a lawn clean-up weekend in which the whole family participates. Weeds are pulled, the lawn is fully manicured, potted flowers and plants arrive on the scene, and sometimes a new piece of lawn furniture surfaces. The days and weeks pass, and then months of warm weather go by. The plants never get taken out of their pots and receive water only occasionally when it rains. The wheelbarrow sits at the front of the house like a lawn ornament for months, and to be sure, when the snow starts to fly, the new piece of furniture will be covered with a white blanket of winter. People like this can drive you crazy, but we all have been this person at one time or other. However, when it's us, we can come up with all kinds of reasons why the project has not yet been completed or has otherwise failed.

Somewhere in my collection of old stuff, I have a pin with the word *tuit* on it. If memory serves me correctly, I think when you wear it, it will prompt someone to ask you what it is. Then you are to say, "Oh, I got a round tuit." It's a play on words, of course, for the expression "When I get around to it." Unfortunately, many of us go through life with a similar attitude. "If it happens, fine. If it doesn't, that's okay too." This indifference in our society has become pervasive in many aspects of our culture. It affects the ability to find enthusiastic workers, the motivation to achieve a meaningful education, the lack of interest in participating in the right to vote, the capacity to be an effective parent, go out of our way to help someone, or to simply be a good role model in society. Holocaust survivor Elie Wiesel once said, "The opposite of love is not hate, it's indifference. The opposite of beauty is not ugliness, it's indifference. The opposite of faith is not heresy, it's indifference. And the opposite of life is not death but indifference between life and death."

I recently read that about one-third of the earth's population is considered to be Christian. This is based upon self-identification, cultural or family tradition, or being credentialed by a Christian group such as membership in a church denomination. I would think that the state of the world would be in much better shape if just a majority of those folks would actively live out their lives as devoted believers rather than with spiritual indifference. There are many who put off having a deeper relationship with the Lord, knowing that it's the right thing to do. They figure there's time to do that later in life when things slow down a bit. Perhaps we have all been guilty of delay in such important matters. But the great prophet of the Old Testament urges what we must do: "Seek the Lord while you can find him. Call on him now while he is near" (Isaiah 55:6 NLT).

When we act half-hearted in our relationship with God, we deceive ourselves and others because we are without the joy our faith should reveal. Those who are lukewarm claim to know God but stroll through life as though He doesn't exist. Paul explains it as "having the appearance of godliness but denying its power. Avoid such people" (2 Timothy 3:5 ESV). When we find that our "religion" is more about customs and tradition than it is about a relationship with the living God, we know it's time to refocus our faith. Otherwise, our complacency and lack of conviction may deny others the heartfelt example we are to exhibit in our journey with Christ. The Apostle Paul says that we should serve with a level of devotion: "Never be lacking in zeal, but keep your spiritual fervor, serving the Lord" (Romans 12:11 NIV). So the next time you find yourself simply existing through one of those many shades of spiritual indifference, instead, let your light shine in such a way that others will observe you glorifying your heavenly Father in all that you do.

Reflection

Have there been times that you have said you were a Christian but your actions did not demonstrate so? What are those barriers in your spiritual journey that have allowed you to become complacent? In what ways do you need to concentrate more on living your Christian life to the fullest, so that you can become an example others will want to emulate?

AUGUST 3
(Y5, D31)

The Apple and the Tree

Imitate God, therefore, in everything you do, because you are his dear children.

—Ephesians 5:1 (NLT)

A friend was recently telling me about her daughter's wedding. When I looked at some pictures from the event, I stated how much the daughter resembled the mother. My friend smiled and said that when she first met her daughter's maid-of-honor, she immediately stated, "You have to be Stacy's mom. As soon as you got out of the car and walked this way, I knew without question who you were because of your mannerisms." It's like that old expression. You know the one: "The apple doesn't fall far from the tree." That can be a good thing, as in, "He graduated at the top of his class, just like his father. I guess the apple doesn't fall far from the tree." Or it can also have a negative connotation. "She has the same nasty disposition as her mother. As they say, the apple"—you get the point!

Imitation is a part of growing up. As children, we try on Mom's jewelry or attempt to fit into Dad's shoes to be just like them. As we get a little older, it becomes fashionable to wear a particular style or look a certain way. This has not significantly changed over time. If you were a flapper or wore a zoot suit, you lived in the 1920s. Donning a poodle skirt or a Beatle cut? Then you must have grown up in the 1950s or 60s. A decade or so later, you would have worn bell-bottom anything. Big hair and denim jackets were part of the 1980s. Grunge, fanny packs, bleached hair, and pierced everything highlighted the culture of the '90's. As we rolled into Y2K and beyond—Crocs, low-rise jeans, and whatever would enhance your "selfie" image took precedence. While fads like these come and go and the memory pictures surface to haunt us years later, in most cases, they are simply a passing fancy. Ultimately, it becomes more about the people we allow in our lives that will make an indelible mark on who we turn out to be.

In Jesus' day, there is perhaps no better example of imitation than the education of Jewish boys who desired to become a rabbi. Only the most outstanding young men were given the opportunity to do so, at times being required to leave home for a period of time to intensely study under one. In such cases, it was not enough to acquire the knowledge of the teacher/rabbi. The disciples of the rabbi noted everything he said and every action he made. Doing his best to imitate, the successful student would replicate the lifestyle and mannerisms so as to become like him in every way. The Apostle John gave the same instruction for followers of Jesus in that "whoever says he abides in him ought to walk in the same way in which he walked" (1 John 2:6 ESV). The New International Version (NIV) of the Bible states it this way: "Whoever claims to live in him must live as Jesus did."

This instruction should give us pause to reflect on who it is we are modeling or with whom we are spending time. Unfortunately, many find themselves "guilty by association" rather than "redeemed by grace." The themes of political candidacies serve to remind us that whatever we did, however we acted, or who we might have hung out with will later haunt us when the photographs, records, and statements are openly released in every attempt to turn a future constituency away from us. Why anyone, these days, would want to run for public office is beyond my comprehension! Lucky for we who recognize that we are sinners to also know that we "are justified by his grace as a gift, through the redemption that is in Christ Jesus" (Romans 3:24 ESV). So who or what is it that you cherish above all others? Is it the latest craze, the love of money, or the attention you receive from others? Or is it something even worse? None of these will protect and preserve your very being. As part of a prayer, David echoed these words: "Keep me as the apple of your eye; hide me in the shadow of your wings" (Psalm 17:8 NIV). In assessing our relationship with God, would anyone venture to look at us and say, "The apple sure doesn't fall far from the tree"? Let it be so in your life. For whenever we make the decision to walk with Jesus, we will find that we are in pretty good company and not at all far from a life-saving, well-rooted tree.

Reflection

Who and what is influencing your life habits? Are these influences drawing you closer to or further away from God? Is there anyone who could say that the time they spent with you was the closest experience they have ever had to walking with Jesus?

AUGUST 4
(Y6, D31)

Dear Diary

Princes persecute me without cause, but my heart stands in awe of Your words.

—Psalm 119:161 (ESV)

With the rise of Adolf Hitler in 1933, Otto Frank and Edith Frank-Hollander, both of German-Jewish heritage, moved their family to Amsterdam to escape the escalating Nazi persecution of Jews. In Holland, Otto ran a successful spice and jam business. In 1942, he began arranging a hiding place in an annex of his warehouse in Amsterdam where his family took shelter out of fear of deportation to a Nazi concentration camp. They occupied a small space where they lived in rooms containing blacked-out windows with another Jewish family and a single Jewish man. The entrance to the secret annex was hidden by a hinged bookcase where former employees of Otto and other Dutch Christian friends delivered food and supplies obtained at high risk. On her thirteenth birthday, Anne, the second daughter of the Franks, began writing a diary relating her everyday experiences and observations about the increasingly dangerous world around her. In June 1944, Anne's spirits were raised by the Allied forces landing at Normandy, and she was hopeful that the long-awaited liberation of Holland would soon begin. She wrote inspirational words once remarking that "we're all alive, but we don't know why or what for; we're all searching for happiness; we're all leading lives that are different and yet the same."

For two years, Anne Frank kept a diary about her life in hiding that is marked with tenderness, humor, and insight. She made her last entry on August 1, 1944. Three days later, on August 4, their seclusion ended after twenty-five months with the arrival of the Nazi Gestapo. Anne and the others had been given away by an unknown informer, and they were arrested along with two of the Christians who had helped shelter them. They were sent to a concentration camp in Holland, and in September, Anne and most of the others were shipped to the Auschwitz death camp in Poland. Otto Frank was the only one of the ten to survive the Nazi death camps. After the war, he returned to Amsterdam and was reunited with one of his former employees who had provided covert support to his family. She handed him Anne's diary, which she had found undisturbed after the Nazi raid. In

1947, her writings were published by Otto in its original Dutch as *Diary of a Young Girl*. An instant best-seller and eventually translated into more than fifty languages, *The Diary of Anne Frank*, as it later came to be known, has served as a literary testament to the nearly six million Jews who were silenced in the Holocaust.

The history of persecution is as old as human life on this earth. Certainly, there were many examples of persecution in the early Christian church. Jesus said that if they persecuted Him, they would do the same to His followers: "They will seize you and persecute you. They will hand you over to synagogues and put you in prison, and you will be brought before kings and governors, and all on account of my name" (Luke 21:12 NIV). The Apostle Paul stated that Christian persecution is to be expected. "In fact, everyone who wants to live a godly life in Christ Jesus will be persecuted" (2 Timothy 3:12 NIV). Today, millions of Christians are being judged, tortured, and even killed for their love of God. It makes praying, reading the Bible, and worshipping with fellow believers perilous to do. It is easy to turn a blind eye when the atrocities of persecution do not happen under our nose, but there may come a time when persecution will be a stark reality for all who choose to live the Christian life. In those situations, it will be difficult to look at the oppression as a blessing when we personally face fear and feel lost.

Jesus reminds us, "Blessed are those who are persecuted for righteousness' sake, for theirs is the kingdom of heaven" (Matthew 5:10 ESV). Even in the times when we face it, we can press on and not become disheartened. In the midst of her own persecution, Anne Frank penned these words: "As long as you can look up fearlessly into the heavens, as long as you know that you are pure within… you will still find happiness." Finding happiness in the midst of persecution requires a strong faith in a loving Creator. Bottom line, He provides three things: a body, a spirit, and a soul. We should begin each day by doing the following—stretch for your body, put a smile on your face for your spirit, and remember to thank God for your soul. Consider it as you begin today's journey by echoing the words "Dear Diary."

Reflection

Why is it important for us to affirm that God is sovereign, even in times when we witness persecution? How can we find "the secret of being content in any and every situation" (Philippians 4:12 NIV)? In what ways can you serve as an example to others by demonstrating happiness during persecution?

AUGUST 5
(Y7, D31)

Moving Mountains

I did this so you would trust not in human wisdom but in the power of God.

—1 Corinthians 2:5 (NLT)

As I drove from my hometown to a neighboring community, I could not help but marvel at the new section of highway being developed. About midway through my thirty-mile trek, the four-lane highway narrows as it navigates through a mountain passage. The tapering of the road from four lanes to two has long been a sticking point for those who experience an inconvenient backup during peak travel times. Extending the four-lane cut through the mountain has been almost impossible for locals to envision, given the existing earthly impediments. But before my very eyes, it was happening. The deep corridor two-lane road barricaded on one side by steep rock formations and on the other by a canyon creek bed had, over the last few years, been widened into the once former mountainside. This could only have been projected by a team of talented civil engineers who had captured a vision before them to move a mountain.

Mountain-moving was the topic of a tough conversation Jesus had with His disciples. When they failed to cast out a demon from a boy whose father had brought him to the disciples, Jesus reprimanded them for their weak faith. Instead "Jesus rebuked the demon, and it came out of the boy, and he was healed at that moment. Then the disciples came to Jesus in private and asked, "Why couldn't we drive it out?" He replied, "Because you have so little faith. Truly I tell you, if you have faith as small as a mustard seed, you can say to this mountain: Move from here to there, and it will move. Nothing will be impossible for you" (Matthew 17:18–20 NIV). It is clear that Jesus didn't intend to declare that mustard seed-sized faith would literally move a mountain. The point of Jesus' comparison was that if the faith of his disciples was stronger, they could have commanded the demon to leave the boy, and it would have been so.

Our faith makes a difference in our lives only because God is the sovereign one who rules over all things. In January, 2015, a rebellious, adopted teenager named John (Ruiz) Smith drowned in Lake Saint Louis after being underwater for fifteen minutes. His lifeless body was retrieved and taken to St. Joseph Hospital West, and for forty-three minutes, CPR was performed on him. But he remained unresponsive. Then the youth's mother, Joyce Smith, pleaded with the Holy Spirit to not let John die, at which point a faint pulse was noted. After John was transferred and put into a medically-induced coma, his parents were warned that there was little hope. Then Joyce began to turn John's possible recovery into an obsession, harassing the health care professionals and clashing with their church's new liberal pastor with whom she eventually bonded. Through their devout faith and the prayerful support received from the community, John was revived, slowly regained consciousness, and regained full cognitive ability. In a short period of time, he was discharged from the hospital and returned to school. His story, labeled as nothing less than a miracle, was made into the 2019 Christian movie entitled *Breakthrough*.

On another occasion, Jesus stated, "I tell you the truth, you can say to this mountain, 'May you be lifted up and thrown into the sea,' and it will happen. But you must really believe it will happen and have no doubt in your heart. I tell you, you can pray for anything, and if you believe that you've received it, it will be yours" (Mark 11:23–24 NLT). We all have obstacles that are so daunting that conquering them seems to be virtually impossible. It is important to understand that if we need a mountain to be moved, then God is certainly capable of doing so. He will do whatever is necessary and right for the fulfillment of His will and plan for our lives. Jesus clearly reminds us that even a little bit of faith—faith the size of a tiny mustard seed—can overcome those mountains we are facing. Trained civil engineers have the vision to aptly build roadways through impossible landscapes. We too must endeavor to capture our own mountain-moving vision. It's quite a humbling task. Simply invite Him to be by your side.

Reflection

Consider the mountains before you at this time. How have you approached them? When you are facing obstacles that seem to be intimidating, do you focus on how you will bring yourself to endure? Or do you give faithful attention to an all-powerful God who can get you to the other side of the storm? In what ways might you be able to change your resolve from dependence on yourself to Him?

AUGUST 6
(Y1, D32)

Grace upon Grace

God saved you by his grace when you believed. And you
can't take credit for this; it is a gift from God.

—Ephesians 2:8 (NLT)

A series of burglaries highlighted a fictional TV story of a small midwestern farm town where items from the general store and several farms had been among the missing. Two preteens who are captivated by a series of detective novels joined forces to solve the mystery. Eventually, it was discovered that a friend of theirs from the neighborhood school had been the burglar all along, stealing to support himself and his ill father who thought the boy had a job. The youngster had also been doing everything he could to read about medical procedures and terminology in hopes of someday becoming a doctor. The revelation brought together an assembly of the men from whom the goods were taken to decide how to handle the matter. As they evaluated the situation, they made the boy aware that they knew what he did. Then he was told that when he someday was that physician they knew he would become, he was to remember that they were owed a free visit. Rather than pressing the matter any further, they demonstrated the true meaning of grace.

Extensions of grace are not commonly offered these days. When we feel wronged, most of us want payback. Our first impulse when we are hurt or offended is to strike out, justifying our anger in the name of fairness. We have become used to the principle of cause and effect; that is, we receive what we earn and we give back what someone deserves. Grace has become a difficult concept to understand, and our teachings and the examples we have seen in our lives don't allow the notion to be rationally considered. Grace is the unmerited favor of God, an unconditional love given to the undeserving. Those who receive and rely on Jesus Christ for salvation receive his grace and respond with gratitude. Part of our grateful response is evidenced whenever we demonstrate God's grace to others. In this spirit, the Apostle Paul told the early Christian church that they should "Let your conversation be always full of grace, seasoned with salt, so that you may know how to answer everyone" (Colossians 4:6 NIV).

At the 1865 surrender of the Civil War between the states, General Grant showed grace by displaying a desire for reconciliation over retribution. President Lincoln had further reinforced this in a meeting only weeks before, urging leniency when the time came. As Grant and Lee drafted the articles of surrender, Lee proposed that Grant allow his men to keep their side arms and horses for use on their farms. Grant agreed and offered very generous terms for the southern soldiers. Lee remarked, "This will have the best possible effect upon the men. It will be very gratifying, and will do much toward conciliating our people." He expressed further concern that many in his army were in severe need of food and supplies, so Grant offered the services of the US commissary and quartermaster to supply the struggling soldiers. As the Union army heard the news of the surrender, spontaneous demonstrations of gun salutes commenced. Hearing them and not wanting to add insult to defeat, Grant sent orders to have them stopped, affirming, "The war is over. The rebels are our countrymen again."

Grace has been demonstrated by powerful figures throughout history. It is a constant theme in the Bible, culminating with the coming of Jesus. John wrote "For the law was given through Moses; grace and truth came through Jesus Christ" (John 1:17 NIV). Grace is God choosing to bless us rather than curse us as our sin deserves. It is His compassion for the undeserving. God is the instigator of grace, and it is from Him that all other grace flows. As Christians, we are charged to show grace to others or face the potential of being tarnished. Paul says, "Look after each other so that none of you fails to receive the grace of God. Watch out that no poisonous root of bitterness grows up to trouble you, corrupting many" (Hebrews 12:15 NLT). If you find yourself in the company of others whose hearts have been captured by grace, count yourself lucky. They love us despite our messy lives, stay connected to us through our struggles, and always hold out for the hope of our recovery through His redemptive spirit. This is sometimes referred to as "grace upon grace" (John 1:16 ESV). We need not only receive it but are called to show it to those who might otherwise be faced with isolation and defeat in their lives.

Reflection

Consider situations in your life where you were shown or wish you had been shown grace. How did that outcome have an effect on the way you treat others? Are there persons you know today to whom you can offer God's gift of grace? What action steps will you take to implement a plan to do so?

AUGUST 7
(Y2, D32)

A Neighbor or Just a Jerk?

"Love the Lord your God with all your heart and with all your soul and
with all your mind and with all your strength." The second is this: "Love your
neighbor as yourself." There is no commandment greater than these.

—Mark 12:30–31 (NIV)

A home repairman was doing a project at my home, and it was taking longer than I had anticipated. Several weeks into the task, he understandably wanted to take a few days off due to the birth of a grandchild. However, I must admit I was growing tired of the mess in my house. A few days after the grandchild was born, he came back to work and informed me that someone else was in immediate need of his help. A water heater had apparently malfunctioned in their home, and they asked if he could get a new one and install it that day. He told them that before he could say that he would, he needed to check with me because, at that time, I was the person for whom he was working. When he asked me, I wanted to say, "Can't they just call a plumber?" I knew, however, that a plumber would be more expensive and they might not be able to get one right away. I also knew that had I been selfish, my conscience would bother me. So rather than be a complete jerk, I told him to go take care of the other people.

When Jesus stated that we should "Love our neighbor as yourself," he was asked, "And who is my neighbor?" Rather than responding by defining one's neighbor as your family, a friend, or the person who lives next door, He told the story of the Good Samaritan found in Luke 10:30–35. As I came to know this Bible story as a child, I always figured that the man who had been robbed was "the neighbor" because he needed help. In other words, I thought Jesus was telling us that our neighbors are all those with whom we come in contact. If we fail to carefully consider the end of the story, we can miss a vital point of His message. For Jesus poses this question: "Which of these three do you think was a neighbor to the man who fell into the hands of robbers?" The expert in the law replied, "The one who had mercy on him." Jesus told him, "Go and do likewise" (Luke 10:36–37 NIV). While Jesus never fully answers, he does reveal that being a neighbor is every bit as important as trying to define who one is. For if a person loves their neighbor as one's self, they will act kindly toward anyone that they happen to meet, even their enemies.

The closest thing I have ever done that even slightly resembles the story of the Samaritan happened quite many years ago. I was using one of those tire pump machines at the front of a local convenience store. Not too far away, a teenager raced into the parking lot on his bike and started doing "wheelies." He was acting rather erratically, and I know it went through my mind that he might be a little hopped up on drugs or alcohol. I continued to work on my tires when all of a sudden, the bike must have hit some loose gravel, and the kid flew off the bike. This caused him to hit his head on the pavement. There was no one else around, and he wasn't moving, so I ran into the store and told the cashier to call for an ambulance. Then I went back outside, propped the boy's head up, and talked with him until the ambulance arrived. I never saw the young man after that, but I knew in my heart that what I had done was the right thing for at that very point in time, he was my neighbor.

One report stated that half of all Americans indicated that they do not even know the names of their neighbors. In many cases, we respond selfishly or aren't sure we want to get involved. I personally knew a lady who lost her life by stopping to help someone, so I suppose that memory is always in the back of my mind. For those who have the heart of a servant, how does one serve if we allow our hearts to become so hardened that we fail to involve ourselves as a neighbor with God's people? A true neighbor is committed to helping persons in need, recognizing that as we do so, it is important to seek discernment and utilize God's wisdom without judgment. Scripture tells us, "There is only one Lawgiver and Judge, the one who is able to save and destroy. But you—who are you to judge your neighbor?" (James 4:12 NIV). With Christ by our side, caring for one's neighbor should not be a process of deliberation. If we allow ourselves to become that bogged down in our consideration to care for one who is in need, we just might miss the opportunity, and then we will become the jerk you never really set out to be.

Reflection

Who do you consider to be your neighbor? In what situations do you classify yourself to be one? Does "loving your neighbor as yourself" explain how Jesus demonstrated love to others? Under what set of circumstances are you reluctant to be a neighbor as Jesus would have defined?

AUGUST 8
(Y3, D32)

God Has Got This One!

Be thankful in all circumstances, for this is God's will for you who belong to Christ Jesus.

—1 Thessalonians 5:18

Sitting in a dugout of a major league baseball field are two pitchers. One is rookie who has just two major league starts under his belt. The other is a ten-year veteran who possesses a ring from a World Series in which he was named the most valuable player. The younger of the two sits on the bench, "picking the brain" of his elder statesman who had, just a few days before, pitched his first no-hitter. And it's a good thing he was able to spend some time doing that because that no-hitter was the last game that the veteran threw for the only team he has never known. Less than a week later, he was dealt to another team, a move that was finalized right at the end-of-July trade deadline. It seems like a very insecure lifestyle to me. However, I suppose when you sign up to play professional sports, the uncertainty of where you might spend your tomorrow is a factor that must be considered.

The ambiguity of our circumstances may at times feel no less protected than that of a major league ball player. But for those who follow Christ, it's not uncommon to hear one say, "I don't know what the future holds, but I know who holds the future." I recall once seeing a social media post by a high school friend who had received a cancer diagnosis. He said, "I have trusted my Savior through this last month with lots of testing that has been done and I know He is with me…never has left my side and I know He never will." I have seen this friend mature deeply in his faith journey since those youthful days in high school when he was a rather happy-go-lucky individual. His life bears out the scripture: "God is love. When we take up permanent residence in a life of love, we live in God and God lives in us. This way, love has the run of the house, becomes at home and mature in us" (1 John 4:17 MSG).

Sometimes in life, we find ourselves facing situations beyond our control in which we allow our thoughts, emotions, and attitudes to prevent us from enjoying the simple joys and peace which God desires for us. During these times, it is important to move beyond our circumstances, not be consumed by them, and allow God to go to work in a way that only He can. I am reminded that years ago, theologian John Baillie wrote these words in his devotional classic, *A Diary of Private Prayer*:

Teach me, O God, so to use all the circumstances of my life today
that they may bring forth in me the fruits of holiness rather than the fruits of sin.
Let me use disappointment as material for patience;
Let me use success as material for thankfulness;
Let me use suspense as material for perseverance;
Let me use danger as material for courage;
Let me use reproach as material for longsuffering;
Let me use praise as material for humility;
Let me use pleasures as material for temperance;
Let me use pains as material for endurance.

Wise words from someone who might just simply tell us not to be blinded by our circumstances. For in doing so, we may easily fail to see the good because we will not be looking for it. The major league pitcher may not like the trade, but when he steps on the mound the first time for his new team, it will be "game on." Oh, and my friend, the one who faced treatments for his cancer, he went on to say: "Please don't feel sorry or sad because I'm not. God has got this one!" And that He does.

Reflection

Have there been times when in the midst of life's unpleasant circumstances that you have asked God where He is? Were you able to move beyond your circumstances and ask what God may want you to learn from them? Can you apply the quote from Martha Washington who said, "The greater part of our happiness or misery depends upon our dispositions and not upon our circumstances"? How would you help another struggling individual to move toward the philosophy, "Let go, let God."

AUGUST 9
(Y4, D32)

Leaning into Safe Mode

In peace I will both lie down and sleep; for you alone, O Lord, make me dwell in safety.

—Psalm 4:8 (NIV)

Several years ago, I had a serious problem with my computer. Somewhere along the line, it must have gotten infected with a virus, commonly referred to as malware. I had a computer geek look at it and try to clean up the problem. However, it was beyond repair, and I ended up having to get a new computer. During this period of time, I was able to get some of my programs to operate. In order to accomplish this, I had to select the "safe mode" function when I booted the system. What was interesting about all of this was that the programs which enabled me to write and post a Christian blog remained functional. While they did not operate as smoothly as they would under normal circumstances, they were able to be used as long as I persevered. In a way, it was symbolic of what we frequently face in life many days; that is, the challenge to struggle through the difficulties and inconveniences with which we are often faced while at the same time trying to maintain a sense of security.

The concepts of safety and security are a common cultural understanding. Parents want to be assured that their children are free of bullying, whether it is on the playground or on social media. Employers lower their risk in certain job categories by requiring that applicants for employment are able to pass a criminal background check. We can purchase monitoring systems for our home in order to enable us to feel safe where we live. Securing national borders and not allowing people into the country who do not have the proper documentation has been a huge part of political discussions. Conversely, in many areas of the world, persons of faith must practice their beliefs in secret or they will risk persecution up to and including death. A prime example is that of a now well-known German Lutheran pastor by the name of Dietrich Bonhoeffer who was executed in a Nazi concentration camp only weeks before the Germans surrendered to the Allied Forces in 1945. His book, *The Cost of Discipleship*, and the practice of his writings no doubt cost him his life. He provided with an example that we must have an "all-in" approach in life, understanding that doing so might not position us in a safe and secure situation.

In our walk with Christ, we come to realize that God eventually leads us where we need to be. Along the way, His provisions are sufficient to keep us safe and secure. We simply need to trust Him. There is probably no better example than when He rescued the children of Israel from Egyptian captivity. During their journey, God sent daily manna for them to eat. The Lord told Moses that He would test them to see if they would follow His explicit instructions (Exodus 16:4–5). Disobeying His command, they took more food than they required for a day (Exodus 16:19–20). On the sixth day, they failed His instruction to save enough to sustain them through the Sabbath (Exodus 16:26–27). The lesson for us here is that the Lord provides exactly what is needed for those who love Him and follow direction, according to His purpose. There are times when we might feel a sense of loss. But like the Apostle Paul, we must conclude, "I count all things to be loss in view of the surpassing value of knowing Christ Jesus my Lord, for whom I have suffered the loss of all things, and count them but rubbish so that I may gain Christ."

We are fortunate to not know exactly where the road of this life will take us. There are some things we can do that will help us feel more protected. Like life itself, however, we will learn that many of these remedies are short-lived. Meanwhile, we can be assured that the Lord will keep us in "safe mode." For wherever we discover in our position in life, scripture reminds us: "Have I not commanded you? Be strong and courageous. Do not be frightened, and do not be dismayed, for the Lord your God is with you wherever you go" (Joshua 1:9 NIV). For many, this life will find little but insecurity, and they will not rest until they "lie down and sleep" (Psalm 4:8 NIV) in the company of God. As the hymnist Elisha Hoffman wrote in her lyrics, when we come to know Him, we will find that we are "safe and secure from all alarm." That kind of solace only exists when we find ourselves "leaning on the everlasting arms" of Jesus.

Reflection

What are some ways you can take a firm stand for Jesus in today's society? In doing so, what are the potential consequences you might face? How do we bring balance to openly expressing our faith with the assurance of knowing that "our help is in the name of the Lord" (Psalm 124:8 NIV)?

AUGUST 10
(Y5, D32)

Reference Check

For there is one God and one mediator between God and mankind, the man Christ Jesus.

—1 Timothy 2:5 (NIV)

There's an old expression known as "vouching for someone." One might say, "Sure, you can extend credit to Pete. I'll vouch for him because I know him to be a stand-up guy. If he says he'll do something, he will. I have no doubt he'll pay you what's due." As years passed, we grew to call it a reference. In one of my work settings, I did a lot of reference checking in conjunction with job applications. In some cases, I found that they were unreliable because oftentimes, the applicant would list people with whom they had worked rather than their supervisor. With that as a reference, you never quite got the full story. Scrutinizing references began to really become a difficult endeavor whenever employers were legally advised to provide restricted information limited to date of hire and position held. It was most unhelpful.

These days, it is not unusual for employers to "snoop" the social media platforms of prospective job candidates. There, a company can find out all kinds of information that most applicants would rather not reveal to a future employer. Thinking that you are sharing information among "friends"—all the posts one has made about calling off from work and how much they hate their current employer are just hanging out there publicly for the world to see. Provocative photos, discriminatory comments, sharing confidential information about clients, or slandering work colleagues and bosses says a lot about who you are and what risk and challenge you will most likely represent to a future employer. It's frequently enough to put your application on the bottom of the pile, provoking any future employer to move on.

One of my interview questions used to be, "Do you know anyone who works here and what would they tell me about you?" I cannot begin to count the number of times that I have gone to a good employee to vouch for one of these "name-droppers," and their response was, "I really don't want to say." When we demonstrate a complete lack of discretion as to how we represent ourselves in today's highly visible culture, we can never be quite sure what will come back to haunt us or who will stand up for us. If that is true for the things of this world, who will advocate for us when it comes to heavenly things which we hope will take us to a place of eternal comfort? The Apostle Paul said to fellow believers, "Since you have been raised to new life with Christ, set your sights on the realities of heaven, where Christ sits in the place of honor at God's right hand" (Colossians 3:1 NLT).

As we set our sights heavenward, it is important that we live a life following the example which Jesus Himself demonstrated for us. Knowing that we would never be without sin, Jesus became the rescuer to liberate us from condemnation. "Therefore, he is able to save completely those who come to God through him, because he always lives to intercede for them" (Hebrews 7:25 NIV). I have always loved the words penned by Carol Gilman in the chorus to the song, "He's Ever Interceding":

And He's ever interceding to the Father for His children;
Yes, He's ever interceding to the Father for His own;
Through Him you can reach the Father, So, bring Him all your heavy burdens;
Yes, for you He's interceding, So, come boldly to the throne.

While Jesus understands that we were incapable of living a life without sin, He does expect that we will work to do so. Some of us want the glory of heaven but not the burden of obedience here on earth. Many will seek the benefit of Jesus' great sacrifice without endeavoring to live like He lived. If we love Him enough that our life has been changed, then we must make the effort to walk the faithful walk. As such, we will build a resume for serving Him alone and have the full assurance that He is the one and only reference we will need for eternal placement.

Reflection

Romans 8:34 (NIV) states, "Who then is the one who condemns? No one. Christ Jesus who died—more than that, who was raised to life—is at the right hand of God and is also interceding for us." How does this passage proved an assurance to us that Jesus is actively advocating on our behalf? How might you help someone who is having a difficult time getting through life that the evidence of their actions (particularly if they claim to be a Christian) may not serve as a good reference?

AUGUST 11
(Y6, D32)

No Greater Legacy

By the grace God has given me, I laid a foundation as a wise builder, and
someone else is building on it. But each one should build with care.

—1 Corinthians 3:10 (NIV)

When I was young, my parents would allow me to provide input into where the family would go for vacation. For a period of several years, I would often reply, "Washington DC." Of course, one of the places you must visit on a trip to the nation's capital is the Smithsonian Institute. In our inexperience, we did not realize that the Smithsonian was not just a building but actually many. Collectively called the Smithsonian Institution, this world-renowned museum and research complex in DC consists of numerous museums, galleries, and a zoo. The Smithsonian came about as a result of a bequest provided by a British scientist who never visited the United States, thereby provoking significant attention on both sides of the Atlantic. James Smithson died in Italy in 1829, leaving behind a will with a peculiar footnote. In the event that his only nephew died without any heirs, Smithson decreed that the whole of his estate would go to "the United States of America, to found at Washington, under the name of the Smithsonian Institution, an Establishment for the increase and diffusion of knowledge." Six years after his death, his nephew, Henry James Hungerford, indeed died without children. In 1836, the US Congress authorized acceptance of Smithson's gift, amounting to a fortune in excess of a half-million dollars. After a decade of debate about how best to spend this bequest to America from an obscure English scientist, President James K. Polk signed the Smithsonian Institution Act into law on August 10, 1846.

These days, boundless opportunities exist for those who have the means to establish a bequest. Most organizations to which one belongs would be blessed to have a portion or all of your estate, deeded in their direction at the time of your passing. Many such organizations have well established "legacy societies" and planned giving staffers who will offer various funding opportunities in exchange for your donation. The truth of the matter is that everyone leaves a legacy whether they plan to or not. Everything we say or do leaves the imprint of our lives on those around us. As long as there is breath in our body, there's an opportunity to leave a negative legacy of despair or a rich legacy of hope. Jesus said:

> Do not store up for yourselves treasures on earth, where moths and vermin destroy, and where thieves break in and steal. But store up for yourselves treasures in heaven, where moths and vermin do not destroy, and where thieves do not break in and steal. For where your treasure is, there your heart will be also. (Matthew 6:19–21 NIV)

Jesus sets the challenge for us to leave a legacy not of material possessions but of spiritual hope as well. King David recognized the importance of passing on a spiritual legacy. When he was on his deathbed, he called on his son, Solomon, who would carry on his reign as king, saying:

> As for you, my son Solomon, know the God of your father, and serve Him with a loyal heart and with a willing mind; for the Lord searches all hearts and understands all the intent of the thoughts. If you seek Him, He will be found by you; but if you forsake Him, He will cast you off forever. (1 Chronicles 28:9 NKJV)

If you had godly parents, you were no doubt deeply affected by their faith. Parents have an awesome opportunity to bestow a spiritual legacy to their children. Proverbs 13:22 (ESV) states, "A good man leaves an inheritance to his children's children." An inheritance is not limited to money. It also includes character qualities such as integrity, trustworthiness, and holiness. This spiritual wisdom can be passed from generation to generation and enables you to stake your claim on your descendants. One great of the great apostles said, "I could have no greater joy than to hear that my children are following the truth" (3 John 1:4 NLT). What a shame it would be to focus on an earthly bequest and not leave behind what you have learned on your faith journey in this lifetime. While carrying out a successful financial strategy to leave something behind for those you care about may be important, the most significant thing we can pass on to others is the riches available to those who love God. Through the sacrificial gift of His Son, Jesus, it would seem that without a doubt there could be no greater legacy.

Reflection

Do you want to leave a legacy for the kingdom of God but feel hindered or inadequate? Are you waiting for something to fall neatly into place, thinking only then God can use you? Consider the words of Paul to his faithful student in 2 Timothy 2:2 (NIV)—"And the things you have heard me say in the presence of many witnesses entrust to reliable people who will also be qualified to teach others." Do this, and the spiritual legacy you leave behind will be rich indeed.

AUGUST 12
(Y7, D32)

Moaning and Groaning

O Lord, hear me as I pray; pay attention to my groaning.

—Psalm 5:1 (NLT)

Have you heard the one about the lady who glued her lips together resulting in her inability to literally get a word in edgewise? It's actually a true story. In 2003, a sixty-four-year-old woman from New Zealand called the emergency services number. When the operator answered, only moans could be heard. Personnel who responded feared they were being contacted by a gagged hostage, so they rushed to her house. It was there where they found a female who could not open her mouth. Having fumbled in the dark for some cold-sore cream in the middle of the night, the woman mistakenly picked up a tube of superglue. Rubbing on the powerful adhesive, she awaited the familiar soothing relief normally provided by the remedy. But it never came. Within minutes, she was, in fact, speechless. When she decided to use the phone to summon for help, moaning and tapping were her only ways to communicate.

Unfortunately, moaning and groaning are not uncommon expressions of the human condition. Some of us spend much of our waking hours groaning about something, while there are those who do so only when they sleep. Still others moan when they move from place to place because they experience some level of discomfort. In reality, how can one see all that is happening today and not sigh and groan at times? We hear about the condition of millions of hungry or sick people, and we feel overwhelmed. Then there's the threat of terrorism or gun violence from just being in the wrong place at the wrong time. Add to that the failure of our elected officials to bring helpful and realistic solutions to our nation's despairs, and it becomes quite easy to find a reason to groan. The expression is often made that rather than doing something, it's just easier to sit back and moan about it. It has become so commonplace that one can even sign up as an honorary member of the Old Boys Moaning and Groaning Society.

Surely, there are times in your life when, even though there were words to express your emotions, those words were inadequate. In these situations, you may have simply groaned rather than

449

voice words that could not satisfy. Scripture reminds us that groaning has forever been a way of communicating to God. The Israelites cried out in their sufferings. "God heard their groaning and he remembered his covenant with Abraham, with Isaac and with Jacob" (Exodus 2:24 NIV). The Psalmist groans and the LORD responds: "'Because the poor are plundered and the needy groan, I will now arise,' says the LORD. 'I will protect them from those who malign them'" (Psalm 12:5 NIV). Paul writes "For we know that all creation has been groaning…we believers also groan, even though we have the Holy Spirit within us as a foretaste of future glory, for we long for our bodies to be released from sin and suffering" (Romans 8:22–23 NLT).

Has suffering and groaning found its way into your life? Are there deep inner agonies you cannot begin to verbalize? If so, your experience is not unique. When one starts to recognize their own shortcomings and those of the world in which they live, they come to see life as it really is. God's Word confirms that "the Spirit helps us in our weakness. For we do not know what to pray for as we ought, but the Spirit himself intercedes for us with groanings too deep for words" (Romans 8:26 NIV). Romans 8:27 (NIV) goes on to state that "He who searches our hearts knows the mind of the Spirit." While we may not always pray in accordance with the will of God, the Spirit does. And God answers. You should not feel guilt-ridden or unspiritual over your groanings if they are guided in the right direction. If your groanings offer you a discontent with this life and give you a hunger for heaven, good for you! That is the work of the Holy Spirit, producing a heart for God in you. Groaning characterizes the life of the Spirit-filled Christian. For those who walk with the Lord, groaning is not a matter of being tongue-tied but more an affirmation that our hope has been directed heavenward to that which we have not yet seen.

Reflection

Have you ever prayed for something so deeply that no words remained to flow from you, only groans that could not be explained or stopped? Can you think of a time in your life when prayer has felt pointless, yet you kept trying to pray? Or maybe a time when you wanted to pray, but circumstances in your life left you wordless? How does an increased understanding of spiritual groaning put your mind at ease that this is not weakness but potentially an increased growth and closeness toward God?

AUGUST 13
(Y1, D33)

Spiritual Blind Spots

Every eye will see him, even those who pierced him.

—Revelation 1:7 (NIV)

Diagnosed with congenital glaucoma at five months old, Italian Andrea Bocelli was only six years old when he began studying the piano. He went on to learn the flute and saxophone and was often asked to sing at family gatherings and at school. Visually impaired from birth, he was totally blind at the age of twelve, following a soccer injury. Bocelli, who rose to fame in 1994, was labeled as an opera singer. Today, he is known as the world's most beloved tenor. While he can sing arias with the best of them, he has also joined to perform duets with well-knowns Tony Bennett, Sarah Brightman, and Ed Sheeran. Though he may be physically blind, one can be certain he does not suffer from spiritual blindness when you hear his versions of "The Lord's Prayer," "Amazing Grace," or "Ave Maria." In fact, Celine Dion, who joined him to perform "The Prayer," stated, "If God would have a singing voice, he must sound a lot like Andrea Bocelli."

Spiritual blindness can be demonstrated in the fictional story of a girl who hated herself because she was blind. She was hateful with everyone, except her loving boyfriend who was always there for her. She told him, "If I could only see the world, I would marry you."

One day, someone donated a pair of eyes to her. When the bandages came off following the surgery, she was able to see everything, including her unexpectedly blind boyfriend for the first time. He asked her, "Now that you can see the world, will you marry me?" As the girl stared at her boyfriend, the sight of his closed eyelids was shocking to her, totally catching her off guard. The thought of looking at them for the remainder of her life led her refusal to marry him. Receiving her response, the boyfriend tearfully departed. Days after, he wrote a note to her, stating, "Take good care of your eyes, my dear, for before they were yours, they were mine."

In John 9:1–12, Jesus confirmed the existence of spiritual blindness when He and his disciples passed by a man who had been blind since birth. They inquired whose fault it was for this man to be blind. Jesus replied that it had nothing to do with his sins or those of his parents. It was, in fact, an opportunity for God to do a very special presentation. It began as Jesus mixed his spit with some earth, making it into a paste to anoint the blind man's eyes. He was then told to go and wash in a public pool called Siloam. As the man received his full sight, those who knew him began to ask whether this was really the beggar they had known and seen all their lives. Then the Pharisees got involved and began to question the man as well. They were furious with Jesus and blamed Him for breaking the Sabbath, being critical of the tremendous good He was doing by releasing people from their afflictions. They knew the Holy Scriptures by heart but did not apply the teachings to their own lives. Filled with their own ego and dreadfully envious of the Son of God who was a threat to their self-elevated positions among the general public, they were truly spiritually blind. Eventually, to silence all of the critics, the man voiced that often-repeated phrase, "One thing I do know. I was blind but now I see" (John 9:25 NIV).

To be spiritually blind is to not see Christ, and not seeing Christ is to not see God. Some are blind to the understanding of who Jesus really is, while others are blind to the reality of our dependence on God. Quite often, they are blind to their own sinful condition. Those who are spiritually blind have a distorted view of the important matters of life. They are blind to the evidence of God as revealed throughout His Word and by the presence of Jesus Christ here on earth. The Apostle Paul stated that "Satan, who is the god of this world, has blinded the minds of those who don't believe. They are unable to see the glorious light of the Good News. They don't understand this message about the glory of Christ, who is the exact likeness of God" (2 Corinthians 4:4 NLT). The lives of the spiritually blind are steeped in the things of the world as they fail to comprehend the Spirit of God. "For this people's heart has become calloused; they hardly hear with their ears, and they have closed their eyes. Otherwise they might see with their eyes, hear with their ears, understand with their hearts and turn, and I would heal them" (Acts 28:27 NIV). Jesus came that we might see clearly. We must allow Him to reveal our blind spots, heal our eyes, and truly see the source of where our sight came from in the first place.

Reflection

Are there times when you find yourself resorting to excuses and rationalizations when it comes to your own sinful behaviors? Do you sometimes feel guilty when you read certain passages in the scriptures? How do you work at showing the light of Jesus to others who are spiritually blind?

AUGUST 14
(Y2, D33)

Rush to Judgment

*These also are sayings of the wise: To show partiality in
judging is not good. (Proverbs 24:23 NIV)*

It was thought that baseball's Colorado Rockies might have a controversy on their hands until they didn't. On one August day in 2021, the Rockies were playing the Miami Marlins. A Marlin's African-American outfielder was seemingly subjected to racial malice during his final at-bat of the game while being called the N-word by a fan. The man yelled loudly several times, apparently aimed in the batter's direction. Picked up by a microphone, it was assumed that broadcast listeners had no doubt heard the remark. One of the team's play-by-play announcers stated, "The level of hate that was displayed has no place in this world. Unfortunately, it's still far too prevalent. We need to be better." The sentiment was similarly echoed among others who were offended by what they thought they heard. After further investigation, it was confirmed that the spectator was trying to get the attention of the team's mascot whose name just happened to be Dinger. Turns out all the fan wanted was a picture with the mascot.

Instances of rushing to judgment are prevalent in today's society. One might recall the 2019 story of a Covington Catholic High School teenager standing in front of a Native American elder who was chanting and beating a drum on the steps of the Lincoln Memorial. The youth had been on a trip with his Kentucky school to Washington DC for the March for Life. When an initial video was released by the media, many perceived the young man to have been mocking the Native American by smirking inches from his face. But full footage showed a more complicated image where the Covington students were not the instigators. The Omaha tribe leader had actually walked up to the Covington school kids after another group began taunting them because they were wearing "Make America Great Again" hats at the anti-abortion rally. The teen was quickly labeled as a racist but spoke out against the backlash which he encountered. Eventually, defamation lawsuits were filed against several media outlets resulting in hundreds of million dollars in settlements in favor of the young student.

Today, many of us are quick to condemn others when we hear or see an allegation, even if proof is lacking. Social media lights up like an electrical storm. It is often filled with hate, hurtful comments, and horrific threats of bodily harm and death toward the accused. Even some professional journalists prejudge before getting all the facts. Verifying information appears to be less important than being the first to publish and take advantage of sensationalism. Bible instruction that we should not judge others does not mean we cannot show discernment. Passing judgment on someone based solely on appearances is not in line with Christian expectations. Jesus gives a direct command how to judge: "Stop judging by mere appearances, but instead judge correctly" (John 7:24 NIV). It's a rare person who is not guilty of judging other people. Jesus would caution us to remember that "you will be treated as you treat others. The standard you use in judging is the standard by which you will be judged" (Matthew 7:2 NLT).

When Jesus said not to judge others, He did not mean that we cannot identify sin for what it is, based on God's definition. But we need to exercise caution. Simon the Pharisee once drew rebuke from Jesus when he passed unrighteous judgment on a woman based on her appearance and reputation. He lacked understanding that the woman had been forgiven (Luke 7:36–50). If it is not our place to judge as it often isn't, then we should keep our opinions to ourselves. Otherwise, we run the risk of overstepping our bounds or even putting ourselves in the place of God who alone has the right to judge. The Message puts it this way:

> So don't get ahead of the Master and jump to conclusions with your judgments before all the evidence is in. When he comes, he will bring out in the open and place in evidence all kinds of things we never even dreamed of—inner motives and purposes and prayers. Only then will any one of us get to hear the praise of God. (1 Corinthians 4:5)

While we can't control what others say or do, we can control our own words and actions. Before we call into question someone else's walk with God, we should scrutinize our own and not give way to what might otherwise be a simple rush to judgment.

Reflection

How fast are you to rush to judgment? Why do you think this has become a norm rather than an exception in our society? Which sensory information should we be cautious about acting upon? How can you pace your decisions about what you see and hear about others to be more appropriate?

AUGUST 15
(Y3, D33)

Not Taking Sides and Glorifying God

I appeal to you, brothers and sisters, in the name of our Lord Jesus Christ, that all of you agree with one another in what you say and that there be no divisions among you, but that you be perfectly united in mind and thought.

—1 Corinthians 10:18 (NIV)

A friend of mine was relating a conversation to me in which she had once participated. She had reached out and was having coffee with a former classmate whose husband had died. The relatively new widow reflected on the past months of her life and how difficult and different it had become. Apparently, she and her ailing husband had moved back home to live with his mother (her mother-in-law) in a house that they owned. After the husband passed away, the ladies found that they were incompatible. This resulted in the mother-in-law deciding to move out of the house where she had made her home for many years. When she did so, the next-door neighbors stopped speaking to the daughter-in law, making it unpleasant for her to continue to live in the neighborhood. What the classmate did not know was that my friend also knew the neighbors and had always found them to be persons of faith. My friend faced an awkward situation, feeling as though she was being pulled into a situation where she might have to take sides.

Unfortunately, life frequently thrusts us into many areas of conflict when we feel ourselves being pulled to one side or another. These vary from having to take the part of a family member to defending someone at work whose job may be on the line. Circumstances grow to be even more personal when friendships become compromised or divisions start to form within the body of the church. You find yourself praying for God's wisdom, wondering if God ever takes sides. And if He does, you sure hope He takes yours. One should further ask: do we ever truly win if in order to do so we must destroy the opposition? And when this occurs, is it even possible to honor God? In his infinite wisdom, Abraham Lincoln was conflicted by this question of God taking sides. He once wrote:

> The will of God prevails—in great contests each party claims to act in accordance with the will of God. Both may be, and one must be wrong. God cannot

be for, and against the same thing at the same time. In the present civil war, it is quite possible that God's purpose is somewhat different from the purpose of either party—and yet the human instrumentalities, working just as they do, are of the best adaptation to effect this.

We must remember that God's ways are not of this world, therefore not comparable to our own. God's side, for the lack of a better understanding, deals with conflict in ways that are very different than the world often teaches or even tries to comprehend. When we study God's Word, there are always persisting conflicts to be found. In the Old Testament, we can read:

> Now when Joshua was near Jericho, he looked up and saw a man standing in front of him with a drawn sword in his hand. Joshua went up to him and asked, "Are you for us or for our enemies?"
> "Neither," he replied, "but as commander of the army of the Lord I have now come" (Joshua 5:13–14 NIV).

In the New Testament, we find there were occasions when Jesus appeared to take sides. In these situations, we often discover Him taking the side of one who is humbling themselves before God rather than one who is proud and boastful (James 4:6).

Is it possible then to be on the right side of an issue from an earthly perspective but wrong in the eyes of God? When attempting to answer this question, it is important that we stand on the side of what He has provided for us—His Word. We may, in fact, be right in truth about a matter, but God may not stand with us if we have not applied His Word as the standard for accomplishment. Through His Word, He has given us rather clear expectations as to how we are to interact with each other. It's not about winning. It's not about pride. It is about the way we behave. If we do take sides, it should be God's side and His alone. Ultimately, one must ask—are there times that rather than taking what appears to be the winning side in a human conflict, God may simply be calling upon us to surrender? Maybe so. For in surrendering to Him, it is quite likely that the world will not understand, but He will be glorified.

Reflection

How can we begin to honor God when in the course of our actions we sometimes destroy others who are His children? Is it possible to say that God is or isn't for someone? If you are currently in a conflict with fellow Christians, is it possible that it might be better to concede than taking sides and creating a division within the family of believers? How would not doing so potentially form a negative image in the eyes of non-Christian bystanders?

AUGUST 16
(Y4, D33)

Going Home

In My Father's house are many dwelling places; if it were not so, I
would have told you; for I go to prepare a place for you.

—John 14:2 (NASB)

A number of years ago, I was on a train coming home from New York City. I don't know about you, but when I have been somewhere aware that my time away has come to an end, I just wish I could snap my fingers and be home. I assume that's how one of my fellow passengers felt when our train began to slow down in the middle of nowhere, less than an hour from my destination. Having no power, we were informed that another engine would have to be dispatched before we would be able to complete our journey. Without power, there was very little anyone could do, so we just tried to keep warm and rest until the new engine arrived. In the midst of the silence, an older gentleman stood up to stretch his legs and resounded these words: "We all would be better off if we'd just stayed home." To this day, when I'm stuck in traffic or out and just want to get to where I am going, I echo his expression.

Home has various meanings for each of us. To Dorothy who walked down the yellow brick road in the Land of Oz, it meant finding the wizard so that he could arrange to get her back to Kansas. For a person who serves in the armed services, the answer to the question "Where are you from?" will usually illicit the response of a place where loved ones await their return. When a person with dementia says they want to go home, they just know that where they are is not where they want to be. Often, home, in their mind, is not where they last lived but rather the place of earlier years where they grew up and lived as children. To most of us, it's that dwelling containing our worldly possessions which has come to be known as our family residence. It's been said, "Home is where the heart is." If that is the case, home is a place of fond memories, not necessarily having anything to do with our current address.

For some, home is not always a place where they feel welcomed or comforted. Not everyone leaves home on good terms, and it often become awkward to return. For these individuals, events like holiday meals or high school class reunions are not the most pleasant recollections. For some who have found success outside of their hometown, they may also find it difficult to adjust or experience acceptance when they go back. They will often relate to the phrase, "You can't go home again," meaning that for whatever reason, they can no longer connect with those who have continued to remain there. When Jesus returned to his hometown, He began teaching in the synagogue. Then they began to recollect who He was: the carpenter's son whose mother was Mary and brothers were James, Joseph, Simon, and Judas. In doing so, they questioned His wisdom and miraculous powers and took offense of Him (Matthew 13:54–56). "But Jesus said to them, 'A prophet is not without honor except in his own town and in his own home'" (Matthew 13:57 NIV). Due to their lack of faith, He was unable to perform many miracles there.

In the mid-1970s, an artist by the name of B. J. Thomas sang these lyrics: "They say that heaven's pretty; And living here is too. But if they said that I would have to choose between the two. I'd go home, going home, where I belong." The song, *Home Where I Belong*, reflects the feelings of many Christians who become homesick for a place they have never been, where they know with confidence they will spend eternity.

> For people who speak thus make it clear that they are seeking a homeland. If they had been thinking of that land from which they had gone out, they would have had opportunity to return. But as it is, they desire a better country, that is, a heavenly one. Therefore, God is not ashamed to be called their God, for he has prepared for them a city. (Hebrews 11:14–16 ESV)

For now, we will continue to travel on this earthly journey. While it is not always happy or nonthreatening, we persevere through each day where we are blessed to bring hope and service to a world that at times feels hurt, helpless, and fearful. We do so with this assurance: "For we know that if the tent that is our earthly home is destroyed, we have a building from God, a house not made with hands, eternal in the heavens" (2 Corinthians 5:1 ESV). And that is a homecoming to which we should look forward with great anticipation.

Reflection

When you think of home, what comes to mind? In what was has the definition of "home" taken on new meanings as you travel through your life journey? How can you help others who have had a difficult home life understand that a loving, permanent home awaits their arrival in God's plan?

AUGUST 17
(Y5, D33)

On Being Offended

Understand this, my dear brothers and sisters: You must all be
quick to listen, slow to speak, and slow to get angry.

—James 1:19 (NLT)

While channel surfing recently, I came across a documentary tour of one of America's state capitol buildings. The narrator included descriptions of the gold painted rotunda and its large entry doors. But what took my eye were the many references to God etched into the walls of the amazing facility. I thought to myself, *I wonder how long it will be until some person or group takes issue with those statements, claims to be offended by them, and then petitions for their removal.* After all, it wasn't that long ago that religious displays in public schools and engravings of the Ten Commandments in government buildings were challenged in the Supreme Court. And later on, statues of historical figures were toppled because intolerant persons were offended by what those folks once represented. Imagine desecrating artifacts or memorials with no allowance for any kind of human frailty as a basis to be offended. It would be almost certain for no statues to remain, as our lessons from history begin to fade.

It seems like it doesn't take much anymore for persons to claim that they have been offended. Once we might have said that these individuals were "thin-skinned." But these days, the wrong comment or a perceived inappropriate act may instantly evoke sufficient anger and toxicity to set the stage for potential violence. Those who allow for such activities should consider the words of Solomon: "The person who strays from common sense will end up in the company of the dead" (Proverbs 21:16 NLT). At the very least, it is not uncommon to find yourself surrounded by those who allow a wound to fester rather than attempt to promote its healing. The late American philosopher Wayne Dyer subscribed to a different philosophy by stating, "When you are spiritually connected, you are not looking for occasions to be offended, and you are not judging and labeling others. You are in a state of grace in which you know you are connected to God and thus free from the effects of anyone or anything external to yourself."

Oftentimes, those who become intolerant and easily offended have cultivated within themselves a degree of moral smugness. They are commonly referred to as the self-righteous and assert that their own beliefs and actions are of far greater virtue than those of the average person. Jesus warned against this as He challenged us, even today with this parable: "Two men went up to the temple to pray, one a Pharisee and the other a tax collector. The Pharisee stood by himself and prayed:

> "God, I thank you that I am not like other people—robbers, evildoers, adulterers—or even like this tax collector. I fast twice a week and give a tenth of all I get." But the tax collector stood at a distance. He would not even look up to heaven, but beat his breast and said, "God, have mercy on me, a sinner." I tell you that this man, rather than the other, went home justified before God. For all those who exalt themselves will be humbled, and those who humble themselves will be exalted. (Luke 18:10–14 NIV)

The Apostle Paul tells his readers that if righteousness could come from our own actions, "then Christ died for no purpose" (Galatians 2:21 ESV). He also stated, "A servant of the Lord must not quarrel but must be kind to everyone, be able to teach, and be patient with difficult people. Gently instruct those who oppose the truth. Perhaps God will change those people's hearts, and they will learn the truth" (2 Timothy 2:24–25 NLT). One must consider that act of being offended is a choice. Pastor Joel Osteen put it this way: "Every day we have plenty of opportunities to get angry, stressed or offended. But what you're doing when you indulge these negative emotions is giving something outside yourself power over your happiness. You can choose to not let little things upset you." As Christians, there are occasions when we must respond by speaking out. At other times, it may be pertinent to engage in some self-reflection asking why or if we have a right to be offended. Or perhaps we just need to get over ourselves.

Reflection

As Christians, what types of situations should offend us? Think of a recent situation when you felt offended. What could you have done differently? When might it be both right and necessary to form an opinion about another? When is it wrong? How can we know the difference?

AUGUST 18
(Y6, D33)

Shopping for Answers

Listen to my voice in the morning, L ORD. Each morning I
bring my requests to you and wait expectantly.

—Psalm 5:3 (NLT)

Through buying goods and then reselling them as a traveling salesman, Aaron Montgomery Ward of Chicago removed the middlemen at the general store. He strategically purchased large quantities of merchandise directly from the manufacturer and in turn resold the items at a lower price to his customers with a "satisfaction or your money back" guarantee. His revolutionary idea led to the concept of a mail order catalog meant for the general public. The very first, published on August 18, 1872, consisted of a one-page sheet boasting 163 items. In 1883, the company's catalog, which became popularly known as the "Wish Book," had grown to 240 pages and 10,000 items. In 1946, a book-lovers' society included a Montgomery Ward catalog on its list of the 100 American books that had most affected American life, noting "no idea ever mushroomed so far from so small a beginning, or had so profound an influence on the economics of a continent, as the concept, original to America, of direct selling by mail, for cash."

Eventually, the extensive use of catalogs was complemented with retail outlets where prospective customers could touch and see items firsthand. At its peak, Montgomery Ward was one of the largest retailers in the United States. With increased competition from other large venders and the expansion of indoor malls, the company ceased its catalog in 1985, eventually closing all of its stores by the turn of the century. Today, what was once one of the most popular ways of shopping is remembered each year on August 18 as National Mail Order Catalog Day. One of the downfalls of the growing catalog business was the ability to sometimes meet demand. At times, customers would be notified that their shipment was out of stock, on delay, or perhaps no longer available. Whenever this occurs, even today, our lack of patience and desire for immediate gratification forces us to simply move on and look elsewhere. Unfortunately, that is true in most aspects of our existence, not the least of which is our prayer life. Sometimes we petition God with our concerns, and when it seems like He isn't going to answer, we become impatient and decide to shop for answers elsewhere.

Jesus said:

> For everyone who asks, receives. Everyone who seeks, finds. And to every-one who knocks, the door will be opened. You parents—if your children ask for a loaf of bread, do you give them a stone instead? Or if they ask for a fish, do you give them a snake? Of course not! So if you sinful people know how to give good gifts to your children, how much more will your heavenly Father give good gifts to those who ask him. (Matthew 7:8–11 NLT)

God always wants what is best for His children. This may be different than our desire, especially when there seems to be a disconnect between what we want and His response or lack of one. Some prayers that seem to go unanswered are simply instances during which God, in His infinite wisdom, knows that what we have asked for is not best for us right now. It may be that our timing is not His timing or He has some far greater purpose in mind. When we pray, we are engaging in the most precious and God-given act of communication with the one to whom we are accountable in all our life activities. While God may at times seem silent to us, He never sends us away empty-handed.

We live in a consumer society and have become accustomed to getting what we want when we want it. Unlike ordering from a catalog that involves our will only, prayer involves God's will also. "This is the confidence we have in approaching God: that if we ask anything according to his will, he hears us" (1 John 5:14 NIV). Even if prayer has not been answered, we must be faithful to continue to "pray without ceasing" (1 Thessalonians 5:17 ESV). With regard to God's answers to our prayer, we should always expect the unexpected. Some of the greatest gifts and deepest joys which God gives us often come wrapped in packages that are nowhere to be found in our wish book. Prayer is a bit different than the typical mail-order business. God doesn't give us what we want; He gives us what we truly need.

Reflection

Are there times you treat your prayer time with God like a "wish book" mail-order catalog? How do you react when your order is not filled or you get something different than what you wanted? Jesus prayed to His heavenly Father, "Nevertheless not My will, but yours, be done" (Luke 22:42 ESV). Are you able to follow His example and do the same?

AUGUST 19
(Y7, D33)

Let Your Yes Be Yes

Fear the LORD your God, serve him only and take your oaths in his name.

—Deuteronomy 6:13 (NIV)

As I watched a favorite TV drama, the show began to concentrate on that historic period in our nation following the attack on Pearl Harbor. Many young men were being called to serve their country, and others who had not yet been called felt it was their patriotic duty to volunteer. The fictional storyline focused on the tension between a father and his youngest son. Because the son was under the age of eighteen, he would have needed parental consent in order to enlist. In this case, the father did not feel his son was mature enough to make this life-affirming decision. But the son was relentless in his pursuit to do so, and the father reluctantly gave his permission. On the day that the headstrong son prepares to leave for the recruiter's office, the elder hopes his son might have a change of heart. So the father provides these parting words: "Remember it's not final until you take that oath." As it turned out, he did not.

The significance of making pledges, taking oaths, and reciting vows has significantly waned over time. Oath-taking has a long history among God's people, with many references found in the Old Testament. There it is said:

> When you make a vow to the LORD your God, be prompt in fulfilling whatever you promised him. For the LORD your God demands that you promptly fulfill all your vows, or you will be guilty of sin. However, it is not a sin to refrain from making a vow. But once you have voluntarily made a vow, be careful to fulfill your promise to the LORD your God. (Deuteronomy 23:21–23 NLT)

There were dire consequences for the Israelites who made and broke vows to God. The story of Jephthah illustrates the foolishness of making vows without understanding the consequences. Before leading the Israelites into battle against the Ammonites, Jephthah—described as a mighty man of valor—made a rash vow that he would give to the Lord whoever first came out to meet him if he returned to his home in triumph. When the Lord granted him victory, the one who came out to meet him was his daughter, an only child. Jephthah remembered his vow and offered her to the Lord (Judges 11:29–40).

In Jesus' time, many rabbis did not consider it a sin to break a vow if it was not made explicitly in the name of God. Jesus pointed out the hypocrisy of this teaching.

> You also say, "If anyone swears by the altar, it means nothing; but anyone who swears by the gift on the altar is bound by that oath." You blind men! Which is greater: the gift, or the altar that makes the gift sacred? Therefore, anyone who swears by the altar swears by it and by everything on it. And anyone who swears by the temple swears by it and by the one who dwells in it. And anyone who swears by heaven swears by God's throne and by the one who sits on it. (Matthew 23:18–22 NIV)

When it comes to taking oaths and making vows, Jesus said: "All you need to say is simply 'Yes' or 'No'; anything beyond this comes from the evil one" (Matthew 5:37 NIV). His teaching is not meant to discourage careful, thought-out promises, such as wedding vows or a legal contract. However, Jesus commands that in most cases our word be sufficient without making vows. When we say "yes" or "no," that's exactly what we should mean. Adding pledges to our words opens us to the influence of Satan whose desire is to trap us and compromise our Christian testimony.

God's Word teaches that our honesty and integrity must be of the highest importance. When we say we are going to do something, we must honor our word. Those who truly walk with Jesus should not find it necessary to make voluntary statements, such as "I would swear on a stack of Bibles" or "Honest to God" as a means of enhancing their trustworthiness. Instead, your dependability should be inherent and displayed in everything you say and do, thereby negating the need for oath-taking. Jesus' teaching leads us to conclude that it is better not to make a vow than to swear an oath that you have no intention of keeping. It also reinforces the point that oaths and vows should not be made on just any occasion, but they should be reserved only for instances of great import and lasting significance. As sojourners with Christ, therefore, we are challenged to be faithful in all circumstances, striving to understand His Word and making it our own. Indeed, wouldn't the world be a better place if we all did just that?

Reflection

How do you think others view your level of sincerity when you make a promise? Do you follow through on the commitments you make? When you make an unnecessary pledge, have you ever stopped to consider if it suggests that you are less than trustworthy under normal circumstances? What does it take for you to trust others at their word?

AUGUST 20
(Y1, D34)

Because He Said He Would

God is not human, that he should lie, not a human being, that he should change his mind. Does he speak and then not act? Does he promise and not fulfill?

—Numbers 23:19 (NIV)

Every four years, the major political parties in the United States come together to announce their candidates for President. Like many others before them who contest for elective political offices, they make unrealistic promises they know they cannot fulfil. For each of us, living up to what we promise often becomes difficult. Yet there are some who take it very seriously. When Bill McCartney retired as the head coach of the University of Colorado Boulder football team in 1994, his reason was not because he was unsuccessful as a coach. His teams had won the national championship, and they had been in the top ten many times. McCartney said that he was retiring because he wanted to reconsider what was important. He stated, "I'm leaving coaching, and I'm going to take a whole year to reevaluate my priorities. Is God first? Is my family second? Is my work third?" When that year was over, Bill McCartney had moved to dedicate his life and talents to Christ, giving importance to Promise Keepers, a Christian men's group which he had founded. Promise Keepers describes its goal as "to bring about revival through a global movement that calls men back to courageous, bold, leadership. We will be the spark that calls men back to God's Word, sharing their faith and caring for the poor and oppressed throughout the world."

In Jesus' day, keeping vows and promises were not always taken seriously. The religious leaders advocated keeping a vow if it was a public vow using God's name. However, if the vow was made in the course of everyday conversation, referencing only heaven or earth or Jerusalem, it was not binding. Therefore, people could lie or exaggerate in their conversations and lend themselves an air of credibility by saying, "I swear by heaven that this is true!" While they could not be held to account because they did not specifically swear by God's name, Jesus disputed that putting forth the idea that if you swear something, it had better be true. Bottom line, your word should be good because His was. One of His chosen stated it this way:

> His divine power has given us everything we need for a godly life through our knowledge of him who called us by his own glory and goodness. Through these he has given us his very great and precious promises, so that through them you may participate in the divine nature, having escaped the corruption in the world caused by evil desires. (2 Peter 1:3–4 NIV)

Inspirational speaker Alex Sheen strongly believes in keeping the promises he makes. In his case, he proposed to honor his late father for whom keeping one's word was a very important character trait, one that he had instilled in his son. Alex was so moved by how his father used this trait as an inner compass that he began a small movement, "Because I Said I Would." He began to spread this teaching to others by encouraging writing promises on small cards and posting them in places as reminders to live up to their commitments, just as he had been taught by his father. As one of the world's foremost experts on accountability and commitment, Alex moved on to become an author, podcast host, internationally-recognized humanitarian and founder of the "Because I Said I Would" crusade. The stories resulting from these "promises made, promises kept" have shared practical life lessons inspiring lives around the world.

Corrie ten Boom, famous for her biography, *The Hiding Place*, once wrote, "Let God's promises shine on your problem." So just how many promises are there? According to one account, there are over 3,500 promises in the Bible. Some of these were limited to certain situations and persons, such as the one to give Abraham and Sarah a son at an old age (Genesis 17:16). However, many more are intended for all believers, like God's promise to never leave or abandon us (Hebrews 13:5). If we claim one of the Lord's promises with the right spirit and pure motives, we will honor Him, receive what we ask, and grow in intimacy with our loving Father. In a changing world where vows are often broken, it's reassuring that followers of Christ serve a God who keeps His word because He will always do what He said He would.

Reflection

What promises are you standing on? Are you seeking this promise with a spirit of submission to the will of God? If you are not holding on to one of God's promises, ask the Lord to show you particular promises that are relevant to your life. What then will be your next steps in applying them each day? How can you instill the value of keeping promises in the lives of others, using biblical promises as a source of hope for others to hold on to?

AUGUST 21
(Y2, D34)

If You Build It, He Will Come

The Kingdom of Heaven is like a treasure that a man discovered hidden in a field.

—Matthew 13:44 (NLT)

Charismatic televangelist Joel Osteen understands that if you build something for the right reasons, dreams may come true. Osteen took over the nondenominational Lakewood Church in Houston in 1999 when his father, its founding pastor, died. With humble beginnings in a converted feed store in 1959, the congregation grew immensely. In 2005, Lakewood Church moved into the former Compaq Center where the Houston Rockets won two NBA Championships in that building which at the time seated 16,000. Initially, a sixty-year lease was signed with the city of Houston. But seven years later, as the city was running low on funds, officials decided to sell off some of their excess properties to fix a budget shortfall. Normally, this type of commercial property would have had a building cost of $400 million, but an appraisal for $7.5 million paved a path for the acquisition. Although there were obstacles along the way, the church now owns their building free and clear with more than 40,000 in attendance each week. Osteen stated, "What could have taken sixty years, God did fifty-three years sooner. He took us further faster."

In the movie, *Field of Dreams*, the main character, Ray Kinsella, is an unseasoned Iowa farmer with a wife and small daughter, struggling to make ends meet. Troubled by a broken relationship with his late father, a devoted baseball fan, he fears growing old without achieving anything. One evening, alone in his cornfield, a voice whispers from the heavens: "If you build it, they will come." In the days ahead, Ray continues to hear the voice, and eventually, he sees a glorious vision of a baseball diamond set in the field. To the astonishment and mockery of his neighbors, he destroys valuable cropland to build a baseball field. Ray is faced with the dilemma of either holding onto his field of dreams or selling the farm to save the life he knows. Although he encounters many interesting persons along his journey of faith, including a gathering of all-star baseball players, one other familiar figure finally appears. It happens to be Ray's late father with whom he became estranged as a youth. Father and son are reconciled, and we observe them playing a game of catch on the baseball diamond nestled by Iowa cornfields.

Ray Kinsella held onto dreams at the high cost of possibly losing all this world has to offer. His field meant everything to him, and he was willing to sacrifice everything for it. His story is similar to one Jesus told about a man who came across a hidden treasure in a field. This treasure was so valuable and attractive that he sold everything he had to buy the field in which he found the treasure. The treasure was attractive and desirable, but there was a cost to obtaining it (Matthew 13:43–46). You may recall other well-known biblical passages which are similar to the reactions Ray experienced from his whispers from the field. Just imagine the neighbors who would have referred to Noah as crazy when God called him to build an ark (Genesis 6:13–14). Then there were those who viewed Abraham as obsessive when he heard and followed the call of God to "go!" (Genesis 12:1). It is likely that family and friends of Peter and Andrew considered them to be compulsive when they heard the call of Jesus to "follow!" And they went (Matthew 4:18–20).

Perhaps you have been thought of as fanatical if you've had a flash of insight and felt compelled act on something that those around you would define as senseless. Regardless, you just knew you had to do it because it gave you the chance to recover something precious you had lost. There are times when the voice of God calls each of us to find that one thing we need to just make sense of our life. He is calling us today to not only remember and enjoy what He has done for us but also to respond by listening for His current call in our life. His voice might be calling you on a new adventure to be the presence of Jesus to those around you as you become modern-day fishers of people. Even as we grow older, we can still hope and imagine all that God desires for our life to be fulfilled. He draws us closer to Him and leads us to an even more wonderful field of dreams full of His presence, full of His peace, and full of a new love of life that's joyful and unafraid. For in the end, what will satisfy the soul are the dreams that God has put in our hearts, promises He has whispered within our spirit. For if you build it, He *will* come.

Reflection

How important is it to your "spiritual listening" that you be ready to position yourself as God's servant? Are there seemingly impossible dreams God might be whispering to you? What are the key things happening in your life today that tomorrow you may wish you'd paid more attention to?

AUGUST 22
(Y3, D34)

It's Just Not Right

Yet I am always with you; you hold me by my right hand.

—Psalm 73:23 (NIV)

These days, it seems like there is a day to honor or celebrate almost anything, including, to my surprise, National Left Handers' Day. I never heard of this before, but why not? It is believed that left-handers represent about 10 to 15 percent of the population. At one point in time, left-handedness was considered a symbol of weakness or evil. At the very least, it could most certainly be regarded as an indication of awkwardness or inconvenience. We all have experienced situations such as being at the family holiday dinner table where, in order to avoid collision, lefties are often placed at the corner of the table. In doing so, they avoid bumping into the righties who are enjoying their Thanksgiving turkey.

Over time, however, many who have favored their left side have gained prominence. At least four of the most recent presidents have been photographed signing those important documents with the pen in their left hand. In some sports, being left-handed can present a tactical advantage which might signify the difference between winning and losing. Although I have always thought of myself as right-handed, I can remember times when left seemed to be a better option. I know it is considered proper to offer one's right hand as a sign of friendship. However, when someone walks up to my table while I am dining at a local restaurant, I find it healthier to extend my left hand in greeting. One time, as I was saying goodbye to a friend who I knew I would not see for a while, I put my right shoulder over hers to give a hug. She pulled away and told me she likes to hug left over left because when you do so, it places both hearts together, symbolizing a special and caring relationship.

In biblical times, being able to use one's left hand was considered to be an extreme advantage. An agile warrior who could fight with his left hand was someone to be feared because he could strike in ways that were not normal or expected. And so in the Old Testament we read, "Among all these soldiers there were seven hundred select troops who were left-handed, each of whom could sling a stone at a hair and not miss" (Judges 20:16 NIV). Likewise in scripture, the right hand is a figure of speech for power. When God told David, "Sit in the place of honor at my right hand until I humble your enemies, making them a footstool under your feet" (Psalm 110:1 NLT). God meant for David to wait patiently and trust that His power would be delivered in order that he would overcome his enemies. David seemed to understand as He wrote: "If I rise on the wings of the dawn, if I settle on the far side of the sea; even there your hand will guide me, your right hand will hold me fast" (Psalm 139:9–10 NIV).

Ultimately, it does not matter to God whether we are a righty or a lefty, but the imagery of the terms throughout His Word is effective. Nothing interweaves the reference to right and left any more than in Jesus' own instruction: "But when you give to someone in need, don't let your left hand know what your right hand is doing" (Matthew 6:3 NLT). The message here seems to be that when God has inclined and equipped us to do works of charity, the knowledge of those offerings should be between us and Him. The term *right* has come to signify that which is correct or proper. C. S. Lewis once said, "Integrity is doing the right thing even when no one is watching." Therefore, what is right has nothing to do with our hand preferences but is more defined by the partialities of experience. The Apostle Paul would tell us that this is where we must place ourselves, "fixing our eyes on Jesus, the pioneer and perfecter of faith. For the joy set before him he endured the cross, scorning its shame, and sat down at the right hand of the throne of God" (Hebrews 12:2 NIV). Although he may have expressed it with tongue in cheek, even Mark Twain seemed to grasp the concept as he said: "Do the right thing. It will gratify some people and astonish the rest." After all, anything less in the eyes of God—well, it's just not right!

Reflection

When you are in a position that no one knows other than you whether you are doing the right thing or not, what ultimately influences your decision? As you find yourself struggling with making such a decision, where do you turn for help? When someone close to you is about to make an error in judgment that you deem to not be right, in what ways might you help influence their thought process?

AUGUST 23
(Y4, D34)

Rest: A Soulful Experience

The Lord replied, "My Presence will go with you, and I will give you rest."

—Exodus 33:14 (NIV)

One year during the summer months, I had two conversations with individuals who had agreed to do outside work for me. The first of these was a person who would only be working an hour or so grinding out the root system of an old tree which had already been removed. The problem was he wanted to come early on a Sunday morning to do the task because he had another job during the week. I informed him that the work he'd be doing would make too much noise for a Sunday, and I did not want to be credited with creating such a disturbance in the neighborhood. The other guy has done odd jobs for me on a more routine basis. He, too, has a day job, and I knew what I was asking him to do would take more than just a few hours. After I described the scope of the work, I told him he was welcome to do it in the evenings or on a Saturday but that I did not want him doing anything on Sundays. After hearing my stipulation, both men agreed on my conditions. While it may have not mattered to anyone else, it would have mattered to me. After all, for those who are Christians, Sunday is the Sabbath, a day for rest.

Rest is promoted in our culture and is big business. Health experts tell us that in order to maintain a good state of physical well-being, it is important that you get a good night's rest. This is reinforced by advertisers who want to sell you the adjustable mattress where you can choose your individual degree of firmness by selecting a number on the provided remote. Or how about that guy who created that perfect pillow and personally guarantees it to be the "most comfortable one you will ever own"? If you have trouble falling and staying asleep, there are prescription medications available. You can purchase machines that play sounds which will relax you, and you can get therapy body oils or lotions to enhance your rest. Assisting us to have a good night's sleep is just one form of rest, but there are many others. Employees are given rest breaks at work. When we are traveling, we might decide to pull over at a rest stop. If we are playing in a band or orchestra, we might take a rhythmical rest as noted in the music. Or if we are going on about something, we may simply be told to "just give it a rest."

Rest is a biblical principle as well. It is so significant that it is part of the creation story. "On the seventh day, God had finished his work of creation, so he rested from all his work. And God blessed the seventh day and declared it holy, because it was the day when he rested from all his work of creation" (Genesis 2:2–3 NLT). When God revealed His commandments to Moses, "Remember the Sabbath day by keeping it holy" (Exodus 20:8 NIV) was on the list. This tradition carried on through the early church. "For somewhere he has spoken about the seventh day in these words: 'On the seventh day God rested from all his works.' There remains, then, a Sabbath-rest for the people of God. For all who have entered into God's rest have rested from their labors, just as God did after creating the world" (Hebrews 4:4, 9–10 NIV). When the Pharisees questioned Jesus about certain activity on the Sabbath, He responded, "The Sabbath was made to meet the needs of people, and not people to meet the requirements of the Sabbath" (Mark 2:27 NLT).

Jesus understood that the concept of rest had many interpretations. Before the feeding of the five thousand, there is this passage: "Then, because so many people were coming and going that they did not even have a chance to eat, he said to them, 'Come with me by yourselves to a quiet place and get some rest'" (Mark 6:31). Ultimately, Jesus was more concerned about a different kind of rest, that which we can only find in Him. He said, "Come to me, all you who are weary and burdened, and I will give you rest (Matthew 11:28). His is the promise of a spiritual rest available to those who repent and believe in Him. When we rest in Jesus, we are assured comfort and peace that He alone can provide. Charles Spurgeon put it this way: "If we can become as He is, we shall rest as He does. The lowly in heart will be restful of heart." Jesus, therefore, extends rest to us as an invitation, not only for the physical relief we might find at the end of a busy day or week but also for that spiritual refuge that is simply ours for the taking. It becomes for us an expression of faith, allowing us to renew our spirit and satisfy the soul.

Reflection

Have there been times in your life when you have been restless? To what have you turned to find peace and comfort? What do you need to do to experience the rest that Christ can provide? How would you help others to understand that it is important to find both physical and spiritual rest?

AUGUST 24
(Y5, D34)

Glimpses of God's Glory

Darkness comes upon them in the daytime; at noon they grope as in the night.

—Job 5:14 (NIV)

Thousands had gathered in anticipation of their arrival. Several hundred reporters, photographers, and cameramen from radio, television, and the press were also standing by. The feverish attention they created was like none ever before. It became labeled as an invasion; others referred to it as "mania." Whatever you called it, riotous-like behavior broke out, the crowd noise became deafening, and police had to close off streets due to the hysteria. It was all caused by the American arrival of four English lads in their early twenties dressed in mod suits and sporting mop-topped haircuts. It was February 7, 1964, and the "Fab-Four" had just arrived at New York's Kennedy Airport via a several thousand-mile flight which had departed only hours before from London's Heathrow Airport. They were, of course, John, Paul, George, and Ringo—better known as The Beatles. To just get a glimpse of them caused many a teenage girl to faint. Listening to their music set the course of rock and roll history for many years to come.

It's not unusual for the world to find themselves in a dither when they are about to see someone or something unusual. On August 21, 2017, people again traveled thousands of miles to witness an incident which had not occurred since February 26, 1979. Then news anchors, Frank Reynolds and Walter Cronkite, reported on the day's events, looking forward to what would not transpire for another thirty-eight years and hoping for "a more peaceful world." Though not at peace, what the world did find were people looking skyward in the middle of the day to catch a glimpse of an event which would last for less than three minutes. Known as a total solar eclipse, it gave a somewhat eerie reference to what many will someday witness. When that time arrives, again looking toward the heavens, they will see Jesus. For "Behold, he is coming with the clouds, and every eye will see him" (Revelation 1:7 ESV).

I am reminded of a story I once heard about a group of salesmen who were attending a convention in one of our larger cities. Arriving late for their flight home, they hurriedly ran through the airport, attempting to make the gate for their departure. In doing so, one of them accidentally caught the leg of a table which held a display of apples. Never looking back, they managed to reach their plane in time, except for one. Observing apples scattered everywhere across the terminal floor, only one of them felt guilty for the mess they had made. Staying behind to offer assistance, he found a sixteen-year-old blind girl groping to recover some of her fruit while, in frustration, tears ran down her face. The salesman knelt to the floor in an attempt to reorganize the display. Then he discovered that many of the apples had become bruised, so he set those aside. When he was done, he asked the young girl if she was going to be okay. He then pulled $40 out of his wallet and requested that she please accept the money as repayment for the damage she had incurred. While beginning to walk away, the blind girl called out to him, "Mister." As he glanced in her direction, she looked up with eyes that could not see and said, "Are you Jesus?"

Has anyone called you Jesus lately? Probably not. But the more pertinent question is, "When was the last time someone saw Jesus in you?" The Apostle Paul offered this challenge: "Imitate God, therefore, in everything you do, because you are his dear children. Live a life filled with love, following the example of Christ. He loved us and offered himself as a sacrifice for us, a pleasing aroma to God" (Ephesians 5:1–2 NLT). Jesus put it this way:

> You are the light of the world—like a city on a hilltop that cannot be hidden. No one lights a lamp and then puts it under a basket. Instead, a lamp is placed on a stand, where it gives light to everyone in the house. In the same way, let your good deeds shine out for all to see, so that everyone will praise your heavenly Father. (Matthew 5:14–16 NLT)

As you allow the heart of Jesus to enter your own, you are lighting your candle in a world of darkness and permitting others to see Jesus in you. Famed singers and eclipses will come and go. However, glimpses of God's glory are lasting and available to us daily. Have you taken a peek lately?

Reflection

One person said, "I read the Bible to catch a glimpse of God's beauty, because that's where God has revealed Himself. Then, as I get to know God, I try to imitate Him, and He begins to make me beautiful like Him." What are some ways you might endeavor to show the world who Jesus is?

AUGUST 25
(Y6, D34)

Losing Sight of the Cross

He made peace with everything in heaven and on earth
by means of Christ's blood on the cross.

—Colossians 1:20 (NLT)

Rumors had abounded for years that a natural cross of snow lay hidden high in the rugged mountains of Colorado. Many claimed to have seen the cross, but others were unable to find it. It, therefore, became known as Colorado's elusive Mount of the Holy Cross. William Henry Jackson, an experienced wilderness photographer who had accompanied wagon trains to California, set out in 1873 to provide reliable proof of its existence. In the pre-dawn hours of August 24, Jackson prepared the heavy camera equipment he had carried up the mountain opposite the cross. He took his photos just as the first rays of the sun angled low across the crevassed face, emphasizing the lines of the cross. The best of the resulting photos became one of Jackson's most famous images, and it ended any further doubts about its existence. Published in well-known mass-circulation magazines, his pictures grew to become immensely popular and showed Americans a rugged western wilderness that most would never see firsthand.

It was discovered that there was nothing miraculous about the cause of the Mount of Holy Cross's formation. After thousands of years of erosion, two deep ravines had formed in the steep rocky face of a mountain peak. Intersecting at a ninety-degree angle, the ravines sheltered the winter snow from the sun well after the rest of the mountain snow had melted away. For a brief time, a nearly perfect cross of snow would appear on the rock face, often melting away later in the summer. It prompted artists to paint and the poet, Henry Wadsworth Longfellow, to pen *The Cross of Snow*. Over time the land formation eroded and shifted the right arm of the cross to visibly fall off, and the image was lost forever. For certain hikers and climbers, the mountain is still a destination. Thus the feeling of any sort of sacred symbol has long departed with the collapse of the cross. All that remains are a series of photographs and a few artistic remnants from a few long dead landscape painters. It stands only in myth, in art, and in an elusive, secluded mountain summit waiting to be climbed by those willing to make the trek.

On one occasion when Jesus was twelve years old, His parents had lost sight of Him while they had been in Jerusalem for the Passover. "After the festival was over, and his parents were returning home, the boy Jesus stayed behind in Jerusalem, but they were unaware of it" (Luke 2:43 NIV). Mary and Joseph had to search for three days to find Him again. But the interesting part of the story is that they, along with others, traveled an entire day before they missed Him. It isn't that they lost their love for Him or their faith. They just lost Him. If Jesus' parents can lose sight of Him, then it is certainly possible for us to do the same. When we first come to Christ, the cross is at the center of our faith. When we are busy with life around us, we become distracted, and often, our spiritual lives are the first things to go. We don't have time to read God's Word. We don't make time to pray, even to offer a brief thanks. We can't afford to give anything to God because we have allowed ourselves to become preoccupied. When we permit the perks to take the place of essentials, we can easily lose sight of the cross.

One wonders what inspired the hymnwriter, Isaac Watts, when he wrote the lyrics of his well-known hymn: "When I survey the wondrous cross; On which the Prince of Glory died. My richest gain I count but loss. And pour contempt on all my pride." The Apostle Paul said, "As for me, may I never boast about anything except the cross of our Lord Jesus Christ. Because of that cross, my interest in this world has been crucified, and the world's interest in me has also died" (Galatians 6:14 NLT). Just as the photographer went to prove the mountain cross in Colorado existed, we too need to "survey" the cross! It is important for us to refocus and appreciate its value in our lives when it begins to dim or gets lost completely. Whenever we lose something, we may retrace our steps and ask where we had it last. If we go back to that place, we often find it again. If you've found that you've lost the sight of the cross in the busyness of life, then you need to find your way back to where you were before. The good news is that even during those periods when we lose sight of Jesus, we can be assured He never loses sight of us.

Reflection

Is your view of the cross of Jesus clear today? What are those things that sometimes cause you to lose sight of it? How might you refocus your routine to maintain a consistently clear view? How would you intercede with another Christian who is seemingly unaware they have lost sight of the cross?

AUGUST 26
(Y7, D34)

Come As You Are

Therefore, if anyone is in Christ, the new creation has
come: The old has gone, the new is here!

—2 Corinthians 5:17 (NIV)

As the preacher of the newly founded church stepped up to deliver his message, he appeared in front of his new congregation in a sweatshirt and torn jeans. While the days of the more formal clerics have gone by the wayside, some did not consider this to be proper attire for giving a sermon in God's House. I remember some of the comments in my own church a while back when several teenage girls took up the offering in shorts and flip-flops during a summer worship service. I can also recall a time when I was conducting interviews for a maintenance position. One of the individuals showed up wearing a dress shirt and necktie. I was actually quite impressed and could tell that he was making an attempt to put his best foot forward. It's been said that clothes make the man, meaning that dressing well helps people to be successful. Depending on your age and point of reference, I'm not so sure this holds true anymore.

Decades ago, people would at times host "come as you are" parties. They would phone their friends and neighbors regarding an impromptu party which was to begin immediately upon their arrival. The idea was that whatever you were wearing when you were called was what you were expected to wear to the party. Older men will no doubt remember a time when certain clubs and restaurants had a rule of "tie and jacket required" before you would be seated. Consider too the first time you saw the sign "No shirt, no shoes, no service" posted on the entrance of your favorite convenience store. Many of us have positioned ourselves to criticize others for wearing what we considered to be inappropriate attire in certain situations. I have always held the philosophy that I should wear the best I have on those occasions where there should be respect shown for a person or while in the presence at a noteworthy event.

Jesus uses attire as in interesting symbol in His Parable of the Banquet. In the story, He compares the kingdom of heaven to a wedding banquet a king is throwing for his son. When those who have been invited refuse to come, the king becomes angry and said they were not worthy. He then summons his servants to extend the invitation to as many as can be found. In that era, appropriate attire would have been furnished for those in attendance.

> But when the king came in to see the guests, he noticed a man there who was not wearing wedding clothes. He asked, "How did you get in here without wedding clothes, friend?" The man was speechless. Then the king told the attendants, "Tie him hand and foot, and throw him outside, into the darkness, where there will be weeping and gnashing of teeth." (Matthew 22:11–13 NIV)

In actuality, neglecting to wear the proper garment had nothing to do with clothing as such. It has a deeper meaning according to Matthew Henry who wrote, "Many are called to the wedding feast, that is, to salvation, but few have the wedding-garment, the righteousness of Christ, the sanctification of the Spirit. Then let us examine ourselves whether we are in the faith, and seek to be approved by the King."

In the case of the King of kings, Jesus would never turn down the opportunity for a relationship with anyone. In fact, He said so: "All those the Father gives me will come to me, and whoever comes to me I will never drive away" (John 6:37 NIV). He wants us to come just as we are with all of our baggage. He understands our imperfections and our sinful nature. While the concept of "come as you are" supports Christ's overall message, the precise phrase is not found in scripture. In modern society, the philosophy has become a bit misrepresented. It has been diluted at times by well-intended Christians who extend the invitation to others to know Christ but somehow give the impression that it's not necessary to change. To the adulterous woman who would have been stoned, had it not been for Jesus' intervention, He said that He would not condemn her for her wrongdoings; however, He also instructs her to "go now, and leave your life of sin" (John 8:11 NIV). Jesus doesn't want His grace to blind us into thinking that it makes no difference how we live. He said, "Come to me, all you who are weary and burdened, and I will give you rest" (Matthew 11:28 NIV). Afterward, He would expect us to act on ridding ourselves of the old while we allow Him to work on creating something entirely new in our life.

Reflection

Have you ever given anyone the impression that any behavior is acceptable as long as they come to the Lord? How might you give serious thought as to how you interpret the gift of God's grace to others?

AUGUST 27
(Y1, D35)

And Pray We Must

Tell God what you need, and thank him for all he has done.

—Philippians 4:6 (NLT)

As I walked to the door of my sunroom, I looked out toward the yard. About twenty-five feet away, there was one of my neighbors crawling on the sidewalk next to the street. He was following his young son, who couldn't be much more than two, doing the same thing. I opened the door and yelled across the lawn, "Where is a camera when you need one?" The neighbor just laughed as his son looked back toward me. Then the boy said, "Come out and crawl with us." Thinking I needed to say something appropriate, I simply replied, "Maybe some other time." As I went back into the house, I chuckled to myself. Then I began thinking how wonderful it was that this father, wearing shorts, would get down on his bare knees and crawl on a cement sidewalk simply to engage in meaningful play with his son.

On one occasion, I was talking with someone about a prayer list I maintain so that I can remember names and situations of those in need. They asked how I find out about these people. "It's interesting," I replied. "When people know you pray for others, they will often give you their specifics and ask you to pray for them as well." There are times I have received names for my list as I take a walk around the neighborhood while allowing myself to become engaged in conversation. It's amazing how often I have been told by an individual for whom I had been praying, "You know I knew someone was because I could feel it." I understood what they meant because there were times when I had been on the receiving end of the prayers of others and could sense them as well. There are those who have told me that they really didn't know how to talk to God as though it was some kind of sophisticated or formalized process. The next time this happens, I will use the example of the neighborhood father and his young son as an illustration. For you see, our conversations with God are not much different than that of a child desiring to be recognized by a loving father who is more than willing to meet them at their level.

When we feel we lack an understanding of how to pray, the Apostle Paul reassures us that the Holy Spirit will search our hearts and pray for us in ways beyond our ability to articulate. He says, "If we don't know how or what to pray, it doesn't matter. He does our praying in and for us, making prayer out of our wordless sighs, our aching groans (Romans 8:26 MSG). The important thing to understand is that God wants us to pray and to recognize that our prayers are not for Him but rather for us. For when we pray to our heavenly Father, we are acknowledging that He is important in our lives. Prayer places the ordinary details of life into divine perspective. In the opening evening of the 2020 Republican National Convention, Cardinal Timothy Dolan of New York began the proceedings with a prayer. Delivered with an image of the New York harbor and the Statue of Liberty in the background, He prayed for our nation with the all-embracing theme "Pray We Must."

In prayer, we are invited by the living God to approach Him in intimate conversation, thereby entering into a deepening relationship with Him. While we should pray specifically for ourselves and for others in need, there will also be times we must pray for the greater good. When we feel that we are living in a nation divided, we must pray for healing. When we hear about missionaries in other countries being persecuted or the right of others to pray in public places being denied, we must pray for those who are suffering for His sake. Who knows how our prayers might serve as comfort to those who are in harm's way such as members of the military, emergency responders, or disaster relief workers? Whether one is a new believer or an established one, prayer is a way to acknowledge who is really in control of our lives. When we become practiced at prayer, it becomes like breathing. Prayer is our primary means of seeing God at work, for "the earnest prayer of a righteous person has great power and produces wonderful results" (James 5:16 NLT). Bottom line, our heavenly Father will meet us where we are when we reach out to Him. If we want to make a difference in our life and the lives of others, pray we must!

Reflection

Have there been times you have stopped praying because you felt that God was not listening? How might you be more intentional in your prayer life, allowing for God's will? Are there occasions when you want to pray for a world situation but think it is too massive to make a difference? In what ways can you instill in others that the collective prayers of a few or many can be powerful?

AUGUST 28
(Y2, D35)

Let Us Do Good

For we are God's handiwork, created in Christ Jesus to do good
works, which God prepared in advance for us to do.

—Ephesians 2:10 (NIV)

Tunnel to Towers' founder, Frank Siller, often shares the story of his brother, an NYC firefighter who died while rescuing others at the attack on the World Trade Center on September 11, 2001. It was nearly twenty years later when he engaged on a 537-mile walk starting at the Pentagon, the site of another attack on the same date. On his way, his trek led him to the Flight 93 Memorial just north of Shanksville, Pennsylvania. Those on that flight were aware that the Trade Center towers and the Pentagon had been hit with commercial planes similar to the one they were on. The forty passengers on Flight 93 knew that the terrorists in the cockpit were going to kill more Americans on the ground, and they weren't going to let that happen. So they took matters into their own hands, making the ultimate sacrifice to control their own destiny in order that another occurrence might be averted. In a brief address at the memorial, Siller stated that "we must never forget. And we must lift them up and walk beside them. Let us do good."

Doing good is relative and certainly results from a variety of motivations. People often do the right thing for at least some of the wrong reasons. For example, they may care for an aging aunt out of compassion but also with an eye on a substantial inheritance. They marry a wonderful person out of love but also because that person will enhance their status in society. They donate generously to good causes of social concern but likewise because they will become known as a charitable individual. There is rarely a perfect motivation. Most of us are resigned to the fact that good actions frequently result from mixed motives. It might appear they are helping others, but in reality, it's sometimes just about them. Jesus had a lot to say about that:

Watch out! Don't do your good deeds publicly, to be admired by others, for
you will lose the reward from your Father in heaven. When you give to someone

in need, don't do as the hypocrites do—blowing trumpets in the synagogues and streets to call attention to their acts of charity! I tell you the truth, they have received all the reward they will ever get. (Matthew 6:1–2 NLT)

Deeds matter, but motives matter more. There is a story once told about a pastor who was preaching at an evening service when a mentally ill man walked down the church aisle, slapped him in the face, pushed over the pulpit, and sent the congregation into a panic. In a seemingly protective act, a church member lunged toward the man, stunning him as he was knocked over, and a further crisis was prevented. The next day, the pastor placed a call to the man commending his bravery. The man responded, "I wasn't trying to protect anyone. I was scared, tried to run away, and accidentally ran into him." What had looked like courage had, in fact, been cowardice. It *is* possible to do the right thing for the wrong reason. Seemingly good deeds can have impure motives. The Pharisees were experts at good deeds. They were trying to keep several hundred commandments and even more restrictions within the expanded Jewish law. But their expertise was in outward conformity rather than purity of heart.

Far too often, even Christians do the right thing for the wrong reason while keeping tally of their good deeds. They mark imagined points on their scorecards to prove that they're living with grace, hoping that a certain number of points will result in more love from Jesus. Scripture is very clear that we are not saved by our good works. Jesus' grace is not something to be won or purchased with points. It is far better when we subscribe to the philosophy that our behavior is an extension of the love with which God has blessed us. In doing so, our motivation becomes one of giving love to everyone unconditionally without making it all about us. Then, as we do good, we offer a sacrifice that pleases God (Hebrews 13:16) and draws others to Him (Matthew 5:16). It begins as we demonstrate our faith in Jesus as our Lord and Savior. But "faith by itself isn't enough. Unless it produces good deeds, it is dead and useless" (James 2:17 NLT). So, my friends, we must understand that doing good in and of itself will not get us into heaven. But it can be a step toward a more blessed life if done for the right reasons.

Reflection

How are you "doing good" as you experience God's plan for your life? If no one ever knows what you are doing (giving, serving, sacrificing), would you continue to do so? If others misunderstand or criticize your good deeds, would you cease doing them? In what ways might you help others understand that we should not become unmotivated to do good if those whom we serve fail to show gratitude?

AUGUST 29
(Y3, D35)

Beyond Belief

Do not let your hearts be troubled. You believe in God; believe also in me.

—John 14:1 (NIV)

As surveys come and go, they are often designed to influence consumer purchasing or political bias. Some have seemingly little significance, asking such things as who you would nominate to have their own reality show or whether you load your toilet paper on the holder in the over or under position. Still others offer trending information which should be concerning for those of us who claim to be believers. Pew Research Center telephone surveys conducted in 2018 and 2019 found that 65 percent of American adults described themselves as Christians when asked about their religion, down 12 percentage points over the preceding decade. Meanwhile, the religiously unaffiliated describing their identity as atheist, agnostic, or "nothing in particular" stood at 26 percent, up from 17 percent in 2009. In another survey, the American Worldview 2020 Inventory concluded that "belief in absolute moral truth rooted in God's Word is rapidly eroding among all American adults, whether churched or unchurched, within every political segment, and within every age group." Shockingly, that included American Christians, those who have historically pointed to biblical scriptures as their source of unqualified truth and their personal guide to how they should live their lives.

Beliefs are important because behavior is important, and your behavior will influence all your beliefs. Everything you do can be traced back to beliefs you hold about the world, and they contribute to how you react to the behavior of others. For Christians, the most important decision in life—trusting in the Lord Jesus Christ—hinges on whether we believe He is who He claims to be. Author Lee Strobel understands that. He was an atheist when he began investigating the biblical claims about Christ after his wife's conversion. Strobel said that he used his knowledge as an investigative journalist and Yale Law School graduate in an attempt to disprove her beliefs. After two years, he concluded that "Jesus just didn't claim to be the Son of God, He backed up His claim by returning from the dead." His best-selling classic, *The Case for Christ*, details his conversion to Christianity. The story of his journey was also made into a full-length movie released in 2017. Someone once said that we should know what we believe and also believe in what we know. Strobel provided confirmation that would become true in his own life.

In the book of Acts, we learn about another conversion. When Paul and Silas were unjustly thrown into a prison in Philippi, they didn't complain about their fate. Scripture states they were up at midnight singing and praising God. The other prisoners were listening, and no doubt, their jailer was also listening.

> Suddenly there was such a violent earthquake that the foundations of the prison were shaken. At once all the prison doors flew open, and everyone's chains came loose. The jailer woke up, and when he saw the prison doors open, he drew his sword and was about to kill himself because he thought the prisoners had escaped. (Acts 16:26–27 NIV)

And when he miraculously saw that Paul and all the prisoners were still there, he was quite shaken and very humbled. He was so open to God that he cried out, "'Sirs, what must I do to be saved?' They replied, 'Believe in the Lord Jesus, and you will be saved—you and your household'" (Acts 16:30–31 NIV). This event was his worst nightmare and could have meant the end of his life. But God intended that these circumstances would be the beginning of a new life. As a result, "the jailer brought them into his house and set a meal before them; he was filled with joy because he had come to believe in God—he and his whole household" (Acts 16:34 NIV). Would he be converted today?

In a country founded upon Christian values, it is obvious beyond the results of surveys that our culture is facing a crisis of belief. Americans look everywhere except to the church for spiritual and moral guidance. And those who express their faith publicly are frequently challenged to defend their beliefs. While appearing on a popular talk program, the Reverend Billy Graham's daughter, Annie Graham Lotz, was once asked, "Are you one of those who believes that Jesus is exclusively the only way to heaven?" Without blinking, she replied, "Jesus is not exclusive. He died so that anyone could come to Him for salvation." Jesus continues to seek people like Lotz who will display His strength, stand up for their convictions, and will do so each and every day—beyond belief.

Reflection

Have you been guilty of holding beliefs that you couldn't defend? How does your understanding of God impact your day-to-day judgments? When you stand at that crossroads of making an important decision, do you hold on to your beliefs? Or will you revert to a more comfortable position?

AUGUST 30
(Y4, D35)

At My Wit's End

But if we look forward to something we don't yet have, we must wait patiently and confidently.

—Romans 8:25 (NLT)

I was unsuccessful at anything I had tried. I wondered if I might be nearing my wit's end following the order of an appliance from a national chain store. Since the appliance was not in stock at my home location, I was informed that it would be delivered to my house the following week. That's when it all began—a series of events that ended up being a comedy of errors during which the anticipated merchandise would not be received. Dealing with the customer service and delivery personnel was horrendous. I attempted exhaustively to work through automated phone calls, responding many times to the same questions over and over again. On one attempt, I did get a "live person" whom I was neither unable to understand or was falsely promised that someone would return my call.

Throughout this sequence of mishaps, I tried to not become angry, but I was at the very least frustrated. While I had desperately desired to act with patience and kindness, the excuses and inattentiveness to provide a solution did at various points cause me to simmer. In times like these, we can either serve as a witness to our faith or provide a poor example of what no one would want to become. On one delivery attempt, I received the wrong appliance, and I took my frustration out on the truck driver. Eventually, I apologized to him for my level of exhaustion. He indicated that he understood and told me the story of a time when he made a delivery to the house of a lady who said she was on her way to church and had very little time. Because the process took longer than anticipated, she became verbally offensive and threw the delivery man's clipboard at him. He said that he calmly picked up the clipboard and said to the lady, "Ma'am, did you just say that you were on your way to church?" Oops!

Motivational speaker and self-help author, Wayne W. Dyer, once wrote: "Anger is a choice, as well as a habit. It is a learned reaction to frustration, in which you behave in ways that you would rather not." An Old Testament scripture puts it this way: "Control your temper, for anger labels you a fool" (Ecclesiastes 7:9). I am always partial to the counsel found in the book of Proverbs which states, "A hot-tempered person stirs up conflict, but the one who is patient calms a quarrel" (Proverbs 15:18 NIV); and "Through patience a ruler can be persuaded, and a gentle tongue can break a bone" (Proverbs 25:15 NIV). The Apostle Paul would challenge us with these words: "Therefore I, the prisoner of the Lord, implore you to walk in a manner worthy of the calling with which you have been called, with all humility and gentleness, with patience, showing temperance for one another in love" (Ephesians 4:1–2 ESV).

I recently heard that even though there are regulations governing the weight and length of the bats players use in major league baseball, some players shave the handles of their equipment. Doing so to an extreme could contribute to what has become an increasing number of broken bats, which combined with a healthy swing will not only fly uncontrollably at other players but also dangerously into the stands toward fans. This example could serve as an analogy for what happens when an individual becomes frustrated, allowing anger to surface to the breaking point where they meet their wit's end. The Bible tells us: "They reeled and staggered like drunkards and were at their wits' end" (Psalm 107:27 NLT). Scripturally speaking, when we reach our wit's end, we waver in our personal devotion to God. It is then that we are no longer able to depend on our own wisdom and what we know to be true. We must rely on our faith, and that's not a bad place to turn. For when we exercise our faith with confidence, God will provide the solution before we ever come close to our breaking point and the reaching of our wit's end. We just have to know when it's time to invite Him in. The sooner, the better.

Reflection

Are there times that your lack of patience has served as a poor example to others? When is the last time you allowed your impatience to turn into anger? Were you able to control your emptions and ask for God's intervention in the situation? How might the words you serve as an example to others the next time you face a difficult situation where you feel like you are not being heard?

AUGUST 31
(Y5, D35)

A Demonstration of True Tolerance

Love does not delight in evil but rejoices with the truth.

—1 Corinthians 13:6 (NIV)

It was good to see my friend as we bumped into each other in the parking lot of a local grocery store. We had developed a friendship when we worked together as colleagues for a former employer for which my friend said she could never work again. When I questioned her, she stated that she had developed an intolerance for the work ethic of some of the persons with whom she had supervised. Finding it difficult to work there, she found another job and was now able to provide services on a one-to-one basis while not compromising her own values. I was happy for my friend, recognizing that not everyone would be in a position to act as she did. Unfortunately, conceding one's personal ethics to a lower standard has become a reality for many who are forced to tolerate today's "anything goes" culture. The word has taken on many meanings over time. Not so long ago, tolerance meant to acknowledge that there are those who have differing beliefs and that they have the right to those beliefs. More recently, however, the word *tolerance* has come to imply you must accept the beliefs that others hold which are different than your own. To do this, you may have to concede in order to keep the peace.

The Lord uniquely created each of us with our own personalities and preferences; therefore, we won't always agree with one another. However, this doesn't mean that we are unable to be loving and respectful to each other despite our differences. Those who consider themselves to be Christians must acknowledge that being labeled intolerant is at times a part of their faith journey. Suffering is expected when you stand up for what you believe is right according to the Word of God. "But in your hearts revere Christ as Lord. Always be prepared to give an answer to everyone who asks you to give the reason for the hope that you have. But do this with gentleness and respect" (1 Peter 3:15 NIV). Tolerance does not require acceptance of all ideas as being true; it is merely a willingness to listen. What is remarkable about those who say Christians are intolerant is that quite often, they actually fit the definition themselves. They are often the ones who are unwilling to grant equal freedom of expression to the beliefs or opinions of others. It is they who endorse the old adage, "It's either my way or the highway."

In the Christian experience, there are occasions when intolerance needs to be exercised. We should not endorse the modern beliefs that all roads lead to God that truth is one's personal concept or that everyone's beliefs are valid. Jesus was loving and associated with all kinds of people. However, He confronted immoral behavior and never instructed us to accept other religions as being true. In some situations, Christ was the most tolerant, broad-minded man who ever lived. But on other occasions, He was quite intolerant. He emphatically stated: "I am the way and the truth and the life. No one comes to the Father except through me" (John 14:6 NIV). We must always keep in mind that there are lost people who need to hear the truth about Jesus. Like the Apostle Paul, we are called to become all things to all people in order that by our words and actions many will come to know the Lord. For he said, "I try to find common ground with everyone, doing everything I can to save some" (1 Corinthians 9:22 NLT).

The Reverend Billy Graham is credited with having told the following story: "Once when we were flying from Korea to Japan, we ran through a rough snowstorm. When we arrived over the airport in Tokyo, the ceiling and visibility were almost zero. The pilot had to make an instrument landing. I sat up in the cockpit and watched him sweat it out as a man in the tower at the airport talked us in. I did not want this man to be broad-minded. I wanted him to be narrow-minded. I knew that our lives depended on it. Just so, when we come in for the landing in the great airport in heaven, I don't want any broad-mindedness. I want to come in on the beam, and even though I may be considered narrow here, I want to be sure of a safe landing there." As followers of Christ, we must give careful thought to show enough open-mindedness to encourage others to consider our faith. However, we must not be so broad-minded that we miss the mark and lead them astray. That, my friend, is effective witnessing. It is also a demonstration of true tolerance.

Reflection

Have you found yourself in situations where your tolerance of the actions of others has put you in conflict with your own Christian values? Would you be willing to take a stand in organizations to which you belong, if you felt there was an inappropriate amount of tolerance shown? How would you make the approach if that organization was your church?

SEPTEMBER 1
(Y6, D35)

All the Right Moves

So he fed them according to the integrity of his heart; and
guided them by the skillfulness of his hands.

—Psalm 78:72 (KJB)

Bobby Fischer is known as one of the greatest and probably the most controversial chess player of all times. At the age of six, he and his sister learned how to play chess using the instructions from a set purchased at a candy store. When the sister lost interest and his mother did not have time to play, Fischer was left to play many of his first games against himself. Once when the family vacationed in Long Island, Bobby found a book of old chess games, studied it intensely, and became a self-taught student of the game. Fischer's interest in chess became more important than school, and as his abilities were noted, he became a member of a chess club. He won the US Junior Chess Championship as the youngest ever Junior Champion at the age of thirteen, thereby gaining national notoriety. Years later on September 1, 1972, Fischer defeated Russian champion Boris Spassky in the most publicized world title match ever played. Bobby Fischer of Brooklyn became the first American World Chess Champion since its establishment in 1866. This allowed the title to pass out of Russian hands for the first time in twenty-five years. Fischer was once quoted to have said, "All that matters on the chessboard is good moves."

There are thousands of different chess moves waiting to be played. For the novice player, it may be difficult to know whether the move you are about to make is the right one. However, most good players are not only anticipating their current move, but they are also strategizing about the road ahead. A player who simply makes the moves he likes and hopes to win by random tactics usually succumbs to the opponent who has a plan behind his moves. When I thought about the concept of personally making every move a good one, my mind reflected on a recent walk I took with a friend of mine. The walking path which we use is along a stream in a local park highly populated with geese and ducks. Many folks from the area stop by the area to feed the ducks. This is fine, but when they do so, they frequently scatter their scraps over the walking path. In their obliviousness, they create

SPIRITUAL UPLIFTS FOR A RAPIDLY CHANGING WORLD

a "hang out" location for the various fowl who not only eat but also "eliminate" on the pathway. I remember smiling to myself, thinking that being cautious where we walk is very typical of life itself. If we don't look ahead and anticipate our next move, we can unexpectantly find ourselves stepping right into a real mess.

As followers of Christ, we are called upon to guard our every step as well. We must set an example for others, realizing that even an inconsiderate act or opinion can cause another to falter. It would be a bad move, for instance, to express a universal condemnation regarding divorce to a prospective church member and later learn that the person to whom you spoke it came from a divorced family. The Apostle Paul put it this way: "Therefore let us stop passing judgment on one another. Instead, make up your mind not to put any stumbling block or obstacle in the way of a brother or sister" (Romans 14:13 NIV). Faithful believers learn through time that life is not a game of chess. While it is prudent to carefully consider each move before we act or speak, long-range plans are really in the hands of God. Most of us will convince ourselves that we have the strategic plan for our lives when, in reality, we often do not.

The only way we can tell the difference between a good game plan and a bad one is in our time with the Lord. We want to be confident that the voice we are hearing is His. Jesus spoke this parallel:

> The one who enters by the gate is the shepherd of the sheep. The gatekeeper opens the gate for him, and the sheep listen to his voice. He calls his own sheep by name and leads them out. When he has brought out all his own, he goes on ahead of them, and his sheep follow him because they know his voice. But they will never follow a stranger; in fact, they will run away from him because they do not recognize a stranger's voice. (John 10:2–5 NIV)

The more we remind ourselves that God establishes our steps and plans, the more we can confidently follow Jesus and trust that with each move, He'll direct us. In a game of chess, the skillful player soon learns that developing an endgame strategy is important. The Old Testament scripture counsels us to "commit your work to the Lord, and your plans will be established" (Proverbs 16:3 ESV). When we master this, we will have learned how to make all the right moves in life.

Reflection

Are you careful to weigh your actions and thoughts in the midst of those you do not know well? Do you listen for God's voice and test the spirits (1 John 4:1) before you make important decisions? How might you use the concept of a chess game to counsel another who is strategizing about their future?

SEPTEMBER 2
(Y7, D35)

And You Visited Me

I will be your God throughout your lifetime—until your hair is white with age.
I made you, and I will care for you. I will carry you along and save you.

—Isaiah 46:4 (NLT)

The conversation I overheard was between two friends, one of whom was caring for her sick mother at home. She was speaking in a terse tone about her cousin who lived in another part of the state. The cousin, her mother's niece, recently drove past the town where they lived and sent a text that she would like to stop by to see her aunt in the next half hour or so. The daughter did not have her cell phone on her person and didn't receive the message until hours later. She was expressing frustration that the cousin could have been more considerate in allowing more notice to respond. The friend remarked that the whole episode looked like an afterthought. The daughter said that to her it seemed more like the cousin wanted to appear as if she was trying to fulfill an obligation but really wasn't all that anxious to visit. It prompted me to recall when my own father was fighting a terminal illness, some of his siblings pulled away. Either they were uncomfortable with his failing or they just didn't know what to say.

I remember the biblical story of Job who the Lord referred to as "blameless and upright, a man who fears God and shuns evil" (Job 1:8 NIV). God allowed Job's faithfulness to be tempted by Satan who said, "But reach out and take away his health, and he will surely curse you to your face!" (Job 2:5 NLT). God used the decline in health as a test and as part of His sovereign plan for Job's life. "When three of Job's friends heard of the tragedy he had suffered, they got together and traveled from their homes to comfort and console him" (Job 2:11 NLT). They stayed with him for seven days and nights and empathized with their friend in silence. Anyone who has spent time with a suffering friend knows how hard it is to remain present without grasping for answers. The silence of these three men did not last forever as they gave a series of speeches which included many inaccuracies, primarily involving why God allows suffering. Their overarching belief was that Job was in misery because he had done something wrong. A prevailing thought existed in that those days that if you were sick, it was a punishment from God. Many centuries later, the teachings of Jesus influenced a new way of thinking: "And the prayer offered in faith will make the sick person well; the Lord will raise them up. If they have sinned, they will be forgiven" (James 5:15 NIV). While Job's friends met their obligation by showing up, empathizing, and giving time, their repeated insistence that he repent so that God would bless him again was condemned by God (Job 42:7). In fact, following Job's suffering, God blessed him with twice as much as he had before (Job 42:10).

Recently, I heard a discussion of a nonfiction book *(Finding Chika)* by author Mitch Albom. While working at a Haitian orphanage, Mitch and his wife, Janine, became attached to a five-year-old girl who they decided to bring to their home in the United States because she had a sickness that could not be cured there. Due to her weakness, it became necessary for Mitch to carry the child from place to place. As time passed, he decided that he needed to return to his primary work. When the child questions him, he tries to explain that he has to do his job. Without hesitation, the little girl says to him that he has to stay because "your job is to carry me." After they embark on a two-year, around-the-world journey to find a cure, Chika ends up becoming a permanent member of the Albom family. Ultimately, there is a profound lesson to be learned from this little one. That is we become defined by what we carry. This includes our physical presence with a hurting friend, an effort that can be a great comfort in and of itself, even if we have no words to say. In one of His parables, Jesus demonstrated how we are to respond toward those who are oppressed in society. One of His central statements is, "I was sick and you visited me" (Matthew 25:36 ESV). When we are willing to enter into the pain of a suffering friend, we follow the example of Jesus. In this one simple act, we provide a living illustration and witness to His sacrifice to bear our pain and suffer in our place. When we absent ourselves from sitting next to one who feels forgotten, we must accept the burden of denying them our visit during their darkest hour.

Reflection

How do you respond when you become aware of someone who is suffering from health concerns? Does visiting those who are sick or incapacitated make you feel uncomfortable? How will you challenge yourself to work toward overcoming these concerns and do what you know to be God's will?

SEPTEMBER 3
(Y1, D36)

What Have You Done for Me Lately?

This is what I have observed to be good: that it is appropriate for a person
to eat, to drink and to find satisfaction in their toilsome labor under the sun
during the few days of life God has given them—for this is their lot.

—Ecclesiastes 5:18 (NIV)

Someone once told me that on the occasion of their retirement, they received the following written note in a card: "After your many years of toiling in the vineyard, you deserve to enjoy yourself by relaxing and reaping the fruits of the harvest and the wine." On first reading, that statement sounded really good, and my friend was sure that the writer meant it to be the highest of compliments after a successful career. But as he got to thinking about it, he wasn't so sure he wanted to rest on his laurels. While on the one hand he was done with the stresses of his lifelong career, he also believed there were many areas of work that would occupy his days ahead. As long as he was physically able to do so, he wanted work to be a part of his daily routine. Most of us work to maintain an adequate living during those years when the mind and body will allow us to be most productive. The ultimate goal is to save enough so that when you reach the golden years of retirement, you no longer have to work to survive.

These days, many workers feel that they are undervalued both in terms of their compensation as well as the manner in which they are treated by their employer. But that may not be new. Jesus told a parable about the workers in a vineyard (Matthew 20:1–7). He used the example of a landowner who went out early in the day to hire men to work in his vineyard. They agreed upon a wage, and the men went to work. At several points throughout the day, he hired additional workers, stating that he would pay them fairly.

That evening he told the foreman to call the workers in and pay them, beginning with the last workers first. When those hired at five o'clock were paid, each received a full day's wage. When those hired first came to get their pay, they assumed they would receive more. But they, too, were paid a day's wage. When they received their pay, they protested to the owner, "Those people worked only one hour, and yet you've paid them just as much as you paid us who worked all day in the scorching heat." He answered one of them, "Friend, I haven't been unfair! Didn't you agree to work all day for the usual wage? Take your money and go. I wanted to pay this last worker the same as you. Is it against the law for me to do what I want with my money? Should you be jealous because I am kind to others?" So those who are last now will be first then, and those who are first will be last. (Matthew 20:8–16 NLT)

Fair treatment and feelings of entitlement have obviously been around since the beginning of time. But never has the entitlement mentality been as rampant in our culture as it is today. The political pundits tell us that as elections draw near, the successful candidates will be those who promise the most free stuff. In doing so, they attempt to answer the question, "What have you done for me lately?" When we allow ourselves to be fooled by this kind of thinking, we should be cautious that it does not also affect our relationship with God; that is, developing an attitude that He owes us something. Just the opposite is true. God owes us nothing, and we should be ever-grateful that He doesn't give us exactly what we deserve. What He provides He gives out of His unbounding love and grace.

As we celebrate yet another Labor Day, we should recognize that there is no job beneath our dignity as long as it is honest work. We are truly blessed when we are able to find work that serves our fellow man and is equally a labor of love for God. The Apostle Paul says that it is not good to be idle. "We never accepted food from anyone without paying for it. We worked hard day and night so we would not be a burden to any of you. We certainly had the right to ask you to feed us, but we wanted to give you an example to follow" (2 Thessalonians 3:8–9 NLT). Those of us who claim to journey with Christ should likewise portray an accurate reflection of God's faithfulness and righteousness to the world. The risk for anyone on a different road is that they risk losing their path to God. They must realize that when they meet Him face-to-face, He may be the one asking the question, "What have you done for me lately?"

Reflection

How do you rationalize working hard in life whenever you see others experience gain from what you might perceive as unfair entitlements? In what ways are you able to express Christian love to these individuals? If you are part of a church or other organization that provides free stuff to those in need, what do you do and how do you avoid judging those who may be taking advantage of the system?

SEPTEMBER 4
(Y2, D36)

Resting in the Blessings of Work

Work willingly at whatever you do, as though you were
working for the Lord rather than for people.

—Colossians 3:23 (NLT)

During one election year, I heard a candidate promising he would implement policies that would improve the infrastructure in our country. This, he claimed, would result in the creation of many jobs. He stated that it was his belief that "most people want to work and be a productive member of society." I am not so sure this is true. While I believe most people want a paycheck, I am not convinced that the majority of people are really dedicated and happy in their work. Work is something which has become less appreciated and is often viewed as more of a burden than it is a blessing. In recent times, parents have come to believe it is their duty to give their children everything they possibly can, possibly attempting to compensate for the time they spend at their own workplace rather than being at home. This has caused at least some children to develop an attitude of entitlement because they have never had to earn their way. On the contrary, those who have learned to develop good work ethics find it is something which will carry them through their entire life, leading them to greater happiness and satisfaction.

When God created humanity, He provided a lush, abundant environment in which to live. "The LORD God took the man and put him in the Garden of Eden to work it and take care of it" (Genesis 2:15). Everything one would need was there for the taking except for the fruit of one tree which was expressly forbidden. But because of greed and defiance of this one rule, man was forced to labor. God said, "Cursed is the ground because of you; through painful toil you will eat food from it all the days of your life" (Genesis 3:17 NIV). Because of an act of defiance in obeying God's rule, this resulted in resources being attained only by hard work. However, the ability to secure what we need has continued to remain a provision from God alone. Even to this very day, we might find the work we do to be difficult and tiring. Nevertheless, we should continue to thank God for it because it His gift to us.

As Christians, we are not called to focus on ourselves or how important our work is or even how much success it will bring to us. We are called to do everything for the glory of God in service to others, including small, ordinary tasks. As you share the burden of your work with fellow believers, you'll find that you can actually accomplish much for the glory of God. In a loving fellowship of those who practice being beneficial to others, one might anticipate that the traps which sometimes result from idleness can be deterred. Paul shows us a way of life that is characterized by growth in Christ, and he presents working and sharing as a way to climb out of a dishonest way of life. "Anyone who has been stealing must steal no longer, but must work, doing something useful with their own hands, that they may have something to share with those in need" (Ephesians 4:28 NIV). The command to work hard and earn enough to give away some of the surplus goes a long way to beginning to understand the true meaning of compassion.

As we have opportunity to provide assistance to our families and in the greater community of which we are a part, we should be encouraged by the fact that Jesus values the time and labor we offer in service. We come to understand that while our work has purpose, we also need to find time for rest. Resting gives us the opportunity to revitalize and reflect. "For all who have entered into God's rest have rested from their labors, just as God did after creating the world" (Hebrews 4:10 NLT). We begin to realize we are not the sum of our accomplishments for our work is not ultimately what provides for our needs. God is our provider, and He is also the source of our true and deepest rest. By taking the opportunity to rest from our work each week, we are publicly declaring to ourselves and others that we depend on God's care. When we are restored, we will find that we are more equipped to make our work matter. As we recognize another Labor Day weekend, we should celebrate by putting our best effort into the blessings of personal work, whatever they may be. In doing so, we will find that it just might turn into a labor of love, and we will learn to deeply appreciate the periods of rest which follow.

Reflection

Do you find that there are times your life has become defined by your work? As you become immersed in the tasks of work, are you neglecting other parts of your life which are equally important? Are you practicing the rest that God intends for you? How will you give purpose to these areas of conflict?

SEPTEMBER 5
(Y3, D36)

Shadowboxing with Your Reputation

A good name is to be chosen rather than great riches, and favor is better than silver or gold.

—Proverbs 22:1 (NIV)

As they pulled the old paneling from the partitions in the basement of their recently purchased home, the young couple discovered that many of the two-by-four boards which had supported those walls for many years had words penciled on them. Occasionally, the words were singular in nature, but others were complete thoughts. It's as if they represented partial conversations. The obvious question was, why would someone write on that framing? If the current occupants knew the history of the house, they just might be able to attach a name to the scriber of those words. In researching the names of prior owners, they would find that they were written by a man who had the reputation of being an excellent carpenter. In his later years, he had lost his ability to speak. While helping to create living spaces in this, his son's home, he would communicate by writing on the boards. Who would guess that in the ensuing years those very words would resurface as a mystery, one which could be easily solved if you only knew the person?

What's so important about a name anyway? Does a name have value? Collectors of art will tell you that it does indeed. Even though there were past artists who rarely signed their work, its authenticity is identified by experts through detailed documentation. Like the house with the message on the wall boards, establishing the chain of ownership of a painting assists in the historical verification of its creator, thereby increasing its value. An artist's name on a print can increase the price by two or more times. Couples sometimes struggle for weeks and even months to find just the right name for their newly anticipated arrival. There are others who take the simpler route of identifying their child as someone's namesake. Two-time heavyweight world champion boxer, George Foreman, explained, "I named all my sons George Edward Foreman so they would always have something in common. I say to them if one of us goes up, then we all go up together, and if one goes down, we all go down together!"

Perhaps Foreman's many years of boxing provided great lessons about maintaining a reputation. He would have understood and implemented the practice of shadowboxing in his daily workouts. The technique involves the fighter literally boxing his shadow for the purpose of training and strengthening his muscles. All this as he primes for an engagement with a competitor in an actual fight. Paul used this analogy as He spoke about the Christian's preparation for the good fight and ultimate path to victory He states it this way: "So I run with purpose in every step. I am not just shadowboxing" (1 Corinthians 9:26 NLT). Acknowledging that his reputation of persecuting Christians would always be under the microscope, he knew that he could not afford to waste his punches by utilizing a lot of time and energy simply beating the air. There would always be those who would remember his past and ask, "Isn't this the same man who caused such devastation among Jesus' followers in Jerusalem?" (Acts 9:21 NLT).

Every so often, I am asked if I know someone to which I frequently reply, "I don't know them well, but I know who they are." Sometimes the manner in which I know them has been tainted by an assumed reputation. It's unfortunately true that what one does or says often burns an impression in another's mind. Once an opinion is formulated, it is difficult to change or erase these imprints from one's memory. The value others place on our name often reflects how sincere they think we are and can also have an effect on how they will interact with us. Knowing you for your true self is never an issue with God. Not only does He know our name, but He knows everything about us. God knows our character, because He understands our intentions and our heart. He knows our every thought, whether we express it out loud, decide to put it in a diary, or write it on a two-by-four. Our name is a marker. It not only identifies who we are but also *whose* we are. Like Paul, we need to stop shadowboxing and simply focus on Him.

Reflection

Do you focus more on what you have heard about someone (their reputation) or on what you have personally observed about them? How much time do you spend on concerns about what others might think about you (your reputation)? Are there ways that you might be more intentional regarding how God sees you (your character)?

SEPTEMBER 6
(Y4, D36)

Out of Respect: Stand Tall

Humble yourselves before the Lord, and he will lift you up in honor.

—James 4:10 (NLT)

"I do so, out of respect." That was the response of an older lady in our community who happened to be the mother of one of my friend's high school classmates. Each time she would see him and especially in his place of business, she would greet him using the title Mister. He reminded her that he had gone to school with her daughter and that she should just call him by his first name. She said that she referred to him as "Mister" out of respect for his position. As this story was related to me, I could tell that my friend was humbled and honored by this act of deference, even though he did not feel he was deserving. Showing respect in almost any form these days is a lost art and practiced by far too few of us.

When San Francisco 49ers quarterback Colin Kaepernick sat during the playing of the National Anthem, twenty-eight-year-old stated that he will continue these public displays out of support for African Americans and other minorities who have been treated unfairly. The athlete's actions were not unique. There is a long history of sports figures who have protested the anthem along with other "unpatriotic" displays. When these protests occur, the opinions are polarizing with regard to the appropriateness and value of their actions. Very few, including the NFL, disagree that in America individuals have the right to express their discontent. However, many verbalize that a team event might not necessarily be the most suitable time for such a demonstration. They argue that when you have been blessed by a nation which provides you with the opportunity to make millions of dollars, acts such as these are disrespectful, especially to those who have sacrificed their lives for our freedom to demonstrate. It does not come down to the question, "Can we do this?" It is better provided by an answer to the question, "Should we?"

Jesus revealed that respect comes in the form of loving those who persecute us (Matthew 5:44). He further explained, "If you are kind only to your friends, how are you different from anyone else? Even pagans do that" (Matthew 5:47 NLT). Love must endure, not only for those who do love us but especially for those who seem to be against us. The Apostle Paul spoke specifically about the Christian's respect for those in power.

> Let everyone be subject to the governing authorities, for there is no authority except that which God has established. The authorities that exist have been established by God. Consequently, whoever rebels against the authority is rebelling against what God has instituted, and those who do so will bring judgment on themselves… Therefore, it is necessary to submit to the authorities, not only because of possible punishment but also as a matter of conscience. (Romans 13:1–2, 5 NIV)

Does this mean that we must always accept what our leaders propose and do? Of course not. But in order to be an example for Christ, we must act in accordance with the direction found in His word.

Every year when we remember another anniversary of 9/11, we are reminded just how vulnerable we are as a nation. Another naïve sports figure made this statement, "When there's significant change and I feel like that flag represents what it's supposed to represent…when this country is representing people the way that it's supposed to, I'll stand." Within days of his words, a flag that was raised by three firemen over the rubble of Ground Zero in Lower Manhattan was returned to be placed in a museum there after being lost for many years. It serves to remind us that the privilege of living in the land of the free does not come without cost. Nor should it come without respect. As followers of Christ, we must lead in setting the example to show reverence for a nation that God established as well as the symbols for which it stands. Any other action should heed this warning: "If you think you are standing strong, be careful not to fall" (1 Corinthians 10:12 NLT). Stand tall, my friend, while you are able to do so.

Reflection

Have there been times when you have said, "I'll show respect when I see significant change"? How does remembering events such as Pearl Harbor and 9/11 help to put feelings and statements like these in perspective? As a person who is on a journey with Christ, what thought processes need to change in your life in order that you are more respectful in the public arena and thereby display a more effective witness for Him?

SEPTEMBER 7
(Y4, D36)

What a Heavenly Season It Will Be

For everything there is a season, a time for every activity under heaven.

—Ecclesiastes 3:1 (NLT)

If we are blessed to live a full life, we come to realize that not so different than nature itself, our life is defined by seasons. Every season is different, each having its own purpose and laying a foundation for the next. While the seasons of nature are somewhat predictable; the seasons of life…well, not so much. In the spring of our life, we are always trying to catch up with our wonderment, the chasing of dreams, and yearning for the hopes of a bright future. Summer is the season of productivity when we attempt to make our mark on the canvas of life. Often, these days pass us by far too quickly, and in our busyness, we seldom pause to take in the warmth of the precious moments. It might not be until autumn when we take the opportunity to reap the harvest. It may only be then that our life begins to reflect a tapestry, an intricate sequencing of events that for the first time begins to make sense. By this time, many have become grandparents, and what they have learned can be passed on to future generations.

In her book, *Everything Beautiful in Its Time: Seasons of Love and Loss*, Jenna Bush Hager, the former first daughter and granddaughter, shares stories about all four of her beloved grandparents. In the course of one year's time, she and her family lost Barbara and George H. W. Bush as well as Jenna Welch, her maternal grandmother and namesake. In her writings, she remembers the past, cherishes the present, and prepares for the future by reflecting on their "passed-on" wisdom that has helped to shape her life. In one passage, she recalls the family tradition of walking to the gate at her grandparents' home in Maine after dinner. Jenna says that there was no purpose for this beyond spending a moment together after a meal, getting a little exercise before bedtime. She writes:

> This is what life is all about. Until it's your time to enter the gates of Heaven
> and join those in your family who have died, you walk to the gates and walk

back. You hope that the sky is clear so that you can see the moon glowing over the ocean. And you hope to always walk with those you love by your side.

Our Christian journey also has its seasons. "Like newborn babies, you must crave pure spiritual milk so that you will grow into a full experience of salvation" (1 Peter 2:2 NLT). No doubt Peter well remembered a time when Jesus used the image of an aging person: "Very truly I tell you, when you were younger you dressed yourself and went where you wanted; but when you are old you will stretch out your hands, and someone else will dress you and lead you where you do not want to go" (John 21:18 NIV). He would caution us to recognize that life is short (James 4:14) and that the beauty of youth is soon gone (1 Peter 1:24). We should take joyful advantage of all the God-given gifts, talents, wisdom, and opportunities with which we are provided. As we transition through life's seasons, we should pause to consider that "the glory of the young is their strength; the gray hair of experience is the splendor of the old" (Proverbs 20:29 NLT). In doing so, we must recognize learning from a righteous elderly person is an honor and a privilege. We should listen to them intently and give them the respect that they deserve.

Christian author and speaker, Joyce Meyer, has stated, "We must remember there are different seasons in our lives and let God do what He wants to do in each of those seasons." Our activity in this world will be meaningful when we rely on His wisdom, His timing, and His goodness. While the seasons of our lives are not predictable in their intensity or length, they do point to one who never changes and is always dependable—the same, year after year (Hebrews 13:8). Even in those seasons of waiting and darkness, God is there walking with us and will never abandon us to face difficult times alone (Deuteronomy 31:8). Eventually, the season of winter will arrive for each of us. As it does, we will know that we have made it through to the conclusive season of this earthly life. Hopefully, we have transitioned well and find ourselves with a firm foundation of faith. Then we realize that our next spring will be one of life eternal as we stand in the presence of He who made us. What a heavenly season it will be!

Reflection

If you examined your life right now, what season would you say you are currently experiencing? Are you seeking ways to redeem your current life season for God's glory? How do you show respect and guidance for those who are in a different season of their life, one that you may not fully comprehend?

SEPTEMBER 8
(Y6, D36)

More Beautiful than You Can Imagine

Look beneath the surface so you can judge correctly.

—John 7:24 (NLT)

There was a time when September meant going back to school, experiencing temperature changes along with shorter days, enjoying football games, and on a particular Saturday night, one could hear the well-rehearsed refrain echoed from the TV: "There she is—Miss America." The song came at the end of the program when only one of fifty women representing each state in the United States was crowned, after each had been judged on their beauty by the millions watching. Originating in Atlantic City on September 8, 1921, as a "bathing beauty revue," the competition has not been without controversy over the years. In 1969, for instance, as the contestants walked across the stage, protestors unfurled a bedsheet from the rafters containing a statement that read "Women's Liberation." Some women shouted "No More Miss America!" over the crowd in the first-ever protest against the pageant. Outside, hundreds of women took over the Atlantic City Boardwalk, carrying signs stating "All Women Are Beautiful." The group condemned the consumerism surrounding the show and how the program valued a woman's beauty more than her personality. This may have resulted in the contestants later being judged on talent performances and interviews without a swimsuit segment or any consideration for physical appearance.

If we are fortunate enough to live very long, we realize that physical beauty wanes over time. This even includes that of former Miss America contestants. I love the story of the gentleman who, after many years of not attending a high school reunion, decided to go to his fiftieth. As he walked into the venue where the event was being held, he opened the door of the gathering area, went in, walked around for a few minutes, then left and went home. As he later relayed his story to a friend of his, the friend asked why he decided to leave so abruptly. He paused and thoughtfully planned his statement: "Well, I decided to attend because I was looking forward to seeing some of my former classmates. But, you know, when I walked into that room, all I saw was old people." No doubt we have all felt or will come to feel that way if we are graced with the gift of age. While we may not be able to see the beauty of age in our contemporaries, we first come to appreciate a different sort of attractiveness in our grandparents. Each September, National Grandparents Day is observed on the first Sunday after Labor Day honoring them and the special role they play in our families and communities. Who better than our grandparents to remind us: "Don't be concerned about the outward beauty of fancy hairstyles, expensive jewelry, or beautiful clothes. You should clothe yourselves instead with the beauty that comes from within, the unfading beauty of a gentle and quiet spirit, which is so precious to God" (1 Peter 3:3–4 NLT).

Someone once said, "Beauty is in the eye of the beholder." Literally translated, this means that the perception of beauty is personal and open to individual preference. What may appear as beautiful to one person may be far less than that to someone else. In this throwaway society, it has become far too easy to discard our relationships when we no longer classify them as attractive. We find that even our own self-esteem is at times based on how we look as we become occupied in a world obsessed with outward appearance. Sometimes we think we are not worth much on the canvas of life. However, nothing in a person's outward appearance impresses God. He looks at our inner beauty, the beauty of one's heart. In those times when you are feeling ugly and downright worthless, remember that you are God's Creation, and He thinks that you are His masterpiece. "Therefore, we do not lose heart. Though outwardly we are wasting away, yet inwardly we are being renewed day by day" (2 Corinthians 4:16 NIV). When you start to believe that you are anything but beautiful, be assured that you are "a keeper" in God's eyes. He sees you as more beautiful than you can imagine, and He is not finished with you yet.

Reflection

The Old Testament prophet tells us, "A voice said, 'Shout!' I asked, 'What should I shout?' 'Shout that people are like the grass. Their beauty fades as quickly as the flowers in a field'" (Isaiah 40:6 NLT). How can we learn to apply this in our life and be confident that we are beautiful to God? As you talk with others who fail to see any personal worth or attractiveness, can you help them understand that Jesus knows the beauty of their heart and He has made a great personal sacrifice for them?

SEPTEMBER 9
(Y7, D36)

Working God's Garden

You shall eat the fruit of the labor of your hands; you shall
be blessed, and it shall be well with you.

—Psalm 128:2 (NIV)

A neighbor of mine told me recently about a new piece of lawn equipment he had purchased. As he began to study the owner's manual, he noticed that every page continued boldly highlighted sentences accentuated with one of two words—*warning* or *danger*. After reading the many cautionary notices, he said that initially he was somewhat intimidated to use his new device. Then he chuckled a little and stated that he also realized it was the company's way of limiting their exposure to lawsuits. After all, if the risks were presented to the purchaser, then the manufacturer would have an argument that they made a good faith effort to "let the buyer beware." His story reminded me of a case I was part of many years ago as I served on jury duty. The situation involved a worker who had become injured while performing normal job duties. The verdict rested on whether or not the employee had received adequate training and had properly applied that training to prevent the injury he had sustained.

One of the greatest warnings ever was issued by God to Adam. "The LORD God placed the man in the Garden of Eden to tend and watch over it. But the LORD God warned him, 'You may freely eat the fruit of every tree in the garden—except the tree of the knowledge of good and evil. If you eat its fruit, you are sure to die'" (Genesis 2:15–17 NLT). A serpent tempts Eve, and through her, Adam, to eat from the tree of forbidden fruit. Because he disobeyed what God had commanded, God said, "By the sweat of your brow will you have food to eat until you return to the ground from which you were made. For you were made from dust, and to dust you will return" (Genesis 3:19 NLT). Note that in both situations, God continues to provide. In Eden, He provided abundantly. But when the earth was cursed (Genesis 3:17) following their temptation, they were banished from the Garden. Then Adam became forced to work the ground from which he had been taken.

Our relationship with Christ should be like a well-tended garden. We have to maintain a daily regime of weeding and watering in whatever labor God has set before us. Sometimes its tedious and tiring, but whatever our status in life, the work which God has placed before us is a gift. Whether we are a physicist or a janitor, a volunteer or a homemaker, a sitter for a young child or a caregiver to an older dependent person, the outcomes of your daily routine most likely benefit someone else. God would again caution us that whenever we are engaged in the task of helping others, we should do it to the best of our ability. Regardless of how menial we might feel about our work, we should never allow the weeds of life to choke out what He is doing for and through us. We should rejoice that every day is Labor Day, and one should "work hard so you can present yourself to God and receive his approval. Be a good worker, one who does not need to be ashamed and who correctly explains the word of truth" (2 Timothy 2:15 NLT).

Just like Adam and Eve, those who do not obey and are ungrateful for His provision will suffer from the consequences. When we are obedient and we choose to follow God's warnings, we will find ourselves in the shelter of His love. Sadly, most of the warnings God sent through His prophets were disregarded, and millions suffered terrible consequences as a result. Bible prophecy indicates that in end-times, our nations will not heed His warnings.

> For a time is coming when people will no longer listen to sound and wholesome teaching. They will follow their own desires and will look for teachers who will tell them whatever their itching ears want to hear. They will reject the truth and chase after myths. But you should keep a clear mind in every situation. Don't be afraid of suffering for the Lord. Work at telling others the Good News, and fully carry out the ministry God has given you. (2 Timothy 4:3–5 NLT)

Our ministry is that which God has set before us. We should regard it as a cherished gift and gratefully work His garden.

Reflection

Norman Vincent Peale once said, "Four things for success: work and pray, think and believe." Can you apply his wisdom to address areas in your life which would enable you to be a more effective servant? In what ways might you ask God to be more sensitive to His warnings and guide you wisely through your daily routine of work?

SEPTEMBER 10
(Y1, D37)

Grandma, Germs, and Grace

Create in me a clean heart, O God, and renew a right spirit within me.

—Psalm 51:10 (NLT)

I don't know about you, but I think grandparents are some of God's best angels here on earth. They are different from our parents, somehow not nearly as strict with us as they probably were with them. Every September since 1978, the first Sunday after Labor Day is celebrated as National Grandparents' Day. When I think of my own, I remember them with a special place in my heart. For a number of years, I have had a copy of a writing entitled *Grandma's Apron.* It talks about the apron which most of our grandmothers had used for many things: "drying tears, cleaning out dirty ears, carrying eggs and kindling as well as apples that fell from the tree, wiping a sweaty brow, as well as a last-minute dusting of the furniture when unexpected company arrived." It ends by stating that: "They would go crazy now trying to figure out how many germs were on that apron. I never caught anything from an apron…but love."

As much as I loved my grandma, I am sure if she was still around and had such an apron that it might make me anxious. I once went to dinner with friends I hadn't seen in a while but with whom I used to travel on a fairly frequent basis. No sooner had we ordered our meal, I pulled out an antibacterial wipe for each of us. It had now been a number of years since we journeyed together, but they laughed remembering how I always obsessed about sanitizing before I eat. Even though I washed my hands immediately before I left for the restaurant, God only knows what I may have touched since then such as my keys, the car, several doorknobs, and the menu. Those who know me well don't even think about playing that "ten-second rule" with me when food is dropped on the floor. And just why would anyone even consider "double dipping" their tortilla chip into the salsa once they had taken a bite off of it?

We do know for sure our world does contain harmful bacteria and viruses that if exposed to our body under the right conditions such as a weak immune system, our physical health may be compromised. Why, then, would we think that our spiritual journey would be any different? There are indeed secular contaminants, including those of doubt and unbelief that can affect our walk with the Lord. I am so fortunate that God doesn't look at me with the same set of eyeglasses through which I sometimes view the world. In fact, when I am unclean by the expressions of sin in my life and confess it, He purifies me with the blood of Christ. For, "In Him we have redemption through His blood, the forgiveness of sins, according to the riches of His grace" (Ephesians 1:7 NIV).

As Christians, we are faced with a dilemma: how to live in the world but also be detached from it. Some commonly referred to as being in the world but not of the world. "Therefore, 'Come out from them and be separate,' says the Lord. 'Touch no unclean thing, and I will receive you'" (2 Corinthians 6:17 NIV). While we are expected to have an influence on those around us and encourage others who are on a journey similar to ours, it is important to be grounded in the Word and pray for wisdom and discernment. Just as Grandma's apron may become physically unclean with the many things it touches each day, we too are affected by spiritual uncleanness resulting from exposure to sin. While water and good detergent may be used to wash away the physical dirt from an apron, the spiritual cleansing we need is not solely of our own doing. "But if we are living in the light, as God is in the light, then we have fellowship with each other, and the blood of Jesus, his Son, cleanses us from all sin" (1 John 1:7 NIV). Just like Grandma's apron reaching out to take us in, it's the ultimate proof that we are loved.

Reflection

Have you come to realize that spiritual cleansing is not something you can achieve on your own? In what ways have you experienced God's grace in your own life? How do you balance being in but not of the world? Would you be able to explain the concept of grace to someone who does not know Christ? In what ways might you be able to use the imagery of physical cleansing to explain the spiritual?

SEPTEMBER 11
(Y2, D37)

Strong Foundations in a Shaken World

When the storms of life come, the wicked are whirled away,
but the godly have a lasting foundation.

—Proverbs 10:25 (NLT)

In June, 2021, a thirteen-story condo in Surfside, Florida, partially collapsed in the middle of the night. Some engineers looking at the failure said the collapse appeared to have begun somewhere near the bottom of the building. Part of the structure first slumped, seemingly falling vertically in one giant piece as if the columns had failed beneath the midpoint of the building. Like a nightmarish avalanche, the failure quickly spread and brought down the entire center. Seconds later, another large section toppled. The catastrophe ultimately claimed ninety-eight lives, ranging from elderly couples to young children. It became the largest non-hurricane related emergency response in the state's history. Reasons for building collapses similar to this one often include poor repairs and maintenance, inadequate inspections, or an overload of structures that have suffered from increasing age and deterioration over time. When this occurs, an otherwise strong foundation can eventually become an unstable one.

Biblical scholars who heard of this event could not help but reflect on what Jesus once said in His parable of "the House on the Rock." He stated:

> Anyone who listens to my teaching and follows it is wise, like a person who builds a house on solid rock. Though the rain comes in torrents and the floodwaters rise and the winds beat against that house, it won't collapse because it is built on bedrock. But anyone who hears my teaching and doesn't obey it is foolish, like a person who builds a house on sand. When the rains and floods come and the winds beat against that house, it will collapse with a mighty crash. (Matthew 7:24–27 NLT)

Jesus teaches the importance of building one's house (our lives) on solid ground. When everything is going well and life is great, a weak or shaky foundation won't reveal itself. But in the real world—stress, anxiety, problems, and struggles come at us almost daily if not more often. It is on those very occasions when the winds are howling and the rain is beating down on our houses that we will become keenly aware of how firm and sure our foundation is or isn't.

On September 11, 2001, the United States of America experienced a massive surprise attack. Foreign terrorists hijacked commercial airplanes and used them as missiles to fly into and topple buildings, including the Twin Towers in New York City. While it grieved the nation to learn of the thousands of lives tragically lost, it did cause some persons to reflect about their total dependence on God. It's easy to take life for granted and assume that we have the power to control our own destiny. We are at times quickly reminded that safety in this world is an illusion, and everything we know can be destroyed in a moment. While worldly circumstances have an effect on us, they cannot control the heart of a believer who understands that security comes only in the arms of an Almighty God. Too often we ignore the words of the prophets until the reality of their words hit home. We read: "Therefore, this is what the Sovereign LORD says: "Look! I am placing a foundation stone in Jerusalem, a firm and tested stone. It is a precious cornerstone that is safe to build on. Whoever believes need never be shaken" (Isaiah 28:16 NLT).

Although we need to have courage to face the fact that our foundations will at times tremor, we must display unwavering faith in God's ability to see us through. It's an opportunity to witness to others that God reigns and provides peace and refuge, even in the midst of panic and fear. Jesus tells us that hearing and living His words will empower us to withstand these forces. In a parallel account of His teaching on the "House on a Rock," we are reminded that "the torrent struck that house but could not shake it, because it was well built" (Luke 6:48 NIV). When we stand on the rock of the one who created, redeems, and sustains us, we will discover when the quaking stops, nothing will have been moved. For the Lord remains on the throne no matter what (Psalm 93:1–2). Bottom line, my friends, hold on to the fact that when the foundations are shaken, what we are hoping for and in is all that will really matter.

Reflection

Can you think of any worldly foundation that cannot be shaken? Consider the foundations of our culture which are being undermined and on shaky ground. What would happen if the moral foundations of our society and biblical standards were destroyed? In what ways will you endeavor to encourage others to formulate and defend strong foundations in their own lives and of those they love?

SEPTEMBER 12
(Y3, D37)

It's All in Who You Know

What is more, I consider everything a loss because of the surpassing worth of
knowing Christ Jesus my Lord, for whose sake I have lost all things.

—Philippians 3:8 (NIV)

As we approach the weekend in which we celebrate Grandparent's Day, I am grateful for having known all four of my grandparents. They were unalike, but there were things I likely learned from each of them. I can appreciate the lyrics of "A Song for Grandma and Grandpa" (Johnny Prill) which, in part, go something like this: "Spending time together, talking on the phone/Happy birthday presents, chocolate ice cream cones/Photographs and memories, picnics and parades/saying that you love me in so many ways." As I reflect on his words, my recollections are similar. I am also conscious of the fact that this celebration falls closely each year to the 9/11 remembrance. I think about the missed relationship opportunities of the grandchildren of the many victims who will never have a chance to have grandparent memories like mine. While the official flower of National Grandparent's Day is the forget-me-not, it would be difficult to apply that to someone you never really knew, except for the legacy that they died far too soon.

As we go through life, we often hear the phrase "It's not what you know, it's who you know." The expression usually has a negative connotation as it applies to what someone has to do to get ahead in the world. I once had a boss who told me that one of my greatest attributes was the ability to surround myself with good people because they, in turn, made me look good. I took that as the compliment I hope she meant it to be. It's always interesting to watch presidential candidates and listen to their responses to some of the questions. When asked about their level of knowledge in certain areas, they often reply that they too would surround themselves with people who are experts in the field since there is not any one person can be expected to know everything. I recall an occasion when one of the candidates was asked to differentiate himself from the front-runner. His response: "I've realized where my success has come from and I don't in any way deny my faith in God. And I think that is the big difference."

These are some pretty fine words from a political candidate and would seem to support the following scripture found in the Old Testament.

> Thus says the LORD, "Let not a wise man boast of his wisdom, and let not the mighty man boast of his might, let not a rich man boast of his riches; but let him who boasts boast of this: that he understands and knows Me, that I am the LORD who exercises loving kindness, justice and righteousness on earth; for I delight in these things," declares the LORD. (Jeremiah 9:23–24 ESV)

As part of His Sermon on the Mount, Jesus spoke of false prophets. He said:

> Thus by their fruit you will recognize them. Not everyone who says to Me, "Lord, Lord," will enter the kingdom of heaven, but he who does the will of My Father who is in heaven will enter. Many will say to me on that day, "Lord, Lord, did we not prophesy in Your name, and in Your name cast out demons, and in Your name perform many miracles?" And then I will declare to them, "I never knew you." (Matthew 7:20–23 NIV)

Will it make a difference who we know? In fact, it does. Our total being is significantly comprised from the influence that others have had upon our lives. If we have been fortunate along our journey to have the opportunity to experience healthy, loving relationships with our parents and grandparents, then we have most certainly been blessed. If we have learned to surround ourselves with good people who bring out the best in us through open and honest interactions, then we have been doubly blessed in this lifetime. Finally, if in our walk we have come to know Jesus in a personal way, then we have been blessed threefold for all of eternity. While praying, Jesus said, "Now this is eternal life: that they know you, the only true God, and Jesus Christ, whom you have sent" (John 17:3 NIV). When Jesus spoke those words, they were for each and every one of us. It does, in fact, matter who you know; it will matter not only for the rest of this life but for the next one as well.

Reflection

Have there been times when your earthly relationships have become more important than heavenly ones? If that has changed, what were the events that caused you to refocus? Moving forward, how will you keep that concentration in proper perspective? In what situations might you share the words of Rick Warren: "You discover your identity and purpose through a relationship with Jesus Christ"?

SEPTEMBER 13
(Y4, D37)

Contentment

That is why, for Christ's sake, I delight in weaknesses, in insults, in hardships,
in persecutions, in difficulties. For when I am weak, then I am strong.

—2 Corinthians 12:10 (NIV)

I had the occasion to run into a guy with whom I used to work. When I asked him how he was doing, he answered positively, stating that in his five years with the same employer he had only missed a few days. I replied with an encouraging statement that maybe he should take some additional courses in order to advance within the organization. His reply to me was brief: "I am content where I am." I'm not sure what that meant to him or if he truly understood what he had said. He is fairly young, so maybe he is just naive. Possibly his remark surfaced because he was with his girlfriend at the time and was in some state of romantic bliss. Or just perhaps he might be a much deeper thinker than I ever thought. However, I did find his use of the word *content* to be an interesting choice.

It's always revealing to hear conversations between parents and their children in times of discontent. In the grocery store, a candy bar at the checkout counter can invoke a plea by the youngster as to how very much they "need" that sweet treat. Many times in life, we fail to distinguish between want and need, and sometimes it gets reinforced at a rather young age. The craving for wants doesn't seem to wane for many of us as we mature. The "gotta have it" mentality has been demonstrated by hundreds who have lined up around the Apple Store in New York City to purchase a product they hadn't even seen. The "keeping up with the Joneses" lifestyle is only heightened when advertisers promote merchandise in which actors who portray neighbors tell us that we can't touch their new car. This is followed by the simple catch phrase "You've got to get your own."

As we navigate through our journey, we often find that when we find ourselves to be discontented, we attempt to fill the void with things. Seldom does the acquisition of stuff make us feel any less empty. Socrates is quoted as having said, "He is rich who is content with the least; for contentment is the wealth of nature." With our basic needs met, we most likely have more than enough but have just not personally endorsed that fact into our way of thinking. For the Christian, the answer should be obvious as to how we find contentment in a world that is full of discontent. We move closer to God. Paul said, "But godliness actually is a means of great gain when accompanied by contentment. For we have brought nothing into the world, so we cannot take anything out of it either. If we have food and covering, with these we shall be content" (1 Timothy 6:6–8 NASB).

While the definition of contentment implies satisfaction with one's situation or with what one has, it does not necessarily mean that we are always happy. After all, can a person who has just received their walking papers or a terminal diagnosis be thrilled? Of course not. There can, however, be an achieved level of acceptance and eventual contentment if one comes to the realization that God is in control. Again, Paul understood this when he wrote to the church at Philippi:

> I am not saying this because I am in need, for I have learned to be content whatever the circumstances. I know what it is to be in need, and I know what it is to have plenty. I have learned the secret of being content in any and every situation, whether well fed or hungry, whether living in plenty or in want. I can do all this through him who gives me strength. (Philippians 4:11–13 NIV)

So it all comes down to this—when our human desires match up with what God desires, only then can we be truly certain that we are content.

Reflection

What are the things of life that make you feel content? Absent from those, how do you work toward a higher level of fulfillment? Consider the following quote: "Until you make peace with who you are, you will never be content with what you have" (Dorothy Mortman). Are there ways you can apply this understanding in your own life? Can you provide an example for others to show you are have been able to find contentment even during the struggles of your personal journey?

SEPTEMBER 14
(Y5, D37)

Absolute Selflessness

Do not withhold good from those who deserve it when it's in your power to help them.

—Proverbs 3:27 (NLT)

The story has been told of a young boy who had a sister with a rare, life-threatening illness not much older than himself. Since the brother once had the same disease and developed antibodies, it was determined that a transfusion using the boy's blood would be beneficial in helping his sister to recover. When the doctor explained the situation to the young child, he carefully assessed the brother's willingness to participate. After processing what he had been told, he said, "Sure, if it will keep my sister from dying." As the staff began to perform the transfusion, the boy rested in bed next to his sister. Thoughtfully, looking up at the doctor, he spoke these words in a trembling voice, "Will I begin to die right away?" Apparently, through all of the detailed information, the boy thought he would have to give all of his blood thereby sacrificing his own life in the process. In his concern for helping someone whom he loved, he failed to understand that his own health would not be affected. What a selfless act.

As we shed the innocence of childhood, we often become more selfish. At times, however, in the wake of a tragedy, there are some caring souls who surprise us. Florida resident Pam Brekke had spent days hunting a generator before 2017's Hurricane Irma made landfall. For her, it wasn't just a matter of convenience—it was a matter of life or death. Then she became aware that an area store had received a shipment of several hundred generators. After driving over thirty miles to buy one, she took her place in line at the store to find that the person immediately ahead of her received the last one. Brekke started crying, thinking about returning home empty-handed to a father who would need oxygen if the power went out. But then a random act of kindness. Without asking a single question, Ramon Santiago walked up to Brekke and handed her his generator. They hugged, and Brekke thanked him for his act of kindness during such a trying time. She said, "God will bless that man." Santiago later stated he did "really believe that God played a role in all of this." He affirmed what Paul wrote to the Church at Philippi: "For God is working in you, giving you the desire and the power to do what pleases him" (Philippians 2:13 NLT).

The story is told in two separate accounts of the New Testament about an observation made by Jesus in the Temple as "he watched the rich people dropping their gifts in the collection box. Then a poor widow came by and dropped in two small coins. 'I tell you the truth,' Jesus said, 'this poor widow has given more than all the rest of them. For they have given a tiny part of their surplus, but she, poor as she is, has given everything she has'" (Luke 21:1–4 NLT). According to Mark 12:41, "Many rich people put in large amounts," so they were bound to be noticed by others. However, Jesus emphasized what no one else saw—the humble offering of a poor widow. The placement of her few coins was the gift that was noted in heaven out of the many who gave that day. She was the one who had sacrificed. What she gave was very little in comparison, but her faith demonstrated confidence that God would use it.

Contrary to what our culture teaches, this life is not about us. It's about Him. The choice we make between selfishness and selflessness has an effect on every part of who we are and how we view life. In our self-focused society, it has become easy to justify those selfless acts are extreme and unnecessary. We then grow comfortable and accustomed to doing the bare minimum in order to make ourselves feel good. It is only when we realize that all we have comes from Him that we can learn to silence our selfish ways. In his devotional classic, *My Utmost for His Highest*, Oswald Chambers penned this thought: "We will never know the joy of self-sacrifice until we surrender in every detail of our lives." Jesus is our example. "He must become greater and greater, and I must become less and less" (John 3:30 NLT). That is absolute selflessness. The boy, the man, and the widow each gave it a try. You can too!

Reflection

Do you consider others before you consider yourself or do you often find yourself at the center of your own universe? When you woke up this morning, did you think about your day as belonging to you or to the one who created you? Would you be willing to ask God to reveal and help you change areas of your life in which you are focused more on yourself than you are on others?

SEPTEMBER 15
(Y6, D37)

Diamond in the Rough

He has shown you, O mortal, what is good. And what does the LORD require of you? To act justly and to love mercy and to walk humbly with your God.

—Micah 6:8 (NIV)

This leading scripture by the Old Testament prophet is said to have been a favorite of Theodore Roosevelt who became the twenty-sixth president of the United States under tragic conditions on September 14, 1901. As the vice-president, he succeeded President William McKinley who died from a gunshot eight days earlier. Theodore Roosevelt came from a high-society New York City family, wealthy descendants of the first Dutch families who settled Manhattan. By the age of twenty-five, he had accomplished more than many men twice his age. Over the prior two years, he had become one of the leading lights of the New York Legislature. But social status could not protect him from personal tragedy. On Valentine's Day, 1884, both Roosevelt's mother, age forty-eight, as well as his twenty-two-year-old wife passed away. Later that year, he relocated to the Dakota Badlands where he hoped to grieve their loss, launch a career as a writer, and mend some personal health issues he had developed as a child. Theodore Roosevelt presented as a rather poor candidate for acceptance into the Western fold; however, ranch life eventually brought him the health and strength that had long eluded him. In his autobiography, Roosevelt wrote of the Badlands, "I owe more than I can ever express to the West, which of course means to the men and women I met in the West."

No doubt you have at one time or other heard the term "diamond in the rough." This phrase is used when someone refers to a person who has exceptional hidden characteristics and future potential but currently lacks the final touches or finesse that would make him or her stand out from the crowd. Perhaps Roosevelt was a bit of a "diamond in the rough" despite his refined cultural upbringing. After all, it was his western experience and developed "cowboy image" that prompted him to conceive and exercise leadership in the Rough Riders cavalry unit at the start of the Spanish-American War in 1898. This experience also prepared him to become President of the United States at the dawn of the twentieth century. Like the cutting and polishing process required to form a precious diamond, Roosevelt's image is sculpted into granite stone at the Mount Rushmore Memorial in South Dakota alongside Presidents George Washington, Thomas Jefferson, and Abraham Lincoln. His friend, historian Henry Adams, once stated: "Roosevelt, more than any other man…showed the singular primitive quality that belongs to ultimate matter—the quality that medieval theology assigned to God—he was pure act."

A diamond doesn't automatically shine and sparkle. When it is uncut, it is rough and not at all like a diamond found in jewelry. It has to be fashioned by someone who is skilled in cutting in order for it to glitter and reflect light. Although diamonds are rare, expensive, and highly prized, they are nothing compared to how God values us. Never forget that Jesus looked at an impulsive, uneducated fisherman named Simon and saw a "diamond in the rough" who he later referred to as "the rock" (Matthew 16:18). This very same Simon Peter said: "As you come to him, the living Stone—rejected by humans but chosen by God and precious to him—you also, like living stones, are being built into a spiritual house to be a holy priesthood, offering spiritual sacrifices acceptable to God through Jesus Christ (1 Peter 2:4–5 NIV). God could have shaped us as beautiful sparkling diamonds. Instead, He allows us to be "diamonds in the rough" because He foresees the ultimate creation of what we can become under His carefully guided hand. Pastor Rick Warren says, "God changes caterpillars into butterflies, sand into pearls and coal into diamonds by using time and pressure. He is working on you too." God charges us to become better, to grow, and to shine. Today, let us consider where we might need a bit of polish and think about areas that need to be cut away. When one yields to the master cutter, you will then be able to "let your light shine before others, that they may see your good deeds and glorify your Father in heaven" (Matthew 5:16 NIV). What was once simply a "diamond in the rough" will be no more!

Reflection

What are some areas of your life that remain like a diamond in the rough? After you have identified these weaknesses with the help of the Holy Spirit, do you trust God enough to grind back the flaws in your character while polishing those surfaces to being more like Him? How can we help others understand each one of us has imperfections that can only improve by the work of the Master's hand?

SEPTEMBER 16
(Y7, D37)

And You Invited Me In

I have never turned away a stranger but have opened my doors to everyone.

—Job 31:32 (NLT)

A sometimes overlooked story occurred on 9/11/2001, one that should never be forgotten. It happened as a result of the terrorist attacks in America but occurred instead in a small Canadian town of Gander on the island of Newfoundland in the North Atlantic Ocean. The village nearly doubled its population when it took in 6,700 people from nearly a hundred countries as thirty-eight planes were grounded following word of the attacks in New York and Washington. The local airport knew it would be impacted as it is the closest point between Europe and the United States. For five days, the townspeople provided meals, offered entertainment, and even invited people into their homes to take showers or make telephone calls. Their simple hospitality to the unexpected house guests (who came to be known as "the Plane People") drew worldwide accolades and even inspired a Broadway musical, *Come from Away*. The passengers who were housed in schools, churches, and community centers tried to compensate their hosts for their many kindnesses. But they were told, "Oh no, you would do the same." Maybe so, maybe not. Here, in this unlikely place, there was witness to the best of humanity on a day when it also evidenced its worst.

In the post-depression family drama, *The Waltons*, which aired for nine seasons in the 1970s–80s, the eleven-member household of three generations offered their home to anyone who needed it. This included runaways, gypsies, orphans, and folks who were stranded. They took them all in. While their offer of comfort and protection was admirable, our culture has dramatically changed since that time. Whether it's the person who rings our doorbell or a foreigner who stands at our nation's border, we have to be cautious these days as to who we let in. It's a bit ironic how one of the buzz terms for those seeking safe harbor has come to be referred to as a "sanctuary" while in the Old Testament, the sanctuary was described as "the Most Holy Place" (1 Kings 8:6). Let us consider that the term *hospitality* might serve as a more appropriate reference for these acts of kindness since there is evidence of its being regarded as an expectation in cultures from biblical times continuing through the early days of our own.

Indeed, hospitality is a virtue that is both commanded and praised throughout Scripture. In the Old Testament, we read of Abraham's humble and generous display of hospitality to three strangers. Wealthy and elderly, Abraham could have called on one of his many servants to tend to the three unannounced visitors. Yet the hospitable and righteous Abraham generously gave them the best he had to offer. And, as it turned out, he entertained the Lord and two angels (Genesis 18:1–8). In the New Testament, Jesus and His disciples depended entirely on the hospitality of others as they ministered from town to town. Jesus discussed the hospitable behavior of those who will inherit the kingdom: "For I was hungry and you gave me something to eat, I was thirsty and you gave me something to drink, I was a stranger and you invited me in" (Matthew 25:35 NIV). The early Christians were welcomed by persons like Gaius of Corinth who not only offered his home for Paul but apparently to the "whole church" as well (Romans 16:23). He was a great example of hospitality while likely doing so at great personal risk.

So how risky is it to be hospitable these days? It is probably not overstated to say that most of us are cautious about entertaining strangers. While we might invite an unfamiliar family from church or a new coworker at our place of employment into our home, we cannot ignore the fact that we are expected to be hospitable to those with whom we have absolutely no connection. As followers of Christ, we emulate His love and compassion when we show hospitality, not only to fellow Christians but even more so to the lonely and less fortunate. The writer of Hebrews reminds us not to "forget to show hospitality to strangers, for some who have done this have entertained angels without realizing it" (Hebrews 13:2 NLT). Biblical hospitality is something a Christlike servant cheerfully provides from the heart. It begins with a good attitude and is given to all without respect of persons. We are challenged these days to balance comfort and caution in doing so. But if we are to follow Christ's directive, we must find a way.

Reflection

What are some "cautious" ways that you might show hospitality to the less fortunate (such as volunteering at a local shelter/food pantry or inviting missionaries sponsored by a local church for dinner)? Will you give consideration to asking the Lord to use your gifts and talents in order to demonstrate hospitality in a way that is pleasing to Him?

SEPTEMBER 17
(Y1, D38)

Jesus for Lord and Savior

God has given no other name under heaven by which we must be saved.

—Acts 4:12 (NLT)

As I was reading the local newspaper, a headline in the "Letters to the Editor" column caught my eye. It simply stated, "Thanks expressed for saving life." Continuing to read on, I discovered that the writer was offering deep appreciation to someone she didn't even know. Apparently, while eating at an area restaurant, she suffered a choking incident. A stranger applied the Heimlich maneuver, dislodging the food blocking her airway. During the course of events which followed, the "hero" exited the establishment while emergency service personnel took over. In the ensuing days, she went back to the restaurant inquiring as to the identity of this individual. But no one there know who he was. Now in a last-ditch effort to offer her appreciation, she penned the letter in hopes he might see it.

While random acts of kindness occur each and every day, it is not often that we have a stranger to thank for our life. Such was the case for major league baseball veteran Neil Walker. During annual Roberto Clemente Day celebrations, the infielder often paused to remember that Clemente "literally saved my life." Neil's father, Tom Walker, pitched parts of six seasons in the big leagues, and he got to know Clemente while playing winter ball in Puerto Rico. He was coming off his rookie season when, on December 31, 1972, Walker was among a handful of ballplayers helping to load a small plane in San Juan with food, clothing, and medical supplies bound for Nicaragua. Clemente was to personally deliver the goods to ensure their safe arrival. Walker begged his idol to let him tag along on the trip, but Clemente urged him and several others to stay. About an hour later, the plane crashed, killing everyone aboard, cutting short the career of one of the best baseball players of his era. Had Tom Walker been on that plane, he would not have fathered a son, Neil, fourteen years later.

When I was rather young, our family and some friends traveled on several occasions to the Jersey shore. I had not yet learned to swim, so my parents insisted that I wear a flotation device around my waist. It helped me to lift over the waves not far off the beachline. In case I would get knocked over, it would also act as a life-saving device. As I grew in maturity and deepened in my Christian faith, I learned that there was another lifesaver whose name is Jesus. I learned to understand that He is the Son of God who came to earth and died in our place so that we might be forgiven and have eternal life. As scripture states, "For God made Christ, who never sinned, to be the offering for our sin, so that we could be made right with God through Christ" (2 Corinthians 5:21 NLT). Accepting Jesus as one's personal Savior means placing your faith and trust in Him. For no one is saved by the faith of others or forgiven by doing certain deeds. In order to receive this gift, one must personally act: "If you declare with your mouth, 'Jesus is Lord,' and believe in your heart that God raised him from the dead, you will be saved. For it is with your heart that you believe and are justified, and it is with your mouth that you profess your faith and are saved" (Romans 10:9–10 NIV).

Speaking of calls to action, the Apostle Jude used a vivid metaphor in describing the critical mission that every true believer has before them; that is to "save others, snatching them out of the fire." It is a paraphrase of what the church calls the Great Commission. Found in Jude 1:23 (ESV), it is also referred to as the "firemen's verse." Jesus calls each of us who have experienced His rescue to willingly put our lives on the line in order to help save others. "This is why we work hard and continue to struggle, for our hope is in the living God, who is the Savior of all people and particularly of all believers" (1 Timothy 4:10 NLT). It's a simple act of gratitude for all who have been given a lifeline to extend it to someone else. As I travel about and observe the front lawns and house windows of others, I find it particularly interesting that every four years at this time, people are boldly willing to place signs in an affirmation of support for a particular presidential candidate. I wonder how many of them know Christ and, if so, would they be willing to display such a public pronouncement for Him? Just imagine the sign as it might appear: "Jesus for Lord and Savior." He's got my vote. Does He have yours?

Reflection

Have you ever considered what is the worst thing that might happen to you by sharing your faith? In your circle of relationships, who might benefit from hearing your story of God's rescue in your life? Will you commit to finding an opportunity to share your story with this person in the coming days?

SEPTEMBER 18
(Y2, D38)

A Model Worthy of Imitation

Therefore I urge you to imitate me.

—1 Corinthians 4:16 (NIV)

Oscar Wilde once said that "life imitates art far more than art imitates life." Whatever the case, one thing we do know is that imitation exists in many forms. This includes jewelry made from raw materials such as inexpensive gemstones and high-end metal instead of silver or gold. Then there's imitation or faux leather which uses a material such as coated fabric or plastic composition manufactured to resemble the genuine product. Artists sometimes copy or imitate the works of other famous artists. Imitation can be controversial as noted by food experts who seldom recommend the use of imitation vanilla in favor of the more expensively produced pure vanilla. The more expensive variety is derived from orchids that produce vanilla beans only grown in a few places around the world. On the other hand, imitation vanilla is made from artificial flavorings which come from wood byproducts. Those with discerning palates usually find that imitation has a slightly bitter aftertaste, and they conclude that the purchase of pure vanilla is definitely worth the additional expense. Bottom line, imitation can be a good or bad thing.

It is recognized that imitation is how children learn. This can sometimes lead to embarrassing experiences for parents when a child repeats a phrase containing words they shouldn't say. Awkward moments can occur when imitation is misinterpreted. The story has been told of a new missionary recruit who went to Venezuela for the first time. While struggling with the language, he decided to visit one of the local churches. Arriving late, he found the church was already packed with the only seat open being on the front pew. So as not to make a fool of himself, he decided to pick someone out of the crowd to imitate. Choosing to follow the man sitting next to him, the missionary tried to do everything this man did. Throughout the service, the preacher used words the recruit didn't understand. During what he perceived to be the announcement period, he observed the man next to him stand up, so he did likewise. Suddenly, a murmuring hush fell over the entire congregation. Seeing that no one else was standing, he quickly sat down. After the service ended, the preacher stood at the door, greeting the congregation. When the missionary stretched out his hand, the preacher said in English: "I take it you don't speak Spanish."

The recruit replied: "No, I don't. Is it that obvious?"

"Well yes," said the preacher. "I announced that the Acosta family had a newborn baby boy and asked if the proud father would please stand up."

We have to exercise caution when we make a decision to imitate another. The Apostle Paul instructed, "Join together in following my example, brothers and sisters, and just as you have us as a model, keep your eyes on those who live as we do" (Philippians 3:17 NIV). On first read, this statement appears to be somewhat arrogant. However, Paul was not a proud man and considered himself the foremost of all sinners (1 Timothy 1:15) whom God saved by grace alone (Ephesians 2:8). He lived his life demonstrating a devout faith in Jesus, placing no confidence in his own humanity (Galatians 2:20). And yet he could say with humility, "Practice what you see in me." Paul is simply asking the people of his day to imitate him by living with the indwelling presence of Christ as the motivating force in their life. In doing so, he imitated the example of Jesus. He delivered this command several times throughout his letters, being the only writer of Scripture to issue such a directive.

We like to think that we are unique, and indeed we are. But it is also true that we all are always imitating someone or something. For that reason, it is important that we surround ourselves with the right people. We are told to imitate Christ, imitate mature believers, and to imitate faithful churches. Once a person becomes a believer, good role models become crucial. They are important for us personally and also as we serve in our witnessing to others. Our challenge then is this—in every context of life where God has raised us up, we should endeavor to serve Him as a model worthy of imitation.

Reflection

How would you respond if one of your leaders actually said, "Be imitators of me as I am of Christ"? Would you react negatively or with conviction? In what ways are you leading others closer to Jesus by what you say and do? If you feel inadequate of setting such an example, then what do you need to change? Which characteristic of Christ would you most like to grow and imitate for others to follow?

SEPTEMBER 19
(Y3, D38)

The Secret Things of God

"Can anyone hide from me in a secret place? Am I not everywhere
in all the heavens and earth?" says the LORD.

—Jeremiah 23:24 (NLT)

When we listen to our political candidates, elected officials, the boss at work, or our teenage children, there is often less concern about what they are telling us than what they are not. Admittedly, in many situations we are provided with information on a "need-to-know" basis. There are times in which we are not privy to facts because we are either not prepared to receive them or because they are not for public release. The Apple Company is notorious for keeping secret information about their new product announcements. In doing so, they create an advertising frenzy in anticipation of the uncertain. Likewise, details of war, employee layoffs, or providing information to a person with dementia about a death in the family are examples in which provided factual information might only create a potentially catastrophic reaction. Some things are best kept secret until the time is right, and that time may never come.

This past summer, I have enjoyed watching butterflies flit on and off my butterfly bush. Seeing them made me think of a story I had heard about an Indian legend that states:

> If anyone desires a wish to come true, they must first capture a butterfly and whisper that wish to it. Since a butterfly can make no sound, the butterfly cannot reveal the wish to anyone but the Great Spirit who hears and sees all. In gratitude for giving the beautiful butterfly its freedom, the Great Spirit always grants the wish. So, according to legend, by making a wish and giving the butterfly its freedom, the wish will be taken to the heavens and be granted.

Oh my, the secret wishes butterflies must have been told over the years!

We can assume that there are lots of secrets in nature beyond legend which are understood only by God. But be assured all of our secrets are known by Him. "Nothing in all creation is hidden from God's sight. Everything is uncovered and laid bare before the eyes of him to whom we must give account" (Hebrews 4:13 NIV). English clergyman and religious writer William Secker put it this way: "A man may hide God from himself, and yet he cannot hide himself from God." God knows our deepest secrets, and yet He continues to love us just the same. When we open our hearts to Him, we come to realize that it is not only the decrees of this world that require our attention but also the provision of spiritual laws which He expects to be obeyed as a demonstration of our love for Him. A great Old Testament passage says: "The secret things belong to the LORD our God, but the things revealed belong to us and to our children forever, that we may follow all the words of this law" (Deuteronomy 29:29 NIV).

To be sure, there are things that God will reveal to us. Then there are others which He will allow to continue to remain a mystery. With all certainty, those who love Him and serve Him faithfully have the privilege of understanding many things that will not be discovered by others. "The secret of the LORD is for those who fear Him, and He will make them know His covenant" (Psalm 25:14 NASB). Meanwhile, there will always be questions which remain: Why would God let that person die? Why would He allow suffering and war to continue? Why does He not answer my prayer? And the questions continue. The Prophet Isaiah provides at least a partial answer: "'For my thoughts are not your thoughts, neither are your ways my ways,' declares the LORD" (Isaiah 55:8 NIV). From this, we are able to conclude that there are just some things for which we are not meant to have answers, at least not in this lifetime. These are the secret things of God, and they provide for the beginning of our faith journey. For now, they only remain wishes that will hopefully one day be further explained by the Great Spirit of the heavens.

Reflection

How have you reconciled the fact that those personal secrets you have kept are known by a God who continues to love you? What are the secrets that seem to be maintained by God that you wish He would reveal to you? Are there ways you might explore biblical truths, in turn asking for God's guidance to provide you with a greater insight for what has seemingly, to this point in time, been hidden from your understanding? How would help others to appreciate that there are some things we just aren't supposed to understand in this lifetime?

SEPTEMBER 20

(Y4, D38)

The Next Chapter

Always be prepared to give an answer to everyone who asks you
to give the reason for the hope that you have.

—1 Peter 3:15 (NIV)

Two legendary broadcasters said goodbye to their posts one week in 2016. Charles Osgood and his ever-present bowtie bid farewell on CBS *Sunday Morning* which only two people had hosted for thirty-seven years. He often used his closing line, "I'll see you on the radio," as he ended the weekly broadcast. Within days, another staple of the microphone, eighty-eight-year-old Vin Scully departed his play-by-play duties for the Los Angeles Dodgers after sixty-seven years. Through all of his reminiscing, he never failed to make a call of what was happening on the field. In their own way, each of these men were exceptional storytellers. They have been succeeded by others, but their poetic voices and reassuring presence will never be replaced. They gave us pause to wondering what accounts might have gone untold as the notorious radio broadcaster, Paul Harvey, often did in his infamous "Rest of the Story" segments.

Great storytellers share the human and vulnerable side of others. They do so in a way that engage the listener to identify with the character, thereby eliciting an emotional, heartfelt, or motivational response. One of the best storytellers was Jesus, who had His own style of presenting a lesson.

His disciples came and asked him, "Why do you use parables when you talk to the people?" He replied, "You are permitted to understand the secrets of the Kingdom of Heaven, but others are not. To those who listen to my teaching, more understanding will be given, and they will have an abundance of knowledge. But for those who are not listening, even what little understanding they have will be taken away from them. Jesus always used stories and illustrations like these when speaking to the crowds. In fact, he never spoke to them without using such parables." (Matthew 13:10–12, 34 NLT)

Throughout God's Word, the stories of individuals who struggled in their relationship with God are unveiled. There are few more life-altering than that of Saul who stated:

> I used to believe that I ought to do everything I could to oppose the very name of Jesus the Nazarene. Indeed, I did just that in Jerusalem. Authorized by the leading priests, I caused many believers there to be sent to prison. And I cast my vote against them when they were condemned to death. Many times I had them punished in the synagogues to get them to curse Jesus. I was so violently opposed to them that I even chased them down in foreign cities. (Acts 26:9–11 NLT)

One day on the road to Damascus, he met Jesus who asked why he was persecuting Him. Subsequently, the converted Saul became the great Apostle Paul. Jesus said to him, "For I have appeared to you to appoint you as my servant and witness. You are to tell the world what you have seen and what I will show you in the future" (Acts 26:16 NLT). Thus, a new chapter in the life of Saul began, and his writings contributed to a substantial part of the New Testament.

We each have a story to tell, and until we take our last breath on this earth, ours is not complete. Your life journey is more than the family you were born into, how you were raised, or your achievements and experiences. It also includes the challenges and hard times you encountered along the way. They are the best part of your story. Chances are it was in one of those times that you first came to God, allowed the grace of His Son to transform you, or experienced a closeness with Him which you will never forget. Your story is unique, and as you travel down the road, you will find that He will interconnect you with others whom He has prepared to hear it. "And I am certain that God, who began the good work within you, will continue his work until it is finally finished on the day when Christ Jesus returns" (Philippians 1:6 NLT). As we draw close to the final chapter of our earthly story, we can be assured that the theme of the next chapter will be that of a happy and joyous life that will have no end.

Reflection

David said, "All the days ordained for me were written in your book before one of them came to be" (Psalm 139:16 NIV). How much do you trust God to write a good life story? Do you believe that he cares about each and every paragraph in the narrative of your life?

SEPTEMBER 21
(Y5, D38)

Could It Be... Satan?

> Stay alert! Watch out for your great enemy, the devil. He prowls
> around like a roaring lion, looking for someone to devour.
>
> —1 Peter 5:8 (NLT)

In the golden age of television, actor Flip Wilson kept America in stitches with his characters—Reverend Leroy, the pompous pastor of the "Church of What's Happening Now," and Geraldine Jones, the sassy lady in a miniskirt. Whenever Geraldine would impulsively buy anything she shouldn't, she excused her urge by uttering the line she made famous, "The devil made me do it!" Only a few decades after Flip Wilson's character first appeared, "the Church Lady" burst onto the scene. Created and played by comedian Dana Carvey, the Church Lady was a pious host of her own TV talk show, a recurring sketch on *Saturday Night Live*. The interviews presented an opportunity for her to call out celebrity guests or portrayals of public figures for their alleged sins who had been frequently in the news. In each case, the interviews culminated with her judgmental reprimand posing the question, "Could it be... Satan?"

These days, it doesn't take a very astute observer to see that the devil is alive and well. In today's world, however, it's far from a joking matter. The following analogy appeared in a December 1992 article from the devotional, *Our Daily Bread*. "In the Australian bush country grows a little plant called the "sundew." It has a slender stem and tiny round leaves fringed with hairs that glisten with bright drops of liquid as delicate as fine dew. Woe to the insect, however, that dares to dance on it. Although its attractive clusters of red, white, and pink blossoms are harmless, the leaves are deadly. The shiny moisture on each leaf is sticky and will imprison any bug that touches it. As an insect struggles to free itself, the vibration causes the leaves to close tightly around it. This innocent-looking plant then feeds on its victim. This is exactly what happens to us when we dare to dance with the devil, who has been referred to by some as the "great deceiver."

The Bible tells us that there was a time when Jesus "was in the desert forty days, being tempted by Satan. He was with the wild animals, and angels attended him" (Mark 1:13 NIV). On three different occasions, the devil wanted to take control of Him, but Jesus knew exactly how to handle the situation. "'Get out of here, Satan,' Jesus told him. For the Scriptures say, 'You must worship the LORD your God and serve only him'" (Matthew 4:10 NLT). There are times in our lives when we must do exactly what Jesus did. Paul understood this and provided this instruction: "Put on the full armor of God, so that you can take your stand against the devil's schemes" (Ephesians 6:11 NIV) for "he will not let you be tempted beyond your ability, but with the temptation he will also provide the way of escape, that you may be able to endure it" (1 Corinthians 10:13 ESV). When we find ourselves in one of these situations, it may be helpful to recall the words of the powerful evangelist, Billy Sunday: "Temptation is the devil looking through a keyhole. Yielding is opening the door and letting him in."

Most of our society fails to accept personal blame when they fall into temptation. Public figures often misconstrue the details of their transgressions, and in our own life, it can become easy to make excuses for our personal wrongdoings. Sentiments like "the devil made me do it" are used far too often to justify our own bad choices. James 1:14 (ESV) declares, "Each person is tempted when he is lured and enticed by his own desire." James continues, "Submit therefore to God. Resist the devil and he will flee from you" (James 4:7 NKJV). If you are a Christian and you commit a sin, the devil did not make you do it. He may have tempted you to do it. He may have even influenced you to do it. But he did not *make* you do it. You still had a choice. The devil is absolutely worthy of blame for much of the evil in the world, but using him as a scapegoat for our own sinful choices is counterproductive to achieving victory over sin. So the next time you feel tempted, you might want to carefully consider your situation and ask the question, could it be Satan? For, yes, it very well could be!

Reflection

In what ways are we being desensitized by the present evil world? Do things that once shocked you now pass us by with little notice? How can a Christian become more attuned to the reality of a personal spiritual conflict? What are some ways you might grow wiser in understanding Satan's schemes? Consider the words of Chuck Swindoll: "Where there is no temptation, there can be little claim to virtue."

SEPTEMBER 22
(Y6, D38)

One Life to Lose

Very rarely will anyone die for a righteous person, though for a
good person someone might possibly dare to die.

—Romans 5:7 (NIV)

Twenty-one-year-old Nathan Hale was forced to make a moral decision. Born in Connecticut in 1755, he was reared in a Christian home. His father, Richard Hale, was deacon in the local congregational church. During Nathan's college years at Yale, the colonists were in constant friction with England. He heard fiery speeches in behalf of freedom. By the time he took his first teaching job, war was a distinct possibility. Hale joined a Connecticut regiment in 1775 and served in the successful siege of British-occupied Boston. By written accounts, it is noted that while in the army, Nathan showed great character. When morale dropped, he divided his extra pay with his men. When his comrades became ill, he visited and prayed with them. When Washington sought a spy to penetrate the British lines to get information, Nathan Hale was the only volunteer. In the summer of 1776, Hale posed as a civilian and crossed behind their held territory on Long Island to spy on the British. Dressed in farm clothes and carrying his Yale diploma, he passed as a Dutchman seeking a school position. He went through the entire British location, estimating their numbers and sketching their fortifications. He took notes in Latin, and while returning with the intelligence information, British soldiers captured him near the American lines and charged him with espionage. He immediately acknowledged his true identity, as his notes were found in his boot. Taken to New York, he was hanged without trial the next day. On the morning of September 22, 1776, Hale wrote a letter to his mother and brother, but the British destroyed them, not wanting it known a man could die with such conviction. As he prepared to die, he calmly spoke. The last words attributed to him were "I only regret that I have but one life to lose for my country."

What are those things for which you would offer your life? Perhaps you would enter into a risky surgery that would save the life of someone you love. As a parent, you would run toward danger when you realize that your child has found themselves in a perilous situation. During your youth, you might fantasize about becoming a fireman or a police officer. Then you grow up to discover that those first responders are potentially placed into harm's way each time they are called to serve. The story was told of how author and speaker Brennan Manning came to better understand the deep love of God. Brennan had a best friend named Ray. They hung around, double-dated, and even bought a car together. In time, they enlisted and served in the same military unit. One day, the two friends were in a foxhole when a hand grenade landed in their midst. Ray looked at Brennan and quickly jumped on top of the bomb. It exploded and killed him instantly. Sometime later, Brennan went to visit Ray's mother. He asked her, "Do you think that Ray loved me?"

She replied by saying something to the effect of, "What more could he have done for you, Brennan?"

Jesus said, "Greater love has no one than this: to lay down one's life for one's friends" (John 15:13 NIV), and then He did just that when He died on the cross for you and me.

The truth of the matter is few of us will ever die for another person; however, all of us have the opportunity to put others first on a daily basis. Making others' needs more important than our own is the sacrifice expected of us when we belong to Christ. "If any of you wants to be my follower, you must turn from your selfish ways, take up your cross daily, and follow me. If you try to hang on to your life, you will lose it. But if you give up your life for my sake, you will save it" (Luke 9:23–24 NLT). Taking up our personal cross is a call to absolute surrender. Evangelist Oswald Chambers once stated, "It is much easier to die than to lay down your life day in and day out with the sense of the high calling of God. We are not made for the bright-shining moments of life, but we have to walk in the light of them in our everyday ways." Taking up our cross daily requires at a minimum that we will lay down our lives for others through sacrificial acts of giving our time, possessions, personal plans, and even asking the question, am I willing to follow Jesus if it means losing my life? As Nathan Hale so profoundly expressed, our only regret then will be that we only had but one life to lose. Except this time, it will be for the one who gave His for us.

Reflection

The Apostle Paul said, "For to me, living means living for Christ, and dying is even better" (Philippians 1:21 NLT). How might you apply his words in your walk with Christ? If there comes a point in your life where you are faced with a choice—Jesus or the comforts of this life—which will you choose?

SEPTEMBER 23

(Y7, D38)

Chasing Happiness

A generous person will prosper; whoever refreshes others will be refreshed.

—Proverbs 11:25 (NIV)

"Now listen to what I said, in your life expect some trouble. When you worry, you make it double." These are just two lines from the lyrics of the well-known Bobby McFerrin song, "Don't Worry, Be Happy." It wasn't only the song's acapella style but also its content to which millions of listeners connected. It seems as if our current culture is hardwired to pursue happiness. We're always looking for it, whether we realize it are or not. If it's bigger, has more bells and whistles, or if it just feels good, we assume that it will bring us happiness, at least for a while. For many, ultimate happiness ends up being based on an accumulation of more stuff, greater wealth, and the freedom to do what we want when we want. Recent surveys on American happiness conducted by the Harris Poll organization revealed that only one in three persons surveyed indicated that they were happy. But interestingly enough, the majority of the respondents shared that their spiritual beliefs were a positive guiding force in their lives.

The United States Declaration of Independence states we are provided by our Creator "with certain unalienable rights, that among these are life, liberty, and the pursuit of happiness." Therefore, happiness is frequently considered to be an entitlement. While Christians and non-Christians would no doubt agree that happiness should be a human goal, they should, however, disagree how this goal is best achieved. God loves nothing more than to make those of us who are chasing happiness truly, deeply joyful. Throughout the Bible, He shows us the path to happiness and joy is contained in the Holy Scriptures. A perfect example is when the psalmist says to God with evident delight: "You make known to me the path of life; you will fill me with joy in your presence, with eternal pleasures at your right hand" (Psalm 16:11 NIV). We must consider that when personal happiness becomes our "be all, end all," it controls the governing principle in our life rather than the Holy Spirit. When we strive for worldly happiness, the thought process in our decision-making is no longer "Is this right and pleasing to God?" but rather "Will this make me happy?" Conversely, the psalmist would attempt to convince us that joy must not be dependent on our circumstances but be reflective of God's Spirit who dwells within us.

Bestselling author Max Lucado provides a personal plan for a life filled with lasting and fulfilling joy, supported by Jesus' teaching and modern research. In his book, *How Happiness Happens: Finding Lasting Joy in a World of Comparison, Disappointment, and Unmet Expectations*, Lucado says that we actually find ourselves in our happiest moments when we are in the process of serving others. His thoughts parallel those of the Apostle Paul who said:

> You yourselves know that these hands ministered to my necessities and to those who were with me. In all things I have shown you that by working hard in this way we must help the weak and remember the words of the Lord Jesus, how he himself said, "It is more blessed to give than to receive." (Acts 20:34–35 ESV)

Both Lucado and Paul would undoubtedly agree that the way to happiness is not through selfishness but selflessness, that we are at our best when we give it all away. A number of years ago, *US News and World Report* explored the subject of happiness. According to the article, researchers have stated that "helping people be a little happier can jump-start a process that will lead to stronger relationships, renewed hope, and general upward spiraling of happiness."

It's tempting to use the promise of happiness as a reason why others should become Christians. Overemphasizing that happiness comes from following Christ can be disillusioning for any Christian when trials hit. Recognize that we don't find happiness, we create it. The Lord's desire is that we live in complete joy. Then, when happy moments, happy relationships, and happy results come to an end, joy remains. During tough moments, painful stages, it's not *our* strength but *His* power that lifts us up and carries us through. Happiness ends in time; joy lasts as long as God's love. He promised:

> As the Father has loved me, so have I loved you. Now remain in my love. If you obey My commands, you will remain in My love, just as I have obeyed My Father's commands and remain in His love. I have told you this so that My joy may be in you and that your joy may be complete. (John 15:9–11 NIV)

We can choose joy when happiness isn't possible, and we should not ever feel the need to chase after it.

Reflection

What are your happiest moments? Do they last? Are you still searching for the "lasting happiness" stage of your life? What keeps you from accepting the eternal gift of joy that God offers? How would you explain to another who is chasing happiness that it should not be a worldly pursuit?

SEPTEMBER 24
(Y1, D39)

A Living Letter from God

See what large letters I use as I write to you with my own hand!

—Galatians 6:11 (NIV)

Somewhere in your home, you may have a box of letters stored away in a forgotten corner. These letters may be filled with happy memories from a loved one or perhaps they are reminders of a painful chapter in your life. But have you ever received a random letter from a stranger? Everyone has heard of people placing a note in a bottle, throwing it into the ocean, and sometimes asking the receiver to reply to a certain address with the date and place they received it. Jeremiah Burke was one of the passengers on board the RMS *Titanic* as it sank in the early morning of April 15, 1912. The nineteen-year-old was traveling to New York with his eighteen-year-old cousin. Both died in the disaster. As the ship sank, Burke quickly scribbled a letter and put it in a bottle. The bottle ended up few miles from his hometown in Ireland a year later. Then there's the oldest-known letter in a bottle which was dated June 12, 1886, and tossed into the Indian Ocean. Researchers believe this bottle may have washed up onto land less than a year after it was thrown into the ocean but became buried in the sand until it was found in 2018.

Letter writing has become a lost art in this age of email, texting, and cell phones. Hannah Brencher didn't know whether her handwritten letters to strangers would have much meaning, but they certainly did. At the age of twenty-two, she moved to New York City for what she thought was a dream job and ended up spiraling into a deep depression. Not a Christian at the time and trying to find a way cope with her sadness, she began writing letters on the 4-Train and leaving them around the city in places like bookstores, coffee shops, and libraries for others to find in the lonely city. Hannah's project took on a life of its own when she made an offer on her blog to handwrite a note and mail it to anyone who wanted one. Her inbox exploded with requests from people all over the world. Nearly 400 handwritten letters later, she started the website "The World Needs More Love Letters." Believing that there is something powerful about receiving a handwritten letter in today's digital era, Brencher states that she partners with God daily as a speaker and author. In her book, *If*

You Find this Letter, her attempts to bring more love into the world chronicles how she rediscovered her faith through the movement she started.

The New Testament includes a lot of letters from spiritual leaders to churches and church leaders. The book of Revelation includes a set of unique letters, identifying the qualities and characteristics of seven church communities. These letters are revealed by Jesus and delivered through His servant, John (Revelation 1:1). Letters played a particular role in the culture of early Christians. A Roman official often carried a letter to a town or province which would give him authority or status as a servant of Caesar. But Paul tells the Church at Corinth that he needs no such letter. He says

> The only letter of recommendation we need is you yourselves. Your lives are a letter written in our hearts; everyone can read it and recognize our good work among you. Clearly, you are a letter from Christ showing the result of our ministry among you. This "letter" is written not with pen and ink, but with the Spirit of the living God. It is carved not on tablets of stone, but on human hearts. (2 Corinthians 3:2–3 NLT)

The letters of Paul and other apostles have become more than ancient documents containing communications to the early church. They serve as teaching documents to all who believe and have relevancy for us today.

Billy Graham once penned these words: "The Bible is God's 'love letter' to us, telling us not only that He loves us but showing us what He has done to demonstrate His love. It also tells us how we should live, because God knows what is best for us and He wants us to experience it." All believers are called to be epistles or letters from Christ in the way we live. As living letters, we can illustrate how Jesus Christ makes a difference in how we treat others and strive to live with integrity. The letters that Jesus is writing these days are not written by hand but, instead, are represented by the words and deeds of His followers. In this way, we won't end up like some floating bottle containing a message that might never be read. We will be an example for all to see, and we will truly become a living letter from God.

Reflection

Can you think of someone who needs encouragement, thanks, or a reminder that you are praying for him or her through an actual handwritten note? Have you ever considered that as a disciple, you are a letter of Christ to the world? What message are you sending through your words and conduct?

SEPTEMBER 25
(Y2, D39)

Don't Quarrel; Agree to Disagree

Avoiding a fight is a mark of honor; only fools insist on quarreling.

—Proverbs 20:3 (NLT)

In interviews with persons having long marital relationships, a common prescription for happiness is offered by many. People who are married for decades say that they resolve their differences before the end of the day. For many, there is deep meaning from years of experience behind this advice. They offer suggestions for "getting over it before you go to bed." Some decide for whom the at-hand issue is most important and then allow that person to win. Others write down their feelings in a "never sent" letter. For some, conceding that the matter is really small stuff, they let it go. Accepting that there is a serious issue that needs to be dealt with and agreeing on future discussion is at times necessary. For the religiously inclined, saying a prayer together is reassuring. Whatever can be done, just do it before the lights go out. For Christians, the advice comes from the wisdom Paul shared with the Church at Ephesus. "Be angry and do not sin. Don't let the sun go down on your anger" (Ephesians 4:26 ESV). At face value, this verse offers a helpful protector against allowing anger to fester into bad decision-making. It also implies that our anger should not last longer than a day, resulting in extended quarreling.

These days, our society produces a constant flow of information often containing thoughtless and heated words. Originating from various media formats, it transfers into cynical rants, frequent false accusations, and useless arguments. While differences of opinion are unavoidable and can even be healthy, nothing good comes from getting into a quarrel. Whether in politics, business, at home, or in community groups and church, quarreling is a destructive force best to avoid. Proverbs 17:14 (NIV) says, "Starting a quarrel is like breaching a dam; so drop the matter before a dispute breaks out." Constructive discussions where differing factions share respect for another's point of view are becoming less valued. Whether we like it or not, we find ourselves living in a "cancel culture" era that often allows little room for a dissenting opinion. Worst of all, there is diminished opportunity for real, enriching communication. Quarreling often persists until a dominating party issues a "my way or the highway" edict.

Many years ago, the story was told of an organ grinder who used to go around in the streets with a dressed-up monkey collecting pennies. It seems he had an especially clever monkey. On one occasion, a big dog broke away from some children with whom it had been playing and made a dash for the monkey. Bystanders were surprised to see that the monkey did not seem the least bit afraid, standing perfectly still in evident curiosity, waiting for the dog to come up to him. This confused the dog, for it would have much preferred engaging in a chase. When the dog reached the monkey, the funny little scarlet-coated creature courteously tipped its cap. Instantly, there was a laugh from the audience. The dog lowered its head, and its tail dropped between its legs. It looked like a whipped mutt, not at all like the fine dog it really was. Turning and retreating back home, the laughing children could not persuade it to return. As for the monkey, he wanted no disagreement, knowing instinctively that it takes two to make a quarrel.

When Paul penned his advice in mentoring Timothy regarding irresponsible controversies, he stated, "Don't have anything to do with foolish and stupid arguments, because you know they produce quarrels. And the Lord's servant must not be quarrelsome but must be kind to everyone, able to teach, not resentful" (2 Timothy 2:23–24 NIV). Paul's instruction warned Timothy and all serious believers to recognize superficial conversations that pretend to be significant but only serve to generate quarrels. Wise people will stay out of such discussions. Nevertheless, they will also learn to recognize when a controversy contains important spiritual issues. When it does, they will carefully and patiently express the truth without quarreling. In doing so, they can be fully confident that God's Holy Spirit alone is able to effectively persuade those in error. Love and gentleness have a way of expressing truth powerfully, and kindness may endear even those with whom we might just simply have to agree to disagree.

Reflection

Can you recall a time when you allowed a quarrelsome spirit enter into your heart? Are there ways you might learn to see disagreements with other Christians as openings to affirm your spiritual unity and mutual joy as servants of Christ? Would you be able to help another individual consider the wisdom in treating each new day as an opportunity to resolve their ongoing quarrel with another?

SEPTEMBER 26
(Y3, D39)

The Reckoning

For we are God's handiwork, created in Christ Jesus to do good
works, which God prepared in advance for us to do.

—Ephesians 2:10 (NIV)

It had been decades since many of them had seen each other. In their own way, every one of them had been successful. They had spent the biggest part of four years together. What would it be like to get together for dinner in that small university town that most likely had changed less than they had? Would there be a preoccupation with their cell phones? Would they try to outdo each other with the trips they had taken, the investments they had made, the cars they were driving, or the houses they had built? Actually, there was none of that. The post-observation comment from the one spouse who attended was that it was obvious that these individuals had actually been good friends and still were. It was evidenced by the fact that they "picked up their conversations and assumed their prior roles just like it was yesterday." Well, I must admit, yesterday has now been a while, and physical appearances somewhat changed. But as I sat there listening, I realized that had I been at another place in the restaurant on that particular evening, I would have recognized every single one of my old friends by their voices.

As we pass through this journey we call life, there are moments in time that we must come to terms with in defining who we are. Unfortunately, this image often becomes defined with how others see us and the roles we have assumed along the way. The various characters we play often become convoluted when we are asked to simultaneously be teacher, friend, parent, boss, and whatever other labels you might like to attach to those stations in life which we have assumed. There are occasions when a soul-searching calculation of who we really have become must be made. Author Beverly Lewis ponders that question with her character Katie Mayfield in a Hallmark made-for-TV movie. The story evolves into a conclusion of a trilogy in which the main character is torn between two worlds. They include the current life she has prepared for herself and the simple one of her heritage as part of the Amish culture in which she was raised. The conflictual narrative is aptly titled *The Reckoning*.

There are likely various points in each of our lives that we are challenged with our own need for a reckoning. As we come to terms with who we are, we must learn to feel comfortable in our own skin. The psalmist said, "I praise you because I am fearfully and wonderfully made; your works are wonderful, I know that full well" (Psalm 139:14 NIV). We learn to age gracefully, recognizing that we are no longer who we once were. If we are lucky enough to acquire some spiritual wisdom along the way, we will be thankful that we are no longer running a race with humanity but learning to walk with Christ. Paul said it this way: "Don't copy the behavior and customs of this world, but let God transform you into a new person by changing the way you think. Then you will learn to know God's will for you, which is good and pleasing and perfect" (Romans 12:2 NLT). If we live long enough, we will be faced with our own mortality and hopefully grasp that what has aged in this life will be made new again. "Therefore, if anyone is in Christ, the new creation has come: The old has gone, the new is here!" (2 Corinthians 5:17 NIV).

Defining who we are isn't always easy, but one thing is apparent. When we pay more attention to what others think of us than what God does, we will always get ourselves into trouble. Bobby Schuller, grandson of the late Robert H. Schuller, has developed this confession for his congregation: "I'm not what I do. I'm not what I have. I'm not what people say about me. I am the beloved of God." When we are young, we are often asked the question, "What do you want to be when you grow up?" It's amazing how many continue to ask that same question through their adult years, never seeming to find an answer or a role that fits. On that evening when I had dinner with my college friends, I recognized that my physical appearance had been altered in those intervening years as well as my thought processes. As I listened closely to their voices one more time, there was another all too familiar one that had joined in. It was my own, and it was the one that I truly understood best of all.

Reflection

In what sets of circumstances do you sometimes feel a competition for social status? What "reckonings" have occurred in your own life that have shaped your view to be more in tune with God? How could you help others who are struggling to accept who they have become in their maturing years?

SEPTEMBER 27
(Y4, D39)

Words that Matter

Let the words of my mouth and the meditation of my heart be
acceptable sight, O Lord, my rock and my redeemer.

—Psalm 19:14 (ESV)

The times are sadly gone when we can take someone at their word. Many a deal was struck by what was known as a gentleman's agreement. Promises that were made over a business handshake and vows of friendship and marriage pledged with carefully chosen words were once taken seriously. Not so much anymore. These days, our TV journalists interview celebrities, athletes, and other public figures frequently having to "bleep" out phrases due to the expletives spoken by these individuals who really should know better. Too often they rationalize that the viewer will accept their language as "an attempt to make a point." In print media, one political candidate creates the headline that their opponent is lying. Days later, the opposition is quoted: "Words matter, unless he's the one speaking them."

It used to be if two people were having a verbal disagreement, we might have been told to just stay out of it. A neutral party might have informed us that they were "just having words." Words have taken on a whole new life today. A person uses one of the many social media platforms to fire off a few choice words about someone they might not know all that well, and the responding comments start flying for all the world to see. Perspective employers have been known to check out how applicants interact with others on their social media page. We forget that what might seem like a personal arena for self-expression can influence how others evaluate us both personally and professionally. When we never hear back about that job opening, we wonder what may have happened. We fail to remember that we may never get a second chance to make a first impression. The late author and syndicated columnist, Earl Wilson, once advised, "If you wouldn't write it and sign it, don't say it." The problem is that we do.

Jesus put it this way:

> A tree is identified by its fruit. If a tree is good, its fruit will be good. If a tree is bad, its fruit will be bad. You brood of snakes! How could evil men like you speak what is good and right? For whatever is in your heart determines what you say. A good person produces good things from the treasury of a good heart, and an evil person produces evil things from the treasury of an evil heart. And I tell you this, you must give an account on judgment day for every idle word you speak. The words you say will either acquit you or condemn you. (Matthew 12:33–37 NLT)

Words have the potential of building someone up or they can cause irreparable harm. Condemning words can affect an individual in unimaginable way while those which console and comfort might shift a life from despair to hope. The choosing of our words can make a powerful difference one way or the other. Nathaniel Hawthorne once stated, "Words—so innocent and powerless as they are, as standing in a dictionary, how potent for good and evil they become in the hands of one who knows how to combine them."

As followers of Christ, we must listen with our heart and realize that there are times when our mere presence speaks more than words themselves. A friend once told me that before going into a stressful situation that may have concluded with a serious consequence, someone had passed on this scripture: "The Lord will fight for you, and you have only to be silent" (Exodus 14:14 ESV). She followed this advice. Instead of the event being life-defeating for her, it ended up being life-affirming. The Word of God offers direction in all that we do and provides a light for our way forward. "Your word is a lamp to guide my feet and a light for my path" (Psalm 119:105 NLT). Allowing His Word to guide us as to how and when we should speak will enable us to voice words that matter. The Apostle Paul advised that we should, "Let your speech always be gracious, seasoned with salt, so that you may know how you ought to answer each person" (Colossians 4:6 ESV). It would serve us well to give thoughtful as well as prayerful consideration before we speak so that the words which flow out of our mouths are acceptable to the Lord. Remember, He is always listening, and so is the world to which we must only express words that matter.

Reflection

Have you ever created an issue because you were slow to hear and quick to speak? In what ways do you seek to weigh the words you express? How can you help others do the same in their journey?

SEPTEMBER 28
(Y5, D39)

Taking a Stand

And they were to stand every morning, thanking and
praising the LORD, and likewise at evening.

—1 Chronicles 23:30 (NLT)

A friend of mine was sharing an experience she had during a visit with her daughter and son-in-law. While she was there, her young grandson had a friend over to their home. When the grandmother (my friend) walked into the room where they were engaged in activity, the boy promptly stood up, held out his hand, and introduced himself. She related that she couldn't have been more impressed with the manners this child demonstrated at such a young age. It seems like it should be simple enough to know that it's polite for us to stand as we greet or say goodbye to someone. Although it was once an instinctive act, changing social norms and rapidly disintegrating signs of respect can oftentimes keep one guessing. Standing when someone comes into your circle sends a signal that you are eager to receive the other person. It demonstrates in a nonverbal way that you've noticed them, and they are worth your effort to rise from a place of comfort in order to welcome them.

On occasion, failure to stand has become politicized at public events during patriotic ceremonies. In an attempt to show discord with leadership or express unrest with how someone may have been treated, those who possess some degree of fame or notoriety have at times chosen to display their discontent. In the United States, it has been tradition to stand for the presentation of the national anthem. The anthem symbolizes a unification of the citizenry around the values of the flag, the country's freedoms, and those who gave their lives so that others might continue to benefit from those liberties. It is a rather basic sign of respect, and it has nothing to do with persons in power or their political positions which may in fact differ from one's own. There is an irony that this type of demonstration is often carried out by those who have profited and gained much from the nation's resources. It is not unlike those who disregard standing in recognition of the very God who has created and provides for them.

The concept of standing is an inherent part of the Christian tradition. In the very first book of the Bible, we read, "Now Abraham arose early in the morning and went to the place where he had stood before the LORD" (Genesis 19:27 NASB). When the Lord spoke to Moses, He said, "Behold, there is a place by Me, and you shall stand there on the rock" (Exodus 33:21 ESV). When the Prophet Ezekiel received his call, God said, "Son of man, stand on your feet, and I will speak with you" (Ezekiel 2:1 ESV). On a visit to Solomon from the Queen of Sheba, she spoke these words: "Blessed are your men, *and* blessed are these servants of yours who stand before you continually *and* hear your wisdom!" (1 Kings 10:8 NASB). In fact, when Jesus was brought before Pilate in His final hours, He also stood (Matthew 27:11). Additionally, the songs of the church make frequent references to standing. They include some of the more traditional hymns such as "Standing on the Promises" and "Stand Up, Stand Up for Jesus" as well as the contemporary chorus, "We Are Standing on Holy Ground."

While nowhere in scripture are we commanded to specifically pay tribute to a patriotic song or salute a national flag, the Bible is clear that we should submit ourselves "for the Lord's sake to every human authority…who are sent by him to punish those who do wrong and to commend those who do right" (1 Peter 2:13–14 NLT). To refuse to participate in showing respect for the nation appears arrogant, disrespectful to its heritage, and contrary to God's teaching. While it may succeed in stirring up controversy, it quite often calls more attention to an individual person than to an actual cause. The Bible says a house divided against itself cannot stand (Mark 3:25). When we all stand for our national anthem, it's a reminder that we are still "one nation under God." In the last stanza of "The Star-Spangled Banner," Frances Scott Key penned these words: "Oh! thus be it ever, when freemen shall stand." The Lord wants us all to take a stand for Him. In this intimidating world, it's much easier to do that when we remain free to be able to make that stand.

Reflection

How do you decide when to take a bold stand and when to be more tactful and polite? What are some Christlike ways to express concerns and motivate change which focus attention on the issue rather than the individual? In what situations might God bless a compromise in order to preserve peace?

SEPTEMBER 29
(Y6, D39)

Where Is God?

O LORD, I will honor and praise your name, for you are my God. You do such wonderful things! You planned them long ago, and now you have accomplished them.

—Isaiah 25:1 (NLT)

Alexander Fleming was a young bacteriologist when an accidental discovery led to one of the great developments of modern medicine. His discovery and isolation of penicillin marks the start of antibiotics which has been hailed by some as "the greatest contribution medical science ever made to humanity." Returning to his lab after a late summer vacation with his family in September 1928, Fleming noticed a patch of "blue mold" with a clear area around it in a culture dish. After some testing, he concluded that the mold had stopped the growth of that particular bacteria. He kept the mold alive and tested it on lab animals. The following year, Fleming published a medical paper stating that this mold could kill disease-causing bacteria with high degrees of resistance and yet was non-toxic to animals. The mold was identified as *Penicillium notatum*, and Fleming named the substance it discharged as penicillin. Fleming lacked the chemical means to turn his discovery into a usable drug, so he moved on to other projects. A decade later, two researchers at Oxford University read the details of Fleming's discovery and conducted extensive tests, proving it was possible to make penicillin in pure form. By 1942, British drug companies began making enough penicillin for military use, saving lives by the hundreds of thousands. The new drug was considered a military secret, and news of its effectiveness was not released officially until war's end. In 1945, along with Fleming, they were awarded the Nobel Prize for Medicine.

The discovery of penicillin is often cited to be by chance. Others, however, are convinced that it was God who planned and directed its finding, just as He did with all of His creation. Fleming seems to support this theory with his own words, "Nature makes penicillin. I just found it." His observation of the growth of a "random deposited mold" emerges as unmistakable evidence of a design in which we can see the finger of God—if we only look. Long before Fleming's miraculous encounter, a French biologist, microbiologist, and chemist by the name of Louis Pasteur who died on September 28, 1895, once stated, "The more I study nature, the more I stand amazed at the work of the Creator. Science brings men nearer to God." By His very own creation, God provided white blood cells in our bodies to fight infections, but some people would still die from them. When the right time had come, He allowed for a new opportunity in our lives through the introduction and use of penicillin. Yet disease processes still occur and new types of infections persist, some of which result in the demise of human lives. Just as we might expect, there will always be those among us who will dare to ask the question, "Where is God in all of this?"

This was the very same question asked by two sisters who were friends of Jesus. When He heard that their brother, Lazarus, was sick, Jesus purposefully delayed travel for two more days (John 11:6). By the time He and the disciples arrived, "Lazarus had already been in the tomb for four days" (John 11:17 NIV). When Martha, one of the sisters, went out to meet Jesus, she said to Him, "If only you would have been here, my brother would not have died" (John 11:21 NLT), as if to say, "Jesus, why did you wait so long?" Jesus ultimately resurrected Lazarus, which was a display of His glory for all to witness. In John 11:40 (NIV), at the end of the Lazarus story, Jesus says, "Did I not tell you that if you believed, you would see the glory of God?" God's delay is not his denial; it is simply an opportunity for Him to be glorified. God's glory is not determined by His timing but rather as He works through the circumstances of our lives. While we fret about the events of today, He is already at tomorrow. One of the prophets gave us these words from our Creator: "Call to me and I will answer you and tell you great and unsearchable things you do not know" (Jeremiah 33:3 NIV). We need never ask where God is. But if we do, we will hopefully hear the voice of Moses in the distance saying to us, "Do not be afraid or discouraged, for the LORD will personally go ahead of you. He will be with you; he will neither fail you nor abandon you" (Deuteronomy 31:8 NLT). Where is God? He is simply revealing a path for you to find and follow.

Reflection

In what ways does God's goodness strengthen your life? When you fail to see evidence of Him working in you, or when you are trying to comfort another who is struggling, how might you find peace in the words, "I have heard your prayer and seen your tears; I will heal you" (2 Kings 20:5 NIV)?

SEPTEMBER 30
(Y7, D39)

Pay Attention to the Small Things

Do not despise these small beginnings, for the LORD rejoices to see the work begin.

—Zechariah 4:10 (NLT)

As I began to reminisce about Aunt Sally, the thought of her brought a smile to my face. She was actually my mother's aunt, but to all the family kids of my generation, she was one special lady. When you were privileged to be a guest in her home, you never got the slightest impression that she may have been engaged by your parents to babysit. From the minute you walked in her front door, she welcomed you with open arms and made you feel really special indeed. Spending a few hours with Aunt Sally meant that she was about to enter your world, not the other way around. She broke out her supply of games, and for however long you were there, you had her undivided attention. She was up in years (at least that was our perception), and she had been widowed for a long time. Her only child lived away with a family of her own, so when any one of us visited, we became her sole focus. She certainly understood what it meant to take care of the small things in life. And that we most certainly were.

God pays attention to the small things and often uses them to accomplish His work. Faithfully following God's instructions, Gideon reduced the size of his army to 300 soldiers to destroy a massive opposition of 135,000 Midianites who prepared to come against Israel (Judges 7). The Lord used a widow's only possession, a small jar of oil, to feed her family for months (2 Kings 4:1–7). When Moses felt inadequate, God turned his rod into a serpent (Exodus 4:1–4), and He used David's meager sling and rock to conquer Goliath (1 Samuel 17:50). Nothing illustrates the concept of "smallness" any better than the boy who gave his lunch to Jesus and ended up feeding five thousand (John 6:9). Then there's the widow who dropped her two coins into the offering and went on her way (Mark 12:42). Neither had any way of knowing what this meant to the Lord or that we would still be talking about them 2,000 years later.

I recently heard a pastor being interviewed on a radio talk show. He explained that his parents introduced the concept of tithing to him at a young age. At first, when his 10 percent was 15 cents of his $1.50 allowance, that didn't seem to be too significant. Years later, when he received his monthly paycheck after accepting his first pastoral appointment, his tithe represented a much larger amount. Giving his tithe would leave little for food and gas after he paid his routine expenses. But he did what he had always done and wrote out a check for God's portion. The next day, the church secretary called to tell him that many families in the congregation wanted to get to know him better, so she took the liberty of scheduling him for dinners each night over the next month. His daily sustenance had been taken care of with lots of leftovers to spare. The problem with most of us is that we don't want to start with the small thing. When we graduate, we have no desire to start at the bottom of the pecking order as we go to work for a new employer. We expect a big salary, a large office, and an important title on the door. After all, we are due these greater things. We feel we have worked hard, sacrificed much, and are ready to collect.

Perhaps there are things you, too, have thought to be too small. The Old Testament Prophet Zechariah reminds us that we should "not despise these small beginnings." Implied in this scripture is the reflection that while we might hold them in disdain, our God is the one who has always used small things to accomplish His purposes. Consider accepting the challenge to tackle what Jesus is calling you to do right where you are. Let your dreams be no bigger than the next person you meet. He would ask us to be more sensitive to others who are facing situations that we might consider to be "no big deal." However, to those individuals, their circumstances may be huge. Your slightest attention to their seemingly small need might have life-altering implications for them. Jesus reminds us, "If you are faithful in little things, you will be faithful in large ones" (Luke 16:10 NLT). When it comes right down to it, nothing is too small for God to use as He cares for His people. So what apparently insignificant situation are you ignoring today? If you give it the attention it deserves, you will discover that the Lord is sufficient to supply all your needs. Learn to pay attention to the small things, my friend. Not only would you make Aunt Sally proud, the Lord will be praised, and your life will be blessed.

Reflection

What are the big goals in your life to which you often give your attention? When you do so, have you considered what small things you are frequently overlooking? How might you refocus some of your priorities in order to let God use these "small things" for the fulfillment of His purposes?

OCTOBER 1
(Y1, D40)

In the Shadow of His Wings

Do nothing out of selfish ambition or vain conceit. Rather,
in humility value others above yourselves.

—Philippians 2:3 (NIV)

In a conversation with a funeral director, he told me about the burial of an underprivileged woman who had lived for years in the county poor house. Over the time she resided there, a portion of her limited funds was set aside for a simple burial. When the time of her passing came, a meager interment would be provided. However, one detail remained—a burial plot needed to be obtained. After much searching of the local cemeteries, an insignificant location was found along a fence in one of the graveyards. In spite of her modest means, the lady received a complete and proper burial, including the marking of the grave with her name. Not long afterward, the funeral director received a phone call from a more prominent member of the community who questioned why he would choose to bury this lady next to her family plot. "How presumptuous," you might say. Perhaps we should pause to ask the question, how often do we look at someone else's life and consider it to be inferior to our own?

On October 1, 2017, Tom McIntosh and his wife were among thousands attending an outdoor country music festival in Las Vegas, Nevada. Suddenly, bullets began flying through the air, while many believed at first that the gun sounds were fireworks. Upon the awareness of what was actually happening, the concertgoers ran for safety. As McIntosh helped his wife and another lady over a barrier wall, he was shot in the leg. As he lowered himself over the other side, he realized that he was badly bleeding. Then James Lawson, a complete stranger, appeared ready to help. He assisted with the placement of a makeshift tourniquet while another stranger transported them to the hospital in the bed of a pickup truck. McIntosh feels he wouldn't have made it if it wasn't for Lawson who unassumingly credited dozens of others like himself performing very similar acts. One of those other helpers, a firefighter, was quoted as saying, "I was in the wrong place at the right time." And this was true for many on that ominous day.

Stories like this serve to validate who we really are. We can run for the hills and never look back or we can become the kind of person God would want us to be. He gave those who helped in Las Vegas the courage to shelter others with their own bodies. When we see someone else's life just as important as our own, we humble ourselves before God. Tragic circumstances are reminders for each of us to consider the fragility of life and our relationship with Him. Jesus was once asked about a tragedy that had occurred in His time. His followers were suggesting that when people die in some kind of arbitrary act, God might be judging them. Jesus responded by saying, "Do you think those Galileans were worse sinners than all the other people from Galilee? Is that why they suffered? Not at all! And you will perish, too, unless you repent of your sins and turn to God" (Luke 13:2–3 NLT). In that regard, we acknowledge that we are all paupers who come with nothing to offer Him but our sin and our need for salvation. In doing so, we recognize our lack of value and our complete inability to save ourselves.

There are always those who will ask, "Where was God in the midst of this tragedy?" In perilous times, God is always present in His role as shepherd and comforter. When David was being hunted by King Saul who wanted him dead, he declared, "In you my soul takes refuge; in the shadow of your wings I will take refuge, till the storms of destruction pass by" (Psalm 57:1 ESV). We long for the day when God wipes away every tear and there is no more death (Revelation 21:4). Until that day comes to pass, the Bible doesn't give us a guarantee of shelter from every kind of harm. The shooting in Las Vegas did not slip past God, for our times continue to be in His hands. The prophet said, "Good people pass away; the godly often die before their time. But no one seems to care or wonder why. No one seems to understand that God is protecting them from the evil to come" (Isaiah 57:1 NLT). When a righteous person dies, they enter into peace and rest. For those of us who remain and continue to be faced with matters of life and death, know that He is there to remind us that we can always take refuge in the shadow of His wings.

Reflection

In what ways might we search for His refuge in everyday situations? How can we seek God's help to grant us humility so that we do not see our life more valuable than that of others? Do you think you can defend this position when you find yourself in the midst of others who are insensitive to the fate of those whose lives are deemed to be insignificant?

OCTOBER 2
(Y2, D40)

Only a Heartbeat Away

LORD, remind me how brief my time on earth will be. Remind me
that my days are numbered—how fleeting my life is.

—Psalm 39:4 (NLT)

I once heard about a Christian mother-to-be who was confronted with devastating news from her obstetrician. Early in her pregnancy, the physician was unable to detect a fetal heartbeat, concluding that a miscarriage had occurred. When the young woman told the father about the situation, he became very upset, earnestly praying that the Lord would save his unborn child. When the couple arrived for the scheduled follow-up procedure, the father insisted that the doctor try just one more time to identify a heartbeat. The doctor counseled the couple that he was highly doubtful and that doing so could potentially cause them senseless grief. But the father remained adamant, and the doctor conceded. Surprisingly, a fetal heartbeat was detected. At the end of what would become a full-term pregnancy, a healthy son was born to the couple. Whether at the beginning or end of our earthly existence, the detection of a heartbeat provides the most basic determination of life as we know it.

Early in our nation's history, Americans expected little from their vice presidents. Therefore, newly elected Vice President John Tyler slipped away unnoticed to his home in Williamsburg, Virginia, shortly after the inauguration of President William Henry Harrison. On April 5, 1841, Tyler was sleeping soundly when Secretary of State Daniel Webster's son, Fletcher, galloped into Tyler's front yard at the crack of dawn and hammered on the front door. He delivered the most shocking news: President William Henry Harrison had died. Because Tyler had been selected only as a means to help balance the ticket, he had harbored no expectations for serving actively in Harrison's administration. Yet Tyler understood instantly the new role thrust upon him resulting from Harrison's death, and he hurried immediately to Washington. John Tyler suddenly became the tenth president of the United States, succeeding Harrison who had served for only thirty-one days. Forcing the nation to confront the death of a president for the very first time, it gave meaning to the phrase that a vice-president is only a "heartbeat away" from the presidency.

The reality is that our life on earth is short, and we are reminded of this throughout God's Word. Moses warned of the curse of disobedience when he stated, "Your life will constantly hang in the balance. You will live night and day in fear, unsure if you will survive" (Deuteronomy 28:66 NLT). As David feared the pursuit of King Saul, he told his friend, Jonathan, "Yet as surely as the LORD lives and as you live, there is only a step between me and death" (1 Samuel 20:3 NIV). Someone once said: "If you live each day as if it was your last, someday you'll most certainly be right." Indeed, no one knows the amount of time we have before we die—the amount of time we have to spend with our family or the amount of time we have to repent and come to the Lord. Most people think that they will grow old before they die. However, we all die in our own due time. It is pertinent, therefore, that we give thanks to the Lord for each new day and live it for Him. Jesus said, "If you try to hang on to your life, you will lose it. But if you give up your life for my sake, you will save it" (Matthew 16:25 NLT).

If we are honest with ourselves, we will admit that we're only too aware of how fragile life is. Whether our life ends by accident, by force, by illness, or by natural causes, one of these days will indeed be our last, and it is impossible to avoid. This mortality face should cause us to be "awake and sober" (1 Thessalonians 5:6 NIV) in the way we spend our time. We need to make every minute count in the things we do and say before our earthly journey is finished. Just imagine how effective Christians could be if they started to view each day as their last. Consider the impact their lives would have because of a conscious choice to prioritize their focus beyond their own selfish and aimless pursuits. As we strive to be as effective as humanly possible in our short lives, perhaps it would be an insightful experience for every believer to ask the question, "If this was the last day of my life, would I want to do what I am about to do today?" Be careful with your answer. It might be only a heartbeat away.

Reflection

Are you living each day as if it was your last? What do you think you would do differently during what might otherwise be a usual day? In consideration of the fact that life as we know it is only a heartbeat away, how does this help you to prepare for eternity?

OCTOBER 3
(Y3, D40)

Spinning Out of Control

Trust in the LORD with all your heart, and do not lean on your own understanding. In all your ways acknowledge him, and he will make straight your paths.

—Proverbs 3:5–6 (ESV)

A neighborhood friend came by the house while she was doing some yard work. The neighbor had been out walking and was invited to sit down for a few minutes on the porch. When asked about her family, the visitor began to open up about her daughter who was in college. Apparently, the daughter and several other students had been arrested on a theft charge stemming from a sorority pledge prank. The neighbor was worried that the charge would become part of a permanent record and could have implications for her daughter's future. Beyond that, she confessed that through this whole incident, she had become quite angry at God. Trying not to be judgmental of her feelings, the host shared that while it was okay to be angry for now, hopefully she would come to realize that God was there for her all the time.

Have you ever been angry with God? We are so conditioned to think in a "cause-effect" mentality that when things don't fall into place as we anticipate, it's often revealing who we hold responsible. At times, it comes in the form of personal guilt for not doing all we might have. Or we place the blame on something or someone else; in this case, God. For those on a faith journey, church attendance, tithing, daily devotions, and good works are often attributed toward having success in certain parts of our lives. While we can be assured that God does bless us for these practices, we cannot then turn around and reject Him when life occurrences become problematic. We come to understand that just as every path is not paved with a smooth surface, God never promised that we would not have trials and tribulations in this life. As a matter of fact, Jesus told us that if we followed Him that it would, in fact, be a difficult road: "I have said these things to you, that in me you may have peace. In the world you will have tribulation. But take heart; I have overcome the world" (John 16:33 ESV).

It's interesting that when the journey appears to be manageable and running smoothly, we frequently take personal credit for our accomplishments. But when life becomes frazzled, we are tempted to move away from the source of the greatest comfort we can find. It is during those most vulnerable times that we can choose God. Or we can harbor our resentment, blame Him, and isolate ourselves from the one who can sustain us. In doing so, we demonstrate a lack of deep faith for the peace and grace we are offered. "And they have no root in themselves, but endure for a while; then, when tribulation or persecution arises on account of the word, immediately they fall away" (Mark 4:17 ESV). We need to confront our emotions by holding on and simply talking to God. In doing so, we acknowledge our desire for His continued presence in our life.

So bottom line, does God expect us to accept our situations where pain and suffering has occurred without question, without hurt, or anger? Charles Spurgeon once wrote, "Christian, remember the good of God in the frost of adversity." God wants us to trust Him not only in the good times but especially through the bad. It's not about finding fault, placing blame, or becoming angry. He wants to shelter us in His loving arms. The psalmist said, "God is our refuge and strength, a very present help in trouble" (Psalm 46:1 ESV). It's so easy to say we trust when things are going well and the path is clear, but God encourages us to really trust in Him in all we do not know. When we walk through our darkest hours and try not to "lean on our own understanding," His light guides us to a place of comfort and rest. For His grace is all that we need (2 Corinthians 12:9) when our life's journey is truly spinning out of control.

Reflection

Do you remember a time when you were angry at God? How long did you allow that anger to remain in your heart? Were you able to overcome these feelings and release them through confession? What did you learn that you will be able to apply in your next "out-of-control" situation?

OCTOBER 4
(Y4, D40)

The Great "I Am"

God said to Moses, "I AM WHO I AM. This is what you are to
say to the Israelites: 'I AM has sent me to you.'"

—Exodus 3:14 (NIV)

Remembered for flexing his muscle and eating spinach, Popeye the Sailor Man is one of the "Greatest Cartoon Characters of All Time" according to a ranking by *TV Guide* in 2002. For decades, he appeared in comic strips and on TV cartoons. He is known for his one-liner, "I am what I am, and that's all that I am." Expressed somewhat more thoughtfully, Frenchman Rene Descartes (known as the father of modern philosophy) once said, "I think, therefore I am." Saying the words "I am" can be lighthearted, philosophical, confident, or just downright egotistical. But given the right set of circumstances, it can also be downright scary. There are far too many times lately when saying those words in affirmation of one's convictions will likely get you killed. A wounded victim of a recent shooting reported that her attempted killer targeted persons of faith by asking the question, "Are you a Christian?" When they positively identified themselves as such, he said, "Good. Because you're a Christian, you are going to see God in just about one second." Throughout the ages, Christians have been persecuted. However, it would appear that targeting them is unfortunately once again on the increase.

I have a friend who has a young grandson who constantly refers to himself by using his name. He will say, "Jack is hungry" rather than "I want something to eat." One day, the "I" word will become more prevalent in his vocabulary. With some individuals, use of "I" referencing can become extreme and sometimes very self-focused. When person utters the words, "I am," they are always followed with an explanation: I am happy, I am a fan of football, I am a man or woman, I am married or single, I am young, or I am growing old. But when God uses those words, the phrase is complete because absent everything else, He is! God alone can say "I am" and nothing more, for He is "the great I Am."

555

In the book of John alone, there are seven "I am" statements expressed by Jesus. They include being the bread of life (John 6:48), the light of the world (John 8:12), the gate (John 10:9), the good shepherd (John 10:11), the resurrection and the life (John 11:25), the way, the truth, and the life (John 14:6), and the true vine (John 15:1). They are significant because Jesus is not being philosophical here but is actually claiming to be these things. His declarations also serve as a source of everlasting hope for those of us who are believers. When confronted by the religious leaders of His day as to who He was, Jesus replied, "Before Abraham was born, I am" (John 8:58 NIV). They understood who He was claiming to be, and they threatened to stone Him. But He hid and escaped.

Because Christ is who He says, He makes the journey whole for all who are Christians. Therefore, we are able to make our own "I am" pronouncements. I am at a peaceful place that is beyond all comprehension (Philippians 4:7). I am complete in Him (Colossians 2:10). I am a recipient of the gift of righteousness (Romans 5:17) and a joint heir with Christ (Romans 8:17). I am forgiven of all my sins and washed in His blood (Ephesians 1:7). Jesus said, "Whoever acknowledges me before others, I will also acknowledge before my Father in heaven" (Matthew 10:32 NIV). So if you are ever asked, "Are you a Christian?" regardless of the situation, you can reply with great certainty, "I am."

Reflection

Are you able to practice your Christianity openly without any fear of reprisal? Have you ever felt persecuted in your own life because of your faith? In what ways might you bring new meaning to the phrase, "It is no longer I who live, but Christ lives in me" (Galatians 2:20 NKJV)? How might you practice using "I am" statements as a witnessing affirmation of your faith?

OCTOBER 5
(Y5, D40)

Brush with Destiny

And Jesus said, "Who was it that touched me?"

—Luke 8:45

Many persons can share their version of a sighting of someone from the rich and famous. Our society longs to be near renowned persons, which is why will we pay excessive prices for a ticket to attend concerts or acquire backstage passes of individuals or groups of whom we already own their recordings. People of means will spend huge sums of money to possess an item that was owned or worn by a star. If they happen to have died, the price is that much higher. A baseball jersey worn by New York Yankees Babe Ruth, circa 1920, sold for more than $4.4 million in 2012. According to the California-based seller, it established a record for any item of sports memorabilia. The cream-colored, silk-satin wedding dress which Elizabeth Taylor wore for the first of her eight marriages sold for around $188,175 in 2013. And the well-remembered blue-and-white gingham dress worn by Hollywood star Judy Garland who played Dorothy in *The Wizard of Oz* sold at auction for more than $1.5 million in November of 2015.

I recall listening to a sports radio talk show during which the hosts were discussing the passing of Arnold Palmer, the American professional golfer regarded as one of the greatest in that sports history. Conversations centered around his popularity and how he was an important trailblazer, one of the first superstars of the early age of televised sports as far back as the 1950s. In the midst of the memories and stories they shared, the question was asked if any of them had ever met this king of golf. One of the hosts spoke up and stated that one time while he was attending a national event, he passed by and brushed the shirt of one whom only minutes later he came to realize was Palmer. He said to this day he occasionally tells the story of how he once had a brush with fame by touching the sleeve of one so well-known. Our society will covet almost anything which at one time or other came in contact with stardom.

One of the most moving stories in scripture involved a woman who suffered from bleeding for twelve years. In her day, she would have been considered an outcast from society. On one occasion, when Jesus was on His way to minister to a dying girl, He had to make His way through the crowds of people. This woman came up behind Him, touched the edge of His garment, and was immediately healed (Luke 8:42–44).

> "Who touched me?" Jesus asked. Everyone denied it, and Peter said, "Master, this whole crowd is pressing up against you." But Jesus said, "Someone deliberately touched me, for I felt healing power go out from me." When the woman realized that she could not stay hidden, she began to tremble and fell to her knees in front of him. The whole crowd heard her explain why she had touched him and that she had been immediately healed. "Daughter," he said to her, "your faith has made you well. Go in peace." (Luke 8:45–48 NLT)

The woman was obviously a person of great conviction.

Contrast this expression of faith with the lack of it shown by a doubting disciple who knew Jesus well. After His death and resurrection, Jesus had appeared to some of the chosen.

> One of the twelve disciples, Thomas, was not with the others when Jesus came. They told him, "We have seen the Lord!" But he replied, "I won't believe it unless I see the nail wounds in his hands, put my fingers into them, and place my hand into the wound in his side." Eight days later the disciples were together again, and this time Thomas was with them. The doors were locked; but suddenly, as before, Jesus was standing among them. "Peace be with you," he said. Then he said to Thomas, "Put your finger here, and look at my hands. Put your hand into the wound in my side. Don't be faithless any longer. Believe!" (John 20:24–27 NLT)

So the question for us becomes, who are we? Do we humbly reach out to touch Jesus with the faith of the sick woman? Or have we come to know Him in a personal way but, like Thomas, allow doubt to enter into our relationship? Are we similar to many in the crowd who bump up against Him but never reach out with faith enough to receive His transforming power? Or do we simply want to follow His stardom because of what we might gain in return? Consider how He has touched your life. Rather than a simple, fleeting brush with fame, the application of your unwavering faith will lead you to a meeting with destiny.

Reflection

With whom do you most identify in this scriptural passage? Have you ever reached out figuratively to touch the hem of Jesus' robe? How does the example of this woman encourage you in your faith journey? How you explain to another that your possession of a souvenir from a famous person or event is insignificant when compared to the importance of your relationship with Christ.

OCTOBER 6
(Y6, D40)

Safe Space

Those who live in the shelter of the Most High will find rest in the shadow of the Almighty.

—Psalm 91:1 (NLT)

Our family has, on more than one occasion, taken shelter in our basement after we became aware of a tornado watch for our area. The warnings from the National Weather Service often call for strong, damaging winds to potentially be accompanied by torrential rainfall. With some blankets and a few battery-operated devices, including a cellphone, we know that in the underground part of the house, we would have better protection from the elements as well as the ability to enjoy TV and have access to a supply of food if the power did not go out. Somehow, it just made sense. Since these alerts are time-limited, a few hours later, we come up the stairs to fortunately discover nothing outside has occurred. But something could have, so it was better to have been safe than sorry. Sometimes the storms of our lives are meteorological; at times, they are man-made. On October 6, 1961, President John F. Kennedy advised American families to build bomb shelters to protect them from atomic fallout in the event of a nuclear exchange with the Soviet Union. Only one year later, true to Kennedy's fears, the world hovered on the brink of full-scale nuclear war when the Cuban Missile Crisis erupted over the USSR's placement of nuclear missiles in Cuba. During the tense thirteen-day crisis, some Americans prepared for nuclear war by buying up canned goods and completing last-minute work on their backyard bomb shelters.

How to save yourself and others from potential adversity has become an obsession of many over time. The doomsday philosophers have created an upswing in interest about how to properly prepare a safe space for almost any crisis, including power grid failures, nuclear disasters, tsunamis, earthquakes, terrorist attacks, or economic collapse. Start-to-finish guides for elaborate bunkers sometimes include cinemas, underground gardens, swimming pools, spas, wine vaults, and whatever other "necessities" you might deem important in order to find comfort during your anticipated apocalypse. Some claim that this frenzy has occurred as we find ourselves in an age of "secular humanism" where those without the security of religion believe their hope lies in working on ways to survive for as long as possible. Predictions about the end of the world have come and gone many times.

Jesus warned that someday this world as we know it *will* come to an end, not because of a war or natural disaster but because God will intervene at an established time only He knows. Jesus said, "It is not for you to know the times or dates the Father has set by his own authority" (Acts 1:7 NIV). Meanwhile, we have been appropriately warned of false prophecies and of Satan's influence in the world situation.

> This is how you can recognize the Spirit of God: Every spirit that acknowl-edges that Jesus Christ has come in the flesh is from God, but every spirit that does not acknowledge Jesus is not from God. This is the spirit of the antichrist, which you have heard is coming and even now is already in the world. You, dear children, are from God and have overcome them, because the one who is in you is greater than the one who is in the world. (1 John 4:2–4 NIV)

Our greatest adversary is alive and well.

As believers, we soon come to realize that wherever we seek safety, it is God's presence with us *in* that place that provides the strength and protection we really need. As he hid in a cave from an enemy who would kill him, David understood that feeling: "Have mercy on me, my God, have mercy on me, for in you I take refuge. I will take refuge in the shadow of your wings until the disaster has passed" (Psalm 57:1 NIV). As humans, we sometimes allow ourselves to view God's protection as a magic force field that keeps us from all harm. Yet Jesus affirmed that the storms of life will always be there. In reality, we will never know how many times God has actually protected us since He works in ways simply beyond our comprehension. Sometimes God's protection comes in the form of peace and strength in the middle of despair. Sometimes it comes in the form of an ending because He sees something more on the horizon that we cannot see. When we come to Christ, we are given new life as well as God's shield in which absolutely nothing can separate us from His love (Romans 8:38–39). The assurance of a safe space such as this will provide all the security we need, regardless of any fallout from the world around us.

Reflection

Consider what you define to be the safe spaces in your life. Do they include a sturdy home where you seek shelter in the event of a storm or the loving arms of a loved one when you are personally attacked? Where does God fit into this picture? How do you challenge yourself and others who sometimes unnecessarily seek safe spaces in their lives when they merely need to exercise faith in God's protection?

OCTOBER 7
(Y7, D40)

Who's in Charge of You?

But I am trusting you, O LORD, saying, "You are my God!" My future is in your hands.

—Psalm 31:14–15 (NLT)

You have no doubt seen the bumper stickers which profess, "God Is My Copilot." The saying was perhaps taken from the 1943 Robert Lee Scott Jr. World War II memoir using these same words and later adapted as a 1945 film. Some in the Christian community have been critical that this expression sends the wrong message. They argue that when we say that God is a "co-anything," it makes Him the same as that with which He is compared. For instance, by saying God is your copilot, you may be giving the impression that you are equal to God. You may also be unintentionally indicating that you don't totally trust God because you are not allowing Him to be fully in charge. In the specific case of an airplane, the copilot fully takes over the controls from the main pilot, only when told to do so. This begs the question, if God is our copilot, do we then do as we please and go where we want and only let God take over when needed? Would it perhaps be better to say, "God Is My Pilot"? It's certainly food for thought.

In her 2019 book, *Nerves of Steel*, author Tammie Jo Shults tells a powerful personal story of landing a damaged Southwest Airliner. On April 17, 2018, Shults was the captain of a routine four-hour domestic flight carrying 148 passengers from the LaGuardia to Dallas airports. Only twenty minutes into the flight at about 32, 00 feet, a piece of a turbine fan blade dislodged and caused catastrophic engine damage. The plane began to violently shudder, and debris shattered one of the passenger windows, releasing air out of the cabin. Passengers screamed, prayed, and began to send messages to their loved ones on the ground. Working together, Shults and her first officer were able to stabilize the aircraft. It was then that Shults made an intercom announcement, stating, "We are not going down. We are going to Philly." When the aircraft was cleared for landing, the captain uttered two words in the form of a question: "Heavenly Father?" It was as if she yielded the control of the plane to a higher authority by asking, "Okay, God, you got this?" With an aircraft that was resisting being steered in every way, Shults knew they had only one shot. And one shot was all that they needed with God as their pilot.

One of the major reasons many Christians consistently fail in their journey is because they want to be in charge using God as a backup when their plans do not work out. This attitude is always a platform for disaster. Consider the times you have tried to maintain control of your own life and ended up in one big mess. On those occasions, you most likely turned to God, ending up being rescued only when you finally surrendered to His will. When we decide to follow Christ, we must unlearn the falsehood that we are not the "captain of our own destiny." Moses instructed Joshua and the people of Israel: "The LORD himself goes before you and will be with you; he will never leave you nor forsake you. Do not be afraid; do not be discouraged" (Deuteronomy 31:8 NIV). In the midst of a life-or-death emergency, the Lord prepared and guided Captain Tammie Jo Shults through an incredible feat. Afterward, passengers said that her one simple reassuring message, "We're not going down," made all the difference. By stating this, the distraught travelers knew that their pilot was in control and that there was a plan and a safe destination awaiting them. As followers of Christ, we must cling to that viewpoint in our spiritual walk as well.

The passengers of the Southwest Airlines Flight quickly learned a lesson that sometimes the road is going to get bumpy. However, if you fully place your trust in the right captain, you will realize that He is in control. Like the Apostle Paul, we are transformed by the turbulent times we experience. "And since we are his children, we are his heirs. In fact, together with Christ we are heirs of God's glory. But if we are to share his glory, we must also share his suffering" (Romans 8:17 NLT). When we say God is our pilot instead of our copilot, we yield to His direction and recognize that because of His grace, we are indeed co-heirs. Someone once said, "If God is your copilot, then switch seats. If the devil is your copilot, then switch planes!" Asking God to guide our vessel is a life-altering decision. So who's in charge of you?

Reflection

Have there been aspects of your life you have released to God's control? What parts have you attempted to personally control? What will it take to for you to fully allow God to be in charge?

OCTOBER 8
(Y1, D41)

Always Ready to Listen

Call to me and I will answer you and tell you great and unsearchable things you do not know.

—Jeremiah 33:3 (NIV)

A few years ago, a good friend from high school was diagnosed with cancer. At that time, I had been in touch and prayed for him regularly. He had recovered, and it had been a while since we talked, so I decided to give him a call. During our conversation, he spoke at length about the journey he had been on since his remission. Then he went on to say, "There are times that I miss that period when I was so sick and receiving treatments." I was somewhat shocked by his comment and gently asked him to clarify what he meant. He said that prior to his illness, he had an established routine. After his diagnosis, he had no regular schedule. There were times that he had to totally rely on the medical professionals and his family for directing his care. It was during this time that he realized how dependent he was on God for healing, if that was to be His will. Now that he has recovered, he has resumed a daily schedule, although different than before. He went on to say, "You know, when you are in a day-to-day routine, it can become monotonous, and you have to be careful you don't lose sight of God." I think I understood.

In the ensuing days, His point of the importance of maintaining a direct line to God became clearer to me. It was during a frustrating attempt to install a new modem-router to alleviate a monthly cable company rental charge that I became more enlightened. After making the purchase and connecting the basic inputs, I followed the provided instructions and called the provider to solicit technical support to activate the new hardware. Bottom line, it took me several hours over the course of three days with four different agents to get everything working properly. In the end, I was finally referred to an individual who resolved my outstanding issues within a short period of time. Here are the lessons learned from this experience: (1) Whatever you pay may not necessarily get you where you want to go; (2) making the right connection is important for everything to function the way it should; (3) you have to find an individual on the other end who is willing to listen and hear the concerns you are facing; and (4) you must ultimately locate someone who has the right level of expertise to be able to address those concerns.

Apply all of this, if you will, to our relationship with God. Take price, for instance. For all who are willing to accept the gift, the cost of that connection has already been paid in full through the sacrificial death of His Son, Jesus. In the words of the Apostle Paul, "For God bought you with a high price" (1 Corinthians 6:20 NLT). There is no separation between God and us as there was in Jesus' day when there was a veil in the temple. It was here that only priests could intervene for us in a place known as the Holiest of Holies. But because of the shed blood of Jesus, "Through him we both have access to the Father by one Spirit" (Ephesians 2:18 NIV). Therefore, when we ask for help, we can be assured of His living presence. "This is the confidence we have in approaching God: that if we ask anything according to his will, he hears us" (1 John 5:14 NIV). While we can always seek the support from "earthly professionals," try finding a better expert to address our needs than the God of Creation. For "it is he who made us, and we are his" (Psalm 100:3 NIV). He understands what we require more than anyone else.

Every one of us has at one time or other made a phone call to the direct line of an individual, needing and fully expecting to get an answer on the other end. Frequently, however, our resulting connection is only to their voicemail. With God, it's far less technical. His "direct line" is only a prayer away; He is practical and has the listening ear that we need. But as is often said, effective communication is a two-way street. Pastor and author, Max Lucado, wrote "The next time you find yourself alone in a dark alley facing the undeniables of life, don't cover them with a blanket, or ignore them with a nervous grin. Don't turn up the TV and pretend they aren't there. Instead, stand still, whisper his name, and listen. He is nearer than you think." Remember that on any ordinary day, the Lord may send a revelation of encouragement, guidance, or instruction to us through the scriptures or another person. As my friend so aptly expressed, we can't allow ourselves to get so consumed in the day-to-day routine that we lose sight of the fact that God is constantly beside us and that He is always ready to listen.

Reflection

Do you take full advantage of your everyday access to God? Or do you wait for those times of desperation to reach out? What are some ways you might draw closer by including Him as a part of your daily routine? How will you monitor your activities to make sure you maintain a regular connection?

OCTOBER 9
(Y2, D41)

Finding the Better Part without Distraction

Looking unto Jesus the author and finisher of our faith.

—Hebrews 12:2 (KJB)

With the overload of information, high level of competition, and the fast-paced nature of our culture, it's easy to become distracted. We've become conditioned to distraction, and it's harming our ability to listen and think carefully, to be still, and to simply be in the moment. It shifts our attention from something of greater importance to something of lesser importance. There is a story involving Yogi Berra, the well-known catcher for the New York Yankees, and Hank Aaron, who at that time was the chief power hitter for the Milwaukee Braves. The teams were playing in the World Series, and as usual, Yogi was constantly chattering, intending to pep up his teammates on the one hand while distracting the opposing batters on the other. As Aaron came to the plate, Yogi tried to sidetrack him by saying, "Henry, you're holding the bat wrong. You're supposed to hold it so you can read the trademark."

Aaron didn't say anything. But when the next pitch came in, he hit it into the left-field bleachers. After rounding the bases and tagging up at home plate, Aaron looked at Yogi Berra and said, "I didn't come up here to read."

A fundamental and most dangerous problem for Christians is when they allow themselves to become distracted. It's hard to stay focused on Jesus when we spend more time concentrating on other things. This happened to Jesus' friend, Martha. Martha was busy in the kitchen while He was teaching in her home. Martha complained that her sister, Mary, wasn't helping because she was sitting at His feet. "But the Lord said to her, 'My dear Martha, you are worried and upset over all these details! There is only one thing worth being concerned about. Mary has discovered it, and it will not be taken away from her" (Luke 10:41–42 NLT). Martha was distracted from Jesus by serving her guests, anxious and wanting to do it to the best of her ability. But Martha didn't recognize her distraction until Jesus helped her to see her heart. He pointed out that her values were disordered and that like her sister, she should choose "the better part." By not doing so, she had shifted her attention from the greater importance to the lesser.

In our busyness, we must learn to recognize our own distractions by challenging ourselves as to whether we are prioritizing our focus on the important things or on something less. Toward the end of 1941, as the Second World War was raging in Europe, the Japanese ambassador was sent to Washington DC, apparently seeking peace; however, back in Japan, the emperor was planning the attack on Pearl Harbor. This was a distraction shrewdly devised by the Empire of Japan so that when the sudden attack on Pearl Harbor took place, the United States was completely surprised. Distraction is a common tactic in warfare. Our enemy is constantly seeking to distract us, both to divert our energies and to keep our eyes off his attack strategy. He wants to distract us from our calling and set us up for the kill. The things of this world can easily allow us to get caught up in endless tasks and issues that are pointless. Renewing our mind requires that we must constantly refocus on the things of this life that truly matter.

Once, when Jesus and His disciples were in Jericho, a blind man by the name of Bartimaeus was sitting and begging by the side of the road. "When Bartimaeus heard that Jesus of Nazareth was nearby, he began to shout, 'Jesus, Son of David, have mercy on me!'" (Mark 10:47 NLT). Many in the crowd tried to silence him, but he persisted. By calling Jesus "Son of David," he gave every indication he knew exactly who He was. "'What do you want me to do for you?' Jesus asked. 'My Rabbi,' the blind man said, 'I want to see!' And Jesus said to him, 'Go, for your faith has healed you.' Instantly the man could see, and he followed Jesus down the road" (Mark 10:51–52 NLT). Bartimaeus was not distracted; even in his blindness, He was focused solely on Jesus. Many things flourish in this world in an attempt to steal our attention away from what is most important. As the hymnwriter Helen Lemmel once wrote, "Turn your eyes upon Jesus, look full in His wonderful face, and the things of earth will grow strangely dim in the light of His glory and grace." As we cultivate a habit of focus, it will result in a new motivation that comes from a clear vision, one that helps us in finding the better part without distraction.

Reflection

Was there a time you can remember when the storm you were in distracted you from recognizing Jesus? Take a look at your life today, and ask if there is something that has been taking away from your relationship with Him. What are some ways you can live intentionally and more focused?

OCTOBER 10
(Y3, D41)

A Line Worth Crossing Over

This they said to test him, that they might have some charge to bring against him. Jesus bent down and wrote with his finger on the ground.

—John 8:6 (ESV)

According to early American folklore, Colonel William Barrett Travis was the command officer at the Alamo in 1836. While faced with a demand to surrender, it is alleged that he drew a line in the sand with his sword. In doing so, he asked that those willing to remain and defend the Alamo to their deaths step across the line. All but one crossed the line and stayed. Each of them died. Over time, this story has remained a symbol for those who will stand for a cause as opposed to those who will not. Even today, whenever world leaders metaphorically draw lines in the sand with other nations, it represents a show of force to make it known that certain acts of aggression will not be tolerated. Likewise, companies often establish mission statements to define their purpose while instituting policies specifically designed to keep their employees in line. In an attempt to strictly discipline their children, parents often set limit lines and propose consequences for disobeying them. And, yes, even churches draw lines in the form of declarations and doctrine to indicate their standards and beliefs.

As new persons in the faith journey, one is often confronted with choosing between denying their former self and embracing one's newfound faith (Matthew 16:24). The struggle often leads to the conflict of a blurred line in which one is faced with attempting to have one foot in the world and the other with God. While in our hearts we have a desire to follow Christ, our heads tell us that if we completely do so, there will be things we have to give up. This results in some adopting an attitude that they will be committed to Christianity just so far, thus drawing their own line of conviction. It doesn't get any easier when we grow to become more grounded, faith deepens, and our path becomes more solidly defined. The dare to "live like Christ within reason" is always there. And it's the debate of reasoning that will sometimes make the journey difficult. It's as though we have a compass that points us in the right direction, but instead, we choose to rely on our instinct and end up getting lost as a result.

Our "true north" must always focus on the teachings of Jesus. In John 8:1–11, Jesus publicly risks his life as he sides with a woman who had been caught in the act of adultery. In doing so, he crossed the line by challenging the authority of the law in His day. Instead, he embraced compassion, mercy, love, and forgiveness. He distorted the line even further by telling the accusers to cast the first stone if they were without sin in their own lives. Of course, no stone was cast. In God's Word, there are evident situations during which a theoretical line in the sand was drawn and choices had to be made. When this occurred, it was quite apparent that the choice differentiated between standing with God or opposing Him. John said it quite clearly, "Do not love this world nor the things it offers you, for when you love the world, you do not have the love of the Father in you" (1 John 2:15 NLT).

So, fellow sojourners, it comes down to this: we cannot straddle the fence because we will eventually fall on one side or the other. If we declare ourselves to be followers of Jesus, we must understand that there is sometimes a line we must step across in order to stand with Him. "Come close to God, and God will come close to you. Wash your hands, you sinners; purify your hearts, for your loyalty is divided between God and the world" (James 4:8 NLT). Ultimately, it's about becoming more like Jesus. Less about me and more about Him. Now there's a line worth stepping over.

Reflection

Where do you draw your line in the sand when it comes to your faith? Do your personal lines reflect truth contained in the Word of God? When it comes to acceptance and forgiveness, have you drawn lines with others you have not dared to cross? What would it take to break down these barriers? What worldly characteristics sometimes inhibit you from becoming more like Jesus?

OCTOBER 11
(Y4, D41)

In His Wheelhouse

Each of you should use whatever gift you have received to serve others,
as faithful stewards of God's grace in its various forms.

—1 Peter 4:10 (NIV)

If you listen to the baseball playoff games and the announcer calling the game says, "I didn't know that was in his wheelhouse," he is most likely speaking of the batter who just had a great hit. When the player gets a pitch that is in his wheelhouse, it means the ball crossed the plate in the perfect zone for that particular batter to exercise his greatest control and power. In other words, the pitch was right where the batter would want it. Likewise, if you are sitting in a brainstorming session somewhere in corporate America, trying to figure out a way to implement a new product, someone at the table might speak up and say, "I'm not afraid to tackle that since its well within my wheelhouse." In this case, the individual using the terminology is applying the slang expression to indicate that they believe the resolution to the project application may be within their area of capability.

In reality, the original definition of wheelhouse is that part of a boat where the skipper has excellent visibility is best able to control the vessel and is prepared to face any perils that might be encountered. The term is commonly used for the pilot house on a steamboat. Applied to a person, a wheelhouse describes one's area of expertise. Those who work with their hands use skills within their wheelhouse to define their work. Many grow to be quite adept at what they do and become known as master craftsmen in their field. Others use their power of reasoning to become excellent teachers, investors, or project designers. Lucky for us that we do not all share the same wheelhouse. If that was the case, the world would most likely cease to function as we know it, and it might be a pretty dull place.

As we traverse the road of life, we hopefully come to realize that everything we have in our personal wheelhouse is a gift from God. The gifts that we have are not ours alone; they are meant to be shared with others. Jesus taught that we should use our gifts wisely. In Matthew 25:14–30, He shares His Parable of the Talents in which a man going on a journey entrusts three servants with various sums of money. Two of the servants make good use of their master's investment. The third hides it, and his master is displeased. Like the three servants in the parable, we, too, are given a wide variety of gifts, not the same degree. The servant who did nothing with the gift was not condemned because he hadn't achieved like the other two but rather because he did nothing with what he had been given. Paul put it this way: "Now there are varieties of gifts, but the same Spirit. And there are varieties of ministries, and the same Lord. There are varieties of effects, but the same God who works all things in all persons. But to each one is given the manifestation of the Spirit for the common good" (1 Corinthians 12:4–7 NASB).

If we are part of the family of God and fortunate to be surrounded by others who are spiritually like-minded, we come to realize that we each play an important and significant role in service to others. The problem with many of us is that we sometimes use our talents for our own glory or do nothing with them at all. We grow to become captain of our own vessel and the manager of our own wheelhouse. We develop possessiveness of that which God has made possible in the first place. Our vision for the journey becomes clouded, and we are at risk of being shipwrecked. When we lose sight of who we are, it's important that we invite God to right the ship. Fortunately for us, God's wheelhouse is filled with grace. We have access to it at any time through faith in Him. There we will be rescued with enough peace, joy, and love to direct us away from the storms of life and put us back on the right course for the voyage ahead.

Reflection

What talents has God provided for your wheelhouse? When you think of the Parable of the Talents, have there been times in your life in which you have played the role of the various servants? When you lose direction, have you found God's grace to be sufficient to get you back on track? Can you apply Philippians 2:13 (NIV), "For it is God who works in you to will and to act in order to fulfill his good purpose" to different phases of your life's journey?

OCTOBER 12
(Y5, D41)

Finding Security in an Insecure World

You will be secure, because there is hope; you will look about you and take your rest in safety.

—Job 11:18 (NIV)

We live in a world filled with fear, uncertainty, and anxiety. It has been a constant law of human nature for thousands of years to somehow gain security against an uncertain future. There are always those who are predicting some major disaster looming on the horizon, threatening to disrupt life as we know it on this planet. Some of this insecurity could occur in nature, ranging from earthquakes to climate change. Then there is international extremism with threats posed by nuclear bombs, chemical warfare and bioterrorism. Even in our own homes, we install security systems and computer software to prevent viruses from hacking our computers. Credit card companies get breeched for personal identity theft, and we are told to pay attention to the financial markets regarding threats of an upcoming economic crash. We learn insecurity at an early age, and most of us carry it through our entire lives. Who of us in our early days has not depended on an object or person for reassurance and comfort, our security blanket of sorts?

First introduced in the *Peanuts* comic strip in 1954, Charlie Brown's best friend, Linus, can be seen carrying his blanket around and sucking his thumb. Ironically, in *A Charlie Brown Christmas*, he sets down his blanket to recite the nativity story which he has memorized. In that instant, Linus laid down what was probably the most precious thing to him to let the other children know about the true meaning of Christmas. He carried his blanket everywhere he went; however, as Linus cites the significant words "fear not," he drops his blanket, the thing that gives him the most comfort. In that moment, Linus forgets his fear and is able to speak up before all of his peers. Charles Shultz, the creator of the *Peanuts* comic, could not be sending a clearer message. With Jesus came the absence of fear. Our security comes from the fact that Jesus Christ was born and died in exchange for our lives. But as creatures of habit, it is only a matter of time before we reach down to reach for a substitute that gives us the most comfort. Much like Linus, we pick up the problems we have laid down because it has become our habit to be insecure.

Throughout historic and scriptural accounts, we find many illustrations where people felt a great sense of insecurity. Their uncertainty may have come from the possibility of famine, so they hoarded grain. When the uncertainty came from the risk of theft, people pursued security by burying their wealth in the ground or by arming themselves. If the uncertainty came from the threat of disease, they created idols and offered sacrifices to various gods, pleading for protection against forces too great. David understood the true source of refuge: "It is God who arms me with strength and keeps my way secure" (2 Samuel 22:33 NIV). The psalmist wrote, "This I declare about the LORD: He alone is my refuge, my place of safety; he is my God, and I trust him" (Psalm 91:2 NLT). And an author in the New Testament stated: "Therefore, we who have fled to him for refuge can have great confidence we hold to the hope that lies before us" (Hebrews 6:18 NLT). The key to living a secure life is knowing who you are in Christ, reaching out and receiving God's love, and basing your worth and value knowing that you are one of His.

As the world reflects on the insecurity resulting from the millions of deaths resulting from COVID, we recognized that the worldwide pandemic that took so many lives was a very insecure period in our lives. During the worldwide spread of the coronavirus and prior to vaccines being available, most of us found our greatest security to be in the comfort of our own home. Emerging new strains have provoked further uneasiness for what any sense of normalcy might mean in the future. Believers cannot escape this insecure world, but we can be secure in the midst of it. Our safety does not lie in any external means of protection but in the knowledge that God is in control and is looking out for us. We need not live our lives masked from fear because He has three prescriptions to protect us. They are faith, hope, and love (1 Corinthians 13:13), and they immunize our hearts against all the diseases of the soul. And when all is well with your soul, you will always find true security in an otherwise insecure world.

Reflection

Where does your sense of security come from? What would you say to someone who proposes that our eternal security is conditional, based on our actions? How could you use the words from Ephesians 2:8–9 to help a nonbeliever understand that their eternal security is not based on works but rather through the redemption of God's love and grace?

OCTOBER 13
(Y6, D41)

A Spiritual Cornerstone

The stone the builders rejected has become the cornerstone.

—Psalm 118:22 (NIV)

The establishment of the United States capital on the banks of the Potomac River was the result of political compromise between the Federalist and the Republican factions of the early republic. The states of Maryland and Virginia relinquished land to form the District of Columbia with work on the new city beginning in 1791. One year later, plans were made for a neoclassical presidential home on Pennsylvania Avenue. On October 13, 1792, the cornerstone of the building, which would later become known as the White House, was laid during a Masonic ceremony overseen by member George Washington who had selected the site. Supposedly, the cornerstone went missing the following day, and no one has seen it since. Many attempts have been made to find it. In the 1940s, then President Harry Truman renovated the building. The rooms were completely dismantled and rebuilt, and a new internal load-bearing steel frame was constructed inside the walls. During this time, a letter was found which uncovered the fact that the first stone was actually laid in the southwest corner of the building. One theory is that the cornerstone might have ended up between two stone walls in the Rose Garden, but so far, nothing has been found there. Its location remains an unsolved American mystery.

The cornerstone is one of a building's most important pieces since it is the first stone to be set and also determines the position of all the pieces to be laid afterward. Cornerstones have been part of building structures for centuries. In the case of the White House cornerstone, it can be assumed that the piece was quite large in size and very heavy, since it was made out of Aquia sandstone from Virginia. Some imagine that the stone was inscribed by the Founding Fathers, while others believe there was a plate on top with the date it was established. Over time, cornerstones have often taken on the purpose of a ceremonial masonry stone. Usually set in a prominent location on the outside of a building, these stones often contain inscriptions indicating the construction dates of the building, sometimes including the names of significant individuals. In years past, a piece of the cornerstone would be hollowed out to act as a type of time capsule to contain artifacts from the era in which a particular building was built. In biblical times, a cornerstone was used as the foundation and standard upon which a building was constructed. Once in place, the rest of the building would conform to the angles and size of the cornerstone. In addition, if removed, the entire structure could be in danger of collapse.

The book of Isaiah makes many references to a coming Messiah. God prophesied through Isaiah that He would place a foundation stone in Jerusalem, "a firm and tested stone. It is a precious cornerstone that is safe to build on. Whoever believes need never be shaken" (Isaiah 28:16 NLT). Hundreds of years later, Jesus identified Himself as this stone: "Didn't you ever read this in the Scriptures? 'The stone that the builders rejected has now become the cornerstone. This is the LORD's doing, and it is wonderful to see" (Matthew 21:42 NLT). It's amazing how the Prophet Isaiah and the Apostle Peter both reference the term of building stones to complete a nice thread that flows from the writing of a heavenly promise in the Old Testament to the New Testament gospel about the one who called this disciple. Peter provides a description that all who believe in Christ are "like living stones...being built into a spiritual house" (1 Peter 2:5 NIV) which hold together as the one edifice of God's people spread throughout the earth.

The illustration of Jesus as the cornerstone upon which the "household of God" was being built would have been well-understood by the early Christians. For those living in societies where people often built their own homes, using construction terminology to explain the priority of Jesus the Messiah as the cornerstone of the household of God provided a clear connecting point that would have made absolute sense. Just as the cornerstone is laid as a guide to line up the rest of a structure, we need to be sure that our life is in alignment with Christ and His teachings. Unlike the one at the White House, the cornerstone of Jesus Christ will never disappear and is one we can be certain to safely build upon.

Reflection

Consider your preferences, experiences, traditions, and values. Do they align your life to establish a cornerstone for your faith? If not, how might you hit the reset button to adjust the substance of your journey on the teachings of Christ? In what ways can you better set an example for others to be "fellow citizens with God's people and also members of his household built on the foundation of the apostles and prophets, with Christ Jesus himself as the chief cornerstone" (Ephesians 2:19–20 NIV)?

OCTOBER 14
(Y7, D41)

Autumn Fingerprints

He made the moon to mark the seasons; the sun knows its time for setting.

—Psalm 104:19 (ESV)

As I look out my window or take a walk through the park, it's easy to see the changing seasons. We are reminded of the ending of the vibrancy of summer as evidenced by the beautiful flowers which have lost their grandeur surrendering to hues of brown and gray. Once thriving leaves drop from their branches, bursting with color, but are now dying. Colder temperatures flow in, and bright, long days full of sunshine move out. When autumn arrives, I am reminded that I have never been a fan. I have often wondered if it somehow stems from my youth when the darkness of the early evening signaled that it was time to put aside playtime and redirect my focus on the more serious task of my studies. Then, too, the arrival of fall meant that when I would go outside, I had to "bundle up so I wouldn't catch cold" as my mother would so aptly put it. Now I find myself using the remaining garden tomatoes and discarding the once-fresh flowers which had been brought in from the yard to escape the pending frost waiting in the wings.

It was the tossing of those wilted flowers that got me to thinking. For the past week or so, they had been held in water contained in an antique vase which has been in our family for generations. As I washed out the vessel, I held it carefully to make sure it would not slip out of my hands and break. I wondered about the many ancestors who had held that vase and reflected as to how long it had been since their fingerprints remained on its surface. Then my mind drifted to those brown leaves on the ground just outside. They had proudly displayed the green of summer and later the colors of early autumn, and now they provide a fingerprint on the earth. Their decay will give nourishment to the soil and, before long, will help to bring forth a new season of beauty. It brings meaning to that familiar scriptural passage, "For everything there is a season, a time for every activity under heaven. A time to be born and a time to die. A time to plant and a time to harvest" (Ecclesiastes 3:1–2 NLT). Certainly, God's creation must have a purpose for the seasons of our life as well. As I watch the leaves dropping one by one, we should consider that perhaps He is simply making room for the future gifts He is preparing for us.

For those of us who have never been crazy about autumn, we might ask what it is that God intends for us to see. When we look at a fallen leaf or disintegrating summer flower, it might be appropriate to reflect on this biblical thought: For "All people are like grass, and all their glory is like the flowers of the field; the grass withers and the flowers fall, but the word of the Lord endures forever" (1 Peter 1:24–25 NIV). We too are a finite and fallen creation soon to pass. Any glory we claim to have is as short-lived as the green leaves of a now-ending season. We seek to accomplish much, but in the end, we disappear from this earth. It would be prudent then for us to ponder what fingerprint we will leave for those generations which follow. We will make our greatest impact if we would strive to understand the Word of God and live out the teachings of Jesus. Unlike the decaying leaves of the season, these will endure because God never changes. He is "the same yesterday and today and forever" (Hebrews 13:8 NIV).

So we find ourselves caught between the abundance of summer and dormancy of winter in the momentary uniqueness of another fall. Autumn is a study in contrasts, and the result is a strange mixture of nostalgia, blessings, and potential. It yields the harvest of seeds we've sown throughout life and braces us for colder days to come. We might find that this a good time to focus on our commitment to God. When life's autumn arrives, we look back and gain a better understanding of the way He has led us. But in this time of transition, we should recognize we still have work to do. We are reminded that we need to let go of anything that would hinder a fresh relationship with Him. During this season, trust God fully as you wait for the harvest. He has a good plan for each life, though some days, the fruit may not be evident. As we watch those dancing leaves fall to the ground and place their fingerprint on the earth, we too must reach an understanding that we must die unto ourselves and become a new creation (Luke 9:23–24). As we do this, we will soon learn that the rebirth of springtime is just around the corner.

Reflection

As you look back at the various seasons of your life, in what ways do you find evidence of God's loving presence? What are you holding on to that is preventing a freshness to the current season ahead? What fingerprints of your life will you leave behind that will positively impact others?

OCTOBER 15
(Y1, D42)

Seen and Unseen

For we live by believing and not by seeing.

—2 Corinthians 5:7 (NLT)

"Now you see it, now you don't." It's a phrase we learned as small children. Perhaps it was related to a series of cups and balls where the balls appeared to be shifted from one cup to the other or disappear entirely. Maybe it was a card trick, when the one you selected ended up in a place you would never have expected. At an early age, it was magic! For me, the phrase took on a whole new meaning recently when I was checking out at the local grocery store. The clerk scanned each of my items as they came up the conveyor belt, while down the line, a girl was packing my groceries. The teller provided my receipt, and I paused to ask her a question about a store gift card. After a brief conversation, I thanked her and turned away to see an empty cart. I asked the young lady who had been bagging where my groceries were, and she looked at me like I had three heads. Apparently, she had loaded my bags into the cart of another customer who had already exited the store, now in possession of a larger order than expected.

We take comfort in and base our understanding on the things that we see on what we believe to be true. We fully expect, for instance, that when we pay for goods or services that we will receive them. Predictability is important to our way of life, and when that doesn't occur, our abilities to rationalize and cope become vulnerable. During the development of the COVID-19 pandemic, many people who had never felt anxious became preoccupied with worry and were not sure what to do next. Viral outbreaks are frightening to many people because you can't see the enemy, in this case the microscopic bacteria that cause you to become infected. However, viruses are not the only things that can't be seen with the naked eye. The Bible reveals that there is an "unseen" world all around us. In fact, scripture tells us that as persons of faith, we must "fix our eyes not on what is seen, but on what is unseen" (2 Corinthians 4:18 NIV). You might wonder how that could be true, but fortunately, the writer, Paul, continues to explain "what is seen is temporary, but what is unseen is eternal." For one who comes to follow Christ rather than the world, this provides a whole new frame of reference.

As believers, we come to realize that he importance of eyesight is true in the physical realm, but it means almost nothing in the spiritual realm. The Israelites saw multiple miracles in the wilderness, but the actual "seeing" seems to not have profited them at all. Consider their experience. There were ten plagues inflicted on Egypt, forcing the Pharaoh to allow them to be freed from slavery. They saw the Red Sea part as well as the pillar of fire at night and a cloud by day to guide them. They saw water coming out of rocks and were provided with manna on the ground daily for forty years. Yet, what they physically saw did not affect their minds because eyesight means almost nothing in terms of the spiritual. Faith is the foundation, the assurance, the substance, the confidence, of things not seen—the invisible realm of God. Faith is trusting God for something to happen which we have not seen or experienced before. It was by faith that Noah was warned by God about things he had not yet seen, but in reverence, he prepared an ark. By faith, Abraham obeyed God and went out not knowing where he was going. By faith, Sarah received the ability to conceive beyond human possibility (Hebrews 11:7–11).

When we were young, we wanted to have faith in magic, if only for a while. Now that we are "grown up," we continue to live with tension between what is seen and unseen. If the things we see are made of things that we cannot see, why then is it so hard to believe that we cannot see the Creator without a proper lens? We must conclude it is only faith that becomes the microscope which satisfies our soul. Saint Augustine brilliantly said, "Faith is to believe what we do not see, and the reward of this faith is to see what we believe." It's often much easier to conform to the commonly held beliefs of our culture than it is to trust in things unseen. But it's the living by faith that God rewards. "Faith shows the reality of what we hope for; it is the evidence of things we cannot see" (Hebrews 11:1 NLT). We may not see everything we want to see. But we can see what we need to until the time is right to see more.

Reflection

When you consider how you view life, are you looking at the things which are seen? Or are you focusing more on those things which are unseen? What would your response be to a skeptic who says, "I don't believe in miracles because I have never seen one?" How would you explain to a person who is new to the faith that not everything has to be seen in order to believe?

OCTOBER 16
(Y2, D42)

Attempting to Cancel Jesus

From eternity to eternity I am God. No one can snatch anyone
out of my hand. No one can undo what I have done.

—Isaiah 43:13 (NLT)

While preparations were being made for Philadelphia's annual Columbus Day parade in 2021, a Christopher Columbus statue in South Philly remained encased in a wooden box for a second year. The location became a site of several violent clashes between opposing protest groups initiated in the previous year. The Italian explorer, often credited with discovering the New World, has a complex legacy. For many Italian-Americans, Columbus is a cultural hero for his courageous exploits and should be admired; but for many others, he is a controversial symbol of violent colonization and oppression. While Italian-Americans have long been accepted as part of the nation's fabric, that very fabric has been torn into shreds by those who can only see the country's flaws. Meanwhile, the City of Brotherly Love found itself playing a part in a "cancel culture cleansing" of time-honored traditions.

The phrase "cancel culture" refers to the practice of discarding someone who doesn't agree with you or may have acted in such a way that what is now considered unacceptable may have once been the cultural norm. Erasing history distorts the facts and negates who we are. Participants in this crusade are not content to stop with tearing down monuments. They are ostracizing entire groups of people, including Christians. While the cancel culture movement is alive and well, it is not new. In the 1960s, prayer was eliminated, and the Supreme Court banned Bible readings in the public schools. It's been a while since nativity scenes have been openly welcomed in the town square. Christians are facing a new battle and wonder how far it might go. As the cancel culture aims to nullify Jesus, believers must consciously consider if they will stay silent or how and when they will exercise their voice in opposition.

Jesus called "cancelled people" his friends. In fact, his circle of followers included a betrayer, a thief, and a prostitute, just to name a few. He was unwilling to abandon the worst of the worst and the guiltiest of the guilty. He moved toward those whom society moved away from. He befriended, loved, and touched the outcast, the misfit, the leper, the liar, and many other shunned persons. He refused to dismiss those who had been dismissed, reject those who had been rejected, denounce those who had been denounced, and shame those who had been shamed. In fact, his closest friends were of such ill-repute that the religious leaders concluded Jesus must be an impostor because no self-respecting man of God would embrace the kinds of people Jesus embraced (Mark 2:16–17). He became a thorn in the side of the major establishment players of his day. They attempted to cancel Him because of it, while instead "He canceled the record of the charges against us and took it away by nailing it to the cross" (Colossians 2:14 NLT).

Any act of canceling a person is essentially attempting to play God, for He is the ultimate authority and judge of all things. When we seek to silence a person or group based on their religious beliefs, we are trying to take away from the only one who has the power to cancel. The Lord understands our sinful nature and knows we are flawed. But He is the God of grace and mercy, and He is not looking to cancel anyone. On the contrary, He wants to extend His redemptive gift of salvation to all. Tullian Tchividjian, grandson of Billy Graham, stated it this way: "The sins and scandals that cancel culture chooses not to forget, Jesus chooses not to remember. That's the big difference between Jesus and cancel culture: while our Culture (including the church) cancels people who have done terrible things, Jesus cancels the horrible things that people are cancelled for." Have no fear, for God himself cannot be canceled because He is the ultimate authority, "the Beginning and the End" (Revelation 22:13). While the cancel culture aims to remove Him from society, He provides the power for His followers to be prayerful and enables them to speak boldly in His name. How we conduct ourselves by what we do and say will provide an opportunity for others to see the glory of God. If we seek unification by loving and treating people as Christ did, we move closer to calling out those who would make any efforts to cancel Jesus.

Reflection

Consider situations when you may have become unintentionally involved in the cancel movement. Are there specific persons whom you have felt to be unworthy of God's love and grace because of something that have said or done? How might you be more inclusive of these individuals?

OCTOBER 17
(Y3, D42)

Anonymous

Beware of practicing your righteousness before other people in order to be seen by them, for then you will have no reward from your Father who is in heaven.

—Matthew 6:1 (ESV)

A young widow goes to her mailbox. It contains several cards, all expressing sympathy for the recent passing of her husband. Among them, one stands out as being a bit unusual. First, it contains one-hundred dollars in cash which will gratefully be used in some way to make payment on the many unexpected bills they have received throughout her husband's illness. But secondly and even more uncommon, after a brief note of condolence, the card is simply signed "A Friend." She wonders who might be so kind as to remember her in this way and what was their reason for not signing the card. The gesture touches her then and even to this day when she recollects the special manner in which it was given.

Following an accident at work which has caused him to be at least temporarily disabled, a man receives a letter containing these words:

> I am aware of your injury through a friend. I want you to know that I am now on the upswing after having passed through a very difficult time in my life. During the long journey back to normalcy, there were those who reached out to me, some whom I knew would do so but also others who surprised me. Among them were those I didn't even know. Now, years later, I run into or are introduced to folks who tell me that during my troublesome journey, they were praying for me. So, my unknown friend, that's what I want you to know. Throughout this dark period in your life, there are those, like myself, whom you do not know who are and will be praying for you.

Anonymity can be good thing if done for the right reasons. The group Alcoholics Anonymous attracts attendance in part because of the confidentiality of its membership. Throughout history, some literary works and famous quotes have been published by that notorious author, Anon. Likewise and to their credit, there are prominent individuals who do wonderful acts of charity choosing to remain anonymous. Others seemed to be motivated in their giving by having their name publicly attached. People of means can dominate many causes, be they political or charitable, and gain recognition for it. In doing so, they exert influence or derive benefit from man-made systems such as the tax law. One political candidate was recently quoted as saying: "I think we need to recognize that it may be time to quit worrying so much about the tax code and start thinking about the truth of the living God, and if it means that we give up tax deductions for charitable contributions, I choose freedom more than I choose a deduction."

Jesus stated it this way:

> So when you give to the poor, do not sound a trumpet before you, as the hypocrites do in the synagogues and in the streets, so that they may be honored by men. Truly I say to you, they have their reward in full. But when you give to the poor, do not let your left hand know what your right hand is doing, so that your giving will be in secret; and your Father who sees what is done in secret will reward you. When you pray, you are not to be like the hypocrites; for they love to stand and pray in the synagogues and on the street corners so that they may be seen by men. Truly I say to you, they have their reward in full. But you, when you pray, go into your inner room, close your door and pray to your Father who is in secret, and your Father who sees what is done in secret will reward you. (Matthew 6:2–6 NASB)

Is it always wrong then to do good works with the awareness of others? Of course not. I recently took a gift of food to a neighbor who had surgery. On the other hand, I once chose to write a weekly devotional blog anonymously. My thought in doing so is that if the reader is blessed in any way from the words I had penned, I would attribute that to God who worked through me in writing them. For you see, "Every good and perfect gift is from above, coming down from the Father of the heavenly lights, who does not change like shifting shadows" (James 1:17 NIV). It's difficult to possess or have your name attached to something without it owning you just a little. For those who choose to walk with Christ, giving anonymously encourages us to serve in kindness and to do so for the right reasons.

Reflection

Are there ways you might need to examine your reasons for giving? How might you allow the words "Give as freely as you have received!" (Matthew 10:8 NLT) to serve as inspiration to giving without expecting anything in return? In what ways might you be able to help others understand that giving anonymously will be blessed in the eyes of God?

OCTOBER 18
(Y4, D42)

A Gift We Don't Deserve

God saved you by his grace when you believed. And you
can't take credit for this; it is a gift from God.

—Ephesians 2:8 (NLT)

While watching one of my favorite TV dramas, I pondered over a line I had just heard spoken by one of the main characters. In the story, the head of an emergency room in a challenged, sometimes understaffed inner-city hospital was questioned by one of the nurses about an order she had just given. Apparently, it contradicted her usual protocol about how to care for a certain type of patient. The director of the ER simply looked at the nurse and made the following response referring to her directive: "He's already paid the ultimate price. I decided to choose grace." This got me to thinking when if at all and in what situations we might be capable of showing grace to another person. Or is that an impossible task for anyone, except for Almighty God? If it is true that when we experience God's grace, we receive favor that we do not deserve, then I think as beings who are created in His image (Genesis 1:27), we must be capable of showing grace at times to others as well.

I remember a friend of mine once telling me that in his work, he would sometimes have to discharge persons after they had broken company policies. He shared that he would always try to allow the person he was releasing to leave with a sense of dignity. If possible, he would supply a reference for them to get another job, even though in order for him to do so, they might be forced to seek employment in another field. While he was obligated to follow the company's employment procedures, he always attempted to put himself in the position of the person he was releasing by showing concern for their future. To me, what he attempted to do was an example of showing grace to others. He went on to say that there were times years later when he would run into some of these individuals who would come up to him and thank him for giving them a new start. He operated by the principle that we need to get along with people without hurting them, even when they challenge us to do otherwise.

I am reminded of a story of a wealthy man who hired an impoverished builder to construct a house. Per the man's instruction, the house was to be magnificent. The builder was given unlimited resources and was told to use the finest material. Instead, the builder decided that he could cut corners by using inferior products. In doing so, he covered up the gaps and masked all of his mistakes. While beautiful in appearance, the home would soon reveal its poor workmanship. It would undoubtedly leak and be unable to keep out the heat and cold. Upon completion, he handed the keys to the man who had commissioned him. However, the wealthy man never meant for the house to be his own. Because he had sensed the need of the poor builder, he had intended that the dream home be a gift for the builder, one that would protect he and his family for years to come. So instead of taking the keys to the house, he gave them back, saying, "I wanted it to be a source of grace and blessing to you and your family."

I wonder how many times we were intended to be the recipient of God's free gift of grace but failed to recognize it as our own. If we look closely at the world around us, we will see many a person who is thirsty for grace. In our journey, we will also soon discover that life's greatest hurts come from other people. They use us, take advantage of us, or turn their backs on us. Yet, if we are going to be like Jesus, we need to love them, even those who are difficult to love. Jesus set the example for us, coming to earth to be one of us and then dying for all of mankind, even for those who hated Him most. "From his abundance we have all received one gracious blessing after another. For the law was given through Moses, but God's unfailing love and faithfulness came through Jesus Christ" (John 1:16–17 NLT). What He provides for us is a gift we don't deserve. To claim this gift, you must sense your own need and receive it with open hands. Now that, my friends, is the true essence of amazing grace. How sweet the sound!

Reflection

Consider the difference between grace and mercy, the latter being defined as the withholding of what we do deserve. Can you think of examples of both in your own life? In what ways can you use your own examples as an encouragement for others who feel unworthy?

OCTOBER 19
(Y5, D42)

Praying in Tight Spots

When I am overwhelmed, you alone know the way I should turn.

—Psalm 142:3 (NLV)

As my friend mentally prepared herself to go for the MRI ordered by her physician, she couldn't help but think of the confined tunnel-like scanning machine into which she would be placed. She understood the diagnostic advantages of having these tests performed. She knew that the MRI machines themselves had certainly been upgraded over the years and were not nearly as unpleasant as they once were. However, that did not help the fact that she was a bit claustrophobic whenever she found herself in tight spaces. Before consenting to the test, she was told that if she felt too anxious a sedative could be administered prior to the procedure. Hoping that this would not be necessary, she traveled to the facility on the day of the scheduled test and was taken to a waiting area where she sat alone. Then out through a door marked "Radiology" came a lady much older than she. Pausing to get a drink at the water cooler, the elder looked over and said, "First time?" to which my friend acknowledged that it was. "Oh it's not so bad, just noisy. You'll be fine. Just think of other things. I sing hymns and say prayers," she shared.

For whatever reason, as my friend entered the scanner, she began to think about the Chilean miners who had been trapped underground quite a few years before. She remembered that they had been down there for several months before they were rescued. Then she rationalized if their plight had been that long, certainly she could endure the next forty-five minutes. It was October 2010 when the world watched those thirty-three who emerge one by one from the earth over a period of two days, having actually been there for sixty-nine. In the aftermath of the rescue, some of those who had been trapped reflected on profound miracles and credited God for protecting them. Many of them said that "He (God) was the thirty-fourth miner." Years later, one of the rescued recounted a time while trapped when one of his colleagues became ill. He attributed the prayers of the other miners for healing him stating, "The next day, he was better. He was doing better than all of us." That power of prayer stayed with the miners throughout their time underground. He elaborated,

"When we prayed, we didn't pray to get rescued; we prayed for the people outside not to abandon us." Of course, that prayer was answered as well.

While fleeing from King Saul who was searching to kill him, imagine how David felt when Saul entered the restricted space of a dark cave where he was hiding. He must have prayed for his own safety or at least for the right thing to do as he was able to get close enough to Saul to kill him. Instead, David only cut off a piece of his robe (1 Samuel 24:4) to later prove that he would bring Saul no harm (1 Samuel 24:10–13). As the destined king, he would not take matters into his own hands but waited patiently for the workings of God to unfold and bring judgment on the house of Saul. Scripture reveals that it was when David was in this very situation that he wrote these words: "I am in the midst of lions; I am forced to dwell among ravenous beasts—men whose teeth are spears and arrows, whose tongues are sharp swords" (Psalm 57:4 NIV). In the strain of being hated and hunted, David shines as an example that we must remain steadfast and hold onto our faith. Probably the last thing we would have expected him to do in this setting would be to write a praise song, but we are blessed that he exactly what he did.

Hopefully, you will never have the experience of being trapped in a cave or underground in a collapsed mine. You might not even have to find yourself in the tight space of an MRI machine. However, there will assuredly be those times when you will be faced with an overwhelming feeling of darkness and despair. As followers of Christ, we are told, "Cast all your anxiety on him because he cares for you" (1 Peter 5:7 NIV). In another cave writing, David teaches us how to pray in such times of desperation. His Psalm 142 concludes with this affirmation: "Set me free from my prison, that I may praise your name. Then the righteous will gather about me because of your goodness to me" (Psalm 142:7 NIV). There is a lesson here: when you find yourself in a tight spot, trapped and alone, you can be confident that it's time to cry out to God, believe in the power of prayer, and feel surrounded by His comfort and love.

Reflection

Why does God allow some of His choicest saints to spend time in dark places? What have you learned from your personal cave experiences? How does prayer provide a sense of peace and hope when you find yourself in one of these situations? What are some ways in which you might better rely on God to be that "ever-present help in trouble" (Psalm 46:1 NIV)?

OCTOBER 20
(Y6, D42)

Maybe Even Today

But about that day or hour no one knows, not even the angels in heaven, nor the Son, but only the Father. Be on guard! Be alert! You do not know when that time will come.

—Mark 13:32–33 (NIV)

The catchphrase "I'll be back" is associated with actor Arnold Schwarzenegger. He used it in his first role as the title character in the 1984 science fiction film, *The Terminator*, high on the rankings of famous movie quotes of all time. The Austrian-American actor once admitted that he had difficulty pronouncing the word *I'll* and would rather have said "I will" but was not permitted to do so. This allowed for various characterizations through the years, always with a great amount of imitation placed on the "I'll" part of the phrase. Schwarzenegger himself used the same line or some variant of it in many of his later films. A similar quote was once used by General Douglas MacArthur who served as chief US military advisor to the Philippines before World War II. Following the bombing of Pearl Harbor, MacArthur was forced to leave the islands due to a Japanese invasion. Months later, he was informed that relief of his forces trapped in there would not be forthcoming. Deeply disappointed, he issued a statement to the press in which he promised his men and the people of the Philippines, "I shall return."

This promise would become MacArthur's mantra during the next two and a half years, and he would often repeat it in public appearances. For his valiant defense of the Philippines, MacArthur was awarded the Congressional Medal of Honor and celebrated as "America's First Soldier." But it was not until September 1944 that the General was poised to launch an invasion of the Japanese-occupied Philippines. After a period of indecision about whether to invade the Philippines or Formosa, the Joint Chiefs put their support behind MacArthur's plan. On October 20, 1944, a few hours after his troops landed, MacArthur waded ashore onto the Philippine Island of Leyte. That day, he made a radio broadcast in which he declared, "People of the Philippines, I have returned!" Over the next months, Japanese forces were cut off, and the Philippine capital of Manila fell. Only one-third of the men MacArthur left behind in March 1942 survived to see his return. "I'm a little late," he told them, "but we finally came."

It's difficult at times to place logical time frames on when it might be possible to see someone again. After Jesus ascended into heaven, the angels declared to the apostles, "'Men of Galilee,' they said, 'why do you stand here looking into the sky? This same Jesus, who has been taken from you into heaven, will come back in the same way you have seen him go into heaven'" (Acts 1:11 NIV). Today, followers of Jesus still await His return, this time not as a suffering servant but rather as the conquering King with the armies of heaven at His side. Modern Christians are often so captivated with the Second Coming that they overlook the ways Jesus comes to us each and every day. When the tragedies around us, the suffering of people we love, and even the stresses of daily life all seem bigger than the fixes on the horizon, we fail to see that Jesus meets people in the midst of these critical events. We discover that God is still at work in the messes of society, and we suddenly receive a reality check that the story isn't always about us. Sometimes it's about God's plan to give time to others who don't yet know His Son.

As the words of Peter remind us:

> But you must not forget this one thing, dear friends: A day is like a thousand years to the Lord, and a thousand years is like a day. The Lord isn't really being slow about his promise, as some people think. No, he is being patient for your sake. He does not want anyone to be destroyed, but wants everyone to repent. (2 Peter 3:8–9 NLT)

Our attachment to this world often keeps us from living in anticipation of Jesus' return as we should. In an increasingly chaotic world, what a hopeful thought that this could be the day or the year Jesus returns. More comforting still is the anticipation that all who trust Him for salvation will be gathered together, relieved from this world's suffering, sorrow, and fear. Our prayer should be that we will always be mindful of His inevitable return. Meanwhile, we should equip others with the knowledge that this world is not all we have and affirm that a blessed eternity awaits all who know Him personally as their savior. Regardless of how or in what manner we pray for Jesus' coming, one thing is sure: He *will* return—maybe even today!

Reflection

Do you eagerly await Christ's return or are you more concerned with storing up earthly treasures? What would you do differently if you knew Jesus was returning today? Would you be motivated and excited? Or frightened and alarmed? Consider these things in prayer, and ask the Lord to make you eager for His return.

OCTOBER 21
(Y7, D42)

Tolerance

Make allowance for each other's faults, and forgive anyone who offends you.

—Colossians 3:13 (NLT)

It was an unusual question, particularly in light of the setting in which it was posed. Nonetheless, the political candidates engaged in questioning were asked, "What friendship have you had that would surprise us? And what impact has it had on you and your beliefs?" Obviously the question was intended to demonstrate that the individuals on the stage had tolerance for those who subscribed to a different political persuasion. Their answers would serve as the conclusion to a three-hour televised debate. Just days before, a former conservative head-of-state was caught on camera laughing with and sitting next to a well-known liberal entertainment personality at a pro-football game. The entertainer was criticized in a social media backlash as to how she could possibly be friends with someone who held partisan views so different than her own. Her response: "Just because I don't agree with someone on everything does not mean I'm not going to be friends with them. When I say be kind to one another, I don't mean only the people that think the same as you do. I mean be kind to everyone."

Our world no longer defines tolerance as an acknowledgement that there are those with a differing belief. Instead, it has come to mean that we are expected to have full acceptance for the beliefs of others. There was a day not so long ago when we would respect individual differences. Not so much in recent times. On one hand, we hear much public discussion about the need for tolerance. On the other hand, those who stand for the truth of their own convictions are often branded as being narrow-minded, intolerant, and judgmental. Unfortunately, this is often the case when it comes to matters of faith. The Lord has uniquely created each of us with our own personalities and preferences. Therefore, we won't always agree with one another. This doesn't mean that we can't still love and respect each other in spite of our varying persuasions and convictions. It's possible with the help of the Holy Spirit to respect those with different opinions. Colossians 4:6 (NIV) instructs us: "Let your conversation be always full of grace, seasoned with salt, so that you may know how to answer everyone." The ability to rise above personal feelings and respectfully treat the intolerant reveals the true measure of our spiritual maturity.

Being labeled "intolerant" for one's Christian faith is an expected part of the journey, and at times, we will suffer when we stand up for the word of God. In fact, the Apostle Paul says that we are to provide for those who may not be very tolerant of us. By doing so, "you will heap burning coals of shame on their heads" (Romans 12:20 NLT). The Lord allows our interaction with people who don't believe in Jesus or who differ in their views about matters of the faith. The key to being Christlike in these situations is to keep your eyes on Him and not the person. We must be careful, however, to not endorse the modern belief that all religions lead to God. For the Christian, Jesus is the truth (John 14:6), and that must not be compromised. We are called to tolerate and even love those whose beliefs (or lack of) are different than our own. In doing so, we place ourselves in a position to become an effective witness for what we believe to be true. Scripture says, "A servant of the Lord must not quarrel but must be kind to everyone, be able to teach, and be patient with difficult people. Gently instruct those who oppose the truth. Perhaps God will change those people's hearts, and they will learn the truth" (2 Timothy 2:24–26 NLT).

Even the most intolerant of individuals can recognize true and unconditional love from Christians. Loving those who are intolerant of the faith empowers the believer to show love, just as Jesus did. If tolerance calls us to be respectful of the beliefs of others, then Christianity is in full agreement. Those who demonstrate true tolerance will seek God's wisdom and discernment before speaking with people who they know will disagree with them (James 1:5). In the end, there are times that you just have to respectfully agree to disagree. It is one thing to have and maintain a differing position; it is quite another to ridicule a person. We must hold fast to the truth while showing compassion to those who question it.

Reflection

What types of personalities trigger your tolerance button? When you are challenged in your Christian belief, do you find that you are respectful or do become defensive? What steps might you take in order to become more tolerant of others who hold positions which are different than your own?

OCTOBER 22
(Y1, D43)

Moving from Facts to Blessings

God is spirit, and those who worship him must worship in spirit and truth.

—John 4:24 (ESV)

Every show began with the same opening: "The story you are about to hear is true. Only the names have been changed to protect the innocent. This is the city. Los Angeles, California. I work here… I carry a badge." These are the immortal words of Sergeant Joe Friday, the fictional detective of the *Dragnet* series first presented on radio, then on TV, and later at the movies. While conducting interviews with his partner, Friday displayed limited patience with the emotional rambling of some of their witnesses. Whenever he had enough, he would look at the person and say, "Just the facts, ma'am."

There are those who have contemplated whether we should be less wordy and more specific in our prayers. In Matthew 6:7 (NIV), we find this passage: "And when you pray, do not keep on babbling like pagans, for they think they will be heard because of their many words." One wonders if the facts alone are sufficient when it comes to fulfilling our faith journey. In the past few years, I have become friends with a gentleman who was a veteran of World War II. Through his time of serving and now in his nineties, he has encountered many physical ailments and life-threatening situations. Recently, he told me that while he practices Christianity and lifts up others in prayer, he claims to have never prayed for himself. He says he tries to live a good life and believes that in doing so, God knows what he needs and will provide. Now that's the bare-bone facts, to be sure. But I believe his personal doctrine is a little off-center from what is contained in God's Word. I doubt if the prayer God rejects is the one in which you pray for yourself. I would rather think that it's the one you pray with a heart full of arrogance and conceit that He will not hear. He doesn't want us to be full of ourselves but simply to be filled with Him.

While there are those who may feel it is selfish to pray for one's self or that they are unworthy of God's attention, scripture reveals that He wants us to engage in a deep personal relationship with Him. One way to have that experience is through an active prayer life. "Call upon Me in the day of trouble; I shall rescue you, and you will honor Me" (Psalm 50:15 NASB). Jesus encourages that we should just ask for what we need. While others rebuked a blind man by the name of Bartimaeus from bothering Jesus with his words for mercy, he persisted in his plea (Mark 10:46–52). Jesus asked the man for specifics of what it was he needed. Of course, the obvious was that he wanted to see. With all we have come to know about Jesus, we can be assured that He already knew that. However, the man's sight was immediately restored not because of his many words but because he asked in faith. God longs for us to come into His presence. In doing so, we acknowledge our dependence on Him as the source of our strength and healing.

It would seem, fellow believers, that our true connections with God increase through prayer, the study of His Word, and participation in worship. Each of these has both a cognitive and an emotional component. The head compiles the thought processes with the understanding that God knows all that we need, everything that is going on in our life, and can predict what we will say even before we attempt to put it into words. It's the truth of the matter, just the facts. But our relationship with Him is not complete without the heart element during which we articulate our feelings and rejoice in all He has provided. These fulfill the spiritual connection and affirm our faith. Remember, Jesus understood the facts. He knew that Bartimaeus wanted to see. However, it was ultimately through the blind man's passion and total reliance on Him that the healing occurred. We are encouraged to "give your burdens to the Lord. He will not permit the Godly to slip nor fall" (Psalm 55:22 NLT). So, in spirit and in truth, give whatever weight you are carrying to Him, for He longs to replace it with a blessing.

Reflection

How does God's truth free you from feelings of insecurity and inadequacy? In what ways can the release of emotions help you develop a stronger spiritual connection? When you allow yourself to fellowship with the Lord in spirit and in truth, do you feel more complete in your relationship with Him?

OCTOBER 23
(Y2, D43)

Searching for Good

Do what is good and run from evil so that you may live! Then the LORD God
of Heaven's Armies will be your helper, just as you have claimed.

—Amos 5:14 (NLT)

As I tuned into a radio talk show already in progress, I couldn't believe what I thought I was hearing. So I did a little Internet browsing, and sure enough, I found the following headline: "Teachers Ordered to Teach the Good Things about the Holocaust Too!" My reaction: You've got to be kidding. But apparently, it was true. As a response, teachers in a Texas school district where this occurred began to strategize how to fight this while allowing their identities to remain obscured. We find ourselves living in a world turned upside down. On one hand, we seek to destroy those whose "bad side" has been exposed. While on the other, we are told that it is imperative to search for "the good" in something which would otherwise be defined as an atrocity against humankind. As a result, we become conflicted, concluding that there are apparently no moral guidelines in attempting to define what is good. Our lives have become blurred between what was once referred to as the good, the bad, and the ugly.

The story has been told about a king in Africa who had a faithful servant with a positive attitude about everything in life. Whether it was good or bad, he would always remark, "This is good." One day, the king and his servant were out on a hunting expedition. When the king fired his weapon, his thumb was blown off because the servant had apparently done something wrong in preparing one of the guns. Examining the situation, the servant remarked as usual, "This is good!"

Angrily, the king replied, "No, this is not good!" and proceeded to send his friend to jail. About three years later, the king was hunting in an unfamiliar area, unaware of cannibals all around him. The cannibals captured him and took him to their village. As they prepared to feast on him, they noticed that the king was missing a thumb. Being superstitious of their prey not being whole, they released and sent him on his way. As he returned home, he was reminded of the event that had taken his thumb and felt remorse for his treatment of his servant. He went immediately to the jail to speak with him. Proceeding to tell the servant all that had happened, he said, "You were right, it was good that my thumb was blown off. And so I am very sorry for sending you to jail for so long. It was bad to do this."

"No," his servant replied, "this is good!"

"What do you mean this is good? How could it be good that I sent you to be in jail for three years?"

"Because if I had not been in jail, I would have been with you. And I am whole. So this is indeed good."

The Bible shares a different story about the King of all kings. As related in Mark 3:1–6, it occurs in a synagogue where Jesus meets a man with a shriveled-up hand. The Pharisees had already challenged Jesus about doing things which they considered to be unlawful on the Sabbath. "Some of them were looking for a reason to accuse Jesus, so they watched him closely to see if he would heal him on the Sabbath" (Mark 3:2 NIV). Jesus forced a confrontation, perhaps suspecting a trap, by asking the religious leaders a question: "'Which is lawful on the Sabbath: to do good or to do evil, to save life or to kill?' But they remained silent. He looked around at them in anger and, deeply distressed at their stubborn hearts" (Mark 3:4–5 NIV). Seeing that the hearts of these religious leaders were far more shriveled than the disabled's hand, Jesus heals the man. What happens to Jesus here is likely to happen to us when we pursue the good of others. We may find ourselves infuriating those who have hardened hearts.

When we first become Christians, we are taught to show love, to do good, and to look for good; in other words, seek good always, first in ourselves and then in others. Every believer will struggle in this effort. God is not looking for good Christians. He's looking for good relationships with His children who will walk with Him. It's your willing heart He wants most. We can truly be good only through the grace of Jesus Christ. As followers, God is constantly working on us, making us more like His Son. I found it interesting that when I searched online for the words "seeking good always," the search engine made the assumption I meant "seeking God always." And therein I found my answer. When we endeavor to search for good, we will likely end up finding God. If we don't, it must not be good.

Reflection

If you are told to look for the good in a bad situation, present or historical, can you test the limits by looking for godliness? Do you toss others aside when their bad qualities surface? What are some ways you can search for good in others rather than being judgmental about their negative qualities?

OCTOBER 24
(Y3, D43)

Losing Our Way

For the Son of Man came to seek and to save the lost.

—Luke 19:10 (NIV)

If you've ever played a game of hide and seek with a very young child, it is quite different than it might be with someone who is a bit older. As your search, it would not be unusual to notice feet sticking out from under the bed or hear giggling from the back of the sofa. It's almost as if the security of being found far outweighs the prospect of becoming missed, even if only for a short time. In October 2014, it was not uncommon for visitors who traversed through the world's largest corn maze at Cool Patch Pumpkins in Dixon, California, to have to call for help to get out. Once inside the sixty-three-acre corn creation, adventurers frequently discovered that what they believed would be an easy maneuver became much more of a challenge than they had anticipated. While inside the maize, they found that as everything begins to look the same and you lose perspective, it becomes easy to panic. In some cases, there were those who reverted to use their cell phones to call 911 as the frustration of being lost wore thin.

In this day and age, it is not infrequent for any one of us to be part of an organization that loses its way. Companies spend valuable energy and dollars hiring consultants to develop mission statements which, by their intent, are to contain the beliefs that define the organization's purpose. In practicality, a company should be able to turn to their mission statement as a source of reference to validate that they are remaining true to their principles or if they have lost their focus. Ideally, a good mission statement should be static and remain true over time. Christian churches often develop mission statements as well, and different from other organizations, they almost universally center on some form of discipleship made possible through the loving grace of Jesus. While companies are not always true to their mission, the Christian church is at times no less accountable. Perhaps they are not all that different. Through the course of time, the church is often viewed by its toughest critics as having become nothing more than another big business which has become lost in the origins of its own creation.

In response to condemnation from the Pharisees who were criticizing Him for welcoming and dining with sinners, Jesus cites three parables of "the lost." They are the lost sheep as well as the lost coin and the lost son, frequently referred to as "the prodigal." In the first of these, Jesus said:

> If a man has a hundred sheep and one of them gets lost, what will he do? Won't he leave the ninety-nine others in the wilderness and go to search for the one that is lost until he finds it? And when he has found it, he will joyfully carry it home on his shoulders. When he arrives, he will call together his friends and neighbors, saying, "Rejoice with me because I have found my lost sheep." In the same way, there is more joy in heaven over one lost sinner who repents and returns to God than over ninety-nine others who are righteous and haven't strayed away! (Luke 15:4–7 NLT)

Jesus made it very clear that His mission was centered on those who were lost.

Throughout the course of our lifetime, it is fair to say that there have been periods when we have been like that lost sheep. As individuals, our personal values attempt to align but can also become in conflict with those organizations to which we belong. It is likely that as we continue on our walk, there will be times in our future when we will feel lost. Getting lost becomes a "rite of passage" for each person in determining who we are. As we do so, we hopefully draw closer to God and learn to always keep an open heart allowing Him to find us. It is not unlike that game of hide and seek engaging that naïve child for the very first time. We want to eventually be found. "In the same way your Father in heaven is not willing that any of these little ones should perish" (Matthew 18:14 NLT). So when we discover ourselves in the midst of a real maze, we come to understand that getting lost may occasionally become an expected part of the journey. Our realization is that we need to know when and who to call for help. Only then can we ultimately become free and once more find ourselves in His loving arms.

Reflection

Try to recall an incident when you were actually lost. What were the steps you took to find your way? Can you apply this recovery to a time when you felt spiritually lost? During those periods in your life when you have felt separated from God, how have you been able to renew your fellowship with Him? What did it take for you to realize that He was there all the time, waiting for your return?

OCTOBER 25
(Y4, D43)

The Lesser of Two Evils

He who justifies the wicked and he who condemns the righteous
are both alike an abomination to the LORD.

—Proverbs 17:15 (ESV)

Suppose that you live in a very rural area. You and your spouse have one young child, and there are few neighbors with children. The potential friends your child's age are limited to two: a boy who has bully-like tendencies and a girl who is known for seldom telling the truth. Which one do you choose to be your child's playmate? Let's make the scenario even more personal. You have been without work for months after having been laid off. You are the sole income earner for several other dependent persons. After many weeks of sending out resumes and being turned down following numerous interviews, you have just been offered two jobs. The one is with a company where the boss is egotistical and has a history of firing people. The head of the other company has a reputation for being deceptive, and if it comes down to defending you, she would most likely let you hang out to dry. Welcome to being caught between a proverbial rock and a hard place where your choice may be limited to the lesser of two evils. Or is it?

The lesser of two evils principle subscribes to the belief that when faced with selecting from two unpleasant options, the one which is least harmful should be chosen. This implies that when confronted with two sources of harm, the act of choosing harm remains. The real quandary is how to do good when we seem to have only immoral choices. Or as some would say, how to make the best of a bad situation. When challenged with this set of circumstances, one must carefully examine all the options and determine if, in any way, our personal values would be compromised. If we are looking for perfection, then we set ourselves up for failure. Short of Christ Himself, we will seldom find an option without inherent negatives. Pray about the possibilities available to you, and seek guidance as to whether every option is corrupt. "A wise man will hear and increase in learning, And a man of understanding will acquire wise counsel" (Proverbs 1:5). You may conclude that not all the available choices are, in fact, evil.

However, when a Christian is confronted with two clearly evil or immoral options, one cannot rationalize to side with immorality just because the alternative appears to be worse. Scripture tells us we will be held accountable not only for the evil deeds we do but also when we "give approval to those who practice them" (Romans 1:32 NASB). Paul warned in his second letter to Timothy that there will be times (he specifically refers to the end-times) when life will be difficult. "For people will love only themselves and their money. They will be boastful and proud, scoffing at God, disobedient to their parents, and ungrateful. They will consider nothing sacred. They will be unloving and unforgiving; they will slander others and have no self-control. They will be cruel and hate what is good. They will betray their friends, be reckless, be puffed up with pride, and love pleasure rather than God. They will act religious, but they will reject the power that could make them godly. Stay away from people like that" (2 Timothy 3:2–5 NLT). Sounds like challenging times we might one day, if not now, be facing!

Nineteenth-century author and Baptist preacher Charles Spurgeon once said that "choosing evil is not an option." We must therefore believe that God always gives us more than a choice of evil. To think less means that we are presented only with options which are dishonorable to God. Honoring God must always be our choice, rather than giving into sin. "The temptations in your life are no different from what others experience. And God is faithful. He will not allow the temptation to be more than you can stand. When you are tempted, he will show you a way out so that you can endure" (1 Corinthians 10:13 NLT). It is clear in Scripture that God's people would follow what they determined to be true to their beliefs, allowing the consequences to be judged by the Lord of history. So "do not be overcome with evil, but overcome evil with good" (Romans 12:21 NIV). For when we find ourselves in a position that we need to defend what we once would have considered disgraceful, we need to be careful we don't lose our self in the process. That's evil in its worse form, and it's not the lesser of anything.

Reflection

What are some decisions in your personal journey that you were uncomfortable making because you sensed your values would be compromised? If it is true that God always gives us a choice of doing good, what are you willing to sacrifice in doing so? Will you need to justify your actions to anyone?

OCTOBER 26
(Y5, D43)

Idols: No Contest for a Pure Heart

But the God of Israel is no idol! He is the Creator of everything that
exists, including his people, his own special possession.

—Jeremiah 51:19 (NLT)

It has been described by some to be one of the most impactful shows in American television history determined by its ratings and the number of stars it had produced. Ever since its first season in 2002, the singing competition series *American Idol* was the place to go to see some of the country's best-hidden talent along with others who thought they had talent but should have just stayed in hiding. The concept of the series involved discovering recording stars from unsigned singers with the viewing audience selecting the winner. Just a few years after its debut, it became the most-watched show on US television, a position it then held for seven consecutive seasons. At the end of the show's first fifteen-year run, its contestants had produced enormous revenue with sales of more than 60 million albums. While there is an innocent tendency to become captivated by the excitement generated around emerging personalities, we have to be cautious about who and what we allow to become our personal idols.

Idol worship was prevalent at the time of the Prophet Jeremiah and caused him to issue this warning to the nation of Israel:

Their ways are futile and foolish. They cut down a tree, and a craftsman carves an idol. They decorate it with gold and silver and then fasten it securely with hammer and nails so it won't fall over. Their gods are like helpless scarecrows in a cucumber field! They cannot speak, and they need to be carried because they cannot walk. Do not be afraid of such gods, for they can neither harm you nor do you any good. (Jeremiah 10:3–5 NLT) As we unveil the latest Halloween costumes each year, it's always interesting to see what characters are on display. Over the years, it seems as though the innocence and fun associated with

Halloween have come to be replaced with evil acts such as vandalism, destructive pranks, glorification of sensuality, death, and demons. Even though idolatry is a topic which many see as antiquated and outdated, it should be obvious from a Christian perspective that these modern practices are alive and well and should fall subject to concern.

An idol is anything or anyone other than God that we allow to influence or control our lives. Idolatry can be practiced in many forms. Evangelist Billy Graham says, "Take, for example, our preoccupation with money and material possessions. These aren't necessarily wrong, of course; we need them to take care of our loved ones and make our lives comfortable. But both can easily become 'idols' that we slavishly follow and allow to become the most important things in our lives." Whenever our needs become focused on the acquisition of what is bigger and better, things that really matter will be pushed away, and God becomes secondary if not forgotten. Paul wrote "For the love of money is a root of all kinds of evil. Some people, eager for money, have wandered from the faith and pierced themselves with many griefs" (1 Timothy 6:10 NIV). There's nothing inherently evil about money, but loving it can lead you into many forms of evil. Jesus warned against the worship of material things. "No one can serve two masters. Either you will hate the one and love the other, or you will be devoted to the one and despise the other. You cannot serve both God and money" (Matthew 6:24 NIV).

If we are to escape modern idolatry, we have to admit that it is rampant and reject it in all forms. We have been given this commandment: "You must not have any other god but me. You must not make for yourself an idol of any kind, or an image of anything in the heavens or on the earth or in the sea. You must not bow down to them or worship them" (Deuteronomy 5:7–9 NLT). We need to examine our lives to determine if we regard our power or possessions as the center of the universe instead of looking to God as the creator and sustainer of all. We must pay careful attention to what we love. For it is only when we love the Lord first and foremost that there will be no room in our hearts for idolatry.

Reflection

Is there anything you feel you cannot live without? Is there anything or anyone in your life whom you love more than God? Consider praying and asking God to reveal the idols which may have crept into your life, even the inherently good things which you've elevated to a higher place than they ought to be. Then make a conscious decision to decide what to do about them.

OCTOBER 27
(Y6, D43)

Yearning to Breathe Free

For I have given rest to the weary and joy to the sorrowing.

—Jeremiah 31:25 (NLT)

Towering above New York Harbor is the Statue of Liberty. That stately lady, with freedom's torch held high, has beckoned millions of people who were suffering from oppression and seeking a better way of life. Drawn to what that monument symbolizes, it is without a doubt one of America's greatest landmarks as it appears against the NYC skyline in images sent around the globe. Once referred to as "The Statue of Liberty Enlightening the World"—it was a gift of friendship from the people of France to the United States. Recognized as a universal symbol of freedom and democracy, the statue was a welcoming sight to immigrants arriving from abroad being processed at nearby Ellis Island. Built in France and shipped overseas in crates, it was assembled on the finished pedestal on what is now known as Liberty Island. It was made with an exterior of copper and originally had a far shinier appearance than its green of today.

The statue's completion was marked by New York's first ticker-tape parade and a dedication ceremony presided over by President Grover Cleveland on October 28, 1886. Inscribed on the Statue of Liberty's pedestal are these words by Emma Lazarus from her 1883 poem, "The New Colossus":

> Give me your tired, your poor,
> Your huddled masses yearning to breathe free,
> The wretched refuse of your teeming shore;
> Send these, the homeless, tempest-tossed, to me:
> I lift my lamp beside the golden door.

Lazarus was one of the first successful and publicly recognized Jewish-American authors. She was born in New York City to a wealthy family who began writing and translating poetry as a teenager by publishing translations of German poems by the 1860s. Lazarus was moved by the fierce persecution of her people in Russia, a frequent topic of her writings, as well as their struggles to assimilate into American culture.

Paralleling the beautiful stanzas inscribed on the base of Lady Liberty are the comforting words of another, articulated many centuries before. They were spoken by Jesus who said, "Come to me, all you who are weary and burdened, and I will give you rest" (Matthew 11:28 NIV). When Jesus said He would give us rest, it meant we wouldn't need to go find it, earn it, or spiritually strive to develop it. It is simply a gift God gives us when we come to Him and openly receive it. This is liberty in its purest form. There is much debate in recent years as to how much automatic freedom should be granted to those who seek refuge in another country. Some argue that such immigrants should follow a lawful process that leads to citizenship. Others feel that there should be open borders and an entitlement for all who come. Perhaps the Apostle Paul, who took advantage of his status as both a Jew and a Roman citizen to minister to both audiences, understood it best when he said, "But our citizenship is in heaven. And we eagerly await a Savior from there, the Lord Jesus Christ" (Philippians 3:20 NIV).

For those who dare to journey with Jesus, we can access His enduring rest and experience everlasting freedom. As Christians in a fast-paced world, we can sometimes find it difficult to relax in God's gift of rest. Instead, we wear busyness like a badge of honor, carry loads we were never meant to bear. And for what? To simply get ahead? When we allow ourselves to pause and take time to be with God, we will receive His rest. In doing so, we may not always be able to avail ourselves of all the earthly riches we might desire. But we will soon discover that there is power in the act of resting. Jesus told His disciples: "Blessed are you who are poor, for yours is the kingdom of God" (Luke 6:20 NIV). Too often we find ourselves becoming part of the huddled masses yearning to breathe free. As you go throughout your day, let your heart treasure that true place of rest, the one which can only be found in His presence.

Reflection

What types of activities cause you to have feelings of weary and burden? As you look at these, how might you prioritize being able to find some time alone with God? Consider reinstating some affirming thing in your life that used to bring you joy. Ask others to support you in this effort if necessary.

OCTOBER 28
(Y7, D43)

One Sweet Life

How sweet your words taste to me; they are sweeter than honey.

—Psalm 119:103 (NLT)

Has anyone ever tried to "sweet talk" you? If you are known to have a competitive edge, were you challenged by the thought of a "sweet victory" ahead? Or have you ever spent a lot of time bargaining for a certain outcome and ended up making "one sweet deal"? As Halloween approaches and children look forward to trick-or-treat activities, those who anticipate sharing in a sampling of the gathered candy might be asked if they have a "sweet tooth." We even find that our music has references to sweetness, from the reassuring lyrics of Neil Diamond's "Sweet Caroline" to the cherished hymn, "Sweet Hour of Prayer." For the most part, the concept of being sweet generally brings forth pleasant feelings. However, a very different impression is created when the words sour or bitter are introduced. In fact, there may have been a time when you may have been prompted to use the phrase "It left a bitter taste in my mouth" if you were involved in something that did not turn out particularly well.

The Bible contains many references to sweetness and bitterness. The leader of the Israelites, Moses, threw a piece of wood God had shown him into water that was bitter, "and the waters became sweet. There He made for them a statute and regulation, and there He tested them" (Exodus 15:25 NASB). The Psalmist declared that "the rules of the Lord are true, and righteous altogether…sweeter also than honey and drippings of the honeycomb" (Psalms 19:9–10 ESV). One of the most interesting stories tells of God commanding the Prophet Ezekiel to speak to the nation of Israel after he consumed a provided scroll. He was "to fill [his] stomach with it" and share the words with its people whom God considered to be "obstinate and stubborn" (Ezekiel 2:4 NIV). In Ezekiel's vision, he eats the scroll God handed him, and we find the creation of an interesting image by which he needs to "fill up and digest God's Word." By Ezekiel following God's direction, he was able to absorb the message before it would be delivered.

Scripture states that both sides of the scroll "were covered with funeral songs, words of sorrow, and pronouncements of doom" (Ezekiel 2:10 NLT). Logic would expect that for any normal person, this unusual request might have been a bitter pill to swallow. But Ezekiel claimed that "when I ate it, it tasted as sweet as honey in my mouth" (Ezekiel 3:3 NLT). Ezekiel seems to have acquired a taste for God's correction. Instead of viewing His reprimand as something to be avoided, Ezekiel recognized that what is good for the soul is sweet. He was a man living in the center of God's Will and in sweet communion with Him. He didn't gloss over the sins of his people and chose to not focus on what little good he might have been able to find within that society. What he did was continue to warn his countrymen with all his heart because that is what God specifically told him to do. Accordingly, he was hated for his testimony.

If we focus on how much God loves us, His challenging truths will begin to taste more like honey. If we are to become one of His messengers, we must first internalize these truths for ourselves before we are equipped to share them with others. As a result, we will encounter those who will accept its sweet aroma while we can anticipate there will always be some who will reject it. Paul put it this way: "Our lives are a Christ-like fragrance rising up to God. But this fragrance is perceived differently by those who are being saved and by those who are perishing" (2 Corinthians 2:15 NLT). As Christians, God wants us to be full of sweet things, and it starts by being filled with His Word and the indwelling of His Holy Spirit. As I assume this in my own life, I can't help but reflect on the lyrics of a chorus I have come to appreciate "there's a sweet, sweet spirit in this place; and I know that it's the spirit of the Lord." There are times in each person's journey when we do our utmost to avoid hearing the truth of God's message. At times, we may find it to be a "bitter pill to swallow." Ultimately, we must begin to recognize that there is one true voice to whom we must listen. Then we will develop a decisive understanding of what it means to begin to live the life He has always had planned for us. That, my friend, is one sweet life.

Reflection

How pleased do you think the Lord is with the aroma you set forth? When you seek spiritual guidance, have you ever found sweetness in challenging words that do not necessarily conform to your way of thinking. Are you able to deliver God's truth to others who seek your advice about lifestyle issues when you do not believe they are in agreement with the teachings of Jesus? How might you apply Proverbs 27:9 (NLT): "The heartfelt counsel of a friend is as sweet as perfume and incense" in these instances?

OCTOBER 29
(Y1, D44)

A Useful Underdog... Just Like You

What, then, shall we say in response to these things? If God is for us, who can be against us?

—Romans 8:31 (NIV)

it's Autumn, and there is nothing better than a football game featuring your favorite college team. It was a Saturday afternoon, and there was no doubt in my mind that my team would triumph. After all, they had dominated this rivalry in recent years, winning nine of the last ten meetings. The opposing team was most certainly the underdog; that is, until the game was tied at the end of the fourth quarter and they went on to win the tie-breaker by one point. Later that evening, I decided to watch the World Series baseball game. The National League participants had not won the Fall Classic for thirty-two years, even after they had been a challenger three times in the last four years. Now they were favored. The American League team did not have any players with household names, but they were known to be scrappers. Amazingly, they managed to stage a two-out, two-strike, come-from-behind recovery following two errors by the favorites to even out the best-of-seven set. So much for leveraging the odds against the underdogs.

Whether we're watching sports, a TV show, or a movie, it's exhilarating to see the "little guy" overcome the odds and win. When Rocky defeated adversity and fought the world's greatest boxer, we cheered. Everybody loves an underdog because they remind us of ourselves. Most of us understand what it's like to go into a game feeling like you don't have a chance, facing a job interview knowing others are more qualified, or stepping into a chapter of life believing that you are far behind. What we don't always recognize is that most heroes start as an underdog, and the heroes in the Bible are no exception. God used ordinary people to show His extraordinary goodness. Childless women. Old men. The youngest sons. Cowards. Stutterers. Daydreamers. Shepherds. Murderers. Slaves. Prostitutes. We can argue that one of the central truths in scripture would be to fully appreciate the theology of the underdog.

There is probably no better example of an underdog than that of King David. Long before he changed the world, led his nation in a new direction, and became known as Jesus' ancestor, he was viewed as insignificant. When we first meet David, he's anything but a person destined to be a king. The Lord sent Samuel to the home of Jesse to find a successor to King Saul. "Jesse had seven of his sons pass before Samuel, but Samuel said to him, 'The LORD has not chosen these'" (1 Samuel 16:10 NIV). This is followed by a conversation between Jesse and Samuel, who asks him if these are all the sons he has. Jesse basically replies:

> "Well, there *is* David, my youngest, nothing more than a shepherd boy. Out of all of my sons, he is the underdog." But God removed Saul and replaced him with David, a man about whom God said, a man about whom He said, "I have found David son of Jesse, a man after my own heart. He will do everything I want him to do." (Acts 13:22 NLT)

When Jesus walked the earth, He surrounded Himself with underdogs. So if you feel like the odds are against you, you're in good company with others who were also told they were nothing special.

While we can learn about the underdog in God's Word, we often dismiss the fact that God is looking for those same qualities in us. He's searching for people who don't have it all together but are willing to let Him take hold of their lives. If we allow this to happen, God's incredible love will use us, regardless of any prevailing opinion that we seem to fall short. Paul said, "Now all glory to God, who is able, through his mighty power at work within us, to accomplish infinitely more than we might ask or think" (Ephesians 3:20 NLT). God will use us in spite of ourselves. Then, by His grace, He transforms our weakness to make a difference in the world. Like a quiet whisper, He orchestrates the ultimate game plan and puts together a roster composed of unbeatable underdogs. If you've been told you won't make the cut or don't measure up, have no fear. God knows exactly what he's doing. Until the game is played, no one knows the outcome. God is the undisputed champion of conquering every issue in our life to make it valuable for His purpose. If then you feel the odds are somehow against you, take hope. God is in the business of using those who seem to be second-rate. He is always preparing to use the next underdog—one just like you.

Reflection

In what ways are underdogs uniquely positioned to listen to the voice of God? What unpolished or awkward traits would you like *to* surrender to God's mighty wisdom? What would you say to a friend who states that they are unable to see where God has any useful purpose for their life?

OCTOBER 30
(Y2, D44)

Speaking Slowly and Deliberately

Even fools are thought wise if they keep silent, and discerning if they hold their tongues.

—Proverbs 17:28 (NIV)

We live in a world of talk. Sometimes way too much. Ours is the age of talk radio, podcasts, and cell phones. Everyone, it seems, wants to be heard. No doubt you have been a part of a committee or workgroup where there are members who love to hear themselves talk. While everyone deserves the right to be heard when one of more persons dominate the conversation, it can be discouraging if not downright demeaning for others. In certain situations, talk becomes way too excessive often without consideration for time and place. I remember once being on a long train ride. Many of travelers had fallen asleep, and the car had become very quiet. Except for one lady, that is, who decided to make a cell phone call to one of her friends. She had one of those voices that carried well and made no effort to attempt to speak in a soft manner. We were subjected to hear about all the distresses and agonies that were part of her life. These included the travel reservations that had initially delayed her trip, the daughter who needs to kick her "no good" husband out of the house, and the detested boss and job to which she would soon be returning. Let's just say they were conversations of which I didn't need to be a part. Ultimately, the types of information we share and when we do so must always be carefully chosen.

A great example of too much information (frequently referred to as TMI) is provided in the story of a plumber who wrote to the National Bureau of Standards. He said he had heard that hydrochloric acid opens plugged pipes quickly and asked whether it was a good thing for a him to use. A scientist at the bureau replied as follows: "The uncertain reactive processes of hydrochloric acid places pipes in jeopardy when alkalinity is involved. The efficiency of this solution is disputable, but the corrosive residue is incompatible with metallic permanence." The plumber wrote back, thanking the bureau for telling him that this method was acceptable. The scientist was disturbed about the misunderstanding and showed the correspondence to his boss, another scientist, who immediately wrote the plumber: "Hydrochloric acid generates a toxic and noxious odor. Consequently, some alternative procedure is preferable."

The plumber wrote back and said he agreed with the bureau: "Thank you. The hydrochloric acid works just fine."

Greatly disturbed, the two scientists took their problem to their top boss. The next day the plumber received an urgent certified letter: "Don't use hydrochloric acid!"

Bottom line, when we use gobbledygook and other gibberish, the heart of the message ends up being drowned in words. If we are more thoughtful, deliberate, and slow to speak in our communication, we can be saved not only from the embarrassment of being wrong but also from creating a misunderstanding or potentially provoking anger. Here, the book of James in scripture can become incredibly relevant. He writes: "Understand this, my dear brothers and sisters: You must all be quick to listen, slow to speak, and slow to get angry" (James 1:19 NLT). Following this advice displays an attribute of humility and serves as an exercise in self-restraint. One should think about the words they are about to speak, determining what kind of impact they will have and whether or not they will accurately convey what they want to say. An incessant talker cannot hear what anyone else says and by the same token will not hear when God speaks to them. Being "slow to speak" signifies obedience to the Word of God.

Talking too much often means listening too little, and it can lead to saying what should not be said. Restraining our lips is an indication of wisdom; not doing so can be detrimental to our Christian witness in the world. Pastor Rick Warren suggests that we consider the acronym THINK before we speak: "T: Is it truthful? Is what I'm about to say the truth? H: Is it helpful? Or will it simply harm the other person? I: Is it inspirational? Does it build up or does it tear down? N: Is it necessary? If it's not necessary, why do I need to say it? K: Is it kind? Will it encourage or discourage?" Being quick to listen, slow to speak, and measured in becoming angry is very hard. To discern the difference between knowing when to speak or be silent, we need to seek the Lord's guidance through prayer, immerse ourselves in Scripture, and ask for His discernment. And if we determine it is time to speak, we must do so slowly and deliberately.

Reflection

Are there ways for you to discern when to speak and when to be silent? How do you slow down and respond properly before speaking in anger? What things in your life are blocking out the voice of God? What measures can you take to help you listen not only to God but also to other wise Christians?

OCTOBER 31
(Y3, D44)

A Spiritual Mulligan

Remember not the former things, nor consider the things of old. Behold,
I am doing a new thing; now it springs forth, do you not perceive it? I
will make a way in the wilderness and rivers in the desert.

—Isaiah 43:18–19 (ESV)

I was sitting in front of the sub shop where I had just made my purchase. As I perceived it, I had three choices. I could throw my food away. I could eat it and hope that there would be no repercussions. Or I could go back into the store and ask for a refund or a replacement. But you don't really know how my story began. It is a fairly simple one, actually. I was hungry, didn't feel like cooking, and decided to stop at a local eatery for a sub. Upon my arrival, I noticed that the only attendant behind the counter was closing with another customer at the cash register. I observed that while handling the money, she was wearing disposable gloves which she did not replace as she took my order and made my sandwich. I was rather stunned at her carelessness but reluctantly allowed her to finish, paid for my order, and exited the establishment. So now I am sitting in my car, feeling angry, and faced with the decision of what to do. Ultimately, I went back into the shop and asked for a do-over.

It is at this time of year we recall the old saying, "Spring forward, fall back." Over the years, it became a way to remember which way we should move the hands on our clocks in changing from Daylight Savings to Standard Time. In doing so, we have always been made to feel that we would somehow regain time that we had lost with a simple reset. Similarly, golfers are familiar with the term mulligan in which a player who blunders a shot is allowed to reset a ball in the same location with no penalty for doing so. While not part of the formal rules, it's a nice do-over opportunity for a member of your foursome who is having a bad day. Just drop another ball, and get on with it. Wouldn't it be nice if life was that simple? Instead, we end up making decisions far too quickly, speak words that perhaps should never have been spoken, or form a judgment about another person using information that wasn't accurate at the source. Consequently, we find ourselves in regretful situations where do-overs seem to be almost impossible.

We are fortunate to have a God who cares so much about us that He created a path for resolution in these and similar matters. "But God demonstrates his own love for us in this: While we were still sinners, Christ died for us" (Romans 5:8 NIV). Lucky for us He is all about fresh starts and new beginnings. His Word is filled with examples of people who messed up and yet were given opportunities to step up in their faith journey. In the Old Testament, we find King David struggling in many ways with His power. Saul of Tarsus became the converted Paul and the prolific author of much of the New Testament after persecuting many followers in the faith. Nonetheless, these individuals were not only offered do-overs but also given new beginnings to serve. So:

> Here is a trustworthy saying that deserves full acceptance: Christ Jesus came into the world to save sinners—of whom I am the worst. But for that very reason I was shown mercy so that in me, the worst of sinners, Christ Jesus might display his immense patience as an example for those who would believe in him and receive eternal life. (1 Timothy 1:15–16 NIV)

In most situations, we cannot change past circumstances. However, we can change how we handle the future. For our God is a God of patient restoration. "Therefore, if anyone is in Christ, he is a new creation. The old has passed away; behold, the new has come" (2 Corinthians 5:17 ESV). By acknowledging that God is the one who looks at our heart and sees the desire for change, He will equip us to walk on a fresh journey. When we realize that we're working through His power, not our own, we understand that we've been given a spiritual mulligan of sorts. In doing so, we experience that special moment of redemption that allows us to be as close as possible to the person He intended us to be all along.

Reflection

If God offers us do-overs in our spiritual journey, why are we sometimes reluctant to make a change and unsure how to go about it? If you are not where you want to be or where you want to stay spiritually, what will it take for you to reach forward to all that God has in store for you? What past circumstance must you get by in order to do so?

NOVEMBER 1
(Y4, D44)

Eligible for Sainthood?

Here is a call for the endurance of the saints, those who keep the
commandments of God and their faith in Jesus.

—Revelation 14:12 (ESV)

It has always intrigued me that the October 31 celebration of Halloween, a festival known for its ghosts and goblins and filled with stories about witches and ghoulishness. All Saints Day on November 1 is a Christian celebration during which we remember those who have labored faithfully in this life in their service to Jesus Christ and who have now have entered into their eternal home. On the other hand, Halloween or All Hallows or All Saints Eve is exclusively pagan in nature according to some scholars. Others claim that its roots are solely Christian, and in many parts of the world, the day includes church services and lighting candles on the graves of the deceased. The relationship of the two observances has raised many questions throughout the ages and will no doubt continue for years to come.

I read an account by a young person of a reluctant visit to a nursing home which he described to be an enlightening one. While assisting some others conduct a worship service, he watched "the joy of those older saints light up." I found his depiction to be interesting, and it made me wonder what it was that caused him to characterize those who lived there as saints. What qualities must one possess to be classified as a saint? Do you have to be a certain age or must you be deceased to qualify? Are there certain accomplishments or good deeds one must do during one's lifetime to be considered as saint-like? We have all heard of the famous saints including St. Patrick, Joan of Arc, St. Thomas Aquinas, and the most well-known and influential of the modern-day saints, Mother Teresa. And who among us at one time or another hasn't known someone with a Saint Christopher medal in their pocket or on a necklace?

Is sainthood reserved only for those who lived an unscathed life? Can you become a saint after having been known for your lack of generosity? The life of St. Thomas Becket would indicate that you can. Known as a coldhearted man of great wealth who shared nothing with those in need, he later gave away all of his possessions and welcomed the poor at his table. Can you hate Christians and even contribute to their slaughter and yet end up being known as a saint? The Apostle Paul, who described himself as the worst of all sinners (1 Timothy 1:15), would be surprised to learn of his own sainthood. Can you abandon your faith, become part of a pagan society, and live with a mistress outside the blessings of a marital relationship and later be called a saint? St. Augustine would tell you that it is possible to do so. In fact, he is quoted as having said, "There is no saint without a past, no sinner without a future."

A saintly life is not a life free from sin but rather from sin's condemning and controlling power. Even the greatest saint was once a sinner saved by the grace of God, and even the worst sinner has a potentially glorious future; that is if we allow our daily life to more closely align itself with the life of Jesus. By virtue of our connection with the Holy One, we are welcomed into the sainthood of His creation, "giving thanks to the Father, who has qualified you to share in the inheritance of the saints in light" (Colossians 1:12 ESV). However, St. Therese of Lisieux would caution that "you cannot be half a saint; you must be a whole saint or no saint at all."

It becomes obvious that as we look at our role in life, we are challenged to consider that it includes "the equipping of the saints for the work of service, to the building up of the body of Christ" (Ephesians 4:12 NASB). Once our earthly excursion come to an end, we will know the inexpressible joys that God has prepared for those who love Him. "They will hunger no longer, nor thirst anymore; nor will the sun beat down on them, nor any heat; for the Lamb in the center of the throne will be their shepherd, and will guide them to springs of the water of life; and God will wipe every tear from their eyes" (Revelation 7:16–17 NASB). We cannot help but personalize the lyrics to that well-known spiritual jazz song as it resonates, "O Lord I want to be in that number—when the saints go marching in." Let it be so for each of us who endeavors to faithfully serve our Lord. Then and only then will we be able to respond to the question, "Eligible for sainthood?" with the answer, "Yes, even me."

Reflection

Who is the worst sinner you have known who turned out to have saintly qualities? What can we learn from the transformation of an individual from sinner to saint? How does such a conversion give us hope for our own life when we fail to be the kind of person God desires for us?

NOVEMBER 2
(Y5, D44)

Earthy Games or Prayers of Passion?

Set your minds on things above, not on earthly things.

—Colossians 3:2 (NIV)

It was a tense time. For over a hundred years, these loyal followers had seen periodic glimmers of hope. But their optimism over the short-term had frequently led to disappointment over the long haul. Through their many years of discouragement, they had tried to be faithful. They displayed their confidence by continuing to support the endeavors of those who could provide signs of encouragement. They knew that one day the world would know them for who they were. Finally, the hour came when they would be delivered. Their long-awaited drought would soon end with a revival that no one now living had ever before witnessed. And so it was on an early November day in 2016 that the curse they had known for over a century would soon be lifted. Once again, coming close to defeat, they looked upward and prayed with all their might that those whom they had followed for so long would now receive their crown and be known as the World Series Champions of Baseball. With one final infield ground ball hit to the third baseman who slipped and nearly made an error toss to first base, the Chicago Cubs rejoiced with praise like they had not been able to do for 108 very long years. The curse had indeed been lifted.

It happens each October when the Boys of Summer pray that they will be blessed to be part of the post-season. As baseball season comes to an end, the weekly gridiron clashes have already established team rankings. In just a few short months, the Super Bowl will be the talk of the town. Between both is another fierce battle at least every four years. It's a fight for power like no other, one that in many ways is even more brutal than colliding with the catcher at home plate or being the quarterback who gets sacked before he ever has a chance to execute his play. It's the vicious game of politics, and it can become downright ugly at times. If we are walking with God, we consider what role we should play in these endeavors. At times, when we look at those who are seeking leadership and examine all that needs to be fixed in our nation, we wonder what it will take to bring even a slight amount of healing to a world that certainly seems to have lost its way. So, once again, we look upward and pray that God will provide for the curse that permeates our society be lifted in a time frame we'd be blessed to witness.

We might question if God answers the prayers of the faithful as they are raised for favorite sports teams or political candidates. Consider how He must feel about the priorities we have set as we spend millions of dollars for seats in sports stadiums or on advertising campaigns for those seeking government leadership positions. Imagine the good these same resources would do for those who are hungry, seeking shelter following a natural disaster, or suffering from a disease they would not have acquired had they been properly vaccinated. I am confident that God always hears the prayers of His people, but I cannot help but wonder if He responds more to His own creation than those of our making. The Apostle Paul provides good guidance.

> I urge you, first of all, to pray for all people. Ask God to help them; intercede on their behalf, and give thanks for them. Pray this way for kings and all who are in authority so that we can live peaceful and quiet lives marked by godliness and dignity. This is good and pleases God our Savior, who wants everyone to be saved and to understand the truth. (1 Timothy 2:1–4 NLT)

Ponder this: rather than praying for your favorite sports team to be the victor, offer a prayer that those who are playing or participating as spectators are spared injury. By all means, vote your conscience in an election, but despite the outcome, offer prayers of respect for those in positions of leadership whom God has given authority over us (Romans 13:1). Whether they happen to be of our political persuasion or not, let us pray that they will surround themselves with good advisers so that we might live in a stable society where we can worship freely. Let us pray that they will seek wise counsel in order that peaceful and quiet lives will flourish, while hate and wars will be averted whenever possible. Let us pray for the right things with the hope that God will turn the hearts of kings (Proverbs 21:1) to be guided from games of fame and power to a passion of love for everyday people and their future.

Reflection

What worldly matters do you offer to God in prayer? In what ways might you be able to refocus your prayers on people in need of basic sustenance or of God's direction? How might you convince others that winners of earthly contests have little relevance to our heavenly Father?

NOVEMBER 3
(Y6, D44)

Finding Truth in a Deceptive World

I write to you, not because you do not know the truth, but because
you know it, and because no lie is of the truth.

—1 John 2:21 (ESV)

It was far from the truth. Some said it was mistake. Others claimed it was a false prediction. On November 3, 1948, the *Chicago Tribune* mistakenly declared New York Governor Thomas Dewey the winner of his presidential race with incumbent Harry S. Truman in a front-page boldly printed headline, "Dewey Defeats Truman." In the weeks before the election, early Gallup polls forecasted the incumbent's defeat. Truman chose not to use the press as a vehicle for getting his message across. Instead, in the summer of 1948, he went directly to the people on an ambitious 22,000-mile "whistle stop" railroad and automobile campaign tour. As the political underdog, Truman asked crowds at every destination to help him keep his job as president. When he went to bed on voting night, he was losing the election. As returns were coming in slowly and the printing deadline at the *Tribune* was approaching, inexperienced workers filling in for staff members out on strike jumped the gun and published the soon-to-be untruthful headline. In a now famous photograph snapped in the early morning hours after the election, a beaming and puzzled Truman is shown holding the *Chicago Tribune* issue that had wrongly predicted his political downfall. When all the tallies were made, Truman eventually defeated Dewey by 114 electoral votes.

Edgar Allan Poe once wrote: "Believe half of what you see and nothing of what you hear." More and more, it seems like those who report the news have come to allow their personal interpretation of details to influence the story rather than simply convey the facts based on truth. It has been said that truth is relative, implying that we can't always trust its accuracy. Unfortunately, our society has grown to accept this kind of distorted truth. The great evangelist Billy Graham once told a story about a clergyman whose friend was employed as an actor. The actor was drawing large crowds of people, and the clergyman was preaching to only a few in the church. He said to his actor friend, "Why is it that you draw great crowds, and I have no audience at all? Your words are sheer fiction, and mine are unchangeable truth." The actor's reply was quite simple. "I present my fiction as though it were truth; you present your truth as though it were fiction." Graham concluded, "I fear that so often we Christians give the idea that the truth is fiction by the way we live and by the lack of dedication to the teachings of our Lord."

The secular world increasingly teaches that all truth is relative, a simple matter of each person's perspective. Some things may appear true to you but may not resonate truth to me. If you believe it, it is true for you. If I don't believe it, it is not true for me. Many people reduce any question of God or religion to this type of conjecture. Paul would confront them with this astounding certainty:

> But God shows his anger from heaven against all sinful, wicked people who suppress the truth by their wickedness. They know the truth about God because he has made it obvious to them. For ever since the world was created, people have seen the earth and sky. Through everything God made, they can clearly see his invisible qualities—his eternal power and divine nature. So they have no excuse for not knowing God. (Romans 1:18–20 NLT)

Those who have come to understand God's intense love for us through His Son, Jesus, recognize that the truth personified by Christ is never relative. The existence of absolute truth is a necessary foundation of Christianity. In John 14:6 (NIV), Jesus said, "I am the way, the truth, and the life. No one comes to the Father except through me." In other words, truth is the very fabric of His being and defines who He is. Conversely, Satan is described as the father of all lies (John 8:44). His mission is to steal, kill, and destroy (John 10:10) and to counterfeit every blessing and promise God has in store for us. The task of every Christian is to declare and demonstrate the truth that can be found only in Jesus. Truth is the only sure foundation on which to build one's life. It is the only stable force capable of withstanding the pressures of this world, one in which we find that the real truth is often deceptive.

Reflection

Can you think of common statements that confuse absolute and relative truth about your faith? How do you compassionately reason that Jesus represents the true path to God? In what ways might neglecting to know and follow God's Word suppress His truth as you interact with others each day? Ask God to reveal the areas in your life in which you are not fully acknowledging His life-giving truth.

NOVEMBER 4
(Y7, D44)

Grounded in a Place of Quiet Rest

Those on the rocky ground are the ones who receive the word with joy when they hear it, but they have no root. They believe for a while, but in the time of testing they fall away.

—Luke 8:13 (NIV)

They worshipped together every Sunday. The service was a simple one with the old hymns of the church, familiar scripture readings, and short prayers of reassurance. To the casual acquaintance, the mother and daughter strongly resembled each other. The younger could recall what her mother looked like in earlier years, and she had to admit that the features of the elder at her age were quite similar. When the mother looked at her daughter, she could not identify her. But there she was, holding the hand of this unnamed other who surrounded her with affection. Perhaps there were hints of recollection of her former self. Or maybe she was just comforted by the presence of the one who visited, knowing somewhere in the tangles of the Alzheimer's disease which she possessed that this lady was indeed very special to her. And although she could not begin to verbalize a name or understand the relationship, when the piano started to play, she effortlessly began to sing, "There is a place of quiet rest."

How is it that one can forget the name of her only daughter but at the very same time know the words of a hymn? While great progress has been made in finding a cure for Alzheimer's disease, some of the mysteries such as "selective memory" continue to baffle us. It is at times amazing to observe a person of deep faith progress through the various stages of the disease. Frequently, those connections which were established at an early age, such as memorization of scriptures and reiteration of prayers, remain intact. Similar experiences are at times true for a person who is dying and seemingly in an unconscious state but who appears to respond to recorded gospel music or scripture reading. The prophet from long ago reminds us:

But blessed are those who trust in the LORD and have made the LORD their hope and confidence. They are like trees planted along a riverbank, with roots that reach deep into the water. Such trees are not bothered by the heat or worried by long months of drought. Their leaves stay green, and they never stop producing fruit. (Jeremiah 17:7–8 NLT)

There is something to be said for those who are grounded in the faith and being able to draw from the comfort it provides during the difficult times.

The concept of being grounded has somehow taken on too much of a negative tone. Children are grounded because they have broken certain rules or need to improve their grades. Flights are grounded due to bad weather, projected threats, or mechanical concerns. However, in each of these cases, the act of being grounded is for our own good. Yet, when it comes to our faith, the idea of grounding through the discipline of daily devotions or Bible readings seems incomprehensible to some. The Apostle Paul said, "Let your roots grow down into him, and let your lives be built on him. Then your faith will grow strong in the truth you were taught, and you will overflow with thankfulness" (Colossians 2:7 NLT). Even those who become ungrateful or who happen to stray from the faith for a time will have something to which they can return if they have developed strong roots in their earlier years.

Increasingly, there are those who claim to be persons of faith but whose lives are easily uprooted when the troubled winds of life prevail. The only way for a believer to become grounded in Christ is to grow in the Word of God. It strengthens and maintains us. His Word is transformative and powerful because it is alive. Jesus explained that seed sown on rocky ground without much depth of soil would wither in the heat of the sun because it lacked root (Matthew 13:5–6). The Word of God provides all of the nutrients and moisture for strengthening to the innermost core of our soul, joining our heart with His very own. And that, my friend, is exactly why the lady who was afflicted with Alzheimer's disease so clearly articulated those words, "There is a place of quiet rest." For she also remembered that the words which followed were "near to the heart of God."

Reflection

What early recollections of scripture do you have that you may have memorized at Bible School or heard repeated time and again by an older person? Is there a part of your daily routine that helps to keep you grounded in the faith? How could you make a case to members in your church who are advocating for change in the worship service that it is also important to maintain the use of some of the old hymns and prayers? What changes might you make this week for sowing seeds to grow deeper roots of faith for yourself and others with whom you come in regular contact?

NOVEMBER 5
(Y1, D45)

The Key to Your Escape

I prayed to the LORD, and he answered me. He freed me from all my fears.

—Psalm 34:4 (NLT)

Inspired by video technology, the concept of an escape game has become a trendy experience. Consisting of an action team positioned in a real-life location, players cooperatively discover clues, solve puzzles, and accomplish tasks in one or more game rooms over a specified but limited period of time. As escape rooms evolved, physical combination locks, hidden keys, and codes found in the rooms have been introduced. The use of technology and elaborate storylines enhance the visitor experience, making the challenge more interactive and theatrical. Participants include family groups, friends, corporate clients interested in team-building, as well as couples. As the concept popularized throughout the world, there has been increased opportunity for risk-taking. In 2019, a psychological film entitled *Escape Room* followed a group of people sent to navigate a series of escape rooms, only to discover that their fates were tied to using their wits to survive a maze of deadly mystery rooms.

Throughout the course of history, humans have been seduced by thrill-seeking, oftentimes increasing the risk to the point of placing their own lives in peril. The world's most exhilarating event takes place each July in the cramped streets of Pamplona, Spain, with the Running of the Bulls. The origin dates back to the fourteenth century when locals began honoring the passing of Saint Fermín who was dragged to his own death by bulls. To this day, adrenaline-seeking contenders sprint down the road, literally running for their lives. The enraged bulls show no mercy to those who slip or fall on the course, making it one of the most dangerous running events of all time. It's not unusual for these daredevils like these to be critical of those who help disengage them from the messes into which they willingly placed themselves. Some who have a faith background have blamed God for not being there to rescue them.

Throughout God's Word, we find assurances like this one from the Apostle Paul: "And he did rescue us from mortal danger, and he will rescue us again. We have placed our confidence in him, and he will continue to rescue us" (2 Corinthians 1:10 NLT). The Old Testament is full of accounts of God being there to rescue His people. On the brink of danger, Moses had led the Israelites to the edge of the Red Sea with Pharaoh and his army hot on their trail. If they caught up to them, it would mean death or a return to slavery for the nation of Israel, but God had a plan. Moses told the people, "Do not be afraid. Stand firm, and you will see the deliverance the LORD will bring you today. The Egyptians you see today you will never see again. The LORD will fight for you; you need only to be still" (Exodus 14:13–14 NIV). Suddenly, the waters of the Red Sea ripped open, and they were able to walk across on dry land. When Pharaoh's army tried to advance after them, they were drowned in the crashing waves of the sea. An equally astounding story (1 Samuel 17:41–51) is revealed when the young, inexperienced David confronted the fierce Philistine, Goliath. Towering above his young combatant, Goliath possessed brute strength and unrivaled weaponry. He challenged Israel to engage in battle, but no one was willing to fight. Imagine the shock when David, carrying only a slingshot, stepped up for the encounter. While everyone else believed Goliath controlled the story, David saw God and demonstrated faith that He loomed larger. And, with a single stone to the giant's forehead, David's faith proved true.

We might place ourselves into dangerous situations, but God will not create inescapable circumstances. He will provide the strength to do what we cannot. "The LORD is my rock, my fortress, and my savior; my God is my rock, in whom I find protection. He is my shield, the power that saves me, and my place of safety" (Psalm 18:2 NLT). At times when there appears to be no means of escape, we allow our fears to control the narrative. However, God can shield us from what might otherwise be a tragic outcome. The blessed reality is that God grants deliverance. This has always been the provision for His people. "The Lord will rescue me from every evil attack and will bring me safely to his heavenly kingdom" (2 Timothy 4:18 NIV). The next time you find yourself in a situation where there appears to be no good ending ahead, dare to ask the question, who is it that holds the key to my escape?

Reflection

Have there been times when you have engaged your life using an "escape game" mentality? Where or when did you give consideration to the fact that you own self-sufficiency might never be enough to be detached from the risk you were taking? How does understanding God's power of deliverance serve to provide strength and reassurance for those uncertain situations in your journey ahead?

NOVEMBER 6
(Y2, D45)

Being Nice Is Not Always Kind

Be kind to one another, tenderhearted, forgiving one another, as God in Christ forgave you.

—Ephesians 4:32 (ESV)

While preparing to go through the checkout line at the local Walmart, I suddenly realized I had neglected to bring my wallet. Fortunately, the person who was with me had $25 in cash. As I looked over my cart, I assumed I was in excess of that amount. So I said to the cashier, "Please scan the items slowly. I just realized I forgot my cards, and I only have $25, so I will have to choose which items I will buy when you reach that amount." Just then, I felt a tap on my shoulder. As I turned around, there was a stranger holding out his hand. In it was a $10 bill. "Take this," he said. "I overheard you saying you had forgotten your wallet." Somewhat overwhelmed and perhaps slightly embarrassed, I responded, "Oh no, thank you." The man said, "Go ahead," to which I responded, "No, really, I appreciate the offer, but there is nothing here I absolutely need." I obviously did not take the money, but I then wondered in what situation some other individual might have taken advantage of this person. Later, I considered if the man was motivated by kindness. Or was he was just trying to be nice? I do believe there is a difference.

Who of us doesn't remember our parents telling us to "play nice" or one of our early teachers correcting a misbehaving student with the phrase "That's not very nice!"? Being nice is expected of schoolyard kids, adult citizens, and especially of declared Christians. We are told, "If you can't say something nice, don't say anything at all." Nice as it relates to being polite, and tactful is certainly behavior we should exemplify. But in doing so, we can become obsessed with not wanting to ruffle feathers, bend the rules, speak honestly, or ever saying no. Our desire to be known as nice urges us to keep the peace at all costs, never allowing our true feelings to show at the expense of trying to please others. Being too nice, almost becoming a doormat for friends, fellow church members, coworkers, and others, comes at a cost if we allow others to take advantage of us. Instead, it is healthier if we simply make it known by our words and actions that we've enacted clear and measurable boundaries. For many of us, we must discredit the belief that being "nice is next to godliness."

But to what degree is "nice" scriptural? To answer this question, consider some examples from Jesus. In counseling His disciples what to do when people would not welcome or listen to them, they should "shake off the dust from your feet as a testimony against them" (Mark 6:11 NIV). Jesus says, move on from them. One time, when He was at Jacob's well, He called out a Samaritan woman for having had several husbands and for currently living with a man who was not her husband (John 4:5–30). On another occasion, a man brought his son to Jesus to be healed, and Jesus exclaimed, "O faithless generation, how long am I to be with you?" (Mark 9:19 ESV). We later learn that Jesus had no patience for unrepentant, greedy men who took advantage of others. When He saw money-changers and merchants selling animals and doves in the temple courtyard, He made a whip, drove them from the temple area, and overturned their tables (John 2:14). One of His last major public discourses was the solemn pronunciation of seven woes against the scribes and Pharisees. In Matthew 23, He tells the crowd that they "preach but do not practice" and that they do everything just for show. He refers to them as hypocrites, blind guides, blind fools, children of hell, extortionists, white-washed tombs, and says that they are filled with iniquity.

Jesus was at times gentle and calm; other times, not so much. However, He was always charitable. Jesus demonstrated the difference between graciousness and personal compromise between speaking truth and needlessly alienating people. He was always thinking of the salvation of souls. Similarly, we need to determine the best approach when speaking to others. We cannot be afraid to tell someone they are wrong. We cannot be afraid to hurt someone's feelings in the short run so that they may repent and be restored to life in Christ in the long run. In 1 Corinthians 13, love is described as patient, kind, not envious, not boastful, not rude, selfless, not easily angered, and ungrudging. "Nice" never shows up on that list; but "kind" does. The difference between niceness and kindness is the difference between tolerating and embracing, political correctness and love, appearance and reality. Unlike niceness, which is focused on outward consequences, kindness comes from inside.

Reflection

What are some ways you have misinterpreted niceness for kindness? How might being more open and honest contribute to kindness? In what ways should you make this happen in your life?

NOVEMBER 7
(Y3, D45)

Amazed... Once Again

Everyone was gripped with great wonder and awe, and they praised
God, exclaiming, "We have seen amazing things today!"

—Luke 5:26 (NLT)

As a child, it may have been when you saw a magic trick, hearing a recorded playback of your voice, or sitting on Santa's lap for the very first time. Those early moments of awe were special ones. I remember my first flight like it was yesterday. I was living on the East Coast at the time, and my destination was California. I had breakfast at home, an early lunch at the Baltimore airport, and was able to eat dinner that evening in Los Angeles. It took a while for me to wrap my mind around the totality of that day, but I recall thinking it was an awesome feat. Then flying became more frequent, and by the time I flew across the Atlantic to Europe a decade later, the magnificence of the experience was less impressive.

The constant stimulation and immediate gratification that we have as a society concerns me because I fear we have come to take for granted any deep sense appreciation for special times. While I am still able to attend a concert of my favorite musician and thoroughly enjoy being in the moment, if I am not careful, I can allow myself to be overly aware of those around me who are making videos of the event. I don't want to lose my admiration for the instrumentation, the back-up vocalization, or the staging and backdrop visuals. For so many, it's just something they have come to expect for the price of a ticket. Being in a state of awe on an occasion like this can attach us to a memory of a person or place that won't easily be forgotten. When we are no longer amazed, impressed, or feel a sense of wonderment, then I believe we have become less than our Maker intended for us to be, and that's just downright sad.

It is difficult, however, to have an awe experience when we are preoccupied with so much around us constantly demanding our attention. We multitask through our hours of the day finding little that we would define as astonishing. But when we do find it, we may experience one of the most significant times in our journey. On those occasions, it would behoove us to nurture it in a way in which we might grow spiritually. When the Lord spoke to the blinded Saul on the way to Damascus, those who were with him were speechless (Acts 9:1–19) as He provided very specific direction as to how Saul's sight would be restored if he obeyed. The miraculous power of God is again demonstrated in the Old Testament when the walls of Jericho fell (Joshua 6:2–5). Here we find that Joshua followed God's direction explicitly. We come to the understand that when we listen for and obey God's Word, we will witness the awesome display of His glory. For then we will witness that "God's voice thunders in marvelous ways; he does great things beyond our understanding" (Job 37:5 NIV). Are you listening for the distant thunder?

Much of our time these days is spent trying to establish the right level of connectivity with the world around us, often neglecting our "out of this world" direct line to God. When our awe of God is lacking, He can and will be replaced by something far less significant if we are not careful. We should never take for granted that "the fear of the LORD is the beginning of wisdom; A good understanding have all those who do His commandments; His praise endures forever" (Psalm 111:10 NASB). Until we rediscover the meaning of awe in our lives, we cannot possibly experience the fullness of a relationship with Him. As we anticipate the upcoming holidays of Thanksgiving and Christmas, they might serve as a wonderful time to renew our search. As we gather together to count our many blessings and reflect on Him as the Christ-child in the manger, He will rekindle our hearts, and we will be amazed once again.

Reflection

What are some of the things in your life that have numbed your relationship with Christ? Are there ways that you and your family might be able to instill a deeper sense of appreciation for God and each other during the holidays ahead? If you are fortunate to have your sense of awe renewed, can you identify a manner in which you might sustain it during the course of the upcoming year?

NOVEMBER 8
(Y4, D45)

Drowning in Busyness

> We are merely moving shadows, and all our busy rushing ends in
> nothing. We heap up wealth, not knowing who will spend it.

—Psalm 39:6 (NLT)

It turned out to be a much different day than I had anticipated. It was light on schedule, almost a free one with only a single appointment arranged for late that afternoon. A friend who was having outpatient surgery had turned down my offer of transportation, so I called an older friend to fulfill a promise I had made the week before. When I got his voicemail, I left a message. I now found myself with several hours of unplanned activity. It was a beautiful autumn afternoon, and I knew that if no one or nothing else was waiting for me, the fallen leaves in my yard were certainly in need of attention. Then, for an hour or so, I raked leaves and had some lunch. Later, my friend who had surgery sent me a text and asked if we could go for a walk. The older friend to whom I had made that promise retuned my call and indicated he would be free later to get together. I completed a quick errand to the grocery store and ran into someone else who wanted to talk. A relative reached out for my help with a small emergency, and suddenly, my unscheduled day was filled with busyness. It happens to all of us from time to time as we allow our days to become consumed with self-imposed schedules which, if we are not careful, can become suffocating.

There is nothing wrong with being busy, but how we prioritize our busyness will determine our life journey outcomes. In our society, busyness has become somewhat of a status symbol. After all, the busier we are, the more important we appear to be. Or so some would think. While our busyness often begins with good intentions, we can become addicted to our routines, and the search for the joys of life become the burdens of our existence. When I once tried to explain to a friend why I hadn't been in touch, I will always remember his response. It was simply, "We make time in our lives for the things that are important." I think his words were wise. That conversation took place years before our default mode became reduced to technology's social media platforms. I hate to think what his comeback might be in today's world when human contact is sometimes limited to a post or a tweet.

Jesus counseled that it is where and on what we spend our time that speaks volumes about who we are. "As Jesus and the disciples continued on their way to Jerusalem, they came to a certain village where a woman named Martha welcomed him into her home. Her sister, Mary, sat at the Lord's feet, listening to what he taught. But Martha was distracted by the big dinner she was preparing. She came to Jesus and said, "Lord, doesn't it seem unfair to you that my sister just sits here while I do all the work? Tell her to come and help me." But the Lord said to her, "My dear Martha, you are worried and upset over all these details! There is only one thing worth being concerned about. Mary has discovered it, and it will not be taken away from her" (Luke 10:38–42 NLT). I think Jesus would tell us that true spirituality is about having real human connections, those which can easily escape us in a world where we have allowed true listening to be reduced to text or sound bites.

God's Word places high value on rest and tranquil living. Much of the time, we become like Martha, losing sight of those things that are really important. We rush around, chasing our tails, and miss the blessings that the Lord has provided all around us. In reality, we learn much more in those calm, restful periods than we ever will in those times when our bodies and minds are on overload. The Lord spoke clearly about this: "Come to me, all you who are weary and burdened, and I will give you rest" (Matthew 11:28 NIV). So the next time you feel troubled with the tasks of the day, and clearing your schedule for a few hours seems to be all but impossible, just learn to listen for these words: "Be still and know that I am God" (Psalm 46:10 NIV). It is when we permit those times of serenity to occur that God reveals Himself to us. Allow yourself to dwell in the Savior's presence and let Him teach you how to follow in Mary's example: to choose what it is better. For when you do so, you will not just experience that peace that passes all understanding, but you will have Him forever as your guide.

Reflection

What are those tasks ahead of you this day that will make you feel like you are drowning under the pressures of life? How might the words reflected in Matthew 6:33–34 (NIV) provide a new vision? They are: "But seek first his kingdom and his righteousness, and all these things will be given to you as well. Therefore do not worry about tomorrow, for tomorrow will worry about itself. Each day has enough trouble of its own."

NOVEMBER 9
(Y5, D45)

Flawed

Even before he made the world, God loved us and chose us in
Christ to be holy and without fault in his eyes.

—Ephesians 1:4 (NLT)

Do you know anyone who is a numismatist? You may be one and not even know it. Do you collect coins or know someone who does? If so, someone might give you this label. Numismatics is the study or collection of currency, including coins. If you get into serious collecting, you will try to find coins that have never been in circulation. However, you will soon realize that to find an old coin in uncirculated condition is a rare and expensive achievement. In the process, you might use the proficiency of a coin-grading service. In their classification system, ratings are used to categorize these never-circulated coins, utilizing factors such as striking strength and luster. Similar services are available for the assessment of precious gems such as diamonds. Unless you have a microscope, the casual observer cannot distinguish between a slightly compromised diamond and one which is perfect, except, of course, when you pay your bill. One company advertises that they are "the perfect source for less than perfect diamonds."

It becomes much more evident to see flaws when we talk about people. In any presidential election, it is not unusual for any candidate of the major political parties to be referred to as "flawed." Americans will frequently voice that one or both candidates are unqualified or undeserving of the office based upon their past. The normal use of the word *flawed* means "blemished, damaged, or imperfect in some way." If we use that as our standard, then we might wonder why any normal person would consider running for office. And if that application follows, the words *imperfect* or *flawed* could define any of us on a given day. It gives us pause to consider the wise counsel of Paul, "For by the grace given me I say to every one of you: Do not think of yourself more highly than you ought, but rather think of yourself with sober judgment, in accordance with the faith God has distributed to each of you" (Romans 12:3 NIV).

In two of the Gospels, Jesus told two different parables about banquet guests. In the book of Matthew, a king prepares a wedding feast for his son. When he sends for the invited guests, they appear to be busy and unable to attend. So he tells his servants, "Go to the street corners and invite to the banquet anyone you find" (Matthew 22:9 NIV). As instructed, the servants invited all sorts of people until the wedding feast was filled. One of the guests insults the king by not wearing the wedding clothes which the host would have provided. The man was thrown out, "For many are invited but few are chosen" (Matthew 22:14 NIV). In Luke's story, the guests are told to be careful not to take the seats of honor "for a person more distinguished than you may have been invited" (Luke 14:8 NIV). It is far better to take "the lowest place so that when the host comes, he will say to you, 'Friend, move up to a better place.' Then you will be honored in the presence of all the other guests" (Luke 14:10–11 NIV). Regardless of where we are seated, we are flawed and must consider it the greatest of all honors to just be invited.

As we sit down to our own feasts this Thanksgiving, we might pause, look around the table, and ask some pertinent questions. Who was invited and did not come? Who is attending out of pure obligation? Did they sit close to or distance themselves from certain people? As we serve the turkey and stuffing, no doubt there is also plenty of heartache and blame to be passed around, enough for each one of us to have a generous portion. Harper Lee, author of *To Kill a Mockingbird*, penned these words: "You can choose your friends but you sho' can't choose your family, an' they're still kin to you no matter whether you acknowledge 'em or not, and it makes you look right silly when you don't." As we set the places at our table, He sets the example for us to offer a seat of honor to our flawed but forgiven family members. And like David, we will respond, "The eyes of all look to you, and you give them their food at the proper time. You open your hand and satisfy the desires of every living thing" (Psalm 145:15–16 NIV). Allow your Thanksgiving to be a perfect reunion for all those who are perfectly made—if only in the eyes of God.

Reflection

How do you allow for imperfection in your own life and in the lives of others without compromising your values? Consider the greater meaning of Matthew 7:3 (NIV): "Why do you look at the speck of sawdust in your brother's eye and pay no attention to the plank in your own eye?" How can you apply this in your own life journey or as you provide counsel to another?

NOVEMBER 10
(Y6, D45)

In the Midst of Any Suffering

We can rejoice, too, when we run into problems and trials, for
we know that they help us develop endurance.

—Romans 5:3 (NLT)

The words "Dr. Livingstone, I presume?" were spoken by Henry Morgan Stanley on November 10, 1871, when he located missionary and physician David Livingstone following several years without anyone hearing from him. Born in Scotland in 1813, David Livingstone's devout Christian parents encouraged their son to pursue whatever he desired as long as it was to the glory of God. At an early age, he had such a passion for souls that he gave his life to go to the untouched and unexplored areas of Africa to reach those that would otherwise not hear the Gospel. He fought lions, buried a child and eventually his wife, suffered tropical illnesses, and endured the hardships of being a pioneer in a strange land for the sake of being able to win people to his Lord. Livingstone did not hide the painful experiences of anxiety, sickness, suffering, and danger. Most any of us would consider these to be sacrifices, but he faced the trials head on. Toward the end of his life, the great missionary returned to his native Scotland to be honored by his countrymen. There was absolute silence as Livingstone told of his experiences in Africa, his left arm hanging limp at his side, the result of being mauled by a lion. He said, "But I return without misgivings and with great gladness. For would you like me to tell you what supported me through all the years of exile among people whose language I could not understand, and whose attitude towards me was always uncertain and often hostile? It was this: 'Lo, I am with you always, even unto the end of the world!'" Livingstone returned there, but his frail body failed in 1873. His native co-laborers found him slumped over the cot where the previous night he had knelt to pray. His well-worn New Testament was open to the same passage he had quoted to the university audience—that of Matthew 28:20.

Livingstone remained committed to his cause for an entire lifetime but emphatically stated that he felt he had never sacrificed. He spoke the way Paul does in Philippians 3:8: "I consider everything a loss because of the surpassing worth of knowing Christ Jesus my Lord, for whose sake I have lost all things." The disciple Peter realized that Jesus called for radical sacrifice when He stated: "In the same way, those of you who do not give up everything you have cannot be my disciples" (Luke 14:33 NIV). In response to Jesus, "Peter spoke up, 'We have left everything to follow you!'" (Mark 10:28 NIV). Jesus quickly rebuked such boasting or self-pity, setting an example for Peter and Livingstone. He established that the sacrifice they had made was not really a sacrifice at all.

> "Yes," Jesus replied, "and I assure you that everyone who has given up house or brothers or sisters or mother or father or children or property, for my sake and for the Good News, will receive now in return a hundred times as many houses, brothers, sisters, mothers, children, and property—along with persecution. And in the world to come that person will have eternal life." (Mark 10:29–30 NLT)

In the bright shadow of David Livingstone's suffering, we are able to understand the point of Jesus' words more clearly—"Following me, you do not make a sacrifice."

When missionary Dr. David Livingstone was working in Africa, a group of friends wrote him: "We would like to send other men to you. Have you found a good road into your area yet?" Dr. Livingstone sent this message in reply: "If you have men who will only come if they know there is a good road, I don't want them. I want men who will come if there is no road at all." Lord knows that our culture lacks that kind of commitment these days, and it all stems from the fact that most of us are not willing to sacrifice. It is evident in our work, our relationships with others and, in particular, our spiritual life. There's a big difference between just being interested in doing something and actually making a commitment to doing it. Just being "interested" allows one the freedom to do it only when circumstances of convenience or notoriety permit. However, actually making a commitment means putting aside our fears and reservations and moving forward until we realize the end-result. If along the way we need to make sacrifices, we will not see them as such because our focus is on that to which we have committed. Nothing else matters. That's the kind of commitment the Lord expects from each one of us, and when we do so, we'll rejoice in the midst of any suffering.

Reflection

When you have made a commitment to a person or project, have you entered into the arrangement with an exit-strategy if one was needed? Through what type of arrangement would you be willing to endure suffering and consider it worth the cost? Does this apply to your relationship with God?

NOVEMBER 11
(Y7, D45)

In Harm's Way

Endure suffering along with me, as a good soldier of Christ Jesus.

—2 Timothy 2:3 (NLT)

It is at this time of the year that we remember those who fought for our country, allowed themselves to be put in harm's way, and who we have come to observe on a special holiday known as Veteran's Day. The phrase "in harm's way" has been attributed to the American Revolutionary War hero John Paul Jones, forever known as the Father of the American Navy. In 1778, American Navy Captain Jones went to France, hoping to persuade the French government to give him a ship to use in the American colonies' rebellion against the British. In a letter dated November 16, 1778, he said, "I wish to have no connection with any ship that does not sail fast, for I intend to go in harm's way." Unfortunately, the best that the American agents in France could find for Jones was a slow, refurbished, fourteen-year-old vessel. Jones proceeded to sail into harm's way with his tub of a ship and motley crew, and that led to his most famous battle. With his ship sinking and burning, guns wrecked, and half his crew dead or wounded, John Paul Jones had a chance to surrender which any normal person would have taken. But Jones himself answered with the call that he had "not yet begun to fight."

Those who serve in our armed forces understand that freedom comes at a cost. And since the birth of our nation, brave men and women have stepped forward, weighed that cost, and have chosen to lay down their lives in service to their fellow countrymen. When one of them dies, the words extended "on behalf of a grateful nation" seem to be inadequate at times. These days, it is not only those in uniform who occasionally march into harm's way. Indeed, that could be any of us who walks into a public building or shops at a local mall. No one would have suspected that attending worship at the First Baptist Church in Sutherland Springs, Texas, would have placed themselves at risk of being among those twenty-six persons who were mortally wounded on that fateful day of November 5, 2017. In those brief minutes after the attacker began to fire his weapon, a mother shielded her four children as best she could by throwing her body over theirs. Only two of the children survived as this mother who sacrificed her life realized they were all in harm's way. A concerned neighbor who heard the massacre unfolding grabbed his rifle and placed himself in danger by opening fire on the shooter and chased him down in a stranger's truck. Reflecting on the event, he later stated, "I'm no hero. I think my Lord protected me and gave me the skills to do what needed to be done."

Undoubtedly, you must like have heard someone say, "Things are going to get worse before they get better." While some may see this as pessimism, others simply view it as a call of preparation. Lest there be any doubt, we live in uncertain times. In the Apostle Paul's last letter to his beloved son in the faith, Timothy, he gave this insight: "But mark this: There will be terrible times in the last days" (2 Timothy 3:1 NIV). In the verses which follow, He goes on to describe what these end times will look like. It is clear that dangerous, harmful, high-risk periods have already arrived. We are living in a generation that faces world threats like no other generation has ever known. The obvious follow up question for any believer then would be, "Now that I know the Lord, what am I to do in perilous times?'" Paul provides this answer: "But you must remain faithful to the things you have been taught. You know they are true, for you know you can trust those who taught you" (2 Timothy 3:14 NLT).

As we face each new day knowing that we will be in a spiritual battle for all that is good and right, it's easy to reflect on the words of the great hymn, "Onward Christian soldiers marching as to war; With the cross of Jesus going on before." Taken from New Testament references to the Christian being a soldier for Christ, none of us know if and when we might be called to stand for our faith. We might march in the ranks of the armed services, engage in the protection of a loved one or neighbor, or come face to face with some other hateful act of this world. We can hold onto those words: "Greater love has no one than this, that he lay down his life for his friends" (John 15:13 NIV). We will sense the presence of His protection and know the assurance of His love as we move to confront whatever places us in harm's way.

Reflection

As a child of God, how can you fully embrace that you are equipped to minister to someone who is suffering? Do you feel overcome with fear or filled with faith as you contemplate facing the special challenges of being in harm's way? Are you heeding the warnings of the Holy Spirit to be spiritually alert?

NOVEMBER 12
(Y1, D46)

Reflectors of Light in a Dark World

Even when I walk through the darkest valley, I will not be afraid, for you are
close beside me. Your rod and your staff protect and comfort me.

—Psalm 23:4 (NLT)

The villages of Rjukan, Norway, and Viganella, Italy, are both situated in deep valleys where mountains block the sun's rays for up to six months every year. To illuminate those darker winter months, the two towns have built gigantic mirrors that track the sun and reflect daylight downward. Viganella completed its huge computer-controlled mirror in 2006, and Rjukan followed suit in 2013 by mounting a mirror that reflects a 6,500-square-foot beam of sunshine into the town below. The idea of the sun mirror was first introduced by Rjukan's founder, Sam Eyde, in 1913. He understood the importance of the sun and tried to create a sun mirror, but unfortunately, his efforts were unsuccessful. This forced the inhabitants of the valley to wait another full century for a brighter tomorrow. In 2005, a local artist began "The Mirror Project" to bring together people who could turn the idea into reality. Eight years later, in October 2013, the mirrors went into action. Residents crowded into the town square to soak up the reflected sunlight.

Sunlight is a crucial aspect when it comes to our health, good mood, and overall well-being. Cities across the world that lack direct sunlight throughout the year have many inhabitants who are in desperate need of Vitamin D which is vital for our health. Living in constant darkness often produces a mild form of malaise, commonly referred to as the winter blues. For a minority of people who suffer from seasonal affective disorder, winter is quite literally depressing. Even many healthy people seem to experience this mood change over the year with their energy level worsening during autumn and winter with a noted improvement in spring and summer. In a spiritual sense, much of the world is like the village of Rjukan—mountains of troubles keep the light of Jesus from getting through. When we walk through the deep valley, we feel swallowed up by its shadow and come face-to-face with fear. The frantic emptiness of our loss threatens the comfort which had previously originated from our trust in God. Consequently, we become vulnerable to become afraid of our future and enjoy a normal life again.

The painting, *A Trail of Light*, by artist Bob Simpich shows a grove of aspen trees with golden leaves lit by the autumn sun. The topmost leaves are brilliantly illuminated while the ground beneath the trees is a mixture of sunlight and shadows. The painter said of this contrast, "I can't resist the light filtered through to the forest floor. It weaves a special magic." When we find ourselves in a darkened valley (as we all do at times) the words expressed by the painter is exactly what God does for us. Slowly at first, but most assuredly, He filters His light through, providing comfort and release from the darkness. Eventually, we escape the valley of the shadow. The Apostle Paul put it this way: "For God, who said, 'Let there be light in the darkness,' has made this light shine in our hearts so we could know the glory of God that is seen in the face of Jesus Christ" (2 Corinthians 4:6 NLT).

In almost every phase of our lives, we strive for the mountaintop experiences. But when it comes right down to it, we spend a significant amount of our days going into or climbing out of the valley or otherwise deep in the valley itself. There are times when it seems that the light of God's face is dimmed because of our difficulty, sorrow, or loss. Yet, even in these dark shadows, we can see evidence of His presence with us. It is also during those times that God strategically places His other children to act as reflectors. As believers, we have opportunities to offer light to those in a valley of darkness. But we must always maintain the perspective that our light is derived from God Himself. We are not the source of the light; we merely reflect it. This challenge, therefore, lies before us: "For once you were full of darkness, but now you have light from the Lord. So live as people of light" (Ephesians 5:8 NLT). Just as sunlight is essential for emotional and physical health, so exposure to the light of Jesus is essential for our spiritual health. When you and I are properly aligned with Christ, His light shines through us in such a way that we become capable of serving as a light to others. In doing so, we act as a prism to become reflectors of God's light in a world of dark places.

Reflection

What gives you the desire to be aligned with Christ so that you might shine His light? In what ways have you acted as a prism for Jesus in your part of the world? If this doesn't apply in your life at the current time, how will you strive to become the kind of light the Lord needs you to be?

NOVEMBER 13
(Y2, D46)

Walking by Faith Alone

My eyes will flow unceasingly, without relief, until the
Lord looks down from heaven and sees.

—Lamentations 3:49–50 (NIV)

Corn mazes have become popular tourist attractions in North America and are a way for farms to generate extra income. Most have a path which embrace a pattern with various false trails diverging from the main path. It's not uncommon for people to panic when they can't find their way out of a maze. Some people daring enough to enter the world's largest corn maze in Dixon, California, have become so lost that they had to call 911 to help get them out of the sixty-acre web. A family trying to find their way through a maze in Massachusetts told one such operator, "We're very worried and we can't find a way out. We came in during the day time and we got completely lost, and now we have no idea where we are. We thought this could be fun. Instead, it's been a nightmare." It turned out the family was just about twenty-five feet from the exit when they were found by a police officer. If you were just able to send a drone over the maze, you would see a distinct route which would provide confident guidance through the path.

The experience of the corn maze can easily be compared to each of us winding our way aimlessly through life. We all encounter twists and turns as well as dead ends and puzzling circumstances, all leading to doubt and uncertainty. Doubt is largely a lack of confidence in a direction. It is fear brought on by a lack of information, experience, or preparation. Doubt can display a lack of faith in God at the many bends in the road, but we can erase those doubts by consciously deciding to trust. We can learn to turn our doubts into destinations. God will never lead us where His grace cannot provide for us or His power cannot protect us. This became a difficult lesson for the Israelites in the Old Testament. God had made a promise to them. He commanded them to take possession of the land that was already theirs. They simply had to trust and obey, but they failed to do so. Although God forgave them, He stated, "They will never even see the land I swore to give their ancestors. None of those who have treated me with contempt will ever see it" (Numbers 14:23 NLT). Rather, they would suffer by wandering in the wilderness for forty years, one year for each of the forty days they explored their land and doubted (Numbers 14:34).

Only the two faithful, Joshua and Caleb, who believed God's promise to give the land over to them survived. Indeed, the Israelites had seen the powerful hand of God at work during the plagues and miracles of the Exodus. Yet, like many of us, they walked by sight and not by faith, and their unbelief displeased God. In Deuteronomy 1:2, we learn that their forty-year wilderness journey should have only taken about eleven days. God reminded this new generation of their ancestor's rebelling, grumbling, murmuring, arrogance, and involvement with worshipers of other gods which collectively lead to aimless wandering and death. He said, "Remember how the LORD your God led you all the way in the wilderness these forty years, to humble and test you in order to know what was in your heart, whether or not you would keep his commands" (Deuteronomy 8:2 NIV). It was in that precarious place called the wilderness where the children of Israel learned to trust God and to believe profoundly in His goodness and mercy.

It was in those days as it is today. Only individuals who believed in God reached the promised land then, and only those who believe in Jesus will receive His promises today. Though the wilderness is a place of darkness and despair, it should be understood that it is also a place where God is. No believer can fully avoid a wilderness experience in our life's path. Without these trials in our lives, it would be difficult for us to appreciate green pastures. While there is not much solace in a wilderness experience, it should bring some comfort for us to realize that every person of faith is subjected to such events. The ultimate purpose of the wilderness is not only to grow a deep transforming faith but also to develop a profoundly rewarding and intimate connection with God. His ultimate desire for us as His children is that we learn to walk by faith alone. In doing so, we'll find "a-maze-ing" destinations ahead.

Reflection

Do you sometimes rebel, doubt, complain, murmur, fear, and then do things God does not want you to do? Has this led you into your own wilderness journey? Will you be faithful to God or will you be like the children of Israel during your experience? How might you help others be prepared for wilderness experiences in their own lives?

NOVEMBER 14
(Y3, D46)

A Good Reference

A good man brings good things out of the good stored up in him, and
an evil man brings evil things out of the evil stored up in him.

—Matthew 12:35 (NIV)

From time to time, I am asked if I will serve as a reference for someone. Sometimes the person and I once worked together. At other times, it is an individual I have known for many years in more of a collegial relationship. Most often, the reference is work-related. Unfortunately, many companies have determined that ability to provide a work reference must be limited to dates of employment and position held with other information needing to be withheld for legal reasons. Once in a while, there are also requests for references where the information requested is more about the person's integrity or character. In these situations, it is often possible to be more open in providing details that will assist the person in becoming a qualified applicant.

What would you do if you were seeking a character reference on an individual and you were provided with the following narrative: "He will do anything you ask of him; in fact, he is fearless. He has had abundant periods of success but has also experienced great failure, including committing adultery and murder. Trouble seems to have a way of finding him." This might be enough to shuffle this particular resume to the bottom of the pile. But what if you listened a little more and read a bit further to learn that additional words used to describe this individual include: devoted, repentant, trusting, humble, and respectful? You might wonder how this could be the same individual. Is it possible that they have a split-personality? What would you think of this person if you knew that the reference was coming directly from God as He described "a man after His own heart" (1 Samuel 13:14)? Would you be surprised to learn that this is how he might likely characterize His loving servant, David, the shepherd boy who became a king?

When people talk about you, do they articulate you to be a person of character? Or might they simply say, "He's quite a character alright!" Scripture tells us, "For where your treasure is, there your heart will be also" (Matthew 6:21 NIV). Regardless of where David's station in life positioned Him,

He found His treasure in God. So it's easy to see how even centuries later he would be remembered by Paul as a man after God's own heart (Acts 13:22). What is it then that defines one's character? It would seem that it might be something that we personally strive for as defined by a framework of values. It might also be defined by others in how they see us demonstrate that system of values in our life. Abraham Lincoln once said that "character is like a tree and reputation like a shadow. The shadow is what we think of it; the tree is the real thing." God sees the tree in all of us, His very own creation.

It is not unusual in our society to witness frequent examples of character assassination. You need to look no further than the personal attacks on the lives of our political candidates. It is evidenced daily in the tabloids and social media as defamations are displayed about public figures as well as common folk who might live right down the block. The Bible says, "There are six things the LORD hates, seven that are detestable to him: haughty eyes, a lying tongue, hands that shed innocent blood, a heart that devises wicked schemes, feet that are quick to rush into evil, a false witness who pours out lies and a person who stirs up conflict in the community" (Proverbs 6:16–19 NIV). God builds character in our lives by allowing us to experience situations where we are tempted to do these things. It is when we choose to do otherwise that we grow in character and become more like Christ. Helen Keller once said that "character cannot be developed in ease and quiet. Only through experience of trial and suffering can the soul be strengthened, ambition inspired, and success achieved." Here's to success, then, for any one of us who is seeking to attain that next good reference.

Reflection

What are those areas of your character that you need to work on? Have you grown in your Christian life in those times when you were faced with trouble, heartache, conflict, disappointment, pain, or misunderstanding? As a result of those difficulties, are there ways that you feel your character was strengthened? How is your character reflected in the ways you serve God?

NOVEMBER 15
(Y4, D46)

Born Again

For you have been born again, but not to a life that will quickly end. Your new life will last forever because it comes from the eternal, living word of God.

—1 Peter 1:23 (NLT)

Late fall is one of my least favorite times of the year. Just as the colors of autumn are beautiful, the dead fallen leaves from the trees cover what not long ago were flowering plants and a bed of green grass. The holidays bring fresh excitement offering warm gatherings for family and friends. But when January arrives and the winter winds begin to howl and snow starts to fly, I start counting the days until the crocus will start to push through the soil once again. I tell myself that even though the daylight hours will soon be at their shortest time, it is right around Christmas when we start gaining back minutes of light with each new day. So rather than rake my leaves, I blow them into a pile and mulch them with my mower, convincing myself that the nutrients will be good for next year's soil. I consider what new bulbs I might want to plant in a few months, recognizing that perennials are one of God's greatest miracles in that while they appear to die, they are "born again" when the earth's warmth returns.

Did you hear the story about the baby who was born twice? Sounds like a headline on the front of one of those tabloids at the grocery check-out counter. But this was the true story of a Texas woman who went for a routine ultrasound in the sixteenth week of her pregnancy. It was discovered that there was a tumor growing from her baby's tailbone. Originally pregnant with twins but having lost one, the mother was now faced with a rare birth defect of the surviving child. She was told that the tumor was stealing the blood supply from the fetus, forcing its survival to become more compromised each day. At nearly twenty-four weeks, fetal surgery was performed requiring that the baby be removed from the womb and then returned. Surgeons were able to detach most of the tumor which had grown nearly as large as the fetus. After five hours, it was replaced back into the mother's womb. After twelve more weeks in utero, LynLee Hope was "born again" at full-term via C-section. Dr.

Darrell Cass, who led the surgical team at Texas Children's Fetal Center, described the procedure as a "kind of miracle." And that it was!

"Surely they cannot enter a second time into his mother's womb to be born" (John 3:4 NIV). These were the words of Nicodemus, a member of the Jewish ruling council. Appearing before Jesus, he was aware of the miracles Jesus had performed and certain Jesus was sent from God. Like many of his time, Nicodemus misinterpreted the plan of God. Correcting Nicodemus' misunderstanding, "Jesus replied, 'I assure you, no one can enter the Kingdom of God without being born of water and the Spirit.'" He went on to explain that "humans can reproduce only human life, but the Holy Spirit gives birth to spiritual life. So don't be surprised when I say, 'You must be born again'" (John 3:5–7 NIV). Nicodemus had a real need. He required a change of heart and understanding—a spiritual transformation. When Jesus spoke with him, He used an illustration that could be easily understood. A newborn baby entering an earthly physical life is a perfect comparison for a person of any age beginning a new spiritual life.

The term "born again" is a commonly used phrase among present-day Christians. The expression literally means "born from above." It is not a spur-of-the-moment decision based on emotion but rather more of a conversion process. The Apostle Paul understood:

> Yes, everything else is worthless when compared with the infinite value of knowing Christ Jesus my Lord. For his sake I have discarded everything else, counting it all as garbage, so that I could gain Christ and become one with him. I no longer count on my own righteousness through obeying the law; rather, I become righteous through faith in Christ. For God's way of making us right with himself depends on faith... I don't mean to say that I have already achieved these things or that I have already reached perfection. But I press on to possess that perfection for which Christ Jesus first possessed me. (Philippians 3:8–9, 12 NLT)

When that happens, it's more perfect than the first buds of spring and more of a miracle than a twice-born child. It's a creation that He alone can bless from above. Unlike the flower that dies, we who are born again will live forever.

Reflection

How would you explain to someone who is considering a journey with Christ what it means to be born again? In what ways has the concept of being a "born-again Christian" received a negative locus? If you were asked if it possible to be a Christian and not be born again, how would you respond?

NOVEMBER 16
(Y5, D46)

Reflecting Who We Are

Imitate God, therefore, in everything you do, because you are his dear children.

—Ephesians 5:1 (NLT)

The little girl stood on the seat of the booth, looking over the divider that separated the eating area and an entrance hallway into the restaurant. Not more than a few years old, she began to smile and giggle. Then she waved as a small child on the other side of the partition waved back. At the urging of her mother, she sat down and ate a few bites of food. As her curiosity got the best of her, she once more stood on the seat and peered over the panel. Again, she giggled, waved, and, as before, the other child did the same. It was amazing how much they looked alike. Indeed, they could have been twins, for one was, in fact, a mirror image of the other. The mother decided to glance over the divider to see what was so intriguing. Then she realized that her daughter had been seeing herself reflected in a mirror on the opposite side of the entrance hallway. As this child grows in age, she will become more focused on others and will learn to reflect that interest in games such as Follow the Leader.

Throughout the history of Judaism, one of the most honored positions for a Jewish man was the privilege of becoming a "follower" of the local rabbi. The decision to ask to be a rabbi's disciple and receive religious training from him was not made lightly. Followers sat at the rabbi's feet as he taught. They would study his words, observed how he acted, and contemplate how he would react to life situations. A student would count it the highest honor to serve his rabbi, even to the point of emulating the rabbi's gestures and mirroring his persona in every aspect of his tradition. A rabbi in the first century would only choose very few, highly promising young men from whom he thought could fully measure up to his standard. A young Jewish lad readily agreed to totally surrender to the rabbi's authority in all areas of interpreting the Scriptures for his life. If a rabbi judged a potential disciple to have the capability to become like him, then he would utter those cherished words of acceptance, "Follow me."

When Jesus used those same words to call His disciples (Matthew 4:19), it was an invitation to be changed by Him and share His passion for all who need a Savior. Jesus deliberately broke the protocol of the traditional rabbi by calling His own disciples. It would seem He had no choice but to do it that way, for no observant young Jewish man would ever have had the courage to ask Jesus to be his rabbi. Following Jesus meant that one didn't simply duplicate His teachings but that they must demonstrate, even with their own imperfections, that one can be faithful. One of his very own put it this way:

> Anyone who listens to the word but does not do what it says is like someone who looks at his face in a mirror and, after looking at himself, goes away and immediately forgets what he looks like. But whoever looks intently into the perfect law that gives freedom, and continues in it—not forgetting what they have heard, but doing it—they will be blessed in what they do. (James 1:23–25 NIV)

Everyone follows something or someone: friends, popular culture, sports, social media, family, selfish desires, or God. We can only effectively follow one thing at a time. To follow Christ means we apply the truths we learn from His Word and live as if Jesus is walking in person beside us. When we decide to follow Jesus, we apprentice our lives with Him. We commit to listening to Him, to obeying Him, and to allowing Him to shape our whole being. No one can imitate Jesus flawlessly, but over time, the disciple begins to reflect the master's influence. "Now we see things imperfectly, like puzzling reflections in a mirror, but then we will see everything with perfect clarity. All that I know now is partial and incomplete, but then I will know everything completely, just as God now knows me completely" (1 Corinthians 13:12 NLT). For like a child, we can look in a mirror and not truly understand who we are. Or instead, we can mature as a faithful disciple and begin to see our image reflect His very own.

Reflection

Are you personally following Jesus? Does your day revolve around Him? Do you start the day seeking Him, go through the day praising Him, spend the day serving Him, and end the day thanking Him?

How might you apply this scripture to your life, "As water reflects the face, so one's life reflects the heart" (Proverbs 27:19 NIV)? Are there ways you might use it as an encouragement to others?

NOVEMBER 17
(Y6, D46)

Imitating His Sacrificial Love

Do not be conformed to this world, but be transformed by the renewal of your mind, that by testing you may discern what is the will of God, what is good and acceptable and perfect.

—Romans 12:2 (ESV)

As a child of the 1930s–40s, he was an avid reader who studied Stalin, Marx, Gandhi, and Hitler, carefully noting the strengths and weaknesses of each. He found making friends difficult, and childhood acquaintances later recalled him as being a "really weird kid who was obsessed with religion… obsessed with death." James Warren Jones became an American religious cult leader who, along with his inner circle, initiated and was responsible for a mass murder/suicide in excess of 900 persons on November 18, 1978. Jim Jones, as he became known, developed a charisma as an ordained Indiana minister in the Christian Church and later established the Peoples Temple in San Francisco in 1956. By the early 1970s, Jones began deriding traditional Christianity as "fly-away religion," rejecting the Bible and beginning his cultlike influence. Jones promised a utopian society that provided for the common welfare of its members. He became a tyrannical leader and exercised that power in a dangerous, manipulative way.

In 1973, an increasingly paranoid Jones began to move Temple members to Guyana, South America, naming the settlement Jonestown in honor of himself. Once free of US law, Jones became a brutal dictator in his isolated and heavily guarded compound where he controlled and employed various mind control techniques on his followers. Concerned ex-members in California brought details of Jones' terror to the attention of Congressman Leo Ryan who, along with some aides and a TV crew, visited the Guyana "paradise" where Jones presented a false show of normalcy for the visitors. Ryan learned that some members wanted to escape, and transportation was offered for those who desired to leave. A vindictive Jones ordered the murder of Ryan, his staff, the TV reporters, and Jonestown escapees as they prepared to board their chartered planes. Back in the compound, he feared a US military rescue mission as a result of killing a congressman, and the cult leader demanded that his trapped followers commit suicide as a revolutionary act. The followers were forced to drink a fatal cocktail of poisoned punch.

As a result of the massacre, "Drinking the Kool-Aid" became a commonly-used phrase to describe blind acceptance of a belief without critical analysis. The reference has been viewed as somewhat unfair to the manufacturer of Kool-Aid since the actual drink used at Jonestown was something else. But it has drawn attention to the reality that there are vulnerable members of society who can become infatuated with a purpose so extreme that they will die for the cause or its leadership. This is quite contrary to the teachings of Christianity. Any follower of Jesus understands that when an act is no longer voluntary, it is no longer Christlike. Jonestown is a bitter reminder of what happens when people surrender their emotional and moral independence and become spiritual slaves to evil leaders who guarantee their own promise of salvation, eternal life, or utopia. Contrast the drink offered by Jim Jones to his followers with the cup offered by Jesus to His disciples during that final Passover meal together. On that occasion, He spoke these words: "This cup is the new covenant between God and his people—an agreement confirmed with my blood, which is poured out as a sacrifice for you" (Luke 22:20 NLT). In this case, the only life that is being sacrificed was that of Jesus. He did this so that we might have eternal life.

So does Jesus not require any sacrifice from us? He does ask that we serve Him. "And so, dear brothers and sisters, I plead with you to give your bodies to God because of all he has done for you. Let them be a living and holy sacrifice—the kind he will find acceptable. This is truly the way to worship him" (Romans 12:1 NLT). These are the words of Paul who also put forth this challenge: "Be imitators of me, as I am of Christ" (1 Corinthians 11:1 ESV). As God's beloved children, we are to imitate Him by loving one another, just as Christ sacrificially loved us. In order to do this, we must understand His ways, study and absorb His Word, and be a beacon of light in the world around us. Test and discern His will for your life, and you will not only learn to imitate Him but also walk in the footsteps of His sacrificial love!

Reflection

Why is it so important for we who imitate Christ to guard in the way we act and speak? Why must we be careful to know God in all His attributes as revealed in His Word? What errors may result if we don't? How would you counsel someone who seems to be caught up in their church leadership more than they are in the Word of God?

NOVEMBER 18
(Y7, D46)

Great Fitting Hand-Me-Downs

Furthermore, because we are united with Christ, we have received an inheritance from God.

—Ephesians 1:11 (NLT)

It was once common for families in which there were numerous siblings to pass down material possessions, particularly clothing, from one child to another. Depending where you were in the pecking order, these garments could be fairly worn or out of style by the time you inherited them. While some may associate this "hand-me-down" philosophy to a lack of wealth or status, it was simply practical to get the most out of items that still had some useful wear. New clothing can become quite expensive, especially for parents whose youngsters who are growing ever so quickly. Many families continue to offer hand-down clothing items to smaller children in the neighborhood or among their friends. Even so, the concept of hand-me-downs does not have a great reputation with certain people. We associate them with things that have lost their value because they were used by or belonged to someone else first. As we grow older, there always comes a time when we will either outgrow or downright reject hand-me-downs and want to make our own choices, individualizing our own sense of what we think is fashionable.

There are streams of Christianity that talk this way about faith as well. They sometimes profess that the only faith having real value is brand-new, acquired by an individual on their own, just for themselves. Faith that evolves from being raised in a family of faith is sometimes viewed as having less value, considered as a hand-me-down that doesn't really belong to you. The Apostle Paul would disagree as he specifically affirmed to Timothy that he, in fact, had kind of faith. He wrote, "I remember your genuine faith, for you share the faith that first filled your grandmother Lois and your mother, Eunice. And I know that same faith continues strong in you" (2 Timothy 1:5 NLT). For Paul, personal sincerity and family heritage aren't in tension with one another but are instead mutually reinforcing. He instructed Timothy to invest his life in faithful followers who would be able to pass on God's truth to the next generation. Paul understood that faith is never something that we earn or accomplish on our own; it is always a gift.

Not everyone is fortunate to possess a legacy of faith similar to that which Timothy received from his mother and grandmother. There are no perfectly functioning families because there are no perfect people. Each of us will encounter persons, sometimes in our own circle, with a level of dysfunction. If those individuals become influencers in our life, we may carry their hand-me-down values into our adult life and relationships. Peter tells us that developing a bond with Christ will help us to overcome those deficits. "For you know that it was not with perishable things such as silver or gold that you were redeemed from the empty way of life handed down to you from your ancestors, but with the precious blood of Christ, a lamb without blemish or defect" (1 Peter 1:18–19 NIV). Remembering that sacrifice, Paul agrees: "For I received from the Lord what I also passed on to you" (1 Corinthians 11:23 NIV). This affirmation is at the heart of the Holy Communion message when a believer receives the sacrament.

As followers of Jesus, He hands down a specific fashion to all those who follow Him:

> Since God chose you to be the holy people he loves, you must clothe your-selves with tenderhearted mercy, kindness, humility, gentleness, and patience. Make allowance for each other's faults, and forgive anyone who offends you. Remember, the Lord forgave you, so you must forgive others. Above all, clothe yourselves with love, which binds us all together in perfect harmony. And let the peace that comes from Christ rule in your hearts. For as members of one body you are called to live in peace. And always be thankful. (Colossians 3:12–15 NLT)

Let me encourage you to wear the clothes Jesus has laid out for you. It's a very personal decision, and no one's going to dress you. Maybe it will make it easier to try them on when you pause to realize that the one you admire more than anyone else. They might just be a great fit, and wearing them will make you appear more like Him.

Reflection

Do you have a faith that is worth handing down? What good habits of your parents have you retained? And what bad traits have you absorbed from those who went before you? Have you ever felt burdened that the faith you may have inherited from others is having a negative impact on your life? What are some ways you might you pass along some divine habit or spiritual hand-me-down?

NOVEMBER 19
(Y1, D47)

Modern-Day Gleaning

And people should eat and drink and enjoy the fruits of
their labor, for these are gifts from God.

—Ecclesiastes 3:13 (NLT)

As we prepare to celebrate another Thanksgiving, we should not only be grateful for God's many blessings, but we should also be willing to share our bountiful harvest with those less fortunate. We read in the Bible that God explicitly ordered property owners to give the poor a chance to "glean" in their fields. Gleaning is the act of collecting leftover crops from farmers' fields after they have been harvested. Gleaning was so important in many past rural societies that it was considered to be sacred. In many parts of Europe, the biblically-derived right to glean the fields continued into modern times. In England and France, the government actually protected the rights of the poor to do so. The provisions for gleaning are stipulated in the Old Testament. One of the scriptures states, "And when you reap the harvest of your land, you shall not reap your field right up to its edge, nor shall you gather the gleanings after your harvest. You shall leave them for the poor and for the sojourner: I am the Lord your God" (Leviticus 23:22). Farmers were commanded to gather their harvest in such a way that there was work left to be done by the poor who needed to secure food for themselves. This practice allowed the less privileged to have the dignity of engaging in meaningful labor. Additionally, it gave the farmers and landowners the opportunity to practice generosity and compassion.

The actual principle of gleaning dominated the social scene between Ruth and Boaz as found in the book of Ruth. There we discover that a poor widowed Moabite girl by the name of Ruth who told her mother-in-law, Naomi, to whom she had been loyal, that she had been gleaning in the fields of Boaz. Naomi's reply was simple, "May the LORD bless him!" Naomi told her daughter-in-law, "He is showing his kindness to us as well as to your dead husband. That man is one of our closest relatives, one of our family redeemers" (Ruth 2:20 NLT). Boaz saw to it that Ruth's needs were fulfilled. When he learned of Ruth's story and her dedication to her mother-in-law, he instructed his field workers to drop extra grain on the ground for Ruth to collect (Ruth 2:15–16). "One day Naomi said to Ruth,

'My daughter, it's time that I found a permanent home for you, so that you will be provided for'" (Ruth 3:1 NLT). By stating such, she encouraged Ruth to pursue Boaz as a suitable husband. Boaz was touched by this widow, blessed her, and eventually announced to the city elders that he would marry her (Ruth 4:9–10). Ruth and Boaz would, in time, have a son named Obed, and Obed would produce a son named Jesse. Jesse would become the father of David and in doing so assumed a direct line in the lineage of Jesus.

The practice of ancient gleaning brought the well-off and poor together. Today, we have food drives and soup kitchens, all designed to help the poor and hungry. While these charitable efforts are an admirable effort, they frequently sidestep personal involvement. It is not possible to practice gleaning today unless we are intentionally paying attention to the otherwise invisible people in our midst; we must choose to stay cognizant of those around us who are vulnerable. The key is to invite them into our community spaces while we treat them with dignity and compassion and bless them through our words of encouragement. In today's society, therefore, gleaning has to be somewhat creative to be successful. Eric Strumberg found that the use of gleaning was a good businesses model. When his Wi-Fi solutions company expanded their workspace, they built extra offices, deliberately setting them aside for nonprofits and less fortunate organizations. In 2019, Strumberg told *Christianity Today*: "This is what the kingdom of God looks like… It's like Boaz—he got people to notice the dignity of the gleaners." Gleaning is an important concept that believers should take to heart. We must remember each time we pause to count our blessings that we must also take stock of how we are sharing our harvest with others. It doing so, we will define a modern-day translation of gleaning to the world around us. There is no better time than Thanksgiving to put it into practice!

Reflection

What does the concept of gleaning look like in your current lifestyle? What corners of your "field" or extra margins could you share? Are there ways to build surplus into your work that would benefit others? Consider the principle of gleaning and how it might apply in organizations to which you belong.

NOVEMBER 20
(Y2, D47)

An Attitude of Gratitude

Let us come to him with thanksgiving. Let us sing psalms of praise to him.

—Psalm 95:2 (NLT)

Researchers have discovered the vast benefits of gratitude, stating it is quite good for our mental and emotional health. Yet so many people struggle to practice it, presumably because we are hardwired to dwell on the bad. The story has been shared about a cowboy who was driving down a road in his pickup truck. His dog was riding in back of the truck and his faithful horse in the trailer behind. The cowboy failed to negotiate a curve and had a terrible accident. Soon, a highway patrolman came on the scene. The patrolman saw the horse first. He was an animal lover, and realizing the serious nature of the horse's injuries, he drew his service revolver and put the horse out of its misery. He walked around the accident and found the dog also critically hurt. He couldn't bear to hear it whine in pain, so he ended the dog's suffering as well. Finally, he located the cowboy off the side of road in the weeds. It was obvious that the driver had suffered multiple fractures. The policeman asked, "Hey, are you okay?" The cowboy took one look at the smoking revolver in the trooper's hand and quickly replied, "Never felt better in my life!"

It's easy to appear to be grateful when fear becomes our primary motivator. As much as we may want to live with a heart rooted in gratitude, we can't flip a switch to make that happen. We often complain about trivial things while resigning ourselves to easily forget how blessed we are. In Luke 17:11–17, we can read the story of the Ten Lepers who collectively approached Jesus as they remained at a distance according to the law. They called out to Him, "Jesus, Master, have pity on us!" Without seeming doing anything to heal them, Jesus merely gave the instruction to go and show themselves to the priests. At the moment, the men were still lepers. No physical change had yet taken place, but in faith, the men obeyed. As they began to walk, they were cleansed. However, only one man, a Samaritan, returned to thank Jesus for the healing. He expressed disappointment that the other nine had not given any thought to praise God for their healing. Even though Jesus did not withhold cleansing from those who did not express appreciation, He made a point of noting their lack of gratefulness (Luke 17:18).

Developing and maintaining an attitude of gratitude is something we need to do with intention. Each new day gives us countless opportunities to do so. Think about it. With everything we see, hear, taste, touch, and experience, we can choose to be grateful. A person who seeks a grateful spirit comes to understand that there are times when good can result out of negative or seemingly hopeless situations. Max Lucado says:

> Gratitude gets us through the hard stuff. To reflect on your blessings is to rehearse God's accomplishments. To rehearse God's accomplishments is to discover his heart. To discover his heart is to discover not just good gifts but the Good Giver. Gratitude always leaves us looking at God and away from dread. It does to anxiety what the morning sun does to valley mist. It burns it up.

An attitude of gratitude forces you to get outside of your problems and look at the bigger picture. Then you will become better prepared to move forward when those challenges occur in your life. In turn, that attitude of gratitude will open up your life for God's will to be done in and through you.

In her book, *Springs in the Valley*, Lettie Cowman tells the story of a man who discovered an old barn. In that barn, he found the seeds that Satan sows into the human heart. There he also saw numerous sacks containing the seeds of complaint. The man questioned Satan, and he learned that the seeds of complaining could be made to grow almost anywhere. But Satan reluctantly admitted that there was one place where he could never get those seeds to take root and grow. The man asked, "Where is that?"

Satan sadly replied, "In the heart of a grateful man." When you're grateful, you'll never ask for anything more than what you have because you're appreciative of having something in the first place. As we celebrate another Day of Thanksgiving, we should pray for a grateful heart. And on Black Friday, when the retail world becomes loud, ask the Lord to speak louder. When your eyes become focused on the newest, shiniest gadgets, ask Jesus to fix your eyes on Him and His gifts. Don't let this season of gratitude get lost in the blur of Christmas fanfare. Make a conscious decision that you will be the one who returns to give thanks. In doing so, you just might display an attitude of gratitude for all the world to see.

Reflection

Can you thank the Lord and proclaim that He is good, no matter what? In what ways might you be able to demonstrate 1 Thessalonians 5:18 ("Be thankful in all circumstances, for this is God's will for you who belong to Christ Jesus") as a model of gratefulness for others to follow?

NOVEMBER 21
(Y3, D47)

A Double Portion

You will possess a double portion of prosperity in your land, and everlasting joy will be yours.

—Isaiah 61:7 (NLT)

Again this year as is the custom, millions of Americans will have the privilege of sitting down to a fine Thanksgiving dinner. Most will not only have a more than adequate plateful of food. They will most likely go back for seconds. Chances are they may even have the opportunity in the following days to enjoy the leftovers. Some might allow their minds to drift between the big meal and the football games to take stock of their blessings or offer a word of gratitude during a prayer before dinner. How would your attitude be different if you just got home after a lengthy hospitalization or from serving in a foreign land, now joining at the dining room table with those familiar faces you call family and loved ones? What if you were recently at a sports event, rock concert, or a downtown city café where terrorists attacked, but you were fortunate to have remained unharmed from a near-death experience? How blessed might you then feel? If you were a loved one of one of these individuals, you might very well echo the words of the Apostle Paul: "Every time I think of you, I give thanks to my God" (Philippians 1:3 NLT).

As the ministry of the great Prophet Elijah was coming to an end, another prophet, Elisha, joined him as his servant. Elisha faithfully followed Elijah, even though Elijah commanded him more than once to stay behind. Near the end of Elijah's life, he said to Elisha: "Tell me, what can I do for you before I am taken from you?" Elisha responded, "Let me inherit a double portion of your spirit" (2 Kings 2:9 NIV). Elisha's request was to be considered as Elijah's successor and bring deliverance to his people. He hoped that he might be empowered with the same Spirit. It was not Elijah's to give; it could only be fulfilled by God (2 Kings 2:10). So he was faithful to Elijah until his time came to an end. Through his passionate service, Elisha was actually serving God's purposes in preparing him to do even greater works than Elijah. In asking for the "double blessing," Elisha was not doing so out of selfish motives. He was simply making this request so that he could accomplish more for God.

Blessings can show up at the most unexpected times. The famous Reformed Baptist minister, Charles Spurgeon, once told the story about once being robbed on the streets of London. When he arrived home and shared his tale, he said "Well, thank the Lord anyway."

His wife countered, "Thank the Lord that somebody stole your money?"

"No, my dear," answered her husband. "First, I'm thankful the robber just took my money, not my life. Secondly, I'm thankful I had left most of our money home and he didn't really rob me of much. Thirdly, I'm thankful to God that I was not the robber." Spurgeon had a true understanding of the words from 1 Peter 3:9 (NIV): "Do not repay evil with evil or insult with insult. On the contrary, repay evil with blessing, because to this you were called so that you may inherit a blessing."

The Prophet Elisha and the preacher, Spurgeon, serve to remind us that as we go through our journey, we can't allow our situation to blind us of the mission ahead. It often becomes easier in life to focus on the things which we do not have rather than to praise God for what He has provided. Vance Havner said, "Too many Christians are stuffing themselves with Gospel blessings while millions have never had a taste." As we gorge ourselves at this year's Thanksgiving table, let us take pause to count our blessings, even if they seem to be few in number. We may come to appreciate that, in fact, He has blessed us more abundantly than we ever thought possible, equipping us in turn to be a blessing to others. For when we come to that realization, we can be certain that we have received a double portion.

Reflection

When is the last time you reflected on your blessings? In what ways has God continued to bless you throughout your life? Are you being faithful with the blessings He has provided? When you sit down to dinner this Thanksgiving, will you be able to think of ways that you might become enthusiastic about your blessings. Consider how you might share a portion of what God has given you with others who are spiritually hungry and may "have never had a taste."

NOVEMBER 22
(Y4, D47)

The Ungrateful Birds

The Lord has done great things for us; we are glad.

—Psalm 126:3 (ESV)

We like to feed the birds in our backyard. We have feeders designed to attract bluebirds and finches and others that contain select seed for enticing cardinals and other colorful specimens. Whenever I have filled them, I almost feel as though I have created the perfect Thanksgiving meal—you know, something for everyone. While we enjoy this activity, there is only one problem. It is not unusual for there to be dozens of birds flocking into our yard and totally emptying these just filled feeders in a matter of days. When they have been emptied, they move on, presumably to another neighborhood feeder. On those occasions, I can find myself thinking, *You ungrateful birds. Look what we have done for you, and you turn around and leave us when it appears that we have nothing more to give.* Then I just smile and think, *I wonder if that's what God sometimes thinks of us when we're ungrateful for His many blessings.*

As we experience Thanksgiving and prepare for the Advent season, we are often more conscious of those around the world who are facing difficult times. I don't need to look any further than my own social circle where several persons whom I know have just been told that their places of employment where they have served faithfully for many years will be moving on without them. Then there are others I know whose very lives are vulnerable with the process of life-threatening diseases. As I once sat at the bedside of one such friend, I found myself making statements like, "We have to be grateful for the good years we have been given." While I know the words that I spoke were true and acknowledged by my friend, I can't help but think that such declarations are more easily spoken when we are not the individual who is at risk. Then I remembered the words of Paul as he wrote: "Be thankful in all circumstances, for this is God's will for you who belong to Christ Jesus" (1 Thessalonians 5:18 NLT). For if we praise God only in the best of circumstances, it would not be faith at all.

Luke tells the story of ten lepers who came to Jesus as He was entering a village. Inflicted with the most isolating disease of their day, they stood at a distance. Calling out to Him as Master in a loud voice, they asked Jesus to have pity on them. "When He saw them, He said, 'Go show yourselves to the priests.' And as they went, they were cleansed" (Luke 17:14 NIV). Only one of the ten, a Samaritan, returned to Him to give thanks. It is then that Jesus asked several pertinent questions, "Didn't I heal ten men? Where are the other nine? Has no one returned to give glory to God except this foreigner?" (Luke 17:17–18 NLT). The one who returned fell at the feet of Jesus and thanked Him. We can imagine that the other nine were also relieved that their bodies had been freed from such a devastating disease. Like we who take God's daily blessings for granted, they failed to show their gratitude to the one who had offered healing. They missed the opportunity to praise God, prompting Jesus to say, "Rise and go; your faith has made you well" (Luke 17:19 NIV). The man who returned received both a physical and a spiritual blessing.

Ralph Waldo Emerson once said that we should "cultivate the habit of being grateful for every good thing that comes to you, and to give thanks continuously. And because all things have contributed to your advancement, you should include all things in your gratitude." Gratitude, therefore, does not need to be reserved just for significant occasions but should be expressed for the little things as well. Thankful people make it a habit to recognize each moment of kindness that comes their way with an attitude of praise and thanksgiving. As we do, we are reminded of the bigger picture that we belong to God and dependent on Him for everything, just like the birds of the field. The difference is that He has given us the capacity to show our gratitude for His infinite love and mercy, even in the tough times. It is a choice we make to acknowledge Him or not. When we fail to do so, we fall short of a relationship with Him and are not much different than the ungrateful birds who feast on their blessings and simply move on.

Reflection

How can you learn to express a spirit of gratefulness during times of sadness, defeat, criticism, regret, and struggle? Would you be able to explain to someone that spiritual healing can come from gratefulness, regardless of the circumstances? Why is it hypocritical for a Christian to move on to the other side of Thanksgiving without ever pausing to be grateful?

NOVEMBER 23
(Y5, D47)

Plenty to Be Thankful For

Give thanks to the LORD, for he is good! His faithful love endures forever.

—1 Chronicles 16:34 (NLT)

I once knew a lady who would respond the same way when she was asked the question, "How are you?" In the time I knew her, her answer never varied. It was always, "Plenty to be thankful for." I am sure she had experienced hardship, suffering, and pain in her lifetime. Yet, one would have never known from a conversation with her. It was obvious that she could continually find something good about her current station in life. From time to time, I offer support to an older lady who in the past few years has lost her husband and a significant amount of her vision. While she can function fairly well in her own home, she is dependent on others to drive her to appointments or shop for things that she needs. Each time I bring her home and get her resettled into her familiar environment, she says, "Thank you, thank you, thank you." Her triple-fold expression of gratitude always humbles me, knowing that her words of appreciation are not just frivolously spoken but are rather a sincere expression of thanksgiving.

On one occasion, when I looked over my prayer list, I became conscious of the fact that many of the persons on it have lost love ones that year. In several cases, it was the father/husband of the family. In another, it was a mother who had been faithfully cared for by her daughter. And in others, it was an adult child who departed this earth far too soon. I thought about the empty chairs that would be around the table at Thanksgiving. Even though in many cases, those chairs would become physically filled by another individual, holidays are exceptionally difficult times to face the absence of a loved one. As the Apostle Paul wrote to the church at Philippi, he stated, "I thank my God every time I remember you" (Philippians 1:3 NIT). When his letter was written, it would be read by the living, but such words can certainly be applied in tribute to those who have passed on to their eternal home. While some share around the Thanksgiving table something for which they are thankful, it would be an even greater blessing simply to be grateful for those who occupy the chairs.

Unfortunately, like many things in our lives, we have come to take our blessings for granted. Charles Dickens once said, "Reflect upon your present blessings, of which every man has plenty; not on your past misfortunes, of which all men have some." In a reading of the Old Testament, one will find that Job's wife, in a moment of despair, encouraged him to give up his loyalty to God because of the many difficulties they had encountered. "But Job replied, 'You talk like a foolish woman. Should we accept only good things from the hand of God and never anything bad?' So in all this, Job said nothing wrong" (Job 2:10 NLT). In other words, Job understood it wouldn't be right to receive the blessings which God sends and not also accept the trials He allows. Likewise, Paul steps in to "be thankful in all circumstances, for this is God's will for you who belong to Christ Jesus" (1 Thessalonians 5:18 NLT).

In the hustle of completing to-do lists and meeting personal deadlines, it has become far too easy to block out the details of the day forgetting that each and every one holds precious gifts. From the air we breathe to the persons we hold dear, there is always something to be thankful for. I once read a thank you letter a lady had published in the local newspaper. She had become acutely ill and needed to be transported to the hospital where she received care for several days. Her letter echoed appreciation to everyone who shared in her service delivery, including not only physicians and nurses but also the housekeepers, food service personnel, and even the ambulance staff. While it sometimes takes a crisis to elicit an attitude of gratitude, we can be moved to incorporate acts of appreciation into our regular routine. William Arthur Ward put it this way: "Gratitude can transform common days into thanksgivings, turn routine jobs into joy and change ordinary opportunities into blessings." Thanksgiving is a choice we can make daily. We simply need to recognize God's wonderful blessings and ask Him to give us a grateful heart. For as one wise woman once reminded me, there is indeed "plenty to be thankful for."

Reflection

Who are those folks for whom you are ever so grateful that you could easily tell them, "I have not stopped giving thanks for you, remembering you in my prayers" (Ephesians 1:16 NIV)? How can we take on some of the characteristics of Christ (such as goodness, love, kindness, and compassion) in order that we might become a more grateful person?

NOVEMBER 24
(Y6, D47)

Thanksgiving Controversies

And now we thank you, our God, and praise your glorious name.

—1 Chronicles 29:13 (ESV)

The tradition of celebrating Thanksgiving became an annual custom throughout New England in the seventeenth century, but it was not until 1863 that President Abraham Lincoln declared the holiday to fall on the last Thursday of November. It was very clear in Lincoln's Proclamation where the gratefulness for our many blessings should be channeled. His opening words state:

> The year that is drawing towards its close, has been filled with the blessings of fruitful fields and healthful skies. To these bounties, which are so constantly enjoyed that we are prone to forget the source from which they come, others have been added, which are of so extraordinary a nature, that they cannot fail to penetrate and soften even the heart which is habitually insensible to the ever-watchful providence of Almighty God.

Lincoln's established tradition continued until 1939 when President Franklin D. Roosevelt created a Thanksgiving controversy. He departed from well-established custom by affirming November 23, the next to last Thursday that year, as Thanksgiving. Some Americans refused to honor Roosevelt's decree, but for the next two years, Roosevelt repeated the unpopular practice. However, in 1941, he admitted his mistake and signed a bill into law, officially making the fourth Thursday in November as the national holiday.

Indeed, Thanksgiving controversies continue not because of any presidential directive but more as a result of our society moving away from what it truly means to be thankful. In most families, Thanksgiving is less about real gratitude and more about overeating, watching football, or getting out the door as soon as possible to do some early Black Friday shopping. Some actually dread the celebration because they're forced to sit in a room with people they really don't enjoy and cautious not to initiate topics such as politics that would be best not discussed. I can remember once talking with a coworker a few days after Thanksgiving, knowing that she had most likely been cooking for her rather large family. By the look on her face, I wished I could take back my question, "How was your Thanksgiving dinner?" It didn't take her long to respond with words of disgust, stating, "Well, I worked hours making a nice meal for a bunch of ungrateful people."

I hardly knew what to say but somehow uttered, "I am so sorry." In years since, I often wondered whether she continued to make Thanksgiving dinner for those same folks. Furthermore, I have also considered how many families go through a similar experience on what should otherwise be a special time together. Although there may be a feeling of inward gratefulness that is simply unexpressed, the whole reason for expressing thanks is to let the giver of a gift know how much you appreciate their effort. Author G. B. Stern once said, "Silent gratitude isn't much use to anyone."

Many of us will have to admit that we do much the same thing with God. The psalmist reminds us that we should "enter his gates with thanksgiving; go into his courts with praise. Give thanks to him and praise his name. For the Lord is good. His unfailing love continues forever, and his faithfulness continues to each generation" (Psalm 100:4–5 NLT). The gates into God's presence are always open. The familiar song of Psalm 100 was an invitation for the Israelites to enter into the presence of God through the temple gates. They were to do so with praise and thanksgiving because of God's steadfast and enduring love. Even when they forgot their identity and wandered away from Him, God remained faithful and still invited them to enter His presence. As a God of consistency, He does the same for us today just as He did for each past generation. As you praise God for who He is and thank Him for what He's done, your perspective of Him grows larger, your problems grow smaller, and you will experience a deeper sense of intimacy with Him.

As we move closer to Christmas, we will find it easy to grumble and voice complaints about the simplest things. But when we are thankful, it's easier to "put on love…and let the peace of Christ rule in your hearts" (Colossians 3:14–15 ESV). We will modify our focus and begin seeing moments of sudden glory through the lens of gratitude and praise—glory moments that were there all along but hidden from the grumbling eye. And then our thanksgiving controversies will pass for yet another year.

Reflection

Do you struggle with how to show expressions of appreciation? Consider Jesus pattern of giving thanks and apply them to a few real examples for improved appreciation toward God and others. If you are around others who appear to be ungrateful this Thanksgiving, in what ways might you encourage them to take stock of their many blessings?

NOVEMBER 25
(Y7, D47)

Why this Waste?

The disciples were indignant when they saw this. "What a waste!" they said.

—Matthew 26:8 (NLT)

I once heard the tongue-in-cheek story about a rich man who was determined to give his mother a birthday present that would outshine all others. He had read about a bird that had a vocabulary of 4,000 words, could speak in numerous languages, and even sing three operatic arias. Locating such a bird, he immediately bought one for $50, 000 and had it delivered to his mother. The next day, he phoned her to see if she had received it. "What did you think of the bird?" he asked.

She replied, "It was delicious." Following your immediate response, your next thought might be, *What a waste*. A more revealing true fact is that during Thanksgiving each year, Americans will discard 35 percent—or several hundred million pounds—of edible turkey meat alone. While this holiday is a time to reflect on our many blessings, much of the bountiful food supply which fills our plates and bellies this season will eventually overflow into our landfills. It has been estimated that the amount of food wasted in the United States each year could feed hundreds of millions of hungry people. These staggering numbers have generated enough sensitivity to sponsor an annual "Food Waste Weekend" nationwide awareness campaign in the faith community.

In God's Holy Word, there are numerous references to waste. In the Old Testament, we read that David was sheltered in a cave. Three of his elite group of fighting men went down to meet him there.

> David was staying in the stronghold at the time, and a Philistine detachment had occupied the town of Bethlehem. David remarked longingly to his men, "Oh, how I would love some of that good water from the well by the gate in Bethlehem." So the Three broke through the Philistine lines, drew some water from the well by the gate in Bethlehem, and brought it back to David. But he refused to drink it. Instead, he poured it out as an offering to the LORD. "The

Lord forbid that I should drink this!" he exclaimed. "This water is as precious as the blood of these men who risked their lives to bring it to me." So David did not drink it. (2 Samuel 23:14–17 NLT)

It would have been easy to ask the question, "Why such waste?" However, it appears that no one questioned David's actions; instead, they were likely inspired. For you see, the gift was too precious for any person to consume it. It belonged to God.

Compare this passage with the story of the alabaster jar in the New Testament. In one account, we observe Jesus dining in Bethany at the home of Simon the leper when a woman enters the scene. She has brought a beautiful alabaster jar containing expensive perfume. She proceeds to break open the jar and pour the perfume on Jesus' head. Realizing the value of the perfume:

Some of those at the table were indignant. "Why waste such expensive perfume?" they asked. "It could have been sold for a year's wages and the money given to the poor." So they scolded her harshly. But Jesus replied, "Leave her alone. Why criticize her for doing such a good thing to me? You will always have the poor among you, and you can help them whenever you want to. But you will not always have me. She has done what she could and has anointed my body for burial ahead of time. I tell you the truth, wherever the Good News is preached throughout the world, this woman's deed will be remembered and discussed." (Mark 14:4–9 NLT). It was immediately after that we hear the story of one of Jesus' own: "Then Judas Iscariot, one of the twelve disciples, went to the leading priests to arrange to betray Jesus to them" (Mark 14:10 NLT).

If we are truly honest with ourselves, we will have to admit that there are times when we have has our own Judas moment. We turn from God's purpose and waste time on what is more comfortable for us. As God does His best to call us back to Him, He might find us preoccupied by what we consider to be an investment in 'more important' activities. Studies have shown that in a lifetime, most individuals will spend over 40 percent of their time staring at some sort of screen, be it a smartphone, laptop, tablet, or TV. By maturing in the faith, we hopefully become more like David recognizing that the gift of a life is just too precious to waste. As we increase our focus on serving the Lord, we will encounter those who do not know or attempt to understand Him. They will dare to look at our acts of service and pass on judgment. Similar to those in Jesus' day, they might look at us and say, "What a waste." But we know better.

Reflection

Is your time well spent? In what ways are you using it to advance the cause of Christ? What would you say to someone who is critical of your relationship with Him as a "total waste of time?"

NOVEMBER 26
(Y1, D48)

The Gift of Presence

And be sure of this: I am with you always, even to the end of the age.

—Matthew 28:20 (NLT)

Throughout my life, I have found it occasionally necessary to attend funeral visitations or services. When my attendance is related to a work situation, I would sometimes take other colleagues with me. When they appeared to be uncomfortable and would ask me what to say, I informed them that I would try to recall a brief memory about the deceased. However, when it came right down to it, I found that the words didn't matter much. While there are times when our words and actions are meaningful, there are just as many occasions when our mere presence will perfectly meet the need. In times of distress, people rarely remember what we say. What they most remember is that we were there. Familiar faces offer strength beyond imagination; they provide comfort for the deep feelings of loneliness setting in from the loss. This gift of presence is one we're all capable of making, even if we're tongue-tied or uncomfortable.

Christmas is near, only a month away. And so we begin the season of Advent. During this four-week period, we seek to encounter and worship Christ. We look for Him in the heavenly host of angels singing to shepherds watching o'er flocks by night. We look for Him in the shining star that led the Magi to the miracle of His birth with their offerings of gold, frankincense, and myrrh. While the thought of Christmas will often remind us of gifts, those *presents* are nothing like the gift of *presence* which He offers to each of us. We are reminded in Matthew 1:23 that it was prophesied 700 years before Jesus' birth that He would be called Immanuel or "God with us" (Isaiah 7:14 NLT). God planned the greatest present for all of us evidenced at the manger scene. This gift was wrapped as a baby, and He was God's presence for the world. Christmas reminds us that God desires an up-close, personal relationship with you and me. Followers of Christ should consider the extreme measures He went through to make that possible.

Throughout the Bible, we become aware of God's presence in the lives of His people. In the Old Testament, we find the promise that He had first made with Moses to accompany him in every situation until he achieved the goal of liberation for the people of Israel (Exodus 33:14). When Solomon dedicated the temple, God did something extraordinary; He filled the building with His presence. It was so powerful the priests were unable to enter (2 Chronicles 7:1–2). Wise men who came out of the east to Jerusalem sought the Son of God, saying, "Where is he who has been born king of the Jews?" (Matthew 2:1–2 ESV). And while they brought presents to honor Him, they were most blessed to simply spend time in His presence. The possessed man from Gadarenes were healed by the presence of Jesus (Matthew 8:28–33). Martha and Mary longed to feel His presence when their brother Lazarus died, and so Jesus came and wept with them (John 11:33–35). Even when the time arrived for Jesus to fulfill His mission, He gave this promise of presence to those who loved Him: "And I will ask the Father, and he will give you another Advocate, who will never leave you. He is the Holy Spirit, who leads into all truth" (John 14:16–17 NLT).

The presence of God in the life of the Christian is constant and permanent. People who offer their presence do so because it's the right thing to do. We have the ability to give deeply of His compassion simply by sharing that same level of concern. Presence is a gift that must simply be received and enjoyed in the time and space in which it is presented. By just being there, our presence offers comfort to the those living in the tender and hurting places. However, it is more than merely a gift of quiet comfort. It will at times provide a window into knowing others more deeply through those things that are unspoken and can only be understood in the midst of just simply being there. Let us be the ones who show up and lean in, even when—and especially when—it is uncomfortable or difficult. In the meantime, may we affirm our learning by deeply experiencing God's presence this Christmas season. For when we do, we will come to truly understand that the beauty of Christmas is not in the presents we receive but more so in the presence that only He alone can give.

Reflection

How have you been impacted by the gift of presence? If so, why do we doubt the powerful presence of God? Strategically consider how you can bring others from not knowing His presence to that point when they will dwell in His house forever. How can we balance gift giving, limit the stress on our budgets, and focus more on being present with our Savior and those most close to us this Christmas?

NOVEMBER 27
(Y2, D48)

Falling for Jesus

I was pushed hard, so that I was falling, but the LORD helped me.

—Psalm 118:13 (ESV)

During a senseless act at Minnesota's Mall of America, a stranger threw a five-year-old boy from a third-floor balcony in 2019. Critically injured with head trauma, the youth miraculously had no brain damage but suffered many injuries including leg and arm fractures. Launched the day after the incident, a fundraising account eventually received more than $1 million from well-wishers to help pay the medical bills while the young boy recovered from the forty-foot fall. Cards and prayers helped to sustain him. He expressed the following comment via social media: "Don't worry, I fell off a cliff, but angels caught me and Jesus loves me, so I'm okay, and you will be too!" A little over seven months later, he was back in school without even a limp. Leaving the house, he would blow kisses at his mom. Whenever she would inquire how he was doing, he told her, "Mom, I'm healed, you don't need to ask anymore." As we enter the Season of Advent, we might consider getting to know Jesus a little better, following the example of this five-year-old boy who seemed to know and understand Him far better than most of us.

For much of our lives, we strive to be independent. Culture says that good parenting will enable us to think for ourselves. As we mature, we realize that there are times we must learn to "stand on our own two feet," so to speak. While we should always embrace those who encouraged, prodded, and loved us through our lifetime, the concept of self-actualization is affirmed by our society. When we invite Jesus into our lives, there can appear to be a contradiction with that which we have been taught. As our culture communicates a need to outgrow dependence on others, followers of Jesus come to realize that they will never outgrow their need for Him. The Apostle Paul tells us that "this will continue until we all come to such unity in our faith and knowledge of God's Son that we will be mature in the Lord, measuring up to the full and complete standard of Christ" (Ephesians 4:13 NLT). Unlike those earthly child-rearing experts, our heavenly Father raises us to depend on Him more each day.

To fall in love with Jesus, we must know Him not superficially but deeply. That kind of knowledge takes time and persistence, just like any good relationship. Jesus invites us to abide in His love, indicating we should not rush through it. In John 15:9 (NIV), He said, "As the Father has loved me, so have I loved you. Now remain in my love." Everything changes when you begin to know Jesus as a real person. When you read in John 8:3–11 about Jesus standing by a shamed woman daring the self-righteous to convict her, one can imagine Him doing that for us. As He dined with sinners (Mark 2:15–17), you can feel His presence in your own home, breaking bread with your family. When Jesus stopped a suffering woman who in faith touched His cloak to be healed (Mark 5:24–31), you know He would also pause for you as well. As we come to embrace these truths, we affirm that Jesus is real, and He loves us. In order for us to experience that love and offer it back, we need to know Him. Really know Him. One who intensely loved Him stated that we must "grow in the grace and knowledge of our Lord and Savior Jesus Christ" (2 Peter 3:18 NIV). When you invite Jesus to live in and through you, He will give you the faith you need to persevere. If you trust Him as you feel broken and vulnerable, God will use this experience to accomplish good purposes in your life. Jesus will be your source of strength when you can't rely on your own.

God is always working in the lives of the those who love Him. When His children fall, He will pick them up and dust them off. He will never forsake His faithful ones, and with His righteous right hand He will hold them up (Isaiah 41:10). Here then is the challenge which lies before you: make a conscious decision to commit to Him, and continue to study and live by His Word. Hold on to God's promises in your heart and know that He is by your side in every situation. For you see, when you fall in love with Jesus, He will put everything in its rightful place. After all, He was there for a little five-year-old boy who was certain his fall was broken by angels, that Jesus loved him, and that he would be okay. As we count our blessings and move toward Christmas, you can be assured that the same will be true for you.

Reflection

Does the love of God create in you a desire to obey, serve, and to pray to Him each day? Where or under what circumstances do you most feel your dependence on Jesus? Are you passionately pursuing your relationship with God by getting to know His Son better? How can we help others fall in love with Jesus and see the Bible as God's love letter to us, not just a rule book of morals to follow?

NOVEMBER 28

(Y3, D48)

For All the World to See

The light shines in the darkness, and the darkness has not overcome it.

—John 1:5 (ESV)

You may not know the name Tom Bodet, but if you were around in the mid-1980s or after, you will remember his famous saying, "We'll leave the light on for you." The voice actor and radio personality used the tagline to close out commercials for Motel 6 that became a successful advertising campaign of the lodging franchise for many years. It reminded us that even in our own homes, it's the polite thing to do when we are expecting company or anticipating the arrival of a family member. Lights are a symbol of welcoming. We are entering that season when the outdoor lights of Christmas are beginning to appear throughout our neighborhoods. Many communities throughout our nation will display lights as a means of public attraction and an opportunity to promote commerce.

For the Christian church, the beginning of Advent is upon us. The term *advent* is derived from a Latin word for "coming," in this case the expectant waiting and preparation for the celebration of the nativity of Jesus at Christmas. Most denominations will use Advent readings during a portion of their services, and a new candle will be lighted weekly for each of the successive four weeks. It is not uncommon for Advent wreaths to be displayed not only in those churches but in the homes of their members as well. The metaphor of light is at the very center of the Christmas message and is reflected in the hymns we will sing. One of the best known is "Silent Night": "Son of God, love's pure light; Radiant beams from Thy holy face, with the dawn of redeeming grace." The words from the great prophet foretold of the coming Prince of Peace and the light He would bring: "The people who walk in darkness will see a great light. For those who live in a land of deep darkness, a light will shine" (Isaiah 9:2 NLT).

Walking in the Light is a recurring theme throughout scripture. "Jesus spoke to the people once more and said, 'I am the light of the world. If you follow me, you won't have to walk in darkness, because you will have the light that leads to life'" (John 8:12 NLT). The world is filled with darkness, and many of us exist in it for a time. It is only through an accepting and growing relationship with Christ that our light can begin to shine. As we mature in Him, we come to experience a very personal journey that commences in Bethlehem and ends on a cross at Calvary. As children, many of us learned the words, "This little light of mine, I'm gonna let it shine." One of my greatest memories of this song is a performance by a church choir in which one of the oldest members, well into her eighties, embraced the tune by letting her body swing melodically from side to side as she sang. She displayed a true understanding of the apostle's writing: "You are the light of the world. A town built on a hill cannot be hidden. Neither do people light a lamp and put it under a bowl. Instead they put it on its stand, and it gives light to everyone in the house. In the same way, let your light shine before others, that they may see your good deeds and glorify your Father in heaven" (Matthew 5:14–16 NIV).

As our walk with Christ deepens, it is important to understand that the Light others will see in us is not our own but a mere reflection of Him. "For once you were full of darkness, but now you have light from the Lord. So live as people of light!" (Ephesians 5:8 NLT). Like the words to the song portray, "It is better to light just one little candle, than to stumble in the dark. Better far that you light just one little candle; All you need is a tiny spark." In many corners of the earth, we can easily be drawn into dark places. Advent is a perfect time to acknowledge or perhaps rekindle that spark of light. And as we nurture it throughout our own spiritual journey, we will once again allow the star over that simple manger many years ago to become a beacon of light for all the world to see.

Reflection

Have you made decisions that have caused the light of Jesus to flicker and grow dim in your life? During this busy Advent season, are there ways that you might pause, reflect, and draw closer to Him? How can you develop your spiritual gifts and share your talents so that others may see a renewed light of Christ in your life?

NOVEMBER 29
(Y4, D48)

Lists of Hope and Expectation

May the God of hope fill you with all joy and peace as you trust in him, so
that you may overflow with hope by the power of the Holy Spirit.

—Romans 15:13 (NIV)

People in chronic illness, recovering from surgery, or facing life-threatening diagnoses. Those who are newly married or others in new jobs or in search of work; families requiring marital healing, coping with a troubled child or in need of discovering a higher power; babies who are beginning their time on this earth, and still others who are facing their final days; one who has experienced bodily harm due to an accident or an individual who is having mental anguish about a situation beyond their control; our country and the world situation; those serving in the armed services or in the mission field; family, friends, neighbors; some who are known well, others of whom I am barely aware; myself—who are these persons? They could be a synopsis of many of the names on any good prayer list. One would hope that they are lives that might be changed or helped in order to better the lives of others. Through faith, we have an expectation that only a loving God can make that happen if it is within His will. So we share those concerns, names and situations of which He already knows as we spend time alone with Him in prayer.

When I was young, my parents would allow me to look at the Wish Book to assist in composing my Santa list. The only problem with that was that I would turn down the corners of almost every page in the toy section. My hope was that I might get all those things, but my expectation was that Santa would bring some of them for sure. When we are young, the excitement around the Christmas season seems to begin earlier each year. Long before the Halloween costumes have ever cleared the store shelves, Christmas decorations have already surfaced. As we mature, our thoughts often turn to meaningful times with family and friends. Upon entering the Advent season, we are filled with a renewed anticipation of the Messiah in the form of the baby Jesus of whom these words were spoken: "Out of the stump of David's family will grow a shoot—yes, a new Branch bearing fruit from the old root" (Isaiah 11:1 NLT).

How can we face hope and expectation in a world that sometimes seems hopeless but expects more and more? The season of Advent gives hope that our lives have meaning beyond our current situation. For if we allow our search for hope to be defined by our present circumstance, then we will always be disappointed. We should pause to remember that in the midst of life-changing circumstances in the Old Testament, the rise and fall of hope also existed. New prophecy for a coming Messiah was often provided as faith began to decline. "Listen well, you royal family of David! Isn't it enough to exhaust human patience? Must you exhaust the patience of my God as well? All right then, the Lord himself will give you the sign. Look! The virgin will conceive a child! She will give birth to a son and will call him Immanuel" (Isaiah 7:13–14 KJB). All of the prophecies pertaining to the first coming of Christ were precisely fulfilled. Since God never changes, we have hope for a future leading us to the expectation that the remaining prophecies will also transpire. Advent represents the spiritual journey of individuals as they affirm that Christ has come, that He is present in the world today, and that He will come again not as a babe in a manger but as a King who will reign with righteousness and power.

Again this year, children will awake on Christmas morning expecting to find gifts under the tree. There may be some disappointment and maybe some surprises as the presents are opened, but the anticipation and excitement will be there nonetheless. "But as for me, I watch in hope for the Lord, I wait for God my Savior; my God will hear me" (Micah 7:7 NIV). During Advent, we long for the renewal of our lives with the hope and expectation that God will be faithful to see our circumstances, to hear our cries, and to know our longings for a better world. Meanwhile, it would be best if we could once again become like little children in anticipation of what is to come. In doing so, we know the best gift we will ever receive doesn't have to appear on a list, for it has already been given.

Reflection

Do you look forward to the four weeks of Advent as much as you do Christmas Day? In what ways might you and your family bring meaning to the celebration of Advent season? How might it be different to show reverence for the baby Jesus, then it will someday be to bow before the King of kings?

NOVEMBER 30
(Y5, D48)

Anticipation: A Contract for All Who Believe

I wait for the LORD, my whole being waits, and in his word I put my hope. I wait for the Lord more than watchmen wait for the morning. (Psalm 130:5–6 NIV)

One of the hardest places to be in life is in a place of waiting. A diagnosis, decision, answer, whatever it is, waiting is just downright difficult for most of us. These days, we wait for nothing. The anticipation of the arrival of Christmas was a little hasty for one Florida homeowner who ended up referring to his homeowner's association as grinches. This occurred following the receipt of a warning for decorating his home too early. Based on the availability of a home decorating company, the family hired the group to put up their outside Christmas lights on November 6. Unaware that doing so would be in violation of the homeowner's association contract, they received a notice stating that they could not put up outside decorations until Thanksgiving. They offered to keep the lights turned off until then, but the association was not receptive to their offer. Stating that they must come down, the household could be fined $100 a day, up to $1,000 if not immediately corrected. Interestingly enough, this was less than what it would have cost to have the decorations removed and put up again.

"The Christmas Song" serves to remind us about the anticipation of the upcoming season. One verse says, "Every mother's child is going to spy to see if reindeer really know how to fly." The lyrics continue to have relevance as children are told the story of Santa Claus and his flying reindeer multiple times during the holidays. But imagine what it must have been like thousands of years ago when every mother's child was told a much different story encouraging even more anticipation. Children in Jewish homes were taught that one day God would send a Messiah, a Deliverer, someone who would rule not just over them but also over the entire world. They even celebrated feasts and holidays to keep this in their minds and to maintain a level of excitement. Years, decades, and centuries went by with the expectation of the coming Messiah. Parents would likely sit with their children and read from the Word of Isaiah: "For unto us a Child is born, unto us a Son is given; and the government will be upon His shoulder. And His name will be called Wonderful, Counselor, Mighty God, Everlasting Father, Prince of Peace" (Isaiah 9:6 NKJV).

The coming of their Prince of Peace was a long time in the making. The prophet of old wrote "But as for me, I will watch expectantly for the Lord; I will wait for the God of my salvation. My God will hear me" (Micah 7:7 NASB). For the people of God, it turned into centuries of anticipating the arrival of their long-awaited Messiah. When the Word was fulfilled, even John the Baptist hesitantly asked the Lord, "Are you the Messiah we've been expecting, or should we keep looking for someone else" (Matthew 11:3 NLV). Most Jews, however, missed His coming. They lost the excitement, their faith waned, or they just weren't waiting with expectation. The promised Messiah was delivered but did so humbly, without fanfare. And after a short time here on earth, they anticipated His return would once again be soon. One of the disciples wrote these words: "Be patient, then, brothers and sisters, until the Lord's coming. See how the farmer waits for the land to yield its valuable crop, patiently waiting for the autumn and spring rains. You too, be patient and stand firm, because the Lord's coming is near" (James 5:7–8 NIV).

These days, as we anticipate Christmas morning, we should look forward to celebrating God's work through Christ and His gift of redemption. We come to realize that Christ's birth was not a one-day event but rather a season of hope and anticipation. In a world filled with big expectations, it would be easy for us to fail to anticipate His return and the hope for the new world He promises. As we live our lives in faith, our expectations during the Christmas season will change as our lives do so. It occurs when we completely believe that God's Word will be assured and the gifts of His faithfulness will be revealed. The one sure reality is that the promise of Jesus' return will not go unfulfilled because God's promises are certain. What a wonderful blessing to be able to bask in the glow of the anticipation of Christmas, give thanks for His coming, and look forward to His return as secured by the contract of all who believe.

Reflection

If you knew that you were going to meet Jesus today, in what ways might your heart be different than it is right now? When you anticipate getting into the Christmas spirit, what controls your context for that reference—parties, gifts, decorations? Have you given consideration as to how you might enable Christmas to be experienced throughout the entire year? In what ways can you help others understand that anticipation of Christ is not just about His birth but also about His ultimate return?

DECEMBER 1
(Y6, D48)

A New Heart for Christmas

And I will give you a new heart, and I will put a new spirit in you. I will take out your stony, stubborn heart and give you a tender, responsive heart.

—Ezekiel 36:26 (NLT)

On December 3, 1967, a fifty-three-year-old South African grocer dying with chronic heart disease received the first human heart transplant. The new heart had functioned normally until eighteen days later the recipient died from double pneumonia. Surgeon Christiaan Barnard, who trained at the University of Cape Town and in the United States, performed the revolutionary medical operation utilizing a technique developed by American researchers in the 1950s. Hope was given to patients with irreparably damaged hearts when heart-transplant operations began, and by the late 1970s, many of Bernard's patients were living up to five years with their new hearts. However, the demand for donor hearts always exceeded availability, and thousands died every year while waiting for healthy hearts to become available. It was only fifteen years after the first transplant that a sixty-one-year-old retired Seattle dentist by the name of Barney Clark in an advanced stage of heart disease became the first recipient of a permanent artificial heart on December 2, 1982. Clark was too old to be a candidate for a heart transplant. His only shot at survival was permanent artificial heart advanced by Dr. Robert Jarvik. The surgery was considered a success since Clark went on to live another 112 days. In the 1990s, the Jarvik-7 was used on more than 150 patients whose hearts were too damaged to be aided by a mechanical pump implant. More than half of these patients survived until they got a transplant, enabling them to celebrate more Christmases.

The ability to get a new heart for Christmas comes in many forms. Released in December 1843, Charles Dickens' novel, *A Christmas Carol*, has never been out of print. It tells the story of Ebenezer Scrooge, a wealthy, stingy man who had developed a calloused heart. Scrooge's catchphrase, "Bah! Humbug!" is often used to express disgust with modern Christmas traditions. One Christmas Eve, he is visited by the ghost of his former business partner and the spirits of Christmases Past, Present, and Yet to Come. After their visits, he is transformed into a kinder, gentler man. His last name,

Scrooge, is synonymous in describing persons who are known to be less-than-generous. Ebenezer Scrooge is arguably one of the most famous characters created by Dickens in all of English literature. Through the visions of Scrooge, Dickens' book is able to capture the universal longing for inner peace felt by each of us. Without self-reflection, we too can easily fall into the role of Scrooge for having a judgmental and cruel attitude.

A young man named Saul once opposed Jesus and His followers with a vengeful spirit. He "began to destroy the church. Going from house to house, he dragged off both men and women and put them in prison" (Acts 8:3 NIV). But, one day, he encountered the risen Christ, and his life became a different story (Acts 9:1–16). In a letter to Timothy, the converted Saul (who became known as Paul) described that life-changing event. "Even though I was once a blasphemer and a persecutor and a violent man, I was shown mercy because I acted in ignorance and unbelief. The grace of our Lord was poured out on me abundantly, along with the faith and love that are in Christ Jesus" (1 Timothy 1:13–14 NIV). A change in behavior begins with Jesus changing our heart. Jesus was born into our world and gave His life so that we can be forgiven and transformed through faith in Him. The medical team operating on Dr. Barney Clark had to remove his disease-ridden heart before they could replace it with a new one. If we are inconsistent in our walk with Christ, we may develop an irregular heartbeat. Over time, our heart can become calloused and our spiritual specialist may need to perform heart surgery. During Advent, we need to improve our heart health by taking a journey to a manger to witness the birth of the King of kings. It's the last place we might expect to find a king, but that is the miracle and gift of God through Jesus Christ. Because of that humble birth of God's Son, we can change our old heart and find a new one that beats only for Him. Amidst the flurry of activities, won't you join me and look at each day as an opportunity to validate Christmas? A heart radiating the love of Jesus is always the perfect gift. And all who receive it will join fellow believers in reaffirming something very special—a new heart for Christmas.

Reflection

What heart conditions do you need God to heal? Throughout this Advent season, what steps will you take to realize the miraculous love of Christ in your life? How might you invite others to journey with you to become more focused on finding a heart-filled Christmas?

DECEMBER 2
(Y7, D48)

A No-Gimmicks-Included Invitation

All those the Father gives me will come to me, and
whoever comes to me I will never drive away.

—John 6:37 (NIV)

This time of year, you get all kinds of invitations without even knowing the people who sent them. Over the last few weeks, I have received email notices for gift cards from numerous major chains. This sounded like something I might be able to use until I figured out the hook. First you must complete a survey, and at the end of the survey, there are numerous purchasing choices from which you must select before you become eligible for the free card. I have also received invitations for new credit cards. Again, there is usually some incentive attached to joining in anticipation I will exceed my ability to pay off my extra holiday spending. In doing so, the company will be able to make some money on my unpaid balance in the new year. My favorite is Publisher's Clearing House who says you need to do nothing to win a huge cash prize. Over the next weeks and months, you will hear from them regularly with envelopes filled with purchasing offers, leading you to believe that you are now one of a very few who may be selected for a big payout. Invitations like these always come at a cost, even if it's just your personal information.

A few years ago, I was invited to the home of former work colleague for a Christmas party. For whatever reason, I decided not to attend and respectfully sent my regrets. That next summer, I ran into this individual and his wife who were doing some shopping. He went on about the wonderful time they had at that now past Christmas party and stated that during the ensuing warm months, they would be hosting a picnic at their home. I was informed that I would again be invited, but I had better attend this time because "once you are a 'no-show' twice, you get taken off the list." My expression or lack thereof must have been a dead giveaway. Either they didn't have the picnic or my invitation got lost in the mail. Having struggled myself with holiday open house guest lists, I tried not to be too critical. There are always considerations such as the capacity of your home and the compatibility of those whom you are including. I would seem that it shouldn't be all that difficult to weed out your list of invitees. But whatever criteria I might use, I am sure glad Jesus doesn't apply that same criterion to His invitation.

At Christmas, we are invited over and again to come to the manger. We do so as we light our Advent candles, stop by the live nativity in the mall, or attend church services Christmas eve. But we must remember that the birth of Jesus was only the beginning. Jesus said, "Come to me, all you who are weary and burdened, and I will give you rest" (Matthew 11:28 NIV). What a great invitation to know that we can simply rest in the arms of Jesus, no matter whether we are carrying guilt from the past, worried about the future, or just exhausted with the weight of the world of everyday life. Still another invitation awaits each of us. Jesus also invites us into fellowship. "Follow me, and I will make you become fishers of men" (Mark 1:17 ESV). Just as Jesus summoned those fishermen of His day to become His disciples, He invites us into discipleship as well. When we accept, we enter into an intimate relationship by becoming Jesus' partner who, in turn, is expected to offer His invitation to others.

The final invitation Christ offers us is to be part of His kingdom. "Remain in me, as I also remain in you. No branch can bear fruit by itself; it must remain in the vine. Neither can you bear fruit unless you remain in me" (John 15:4 NIV). Those who do so are the recipients of His love and affection. No invitation of any kind in this world can compare with fact that you belong to God and are identified with Him. We can have joy in knowing that it's not a temporary membership. His invitation is neither conditional nor time-limited. He has paid our dues for all of eternity with His journey from a simple manger in Bethlehem to a lonely, horrifying death on the cross at Calvary. That is a real invitation, my friend, and it comes with a promise that if you remain in Him, you will never be taken off the guest list. Jesus is the Master of inclusion. He is Lord of all, and His invitation is for everyone—no gimmicks included.

Reflection

How do you think others feel when they are invited to your home? Have you ever had to exclude or been excluded from an invitation list? In what ways might you show appreciation to Jesus for the many invitations and gifts He extends to you this Christmas?

DECEMBER 3
(Y1, D49)

The Gift of Wonder

Blessed be the LORD, the God of Israel, who alone does wondrous things.

—Psalm 72:18 (ESV)

When I was quite young, our family traveled to the Jersey shore for a week of summer vacation. Shortly after we arrived, we went to the boardwalk where I had my first-ever view of the ocean. I was in awe of the waves, so much that when we went back to the beach the next day, I ran slightly ahead of my parents. I was so excited that I hurried, returning to say, "Come, look, they turned the waves on again." Oh, the wonderment of childhood. Even as we grow older, there are times that we have a sense of amazement. I can recall the first time I took a cross-country flight. I couldn't quite imagine the fact that it was possible to have breakfast on the east coast and later that day have dinner in California. Although I have made that journey several times since, I have not lost that wonderment for the possibilities of life, and I hope I never do. For when we find wonder, we learn the essence of who we are by realizing that it's right there in front of us if we only pause long enough to see it.

When Moses led the Israelites out of Egypt, they were no doubt speculating, "How am I going to be fed and survive in this wilderness?" Imagine their logistical nightmare: an incalculable quantity of food and water would be needed for the hundreds of thousands to survive in the desert. Where would it come from? Yet, in this seemingly impossible situation, God provided manna from heaven. "When the Israelites saw it, they said to each other, 'What is it?' For they did not know what it was. Moses said to them, 'It is the bread the LORD has given you to eat'" (Exodus 16:15 ESV). But we know what happened as time passed. The people got used to this provision, began to take it for granted, and even became bored with it. As a result, Israel lost sight of the miracle that God was doing in their lives every day. Many years after, Peter healed a lame man in the name of Jesus. The people who witnessed it "recognized him as the same man who used to sit begging at the temple gate called Beautiful, and they were filled with wonder and amazement at what had happened to him" (Acts 3:10 NIV). Every day is a miracle from God. We walk through a world filled with gifts of wonder from the Lord, if we only choose to recognize them.

As the days draw closer to the celebration of the birth of the Savior, our minds turn to thoughts of that glorious time when God became a man. When the angel first spoke to Mary, she was also filled with wonder as she learned of God's plan (Luke 1:29). Even in her young age, she was reflective and deliberated with a deep sense of meditation. After she gave birth to the Son of God, shepherds visited the baby Jesus in the manger. Afterward "they spread the word concerning what had been told them about this child, and all who heard it were amazed at what the shepherds said to them. But Mary treasured up all these things and pondered them in her heart" (Luke 2:17–19 NIV). Then later, Magi from the east felt the presence of God and followed the star they had seen (Matthew 2:1–2). Their amazement to see this newborn King of the Jews is reflected in the song lyrics, "O star of wonder, star of night, star with royal beauty bright. Westward leading, still proceeding, guide us to thy perfect light."

As we age and gain life experience, we so often lose our sense of wonder with how the world operates. And in losing this wonder, we also forfeit the ability to see the possibility or the richness of any given situation. In the story *The Little Prince*, there is a line which says, "All grown-ups were once children...but only few of them remember it." And so when we search for wonder, we must recall those youthful memories of the waves of the sea and a ride above the clouds. We learn that God's creation can be full of patient wonder not to be found in a thirty-minute sitcom that resolves a superficial crisis. The real wonder of Christmas is revealed in the Christ child who came to Bethlehem and in the fact that He has also come to each one of us. We must be determined to not allow the busyness of the season rob us of our moments of wonder. And when those moments come, we must embrace them and thank God for such an incredible message of hope. May we count ourselves among the few who remember. For only those who remember that the gift of wonder comes from God can participate in it with Him.

Reflection

Give consideration to the everyday occurrences that are capable of bringing wonderment to your life. How can we avoid losing our sense of wonder for all that He has done and provided for us?" As we approach Christmas, what are some ways that we might bring new life to story of His birth?

DECEMBER 4
(Y2, D49)

Faith's Beginning: Making Room for Jesus

If we are faithless, he remains faithful, for he cannot disown himself.

—2 Timothy 2:13 (NIV)

Have you ever wondered what would be missing from your life if there was no Christmas? That very question was given at least some consideration in the classic children's book, *How the Grinch Stole Christmas*, by Dr. Seuss. The main character, known as the Grinch, was a mean, nasty, and vindictive person. He lived to the north of Whoville, a small town where people had hearts as sweet as sugar pops. In the story, the Grinch goes down to Whoville and steals every present from each house. He also steals the Christmas food for the feast and the decorations, taking away every material tradition that symbolized Christmas. There are lessons to be learned from the people of Whoville. To the Grinch's utmost surprise, Christmas came anyway. The Whos had none of their stuff. The day certainly didn't look as they may have planned, but they were happy anyway. Without any remorse or sadness, they sang and danced, exuding joy and happiness despite any of the Grinch's efforts. The true spirit of the holiday existed within their hearts, and for them, this was all that mattered.

If there was no Christmas, what would we be missing in your life? No gifts, no colorful lights, no special dinners, no holiday spirit of giving? But more important, there would be no reason for the season, no revelation of Jesus, no Good News, no bridge to heaven, no grace, no mercy, no forgiveness, no miracles, no defeating death, no Savior, no hope, and no love. And yet this is the way many live, without any purpose in their lives. I don't know about you, but for me, this thought is scary. Because of Jesus Christ, we do have Christmas! Yes, because of Christ's willingness to come, His willingness to be born in a stable, and His willingness to die on the cross for us, we not only have all those things mentioned above but far more. The truth is because of Christmas, we really do get an endless array of heavenly gifts. Jesus did come, and He gave us the greatest gift of all. But do we have room for Him in our hearts?

Whenever Christmas pageants are talked about, someone is sure to mention the name of Wallace Purling. Wally was nine and in the second grade, though he should have been in the fourth. He was big and awkward, slow in movement and mind. Wally wanted to be a shepherd in the Christmas pageant, so the director assigned him an important role as the innkeeper with few lines. Additionally, Wally's size would make his refusal of lodging more forceful. As the performance unfolds, Joseph appears, slowly, tenderly guiding Mary to the door of the inn. Wally swung the inn door open with a brusque gesture, "What do you want?"

"We seek lodging," Joseph says.

"Seek it elsewhere," Wally spoke vigorously. "The inn is filled."

Joseph persists, "Sir, we have asked everywhere in vain, have traveled far, and are very weary."

"There is no room in this inn for you." Wally looked properly stern.

"Please, good innkeeper, this is my wife, Mary. She is heavy with child and needs a place to rest. Surely you must have some small corner for her."

"No!" Wally repeated.

Joseph sadly placed his arm around Mary who laid her head upon her husband's shoulder while the two of them started to move away. The innkeeper did not return inside. His brow creased with concern, his eyes filling unmistakably with tears. And, suddenly, this Christmas pageant became different from all others. "Don't go, Joseph," Wally called out. "Bring Mary back." And Wallace Purling's face grew into a bright smile. "You can have my room."

If there had never been a Christmas, the world would be far different than it is today in ways we might never imagine or wish to consider. The only reason for recognizing Christmas is that you must have faith to believe that God decided to come and live among us. Before you can have faith in Christmas, you have to have faith to believe that you actually matter to God. One can't read the biblical account about Jesus' birth without encountering the word *Savior*—yes, "the Messiah, the Lord" (Luke 2:11 NLT). The only reason a savior being born is good news is that somebody needed to be saved. Believe it or not, that somebody was you and me. When you let Him in and accept Him as your very own, you can be assured He will never leave you (Matthew 28:20). That's simply the beginning of faith. As with Wally, the pageant innkeeper, we just have to find a way to make room for Jesus in our life.

Reflection

Do you have faith this Christmas? Do you believe God actually intervened in the life of humanity? Do you believe God is still interested in making a difference in your life? If so, are you able to approach the holiday regardless of how others might attempt to steal your Christmas? In what ways might you help others personally recognize their need to make room for Jesus in their lives?

DECEMBER 5
(Y3, D49)

Three Wise Women

After Jesus was born in Bethlehem in Judea, during the time of
King Herod, Magi from the east came to Jerusalem.

—Matthew 2:1 (NIV)

Several years ago, I was involved with helping to arrange a special afternoon Advent service for residents at a local nursing home. Part of my responsibility was to secure a pianist to accompany the hymn singing. The night before, I had a call from Barb who had weeks before committed to play. As sometimes happens, a family crisis would prevent her from being there. The next morning, I called Sandy, an old friend, who I was sure would be at her own church that morning. I left a voice message, told her my situation, and asked if she could help me out. I also stated that due to the fact it was last-minute, I did not know of anyone else I would feel comfortable asking. I did not hear back from her but felt that my prayers were answered when I arrived at the nursing home about an hour before the service. Sitting at the piano in the facility's chapel was Michelle who was playing some music for her mother, a resident there. I knew Michelle by reputation as an excellent pianist, so I proceeded to explain my predicament. Long story short, she agreed to play for the service in less than an hour. All was well.

Prior to the service, several of us began to visit with and assist residents of the nursing home to its chapel. Michelle had already seated herself at the piano and had started to play some beautiful prelude music. On my final round to gather residents, I came down the hall to find Barb outside the chapel with the pastor, clarifying why it was not she who was playing. Apparently, her crisis had been temporarily resolved, and she thought it would be best to check in and make sure we had found someone. As I greeted her, I looked off to the side, and there was Sandy coming down the hall. There they all were, three wise women. One came because she had obligated herself to a promise she had not wanted to break. The second, no doubt, had other things on her agenda that Sunday but had felt God's call. And the third came with only one purpose in mind but had been unexpectedly asked to share her talent.

Scripture tells us about the Magi who searched to find Jesus after they knew of His birth. We often hear them referred to as the three wise men. Although there is no reference to the exact number, we can assume that there were at least three because of the gifts that they brought, that of gold, frankincense, and myrrh. We can also be assured that they were wise. We know this because they sought Jesus by following the star (Matthew 2:9), they were joyful in their understanding of who He was (Matthew 2:10), they were humbled as they bowed down before Him (Matthew 2:11), and they followed God's direction in a dream as they traveled back home (Matthew 2:12). It's obvious that their journey was inspired and guided by divine intervention.

As we move through the season of Advent toward the celebration of Christmas, it is important for us to ask what motivates us to come to the manger? For many of us, it is part of our heritage, it's tradition. No doubt for others who are home to be with family and perhaps get pulled into church on Christmas Eve, it may be nothing more than an obligation. To those who have not yet come to know the Christ-child, it may be the sense of awe one initially feels when they pass a live nativity scene reenacted by a local church or when they experience the dramatic portrayal at an event such as New York's Radio City Christmas Show. It may be that you simply view it as part of a promise, the feeling of a call from God, or the sharing of a talent that only He alone can instill. Just ask my friends. You know, my friends—the three wise women. They'll help you to understand why they came. It's part of the awareness in their own personal journey, not just at Christmas but all year long.

Reflection

So what is it that you bring to Jesus this Christmas? Why not consider the lessons from the three wise women: keeping a promise, feeling God's call, and sharing your gifts? In what ways can these be used as a response to God's love? With whom will you share your journey to the manger? How do we extend the invitation to those who might not otherwise feel welcome?

DECEMBER 6
(Y4, D49)

The Need for a Savior

I, even I, am the LORD, and apart from me there is no savior.

—Isaiah 43:11 (NIV)

I was decorating my light post and the bushes in front of my home for Christmas. A former work colleague saw me as he was driving by pulled over, got out of the car and, after greeting me, began to reminisce. The weather was fairly mild, so we stood outside and talked for a while. About halfway through the conversation, there was an attempt by my friend to turn the conversation toward politics. I rather promptly shut down the subject by simply stating that I didn't like to get into political discussions. Then I concluded by saying, "Quite frankly, I have come to the conclusion that the world is a mess." My visitor could not resist in agreeing that my statement contained a lot of truth. As I reflected on this dialogue later, I decided that my attitude was a rather gloomy way to feel as we enter into the four weeks of Advent which prepare us for Christmas. Then I thought there undoubtedly have been many Christmas seasons during which mankind must have found themselves in a dark state of unrest.

One of those was in December 1941, when much of the world was at war. On December 6 of that year, President Franklin D. Roosevelt issued a personal appeal to Japanese Emperor Hirohito to use his influence to avoid war. One day later, America was caught off-guard when the Imperial Japanese Navy Air Service attacked Pearl Harbor. The surprise attack, which killed 2,403 US citizens with another 1,178 wounded, came as a profound shock to the American people and led directly to the nation's entry into World War II. For the next three years, young men were called to serve, and the United States and their allies were at war during Christmas. "Peace on Earth" was not just a nice phrase found on holiday cards, but it was also the number one wish of all people throughout the world. The season gave hope that maybe next year the war would be over while song lyrics like "I'll be home for Christmas…if only in my dreams" topped the charts.

Throughout much of history, we find the world searching for some kind of peace. We should not be surprised then to realize that even the birth of Jesus occurred during a dark time in a turbulent land. Anticipating the coming of the Christ-child centuries before His arrival, the great Prophet Isaiah wrote, "The people who walk in darkness will see a great light. For those who live in a land of deep darkness, a light will shine" (Isaiah 9:2). When we consider that Christ came to bring light to a deeply troubled world, the image we form is one which is awe-inspiring and beautiful. For we all face seasons of darkness, and God in the flesh ("the Incarnate") knows exactly how that looks and feels. God sent His Son into the darkness as one of us when He had every reason to refrain from doing so. His justification: "For God so loved the world, that he gave his only Son, that whoever believes in him should not perish but have eternal life" (John 3:16 NIV).

So we find ourselves in a fallen world as fallen persons looking for some kind of salvation. Henry David Thoreau once wrote, "The mass of men lead lives of quiet desperation." Here, he describes the void we each sometimes feel in our lives. The effortless search to find a savior will never be satisfied until we find the one true source of light in this dark world. Jesus himself said, "For many will come in my name, claiming, 'I am the Messiah,' and will deceive many. You will hear of wars and rumors of wars, but see to it that you are not alarmed. Such things must happen, but the end is still to come" (Matthew 24:5–6). In the hours of our greatest doubt, fear, pain, and worry, Jesus was born to take up residence in our lives. "For the Son of Man came to seek and save those who are lost" (Luke 19:10 NLT). It's okay, then, to conclude that this world is in a real mess. It will continue to be that way until Jesus returns. Until then, we will receive confidence that only the one true God can provide through the Holy Spirit and His Word. As we do so, we can rest assured that the hope of the Advent season will deliver the only Savior we need.

Reflection

How do you presently feel about the state of the world? Are there ways you might use this season of preparation to remind you that "greater is He who is in you than he who is in the world" (1 John 4:4 KJB)? As you interact with others over the next few weeks, how might you be able to lead those who have a need for a savior to the birth of the one who came to save and sustain?

DECEMBER 7
(Y5, D49)

With Awe and Amazement

The whole earth is filled with awe at your wonders; where morning
dawns, where evening fades, you call forth songs of joy.

—Psalm 65:8 (NIV)

"Godspeed, John Glenn," were the infamous words that were spoken by astronaut Scott Carpenter as his fellow *Mercury 7* astronaut was launched into space from Cape Canaveral on April 12, 1961. It was a solo mission which only lasted just shy of five hours, but Glenn will always be remembered as the first American to orbit the earth. He did so at the age of forty. He once said, "There is still no cure for the common birthday." However, thirty-seven years later in 1998, he ventured into space again, this time for nine days, testing the effects of space travel on an aging body. Having become fascinated with flying at a young age, he piloted his own personal plane until he was ninety. On December 8, 2016, he left earth for the final time, marking his passing at the ripe old age of ninety-five. Those who were part of the generation serving witness to his pioneering into space will remember his missions with awe and amazement.

These days, I consider if we view much of anything with the same sense of awe and wonder that we once did. I can remember my early Christmases with what must be a much different perspective than that of today's children. Then there was a feeling of anticipation that doesn't seem to exist much today. These days, children are barely back in school from summer break when Christmas trees and other decorations start to populate the stores. By the time Christmas Day arrives, they have no doubt seen dozens of trees over the course of the past months. What was once new and exciting has now become familiar and assumed. Not so long ago, the tree was as much a part of Christmas morning as the gifts and the evidence that Santa must have somehow shimmied his way down that chimney one more time. It is no surprise that by Christmas day, many are tired of it all and ready to pack it up soon after.

Awe and wonder are at the very root of our Christian walk. In the Holy Scriptures, Luke tells the story of a paralyzed man who was brought to Jesus by some men and lowered into a house from the roof on a mat because of the crowds. Seeing their faith, Jesus forgave the man of his sins but was criticized by the religious rulers of the day.

> Jesus knew what they were thinking, so he asked them, "Why do you question this in your hearts? Is it easier to say 'Your sins are forgiven' or 'Stand up and walk'? So I will prove to you that the Son of Man has the authority on earth to forgive sins." Then Jesus turned to the paralyzed man and said, "Stand up, pick up your mat, and go home." And immediately, as everyone watched, the man jumped up, picked up his mat, and went home praising God. Everyone was gripped with great wonder and awe, and they praised God, exclaiming, "We have seen amazing things today." (Luke 5:22–26 NLT)

It's been said that when we allow our focus to be diverted away from God, we will cease to be amazed. How very true that is for many today.

After seeing the baby Jesus, the shepherds began to spread the word of what they had been told and themselves witnessed. "And all who heard it were amazed at what the shepherds said to them" (Luke 2:18 NIV). A sense of awe for what they had seen led them to glorify and praise God (Luke 2:20). Max Lucado put it this way:

> Off to one side sits a group of shepherds. They sit silently on the floor, perhaps perplexed, perhaps in awe, no doubt in amazement. Their night watch had been interrupted by an explosion of light from heaven and a symphony of angels. God goes to those who have time to hear him, and so on this cloudless night he went to simple shepherds.

When nothing impresses us anymore, it becomes quite important that we spend time with God. For when we rest in Him, even in the busiest of seasons, our eyes become more like those of the astronaut: focused beyond the things of this world and renewed once again with awe and amazement.

Reflection

What experiences elicit a sense of awe and wonder for you? How can you allow the season of Advent to revitalize your relationship with Jesus? Are there ways in which you can reach out to others this Christmas and help them to also find new wonderment in their life?

DECEMBER 8
(Y6, D49)

Freedom from All Your Fears

The LORD is for me, so I will have no fear. What can mere people do to me?

—Psalm 118:6 (NLT)

As America's Pacific fleet lay in ruins at Pearl Harbor, President Franklin Roosevelt delivered perhaps the most memorable speech of his career on December 8, 1941. The day before, Japanese pilots had bombed the US naval base at Pearl Harbor with raids that killed 2,403 people and wounded nearly 1,200 others. Although Roosevelt and his advisers had received intelligence reports indicating an imminent attack by Japan days before, he had hoped that a peaceful solution could be found. He was infuriated to realize that while American and Japanese diplomats engaged in negotiations, Japanese aircraft carriers had been steaming toward Hawaii intent on attack. His words on December 8 relayed his personal indignation and anger. The speech, in which he called Japan's act a "deliberate deception," received thunderous applause from Congress and, soon after, the United States officially entered the Second World War. The same president who once said, "The only thing we have to fear is fear itself" declared with equal conviction that his nation and the "unbounding determination of our people, will gain the inevitable triumph—so help us God." Reports on supposed spy activity on the part of Japanese Americans began pouring into Washington. In some areas of the country, Japanese nationals were rounded up and held in custody as fear mounted.

Fear is one of the most debilitating emotions known to the human race. It is unbelievably powerful. It penetrates the heart, poisons the spirit, and paralyzes the soul. It can affect you not only emotionally, mentally, and spiritually, but it can also distress you physically. For Christians, the antidote to fear is faith in a God who is actively involved in the lives of His people, a God who is present with us. It is helpful to remember that some form of "fear not" is one of if not the most common address to us in Scripture. Our most helpful counsel about fear comes in the form of an angel ministering to Mary when she learned she was pregnant with the one who was to be the Savior of the world. Totally baffled and devastated, no words could have meant more. "Do not be afraid, Mary, for you have found favor with God" (Luke 1:30). The angelic greeting comes with incredible consistency throughout the long-awaited story about the coming of the Messiah. The story carries the same message, the same command repeated over and over again: "Fear not." When Joseph became aware that Mary was with child, he "resolved to divorce her, quietly. But as he considered these things, behold, an angel of the Lord appeared to him in a dream, saying, 'Joseph, son of David, do not fear to take Mary as your wife, for that which is conceived in her is from the Holy Spirit" (Matthew 1:19–20 ESV). Likewise, when God announced the birth of His Son to a group of humble shepherds, an angel appeared before the stunned men. "But the angel said to them, 'Do not be afraid. I bring you good news that will cause great joy for all the people. Today in the town of David a Savior has been born to you; he is the Messiah, the Lord'" (Luke 2:10–11 NIV). In each case, the message was simple and yet so profound: "Don't be afraid… The Lord is with you."

Therein lies the message of Christmas. As we consider the good news of the birth of Jesus, we come to understand the true meaning of Immanuel, God with us (Matthew 1:23). He sustains us through all things because He is the author and finisher of our faith. We need to become more like the main characters of the Christmas story and walk on our journey by faith and not by sight. With messages like the angels' visits to Mary, Joseph, and the shepherds, the words "fear not" assure us that God will always give us the guidance we need to reject fear. Listen to the message from the psalmist, David, who was born in the same city as Jesus many years and generations before: "The LORD is my light and my salvation—whom shall I fear? The LORD is the stronghold of my life—of whom shall I be afraid?" (Psalm 27:1 NIV). God is still present and active in this world. And because we know that He keeps his promises, we don't have to be overcome by the fears of the moment. When Christ becomes our central focus, confidence replaces all of our anxieties. As you prepare your heart for Christmas this year, may you experience the fullness of His joy. As a result, you are destined to find true freedom from all your fears.

Reflection

What fears are threatening to overwhelm you this Christmas season? How might focusing on Jesus help you to live more confidently? In what ways might you use the message of freedom from our fears to bring peace to others who are struggling with their own doubts and uncertainties?

DECEMBER 9
(Y7, D49)

All Roads Lead TO Bethlehem

But you, O Bethlehem…are only a small village… Yet a ruler of Israel, whose
origins are in the distant past, will come from you on my behalf.

—Micah 5:2 (NLT)

Each year, as I carefully unpack each piece of my nativity set, I think about the placement of the figures and justify in my mind where they should be. My homemade creche houses a few animals where the manger holding baby Jesus, Mary, and Joseph take center-stage. The shepherds receive a prominent spot, revealing that they "came with haste" (Luke 2:16 KJB) to Bethlehem "to see this thing that has happened, which the Lord has told us about" (Luke 2:15 NIV). The wise men with their gifts are grouped facing the Christ-child, fulfilling the scripture that they "bowed down and worshiped Him" (Matthew 2:11 NIV), although likely at a later time according to most accounts. It is safe to say that the companies which create nativity scenes have taken great liberties over the years to include more characters, making it appear as though there were more persons present at the birth of Jesus than there actually was. With these additional personas evolving from storytellers, songwriters, and mythology, the purchase of a fine nativity set is often far pricier than it would need to be, especially if the pieces are separately purchased.

While some people imagine the manger scene with snow, singing angels, and many other worshippers, none of that is actually found in the biblical account. I must admit that my own set contains a drummer boy. He no doubt represents the fictitious character in "The Little Drummer Boy," a well-known Christmas song from by Katherine Kennicott Davis. It was written in 1941 and became popularized in the 1950s by several groups. In the lyrics, the songwriter tells of a poor young boy called by the Magi to the nativity where he played his drum, the only gift he had to offer to the baby Jesus, with Mary's approval. When I place the pieces of my nativity set, the drummer boy is right there, hanging out with the other visitors just as if he belongs there—and maybe he does, at least for conversation's sake.

In my own life's journey, I have heard about that trip to Bethlehem for many years now. I have had several occasions to see and actually participate in live nativity modernizations. One of the most moving I have seen is in the concluding act of the Radio City Music Hall Christmas Show which has elaborate staging, beautiful music, and even live camels on stage. Such reenactments, as one might call them, often take their own liberties which also frequently stray from scripture. I am challenged to think about what it must have been like to really be there in that town of David's birth (Luke 2:11) where there was no room for the Son of God to be born except in a humble stable (Luke 2:7). God chose some small, quiet, out of the way place, and it is there that the course of history is changed for all of eternity. To be sure, love came down at Christmas. "God showed how much he loved us by sending his one and only Son into the world so that we might have eternal life through him" (1 John 4:9 NLT).

In many ways, I can reflect upon and identify with that little drummer boy in my own nativity set. He actually has no business being there in the first place. But then I hear the voice of Jesus saying, "No, you belong here too." For it is here in Bethlehem that God makes Himself meek and helpless. It is here at the nativity where He invites all of His children throughout the world to love Him. This is where we also belong—beside the manger. For here, we behold this child who is of God, adoring Him as King of kings and Lord of lords. Perhaps we each need to look in that hidden part of ourselves where we are also searching for God. There we will find our own inner Bethlehem, the place in us where He comes alive. We simply have to trust that God will lead and guide us as He did for the Holy Family. The Advent journey is nothing less than making your heart and home a place for Christ to be born. In doing so we come to realize that all roads lead to Bethlehem. We simply have to find our way there.

Reflection

With what character do you identify in the Nativity? Does the scene draw you in, or do you think there is no place for you there? Do you fully recognize that God loves you so much that He was willing to become like one of us? Are there ways in which you might journey to Bethlehem and once again feel close to the Christ-child during this season of Advent?

DECEMBER 10
(Y1, D50)

Withholding Christmas

And then he told them, "Go into all the world and preach the Good News to everyone."

—Mark 16:15 (NLT)

"Now you'd better be good because Santa's coming in a few weeks. If you don't act the way you should, instead of those presents you want, he'll bring you a lump of coal." As children become excited about the anticipated visit from the man with the white beard in the red suit, parents will sometimes say or do almost anything to mellow their restless behavior. The lump of coal legend is one that has been around for generations. However, the threat of withholding Christmas, in whatever form, is an act of manipulation which often works and sometimes surpasses the innocence of childhood. I recently heard the story of a young man who lives in a different state than most of his relatives. For years, unresolved tension has existed with his parents, even though they have tried to make amends. Again, this Christmas, the son will travel to his hometown to visit with siblings, aunts, uncles, and cousins but will withhold Christmas from his parents by purposefully making no effort to spend time with them.

Several years ago, a consultant to a company for which I was employed decided that he would no longer be able to serve our organization in the upcoming year. It had been our usual custom to purchase Christmas gifts for individuals who had provided services to the establishment. The individual who purchased these gifts for the company pursued my opinion as to whether we should provide a gift to the person who would be discontinuing his services. My reply was that this individual should be treated the same as all the others because I had always viewed the gifts as a token of appreciation for what had already been done. To be honest, I suppose I also did not want to burn any bridges not knowing what the future might bring. Therefore, gifts were purchased and delivered to everyone. A few days later, I took a phone call from the consultant humbled that he had received a gift after tendering his resignation. I extended my gratefulness for the services he had rendered. Christmas is about giving, not withholding.

These stories beg the question, have you ever withheld Christmas from another person? My guess is that you have more times than you would dare to imagine. I know this is true in my life as well. For, you see, there are many ways to withhold Christmas. It doesn't have to take the form of not giving a gift or deciding to exclude someone from your visitation schedule. Every time we have an opportunity to share the Good News of Jesus and fail to do so, we are doing just that. When the angel of the Lord announced the birth of Christ to the shepherds, these words were spoken: "'Don't be afraid!' he said. 'I bring you good news that will bring great joy to *all* people'" (Luke 2:10 NLT). Notice that the angel said that the good news was for everyone. That, my friends, means not just you and me. It's also the guy you regularly see eating alone in the diner you frequent. *All* refers to the neighbor who often disturbs your day with the noisy dog and the loud motorcycle. It means the person you intentionally omitted from your Christmas party invitation list for whatever reason. No doubt you can think of more.

Jesus came that we might have life and have it abundantly (John 10:10). It was a point He tried to make to the religious leaders of His time, but it escaped their understanding. It sometimes escapes ours as well, for we have come to define abundance in the form of material possessions rather than spiritual gifts. It is important that we are passionate about the unique gifts God has given us and be ready to share His Good News. Sometimes we feel we don't have the right words, but readiness includes a state of willingness. So simply be a good example in the community and an authentic witness to the faith that is within you. "And I am praying that you will put into action the generosity that comes from your faith as you understand and experience all the good things we have in Christ" (Philemon 1:6 NLT). This Christmas we can fill the needs of the lonely, bring joy to those who are sad, and give hope to the depressed. Christ has commissioned us to share the Good News of His birth with all persons. We are called not just to the world of those we love but also to the wider world of the hurting who need to be uplifted at this time of year. Jesus stated it this way, "Peace be with you. As the Father has sent me, even so I am sending you" (John 20:21 ESV). In taking up His call, we will never withhold Christmas again.

Reflection

Why do you think Christmas remains one of the most likely times of the year for nonbelievers to consider matters of faith? What are some practical ways you might allow God to use you to bring hope to others this Christmas? What obstacles might you have to overcome in order to do so?

DECEMBER 11
(Y2, D50)

The Gift of Patience

Be still before the LORD and wait patiently for him.

—Psalm 37:7 (NIV)

My grandfather was not the most patient person, although as I was growing up, he always showed a great deal of love and caring in my behalf. He also demonstrated a great deal of patience when he was forced to be a caregiver to my grandmother after she suffered a stroke in her later years. However, when my mom was young, there *was* that one Christmas that his level of patience went by the wayside. As she related the story, her dad went out to find a Christmas tree. After he brought it home, apparently the ladies of the household could find very little right with it. So my grandfather proceeded to remove the tree, took it outside, and chopped it up for firewood. His concluding words were, "Now you can go out and get your own tree." And that was the last Christmas tree he ever brought home. For many of us, Christmas can become a time of irritability. During the Christmas season we wait, often impatiently. We wait in traffic and checkout lines. We wait for family to arrive. We wait to gather around a table filled with our favorite foods. We wait for others to open their presents so that we can open ours.

God's Holy Word is filled with stories about His people in waiting. Jacob waited seven years for a wife and then worked seven more after being tricked by her father (Genesis 29:15–20). Moses waited four decades for the call to lead the Israelites, then four more decades for a promised land he would never enter (Deuteronomy 32:51–52). At the time of the birth of Jesus, there are stories of people in waiting as well. There was a prophetess by the name of Anna, a widow who was eighty-four years old. Scripture says that "she never left the Temple but stayed there day and night, worshiping God with fasting and prayer" (Luke 2:37 NLT). Her many years of patience, sacrifice and service were worth it all when she saw the Messiah, the One for whom she had waited so long. Shortly after His birth, the parents of Jesus arrived at the temple to present Him before God and make the customary purification offering. It was then that Anna "came along just as Simeon was talking with Mary and Joseph, and she began praising God. She talked about the child to everyone who had been waiting expectantly for God to rescue Jerusalem" (Luke 2:38 NLT). Anna had been rewarded for her patience.

All of this waiting can be a reminder to Christians that the annual event is a celebration of waiting for something much more important than our holiday traditions. Once we have welcomed Him into our lives as Savior and Lord, we find that we must have patience to continue to wait on Him once more. Although He already came as the long-awaited Messiah, He has not yet come as ruler over all the earth. We must remember that "the LORD is good to those whose hope is in him, to the one who seeks him; it is good to wait quietly for the salvation of the LORD" (Lamentations 3:25–26 NIV). So, today, we wait for Christ's Second Coming. What seems to us like God's slowness in coming is instead His patience in waiting. It is written, "The Lord is not slow in keeping his promise, as some understand slowness. Instead he is patient with you, not wanting anyone to perish, but everyone to come to repentance" (2 Peter 3:9 NIV).

You may have heard the tongue-in-cheek prayer: "Lord, make me more patient—and do it now!" As our minds try to wrap themselves around a world turned upside-down, times get stressful, and patience often goes into hiding and somehow gets lost in the shadows. For the Christian, patience is a sign of spiritual maturity, a quality that can develop only through the passing of time. Patience is essentially "waiting with grace." Part of being Christian is having the ability to accept unfortunate or delayed circumstances gracefully while having faith that we will ultimately find resolution in God. Patience is not just a virtue, it's a fruit of the Spirit (Galatians 5:22). If patience is a virtue, then waiting is the best means by which the Holy Spirit will grow patience in us. Patience is a gift that that can work incredible magic on us, and our attitude becomes transformed by it. The next time you find yourself becoming impatient, stop and remember that the ability to patiently wait is a gift from God. Receive that gift and allow it to bring the calm, peace, joy, and yes, endurance that only He alone can give.

Reflection

What does it mean to wait quietly without complaint? Do you set an example of waiting quietly? Or do you make sure everybody knows how unhappy you are? Think of the things in your life that you could develop patience toward, and ask the Lord to help you with them as you prepare for Christmas.

DECEMBER 12
(Y3, D50)

In the Presence of Angels

For he will command his angels concerning you to guard you in all your ways.

—Psalm 91:11 (NIV)

For nine seasons, we came to know her as the angel who sometimes needed some tough guidance with her earthly assignments. Her TV character, Monica, was played by the Irish actress, Roma Downey. Sometimes her kindheartedness got in the way of a smooth mission, but her wise, more experienced supervisor, Tess (Della Reese), was always able to redirect her through her assignment. This sometimes included an intersection with Andrew, the Angel of Death, when it was someone's time to pass on to their heavenly Home. Together, the trio always managed to provide a message of hope and let folks know that God hadn't forgotten about them. In the end, the story characters along with the viewer became inspired because, after all, we had all been *touched by an angel.* The series left many wondering if angels might, at times, be dispatched along the way to help us though our troubled times.

A story is told of a nineteenth-century English Bishop who early in his ministry was called out late to visit a dying man. The journey into the dark of night several miles from his home turned out to be a wild goose chase and left the young pastor a bit mystified. Years later, he found himself on another visit, this time to a prison. During conversation, the condemned man asked the bishop if he remembered his useless walk many years before. "It was I who gave you the false message," said the man, "to lure you out that I might rob you." The bishop asked why he hadn't carried out his plan. "When you came near," said the man, "I saw you were not alone. There was a mysterious looking stranger walking close behind you, and he followed you to your home and then disappeared." An angel from God? Probably so.

Here we are, Christmas is just days away. Once again, we not only hear the account of the birth of Jesus but also the role the many angels played in the narrative. They are some of the most pivotal players. The angel Gabriel informs Mary that she is highly favored and will receive a diving blessing from God (Luke 1:26–38). In Matthew 1:18–25, an angel speaks to Joseph who trusts and follows

God's direction. When Jesus is born, the angels enlighten the shepherds of good news and great joy (Luke 2:8–10). And following the visit from the wise men, an angel sends a warning to Joseph in a dream, and he obeys (Matthew 2:13–14). Their role in the Christmas drama has been practically immortalized by the writers of our hymns. While angels play a prominent role in the events surrounding the birth of Jesus, they appear on rare occasions throughout significant times in scripture in unpredictable ways.

This raises a question from the modern-day Christian as to whether there is a presence of angels along our personal journey. Hebrews 1:14 (NIV) explains, "Are not all angels ministering spirits sent to serve those who will inherit salvation?" Just as angels protected God's people in the past, we can be assured that they are guarding us today. "Do not forget to show hospitality to strangers, for by so doing some people have shown hospitality to angels without knowing it" (Hebrews 13:2 NIV). We are heartened by the knowledge that God's angels are at work, and the reality of His angels should provide promise for us in our daily walk. Billy Graham stated, "Every believer should be encouraged and strengthened! Angels are watching; they mark your path. They superintend the events of your life and protect the interest of the Lord God, always working to promote his plans and to bring about his highest will for you." And for those who have not yet joined us on the journey, hope remains. For "in the same way, I tell you, there is rejoicing in the presence of the angels of God over one sinner who repents" (Luke 15:10 NIV). God provides the angels that we need when we need them, and for that, we should all rejoice.

Reflection

As you hear the words of the angels in the Christmas story this year, will you share their joy at the birth of Jesus? How does the presence of angels in the scriptures reassure us that God is faithful to His people? In what ways has your path been marked by angels?

DECEMBER 13
(Y4, D50)

Beware of the Wrapping

That night there were shepherds staying in the fields nearby, guarding their flocks of sheep.

—Luke 2:8 (NLT)

His name was Bill, and for a number of years, we attended the same church. He was a motorcycle enthusiast, to say the least, and it was not unusual for Bill to come to worship wearing jeans and a Harley-Davidson t-shirt. Before the service began, he would be up and down the aisles, welcoming people. On occasion, he would take the pulpit to share something that had happened in his life or promote a mission or an upcoming activity in the church. I would criticize him for being far too wordy and would usually roll my eyes when I knew he was getting up to speak. He pretty much drove me crazy. Then I went through a difficult time in my life, and one day, when I went to the mailbox, there was a card from Bill. In the card, he wrote a personal note of encouragement and offered to come to my home and pray with me if I desired him to do so. I never took him up on his offer, but months later, I saw him and told him how much I had appreciated his card. About a year later, I opened the newspaper one morning and saw his obituary. I realized that Bill had given me a gift of joy. There are other persons who would not have surprised me to reach out during that time, but "Harley" Bill? Never would have expected it!

The adage "Don't judge a book by its cover" seems to apply here. The Gospel of John reminds us: "Look beneath the surface so you can judge correctly" (John 7:24 NLT). In the Old Testament, the story is told of Samuel who was commissioned by the Lord to go to Jesse of Bethlehem in search of a new king. Jesse had seven of his sons pass by Samuel. However, none of them fulfilled the words of the Lord: "Do not look on his appearance or on the height of his stature, because I have rejected him. For the LORD sees not as man sees: man looks on the outward appearance, but the LORD looks on the heart" (1 Samuel16:7 ESV). It was not until Jesse sent for his youngest, a shepherd boy named David, that the Lord's words were satisfied. We should not be surprised as we prepare for another Christmas that we find the baby Jesus in this very same city of Bethlehem, the City of David, being visited by the shepherds,

Isn't it interesting that out of all of Jerusalem society, God picked a band of shepherds to hear the news of Jesus' birth? They would have been among the lowest and most despised social groups of their day and would have no doubt been dirty, smelly, and unkempt. But Luke tells us that "they hurried off and found Mary and Joseph, and the baby, who was lying in the manger" (Luke 2:16 NIV). Depicted in several versions of the painting entitled *The Adoration of the Shepherds*, they are shown kneeling before the crib, hands raised in gestures of prayer and amazement, reflecting what that had been told by the angel: "I bring to you good news of great joy that will be for all people" (Luke 2:10 ESV). More significant, they came to see Him the night He was born and, despite the many versions of the story that are told, most likely, no one else did. They were the first eyewitnesses who spread the word of His birth, "and all who heard it were amazed at what the shepherds said to them" (Luke 2:18 NIV).

As we find ourselves in another week of the Advent season, we should be aware that joy proclaims itself in many different ways. Sometimes, it comes as an enthusiastic follower attired with a Harley insignia. It can be seen in the shepherds as they enter with haste and use their staff to kneel in the presence of the newborn king. Or maybe we find it in the words of a carol reflected by our own desire to feel in our hearts once more the true meaning of Christmas. But don't be fooled; it is there, waiting for you. Just be aware of the wrapping, for it doesn't always appear in a way you might expect.

Reflection

Are there times in your life when you have received unanticipated joy from someone whom you least expected? Is there a person you know who might have a heart very different than what you might be judging by their external persona? How might you work at discovering new joy this Christmas?

DECEMBER 14
(Y5, D50)

Tradition

I praise you for remembering me in everything and for holding
to the traditions just as I passed them on to you.

—1 Corinthians 11:2 (NIV)

There is probably no holiday that highlights the practice of tradition more than Christmas. One family saves their Christmas tree following the season. As the wood begins to dry out, it is cut into logs which are saved to burn in their fireplace the following Christmas Eve. A newly established tradition at our home was initiated several years ago following a visit to the Epcot theme park at Walt Disney World. There I purchased a pickle ornament from a store in the Germany attraction. I learned that it is German tradition for parents to hide this ornament on their tree for the children to find on Christmas Eve. The child who locates the special decoration receives an extra gift from Saint Nicholas as most observant child. When I was in my teens, my family was invited to attend Christmas Eve service. The church held their program at 11:00 p.m., so by the time you were singing the last hymn, it was Christmas Day. During the numerous choruses of "Silent Night," candles were lit all over the sanctuary by each attendee. As the service concluded, participants were encouraged to make it home with their candle still burning. In this way, you were carrying the light of Christ out into the world and also bringing His light into your own home. In the last few years we attended, this practice was discouraged. Even though protectors had been provided for each candle, apparently, too much wax was being dripped onto the carpet in the church. I suppose it was a practical consideration, but the significance of the candle lighting and the challenge to get it home somehow forfeited a tradition that, for me, was never quite the same.

In the Broadway musical, *Fiddler on the Roof*, the main character, Tevye, sets a major theme for the play. He says:

Because of our traditions, we have kept our balance for many, many years…
For instance, we always keep our heads covered and always wear a little prayer

shawl. This shows our constant devotion to God. You may ask, how did this tradition get started? I'll tell you… I don't know. But it's a tradition. And because of our traditions, every one of us knows who he is and what God expects him to do.

We all try to hold on to our traditions as the world around us is constantly changing. Sometimes we have no idea why they were started. Jesus rebuked the judgment of the religious leaders and teachers of the law who were making accusations about His disciples not following the ceremonial practices of the day. His response to them was, "These people honor me with their lips, but their hearts are far from me. They worship me in vain; their teachings are merely human rules. You have let go of the commands of God and are holding on to human traditions." And he continued, "You have a fine way of setting aside the commands of God in order to observe your own traditions!" (Mark 7:6–9 NIV).

Traditions can be comforting to us on many levels, and sometimes they will be questioned by those who challenge the sincerity of our faith. For instance, in Jeremiah 10:3–4 (ESV), we read: "A tree from the forest is cut down and worked with an axe by the hands of a craftsman. They decorate it with silver and gold; they fasten it with hammer and nails so that it cannot move." At first glance, it might seem that this passage is referring to Christmas trees. But a more careful look at the entire passage makes it clear that God is talking about making a carved image—or idol—made from the trunk of a tree. Unless one is worshiping their Christmas tree, there would be no logical reason to discontinue this tradition. In fact, Martin Luther taught that the fir tree represented the everlasting love of God because he was so struck by its beauty. Believers in Christ should give serious thought as to whether any of their traditions contradict or distracts them from God's Word. Paul said, "See to it that no one takes you captive through hollow and deceptive philosophy, which depends on human tradition and the elemental spiritual forces of this world rather than on Christ" (Colossians 2:8 NIV). There you have it. As long as your holiday customs are not separating you from your walk with Christ, then they are just simply that—tradition.

Reflection

Is your religious experience based upon family tradition or on a personal relationship with Jesus Christ? Have you blindly accepted traditions not of your own making without consideration as to whether they are supported in God's Word? Have some of your traditions influenced the way you practice your faith? Are there any of your personal or family traditions that might require closer examination?

DECEMBER 15
(Y6, D50)

Leaning in the Right Direction

By doing this they will be storing up their treasure as a good foundation
for the future so that they may experience true life.

—1 Timothy 6:19 (NIV)

A must-see for tourists visiting Italy is the Leaning Tower of Pisa in Tuscany. The eight-story cathedral bell tower was completed in the twelfth century. While construction was still in progress, the tower's foundation began to sink into the soft, marshy ground, causing it to lean to one side. Its builders tried to compensate for the lean by making the top stories slightly taller on one side, but the extra masonry only made the tower sink further. By the time it was completed in 1360, modern-day engineers say it was a miracle that it didn't fall down completely. By the twentieth century, the 190-foot-high white marble tower leaned a dramatic fifteen feet off the perpendicular. Engineers were eventually able to reduce the lean nearly seventeen inches by removing earth from underneath its foundation. On December 15, 2001, Italy's Leaning Tower of Pisa reopened after a team of experts spent eleven years and $27 million to fortify the tower without eliminating its famous lean. Though entrance to the tower is now limited to guided tours, hordes of tourists can still be found outside striking the classic pose for photos next to the tower pretending to hold it up. Today, the top of that tower is nearly thirteen feet off center. Engineers annually measure its slow descent, calculating that at its current rate of decline, it will one day collapse.

Nothing is more important in construction work than making sure you have the foundation right. If you don't get that correct, then nothing else will matter. It may be more fun to decide what color to paint the rooms or how you will decorate the finished structure, but without a proper foundation, nothing else you do will last long enough to make any difference. How many lives have been erected in a similar manner? Instead of building them on something solid, many in today's society will try all kinds of fads and gimmicks. They will spend precious time and energy compensating for a life that is not instituted on a firm foundation in the first place. Jesus said:

> Therefore everyone who hears these words of mine and puts them into practice is like a wise man who built his house on the rock. The rain came down, the streams rose, and the winds blew and beat against that house; yet it did not fall, because it had its foundation on the rock. But everyone who hears these words of mine and does not put them into practice is like a foolish man who built his house on sand. (Matthew 7:24–26 NIV)

Smart and successful Christians build their lives on the right foundation. Man tries to change life from the outside, hoping the inside will be altered. God changes it from the inside, and then the outside will ultimately be transformed. Scripture makes it clear that there is only one foundation possible for a sound spiritual life: "For no one can lay any foundation other than the one we already have—Jesus Christ" (1 Corinthians 3:11 NLT). The amount of renovation we can anticipate is reliant on one's degree of obedience to God's commands found in His Word. As we prepare to celebrate Christmas, many will strive for perfection in all they feel they must do to be ready for the big day. This mindset brings additional stress especially at this time of year, and it can only lead to arguments, discontent, and frustration. But in our day-to-day lives, we do not always seek that same level of perfection; nor are we able to attain it. But the very fact that we seek perfection is an indication of our longing for something beyond what this world provides. Ultimately, perfectionism leads us to failing in our own efforts to accomplish that which only God is able to do. And that, my friends, is why Jesus was sent into the world. The Lord does not change with the whims of culture; He sets the standard. A wise man once wrote: "Trust in the LORD with all your heart, and do not lean on your own understanding" (Proverbs 3:5 ESV). Build your life around the Word of God. It is as true today as when it was first written. If you take it into your heart and apply it to your life, you will discover a firm foundation that will always keep you leaning in the right direction.

Reflection

What factors in your life push you to lean in the wrong direction? In what ways might you be able to make time to build a stronger foundation for Christ? Are there activities this Christmas season which might allow you opportunities to implement these changes? Establish a plan to do just that!

DECEMBER 16
(Y7, D50)

The Gift of Our Worth

God sent his Son into the world not to judge the world, but to save the world through him.

—John 3:17 (NLT)

In the United States, the right to be counted is an important one. Each citizen who meets their state's residency requirements and is at least eighteen years of age is eligible to vote in elections. The issue of voting rights in the United States has, at times, been contested. For instance, women could not vote until 1920, after decades of protests and struggle by the Suffrage Movement. Until the Voting Rights Act of 1965 was signed into law, there were legal barriers at state and local levels preventing African Americans from exercising their right to vote. Individuals from both groups were simply not counted. There have also been other challenges in obtaining accurate counts. It is mandated that everyone living in the United States and its territories is counted through a census completed every ten years. The data collected by the census bureau determines the number of seats each state has in the US House of Representatives, and it is also used to distribute federal funds to local communities. According to the Constitution, all residents, regardless of citizenship status, are persons who must be counted. It is a challenge to do so.

Likewise, in the days prior to the birth of Jesus, "Roman emperor, Augustus, decreed that a census should be taken throughout the Roman Empire" (Luke 2:1). Scripture reveals that:

> All returned to their own ancestral towns to register for this census. And because Joseph was a descendant of King David, he had to go to Bethlehem in Judea, David's ancient home. He traveled there from the village of Nazareth in Galilee. He took with him Mary, to whom he was engaged, who was now expecting a child. And while they were there, the time came for her baby to be born. (Luke 2:3–6 NLT)

Other than the census, there was no reason for Joseph and Mary to be in Bethlehem at that particular time. Yet nearly eight centuries before, a prophet predicted that is exactly where the Messiah would be born. "But you, O Bethlehem Ephrathah, are only a small village among all the people of Judah. Yet a ruler of Israel, whose origins are in the distant past, will come from you on my behalf" (Micah 5:2 NLT). So it was time for all to declare, "Here I am," both the Son of God wrapped in swaddling clothes as well as all those who lived within the governance of the Roman Empire. They appeared on the scene to be counted, at least most of them.

The story of Jesus' birth unfolds among those who had worth, and in so doing, it rearranges a new sense of perception on who lacked it. If you grew up in a church, chances are that at one time, you may have had the opportunity to be a shepherd in a Christmas pageant. Unlike the roles of Mary and Joseph, the shepherds are not equal in importance as nativity story roles. Yet they are an essential part of the narrative. After all, it is the shepherds to whom an important announcement is made: "The Savior—yes, the Messiah, the Lord—has been born today in Bethlehem, the city of David" (Luke 2:11 NLT). An historical perspective reveals that most shepherds at the time of Jesus' arrival were not treated as desirable people. To be sure, their testimony would not necessarily have been considered to be reliable. Shepherds found themselves to be on the bottom rung of the social ladder, and shepherding had lost its widespread appeal. Some shepherds earned their poor reputations, but others became victims of cruel stereotypes. So there is great irony in the fact that a handful of shepherds, counted as nothing by the social and religious elite, were chosen to break the silence of centuries as they proclaimed the Messiah's birth.

Now therein lies a great contradiction; receiving the good news of Jesus' birth means opening our eyes and ears to receive those who seemingly don't count. Our value doesn't come from what we do or how perfect we are; it comes from God's valuation of us. Our self-worth is too often based on what other people say about us, but in reality, the one true authority on our self-worth is found in Jesus Christ. God demonstrated His extreme love for us by sending His Son into the world who would come to die for us. The birth of Jesus Christ at Christmas represents a gift of great value. However, it must be opened, received, and reflected in our lives as we acknowledge His sacrificial gift of our worth.

Reflection

Do you sometimes feel worthless? Or, at times, have you been slighted or treated as though you were of little value? How should we set a value upon each other's lives? Are we prepared to receive the testimonies of those who, in our opinion, shouldn't or just don't count?

DECEMBER 17
(Y1, D51)

There's Just Something about that Name

A good name is more desirable than great riches; to be esteemed is better than silver or gold.

—Proverbs 22:1 (NIV)

When my friend got word that the place where she worked for many years of her life was sold, she was somewhat upset. She had actually left this establishment for a while but had decided to return because she felt she had more to give. In many ways, it felt like she was coming home to this non-profit organization where its services had been utilized by thousands from the community. As a matter of fact, prior to its opening, the facility was named by a local resident who had participated in a selection contest. This was what upset my friend more than anything else. She could rationalize to some degree that the sale was purely a business decision. But she could not understand why the soon-to-be owner would institute a new name which appeared to be purely arbitrary, having nothing to do with the company itself. Names usually have purpose and meaning, but in this case, there appeared to be none.

While most names have significance, there appears to be a lack of deep thought in some instances. This was the situation of former boxer George Foreman who named each of his five sons George Edward Foreman. Although individually they have inherited their own nicknames, Foreman once said, "If you're going to get hit as many times as I've been hit, you're not going to remember many names." Yet, for countless individuals, our name will come to define us. When parents give a name to their child, it is usually chosen with much though and intention. Naming children in biblical times was important business. Names were not given to children just because they sounded good or because it was a popular name of the day. Names for children in past days had great significance and strong meaning. The names placed upon children had power to set a child's character or even their future. Regardless of when, why, or how often it happened, the giving and receiving of a name was an event of major importance.

Jesus is a Jewish name, Yeshua, which is derived from the word meaning "to rescue/deliver." When an angel of the Lord spoke to Joseph in a dream about Mary being with child, He was told "she will have a son, and you are to name him Jesus, for he will save his people from their sins" (Matthew 1:21 NLT). Therefore, Joseph named the child Jesus. There are times the name given at birth is only one of several names a person will bear throughout their life. This was the case of Jesus. Matthew describes Jesus as Immanuel, which means "God with us" (Matthew 1:23) because it highlights the essential truth that Jesus was indeed God himself dwelling with mankind. Additionally, Jesus was referred to as "the Christ" (John 1:41), the "Lamb of God" (John 1:29), the "Messiah" (Matthew 16:20), the "Light of the World" (John 8:12), the "Bread of Life" (John 6:35), and "the Good Shepherd" (John 10:11). In fact, Jesus also referred to Himself with many "I am" references, including "God's Son" (John 10:36), "the resurrection and the life" (John 11:25), "the way, and the truth, and the life" (John 14:6), and "the true vine" (John 15:1). Jesus is not just a name of unmatched humility; His name is glorified far above every other name.

Even today, many Christian parents bless their children with biblical names, perhaps as a sign of the spiritual heritage they hope for their offspring. Look at what Jesus promised to all who believe in Him: "I will give to each one a white stone, and on the stone will be engraved a new name that no one understands except the one who receives it" (Revelation 2:17 NIV). When God changes a name, it indicates that something new has happened or will happen to that person—a new relationship, a new character quality, or a new phase of life. Jesus is the name that shakes the foundations of heaven and earth, welcomes the stillness of peace into our minds, and the greatness of His love into our hearts. The name of Jesus makes the cold and darkness of winter pass and the pounding rains from the storms of life over and gone. His name shines the brightness of spring into our hearts bringing an end to our troubled winter. His name is the dew in the garden of our hearts that sprouts forth the roses of beauty and splendor with an elegant fragrance that draws us near unto Him. When we consider His entirety—Jesus, Jesus, Jesus—there is just something about the name that naturally flows from our lips.

Reflection

When we sing "All Hail the Power of Jesus' Name," what exactly does that mean to you? How does knowing the present-tense Christ help you to stay calm in the storms of life? As Christmas nears, in what ways might you help others to fully understand the light of Jesus in a dark world?

DECEMBER 18
(Y2, D51)

Now that Is Good News

How beautiful on the mountains are the feet of the messenger who brings good news,
the good news of peace and salvation, the news that the God of Israel reigns!

—Isaiah 52:7 (NLT)

"It was the best of times, it was the worst of times, it was the age of wisdom, it was the age of foolishness, it was the epoch of belief, it was the epoch of incredulity, it was the season of Light, it was the season of Darkness, it was the spring of hope, it was the winter of despair." These are the words of Charles Dickens in the opening of the novel, *A Tale of Two Cities*. This same language could easily be spoken by someone today. I have friends who intentionally don't watch the news, and even though I like to be aware of what's happening, I understand the feeling of sometimes just wanting to ignore the dismal and disheartening stories of today's world. The eleven o'clock news is no longer something you want to watch before you go to bed, and who wants to start your day with depressing stories of doom and gloom?

But once in a while, if you listen for it, you find a news release that restores your faith in humanity at least for a time. Such is the real-life narrative of a single mother in Central Pennsylvania who was informed last spring that she had terminal liver cancer. Facing the diagnosis was difficult enough, but her main concern was who would care for her eight-year-old son because she had no family who would be capable of raising him? So she asked her favorite nurse and the nurse's husband who had recently applied to become adoptive parents through the foster care system. As time progressed, the forty-five-year-old mother became weakened by the disease and treatment process. Her nurse not only made a home for the son but also for his mother, now her former patient. Together, they became a family. Although the prognosis was poor, it is believed the love and care received in their new home extended her life for months, including a wonderful summer vacation. Ultimately, the mother entered a hospice for her final days, but she was at peace knowing that her son was loved and would be well cared for.

Over two-thousand years ago, shepherds attending to their flock also heard some wonderful news.

> An angel of the Lord appeared to them, and the glory of the Lord shone around them, and they were terrified. But the angel said to them, "Do not be afraid. I bring you good news that will cause great joy for all the people. Today in the town of David a Savior has been born to you; he is the Messiah, the Lord. This will be a sign to you: You will find a baby wrapped in cloths and lying in a manger." (Luke 2:9–12 NIV)

As the baby Jesus grew into manhood, He began His mission here on earth. "But he said to them, 'I must preach the good news of the kingdom of God to the other towns as well; for I was sent for this purpose'" (Luke 4:43 ESV). The birth of our Lord Jesus Christ is the gospel, meaning "good news." As His followers, we have also been called to proclaim this gospel to others so that they might believe. "And then he told them, 'Go into all the world and preach the Good News to everyone'" (Mark 16:15 NLT).

So in a day when we so often hear the expression, "No news is good news," Max Lucado said it this way:

> Perhaps Jesus, the only Son of God, was born in a stable to give hope to all whose lives look like one. We sure do make a mess of things. Sometimes our actions stink. And though we try to make the best of it, the winter wind still sneaks into the corners of our lives, and the nights get cold and dark. Too many days too far from God? Too many years too hard on others? Too much mess? God knows…and he has some amazing words for you.

It should provide reassurance to know that those words are sometimes heard. For there was that day not so long ago when a mother asked someone to care for her child so that in her dying days, she might have hope and peace. Isn't it amazing that a similar story occurred thousands of years before? It was then recorded that an angel of God spoke to a young virgin, asking that she might care for His son, knowing that He would be the one to die in order that peace and everlasting hope would be brought into the hearts of all those who would believe. Different time and place but a parallel theme. Bottom line, both, my friends, are good news indeed!

Reflection

In a culture that is often preoccupied with negativity, in what ways do you strive to search for positive stories? How can the preparation for Christmas reassure us that the good news of the birth of Jesus supersedes the passage of time? During the celebrations ahead, are there opportunities to compare and affirm the good news of Jesus with the good news that can be found in today's world?

DECEMBER 19
(Y3, D51)

Finding Peace Once More at Christmas

The LORD gives his people strength; the LORD blesses them with peace.

—Psalm 29:11 (NLT)

A few years ago, a friend of mine and her teenage daughter sat at my kitchen table just a few weeks before Christmas. About a month later, my friend told me that her daughter, who was in her final year of high school, was pregnant. The mother went through many emotions ranging from anger to empathy, knowing how increasingly difficult her daughter's life might become if the child remained in her life. For a brief time, the option of giving up the baby for adoption was discussed. But no matter how complicated a newborn might change their lives, it was decided that the child would be welcomed and remain with this family. I must say when I first heard the news, my goal was to help my friend accept the situation and comfort her with the understanding that while this may have been a mistake on her daughter's part—God doesn't make mistakes. Now looking back, I think about how scared the daughter must have been halfway through her pregnancy knowing that soon not only her parents would be aware of her situation but it would also become very public. How she ever had peace that Christmas, I will never know.

Over two-thousand years ago, another teenage girl found herself with child. Although it was under very different circumstances than the daughter of my friend, she too must have been frightened. Scripture says that Mary was "greatly troubled" (Luke 1:29 NIV). "But the angel said to her, 'Do not be afraid, Mary; you have found favor with God'" (Luke 1:30 NIV). Mary felt acceptance, stating, "I am the Lord's servant. May everything you have said about me come true" (Luke 1:38 NLT). She had her own prayerful song of praise having found peace in her situation (Luke 1:46–55). Her husband, Joseph, also had to find his own peace because when he first found out Mary was pregnant, "he had in mind to divorce her quietly" (Matthew 1:19 NIV). But an angel of the Lord appeared to him in a dream explaining that he should not be afraid to take Mary home as his wife, "For the child within her was conceived by the Holy Spirit. And she will have a son, and you are to name him Jesus, for he will save his people from their sins" (Matthew 1:20–22). So Joseph did what the angel asked of him.

Finding peace in our lives can at times be very difficult, especially when one is engaged in any battle. On Christmas eve over a hundred years ago in the midst of a world war, it is reported that thousands of British, Belgian, and French soldiers stepped out of their trenches and spent Christmas in a truce mingling with their German enemies. It is written that it all began with carol singing first from one side and then the other, each melodiously sharing the familiar tunes in their own language. The next morning, German soldiers emerged from their trenches saying, "Merry Christmas" in English while Allied soldiers hesitantly came out of hiding to greet them. Gifts such as cigarettes and chocolate bars were exchanged, and some say makeshift soccer games and other signs of human comradery broke out. While it was only a truce, it proves that the wars of our nations are about the ideologies of those in control while the greater power finds its place in the hearts of mankind who desires peace and goodwill for all.

What is the battle that is preventing you from finding peace this Christmas? Are you my neighbor who is lying in a hospital bed, waiting for an answer as to how your recently diagnosed cancer will be treated? Are you my work colleague who was given notice that if the financial situation doesn't improve in the new year, he will be the first of many to be laid off? Or are you like the lady I visited this week who is only a few birthdays away from a hundred, wondering whether your life still has purpose? My prayer is that each of you will find your own path to the manger this Christmas. There you will be introduced to the Prince of Peace (Isaiah 9:6). In a world filled with turmoil, each of us struggles to find peace along our own journey, no matter what the conflict. But like my friend who describes her new granddaughter as "the light" of their family, the baby Jesus would years later refer to Himself as the light of the world (John 8:12). As we grow closer and walk with Him daily, we will hear the angels say once more, "Glory to God in highest heaven, and peace on earth to those with whom God is pleased" (Luke 2:14 NLT).

Reflection

Are you allowing God to work within you in accomplishing His will or are you fighting through a situation, finding you are distancing from Him? How might you renew your relationship with the Savior so that you can experience the peace that passes all understanding (Philippians 4:7)?

DECEMBER 20
(Y4, D51)

Joy and Sorrow

When they saw the star, they were filled with joy!

—Matthew 2:10 (NLT)

As I sat in the home of a friend who was dying, I doubted very much if he would make it until Christmas. Becoming engaged in conversation with his spouse as he went in and out of consciousness, I learned that his brother was also terminally ill. Here was a family soon to be filled with sorrow. On my prayer list, there are at least a dozen families who will be going through their first Christmas without a loved one. The Christmas season has become a difficult time for many in our society, prompting one to ask the question, is sorrow more plentiful at this time of year? Or are we just more conscious of it? According to the National Institute of Health, during Christmas, people experience a high incidence of depression. For those of us who don't have these difficulties at present, it certainly provides an opportunity to reach out. Those who do so will discover that "real joy comes not from ease or riches or from the praise of people, but from doing something worthwhile" (Wilfred T. Grenfell).

One would think that joy and sorrow are polar opposites. However, it seems more like they are close-knit companions with one taking dominance over the other. Just as we can't appreciate the light if we haven't spent time in darkness, joy and sorrow are much the same way. One thing is true: each of us has those days and moments when we must look a little harder to see the joy scattered within our sorrow. But joy is there, and we can always find it again. We just need to know where to look. Ultimately, we may learn that it is impossible to know joy unless we go through periods of sorrow. Whenever we seek God's direction during our suffering, we often see Him more clearly, and our joy is made full. Consider this thought from Philip Bernstein: "We have no right to ask when sorrow comes, 'Why did this happen to me?' unless we ask the same question for every joy that comes our way."

This story is told in a 1980 excerpt *Our Daily Bread*. Many years ago, a Salvation Army officer was preaching in Chicago when a man spoke out in front of the crowd, "You can talk about how

Christ is dear to you, but if your wife were dead, as my wife is, and you had babies crying for their mother, you couldn't say what you are saying." A few days later, that preacher's wife was killed in a tragic train accident. At the funeral service, the grieving husband stood beside her casket and said, "The other day when I was preaching in this city, a man said that if my wife were dead and my children were crying for their mother, I couldn't say that Christ was sufficient. If that man is here, I'd tell him that Christ is sufficient! My heart is crushed, bleeding, and broken. But there is also a song in my heart, and Christ put it there. The Savior speaks comfort to me today." The man who had raised the objection was present, and he surrendered his life to Christ.

"And the angel said to them, 'Fear not, for behold, I bring you good news of great joy that will be for all the people. For unto you is born this day in the city of David a Savior, who is Christ the Lord'" (Luke 2:10–11 ESV). This was the best possible news, for we who trust that Jesus holds our future and for those who have died in the Lord, His birth will always be "good news." Late in His ministry when His time had come, Jesus told His disciples that He would turn their sorrow into joy. By using the analogy of a woman in labor, He said: "She forgets the anguish because of her joy that a child is born into the world" (John 16:21 NIV). Paul reflected a similar message when he stated, "Yet what we suffer now is nothing compared to the glory he will reveal to us later" (Romans 8:18 NLT). The Messiah also needed first to suffer and then enter His glory for the sake of His kingdom. By doing so, He prepared a place for each of us where pain and sorrow is relieved and only joy remains for all of eternity. If you believe that, you have captured a true understanding of why love came down at Christmas. Like the Magi, we too should be filled with joy every time we think of that star over Bethlehem (Matthew 2:9–10).

Reflection

Think of a time when you experienced great sorrow and then found renewed joy. If you were asked to define biblical joy to someone, what would you say? How might you be able to help another person begin to search for joy in the midst of their sorrow this Christmas?

DECEMBER 21
(Y5, D51)

Divine Interruption

Therefore the Lord himself will give you a sign: The virgin will conceive
and give birth to a son, and will call him Immanuel.

—Isaiah 7:14 (NIV)

It was Black Friday, the busiest shopping day of the year. I was checking online for the prices of TVs, trying to decide if I had the best price or whether I should wait until Cyber Monday. Finally, I decided to go for it, and I placed my order with a large retailer that deals in electronics. Immediately, I received an email confirmation and was able to arrange my delivery date through the website. I chose December 5, between 8:00 a.m. and noon. On December 4, I received an email reminder stating, "We'll see you tomorrow." On December 5, I woke up to receive another email. Guess what it said? "Today is the day." It wasn't long until I got a phone call from the company, giving me their estimated delivery time. I no sooner hung up the phone when I noticed an email in my inbox stating, "You can expect Matthew to arrive at approximately 10:35 a.m." About a half hour later, I looked at my watch. It was just after 10:30, and almost like a little child expecting Santa, off to the window I flew like a flash. There he was, pulling up in front of my house. Santa? No, Matthew, of course, with my package just as I expected.

In these days of instant notification, we can track our pizza delivery order being fulfilled or we can find the location of our online order and its projected appearance at our front door. Likewise, young children are able to use the NORAD tracker to find out exactly how much time remains before Santa leaves the North Pole. In the case of my TV delivery, everything worked just like clockwork with nothing left to the imagination. The anticipation of my Christmas gift had been fulfilled. The first Christmas, however, was a bit different. The testimony of the Old Testament prophets provided a long history of faithfulness that the Jewish people would at some future point receive their long-awaited promise of a Messiah (Isaiah 9:6; Jeremiah 23:5; Micah 5:2). This was followed by four-hundred years during which the prophets appear to be silent. Then, one day, a teenage girl by the name of Mary experienced a divine interruption when an angel appeared to her (Luke 1:26-38).

Mary's response was not only humble, it was also courageous. When Joseph discovered his betrothed was with child, who would not have questioned how God would have anything to do with this sudden turn of events? It was an interruption for certain to the matrimony plans he was anticipating. He could have been bitter, yet through his faith, God assured him that this child would bless mankind and "save His people from their sins" (Matthew 1:21 NIV).

If somewhere in your lifetime you experienced a divine interruption, then you are in remarkable company. Selected individuals in God's Word were simply leading normal lives which were deliberately interrupted to fulfill a greater purpose. The Apostle Paul said, "And we know that in all things God works for the good of those who love him, who have been called according to his purpose" (Romans 8:28 NIV). Joel Osteen stated it this way:

> We all have times when our plans don't work out. We get delayed, interrupted and inconvenienced. It's easy to get frustrated and fight against everything that doesn't go our way. But, not every interruption is bad. Every closed door doesn't mean you're doing something wrong. Every delay doesn't mean you're not where you're supposed to be... The next time you're interrupted, delayed or inconvenienced, don't start thinking, *This is a pain. This is getting me off schedule.* No, get a new perspective. Look for what God wants to do, because it could be divine interruption or divine protection. Trust Him today because He is directing your steps.

Christmas is a time for remembering the greatest interruption which ever occurred. After all, the small hands of the innocent Christ-child born in a stable in Bethlehem were the same ones which only a few decades later would be nailed to a cross on Calvary as He fulfilled His mission as the Savior for all mankind. Like Jesus, when we surrender to God's interruptions, we can rest in the knowledge that He always has a higher purpose for us. Little do we sometimes know that when our lives are divinely interrupted, what may appear as a tragic ending may only serve to become a beautiful beginning.

Reflection

Can you attest to having experienced a divine interruption at some point in your life? How did you become a different person as a result? Or have you drifted back into your old self? Are there ways that you might cause your own interruption to start anew this Christmas and serve Him more profoundly?

DECEMBER 22
(Y6, D51)

One Silent Night

He came and preached peace to you who were far away and peace to those who were near.

—Ephesians 2:17 (NIV)

Our family recently received an animated e-card from an old friend. It portrayed characters passing the light of a candle one to the other with a hymn playing in the background, just as many will experience on Christmas Eve. A personalized message from our friend at the end said, "Sending you one of my favorite songs to wish you Merry Christmas." The song "Silent Night" has become one of the most cherished Christmas carols of all time. It was first performed on Christmas Eve, 1818, at St. Nicholas parish church in Oberndorf, a village in Austria. A young priest, Father Joseph Mohr, had come there one year earlier. He had written the lyrics of the song "Stille Nacht" in 1816. Mohr brought his words to Franz Gruber, a musician friend, and asked him to compose a melody and guitar accompaniment for that year's Christmas Eve mass. According to Gruber, an organ builder and repairman was enamored with the song after he heard it performed, and he took a copy of the composition home with him. From there, the carol began an unexpected journey as it slowly circulated around the world. Because the original document had been lost, Mohr's name was forgotten, and it was assumed the melody was compiled by one of the many famous composers of that era. It was not until 1995 that a manuscript was discovered in Mohr's handwriting confirming that he wrote the lyrics in 1816—a poem about the night when angels announced the birth of the long-awaited Messiah to shepherds on a hillside.

We sometimes forget that God moves powerfully in quiet, humble settings. Perhaps He sent the gentle whisper of an angel to allure the emotion of an organ repairman with a new song who sent it on a journey and into the hearts of people everywhere. Its words flowed from the imagination of a modest poet. The music was composed by a musician who was not known outside his village. However, there was no celebrity to sing at its world premiere. In that same quiet manner, God stepped into our world through a baby born in an obscure village. It was there that a host of angels praised Him from the heavens before a group of unnoticeable shepherds delivering a powerful message of heavenly peace (Luke 2:13–14). We must never be surprised to learn that when God is involved in the details, we should come to expect the unexpected. Consider that Joseph, a humble carpenter, and Mary would have barely had enough money to make the round trip from Nazareth to Bethlehem to register for the census (Luke 2:1–5). Unpredictably, their plans changed when "an angel of the Lord appeared to Joseph in a dream. 'Get up, ' he said, 'take the child and his mother and escape to Egypt. Stay there until I tell you, for Herod is going to search for the child to kill him'" (Matthew 2:13 NIV). One might logically ask the question as to how they could have afforded this unexpected trip? But don't forget! They were given three gifts from the Magi, otherwise known as the wise men. While their gifts had spiritual significance, they were also practical and would have had financial value. It would have been easy to exchange gold, and the aromatic spices could have been sold at market. Some scholars believe these gifts were simply God's provision for the funds which would have been needed to flee to Egypt and to begin raising a baby in a foreign land. However it occurred, be assured it was quietly touched and directed by an angel from God.

So often, our Christmas celebrations are anything but silent. There was undoubtedly some commotion as well on that first Christmas night. Anyone who has experienced the miracle of child-birth knows there can be a lot of noise involved in welcoming a newborn into the world. It's beautiful, even sacred, but it is not quiet, while in many ways, this was an ordinary family in an ordinary town tucked away in a very ordinary stable. And yet there was nothing ordinary about this birth, this night, or this boy. If we dare to take time to retreat from our personal chaos and imagine what it would have been like to join the shepherds at the manger, then perhaps we will hear a new call to silence. He sings our souls to sleep and gives us rest in the peace only He can provide. And when we wake in the morning, we will once again meet the dawn of redeeming grace, all because of a precious birth one silent night.

Reflection

When, if at all, have you experienced silence in your celebrations of Christmas? Why is finding silence an appropriate response to God's holiness? What changes might you have to make in your holiday traditions in order to find the peace and silence necessary to find the true reason for the season?

DECEMBER 23
(Y7, D51)

Who Are We in Yonder Stall?

And she gave birth to her firstborn son and wrapped him in swaddling cloths
and laid him in a manger, because there was no place for them in the inn.

—Luke 2:7 (ESV)

Over the past few Christmases, I have developed a fondness for the song, "Who Is He in Yonder Stall?" It was written by Benjamin Russell Hanby who, in addition to being a composer, was also an educator and a pastor. He is said to have written about eighty songs in his brief thirty-three years, including "Up on the House Top" and "Jolly Old Saint Nicholas." In 1866, a year before he died, he penned the words to his final song. Often sung as a musical response to a series of questions, each is followed by the answer in this refrain: "'Tis the Lord, O wondrous story! 'Tis the Lord, the King of glory! At His feet we humbly fall, Crown Him, crown Him Lord of all!" In years past, the hymn was often utilized by those who taught children in the church because it so visibly outlined the key aspects of the life of Jesus. If like me you escaped remembering this hymn while growing up, no doubt you were exposed to Christmas pageants, most of them ending with a nativity play. As a child, you would perhaps feel honored if you were chosen to represent one of the main characters.

Consider as an adult if you were asked to play a role in a live nativity, what persona would you need to assume to be Joseph? He usually stands quietly next to the manger, almost playing a secondary part in the story. Far from being a minor character, he was a silent hero demonstrating courage, despite facing personal embarrassment and societal ostracism. He believed God and thus cared for his young fiancé who was carrying a child that was not his own. Joseph "did what the angel of the Lord had commanded him and took Mary home as his wife" (Matthew 1:24 NIV). He was a rugged and brave man whom God chose to lead her safely along the dangerous roads to Bethlehem, Egypt, and eventually back home to Israel. God selected Joseph to protect the infant Jesus in the dangerous first years of his life.

Might you be Mary? She gives us a wonderful example of how to respond to the seemingly impossible circumstances of life. She was a young ordinary Jewish girl, looking forward to marriage.

715

Suddenly, her life would forever change. As a virgin who is told she will give birth to the "Son of God" (Luke 1:35), she demonstrates a willingness to listen, believe, and be used in a situation in which she found "favor with God" (Luke 1:30). Her response: "I am the Lord's servant... May your word to me be fulfilled" (Luke 1:38 NIV). Although Mary's calling held great honor, it would demand great suffering too. There would be pain in the privilege of being the mother of the Messiah.

So if not Mary, you might be requested to portray one of the Magi. What we know about them is that they came bearing precious gifts (Matthew 2:11). They had seen an unusual star in the sky and knew that it told of the birth of a special king in Israel (Matthew 2:6, 9). As "wise men" indeed, they traveled a great distance to worship the one about whom they would have gained knowledge from religious prophecy. Although their presence is depicted in most nativity scenes, biblical scholars believe that they caught up with Jesus and His parents sometime later. They are, however, a somewhat fascinating addition to the Christmas story because their presence indicates that Jesus wasn't born as Savior only for the Jews. Rather, He had come as the Savior for the entire world.

That leaves the shepherds who are included in every nativity display. Today, we embrace them as key characters in the story of Jesus' birth, yet at that time, they would have been viewed as culturally insignificant. Unlike the Magi, they did not have exquisite gifts to offer the Christ-child. Receptive to the good news delivered from an angel, they decided to go immediately and see for themselves (Luke 2:15). Later, they become God's messengers, for "when they had seen him, they spread the word concerning what had been told them about this child" (Luke 2:17). You might identify most with the shepherds for they represent those who are frequently overlooked, whom Jesus would later refer to as "the least of these" (Matthew 25:40). They are those who oftentimes come to understand Him the best. For they know the answer to the question: "Who is He in yonder stall...at whose feet the shepherds fall?"

Reflection

How does Joseph's decision to please God rather than men give you pause for consideration in your own life? Can you be like Mary and accept God's plan for your future, knowing it could cost you dearly? If you were asked to be one of the Magi, what gift would you bring to share with Him? How could you be more like the shepherds through sharing the story of Christ's birth with others?

DECEMBER 24
(Y1, D52)

Seeing the Face of God

Blessed are the pure in heart, for they shall see God.

—Matthew 5:8 (ESV)

While at a mall a number of years ago, four-year-old Spencer saw kids lined up to see Santa Claus. Having been taught as a toddler that Christmas is the holiday that Christians celebrate the birth of Jesus, he asked his mom, "Where's the line to see Jesus?" His mom mentioned this to her father who immediately became inspired and quickly jotted down words to a song. After putting music to the words and doing a home recording, he received a great response from friends. Then he sent the song off to Nashville and received feedback from a Christian song writer. It took an investment of time and energy, but eventually, Becky Kelley (Spencer's aunt) recorded the song. Having seen it on YouTube, thousands of Christians came together to remember the true meaning of Christmas. Becky stated, "Hopefully, Spencer's observation will cause people all over to reflect on the love of Jesus and that one day we will all stand in line to see Him." At the time of Jesus birth, there certainly was no line to see Him. The exception was a few lowly shepherds and some Magi who later came along. But because of what happened in a stable at Bethlehem, God had a face. It was there that a remarkable gift arrived in an unremarkable package. No one expected God to come the way he did. Yet the way He came was every bit as important as the coming itself. The season leading up to that first Christmas certainly wasn't what Mary hoped for, but it was a miracle in the making. In spite of and out of Mary's chaos and hardships, Christ came. At the most unexpected time and place, Mary saw the face of God in baby Jesus.

In his book, *Because of Bethlehem Love Is Born, Hope Is Here*, Max Lucado shares a story about Dr. George Harley who founded a medical mission among the Mano tribe of Liberia in 1926. The locals were receptive to the doctor and helped him construct a clinic and a chapel. During the first five years, not one person from the tribe visited his chapel. The Harleys young son, Bobby, grew up on the edge of a forest familiar to the natives. Shortly before turning five, he developed a tropical fever. Dr. Harley tried every treatment he knew, but the disease took his life, leaving his parents distraught with grief. After building a coffin in his workshop, the missionary went out to find a place to bury his son. One of the old men in the village saw him and asked about the box he carried. When Harley explained that his son had died, the man offered to help him. They eventually found an appropriate clearing in the forest. Realizing he was 8,000 miles from home and relatives, Harley sank to his knees and began to weep. The elder was stunned in amazement and for a long time sat there, listening to Harley cry. Then, suddenly, he leaped to his feet and went running back up the trail through the jungle, screaming at the top of his voice, "White man—he cries like one of us!" That evening, there was a knock at the door of his cottage. Harley opened it to find the chief and almost every man, woman, and child in the village. The next Sunday, they overfilled the chapel. Lucado states, "Everything changed when the villagers saw the tears of the missionary, just like everything changes for us when we see the face of God."

Toward the end of His ministry, one of Jesus' disciples (Philip) said to Him:

> "Lord, show us the Father, and we will be satisfied." Jesus replied, "Have I been with you all this time, Philip, and yet you still don't know who I am? Anyone who has seen me has seen the Father! So why are you asking me to show him to you? Don't you believe that I am in the Father and the Father is in me? The words I speak are not my own, but my Father who lives in me does his work through me." (John 14:8–10 NLT)

We must understand that what seems to be quite blurred at times will one day become crystal clear. Faith will become sight when one day we, too, will see Him face-to-face. "For God, who said, "Let there be light in the darkness," has made this light shine in our hearts so we could know the glory of God that is seen in the face of Jesus Christ'" (2 Corinthians 4:6 NLT). During these final days before Christmas, we might look closer to recognize the true presence of Christ in the persons we encounter and are called to serve. If we pause and look closely enough, we might just see the face of God.

Reflection

When you find yourself waiting a in long checkout line or perhaps to see Santa, would you consider waiting in one to see a nativity scene? As you reflect on both your hopes and the difficulties you are facing at this time, might you respond like Mary to the idea that your circumstances could be a miracle in the making, leading you in some way to seeing the face of God?

DECEMBER 25
(Y2, D52)

And That's My Final Answer

But to all who believed him and accepted him, he gave the right to become children of God.

—John 1:12 (NLT)

Many of you will recognize the title of this devotion as the tagline from the game show, *Who Wants to Be a Millionaire?* In this game show studio, contestants are seated opposite the host and answer multiple-choice questions with increasing difficulty and value, leading up to the ultimate one-million-dollar question. As they consider four possible answers to the questions, they can walk away anytime. The contestant has three one-time lifelines available to them—phone a friend, fifty-fifty, or they can ask the audience. As they eliminate their options and make a selection, the host asks, "Is that your final answer?" The player must respond affirmatively in order to "lock it in." When the contestant responds "final answer," there is no turning back, and their fate is sealed. By successfully answering all the questions, he or she wins the jackpot of one million dollars. It is easy to identify with the contestants on this show because most are common people forced into a position to make daily choices just like you and me.

What would your answer be if God intervened with this host at the end of your life to ask one final question: "Why should God let you into heaven?" The potential answers provided are: (A) I tried to live a good life; (B) I grew up in church; (C) Jesus is God's Son; (D) Jesus is my Savior. Before we leave this world, God needs to be certain of our answer. As you consider your response, we are reminded of a particular passage of Scripture when Jesus asks his disciples, "'Who do people say the Son of Man is?' They replied, 'Some say John the Baptist; others say Elijah; and still others, Jeremiah or one of the prophets.' 'But what about you?' he asked. 'Who do you say I am?' Simon Peter answered, 'You are the Messiah, the Son of the living God'" (Matthew 16:13–16 NIV). When it comes to our relationship with Jesus, we cannot poll the audience or phone a friend. Although those are helpful tools in seeking spiritual advice and wise counsel, at the end of your lifetime, only you can give the final answer to this question.

There are questions that both the Christian and the skeptic will likely ponder at some point in their lives. Young and old, rich and poor, male and female will all ask themselves, "Does God really love me no matter what? How long will His love endure? Is there anything that can separate me from His love?" One of the beauties of Christmas is that God answered these questions before we could even ask them. He lit the night sky with a star so that we would see His answer. To make sure we heard it, He sent a choir of angels to pierce the silence, filling the crevices of uncertainty with hope. And so that we would believe His answer, God did what no one could have ever imagined—He became flesh and dwelt among us. From the beginning of Creation, He has desired a personal relationship with each of us. He loves us no matter what, and His love endures forever. The miracle of Christmas is not only that God loves us but that He also made a way for us to love Him. He provided the gift of that sweet baby in the manger as our way to Him. Jesus' birth was God implementing his plan to save us. It was the start of the biggest miracle ever, and it culminated in the biggest "I love you" statement of all time.

The Apostle Paul stated it like this:

> He gave up his divine privileges; he took the humble position of a slave and was born as a human being. When he appeared in human form, he humbled himself in obedience to God and died a criminal's death on a cross. Therefore, God elevated him to the place of highest honor and gave him the name above all other names, that at the name of Jesus every knee should bow, in heaven and on earth and under the earth, and every tongue declare that Jesus Christ is Lord, to the glory of God the Father. (Philippians 2:7–11 NLT)

If you can honestly say that Jesus is your Savior and the Lord of your life, then you should praise Him today. If you have any other answer, there is still time to change it. If you have never trusted Jesus as Lord and Savior, you should know that He is your one and only lifeline. If you feel Him calling you, now is the perfect time. At this moment, you may be wondering, "What should I do with Jesus?" However, one day, the question will be, "What will Jesus do with me?" So the next time someone asks one of those unanswerable questions about faith, just look them straight in the eye and tell them, "I don't know, but God knows…and that's my final answer."

Reflection

Who is Jesus to you? Do you declare His authority as the Son of the Living God and your Savior? How would you explain Jesus as God's way of seeking a personal relationship with you? When we celebrate Christmas, why is it difficult to forget His ultimate sacrifice and resurrection at Easter?

DECEMBER 26
(Y3, D52)

Standing at the Door

Here I am! I stand at the door and knock. If anyone hears
my voice and opens the door, I will come in.

—Revelation 3:20 (NIV)

The concept of doors can be fascinating to explore. They were certainly made popular on the game show *Let's Make a Deal* where contestants frequently got to choose from three blind-panel doors, at least one of them containing a nice prize. Behind the other doors, there were often surprises encompassing less desirable items. During one Christmas season, I enjoyed watching the reaction of people who were shopping as I would courteously hold the store entrance door open for them. It's always interesting to see who expresses appreciation. While it is not unusual for an older person to pause to say "Thank you," sometimes a person younger than myself smiles and nods as if to say, "I should be holding the door for you." On one occasion, as I was leaving a store, I held the door open for a lady who appeared to have her hands full. She passed through, and so did at least four children, none of them offering to give me as much as the time of day while I delayed in their behalf. Oh well, my purpose was to express a caring attitude toward others, and I must admit, it has also become a bit of a social experiment as well.

I have personally used the analogy of a door in many situations. A frequent example I can recall is when someone asks me if they should go for a job interview. I will often find myself saying, "Why not walk through the door? If the interview doesn't go well, then you will probably forfeit the opportunity, and the door will close. However, if you are offered the position, then you have the choice to close the door by refusing the job or you can pass through it again in acceptance." In other words, what does one really have to lose in a situation like that? If it was a different set of circumstances like a marriage which required a binding commitment, I'm sure my advice would not be quite so relaxed.

Jesus said, "I am the door. If anyone enters by me, he will be saved and will go in and out and find pasture" (John 10:9). He is making it clear that the path to eternal life is His alone. He *is* the way, the only door to salvation, enabling us to live without fear and remorse. He uses the familiar imagery of a shepherd guarding the entrance to a pen in the countryside or at a public sheepfold in a town where the flock would be herded at night for protection.

> Truly, truly, I say to you, he who does not enter the sheepfold by the door but climbs in by another way, that man is a thief and a robber. But he who enters by the door is the shepherd of the sheep. To him the gatekeeper opens. The sheep hear his voice, and he calls his own sheep by name and leads them out. When he has brought out all his own, he goes before them, and the sheep follow him, for they know his voice. A stranger they will not follow, but they will flee from him, for they do not know the voice of strangers. (John 10:1–5 ESV)

As we move on from another Christmas and begin a New Year, our world does not offer much optimism and harmony. We have every right to sometimes be afraid. Then somewhere along our path, we remember a stable in Bethlehem where God sent His son Jesus, who the Prophet Isaiah referred to as Immanuel, meaning "God is with us" (Isaiah 7:14 NLT). That, my friends, is the purpose of Christmas. Jesus came to offer hope and peace to a world which might otherwise serve to destroy us. He gave us the gift of protection so that we might come to know Him for all of eternity. We have this assurance: "I know your works. Behold, I have set before you an open door, which no one is able to shut. I know that you have but little power, and yet you have kept my word and have not denied my name" (Revelation 3:8). As Christ fulfilled the will of God, so do we who journey with Him in faith. Like the sheep guarded by the shepherd, we can be certain that we are secure in all His purposes and plans as we turn the calendar for another New Year. He stands at the door and knocks (Revelation 3:20 ESV). Will you answer?

Reflection

Consider the many doors (both physical and spiritual) you have walked through in your life. Which of those have provided an opportunity for a positive outcome? Which ones have been lasting? How can you use the concept of doors to encourage others who appear to be indecisive about decision-making?

DECEMBER 27
(Y4, D52)

New and Improved

Do not remember the former things. Nor consider the things of old. Behold, I
will do a new thing. Now it shall spring forth. Shall you not know it?

—Isaiah 43:18–19 (NKJV)

Just a few months before, he publicly announced that he had been diagnosed with brain cancer. Then after a series of radiation treatments and undoubtedly a great deal of prayer, he was later able to state that he was cancer-free. Now the former president of the United States, standing in the presence of members of his church, delivered the news that his twenty-eight-year-old grandson had passed away the day before. Although visibly shaken, our thirty-ninth president, Jimmy Carter, then went on to teach the Sunday School lesson he had prepared. Known to be a devout Christian, he urged the congregation to "be filled with a sense of joy and thanksgiving" despite his own personal family tragedy. What did the former President recognize that many others do not? Maybe he understood the full impact of the message of the Apostle Paul when he said, "Therefore we do not lose heart. Though outwardly we are wasting away, yet inwardly we are being renewed day by day" (2 Corinthians 4:16 NIV).

Did you ever notice how many people seem to be going through a tough time in their lives at Christmas? I have often wondered whether things happen with greater frequency or if our sensitivity to care just increases at this time of the year. In the midst of what many experience as holiday cheer, going through a difficult situation can be very frightening and disconcerting, especially for those who do not truly understand "the reason for the season." When we are faced with having to let go of the comfort and familiarity of what we know, feelings of depression and loss of hope can surface as we are challenged by the prospect of having to embrace the unknown. But there is a new beginning that we will come to regard as a blessing, sometimes undeserved but always welcome. If we have journeyed to the manger this Christmas, we found it in the presence of the Christ child who came to earth to offer Himself as a living sacrifice for each of us. We come to understand: "Therefore, if anyone is in Christ, he is a new creation. The old has passed away; behold, the new has come" (2 Corinthians 5:17 ESV).

Our society offers a vision that many times clouds the judgment of an already confused world. In a variety of forums, advertisers try to fool us with catchphrases such as "new and improved." How can that be? If something is new, we have not experienced it before. If it is improved, then it's just a revision of what already existed. It cannot be both. There is only one presence who can make that claim, and He is reflected in the arrival as the long-awaited Messiah. Through His gift of salvation, He offers us a new covenant as He becomes a living sacrifice for our sinfulness. And He promises that there will come a day in which "He will wipe away every tear from their eyes; and there will no longer be any death; there will no longer be any mourning, or crying, or pain; the first things have passed away. And He who sits on the throne said, 'Behold, I am making all things new'" (Revelation 21:4–5 NASB).

At the beginning of a calendar year, some people make resolutions. Perhaps you are one of those. For many, the start of a new year seems to be a time to wipe the slate clean. We vow to give up bad habits, go on a diet, or otherwise change our ways. Let's face it, resolutions can only go so far. The heartache and pain that many folks feel at this time of year are not going to somehow instantly change by the flipping of a page. At the threshold of the New Year, let us make our first resolution to hear those words of extraordinary promise which began in a manger in Bethlehem. Then we will experience a precious transformation leading to new hope, new joy, and new life. Henry Ward Beecher once said, "Every man should be born again on the first day of January. Start with a fresh page." Like Jimmy Carter, I think he understood the true essence of the fact that "new and improved" can only be found when we invite Jesus to take up residence in our hearts and in our homes so that we can indeed begin anew.

Reflection

What plans will you put in place to make sure that Jesus is part of each day of the New Year? If you know someone who is facing a difficult time, in what ways can you help them find purpose? How might you lead them on a path in search of Jesus to find a new and improved life?

DECEMBER 28
(Y5, D52)

Worthy and Lasting Praise

Praise him for his mighty deeds; praise him according to his excellent greatness!

—Psalm 150:2 (ESV)

When I once went to visit the grieving parents of a young man who had died, I recalled the last words I had shared with him. They were "I am proud of you" verbalized on the occasion of another relative's passing when he had spoken quite eloquently. He seemed pleased to receive my praise. As I remembered, it also made me happy that those words were the final ones I would have spoken to him. However humble we might profess to be, we all like to be the recipients of heartfelt praise acknowledging those things we have done well. God loves it, too, when we express our adoration and gratitude to Him for His creation. When we praise God, it enhances our fellowship with Him by indicating that we understand and value the power of His presence over our lives. "Through Jesus, therefore, let us continually offer to God a sacrifice of praise—the fruit of lips that openly profess his name" (Hebrews 13:15 NIV).

In her book, *In My Father's House*, Corrie Ten Boom told a story about an old monk who sang every Christmas Eve for all the monks in the monastery as well as for the visitors who would come from the village for the special services. The monk's voice was unpolished. But he loved the Lord and truly sang from his heart. One year, the director of the cloister said, "I'm sorry, Brother, we will not need you to sing this Christmas Eve. We have a new monk who has a marvelous voice."

The new monk sang stunningly, and everyone was happy. But later that night, an angel came to the superior and said, "Why didn't you have a Christmas Eve song?"

The superior was very surprised. "We had a beautiful song that was inspirational. Didn't you hear it?"

The angel shook his head sadly. "It may have been inspiring to you, but we did not hear it in heaven. The old monk with the raspy voice had Christ in his heart, and he sings from his heart. The young monk was singing for his own benefit."

We can't expect the entire world to celebrate their feelings about Christmas in the same way, but we can pray that somehow the true heart of Christmas might help them to understand what God has done for them. Simeon understood the significance of Jesus birth when, after forty days, Joseph and Mary entered the temple in accordance with the Law of Moses. Scripture shares:

> At that time there was a man in Jerusalem named Simeon. He was righteous and devout and was eagerly waiting for the Messiah to come and rescue Israel. The Holy Spirit was upon him and had revealed to him that he would not die until he had seen the Lord's Messiah. That day the Spirit led him to the Temple. So when Mary and Joseph came to present the baby Jesus to the Lord as the law required, Simeon was there. He took the child in his arms and praised God, saying, "Sovereign Lord, now let your servant die in peace, as you have promised. I have seen your salvation, which you have prepared for all people. He is a light to reveal God to the nations, and he is the glory of your people Israel!" (Luke 2:25–32 NLT)

In some Christian traditions, a remembrance of this meeting (known as Candlemas) is celebrated each February.

Simeon provides a note of hope and expectation. His praise makes a pronouncement that the baby Jesus, whom he held in his arms, was God's promise fulfilled. It is unmistakably clear that the Wise Men also understood who He was when they shared their gifts in praise. "After Jesus was born in Bethlehem in Judea, during the time of King Herod, Magi from the east came to Jerusalem and asked, 'Where is the one who has been born king of the Jews? We saw his star when it rose and have come to worship him'" (Matthew 2:1–2 NIV). Without a doubt, the chosen twelve spoke of praise for who He was. Peter, one who was closest to Jesus, said, "If anyone speaks, they should do so as one who speaks the very words of God. If anyone serves, they should do so with the strength God provides, so that in all things God may be praised through Jesus Christ" (1 Peter 4:11 NIV). As we celebrate Christmas with great food, presents, and parties, it is important that we move beyond the tinsel. When we get to that heart of the events surrounding Jesus' birth, we find deep significance of how God chose to orchestrate His coming into our world. Then we will come to realize that the praise we give for Jesus will always be worthy and lasting.

Reflection

When you think about your Christmas traditions, how many of them are done for your benefit as opposed to those reserved for praising God? In what ways could you consider reprioritizing how you celebrate the birth of Jesus? How might you invite others to join you in your praise revisions?

DECEMBER 29
(Y6, D52)

New Light

He came as a witness to testify concerning that light, so that through him all might believe.

—John 1:7 (NIV)

Though Thomas Edison is usually credited with the invention of the light bulb, the famous American inventor wasn't the only one who contributed to the development of this revolutionary technology. The first incandescent lamp had been produced forty years earlier, but no inventor had been able to come up with a practical design until Edison embraced the challenge in the late 1870s. After countless tests, he developed a high-resistance carbon-thread filament that burned steadily for hours as well as an electric generator sophisticated enough to power a large lighting configuration. In 1878, Edison began working on a system of electrical illumination which he hoped could compete with gas and oil-based lighting. It was during this time that he said, "We will make electricity so cheap that only the rich will burn candles." Edison made the first public demonstration of his incandescent light bulb on December 31, 1879, in Menlo Park, New Jersey. The Pennsylvania Railroad Company ran special trains to Menlo Park on the day of the demonstration in response to public enthusiasm over the event. Today, lighting choices have greatly expanded, and we have a wide-ranging variety of light bulb choices available to us.

Edison would no doubt be amazed at the public displays of lights these days. Nothing highlights this more profoundly than *The Great Christmas Light Fight* which debuted in 2013 as an American reality competition show. It features a series of families or groups who create elaborate Christmas light exhibitions for monetary prizes. In many American towns, outside light displays are fairly common during the holidays. In my own neighborhood, many of the homes on our block have some kind of exterior decorations each year. That is except for one home owner, who on occasion displays their Halloween decorations which have been placed months before. While I fully understand that not everyone celebrates Christmas or might not be capable of providing a seasonal display, what appeared in the window of this home one year was just downright creepy. Written in large letters were these words: "Help! Do NOT ENTER." Maybe these folks are nonbelievers or perhaps they have a different understanding of Christmas than me, but I found the lingering words from the presumed "ghosts of Halloween past" to be a little too dark for the rejoicing of that new light who came into the world at Christmas (John 1:9).

Jesus said, "I am the Light of the world; he who follows Me will not walk in the darkness, but will have the Light of life" (John 8:12 NASB). The fact that God is light sets up a natural contrast with darkness. Those who know Him understand it is His plan that believers shine forth His light, striving to be more like Christ every day. The Apostle Paul said, "You are all children of the light and children of the day. We do not belong to the night or to the darkness" (1 Thessalonians 5:5 NIV). To walk in the light means to know God, understand His truth, and live in righteousness. Believers in Christ must confess any darkness within themselves and allow God to shine His light through them. Norman Vincent Peale once shared a story about Thomas Edison:

> I knew his widow, and one day when I was in her home, I said to her, "Tell me about your husband. What sort of mind did he really have?"
>
> She said, "Exactitude was the mark of my husband's mind. He was not sentimental. He had to know something for sure before he would say it or record it. It had to be proven." Then she told me that when her husband was dying, he could barely speak.
>
> His doctor, who was also a family friend, noticed that the great inventor was trying to say something. He leaned close and heard Edison whisper, "It's very beautiful over there." Those were his last words.

Edison had seen the one true Light. Hopefully my neighbors will someday as well.

Reflection

In scripture, it is written, "For God, who said, 'Let light shine out of darkness,' made his light shine in our hearts to give us the light of the knowledge of God's glory displayed in the face of Christ" (2 Corinthians 4:6 NIV). How can we carefully use the knowledge of our hearts to let the light of God shine forth in us and bring others to Christ? What changes will you make in your life so that you can be an effective witness for Christ in the new year ahead?

DECEMBER 30
(Y7, D52)

A Wonderful Ending

Open my eyes, that I may behold wondrous things out of your law. I am a
sojourner on the earth; hide not your commandments from me!

—Psalm 119:18–19 (ESV)

Another version of the *Christmas Crier*—you know those full-page typed summaries of everything that happened in the life of one's family in the past year. Fortunately, those documents have come and gone with most generations, but there are a few who hold on for dear life. I continue to receive the annual updates from a few college friends, and because they send, I somehow feel obligated to read them. For the most part, they contain far too much information. I really don't need to know that the puppy is now full-grown or the specifics of the family's daily exercise routine. One of my friends actually had a serious health scare which could have resulted as cancer. Okay, I was interested in that, most gratefully, her procedure had gone well and that she was healthy. But what I didn't care to hear about was that she and her husband missed out on their European cruise due to the surgery. *Good grief,* I thought, *be grateful you are okay. How many cruises have you been privileged to take, without incident, in the last few years?* I'm sorry, but I guess I get a little impatient when I feel folks are just a little too self-absorbed.

Speaking of being self-absorbed, I read a statistic that nearly 6,000 pedestrians died over a two-year period. A significant number of these figures was attributed to individuals who were preoccupied while they were walking. One analyst said that if you take a distracted walker, combine it with an inattentive or impaired driver, and introduce a slightly decreased vision from a foggy or poorly illuminated environment, it can only set up a hypothetically deadly combination. There are communities which have passed ordinances to outlaw the use of smartphones while strolling. The opinion of some is that even widespread laws against distracted walking probably won't prevent people from accidentally wandering onto the road. You simply can't regulate individuals who are so self-absorbed that their lack of focus becomes a public nuisance and a potential fatality simply waiting to happen.

Unfortunately, the preoccupation with one's self has become a disastrous flaw in our society as a whole. In its rawest form, selfishness and self-interest deny us the opportunity to carry out God's plan for our lives. By doing so, we fail to be useful in the offering of our talents and encouragement to those who need it. Furthermore, we allow ourselves to become detached from providing service in His name. When Jesus was challenged by the Pharisees to answer questions regarding the kingdom of God, one of His profound statements was this: "If you cling to your life, you will lose it, and if you let your life go, you will save it" (Luke 17:33 NLT). I recently hard about a woman who had been dedicated to a life of service attributed her motivation to something she had been told in her youth by a relative. That motivation: "Do something that God will notice or else you'll get lost in the big shuffle of life."

Paul provided this counsel: "Do nothing out of selfish ambition or vain conceit. Rather, in humility value others above yourselves, not looking to your own interests but each of you to the interests of the others" (Philippians 2:3–4 NIV). Self-centeredness is a sin because it leads to being devoted to self-gratification and overlooking other people's needs. Jesus strikes at the very heart of the sin of self-centeredness with this unmistakable declaration: "If any of you wants to be my follower, you must give up your own way" (Matthew 16:24 NLT). Do you find that you habitually hold yourself and your desires accountable to helping others? If your first response is to obey any prodding from the Holy Spirit, it is a sure sign that the self-consumed attitude of the world does not have a place in your heart. If, however, you find it hard to say no to your own comforts and regularly ignore His invitation to help someone else, you can be assured that the attitude of the world is working its way into your heart and soul. As we prepare to enter a new year, we should take every opportunity to "deny one's self." In doing so, we make a conscious turn from self-centeredness to God-centeredness. We are no longer in charge—God is. What a wonderful ending to another celebration of Christmas, knowing that Christ is the one ruling our hearts.

Reflection

When you look at the world around you today, do you see a high level of selfishness and self-centeredness permeating every sphere of society? How do you measure whether you have fallen into this very same trap? What steps will you consciously take to be less self-absorbed? As you enter a new year, how might you consider using the counsel of others in holding you to be more accountable?

DECEMBER 31
To Be Continued

And surely I am with you always, to the very end of the age.

—Matthew 28:20 (NIV)

It's that time of the season when many of us subscribe to the old adage, "Out with the old, in with the new." For many, it's a chance to have an imaginary clean slate. I don't know about you, but for the most part, I like to be able to visualize things coming to a conclusion. At work, I am pleased when a project has a successful ending. At home, I get a sense of satisfaction when I am able to cross items off of my "to-do list." Whenever I am watching a really good episode of one of my favorite TV programs, I resent it when the program is coming to an end and the words "To be continued" flash on the screen. Of course, that's how the producers get you hooked so you keep watching. After all, the *Star Wars* franchise didn't become a megabillion-dollar operation overnight. But with its sequels and prequels since its debut in 1977, "The Force" had a successful run for a very long time.

In life, we do find that there are some things worth holding on to. I once heard a story about a fire that occurred a number of years ago in the Black Forest of Colorado. Upon returning to a leveled home following the fire, only the brick fireplace appeared to have survived. As the owner began to look through the charred rubble, he started to search for a very small ceramic figurine. It was a statuette of the baby Jesus which had been made years before by his wife. Of all the things he had lost, this would be the treasure he would hope to recover. It was an established family tradition that his wife would hide the Jesus figure and not allow other family festivities to commence until it was found. He paused and asked the question, "Is the baby Jesus still here?" As he continued the search in the area of what would have been the garage of their home, he located some burned remnants of a nativity scene. It was there that he found the baby Jesus figurine, undamaged by the fire. The owner had described the state of his property as bleak, but the small statue served as a new symbol of hope for him and his family.

When we think about the scene of the original nativity at first look, it appears to be a rather tranquil one. The kneeling shepherds, the lowing cattle, and the amazement of the birth of an innocent child now lying in the manger collectively represent a peaceful celebration of the newborn King. Following a visit from the wise men, however, there would be no peace for the family of Jesus. "After the wise men were gone, an angel of the Lord appeared to Joseph in a dream. 'Get up! Flee to Egypt with the child and his mother,' the angel said. 'Stay there until I tell you to return, because Herod is going to search for the child to kill him'" (Matthew 2:13 NLT). Only when it was safe again did the family go back home to Nazareth. Once again, Joseph had a dream in which he was told, "'Get up!' the angel said. 'Take the child and his mother back to the land of Israel, because those who were trying to kill the child are dead'" (Matthew 2:20 NLT). The stories move forward from the birth of Jesus to His brief earthly ministry: the calling of disciples, what He taught, the miracles He performed, His death, His resurrection, and how we as His modern-day disciples must respond to the events in today's world.

What gives meaning to Christmas isn't simply God taking on human flesh and being born as a baby. Fortunately for us, the narrative continued with Christmas as just the prelude. Good Friday and Easter become the pivotal point of His story. In explaining Christ's life here on earth to his student Timothy, the Apostle Paul said, "Without question, this is the great mystery of our faith: Christ was revealed in a human body and vindicated by the Spirit. He was seen by angels and announced to the nations. He was believed in throughout the world and taken to heaven in glory" (1 Timothy 3:16 NLT). Our story will conclude as we are called to enter our eternal home or when He returns. God's Word says, "So Christ was sacrificed once to take away the sins of many; and he will appear a second time, not to bear sin, but to bring salvation to those who are waiting for him" (Hebrews 9:28 NIV). The days following Christmas give us an opportunity to think about how our story will be reflected along with His. It's not an end but just a new beginning of His work to be continued through us here on earth with each new year.

Reflection

How will you live out your faith story in the days ahead? Are there changes you might consider? What are the ways you might view the new year as a continuation of your journey with Christ?

CPSIA information can be obtained
at www.ICGtesting.com
Printed in the USA
BVHW020617140223
658412BV00012B/316

9 798886 852820